Microsoft® Outlook® 2010 Inside Out

Jim Boyce

Published with the authorization of Microsoft Corporation by:
O'Reilly Media, Inc.
1005 Gravenstein Highway North
Sebastopol, California 95472

ISBN: 978-0-735-62686-7

2 3 4 5 6 7 8 9   QG   6 5 4 3 2 1

Printed and bound in the United States of America.

Microsoft Press titles may be purchased for educational, business or sales promotional use. Online editions are also available for most titles (*http://my.safaribooksonline.com*). For more information, contact our corporate/institutional sales department: (800) 998-9938 or *corporate@oreilly.com*. Visit our website at *microsoftpress.oreilly.com*. Send comments to *mspinput@microsoft.com*.

Acquisitions and Development Editors: Juliana Aldous and Kenyon Brown
Production Editor: Loranah Dimant
Editorial Production: Custom Editorial, Inc.
Technical Reviewers: Vincent Averello
Indexing: Potomac Indexing, LLC
Cover: Karen Montgomery
Compositor: Ron Bilodeau
Illustrator: Robert Romano

[2011-10-07]

Contents at a Glance

Table of Contents

What do you think of this book? We want to hear from you!

Microsoft is interested in hearing your feedback so we can continually improve our books and learning resources for you. To participate in a brief online survey, please visit:

microsoft.com/learning/booksurvey

Part 2: Email and Other Messaging

Part 3: Working with Contacts

Part 4: Managing Your Time and Tasks

Part 7: Collaboration

Part 8: Using Outlook with Exchange Server

Part 9: Mobility

What do you think of this book? We want to hear from you!

Microsoft is interested in hearing your feedback so we can continually improve our books and learning resources for you. To participate in a brief online survey, please visit:

microsoft.com/learning/booksurvey

Acknowledgments

I've authored and contributed to more than 50 books, and each project has been much the same in terms of compressed schedules and tight deadlines. This book was no different in that respect, but what made it very enjoyable and possible to accomplish was the phenomenal dedication to the project shown by everyone involved.

I offer sincere thanks to Kenyon Brown, who helped launch the project and kept it and the people involved all moving forward as a team. My sincere thanks also go to Juliana Aldous Atkinson for the opportunity to do the project and for her help in getting the project rolling. Carole McClendon, my agent at Waterside Productions, gets a well-deserved thanks, as well.

A very big nod of appreciation goes to Vince Averello, technical reviewer, who did a phenomenal job of checking the accuracy of the content and being my safety net. I thank Linda Allen, who served as copyeditor and did a great job tightening up and clarifying the manuscript. Thanks also to Loranah Dimant, production editor, for keeping everything rolling along, and managing the production side of things.

Although I did all of the revisions to this edition myself, many other authors have helped out with previous editions. This is therefore a cumulative and collaborative work, so many thanks go to the other authors who contributed to this book: Beth Sheresh and Doug Sheresh, Rob Tidrow, Bill Zumwalde, and Sharyn Graham for the 2007 edition; Blair Rampling, Rob Tidrow, Deanna Maio, Tyler and Rima Regas, Dan Newland, John Durant, Matthew Nunn, and KC Lemson for their contributions to the previous edition. All of them poured heart and soul into their contributions.

I also express sincere thanks to Westley Annis, who took the rough script code I developed for the CustomContactPrint and CustomMessagePrint scripts and performed a major overhaul of the code to make the scripts functional and presentable.

I offer my appreciation and admiration to the Microsoft Outlook development team for their efforts in making a great program even better!

Last but not least, I extend my deepest love and appreciation to my wife, Julie, for her tolerance of my obsessive work habits and understanding of my myriad other annoying character traits and bad habits.

Conventions and Features Used in This Book

This book uses special text and design conventions to make it easer for you to find the information you need.

Text Conventions

Convention	Feature
Abbreviated menu commands	For your convenience, this book uses abbreviated menu commands. For example, "Choose Tools, Forms, Design A Form" means that you should click the Tools menu, point to Forms, and select the Design A Form command.
Boldface type	Boldface type is used to indicate text that you enter or type.
Initial Capital Letters	The first letters of the names of menus, dialog boxes, dialog box elements, and commands are capitalized. Example: The Save As dialog box.
Italicized type	Italicized type is used to indicate new terms.
Plus sign (+) in text	Keyboard shortcuts are indicated by a plus sign (+) separating two key names. For example, Shift+F9 means that you press the Shift and F9 keys at the same time.

Design Conventions

> **Note**
> Notes offer additional information related to the task being discussed.

Cross-references point you to other locations in the book that offer additional information on the topic being discussed.

> **CAUTION**
> Cautions identify potential problems that you should look out for when you're completing a task, or problems that you must address before you can complete a task.

INSIDE OUT
This statement illustrates an example of an "Inside Out" problem statement

These are the book's signature tips. In these tips, you'll get the straight scoop on what's going on with the software—inside information on why a feature works the way it does. You'll also find handy workarounds to different software problems.

TROUBLESHOOTING
This statement illustrates an example of a "Troubleshooting" problem statement

Look for these sidebars to find solutions to common problems you might encounter. Troubleshooting sidebars appear next to related information in the chapters. You can also use the Troubleshooting Topics index at the back of the book to look up problems by topic.

Sidebar
The sidebars sprinkled throughout these chapters provide ancillary information on the topic being discussed. Go to sidebars to learn more about the technology or a feature.

Your Downloadable eBook

The eBook edition of this book allows you to:

- Search the full text
- Print
- Copy and paste

To download your eBook, please see the instruction page at the back of this book.

Introduction

Fifteen years ago, the average computer user spent most of his or her time using productivity applications such as Microsoft® Word or Microsoft Excel®. In the ensuing years, users have become more sophisticated, network implementations have become the rule rather than the exception, and collaboration has become a key facet of a successful business strategy. Perhaps the most significant change of all has been the explosive growth of the Internet. All these factors have led to a subtle but significant shift in the way people work. Today, most users of the 2010 Microsoft Office system spend a majority of their time in Microsoft Outlook® 2010. That change alone signifies a shift toward information management as an increasingly important everyday task. Getting a handle on daily information management can be critical to your productivity, success, and sanity.

Outlook® 2010 is an extremely versatile program. Most of the other applications in the Microsoft Office system suite have a fairly specific purpose. Outlook 2010, however, serves as personal information manager (PIM), calendar, e-mail application, task manager, and much more. With so much power and flexibility at your fingertips, you need to have a good understanding of the Outlook 2010 features. Understanding the ins and outs will not only help you get the most from this program but will also have a positive impact on your work day.

Who This Book Is For

Understanding all of the Outlook 2010 features and putting them to work is the focus of *Microsoft® Outlook® 2010 Inside Out*. Most Outlook 2010 books act mainly as how-to guides for users who want to learn about the software. This approach leaves out workgroup managers and administrators when it comes to deployment, collaboration, server-side issues, and administration. *Microsoft Office Outlook 2010 Inside Out* offers a comprehensive look at the features most people will use in Outlook 2010 and serves as an excellent reference for users who need to understand how to accomplish what they need to do. In addition, this book goes a step or two further, providing useful information to advanced users and IT professionals who need to understand the bigger picture. Whether you want to learn Outlook 2010 for your own use, need to support Outlook 2010 on a peer-to-peer network, or are in charge of supporting Outlook 2010 under Microsoft Exchange Server, you'll find the information and answers you need between the covers of *Microsoft Office Outlook 2010 Inside Out*.

This book makes some assumptions about the reader. You should be familiar with your client operating system, whether it's Microsoft Windows® XP, Windows Vista™, or Windows 7. You should be comfortable working with a computer and have a good understanding of how to work with menus, dialog boxes, and other aspects of the user interface. In short, *Microsoft Office Outlook 2010 Inside Out* assumes that you're an experienced computer user who might or might not have an understanding of Outlook 2010 and what it can do. The purpose of this book is to give you a comprehensive look at what Outlook 2010 can do, how to put Outlook 2010 to work, and how to manage Outlook 2010 at the user, workgroup, and server levels.

How This Book Is Organized

Microsoft Office Outlook 2010 Inside Out offers a structured, logical approach to all aspects of using and managing Outlook 2010. Each of the 10 parts of this book focuses on a specific aspect of Outlook 2010 use or management.

Part 1—Working with Outlook

Part 1 starts with the basics. Chapter 1 takes a look at the features that are new in Outlook 2010. Chapter 2 takes a look at the Outlook 2010 architecture and startup options. In Chapter 3, you'll learn how to perform advanced setup and configuration tasks such as setting up e-mail accounts, using profiles, making Outlook 2010 work with other e-mail services, configuring receipt and delivery options, and using add-ins that extend the Outlook 2010 functionality. Chapter 4 gets you up to speed using Outlook 2010 to send and receive messages, manage your workday, locate information on the Internet, and perform other common tasks. Chapter 5 rounds out Part 1 with a detailed look at how you can use categories to organize your data in Outlook 2010.

Part 2—E-Mail and Other Messaging

Part 2 delves deeper into the Outlook 2010 e-mail components and features. In Chapter 6, you'll learn how to manage address books and distribution lists. Chapter 7 explains how to set up Internet e-mail accounts. Chapter 8 will help you start to manage the e-mail features in Outlook 2010. Chapter 9 will make you comfortable with the range of features Outlook 2010 provides for creating messages both simple and complex. In Chapter 10, you'll learn how to find and organize your messages. Chapter 11 explains how to apply filters and rules to process messages automatically. Chapter 12 will help you exclude junk and spam e-mail senders. Look to Chapter 13 to learn how to generate automatic responses to incoming messages.

Because security is an increasingly important topic, Chapter 14 will help you secure your system and your data, send messages securely, and prevent others from impersonating you to send messages. Chapter 15 offers a comprehensive look at how the Outlook 2010 remote mail features can be indispensable for managing your mail online and offline. Chapter 16 explains how to use the new Really Simple Syndication (RSS) features to subscribe to and read RSS feeds in Outlook 2010. Chapter 17 rounds out the section with an explanation of Lightweight Directory Access Features (LDAP) features in Outlook 2010.

Part 3—Working with Contacts

Part 3 explores the Outlook 2010 features for managing your contacts. Chapter 18 starts with a look at how to manage contact information, including addresses, phone numbers, e-mail addresses, fax numbers, and a wealth of other information. You'll also learn how to sort, filter, and categorize your contacts, as well as share contact data with others.

Part 4—Managing Your Time and Tasks

Part 4 covers scheduling, one of the most widely used features in Outlook 2010. Chapter 19 provides an in-depth look at the Outlook 2010 appointment-scheduling capabilities. You'll learn how scheduling works, and you'll learn how to schedule appointments, create recurring appointments, use color effectively to manage your schedule, allow others to access your schedule, and publish your schedule to the Web. Chapter 20 takes a look at scheduling meetings and resources using Outlook 2010 and explains the subtle differences between scheduling appointments and scheduling meetings. Chapter 21 examines all aspects of managing tasks with Outlook 2010. You can use the Outlook 2010 Tasks folder to keep track of your own tasks as well as assign tasks to others. Integrating your tasks in Outlook 2010 can help you ensure that your tasks get done on time and are allocated to the appropriate person to complete them.

Chapter 22 offers a look at journaling, an important feature in Outlook 2010 that allows you to keep track of time spent on projects and documents and to track contacts and other items of interest. Chapter 23 takes a look at notes, a useful feature in Outlook 2010 that will help you get rid of those little slips of paper cluttering your desk and the sticky notes taking over your monitor. You'll learn how to create notes, assign categories to them, change their color, move them to other applications, put them on your desktop, and much more. Chapter 23 also explores Microsoft OneNote, which you'll find a much better alternative to the Notes folder in Outlook for keeping notes and related information.

Part 5—Customizing Outlook

Customizing an application or the user interface for your operating system isn't just a matter of picking and choosing your personal preferences. Your ability to customize the way an application functions or appears can have a profound impact on its usefulness to you and to others. In short, the ability to customize an application allows you to make that application do what you want it to do in the way that makes the most sense to you. Chapter 24 starts the coverage of customization with a look at templates and how they can simplify the creation of e-mail messages, appointments, events, and other Outlook 2010 objects. You'll learn not only how to create and edit templates, but also how to share those templates with others.

Chapter 25 provides the detailed information you need to customize the Navigation Pane, the toolbar that appears by default to the left of the Outlook 2010 window and gives you quick access to the Outlook 2010 components. Chapter 25 also helps you customize the other aspects of the Outlook 2010 interface, including toolbars, Outlook Today view, and folders. Chapter 26 explains how to create custom views and print styles for organizing and displaying your Outlook 2010 data. Chapter 27 takes a look at creating and using custom forms for a variety of tasks. Chapter 28 gives you a look at a host of ways you can automate tasks in Outlook 2010.

Part 6—Managing and Securing Outlook

Part 6 begins the transition to more advanced topics of interest to users, administrators, and IT professionals. In Chapter 29, you'll learn how Outlook 2010 uses folders to store your data and how to manage those folders. Chapter 29 also offers in-depth coverage of how to organize and archive your important data. In Chapter 30, you'll learn how to archive, back up, and restore your Outlook 2010 data. The chapter not only covers the importance of a sound backup and recovery strategy but will also help you develop and implement your own strategy that takes into account the unique requirements of Outlook 2010 and Exchange Server.

In Chapter 31, you'll learn how to move data in an out of Outlook 2010 using the program's import and export features. Chapter 32 will help you get a handle on all of your Outlook 2010 data, with a discussion of the new Instant Search feature and other features in Outlook 2010 for finding and organizing data. Chapter 33 includes an analysis of the importance of virus protection and how to guard against virus infections and outbreaks. You'll read about both client-side and server-side solutions. Because up-to-date virus definitions are the key to successful prevention, Chapter 33 takes a close look at developing a virus definition update strategy. You'll also find a detailed discussion of how to configure attachment blocking at the server as well as in Outlook 2010 itself.

Part 7—Collaboration

Chapter 34 will help you simplify your life by teaching you how to delegate many of your responsibilities—including managing your schedule—to an assistant. Chapter 35 will help you coordinate your schedule with others by teaching you to share your calendar. Chapter 36 explains how to integrate Outlook 2010 with other Microsoft Office system applications, such as performing a mail merge in Microsoft Office Word 2010 based on contacts stored in Outlook 2010. Chapter 37 explores Office Communicator and Office Communications Server, focusing on the integration between OCS, Outlook, and SharePoint. Chapter 38 explores online collaboration with SharePoint and how you can use Outlook to interact with SharePoint sites and data. You'll learn how to work with shared contacts, set up and use alerts, work with shared documents, link a team calendar to Outlook 2010, and more.

Part 8—Using Outlook with Exchange Server

Outlook 2010 can be an effective information management tool all by itself, whether you use it on a stand-alone computer or on a network in collaboration with other users. Where Outlook 2010 really shines, however, is in its integration with and as a client for Microsoft Exchange Server. Part 8 steps up to a more advanced level to explain a broad range of Outlook 2010/Exchange Server integration topics. Chapter 39 turns the focus to the client, explaining how to configure Outlook 2010 as an Exchange Server client. Chapter 40 explores the wealth of features in Outlook 2010 specifically geared toward messaging with Exchange Server, such as the ability to recall sent messages before they are read, prioritize messages, and much more. This chapter also contains a detailed look at voting, an interesting feature in Outlook 2010. You can use Outlook 2010 as a tool to solicit input from others on any issue or topic, receiving and tallying their votes quite easily. Chapter 41 helps you continue working when you're away from the office or when your server is offline, covering how to use remote features to access and manage your Outlook 2010 data.

Part 9—Mobility

Life isn't just about working in the confines of your office, and Part 10 takes that into account. For example, Chapter 42 explains how to connect to Exchange Server using a Web browser such as Microsoft Internet Explorer® and Outlook Web App (OWA). Chapter 43 completes this part of the book with a look at the mobility-related features in Outlook 2010—which you can use with Exchange Server 2003 and later—to take your Outlook 2010 data on the road.

See the section "Conventions and Features Used in This Book" for a list of some of the features you will find used throughout this book.

PART 1

Working with Outlook

What's New in Outlook 2010

Mᴵᶜᴿᴼˢᴼᶠᵀ Outlook 2010 sports a lot of new features that improve usability and add functionality. What's more, many of the familiar features in earlier versions have been revamped or fine-tuned in Outlook 2010. All these changes come together to make Outlook 2010 an outstanding tool for communication, time and information management, and collaboration. If you are one of those people who gauges the productivity of your day by how many emails you've cleaned out of your Inbox, you'll really appreciate the new features in Outlook 2010.

If you are an experienced Outlook user, one of your first questions undoubtedly is, "What's new in Outlook 2010, and how do I find all of these new features?" That's what this chapter is all about. While we don't cover every little change or nuance of the new Outlook 2010 interface or new and improved features here, we offer a broad overview of the new features in Outlook 2010 to help you get up to speed quickly. Let's start with the most obvious—the user interface.

A New Look and Feel

Microsoft has made some significant changes to the look and feel of Outlook's user interface over the last several versions, but those changes have largely been evolutionary rather than revolutionary. That trend continues in Outlook 2010 with the extension of the ribbon interface across the application, along with a handful of other changes, described in the following sections.

The Ribbon

The ribbon is one of those user interface features that you either love or hate (although you can certainly customize it to suit your preferences, as explained in Chapter 25, "Customizing the Outlook Interface"). When it was introduced, the ribbon was something of a paradigm shift, replacing a linear menu list of commands with features organized into groups on multiple tabs. Unless you are moving to Outlook 2010 from a version of Outlook prior to Outlook 2007, you are probably familiar with the ribbon. The difference in Outlook 2010 is that the ribbon is now present throughout the Outlook interface (see Figure 1-1), rather than being limited to certain forms as in Outlook 2007.

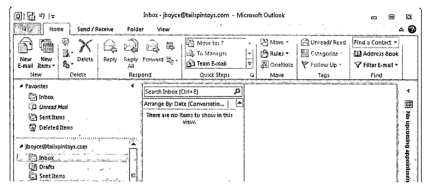

Figure 1-1 The ribbon makes commands and features easily discoverable.

There are four tabs by default for each of the main Outlook folders (Mail, Calendar, etc.), and each tab contains multiple groups of controls that you can use to work with Outlook's options and features. The presence of these controls in the ribbon makes it easier to create new items (such as meeting invitations) and access features more quickly. There is also an optional Developer tab that you can turn on that gives you easy access to Microsoft Visual Basic and macros, add-ins, and custom forms. If you have any third-party add-ins installed, you'll also see an Add-Ins tab.

For the most part, the ribbons on the individual item forms (new message, new meeting invitation, etc.) are essentially the same as they are in Outlook 2007. The one notable difference is that the proofing tools are now on their own Review tabs in the ribbon.

Navigation Pane

You won't find significant changes in the Navigation pane in Outlook 2010 (see Figure 1-2), but there are some subtle usability changes. First, a lot of the lines, gradients, and headers are gone, giving the Navigation pane a cleaner, sleeker look. The folders have also been rearranged to put the most commonly used folders—Inbox, Drafts, Sent Items, and Deleted Items—at the top of the list, with other folders listed below in alphabetical order. The mailbox name has also changed to show your email address, which helps you identify accounts quickly when you have more than one email account in Outlook. Windows-style expand/collapse widgets have replaced the older style + / - widgets for expanding and collapsing folders.

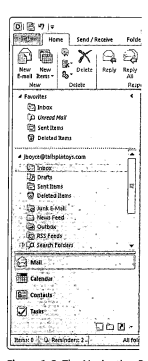

Figure 1-2 The Navigation Pane has been streamlined and rearranged a bit.

Backstage

As I mentioned previously, the most significant visual change in Outlook is the implementation of the ribbon across the application. This means that some of the features and commands that were previously accessible through the Navigation pane are moved to the ribbon, as are the majority of the commands from the menus.

In particular, the Backstage replaces the File menu in Outlook 2010. To get to the Backstage, click the File tab. The Backstage offers categories on the left, a content pane in the middle, and a preview pane at the right (see Figure 1-3). Click a category on the left to view the commands and options for that category. To get back to your Outlook folders from the Backstage, just click a tab name.

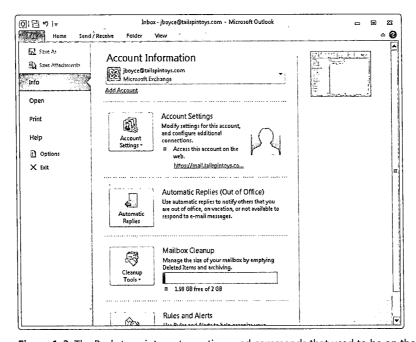

Figure 1-3 The Backstage integrates options and commands that used to be on the File menu.

Other Changes

As you work through the new interface, you'll find some other, subtle changes. For example, the color scheme is a little different, some of the icons and controls have a slightly different look, the Help button sits on its own at the right of the ribbon, and so on. You'll also find some more significant changes, such as the People pane, discussed a little later in this chapter.

Conversation Management

A great new feature in Outlook 2010 is the way the program handles message threads, or conversations. On the View tab, you'll find a new Date (Conversations) view that, when selected, causes all related messages in a conversation to be grouped together. So, for example, you'll see the original message, with all the replies from you and from other recipients in a single group (see Figure 1-4). This view pulls together related messages regardless of whether they are still in your Inbox or have been moved (or reside in Sent Items).

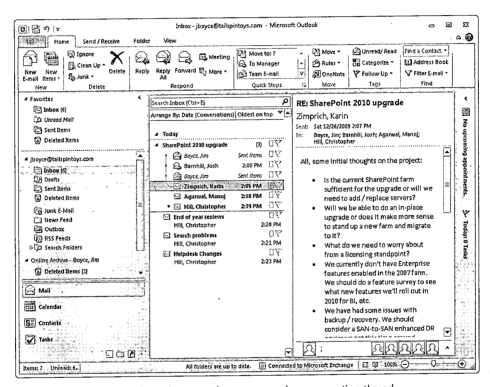

Figure 1-4 The Conversations view organizes messages by conversation thread.

The Conversations view is a great tool for finding and viewing related messages. In addition, the view shows you how the messages relate to one another. For example, you can see who replied to whom and follow the message trail.

Perhaps just as useful is the ability to work with the messages in a conversation as a group. For example, if you want to file an entire group of messages, just drag the top item in the conversation thread to a destination folder and all the messages will be moved there. Note that this applies only to messages in the current folder, so the messages in your Sent Items folder that show on the conversation thread, for example, will remain in the Sent Items folder.

Another handy aspect of the Conversations view is the capability to clean up a lot of the duplicated messages. To clean up a conversation, select a conversation and then click Clean Up, Clean Up Conversation in the Delete group on the Home tab. Doing so will move all older, redundant messages in the conversation to the Deleted Items folder. You can also ignore a conversation, which moves the conversation and any future replies to the Deleted Items folder. To do this, right-click the conversation and choose Ignore.

Search

Search is improved in Outlook 2010 primarily by giving you quick access to tools and options that will help you refine a search scope, work with recent searches, and locate search options. When you click in the Search box, a new Search tab appears (see Figure 1-5) that lets you easily select the target for the search, specify search criteria like subject or categories, and change other options for the current search. You can also quickly open recent searches and access search tools, such as Advanced Find, Search Options, and Indexing Status.

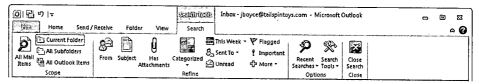

Figure 1-5 The Search tab integrates search options and commands into a single place.

Calendar Preview

Another new feature that is a great addition for people who have a busy calendar is Calendar Preview, which shows a preview of a meeting in your Inbox so that you can see adjacent and conflicting meetings or appointments without having to open the Calendar (see Figure 1-6). Use the Accept, Tentative, or Decline drop-down menu to process the meeting request.

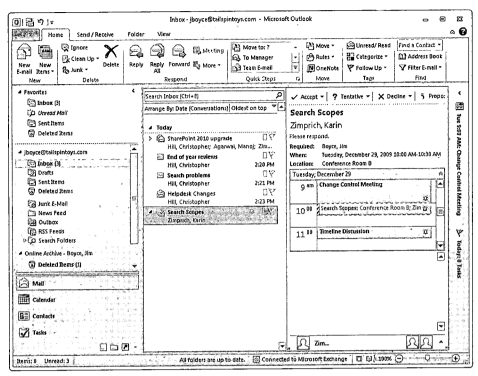

Figure 1-6 Calendar Preview makes it easy to see if a meeting request conflicts with your schedule.

Quick Steps

Quick Steps are a lot like multi-step rules, or in the Microsoft SharePoint world, a lot like a workflow. You can initiate them with a single click to have them perform the actions defined in the Quick Step. Outlook 2010 includes a small set of predefined Quick Steps, and you can easily create your own. For example, you might create a Quick Step that moves messages that meet certain criteria to a folder, sets the importance level to Low, and marks the message as Read. Or, maybe you would like to have Outlook automatically reply to a message, then move the message to a folder and mark it as Read. The Quick Steps group appears on the Home tab when you open the Mail folder. Click More and choose Manage Quick Steps to view the Manage Quick Steps dialog box, shown in Figure 1-7.

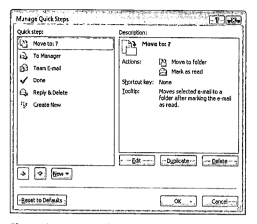

Figure 1-7 Use Quick Steps to perform multiple actions on a message with one click.

TIP

Quick Steps are covered in detail in Chapter 13, "Responding to Messages Automatically."

People Pane

Several Microsoft server applications—including Microsoft Exchange Server, Microsoft Office Communications Server, and SharePoint—work together in concert with Office to provide a unified communications and collaboration environment. One aspect of a good collaboration environment is the capability to readily identify others with whom you want to collaborate, and to simplify the process of connecting with those people to work on documents, chat, and so on.

You are probably familiar with presence features in previous versions of Outlook, which provide an indication of whether others are online. For example, you can see an indicator beside a user's name in the To field of an email message when that person is online (and potentially available for an online chat session).

The People pane in Outlook 2010 (see Figure 1-8) is the visible part of the Outlook Social Connector, which connects Outlook 2010 to social networking sites like SharePoint, LinkedIn, and others. The Outlook Social Connector integrates with these services to show not only online status, but other information about the selected person, such as attachments that you've received from him or her or upcoming appointments.

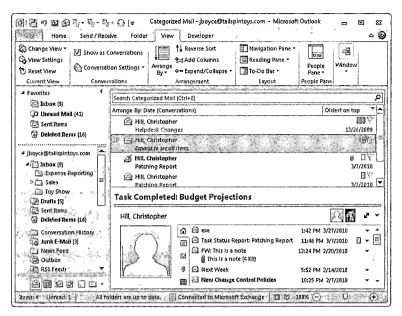

Figure 1-8 The People pane links you to information about others.

Exchange Server Improvements

Outlook is a great messaging and information management tool when used with almost any type of email account, but it really shines when used as a client for an Exchange Server account. This is particularly true when using Outlook 2010 with Exchange Server 2010. The following sections briefly describe many of the features that are new or improved in Outlook for Exchange Server.

> **NOTE**
>
> This section does not cover all the Exchange Server 2010 enhancements; rather, it focuses on the ones you'll probably deal with most often in Outlook 2010.

Calendar Features

Exchange Server supports federation among organizations, enabling those organizations to share availability, calendars, and contacts. For example, you might use federation to enable your closest business partners or customers to view your users' free/busy data and vice versa, simplifying scheduling among the organizations. You can also use federation in large

Chapter 1

enterprises where, for example, multiple business units have their own Exchange Server environments.

Group scheduling is also improved. You can create calendar groups that contain the calendars for multiple people, and view free/busy times as a group. Outlook 2010 automatically adds a group calendar for all of your direct reports, as well as your peers (those people who share the same manager). Figure 1-9 shows these team calendars.

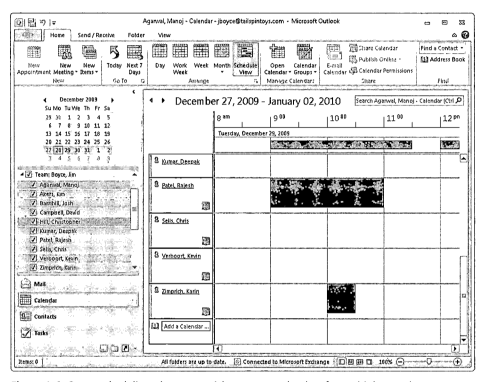

Figure 1-9 Group scheduling gives you quick access to calendars for multiple people.

Integrated Email Archive

Exchange Server 2010 includes a Personal Archive feature that can help eliminate personal folder (.pst) files on the users' computers. When an Exchange Server 2010 mailbox is archive-enabled, an additional branch appears in the Navigation pane, as shown in Figure 1-10. As Exchange Server archives messages to a user's archive based on the retention policy assigned to the mailbox, folders will appear under this branch in Outlook that correspond to the folder from which the archived message came.

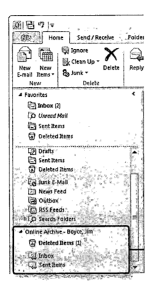

Figure 1-10 The Personal Archive can be used to move messages to an archive mailbox automatically.

The advantages of the Personal Archive are that the user has easy access to the archived items right from Outlook, the Exchange Server administrator can control when messages are moved out of users' mailboxes, and the security risk inherent in .pst files on the users' computers is eliminated.

MailTips

The MailTips feature can keep users from making common email mistakes such as send-ing a message to too broad a range of recipients. They can also indicate to the user when a recipient's email address is outside the organization, when a recipient is out of the office, or an email address is not valid. MailTips doesn't prevent you from sending a message, but instead displays a warning message in an InfoBar on the message form indicating the potential problem.

Multiple Exchange Server Accounts

A handy new feature for anyone who has more than one Exchange Server mailbox they need to work with or monitor is the capability of Outlook 2010 to add multiple Exchange Server mailboxes to a single profile. In previous versions, you could open another mailbox from the same Exchange Server environment, subject to your permissions for that mailbox, and the mailbox would show up in the Navigation pane along with your own. You added the additional mailboxes through the properties for your primary mailbox.

In Outlook 2010, you can add the mailbox as a separate account in your profile. What's more, the mailbox can reside in a completely separate Exchange Server environment from your other mailbox(es). For example, perhaps one of your primary business partners or customers has created an Exchange Server mailbox for you to use for collaboration, scheduling, and messaging. Rather than have two Outlook profiles and switch between them, or have your messages forwarded from one mailbox to the other, you can simply add both mailbox accounts to your profile and work with them in the same Outlook session.

Because Outlook imposes no boundaries between the mailboxes, you can move items between them just as you can from an Exchange Server mailbox to a local .pst file. This can be a good thing, but it can also pose a risk. You might not want to move messages accidentally from your primary work mailbox to a customer-supplied mailbox, but it's certainly possible to do so. If you want to use multiple Exchange Server mailboxes, give some thought to the risks and potential problems you might face before doing so.

Other Improvements for Exchange Server

There are several other new features for Exchange Server 2010 and Outlook 2010, not discussed here, which include additional voice mail features, text messaging through Exchange ActiveSync, improved Internet Message Access Protocol (IMAP) support, and lots more. Many of these additional features are covered to some degree in other chapters of this book where appropriate.

Extended Browser Support

If you happen to be a Firefox user, you'll be happy to know that Microsoft has extended browser support for Outlook Web Access (OWA) with Exchange Server 2010, and Firefox will work well with both SharePoint and OWA. In fact, most popular browsers should work with both SharePoint and OWA.

SharePoint Workspace

As discussed in Chapter 38, "Collaboration with Outlook and SharePoint," SharePoint provides some great integration features with Outlook. These include the capability to synchronize SharePoint calendars and other types of items to Outlook, pull Really Simple Syndication (RSS) feeds into Outlook from SharePoint lists, send and receive document links in Outlook, and more. Many of these features have the goal of making SharePoint content available in Outlook so you can work with that content without opening the SharePoint site.

Office 2010 introduces a new application called SharePoint WorkSpace, formerly known as Groove. SharePoint Workspace enables you to work with SharePoint content offline, and then synchronize the content back to SharePoint when you are connected to the network again. While not an Outlook feature, SharePoint Workspace is worth mentioning because you might find it an alternative to Outlook for working with your SharePoint sites.

What's Out

Several features previously in Outlook have been removed, either because they are obsolete or because they have been replaced by other functionalities. The following list summarizes the features that have been removed from Outlook.

- **ANSI OST files**   Outlook creates Unicode .ost files by default, and ANSI OST files can be created only by modifying group policy for Outlook. ANSI .ost files do not work for profiles containing multiple Exchange Server accounts.

- **AutoArchive-based retention**   The capability to deploy AutoArchive-based reten- tion settings through Group Policy has been removed. The Messaging Records Man- agement features in Exchange Server 2007 and later offer an alternative.

- **Calendar rebasing tool**   This tool, introduced in Outlook 2007, has been removed. Outlook 2010 can display start and end times correctly for items in the calendar and no longer needs time zone rebasing. The Time Zone Data Update Tool, which can be used to rebase older Outlook clients and servers, is available as a download from Microsoft.

- **Activities-based Search Folders**   The capability to customize the list of folder groups available to search from the Activities view in a contact item has been removed (the Activities tab of the Contacts folder properties is removed).

- **DAV for HTTP accounts**   Distributed Authoring and Versioning (DAV) connectivity for Hypertext Transfer Protocol (HTTP) accounts (such as Hotmail) has been removed from Outlook 2010. You can use the new Outlook Connector to synchronize your Hotmail account to Outlook 2010.

- **Exchange Server 2000**   Outlook 2010 will not connect to Exchange Server 2000 or earlier versions of Exchange Server.

- **Most Recently Used (MRU) list**   The MRU list (File, Open, Other User's Folder) has been removed.

- **Outlook integrity check tool (ost)**   The Scanost.exe tool is not included with Out- look 2010. You can resynchronize manually individual folders that have an issue, or simply delete the OST file and let Outlook download the content from the server again.

- **Photo resizing**   The option to resize an attached image file has been replaced with resizing options on the ribbon.

- **Postmarking**   This feature, which previously postmarked a message to help distinguish it from junk email, has been removed from Outlook 2010.

- **Preview of published Office Online calendars**   This feature, which enabled users to view and managed shared Office Online calendars without having to subscribe to the published calendar, has been removed. Now, users must subscribe to the calendar to view it in Outlook, or subscribe to the calendar in Windows Live Calendar.

- **Remote mail**   This feature is removed from Outlook 2010 and is replaced by Cached Mode.

- **Search Toolbar add-in**   This add-in, which enabled local indexing of online Exchange Server mailboxes through Windows Desktop Search, has been removed to reduce Exchange Server bandwidth and improve Outlook startup and shutdown. You can still search Exchange Server mailboxes in Cached Exchange Mode or use the Exchange Search feature in Exchange Server 2007 or later.

- **Send Link To This Folder**   The Send Link To This Folder option on the context menu for an Exchange Server public folder has been removed as a result of a shift from Exchange Server public folders to SharePoint for collaboration.

- **Send Options**   This option, available in Outlook 2007 by right-clicking an address in the To field and choosing Send Options, is removed. This feature previously enabled you to choose between Multipurpose Internet Mail Extensions (MIME) and Plain Text/UUEncode formats for outgoing messages.

- **Third-party Exchange Server client extensions do not load**   Outlook 2010 does not load these extensions. Contact the third-party vendor in question for updated solutions (and note that some of the provided features might be incorporated into Outlook or in Exchange Server natively).

And More...

The features briefly explored in this chapter are the main new features introduced in Outlook 2010. As you become familiar with Outlook 2010, you'll find lots of additional features that increase ease of use, make Outlook 2010 more reliable, simplify collaboration with others, and in general, make it easier to use Outlook 2010 to manage your contacts, schedule, email, and other information. You'll find coverage of all these new features throughout the rest of *Microsoft Outlook 2010 Inside Out*.

Outlook Overview and Startup

THIS chapter provides an overview of Microsoft Outlook 2010 to help you learn not only how Outlook 2010 works but also how it stores data. If you are relatively new to Outlook, this chapter will give you a quick overview of what it can do, what types of email accounts you can manage with Outlook, and how Outlook stores your data.

This chapter also explains the different options that you have for connecting to email servers through Outlook 2010 and the protocols—Post Office Protocol 3 (POP3) and Internet Message Access Protocol (IMAP), for example—that support those connections. In addition to learning about client support and the various platforms on which you can use Outlook 2010, you'll also learn about the options that are available for starting and using the program.

If you're anxious to get started using Outlook 2010, you could skip this chapter and move straight to Chapter 3, "Configuring Outlook Profiles and Accounts," to learn how to configure your email accounts and begin working with Outlook 2010. However, this chapter provides the foundation on which many subsequent chapters are based, and reading it will help you gain a deeper understanding of what Outlook 2010 can do so that you can use it effectively and efficiently.

Overview of Outlook

Outlook was once primarily a tool for managing personal information such as contacts and email, scheduling, and tasks. Today, Outlook 2010 provides all these features but adds the benefits of enhanced collaboration. This collaboration comes in the form of group scheduling, data sharing, shared calendars, Microsoft InfoPath forms integration, and Microsoft SharePoint integration. While the capability to manage your email, contacts, calendar, and tasks is still important, the ability to collaborate with your coworkers and business partners can be even more important.

Outlook 2010 provides a broad range of capabilities to help you manage your entire workday. In fact, a majority of Office system users work in Outlook more than 60 percent of the time. An understanding of the Outlook 2010 capabilities and features is important not only for using the Office system effectively but also for managing your time and projects. The following sections will help you learn to use the features in Outlook 2010 to simplify your workday and enhance your productivity.

Messaging

One of the key features that Outlook 2010 offers is messaging. You can use Outlook 2010 as a client to send and receive email through a variety of services (see Figure 2-1). Outlook 2010 offers integrated support for the email services covered in the sections that follow.

> **Note**
>
> A client application is one that uses a service provided by another computer, typically a server.

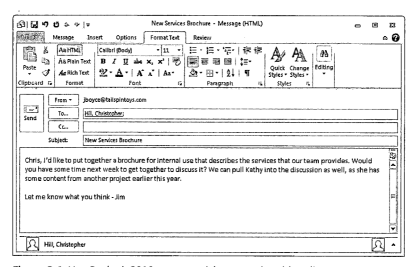

Figure 2-1 Use Outlook 2010 to create rich-text and multimedia messages.

Exchange Server

Outlook 2010 integrates tightly with Microsoft Exchange Server, which means that you can take advantage of workgroup scheduling, collaboration, and other features offered through Exchange Server that aren't available with other clients. For example, you can use any POP3 email client (such as Microsoft Outlook Express, Windows Mail, or Windows Live Mail), to connect to a computer running Exchange Server (assuming that the Exchange Server administrator has configured the server to allow POP3), but you're limited to email only. Advanced workgroup and other special features—being able to recall a message before it is read, use public folders, view group schedules, and use managed folders for archiving and retention, for example—require Outlook.

POP3 and IMAP Email

Outlook 2010 provides full support for Internet email servers, which means that you can use Outlook 2010 to send and receive email through mail servers that support the Internet-based POP3 and IMAP standards. What's more, you can integrate Internet mail accounts with other accounts, such as an Exchange Server account, to send and receive messages through multiple servers. For example, you might maintain an account on Exchange Server for interoffice correspondence and use a local Internet service provider (ISP) or other Internet-based email service for messages outside your network; or perhaps you want to monitor your personal email along with your work-related email. In that situation, you would simply add your personal email account to your Outlook 2010 profile and work with both simultaneously. You can then use rules and custom folders to help separate your messages.

For more information about messaging protocols such as POP3 and IMAP, see the section "Understanding Messaging Protocols and Standards," on page 32.

HTTP-Based Email

Previous versions of Outlook supported email accounts based on the Hypertext Transfer Protocol (HTTP), and while Outlook still technically supports HTTP-based email, it only does so for Hotmail with the Outlook Hotmail Connector, a separate downloadable add-on for Outlook 2010. In addition, Outlook 2010 also supports access through HTTP/HTTPS for Exchange Server accounts through Outlook Anywhere (formerly called RPC-over-HTTP) in Exchange Server. If you have a different HTTP-based email service, contact your mail provider to determine if it offers an add-on to support Outlook 2010.

Text Messaging and Notifications

Outlook 2010 includes built-in support for text messaging, enabling you to send text messages from Outlook just as you send emails. To use this feature, you must have a text messaging service provider configured in Outlook that supports your mobile operator. Then, to send a text message, you simply choose Text Message from the New Items button in the ribbon, compose the text message in the resulting window, choose a recipient or type a mobile number, and click Send (see Figure 2-2).

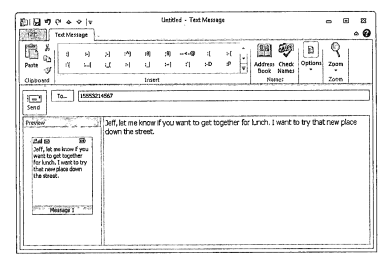

Figure 2-2 Send text messages from Outlook.

In addition to sending text messages through a Short Message Service (SMS) service provider, Outlook 2010 can integrate with messaging and notification features in Exchange Server to send notifications to your mobile phone. For example, Exchange Server can send you notifications when your calendar is updated, send meeting reminders, or send a daily calendar agenda that summarizes your schedule. You can also configure email notifications so that you receive notifications on your mobile device when messages arrive in your Inbox that meet rule criteria that you specify (see Figure 2-3). For example, you might want to receive a mobile notification when an email arrives with a priority setting of High.

Exchange Server

Outlook 2010 integrates tightly with Microsoft Exchange Server, which means that you can take advantage of workgroup scheduling, collaboration, and other features offered through Exchange Server that aren't available with other clients. For example, you can use any POP3 email client (such as Microsoft Outlook Express, Windows Mail, or Windows Live Mail), to connect to a computer running Exchange Server (assuming that the Exchange Server administrator has configured the server to allow POP3), but you're limited to email only. Advanced workgroup and other special features—being able to recall a message before it is read, use public folders, view group schedules, and use managed folders for archiving and retention, for example—require Outlook.

POP3 and IMAP Email

Outlook 2010 provides full support for Internet email servers, which means that you can use Outlook 2010 to send and receive email through mail servers that support the Internet-based POP3 and IMAP standards. What's more, you can integrate Internet mail accounts with other accounts, such as an Exchange Server account, to send and receive messages through multiple servers. For example, you might maintain an account on Exchange Server for interoffice correspondence and use a local Internet service provider (ISP) or other Internet-based email service for messages outside your network; or perhaps you want to monitor your personal email along with your work-related email. In that situation, you would simply add your personal email account to your Outlook 2010 profile and work with both simultaneously. You can then use rules and custom folders to help separate your messages.

For more information about messaging protocols such as POP3 and IMAP, see the section "Understanding Messaging Protocols and Standards," on page 32.

HTTP-Based Email

Previous versions of Outlook supported email accounts based on the Hypertext Transfer Protocol (HTTP), and while Outlook still technically supports HTTP-based email, it only does so for Hotmail with the Outlook Hotmail Connector, a separate downloadable add-on for Outlook 2010. In addition, Outlook 2010 also supports access through HTTP/HTTPS for Exchange Server accounts through Outlook Anywhere (formerly called RPC-over-HTTP) in Exchange Server. If you have a different HTTP-based email service, contact your mail provider to determine if it offers an add-on to support Outlook 2010.

Text Messaging and Notifications

Outlook 2010 includes built-in support for text messaging, enabling you to send text messages from Outlook just as you send emails. To use this feature, you must have a text messaging service provider configured in Outlook that supports your mobile operator. Then, to send a text message, you simply choose Text Message from the New Items button in the ribbon, compose the text message in the resulting window, choose a recipient or type a mobile number, and click Send (see Figure 2-2).

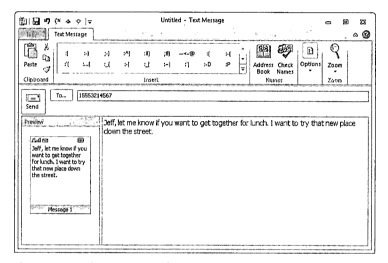

Figure 2-2 Send text messages from Outlook.

In addition to sending text messages through a Short Message Service (SMS) service provider, Outlook 2010 can integrate with messaging and notification features in Exchange Server to send notifications to your mobile phone. For example, Exchange Server can send you notifications when your calendar is updated, send meeting reminders, or send a daily calendar agenda that summarizes your schedule. You can also configure email notifications so that you receive notifications on your mobile device when messages arrive in your Inbox that meet rule criteria that you specify (see Figure 2-3). For example, you might want to receive a mobile notification when an email arrives with a priority setting of High.

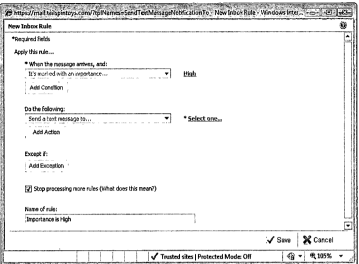

Figure 2-3 Configure text alerts to your mobile device using email notification rules.

Fax Send and Receive

Outlook 2010 includes a Fax Mail Transport provider, which allows you to send faxes from Outlook 2010 using a fax modem. In addition, third-party developers can provide Messaging Application Programming Interface (MAPI) integration with their fax applications, allowing you to use Outlook 2010 as the front end for those applications to send and receive faxes. Microsoft Windows XP, Windows Vista, and Windows 7 include built-in fax services that support sending and receiving faxes. These fax services can print incoming faxes and deliver a copy to a file folder, but neither will deliver faxes to your Outlook mailbox.

If you need to be able to deliver incoming faxes to your mailbox, you must use a third-party, MAPI-capable fax application. Alternatively, if you use Exchange Server, you can choose a server-side fax application to provide fax support and delivery.

Calendars and Scheduling

Scheduling is another important feature in Outlook 2010. You can use Outlook 2010 to track both personal and work-related meetings and appointments, as shown in Figure 2-4, whether you are at home or in the office—a useful feature even on a stand-alone computer.

Where the Outlook 2010 scheduling capabilities really shine, however, is in group scheduling. When you use Outlook 2010 to set up meetings and appointments with others, you can view the schedules of your invitees, which makes it easy to find a time when everyone can attend. You can schedule both one-time and recurring appointments. All appointments and meetings can include a reminder with a lead time that you specify, and Outlook 2010 will notify you of the event at the specified time. You can process multiple reminders at one time, a useful feature if you've been out of the office for a while.

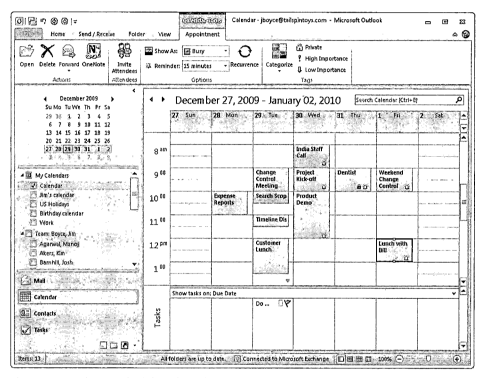

Figure 2-4 Track your schedule with Outlook 2010.

Outlook 2010 also provides integration with SharePoint calendars, enabling you to view and manage SharePoint calendars in Outlook and synchronize changes between Outlook and SharePoint (for example, create a calendar event in a SharePoint calendar using Outlook). This is a very useful feature that enables you to view group, project, and other types of schedules from multiple sources in a single place—Outlook. Figure 2-5 shows a SharePoint vacation calendar displayed in Outlook next to my work calendar.

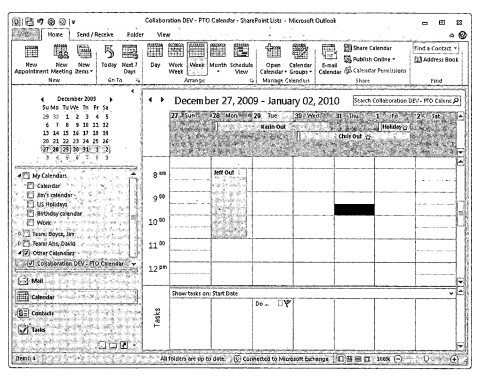

Figure 2-5 You can integrate SharePoint calendars and other SharePoint content in Outlook.

Organizing your schedule is also one of the strong suits of Outlook 2010. You can use categories to categorize appointments, events, and meetings; to control the way they appear in Outlook 2010; and to perform automatic processing. Colored labels allow you to identify quickly and visually different types of events on your calendar.

In addition to managing your own schedule, you can delegate control of the schedule to someone else, such as your assistant. The assistant can modify your schedule, request meetings, respond to meeting invitations, and otherwise act on your behalf regarding your calendar. Not only can others view your schedule to plan meetings and appointments (with the exception of items marked personal), but also you can publish your schedule to the web to allow others to view it over an intranet or the Internet, as shown in Figure 2-6.

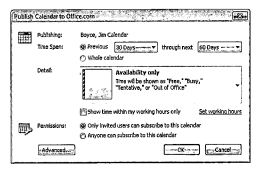

Figure 2-6 You can publish your schedule to the web easily.

Contact Management

Being able to manage contact information—names, addresses, and phone numbers—is critical to other aspects of Outlook 2010, such as scheduling and messaging. Outlook 2010 makes it easy to manage contacts and offers flexibility in the type of information that you maintain. In addition to basic information, you can also store a contact's fax number, cell phone number, pager number, web page Uniform Resource Locator (URL), and more, as shown in Figure 2-7. You can even include a picture for the contact.

In addition to using contact information to address email messages, you can initiate phone calls using the contacts list, track calls to contacts in the journal, add notes for each contact, use the contacts list to create mail merge documents, and perform other tasks. The Contacts folder also provides a means for storing a contact's digital certificate, which you can use to exchange encrypted messages for security. Adding a contact's certificate is easy—when you receive a digitally signed message from the contact, Outlook 2010 adds the certificate to the contact's entry. You can also import a certificate from a file provided by the contact.

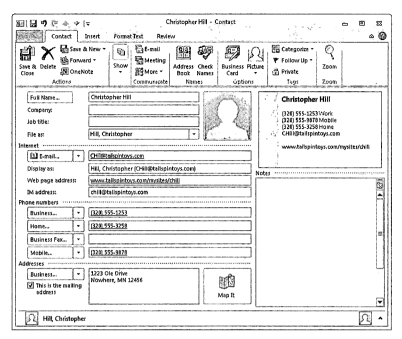

Figure 2-7 You can manage a wealth of information about each contact with Outlook 2010.

For details about digital signatures and encryption, see the section "Message Encryption," on page 39. For complete details on how to use the journal, see Chapter 22, "Tracking Documents and Activities with the Journal."

In an Exchange Server environment, Outlook integrates with the organization's Active Directory Domain Services (AD DS) and Exchange Server Global Address List (GAL), enabling you to browse and select addresses or contact information for other people in your organization easily. There is nothing you need to do in Outlook to make these contacts or addresses available—all the necessary configuration happens automatically when you add an Exchange Server account to your profile, and the GAL downloads to your computer when you open Outlook.

As with calendars, you can also work with SharePoint Contacts lists from within Outlook, enabling you to view and manage a shared Contacts list in Outlook. Changes that occur in Outlook appear in SharePoint, and vice versa.

Task Management

Managing your workday usually includes keeping track of the tasks you need to perform and assigning tasks to others. Outlook 2010 makes it easy to manage your task list. You assign a due date, start date, priority, category, and other properties to each task, which makes it easier for you to manage those tasks, as shown in Figure 2-8. As with meetings and appointments, Outlook 2010 keeps you informed and on track by issuing reminders for each task. You control whether the reminder is used and the time and date it's generated, along with an optional, audible notification. You can designate a task as personal, preventing others from viewing the task in your schedule, just as you can with meetings and appointments. Tasks can be one-time or recurring events.

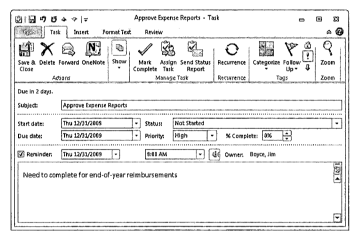

Figure 2-8 Use Outlook 2010 to manage tasks.

If you manage other people, Outlook 2010 makes it easy to assign tasks to other Outlook 2010 users. When you create a task, simply click Assign Task, and Outlook 2010 prompts you for the assignee's email address. You can choose to keep a copy of the updated task in your own task list and receive a status report when the task is complete.

To learn more about how to assign tasks, see the section "Assigning Tasks to Others," on page 547.

Tasks are another area of integration with SharePoint. You can use Outlook to view and manage tasks in a SharePoint Tasks list, including creating new tasks in SharePoint from Outlook. This means you don't have to open a browser and navigate to the SharePoint site—just open the SharePoint list in Outlook and create the task as you would any other task in Outlook.

Tracking with the Outlook Journal

Keeping track of events is an important part of managing your workday, and the Outlook 2010 journal makes it simple. The Journal folder allows you to keep track of the contacts that you make (phone calls, email messages, and so on), meeting actions, task requests and responses, and other actions for selected contacts, as shown in Figure 2-9. You can also use the journal to track your work in other Office system applications, giving you a way to track the time that you spend on various documents and their associated projects. You can have Outlook 2010 add journal items automatically based on settings that you specify, and you can also add items manually to your journal.

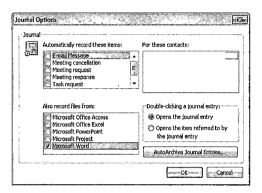

Figure 2-9 Configure your journal using these Outlook 2010 options.

When you view the journal, you can double-click a journal entry to either open the entry or open the items referred to by the entry, depending on how you have configured the journal. You can also configure the journal to archive items automatically in the default archive folder or in a folder you choose, or you can have Outlook 2010 regularly delete items from the journal, cleaning out items that are older than a specified length of time. Outlook 2010 can use group policies to control the retention of journal entries, allowing administrators to manage journaling and data retention consistently throughout an organization.

Organizing Your Thoughts with Notes

With Outlook 2010, you can keep track of your thoughts and tasks by using the Notes folder. Each note can function as a stand-alone window, allowing you to view notes on your desktop outside Outlook 2010, as shown in Figure 2-10. You can copy or move them to other folders, including your desktop, or easily share them with others through network sharing or email. You can also incorporate the contents of notes into other applications or other Outlook 2010 folders by using the Clipboard. For example, you might copy a note regarding a contact to that person's contact entry. As you can with other Outlook 2010 items, you can assign categories to notes to help you organize and view them.

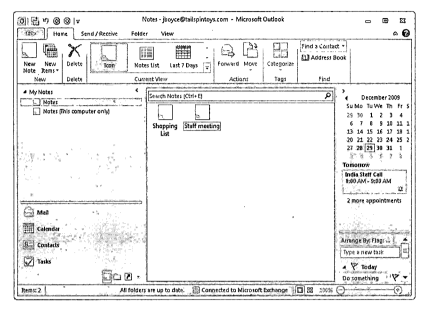

Figure 2-10 Use notes to keep track of miscellaneous information.

Although the Notes folder has always been a part of Outlook, its usefulness is honestly limited for most people. You should consider instead using Microsoft OneNote to manage your notes and related data. OneNote is a separate application included with Office that lets you organize notes into multiple notebooks with multiple sections, complete with graphics, audio, video, formulas, and much more. Check out Chapter 23, "Notes and One-Note Integration," for details on the integration features between OneNote and Outlook.

How Outlook Stores Data

If you work with Outlook 2010 primarily as a user, understanding how the program stores data helps you use it effectively to organize and manage your data on a daily basis, including storing and archiving Outlook 2010 items as needed. If you're charged with supporting other Outlook 2010 users, understanding how Outlook 2010 stores data allows you to help others create and manage their folders and ensure the security and integrity of their data. Finally, because data storage is the foundation of all the features of Outlook 2010, understanding where and how the program stores data is critical if you're creating Outlook 2010–based applications—for example, a data entry form that uses Outlook 2010 as the mechanism for posting the data to a public folder.

You're probably familiar with folders (directories) in the file system. You use these folders to organize applications and documents. For example, the Program Files folder in the Microsoft Windows operating system is the default location for most applications that you install on the system, and the My Documents folder (called Documents in Windows Vista and Windows 7) serves as the default location for document files. You create these types of folders in Windows Explorer.

Outlook 2010 also uses folders to organize data, but these folders are different from your file system folders. Rather than existing individually on your system's hard disk, these folders exist within the Outlook 2010 file structure or within your Exchange Server mailbox. You view and manage these folders within the Outlook 2010 interface, not in Windows Explorer. Think of Outlook 2010 folders as windows into your Outlook 2010 data rather than as individual elements that exist on disk. By default, Outlook 2010 includes several folders, as shown in Figure 2-11.

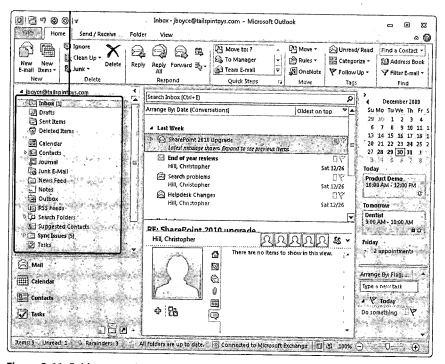

Figure 2-11 Folders organize your data in Outlook 2010.

Personal Folders—.pst Files

If your Outlook 2010 folders aren't stored as individual folders on your system's hard disk, where are they? The answer to that question depends on how you configure Outlook 2010. As in earlier versions of Outlook, you can use a set of personal folders to store your Outlook 2010 data. Outlook 2010 uses the .pst extension for a set of personal folders, but you specify the file's name when you configure Outlook 2010. For example, you might use your name as the file name to help you easily identify the file. The default .pst file contains your Contacts, Calendar, Tasks, and other folders.

You can use multiple .pst files, adding additional personal folders to your Outlook 2010 configuration, as shown in Figure 2-12. For example, you might want to create another set of folders to separate your personal information from work-related data. As you'll learn in Chapter 3, you can add personal folders to your Outlook 2010 configuration simply by adding another .pst file to your profile.

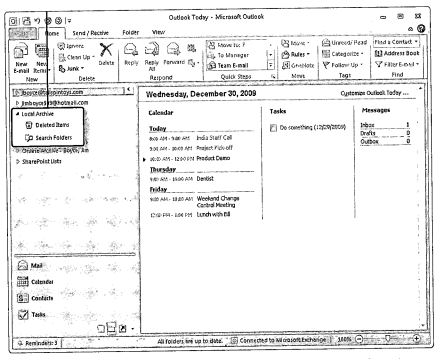

Figure 2-12 You can add multiple sets of folders to your Outlook 2010 configuration.

Options for Working Offline

If you use Outlook 2010 with Exchange Server and do not use local .pst files to store your data, you have two options for working with your mailbox data offline, and these methods differ only in the way synchronization occurs.

An .ost file allows you to work offline. The .ost file acts as an offline copy of your data store on the computer running Exchange Server. When you're working offline, changes that you make to contacts, messages, and other Outlook 2010 items and folders occur in the offline store. When you go online again, Outlook 2010 synchronizes the changes between the offline store and your Exchange Server store when you perform a send/receive for the account. For example, if you've deleted messages from your offline store, Outlook 2010 deletes those same messages from your online store when you synchronize the folders. Any new messages in your Inbox on the server are added to your offline store. Synchronization is a two-way process, providing the most up-to-date copy of your data in both locations, ensuring that changes made in each are reflected in the other.

For detailed information about important offline and remote access topics, see Chapter 41, "Working Offline and Remotely." For a discussion of the differences between remote mail and offline use, see Chapter 15, "Receiving Messages Selectively."

Outlook 2010 includes a feature called Cached Exchange Mode. This mode works much the same as offline synchronization with an .ost file. In fact, Outlook 2010 uses an .ost file for Cached Exchange Mode. The main difference is that with Cached Exchange Mode, Outlook 2010 always works from the copy of your mailbox that is cached locally on your computer. Outlook 2010 then automatically handles synchronization between your offline cache mailbox and the mailbox stored on the server. With Cached Exchange Mode, you don't need to worry about synchronizing the two—Outlook 2010 detects when the server is available and updates your locally cached copy automatically.

When you create an Outlook 2010 storage file, Outlook 2010 defaults to a specific location for the file. The default location is the Local Settings\Application Data\Microsoft\Outlook (Windows Vista) or AppData\Local\Microsoft\Outlook (Windows 7) folder of your user profile.

INSIDE OUT   Find your data store

If you're not sure where your Outlook storage files are, open Outlook and click File, Account Settings, and Account Settings, and then click the Data Files tab. This tab lists the data files associated with your current Outlook profile, as well as their location on disk.

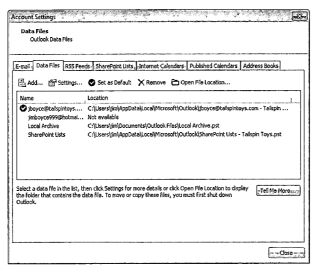

Figure 2-13   Locate your data files by using the Data Files tab of your account settings.

Understanding Messaging Protocols and Standards

A messaging protocol is a mechanism that messaging servers and applications use to transfer messages. Being able to use a specific email service requires that your application support the same protocols the server uses. To configure Outlook 2010 as a messaging client, you need to understand the various protocols supported by Outlook 2010 and the types of servers that employ each type. The following sections provide an overview of these protocols.

SMTP/POP3

Simple Mail Transport Protocol (SMTP) is a standards-based protocol used for transferring messages and is the primary mechanism that Internet- and intranet-based email servers use to transfer messages. It's also the mechanism that Outlook 2010 uses to connect to a mail server to send messages for an Internet account. SMTP is the protocol used by an Internet email account for outgoing messages.

SMTP operates by default on TCP port 25. When you configure an Internet-based email account, the port on which the server is listening for SMTP determines the outgoing mail server setting. Unless your email server uses a different port, you can use the default port value of 25. If you want to use Outlook 2010 for an existing Internet mail account, confirm the SMTP server name and port settings with your ISP.

POP3 is a standards-based protocol that clients can use to retrieve messages from any mail server that supports it. Outlook 2010 uses this protocol when retrieving messages from an Internet- or intranet-based mail server that supports POP3 mailboxes. Nearly all ISP-based mail servers use POP3. Exchange Server also supports the use of POP3 for retrieving mail.

POP3 operates on TCP port 110 by default. Unless your server uses a nonstandard port configuration, you can leave the port setting as is when defining a POP3 mail account.

To learn how to set up an Internet email account for an SMTP/POP3 server, including setting port numbers, see the section "Using Internet POP3 Email Accounts," on page 160.

IMAP

Like POP3, IMAP is a standards-based protocol that enables message transfer. However, IMAP offers some significant differences from POP3. For example, POP3 is primarily designed as an offline protocol, which means that you retrieve your messages from a server and download them to your local message store (such as your local Outlook 2010 folders). IMAP is designed primarily as an online protocol, which allows a remote user to manipulate messages and message folders on the server without downloading them. This is particularly helpful for users who need to access the same remote mailbox from multiple locations, such as home and work, using different computers. Because the messages remain on the server, IMAP eliminates the need for message synchronization.

INSIDE OUT   Keep POP3 messages on the server

IMAP by default leaves your messages on the server. If needed, you can configure a POP3 account in Outlook 2010 to leave a copy of messages on the server, allowing you to retrieve those messages later from another computer. (To learn how to configure a POP3 account, see the section "Using Internet POP3 Email Accounts," on page 160.) IMAP offers other advantages over POP3 as well. For example, with IMAP, you can search for messages on the server using a variety of message attributes, such as sender, message size, or message header. IMAP also offers better support for attachments because it can separate attachments from the header and text portion of a message. This is particularly useful with multipart Multipurpose Internet Mail Extensions (MIME) messages, allowing you to read a message without downloading the attachments so that you can decide which attachments you want to retrieve. With POP3, the entire message must be downloaded.

Security is another advantage of IMAP because it uses a challenge-response mechanism to authenticate the user for mailbox access. This prevents the user's password from being transmitted as clear text across the network, as it is with POP3.

IMAP support allows you to use Outlook 2010 as a client to an IMAP-compliant email server. Although IMAP provides for server-side storage and the ability to create additional mail folders on the server, it does not offer some of the same features as Exchange Server, or even POP3. For example, you can't store contact, calendar, or other nonmessage folders on the server. Also, special folders such as Drafts and Deleted Items can't be stored on the IMAP server. Even with these limitations, however, IMAP serves as a flexible protocol and surpasses POP3 in capability. Unless a competing standard appears in the future, it is possible that IMAP will eventually replace POP3. However, ISPs generally like POP3 because users' email is moved to their own computers, freeing space on the mail server and reducing disk space management problems. For that reason alone, don't look for IMAP to replace POP3 in the near future.

For information about other advantages and disadvantages of IMAP and how they affect Outlook 2010, see the section "Using IMAP Accounts," on page 169. For additional technical information about IMAP, go to www.imap.org.

MAPI

MAPI is a Microsoft-developed application programming interface (and) that facilitates communication between mail-enabled applications. MAPI support makes it possible for other applications to send and receive messages using Outlook 2010. For example, some third-party fax applications can place incoming faxes in your Inbox through MAPI. As another example, a third-party MAPI-aware application could read and write to your Outlook 2010 Address Book through MAPI calls. MAPI is not a message protocol, but understanding its function in Outlook 2010 helps you install, configure, and use MAPI-aware applications to integrate Outlook 2010.

LDAP

Lightweight Directory Access Protocol (LDAP) was designed to serve with less overhead and fewer resource requirements than its precursor, Directory Access Protocol. LDAP is a standards-based protocol that allows clients to query data in a directory service over a Transmission Control Protocol (TCP) connection. For example, Windows Server uses LDAP as the primary means for querying AD DS. Exchange Server supports LDAP queries, allowing clients to look up address information for subscribers on the server. Other directory services on the Internet employ LDAP to implement searches of their databases.

Like Outlook Express, Windows Mail, and Windows Live Mail, Outlook 2010 allows you to add directory service accounts that use LDAP as their protocol to query directory services for email addresses, phone numbers, and other information regarding subscribers.

To learn how to add and configure an LDAP directory service in Outlook 2010, see the section "Configuring a Directory Service Account in Outlook," on page 423.

RSS

Real Simple Syndication (RSS) is a set of web feed formats that enable publishing and updating of frequently updated content. Outlook 2010 can function as an RSS feed reader, pulling in news items, blog posts, and other data from online sites and services that offer the RSS feeds. See Chapter 16, "Using RSS Feeds," to learn more about RSS and Outlook 2010.

MIME

MIME is a standard specification for defining file formats used to exchange email, files, and other documents across the Internet or an intranet. Each of the many MIME types defines the content type of the data contained in the attachment. MIME maps the content to a specific file type and extension, allowing the email client to pass the MIME attachment to an external application for processing. For example, if you receive a message containing a WAV audio file, Outlook 2010 passes the file to the default WAV file player on your system.

S/MIME

Secure/Multipurpose Internet Mail Extensions (S/MIME) is a standard that allows email applications to send digitally signed and encrypted messages. S/MIME is therefore a mechanism through which Outlook 2010 permits you to include digital signatures with messages to ensure their authenticity and to encrypt messages to prevent unauthorized access to them.

For a detailed discussion of using Outlook 2010 to send digitally signed and encrypted messages, as well as other security-related issues such as virus protection and security zones, see Chapter 14, "Securing Your System, Messages, and Identity."

MHTML

MIME HTML (MHTML) represents MIME encapsulation of HTML documents. MHTML allows you to send and receive web pages and other HTML-based documents and to embed images directly in the body of a message instead of attaching them to the message. See the preceding two sections for an explanation of MIME.

iCalendar, vCalendar, and vCard

iCalendar, vCalendar, and vCard are Internet-based standards that provide a means for people to share calendar information and contact information across the Internet. The iCalendar standard allows calendar and scheduling applications to share free/busy information with other applications that support iCalendar. The vCalendar standard provides a mechanism for vCalendar-compliant applications to exchange meeting requests across the Internet. The vCard standard allows applications to share contact information as Internet vCards (electronic business cards). Outlook 2010 supports these standards to share information and interact with other messaging and scheduling applications across the Internet.

Security Provisions in Outlook

Outlook 2010 provides several features for ensuring the security of your data, messages, and identity. This section presents a brief overview of security features in Outlook 2010 to give you a basic understanding of the issues involved, with references to other locations in the book that offer more detailed information about these topics.

Protection Against Web Beacons

Many spammers (people who send unsolicited email) use web beacons to validate email addresses. The spammers send HTML-based email messages that contain links to external content on a website (the web beacon), and when the recipient's email client displays the remote content, the site validates the email address. The spammer then knows that the address is a valid one and continues to send messages to it.

Outlook 2010 blocks web beacons, displaying a red X instead of the external image. You can view blocked content selectively, on a per-message basis, or you can configure Outlook 2010 to view all content but control access to HTML content in other ways. You can also turn off web beacon blocking, if you want, and control external HTML content in other ways.

See Chapter 14 for an explanation of how to configure HTML message-handling options.

Attachment and Virus Security

You probably are aware that a virus is malicious code that infects your system and typically causes some type of damage. The action caused by a virus can be as innocuous as displaying a message or as damaging as deleting data from your hard disk. One especially insidious form of virus, called a worm, spreads itself automatically, often by mailing itself to every contact in the infected system's address book. Because of the potential damage that can

be caused by viruses and worms, it is critically important to guard against malicious code entering your system.

There are multiple possible points of defense against viruses and worms. For example, your network team might deploy perimeter protection in the form of one or more firewalls that scan traffic coming into your network and leaving it. Your mail administrators might have virus protection at the server level. You probably have a local antivirus client that checks the files on your computer and potentially also checks attachments that come into your Inbox. All of these are important options for protecting your network and your computer from infection.

CAUTION

Your virus scanner is only as good as its definition file. New viruses crop up every day, so it's critical that you have an up-to-date virus definition file and put in place a strategy to ensure that your virus definitions are always current.

Most viruses and worms propagate through email attachments, so to provide protection against them, Outlook 2010 controls how attachments are handled, blocking certain types of files (such as program executables) from being opened at all. For selected other files that offer less risk, Outlook requires you to save the file to disk and open it from there, rather than from Outlook. These behaviors and the types of files applicable for each can be controlled either by the end user or by an administrator, depending on your environment.

See Chapter 33, "Security and Virus Protection," to learn how to configure attachment blocking in Outlook.

An additional security feature that is new in Office 2010 is Protected View. When you open an attachment that is an Office file type (a Microsoft Word document, a Microsoft Excel spreadsheet, etc.), the document opens in a separate sandbox instance of the application. For example, assume that you have Word open and are working on a document that you created. Then, you switch over to Outlook and open a Word document that arrived as an attachment to an email. Word opens a separate version to display that attachment, but this sandbox version of Word operates with greater restrictions and fewer rights and privileges than the version that you are using to modify your own document. You can't save the file or edit it while it is running in this version, so the application displays a banner across the top labeled Protected View (see Figure 2-14), and provides a button labeled Enable Editing that, when clicked, enables you to edit the document, save it, and so on.

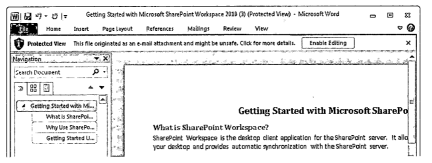

Figure 2-14 Protected View is actually a separate, lower-privileged instance of the application.

The combination of attachment blocking and Protected View will protect your computer from a wide variety of potential threats, but that combination can't protect against all threats. For that reason, you should ensure that you have an updated antivirus client running on your computer as well as at your mail server. Adding protection at the perimeter of the network is a good idea as well.

Digital Signatures

Outlook 2010 allows you to add a certificate-based digital signature to a message to validate your identity to the message recipient. Because the signature is derived from a certificate that is issued to you and that you share with the recipient, the recipient can be guaranteed that the message originated with you, rather than with someone trying to impersonate your identity.

For information about how to obtain a certificate and use it to sign your outgoing messages digitally, see the section "Protecting Messages with Digital Signatures," on page 360.

In addition to signing your outgoing messages, you can use secure message receipts that notify you that your message has been verified by the recipient's system. The lack of a return receipt indicates that the recipient's system did not validate your identity. In such a case, you can contact the recipient to make sure that he or she has a copy of your digital signature.

> **Note**
> Although you can configure Outlook 2010 to send a digital signature to a recipient, there is no guarantee that the recipient will add the digital signature to his or her contacts list. Until the recipient adds the signature, digitally signed messages are not validated, and the recipient cannot read encrypted messages from you.

Message Encryption

Where the possibility of interception exists (whether someone intercepts your message before it reaches the intended recipient or someone else at the recipient's end tries to read the message), Outlook 2010 message encryption can help you keep prying eyes away from sensitive messages. This feature also relies on your digital signature to encrypt the message and to allow the recipient to decrypt and read the message. Someone who receives the message without first having the appropriate encryption key from your certificate installed on his or her system sees a garbled message.

To learn how to obtain a certificate and use it to encrypt your outgoing messages, as well as how to read encrypted messages you receive from others, see the section "Encrypting Messages," on page 389.

Options for Starting Outlook

Office offers several options to control startup, either through command-line switches or other methods. You can choose to have Outlook 2010 open forms, turn off the Reading pane, select a profile, and perform other tasks automatically when the program starts. The following sections describe some of the options that you can specify.

Normal Startup

When you install Outlook 2010, Setup places a Microsoft Outlook 2010 icon on the Start menu. You can start Outlook 2010 normally by clicking the icon. You also can start Outlook 2010 by using the Programs menu (choose Start, All Programs, Microsoft Office, and Microsoft Outlook 2010).

Outlook uses a profile to store account settings and configure Outlook for your email servers, directory services, address books, data files, and other settings. You can configure Outlook to either prompt you to choose a profile (if multiple profiles exist) or have it use a specific one by default. Figure 2-15 shows Outlook prompting to choose a profile.

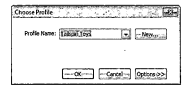

Figure 2-15 Outlook 2010 prompts you to choose a profile at startup.

To use an existing profile, simply select it in the drop-down list in the Choose Profile dialog box and then click OK. Click New to create a new profile (covered in Chapter 3). Click Options in the Choose Profile dialog box, shown in Figure 2-13, to display the option Set As Default Profile. Select this option to specify the selected profile as the default profile, which will appear in the drop-down list by default in subsequent Outlook 2010 sessions. For example, if you maintain separate personal and work profiles and your personal profile always appears in the drop-down list, but you want the work profile to show up by default instead, select your work profile and then choose Set As Default Profile to make the work profile the default.

For an in-depth discussion of creating and configuring profiles, see the section "Understanding Profiles," on page 52. The details of configuring service providers (such as for Exchange Server) are covered in various chapters where appropriate—for example, Chapter 7, "Using Internet Mail Accounts," explains how to configure POP3 and IMAP accounts, and Chapter 39, "Configuring the Exchange Server Client," explains how to configure Exchange Server accounts.

Safe Mode Startup

Safe mode is a startup mode available in Outlook 2010 and the other Office system applications. Safe mode makes it possible for Office system applications to recover automatically from specific errors during startup, such as a problem with an add-in or a corrupt registry setting. Safe mode allows Outlook 2010 to detect the problem and either correct it or bypass it by isolating the source.

In certain situations, you might want to force Outlook 2010 into safe mode when it would otherwise start normally—for example, if you want to prevent add-ins or customized toolbars or command bars from loading. To start Outlook 2010 (or any other Office system application) in safe mode, hold down the Ctrl key and start the program. Outlook 2010 detects the Ctrl key and asks whether you want to start Outlook 2010 in safe mode. Click Yes to start in safe mode or No to start normally.

See the section "Startup Switches," on page 45, to learn how to use safe mode switches as an option to holding down the Ctrl key when starting Outlook.

If Outlook is running in safe mode and you want to view and/or enable a disabled add-in, click File, Options, and click Add-Ins in the left pane of the Outlook Options dialog box. Near the bottom of the dialog box, choose Disabled Items from the Manage drop-down list, then click Go. Outlook displays the Disabled Items dialog box, which lists the disabled items and lets you enable them. Given that Outlook disabled the items for a reason, you should generally re-enable them only if you know that they will not cause a problem.

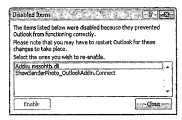

Figure 2-16 Use the Disbaled Items dialog box to view and manage disabled items.

If you start an application in safe mode, you cannot perform certain actions in the application. The following is a summary of these actions (not all of which apply to Outlook 2010):

- Templates can't be saved.

- The last used web page is not loaded (Microsoft FrontPage).

- Customized toolbars and command bars are not opened. Customizations that you make in safe mode can't be changed.

- The AutoCorrect list isn't loaded, nor can changes that you make to AutoCorrect in safe mode be saved.

- Recovered documents are not opened automatically.

- No smart tags are loaded, and new smart tags can't be saved.

- Command-line options other than /a and /n are ignored.

- You can't save files to the Alternate Startup Directory.

- You can't save preferences.

- Additional features and programs (such as add-ins) are not loaded automatically.

To start Outlook 2010 normally, simply shut down the program and start it again without pressing the Ctrl key.

Starting Outlook Automatically

If you're like most Microsoft Office system users, you work in Outlook 2010 a majority of the time. Because Outlook 2010 is such an important aspect of your workday, you might want it to start automatically when you log on to your computer, saving you the trouble of starting it later. Although you have a few options for starting Outlook 2010 automatically, the best solution is to place a shortcut to Outlook 2010 in your Startup folder.

To start Outlook 2010 automatically when you start Windows, simply drag the Outlook icon from the Start menu or Quick Launch bar to the Startup folder in the Start menu.

INSIDE OUT   Create a new Outlook 2010 shortcut

If you have no Outlook 2010 icon on the desktop, you can use the Outlook 2010 executable to create a shortcut. Open Windows Explorer and browse to the folder \ Program Files\Microsoft Office\Office14. Create a shortcut to the executable Outlook. exe. Right-click the Outlook.exe file, and then choose Create Shortcut. Windows asks whether you want to create a shortcut on the desktop. Click Yes to create the shortcut.

INSIDE OUT   Change the Outlook Shortcut Properties

If you want to change the way Outlook 2010 starts from the shortcut in your Startup folder (for example, so you can add command switches), you need only change the shortcut's properties. For details, see the section "Changing the Outlook Shortcut," below.

Pinning Outlook to the Start Menu and Taskbar (Windows 7)

Windows 7 enables you to pin programs to the Start menu and Windows taskbar, making the programs easily accessible. You can then simply click the program's icon on the Start menu or taskbar to open the program. To pin Outlook to the Windows 7 Start menu or taskbar, click Start, All Programs, and Microsoft Office, and then right-click Microsoft Outlook 2010 and choose Pin To Start Menu or Pin To Taskbar.

Changing the Outlook Shortcut

Let's assume that you've created a shortcut to Outlook 2010 on your Quick Launch bar or in another location so that you can start Outlook 2010 quickly. Why change the shortcut? By adding switches to the command that starts Outlook 2010, you can customize the way that the application starts and functions for the current session. You can also control the Outlook 2010 startup window state (normal, minimized, or maximized) through the shortcut's properties. For example, you might want Outlook 2010 to start automatically when you log on, but you want it to start minimized. In this situation, you would create a shortcut to Outlook 2010 in your Startup folder and then modify the shortcut so that Outlook 2010 starts minimized.

> **Note**
> You cannot add switches to the Outlook icon that is pinned to the Start menu or the
> Windows 7 taskbar. Instead, you must create a shortcut on the desktop or in another
> folder, such as the Quick Launch taskbar, and modify the settings there.

To change the properties for a shortcut, locate the shortcut, right-click its icon, and then
choose Properties. You should see a Properties page similar to the one shown in Figure
2-17.

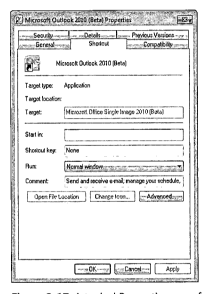

Figure 2-17 A typical Properties page for an Outlook 2010 shortcut.

The following list summarizes the options on the Shortcut tab of the Properties page:

- **Target Type**   This read-only property specifies the type for the shortcut's target,
  which in the example shown in Figure 2-17 is Application.

- **Target Location**   This read-only property specifies the directory location of the target executable.

- **Target**   This property specifies the command to execute when the shortcut is
  executed. The default Outlook 2010 command is "C:\Program Files\Microsoft Office\
  Office14\Outlook.exe" /recycle. The path could vary if you have installed Office in a
  different folder. The path to the executable must be enclosed in quotation marks, and

any additional switches must be added to the right, outside the quotation marks. See the section "Startup Switches," on page 45, to learn about additional switches that you can use to start Outlook 2010.

- **Start In** This property specifies the startup directory for the application.

- **Shortcut Key** Use this property to assign a shortcut key to the shortcut, which allows you to start Outlook 2010 by pressing the key combination. Simply click in the Shortcut Key box, and then press the keystroke to assign it to the shortcut.

- **Run** Use this property to specify the startup window state for Outlook 2010. You can choose Normal Window, Minimized, or Maximized.

- **Comment** Use this property to specify an optional comment. The comment appears in the shortcut's tooltip when you position the mouse pointer over the shortcut's icon. For example, if you use the Run As Different User option, you might include mention of that in the Comment box to help you distinguish this shortcut from another that starts Outlook 2010 in the default context.

- **Open File Location** Click this button to open the folder containing the Outlook.exe executable file.

- **Change Icon** Click this button to change the icon assigned to the shortcut. By default, the icon comes from the Outlook.exe executable, which contains other icons that you can assign to the shortcut. You also can use other .ico, .exe, and .dll files to assign icons. You'll find several additional icons in Moricons.dll and Shell32.dll, both located in the %SystemRoot%\System32 folder.

- **Advanced** Click this button to access the following options:

- **Run In Separate Memory Space** This option is selected by default and can't be changed for Outlook 2010. This provides crash protection for other applications and for the operating system.

- **Run as Administrator** Select this option to run Outlook 2010 in the administrator user context.

When you're satisfied with the shortcut's properties, click OK to close the Properties dialog box.

Startup Switches

Outlook 2010 supports a number of command-line switches that modify the way the program starts and functions. Although you can issue the Outlook.exe command with switches from a command prompt, it's generally more useful to specify switches through a shortcut, particularly if you want to use the same set of switches more than once. Table 2-1 lists some of the startup switches that you can use to modify the way Outlook 2010 starts and functions.

For an explanation of how to modify a shortcut to add command-line switches, see the section "Changing the Outlook Shortcut," on page 42. See "Command-Line Switches for Microsoft Outlook 2010" in the Outlook Help content for a complete list of switches.

Table 2-1 Startup Switches and Their Uses

Switch	Use
/a <filename>	Opens a message form with the attachment specified by <filename>
/c ipm.activity	Opens the journal entry form by itself
/c ipm.appointment	Opens the appointment form by itself
/c ipm.contact	Opens the contact form by itself
/c ipm.note	Opens the message form by itself
/c ipm.stickynote	Opens the note form by itself
/c ipm.task	Opens the task form by itself
/c <class>	Creates an item using the message class specified by <class>
/CheckClient	Performs a check to see whether Outlook 2010 is the default application for email, calendar, and contacts
/CleanFreeBusy	Regenerates free/busy schedule data
/CleanReminders	Regenerates reminders
/Safe	Starts Outlook without the Reading pane or toolbar customizations and with native and COM add-ins disabled
/safe:1	Starts Outlook with the Reading pane off
/safe:3	Starts Outlook with native and COM add-ins disabled

Choosing a Startup View

When you start Outlook 2010, it defaults to using the Inbox view, but you might prefer to use a different view or folder as the initial view. For example, if you use Outlook 2010 primarily for scheduling, you'll probably want Outlook 2010 to start in the Calendar folder. If you use Outlook 2010 mainly to manage contacts, you'll probably want it to start in the Contacts folder.

To specify the view that should appear when Outlook 2010 starts, follow these steps:

1. Start Outlook 2010, click the File tab, and then click Options.

2. Click Advanced to display the Advanced Options page, as shown in Figure 2-18.

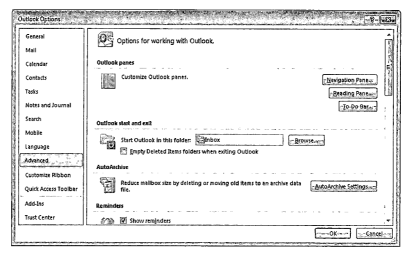

Figure 2-18. Use the Advanced Options dialog box to specify the Startup view.

3. Under Outlook Start And Exit, click Browse, select the folder that you want Outlook 2010 to open at startup, and click OK.

4. Click OK, and then close the dialog box.

If you switch Outlook 2010 to a different default folder and then want to restore Outlook Today as your default view, you can follow the preceding steps to restore Outlook Today as the default.

Simply select Outlook Today in the drop-down list or follow these steps with the Outlook Today window open:

1. Start Outlook 2010, and then open the Outlook Today view.

2. Click Customize Outlook Today at the top of the Outlook Today window.

3. In the resulting pane, select When Starting Go Directly To Outlook Today, and then click Save Changes.

Creating Shortcuts to Start New Outlook Items

In some cases, you might want to create new Outlook 2010 items directly from the Start menu, the taskbar, or a shortcut icon without first opening the Outlook program window. For example, perhaps you would like an icon that starts a new email message and another icon that starts a new appointment item. With Outlook 2010, you can access these items right from the Start menu without any additional setup. Just click Start, pause the mouse over Outlook 2010 (or click the Expand button at the right of the menu), and choose the type of item that you want to create from the cascading menu that appears. If Outlook is pinned to the taskbar in Windows 7, you can also right-click the Outlook icon in the taskbar and, from the Tasks section of the menu, choose the type of Outlook item to create.

You can also create a shortcut to a mailto: item on the desktop or on the Quick Launch bar to make it easy to create a new email message. Here's how to create the shortcut:

1. Right-click the desktop, and then choose New, Shortcut.

2. In the Create Shortcut dialog box, type mailto: as the item to start, and then click Next.

3. Type New Mail Message as the shortcut name, and then click Finish.

4. Drag the shortcut to the Quick Launch bar to make it quickly accessible without minimizing all applications.

When you double-click the shortcut, Outlook 2010 starts and prompts you for a profile unless a default profile has been set. However, only the new message form appears—the rest of Outlook 2010 stays hidden, running in the background.

You can use the Target property of an Outlook 2010 shortcut to create other types of Outlook 2010 items. Refer to the section "Changing the Outlook Shortcut," on page 42, to learn how to create an Outlook 2010 shortcut. See Table 2-1 on page 45 for the switches that open specific Outlook 2010 forms. For example, the following two shortcuts start a new message and a new appointment, respectively:

```
"C:\Program Files\Microsoft Office\Office12\Outlook.exe" /c ipm.note
```

```
"C:\Program Files\Microsoft Office\Office12\Outlook.exe" /c ipm.appointment
```

> **Note**
>
> You can use the /a switch to open a new message form with an attachment. The following example starts a new message and attaches the file named Picture.jpg:
>
> "C:\Program Files\Microsoft Office\Office14\Outlook.exe" /a Picture.jpg

B ECAUSE Microsoft Outlook 2010 has so many features, configuring the program—particularly for first-time or inexperienced users—can be a real challenge. However, after you master the basic concepts and experiment with the configuration process, it quickly becomes second nature.

This chapter examines Outlook 2010 setup issues, including what you see the first time you start Outlook 2010 and how to use the Add New Account Wizard to create, modify, and test email accounts. You'll also learn about user profiles, including how to create and modify them, how to use multiple profiles for different identities, how to copy profiles, and how to configure profile properties.

After you have a solid understanding of profiles, you're ready to tackle configuring the many email and data file services that Outlook 2010 offers. This chapter discusses configuring both online and offline storage and will help you add, modify, and remove personal message stores (personal folders) for a profile.

In addition, you'll learn how to configure Outlook 2010 to maintain an offline copy of your Microsoft Exchange Server mailbox and folders so that you can work with your account while you are disconnected from the network. You'll also learn how to change the storage location for your data and how to set options to control mail delivery.

Configuring Accounts and Services

Outlook 2010 provides a wizard to help simplify the setup and configuration of email accounts, data stores, and directory services. You use the Add New Account Wizard to add new email accounts. If you are starting Outlook for the first time, or Outlook can't find any profiles in the registry, Outlook will prompt you for a profile name and then show the Add New Account Wizard. In many cases, the wizard can configure your email account for you automatically after you give it only your name, email address, and mailbox password.

> **Note**
>
> If you upgraded to Outlook 2010 from an earlier version, Outlook 2010 automatically migrates your accounts, preferences, and data the first time you run it. This means that you don't have to perform any other tasks before working with Outlook 2010 unless you want to add other accounts or take advantage of features not provided by your current profile settings. In the following section, you'll learn how to add other services and accounts to your current Outlook 2010 profile.

Follow these steps to get started in setting up email accounts:

1. Start Outlook 2010. When the Outlook 2010 Startup Wizard appears, click Next. If the wizard does not start automatically, choose File, Account Settings, Account Settings, and then click New on the E-Mail tab.

2. On the E-Mail Accounts page, select Yes, indicating that you want to set up an email account, and then click Next.

3. The Add New Account Wizard displays, as shown in Figure 3-1. Fill in your email account information to have Outlook 2010 attempt to locate your email account automatically.

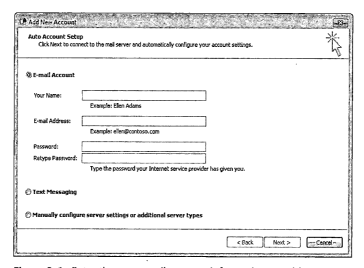

Figure 3-1. Enter the new email account information to add an account to Outlook 2010.

4. Type the password as required, and then click Next.

5. Click Finish on the last page of the wizard.

For a discussion of user profiles and how Outlook 2010 uses them to store your account settings, see the section "Understanding Profiles," on page 52.

Note

If you select Manually Configure Server Settings Or Additional Server Types on the Auto Account Setup page, the wizard prompts you for the email service type. The action that the wizard takes at this point depends on the type of account or server you select. Rather than cover account configuration here, outside the context of using each type of account, this book covers the specifics of each account type in the associated chapter. The following list helps you locate the appropriate chapter and section:

- Exchange Server   See Chapter 39, "Configuring the Exchange Server Client."

- Internet Email (POP3 or IMAP)   See the section "Using Internet POP3 Email Accounts," on page 160.

- Other (Fax Mail Transport or Hotmail)   See Chapter 7, "Using Internet Mail Accounts," to configure the Outlook Hotmail Connector. The Fax Mail Transport is not covered in detail in Microsoft Outlook 2010 Inside Out.

- Text Messaging (SMS)   See Chapter 43, "Making Outlook Mobile," to learn how to configure Short Message Service (SMS) accounts in Outlook.

You can easily add an email account to your Outlook 2010 profile after Outlook 2010 is installed. Just click File, and then click Add Account to start the Add New Account Wizard.

Note

If your system includes multiple profiles, select the one to which you want to add accounts. Open the Mail item from Control Panel. Click Show Profiles, locate and select your profile, click Properties, and then select E-Mail Accounts.

TROUBLESHOOTING

Outlook 2010 can't find your email server

If Outlook 2010 can't seem to locate your email server, you can check a handful of settings to determine the problem. First, make sure that your computer is connected to the network or the Internet, depending on where the server is located. If you're specifying a server on the Internet, make sure that you have specified the correct, fully qualified domain name (FQDN) of the server, such as mail.tailspintoys.com. If you specify the correct name but Outlook 2010 still can't find the server, try pinging the server by name. Open a command prompt window and type the following command, where <server> is the FQDN of the server:

PING <server>

If this results in an unknown host error, it's likely that the Domain Name System (DNS) is not configured or working properly on your computer (or the host name is wrong). Check the DNS settings for your Transmission Control Protocol/Internet Protocol (TCP/IP) protocol to make sure that you are specifying the correct DNS server. If you know the IP address of the server, ping the address. If you are able to ping the address but not the host name, you definitely have a DNS problem or are specifying the wrong DNS name. If the ping fails, you have a network connectivity or TCP/IP stack problem. If you are connecting to a computer running Exchange Server using Outlook Anywhere, you must be able to resolve the autoconfigure host for your Exchange Server environment (such as autoconfigure.tailspintoys.com). Try pinging that FQDN as well. If you still have no luck, consult your network support staff. Your configuration needs to be verified (and changed, if an incorrect value has been specified). If you have faulty hardware, it needs to be replaced.

Understanding Profiles

In Outlook 2010, profiles store the configuration of email accounts, data files, and other settings that you use in a given Outlook 2010 session. For example, your profile might include an Exchange Server account, an Internet mail account, and a set of personal folders. Outlook 2010 either prompts you to select a profile at startup or selects one automatically, depending on how you've configured it.

In most cases, you'll probably use only one profile and will configure Outlook 2010 to select it automatically. In some situations, however, multiple profiles can be useful. For example, you might prefer to keep your work and personal data completely separate on your notebook computer because of privacy concerns or office policies. In this situation, you maintain two profiles: one for your work data and a second for your personal data.

You then configure Outlook 2010 to prompt you to choose a profile at startup. The profile controls which set of data files and configuration settings are used for that specific session. For example, when you're working at the office, you use the office profile, and when you're using the computer at home, you use the personal profile.

It's important to understand that Outlook 2010 profiles have no relationship to the other types of profiles that you'll find in a Microsoft Windows operating system, which include hardware profiles and user profiles. Hardware profiles store hardware settings and allow you to switch between different hardware configurations without reconfiguring your system. User profiles store the unique working environment (Desktop, Documents, and so on) that you see when you log on to your computer. Outlook 2010 profiles, in contrast, apply only to Outlook 2010.

Note

Unless otherwise noted, the term profile in this book refers to an Outlook 2010 profile.

Each profile can contain multiple accounts and services, which means that you can work with different email servers at one time and use multiple sets of data files (such as a set of personal folders, or .pst files). The following list describes the items stored in an Outlook 2010 profile:

- **Services**   These include email accounts, directory services, and data files, along with their settings. For example, your profile might include an Exchange Server account, two Internet email accounts, a .pst file, and a directory service account. When these accounts are in a single profile, you can use all of them in the same Outlook 2010 session.

- **RSS feeds**   The profile stores the list of Really Simple Syndication (RSS) feeds that you have configured in Outlook. You don't need to open the profile to add the feed; instead, you can simply subscribe to it and allow Outlook to add the feed to your profile for you.

- **SharePoint lists**   SharePoint lists (such as calendars and task lists) that you have connected to Outlook appear in your profile. You add these from the SharePoint site, rather than from Outlook.

- **Internet calendars**   You can add Internet calendars to Outlook from your profile and view those calendars alongside your own.

- **Published calendars** The profile lists the calendars that you have published to Office Online or another online calendar server. You can change the account and other settings for the published calendar from the profile.

- **Delivery settings** The profile specifies the store to which Outlook 2010 should deliver new mail when it arrives. You also can specify the order in which Outlook 2010 processes accounts.

  To learn how to configure these delivery properties for a given profile, see the section "Setting Send and Delivery Options," on page 65.

- **Address settings** You can specify which address book Outlook 2010 displays first, where Outlook 2010 should store personal addresses, and the order of the address books that Outlook 2010 uses to check email addresses when the profile includes multiple address books.

  For detailed information about configuring and using address books in Outlook 2010, see Chapter 6, "Managing Address Books and Distribution Lists."

The first time you run Outlook 2010, it creates a profile named Outlook even if you don't add any email accounts to the profile. If you do add an email account, Outlook 2010 uses the name that you specify in the account settings as the name for the profile.

As mentioned earlier, you can use multiple profiles. The following sections explain how to create new profiles, copy existing profiles to new profiles, and perform related operations.

Creating Profiles

You don't have to be in Outlook 2010 to create a profile—in fact, you can't create one in Outlook 2010. You can create profiles through the Control Panel. In addition to specifying a profile name, you can also (optionally) add email and other services to the profile. You can create a profile from scratch or copy an existing profile to create a new one.

Creating a Profile from Scratch

When you have no existing Outlook profile or no profile that contains the accounts or settings you need, you must create a profile from scratch.

Follow these steps to create a new profile:

1. Open the Mail item from the Control Panel.

2. In the Mail Setup dialog box, shown in Figure 3-2, click Show Profiles. If no profiles exist, the Mail dialog box appears; continue with step 3.

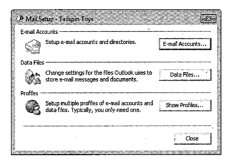

Figure 3-2 You access the current profile's settings as well as other profiles in the Mail Setup dialog box.

3. Click Add, specify a name for the profile in the New Profile dialog box, and then click OK.

4. The Add New Account Wizard starts. Add accounts and other services to the profile. Enter requested data, such as email address and password. To create a new profile without adding any services (useful if you are not using Outlook 2010 for email), click Cancel, and then click OK. In this situation, Outlook 2010 automatically creates a set of personal folders (a .pst file) to store your Outlook 2010 data.

Copying a Profile

In addition to creating profiles from scratch, you can also create a profile by copying an existing one. When you copy a profile, Outlook 2010 copies all the settings from the existing profile to the new one, including accounts and data files.

Follow these steps to copy an existing profile:

1. Open the Mail item from the Control Panel.

2. In the Mail Setup dialog box, click Show Profiles.

3. Select the existing profile that you want to use as the basis for the new profile, and then click Copy.

4. In the Copy Profile dialog box, specify a name for the new profile and click OK.

Modifying or Removing a Profile

You can modify a profile at any time to add or remove services. You can also remove a profile altogether if you no longer need it.

Follow these steps to modify or remove an existing profile:

1. Open the Mail item from the Control Panel.

2. In the Mail Setup dialog box, click Show Profiles.

3. Select the profile to be modified or removed.

4. Click Remove if you want to remove the profile, or click Properties to modify the profile settings.

Setting a Default Profile

You can configure Outlook 2010 either to use a specific profile automatically or to prompt you to select a profile at startup. If you use the same profile most of the time, you can configure Outlook to start automatically with that profile.

Follow these steps to specify the default profile and use it automatically when Outlook 2010 starts:

1. Open the Mail item from the Control Panel.

2. In the Mail Setup dialog box, click Show Profiles.

3. In the Mail dialog box, on the General tab, select Always Use This Profile, as shown in Figure 3-3. In the drop-down list, select the default profile that you want Outlook 2010 to use.

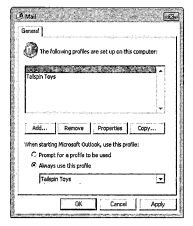

Figure 3-3 You can specify a default profile on the General tab.

4. Click OK.

Choosing a Profile

If you work with multiple profiles and switch profiles relatively often, you'll probably want to configure Outlook 2010 to prompt you to choose a profile at startup. This saves you the trouble of changing the default profile each time you want to switch. For example, assume that you use one profile for your personal accounts and another for your work accounts. Have Outlook 2010 prompt you for the profile when the program starts, rather than configuring the settings each time to specify the default profile.

Follow these steps to configure Outlook 2010 to prompt you to choose a profile:

1. Open the Mail item from the Control Panel.

2. In the Mail Setup dialog box, click Show Profiles.

3. In the Mail dialog box, select Always Use This Profile, select the profile that you want Outlook 2010 to display as the initial selection in the list, and then select Prompt For A Profile To Be Used.

4. Click OK.

INSIDE OUT   Set the initial profile

You probably noticed in step 3 of the preceding procedure that you enabled an option and then immediately disabled it by selecting Prompt For A Profile To Be Used. In effect, you've accomplished two tasks: setting the default profile and also configuring Outlook 2010 to prompt you for a profile. In the drop-down list, select the profile that you use most often, which saves you the step of selecting it when prompted at startup.

Configuring Online and Offline Data Storage

The preceding section explained how to add email account services and introduced data stores. This section provides a more detailed look at storage options in Outlook 2010 and shows how to configure those options.

Like earlier versions of Outlook, Outlook 2010 offers three options for storing data: your Exchange Server mailbox, .pst files, and offline folder (.ost) files. Like Outlook 2007, Outlook 2010 can use Cached Exchange Mode in conjunction with an .ost file to create a local copy of an Exchange Server mailbox. With Cached Exchange Mode, Outlook 2010 works from the cached local copy of the mailbox and automatically handles synchronization between the local profile and the server. Your mailbox is therefore always available, even when the server is not. When you connect to the network, Outlook 2010 automatically detects server connection status and synchronizes the Outlook 2010 folders.

See Chapter 39 to learn how to configure a client running Exchange Server, including enabling and disabling Cached Exchange Mode.

For detailed information about configuring and using IMAP accounts and how Outlook 2010 stores IMAP folders and messages, see the section "Using IMAP Accounts," on page 169.

An Outlook profile can contain multiple data files (also called stores). For example, if your profile contains an Exchange Server account and a POP3 account, the Exchange Server account probably uses an .ost file to store an offline copy of your Exchange Server store, and the POP3 account probably uses a .pst file for its items. Add an Internet Message Access Protocol (IMAP) account to that same profile and you'll get another .pst file to contain the items for that account. What's more, you can add a data file to a profile without associating it with an email account. For example, you might add a data file to use as an archive for old messages. In fact, Outlook does that very thing for you when you use its archive features (discussed in Chapter 29, "Managing Outlook Folders and Data").

Whatever your situation, you need to decide which type of data file is right for your situation (and how many you need). Let's get started with a look at .pst and .ost files.

Personal Folders and Offline Folders

A .pst file is a special Outlook file that stores Outlook folders and the items in those folders (emails, tasks, etc.). Each .pst file that you add to your profile or open separately shows up as a folder branch in the Navigation pane.

> **Note**
> The native .pst format of Outlook 2010 is not compatible with Outlook 2002 or earlier. The Outlook 2010 .pst format provides better support for multilingual Unicode data and eliminates the 2-GB file size limit imposed by the .pst format in Outlook 2002 and earlier.

You can password-protect .pst files for greater security, although utilities available on the web can bypass the password security. The .pst files offer encryption, providing an additional level of security. The .pst files do not have a built-in capability for synchronization with an Exchange Server mailbox, although you can work offline if a .pst file is configured as the default store location rather than the Exchange Server mailbox. If the Exchange Server mailbox is your default store (which is recommended), you must use an .ost file to work offline, whether in normal offline mode or in Cached Exchange Mode.

INSIDE OUT   Make your .pst file available when you're roaming

If you use a roaming Windows profile to provide a common desktop configuration regardless of the computer from which you log on, consider placing the .pst file (if you use one) on a network share that is available from all your logon locations. This eliminates the need to copy your .pst file across the network each time you log on, reducing network utilization and speeding logon time. Microsoft doesn't recommend placing .pst files on a network share because of performance issues, but we have found that this is a workable solution that offers enough advantages to balance any performance issues. Naturally, performance depends on the size of a user's mailbox and available network bandwidth. A great alternative is to enable and use Outlook Web Access (OWA) to access your mailbox.

You can choose the format of a .pst file only when you create the .pst file—you can't convert an existing .pst file to the new format. You can, however, simply export all the items in an existing .pst file to a new .pst file that does use the new format. Start Outlook 2007, choose File, Import And Export, and then follow the wizard's prompts to export to a .pst file. The wizard creates an Outlook 2007 native format .pst file by default.

To decide which .pst file format you should use, consider whether you need to use the .pst file with an earlier version of Outlook. If not, the Outlook 2010 native format is the best choice. If you need to export items from an Outlook 2010 .pst file to an earlier version, simply export the items to a .pst file that you created with an earlier version of Outlook, or create the pre–Outlook 2003 .pst file in Outlook 2007. To do so, choose the Office Outlook 97-2002 Personal Folders File option when creating the .pst file.

So much for .pst files—what about .ost files? An .ost file is essentially the same as a .pst file, except that Outlook uses the .ost file for offline storage and synchronizes changes up to Exchange Server when Outlook is connected to the server. The main difference is that the .ost file does not show up as a separate set of folders in the Navigation pane as .pst files do.

Adding Other Data Stores

Outlook 2010 uses a particular store as your default store to contain your Outlook 2010 data and email, but you can add other store files to help you organize, separate, or archive your data.

When you add an email account to a profile, Outlook gives you the option of creating a new .pst file for the account or choosing an existing .pst file. If you choose the existing .pst file, Outlook places new email that arrives from that account into that existing .pst file.

Otherwise, Outlook creates a new .pst file and stores the incoming email for that account in that new .pst file.

You can also add another .pst file without adding another email account. For example, you might want to use the new .pst file as your local archive file.

Adding another store is easy. Just follow these steps:

1. Open the Mail item from the Control Panel, click the appropriate profile (if you have multiple profiles), and click Data Files. Or, if Outlook 2010 is running, choose File, Account Settings, Account Settings, and Data Files. The current storage files are listed on the Data Files tab.

2. Click Add, enter the file name, select the type of personal folder file to create, and then click OK.

3. To change other settings for the .pst file that you just created, select the new data file from the list and click Settings to display the Outlook Data File dialog box, shown in Figure 3-4. Configure settings as necessary based on the following list:

   - **Change Password** Specify an optional password (and type it a second time to verify it) to protect your .pst file from access by others.

   - **Save This Password In Your Password List** Select this check box to have Outlook 2010 save the password for your .pst file in your local password cache. This eliminates the need for you to enter the password each time you open the .pst file. Clear this check box if you want Outlook 2010 to prompt you each time (providing greater security).

   - **Compact Now** This option doesn't apply to new .pst files, which need no cleanup. However, you can use this option to compact a large .pst file.

Figure 3-4 Use the Create Microsoft Personal Folders dialog box to add a .pst file.

4. Click OK to close the Create Microsoft Personal Folders dialog box.

> **Note**
>
> It's possible for others to gain access to your .pst file even if you use a password for it, if they can get physical or network access to your computer. For that reason, if you have an Exchange Server account and are concerned with the potential for data theft, you should keep your email in your mailbox on the server running Exchange Server and not use an offline file. If that isn't practical, or you don't use Exchange Server, consider implementing whole disk encryption on your computer using Microsoft's BitLocker or a third-party encryption tool like PGP (www.pgp.com).

INSIDE OUT   Add an existing .pst file to a profile

You can add an existing .pst file to a profile so that you can work with its contents in Outlook 2010, either permanently or temporarily. For example, you might want to open an archived .pst file to find an old message or two and then "disconnect" the .pst file when you have finished using it. Just start Outlook 2010, choose File, Open, and Open Outlook Data File, and then choose the .pst file. When you have finished using the file, right-click its root in the folder list, and then choose Close to remove the .pst file from the folder list.

Removing Data Stores

Occasionally, you might want to remove a data store from a profile—for example, perhaps you've been using a .pst file as your primary store and are now moving to Exchange Server with an .ost file for offline use.

To remove a data store from a profile, you use steps similar to those you followed to add a store:

1. Open the Mail item from the Control Panel, select the appropriate profile, click Properties, and then click Data Files.

2. Select the data file to remove from the profile, click Remove, and then click Yes to verify the action.

3. Close the remaining dialog boxes.

When you remove a data file from a profile, Outlook 2010 does not delete the file itself. This means that you can add the file back to a profile later if you need to access its contents. If you don't need the data stored in the file, or if you've already copied the data to a different store, you can delete the file. Open the folder where the file is located, and then delete it as you would any other file.

Configuring Offline Storage

Configuring an offline store allows you to continue working with data stored in your Exchange Server mailbox when the server is not available (if your computer is disconnected from the network, for example). As soon as the server becomes available again, Outlook 2010 synchronizes the data either automatically or manually, according to the way in which you have configured Outlook 2010.

For a detailed explanation of folder synchronization, see the section "Controlling Synchronization and Send/Receive Times," on page 197.

Like earlier versions of Outlook, Outlook 2010 supports the use of an .ost file to serve as an offline cache for Exchange Server.

Using an .ost File

You can use an .ost file to provide offline capability for your Exchange Server mailbox. You do not need to use a .pst file in conjunction with the .ost file—the .ost file can be your only local store file, if you want. However, you can use other .pst files in addition to your .ost file.

This section assumes that you are working with an Exchange Server account that has not been configured to use Cached Exchange Mode. When you add an Exchange Server account in Outlook 2010, the Add New Account Wizard enables Cached Exchange Mode by default. This section helps you create and enable an offline store for a profile that has not had Cached Exchange Mode enabled previously.

> **Note**
> The .ost file does not appear as a separate set of folders in Outlook 2010. In effect, the .ost file is hidden and Outlook 2010 uses it transparently when your computer is offline. For more information, see Chapter 41, "Working Offline and Remotely."

Follow these steps to configure offline storage with an .ost file:

1. Open the Mail item from the Control Panel, select the appropriate profile, and then click E-Mail Accounts. Or, if Outlook 2010 is running, click File, Account Settings, and Account Settings.

2. On the E-Mail tab, select the account, and then click Change.

3. Click More Settings to display the Microsoft Exchange Server dialog box. Click the Advanced tab, and then click Outlook Data File Settings to open the dialog box shown in Figure 3-5.

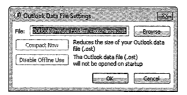

Figure 3-5 Specify the file name and other settings for the .ost file.

4. Specify a path and name for the .ost file in the File box, and then click OK.

5. Click OK to close the Outlook Data File Settings dialog box.

6. Click Next, and then click Finish.

Configuring Cached Exchange Mode

When you add an Exchange Server account to a profile in Outlook 2010, Outlook enables Cached Exchange Mode by default and creates the .ost file that Cached Exchange Mode will use to store the local copy of the mailbox. If you originally added the Exchange Server account without Cached Exchange Mode, you can still enable it by following these steps:

1. Exit Outlook 2010, and then open the Mail item in Control Panel.

2. Select the profile if needed, and then click E-Mail Accounts in the Mail Setup dialog box.

3. Select the Exchange Server account, and then click Change.

4. Select Use Cached Exchange Mode, click Next, and then click Finish.

Outlook 2010 creates the .ost file the next time you start the program and begins the synchronization process if the server is available.

Changing Your Data Storage Location

On occasion, you might need to move a data file from one location to another. For example, perhaps your C: drive is filling up and you want to put your .pst file on another hard disk. Or, you've been using a local .pst file file and now want to place that file on a network share for use with a roaming profile so that you can access the file from any computer on the network.

Moving a .pst file is a manual process. You must exit Outlook 2010, move the file, and then reconfigure the profile accordingly.

Follow these steps to move a .pst file:

1. Exit Outlook 2010 and open the Mail item from the Control Panel.

2. Select a profile if necessary, and then click Data Files to display the Data Files tab in the Account Settings dialog box, shown in Figure 3-6.

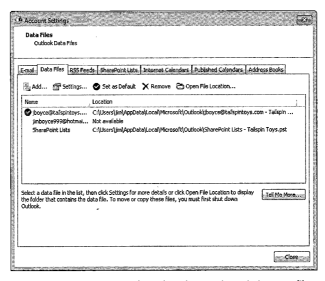

Figure 3-6 Use the Data Files tab to locate the existing .pst file.

3. Select the .pst file that you want to move, and then click Open File Location. Outlook 2010 opens the folder where the .pst file is located and selects the file's icon.

4. Drag the file or use the Clipboard to move the file to the desired location, and then close the folder.

5. On the Data Files tab, click Settings. Outlook 2010 displays an error message, indicating that it can't find the file. Click OK.

6. Browse to the new location of the .pst file, select it, click Open, and then click OK.

7. Click Close to close the Outlook Data Files dialog box, and then click Close again to close the Mail Setup dialog box.

Setting Send and Delivery Options

Outlook 2010 uses one data store location as the default location for delivering messages and storing your other Outlook 2010 items. You can change the store location if needed. You also can specify the order in which Outlook 2010 processes email accounts, which determines the server that Outlook 2010 uses (where multiple servers are available) to process outgoing messages. The order also determines the order in which Outlook 2010 checks the servers for new messages.

For example, assume that you have an Exchange Server account and a POP3 account for your personal Internet mail. If the Exchange Server account is listed first, Outlook 2010 sends messages destined for Internet addresses through Exchange Server. In many cases, however, this might not be what you want. For example, you might want all personal mail to go through your POP3 account and work-related mail to go through your Exchange Server account.

You have two ways to change the email service that Outlook 2010 uses to send a message: You can configure the service order, or you can specify the account to use when you create the message.

Follow these steps to configure the service order for your email:

1. Open the Mail item from the Control Panel and click E-Mail Accounts, or in Outlook 2010, choose Tools, Account Settings, and Account Settings to display the E-Mail tab in the Account Settings dialog box, shown in Figure 3-7.

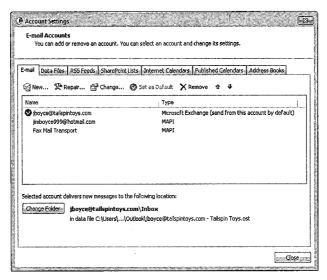

Figure 3-7 Use the E-Mail Accounts tab in the Account Settings dialog box to configure account order.

2. Use the Move Up and Move Down buttons to change the order of the accounts in the list.

3. Click Close.

> **Note**
>
> The account at the top of the list is the default account. Choosing an account and clicking Set As Default moves the account to the top of the list. You can also set the default account simply by using the up arrow button to move it to the top of the list.

When you compose a message, you can override the default email service that Outlook 2010 uses to send messages simply by selecting the account before sending the message.

To select the account, follow these steps:

1. Start a new email and then click the From button in the message window.

2. Select the account that you want to use to send the message.

3. Compose the message, make any other changes to options as needed, and then click Send.

F you've used earlier versions of Microsoft Outlook, you'll find that the interface in Outlook 2010 has both changed and stayed the same. Many elements are the same or similar to previous versions, but there are some big changes, such as the presence of the ribbon throughout the program. If you have worked with Office 2007 or with other Office 2010 applications, you're no doubt familiar with the ribbon and can make the transition in Outlook without too much trouble. If you're new to Outlook 2010 entirely, you need to become familiar with its interface, which is the main focus of this chapter.

Outlook 2010 presents your data using different views, and this chapter shows you how to customize the way those views look. This chapter also examines other standard elements of the interface, including the ribbon, toolbars, the Navigation pane, the Folder list, and the Reading pane. You'll also learn how to use multiple Outlook 2010 windows and views and navigate your way through the Outlook 2010 interface.

This chapter looks at the various ways you can configure Outlook 2010, explaining settings that control a broad range of options, from email and spelling to security. In addition, you'll learn about settings in your operating system that affect how Outlook 2010 functions. Where appropriate, the text refers you to other chapters where configuration information is discussed in detail in the context of a particular feature or function.

This chapter also examines web integration in Outlook 2010. You'll learn about browsing the web with Outlook 2010 and about accessing your Microsoft Exchange Server email through a web browser. Later in the chapter, you'll find a discussion of add-ins, which can enhance Outlook 2010 functionality.

Using the Ribbon

Before diving into Outlook folders and how to use them, let's take a look at the most obvious interface change in Outlook 2010, the ribbon. Unlike previous versions of Outlook that used a combination of menus and toolbars, Outlook implements the full Office ribbon interface to give you access to commands, options, and tools in Outlook 2010. The ribbon is shown in Figure 4-1.

Figure 4-1 The ribbon provides quick access to context-sensitive commands and features.

The ribbon is something of a paradigm shift. Rather than provide a linear, menu-based list of commands, the ribbon places features onto individual tabs, each of which comprises tools with related functions. For example, all the tools that relate to inserting items into a new message are located together on the Insert tab of the new message form.

Each ribbon tab is divided into groups, and each group organizes the features for a specific function. On the Message tab of the new message form, for example, the Basic Text group organizes the tools you use to format text in the message.

The ribbon operates in the context of the currently selected folder. For example, when you have the Inbox open, the tabs and commands in the ribbon apply primarily to the Inbox. For example, when the Inbox is open, the New group on the Home tab shows a New E-mail button that, when clicked, starts a new email message. Likewise, when the Calendar folder is open, the buttons offered are New Appointment and New Meeting. Other tabs and commands change as well, such as the commands on the View menu, which show view choices for the selected folder.

You'll see at least four tabs in the ribbon regardless of which folder is open, and the Search tab appears when you click in the Search box. These tabs include:

- **Home**   This tab is the place to go to create new items and access the most common commands for items in the selected folder. For the Inbox, for example, the Home tab contains commands for replying to messages, creating and using Quick Steps, moving messages, and other common email tasks.

- **Send/Receive**   Use this tab to synchronize folders (send/receive email, for example), show send/receive status, and set connection and download preferences.

- **Folder** Use this tab to access folder-specific tasks such as setting permission for a folder, cleaning up the folder, recovering deleted items, and so on.

- **View** Use the View tab to access various views for the current folder, create and manage views, and set options for the various interface panes (such as the Navigation pane).

- **Search** This tab appears only when you click in the Search box, and it offers options that you can use to define your search criteria and access search options and other tools.

In addition to these tabs, Outlook will show other tabs as appropriate. For example, when you click an appointment in the Calendar, Outlook displays the Calendar Tools/Appointment tab, which includes commands that are specific to the appointment. If you click a meeting, Outlook shows the Calendar Tools/Meeting tab. The important point is that these tabs are context-sensitive and apply to the selected item.

Using Backstage View

As described briefly in Chapter 1, "What's New in Outlook 2010," like the other Office applications, Outlook uses the Backstage view (see Figure 4-2) to give you access to commands and options formerly found on the File menu, and it also integrates many of the commands from the former Tools menu. For example, you can access account settings, open files, print, set up Out of Office replies, clean up the mailbox, and access rules and alerts from the Backstage view.

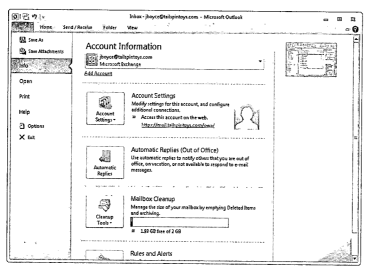

Figure 4-2 Use the Backstage view to access account settings and other general Outlook options and commands.

The Backstage view is fairly self-explanatory. Individual items are covered where applicable throughout this book. To return to your Outlook folders, just click one of the other ribbon tabs.

Using the Quick Access Toolbar

Outlook, like the other Office applications, provides a Quick Access toolbar that, as its name implies, gives you quick access to commonly used commands and options (see Figure 4-3). By default, the Quick Access toolbar contains only two commands: Send/Receive All Folders and Undo. To use one of these commands, just click its button. If you want to move the toolbar below the ribbon instead of above it, click the small arrow button at the right of the toolbar and choose Show Below the Ribbon. Click the button again and choose Show Above the Ribbon to move it back to its default location.

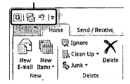

Figure 4-3 Use the Quick Access toolbar to access common commands.

> **Tip**
> As you might expect, you can customize the ribbon to suit your liking. See Chapter 25, "Customizing the Outlook Interface," for details on customizing the ribbon and the Quick Access toolbar.

Understanding the Outlook Folders

Outlook 2010 uses a standard set of folders to organize your data. Once you're comfortable working with these standard folders, you'll be able to change their location, customize their appearance, or even create additional folders, as you'll learn throughout this book.

The following list describes the default Outlook 2010 folders:

- **Calendar** This folder contains your schedule, including appointments, meetings, and events.

- **Contacts**   This folder stores information about people, such as name, address, phone number, and a wealth of other data.

- **Deleted Items**   This folder stores deleted Outlook 2010 items of various types (contacts, messages, and tasks, for example). You can recover items from the Deleted Items folder, giving you a way to "undelete" an item if you've made a mistake or changed your mind. If you delete an item from this folder, however, the item is deleted permanently.

- **Drafts**   Use this folder to store unfinished drafts of messages and other items. For example, you can use the Drafts folder to store a lengthy email message that you haven't had a chance to finish yet. Or you might start a message, have second thoughts about sending it, and place it in the Drafts folder until you decide whether to send it.

- **Inbox**   Outlook 2010 delivers your email to this folder. Keep in mind that, depending on the types of email accounts in your profile, you might have more than one Inbox in locations other than your default information store. For example, if you have a Hotmail account and an Exchange Server account, you'll have an Inbox folder for each.

- **Journal**   This folder stores your journal items, allowing you to keep track of phone calls, time spent on a project, important email messages, and other events and tasks.

- **Junk E-Mail**   This folder contains items that have been placed there by the Outlook Junk E-Mail Filter. This filter is designed to divert the most obvious spam, and you can customize it to suit your needs.

- **News Feed**   This folder stores news feed items delivered through the Outlook Social Connector.

- **Notes**   This folder stores and organizes notes. You can move or copy notes to other folders in Outlook 2010, as well as to folders on disk. You can also create shortcuts to notes.

- **Outbox**   The Outbox stores outgoing messages until they are delivered to their destination servers. You can configure Outlook 2010 to deliver messages immediately after you send them or have the messages wait in your Outbox until you process them (by synchronizing with the computer running Exchange Server or by performing a send/receive operation through your POP3 account, for example).

- **RSS Feeds**   This folder stores Really Simple Syndication (RSS) content. RSS is a way for content publishers to make news, blogs, and other content available to subscribers.

- **Search Folders**   Search folders are special virtual folders that you can use to search for and display messages in a familiar folder structure. The folders look like regular Outlook folders, but the messages that appear in them can actually be located in multiple places.

- **Sent Items**   This folder stores copies of the messages you have sent. You can configure Outlook 2010 to store a copy of each sent item in this folder automatically.

- **Suggested Contacts**   This folder shows the email addresses for people who have emailed you or who you have emailed that are not already in your Contacts folder.

- **Sync Issues**   This folder contains synchronization status messages (essentially a log of mailbox synchronization errors).

- **Tasks**   This folder lists tasks that have been assigned to you or that you have assigned to either yourself or others.

Working with the Standard Outlook Views

Before you can become proficient at using Outlook 2010, you need to be familiar with its standard views and other elements of its interface. This section introduces you to the Outlook 2010 standard views and includes information about how to work with these views and customize them to meet your needs.

Outlook Today

Outlook 2010 provides default views of its standard folders as well as one additional view that is a summary of your schedule, tasks, and email for the current day—Outlook Today. To switch to Outlook Today view if you are working in another folder, click the root of your default mail store in the Navigation pane, which is identified in the Folder pane by your email address (in other words, click your email address in the Navigation pane). Figure 4-4 shows a typical Outlook Today view. In the Calendar area on the left, Outlook 2010 summarizes your schedule for the current day, showing each appointment with time and title. You can view the details of a particular appointment easily by clicking the appointment time or title to open it.

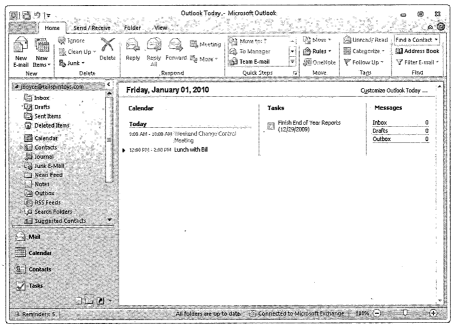

Figure 4-4 Outlook Today lets you see your day at a glance.

In the Tasks area, Outlook Today lists your tasks for the current day, including overlapping tasks with a duration of more than one day. The list includes a title and completion date for each task, along with a check box. You can mark the task as completed by selecting the check box; doing so crosses out the task on the list. If the check box is cleared, the task is incomplete.

In the Messages area, Outlook Today lists the number of unread messages in your Inbox and number of messages in the Drafts and Outbox folders.

For details on customizing the Outlook Today view to display additional information, including the use of Hypertext Markup Language (HTML) code in such customization, see Chapter 25.

Inbox

The Inbox displays your default message store, as shown in Figure 4-5. For example, if you use an Exchange Server account, the Inbox view shows the Inbox folder in your Exchange Server mailbox. If you are using a mail account that stores data in a local .pst file, the Inbox view shows the contents of the Inbox folder in that store.

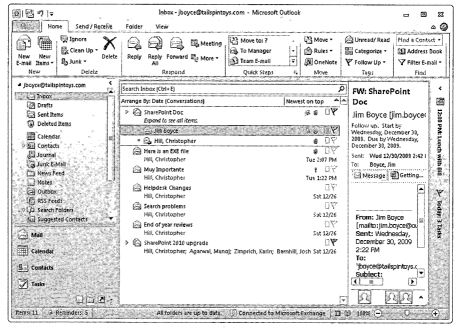

Figure 4-5 The Inbox view shows the contents of the Inbox folder of your default store.

As you can see, the Inbox view shows the message header for each message, including such information as sender, subject, and date and time received in various columns. These columns are not always visible, however, because the default configuration includes the Reading pane on the right in the Outlook 2010 window, which hides many of the columns on a typical display. If you turn off the Reading pane or move it to the bottom of the window, you can view the message header columns.

You can sort messages easily by clicking the column header for the column you want to use as the sort criterion. For example, to locate messages from a specific sender quickly, you can click the From column header to sort the list alphabetically by sender. To switch between ascending and descending sort, simply click the column header again. An up arrow next to the column name indicates an ascending sort (such as A to Z), and a down arrow indicates a descending sort (such as Z to A).

To learn how to add and remove columns and change their appearance and order, see the section "Customizing the Inbox View," on page 78.

By default, Outlook 2010 shows the following columns in the Inbox view when the Reading pane is either off, displayed at the bottom of the window, or taking a minimal amount of space on the right in the window:

- **Importance**   This column indicates the level of importance, or priority, that the sender has assigned to a message—Low, Normal, or High. A high-priority message is accompanied by an exclamation point, whereas a down arrow marks a low-priority message. No symbol is displayed for a message of normal importance.

> **Note**
> After you've received a message, you can change its priority status by right-clicking the message header, choosing Message Options, and then specifying a new importance level.

- **Reminder**   This column indicates whether messages have a reminder associated with them (a bell icon indicates a reminder).

- **Icon**   This column indicates the type of message and its status. For example, unopened messages are accompanied by a closed envelope icon, and opened messages are accompanied by an open envelope icon.

- **Attachment**   This column displays a paper clip icon if the message includes one or more attachments. Right-click a message and choose View Attachments to view the attachments, or simply double-click an attachment in the Reading pane.

CAUTION

> Although Outlook 2010 provides protection against viruses and worms by preventing you from opening certain types of attachments and opening Office file types in Protected View, this is no guarantee against infection. Your network administrator might have modified the blocked attachment lists, or you might have modified your blocked attachment list locally to allow a specific attachment type that may be susceptible to infection to come through. So you should still exercise caution when viewing attachments, particularly from unknown sources. It's a good practice to save attachments to disk and run a virus scan on them before opening them.

- **From**   This column shows the name or address of the sender.

- **Subject**   This column shows the subject, if any, assigned by the sender to the message.

- **Received**   This column indicates the date and time that Outlook 2010 received the message.

- **Size** This column indicates the overall size of the message, including attachments.

- **Categories** This column shows the color indicators for color categories assigned to the message.

- **Flag Status** In this column, you can flag messages for follow-up action. For example, you can flag a message that requires you to place a call, to forward the message, or to respond at a particular time. You specify the action, date, and time for follow-up.

For detailed information about flagging messages for follow-up and other ways to manage and process messages, see the section "Flagging and Monitoring Messages and Contacts," on page 293.

INSIDE OUT   Time is relative

The date and time displayed in the Inbox's Received column can be a little deceiving. This data reflects the time the message was placed in your message store (received by the server). If you're working online with an Exchange Server account, for example, Outlook 2010 shows the time the message was placed in the Inbox folder for your mailbox on the computer running Exchange Server. If the time on your computer isn't coordinated with the time on the server, the time you actually receive the message could be different from the time reflected in the message header. For sent messages (in the Sent Items folder), the time indicated is the time the message was placed in your Outbox. If you're working offline, that time could differ from the time the message is actually sent.

Previewing Messages

Another part of the Inbox view is the Reading pane, which appears on the right in the Inbox view. You can use the Reading pane to preview messages without opening them in a separate window, as well as preview attachments without opening them. The scroll bar on the right of the Reading pane lets you scroll through the message or attachment. The top of the Reading pane presents information about the message, such as sender, recipient, subject, and attachments.

You can double-click most of the items in the Reading pane header to see detailed information about the items. For example, you can double-click the name of the sender to display information about the sender, as shown in Figure 4-6. Use this method to view quickly other information about the contact, such as phone number. You can also double-click attachments to open them. Right-clicking an item opens its shortcut menu, on which you can choose a variety of actions to perform on the item—for instance, you can right-click an attachment and choose Save As to save the attachment to disk. Experiment by right-clicking items in the Reading pane to see which actions you can take for specific items.

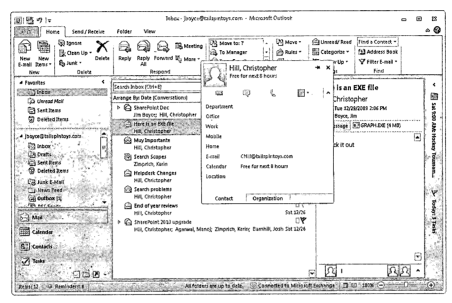

Figure 4-6. After you double-click a sender's address in the Reading pane, Outlook displays information about the sender.

Note

The information that Outlook 2010 displays when you double-click the name of the sender of an email message in the Reading pane depends on whether the sender is in your Contacts folder, in the Global Address List (GAL; Exchange Server accounts), or not in either.

Note

If a message has been flagged for follow-up, information about the follow-up (the specific action, the date due, and so on) also appears in the Reading pane header.

> **Note**
> To turn the Reading pane on or off, click the View tab, click Reading Pane, and then choose Right, Bottom, or Off. To change the location of the Reading pane, click the View tab, click Reading Pane, and then choose Right or Bottom.

For detailed information about using and customizing the Reading pane in various folders, see the section "Using the Reading Pane," on page 104.

On the View tab of the ribbon, you'll find a Change View button in the Current View group. Clicking Change View displays the following three options:

- **Compact**   This view shows the From, Subject, Received, Quick Click Category, and Flag Status columns in two lines for each message. This is the same as the two-line view option in previous versions of Outlook.

- **Single**   This view shows the default columns described previously in this chapter using a single line for each message.

- **Preview**   This view turns off the Reading pane and shows a single-line view of your message headers with the first few lines of the message text displayed below the header. This is essentially the same as the AutoPreview view in previous Outlook versions.

Customizing the Inbox View

Outlook 2010 offers a wealth of settings that you can use to control messaging. In addition, you also have quite a bit of control over the appearance of the Inbox and other message folders. For example, you can change the column headings included in the Inbox or add and remove columns. The following sections explore specific ways to customize the Inbox (which apply to other message folders as well).

For detailed information about configuring messaging and other options, see the section "Configuring Outlook Options," on page 107.

Adding and Removing Columns

By default, Outlook 2010 displays only a small subset of the available fields for messages. You can add columns for other fields, such as CC or Sensitivity, to show additional informa-tion. However, the Inbox behaves differently depending on the location and size of the Reading pane. Essentially, the view adjusts to accommodate the Reading pane; as you make the Reading pane larger, making less room available to show message headers, Outlook 2010 switches to Compact view.

When displaying Compact view, Outlook 2010 also provides two column headers above these message columns that you can use to change views or change the sort order. For example, the default view is Arranged By: Date. You can click this header to choose a different property by which to group the view.

The other column header sorts by ascending or descending order and changes the name depending on the Arrange By criteria. For example, it might say either Newest On Top or Oldest On Top, depending on whether the folder is sorted in ascending or descending order by date. Or, if you are arranging by Subject, for example, the column reads A On Top or Z On Top. Whatever the case, you can click this column to switch between the two sort options.

The number of columns in the message pane depends on the amount of space available in the window. The more space that is available, the more columns Outlook 2010 displays. For example, continue to drag the left edge of the Reading pane to the right, and Outlook 2010 eventually shows additional columns. You have to experiment with the size of the Reading pane to find a layout that suits you because the amount of available space depends on your system's display resolution. Alternatively, simply position the Reading pane at the bottom of the window to maximize the amount of space available for message pane columns.

To add and remove columns, follow these steps:

1. Open the folder that you want to modify in either Single or Preview view, right-click the column header bar, and choose Field Chooser to display the Field Chooser dialog box, shown in Figure 4-7.

Figure 4-7. Add or remove columns by using the Field Chooser dialog box.

2. Locate the name of the field you want to add, and then drag the field from the Field Chooser dialog box to the desired location on the column header bar. Outlook

2010 displays a red arrow at the top of the column header bar to indicate where the column will be inserted.

3. Add other fields as necessary.

4. To remove a field, drag the field from the column header bar.

5. Close the Field Chooser dialog box.

You can choose other types of fields by selecting a type from the drop-down list at the top of the Field Chooser dialog box. You can also use this dialog box to create custom fields.

Outlook 2010 also provides another method for adding and removing columns in message folders. Perform the following steps:

1. Click View Settings on the View tab, and then click Columns to display the Show Columns dialog box, as shown in Figure 4-8.

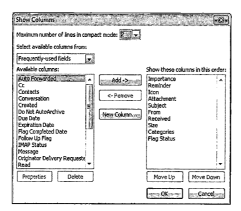

Figure 4-8. You can also use the Show Columns dialog box to add or remove columns.

2. To add a column, select the column in the Available Columns list, and then click Add.

3. To remove a column from the folder view, select the field in the Show These Columns In This Order list, and then click Remove.

4. Click OK to have your changes take effect.

5. Click OK to close the Advanced View Settings dialog box.

Changing Column Order

In a message folder, Outlook 2010 displays columns in a specific order by default, but you can change the order easily. The simplest way is to drag a column header to the desired location. You also can right-click the column header bar, choose View Settings, click

Columns to display the Show Columns dialog box (shown in Figure 4-5), and then use the Move Up and Move Down buttons to change the column order.

Changing Column Names

Outlook 2010 uses a default set of names for the columns that it displays in message folders. However, you can change those column names—for example, you might want to rename the From column to Sender.

To change a column name, follow these steps:

1. Click View Settings in the View tab of the ribbon and then click Format Columns to display the Format Columns dialog box, shown in Figure 4-9.

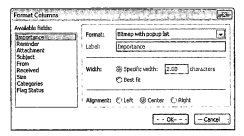

Figure 4-9. You can change several column characteristics, including column header name.

2. In the Available Fields list, select the field for which you want to change the column header.

3. In the Label box, type the label you want displayed in the column header for the selected field.

4. Repeat steps 2 and 3 for the other fields you want to change.

5. Click OK to apply the changes.

6. Click OK to close the Advanced View Settings dialog box.

Note

Four columns will not allow you to change the label: Importance, Reminder, Flag Status, and Attachment. However, you can switch between using a symbol or text in the Importance and Flag Status columns. You can change the Attachment column to display either a paper clip icon or the text True/False, On/Off, or Yes/No, depending on whether the message has an attachment.

Changing Column Width

If a column isn't wide enough to show all the information for the field or if you need to make room for more columns, you might want to change the column width. The easiest way to change the width of a column is to drag the edge of the column header in the column header bar to resize it. Alternatively, you can right-click the column header bar, choose View Settings, Format Columns, and specify a column width in the Format Columns dialog box (shown in Figure 4-6).

INSIDE OUT   Size columns automatically

Use the Best Fit option in the Format Columns dialog box to size the selected column automatically based on the amount of data that it needs to display. Outlook 2010 examines the data for the field in the existing messages and resizes the column accordingly.

Changing Column Alignment

By default, all the columns are left-aligned in message folders, including the Inbox. You can, however, configure the alignment to display the columns as left-justified, right-justified, or centered. For example, you might want to change the format for the Size column to show only numbers and then display the column right-justified. Simply click View Settings in the View tab on the ribbon and then click Format Columns. In the Format Columns dialog box (shown in Figure 4-6), select the column to change, and then, under the Alignment option, select Left, Center, or Right, depending on the type of justification you want.

Changing Column Data Format

Each default column in a message folder displays its data using a particular format. For example, the From column shows only the sender, not the recipient. Although in most cases, the specified recipient is you, that isn't the case when the message you've received is a carbon copy. You might then want to change the data format of the From column to also display the person specified in the To field of the message. Other columns also offer different formats. For example, you can change the data format used by time and date fields such as Received or Sent to show only the date rather than date and time.

To change the data format used for a particular column, right-click the column header bar and choose View Settings, or click View Settings in the View tab on the ribbon, and then click Format Columns. In the Format Columns dialog box (shown in Figure 4-6), select the column for which you want to change the format, and then select the format in the Format drop-down list. The available formats vary according to the field selected.

Grouping Messages

Outlook 2010 offers many ways to organize and display your data. A good example of this flexibility is the option of grouping messages based on a hierarchy of criteria. For example, you might want to group messages in your Inbox first by subject, then by sender, and then by date received, as shown in Figure 4-10.

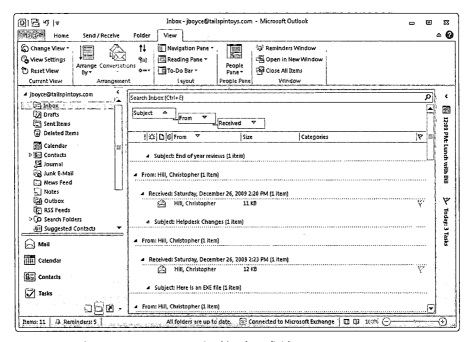

Figure 4-10 These messages are organized by three fields.

To organize your messages based on a particular column, you can simply right-click the column and choose Group By This Field. If the folder is showing the Arranged By column (Compact view), click this column header, and then choose the field by which you want to group the messages.

For more complex groupings, follow these steps:

1. Right-click the column header bar, and then choose Group By Box to display the Group By box above the column header bar.

2. To set up a grouping, drag a column header from the column header bar to the Group By box.

3. To set up an additional level of grouping, drag another column header to the Group By box. Repeat this process until you have as many levels of grouping as you need.

> **Note**
> If you are unable to drag an additional column to the Group By box, click the More button on the Arrangement group in the ribbon, and then choose Show In Groups to turn off grouping.

4. To remove a grouping, drag the column header from the Group By box to the desired location on the column header bar.

To hide or show the Group By box, right-click the column header bar, and then choose Group By Box again. To expand or collapse your view of a group of messages, click the triangle button next to the group or message.

For a detailed explanation of grouping and sorting, along with several other topics that will help you organize your data, see the section "Grouping Messages by Customizing the Folder View" on page 298.

Applying View Customizations to Other Folders

Let's say you've just spent an hour fine-tuning your default Inbox view and have discovered that the customization doesn't apply to the subfolders in your Inbox. Or, you want to apply the same settings to the Inbox folder for your other mail accounts, Microsoft SharePoint lists, and so on. Fortunately, you don't have to go through the customization process again for each one.

In the customized view, click Change View on the View tab in the ribbon, then choose Apply Current View to Other Mail Folders to open the Apply View dialog box (see Figure 4-11). Place a check beside the folders where you want the view applied, and make sure to choose the Apply View To Subfolders check box to have the view settings applied to sub-folders. Then, click OK to apply the view settings.

Figure 4-11 Apply view settings to other views with the Apply View dialog box.

Calendar

In the Calendar folder, you can look at your schedule in several different ways. By default, the Calendar view shows the current day's schedule as well as the Date Navigator (a monthly calendar) in the upper-left corner of the Navigation pane. The To-Do Bar, which displays tasks that overlap or fall on the current day, is shown in Figure 4-12. With the To-Do Bar turned on, the Date Navigator moves to the upper-right corner of the To-Do Bar. You can configure the To-Do Bar to show other tasks as well. In addition, the Task List can appear at the bottom of the window in Day and Week views.

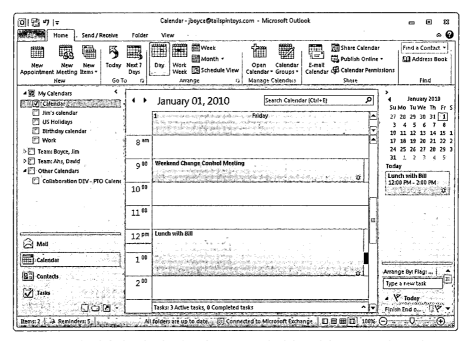

Figure 4-12 The default Calendar view shows your schedule and the Date Navigator, but you can also view tasks.

Your schedule shows the subject for each scheduled item—a brief description of a meeting or an appointment, for example—next to its time slot, blocking out the time assigned to the item. Items that overlap in the schedule are displayed side by side, as shown in Figure 4-13.

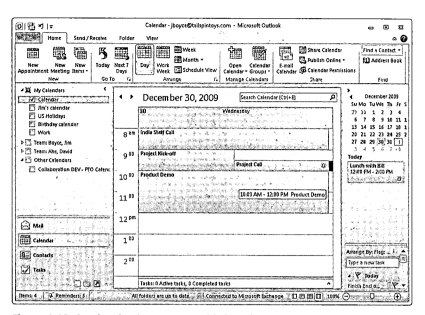

Figure 4-13 Overlapping items appear side by side in your schedule.

Working with the Schedule

By default, the Calendar view shows only the subject for each item scheduled in the period displayed. You can open the item to modify it or view details about it by double-clicking the item, which opens its form, as shown in Figure 4-14.

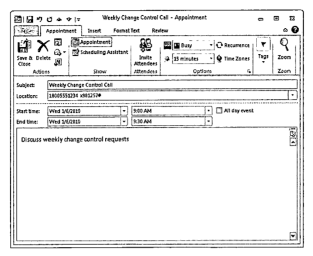

Figure 4-14 An appointment form shows details for a selected appointment.

You can add an item to your schedule using one of these methods:

- Double-click the time slot of the start time that you want to assign to the item.

- Right-click a time slot, and then choose the type of item to create (an appointment, a meeting, or an event).

- Select a time slot, and then click an item type in the New group on the Home tab of the ribbon.

- Click New Items on the Home tab of the ribbon, and then select the item type.

The first method opens an appointment form. The form opened by the other three methods depends on the type of item you select.

It is also easy to change the start or end time for an item in the schedule. To move an item to a different time without changing its duration, simply drag the item to the new time slot. To change the start or end time only, position the mouse pointer on the top or bottom edge of the item, and then drag it to the desired time.

Using the Calendar's Reading Pane

Like the Inbox and other message views, Calendar view has a Reading pane that lets you preview appointments and other items in your schedule without opening them. To turn the Reading pane on or off, click the View tab on the ribbon, click Reading Pane, and then choose either Right, Bottom, or Off. Click the item to display it in the Reading pane, as shown in Figure 4-15. To display more or less information in the pane, drag the edge of the

Reading pane to resize it. You can also make other changes to the displayed item—such as subject and times—through the Reading pane.

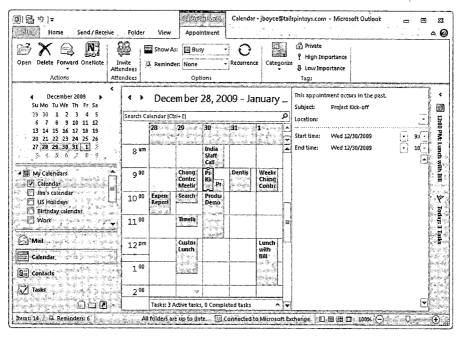

Figure 4-15 Use the Reading pane in the Calendar view to preview scheduled items.

Using the Task List

The Task List displays a list of your tasks on the To-Do Bar. You can turn the Task List on or off on the To-Do Bar. If the To-Do Bar is not shown, click the View tab, click To-Do Bar, and then click Normal or Minimized. By default, the Task List shows the tasks for the current day. As you can in the Inbox and other views, you can change the options and the items displayed on the To-Do Bar: right-click the To-Do Bar column header bar, and then choose the items you want to include, or choose Options to customize how these items are displayed.

For more information about the To-Do Bar and the features Outlook 2010 provides for working with and assigning tasks, see Chapter 21, "Managing Your Tasks."

Using the Date Navigator

The monthly calendars in the upper-right area of the To-Do Bar are collectively called the Date Navigator. When the To-Do Bar is hidden, the Date Navigator appears at the top of the Navigation pane.

The Date Navigator is useful not only as a calendar but also as a way to provide a fast glance at which days include appointments. Days with a scheduled item appear in bold, and those without scheduled items appear in a normal font. You can view a particular day by clicking it. Click the arrow at the left or right of the Date Navigator to change which months are displayed. You can also click and hold on the month name to choose from a shortcut menu which month to view.

INSIDE OUT   Specify the font of the Date Navigator

You can configure the Date Navigator to display all dates in normal text rather than using bold for days that contain items. To do this, click View Settings on the View tab of the ribbon, and then click Other Settings in the Advanced View Settings dialog box. Clear the Bolded Dates In Date Navigator Represent Days Containing Items check box, and then click OK. Click OK to close the dialog box.

You can change the number of months displayed by the Date Navigator by resizing the Reading pane, resizing the Calendar pane, changing the width of the Navigation pane or the To-Do Bar, or changing the font used by the Date Navigator. Assign a smaller font to show more months.

Customizing the Calendar View

Although the default Calendar view shows only the subject for a scheduled item, you can configure the view to show additional detail—or you can change the view completely. For example, you can switch from a daily view to one that shows the work week, the calendar week, or the month. You can see examples of the Work Week view in Figure 4-16, the Week view in Figure 4-17, and the Month view in Figure 4-18. To select a particular view, click the Day, Work Week, Week, or Month button on the Home or View tab of the ribbon.

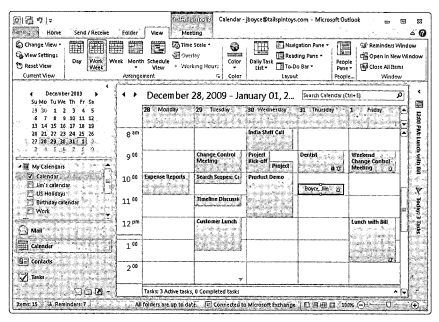

Figure 4-16 Use the Work Week view to organize your work schedule.

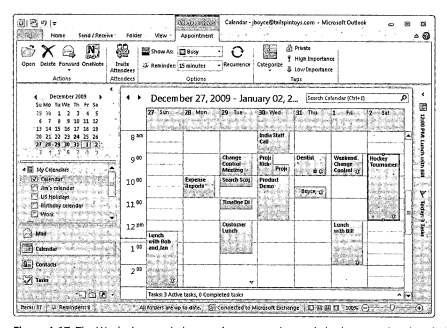

Figure 4-17 The Week view can help you plan your entire week, both personal and work time.

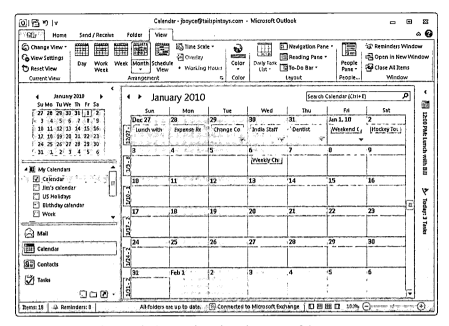

Figure 4-18 Use the Month view to plan a broader range of time.

You have additional options for viewing your schedule in the Calendar folder. Click Change View on the View tab of the ribbon, and then choose one of the following to change the view:

- **Calendar** Show the items in a calendar format with the Reading pane turned off.

- **Preview** Show the items in a calendar format with the Reading pane turned on.

- **List** Show items in a list rather than Calendar view.

- **Active** Show only items that have not yet occurred.

- **Active Project Related-Related Appointments** Show only items that occur in the future and that are related to projects.

- **Active Non-Project-Related Appointments** Show only items that occur in the future and are not related to projects.

For additional information about customizing the way Outlook 2010 displays information in the various calendar views, see Chapter 19, "Scheduling Appointments."

Applying Calendar Views to Other Folders

As you can with mail folder views, you can apply customized view settings from one cal-endar folder to other calendar folders. After you are satisfied with the custom view set-tings, click the View tab in the ribbon, click Change View, and then choose Apply Current View to Other Calendar Folders. Outlook displays an Apply View dialog box similar to the one shown previously in Figure 4-8. Place a check by the folders where you want the view applied and click OK.

Contacts

The Contacts folder stores all your contact information. By default, the Contacts folder displays the Business Cards view, shown in Figure 4-19, which shows the name for each contact along with other selected fields (address and phone number, for example). You can view the details for a contact by double-clicking the contact's business card, which opens the contact form, shown in Figure 4-20. Using this form, you can view or make changes to the contact's data or perform other tasks, such as calling the contact, generating a meeting request, or viewing a map of the contact's address. If you have a large number of contact entries stored in the Contacts folder, you can click the buttons at the right edge of the view to select which portion of the contacts list to show.

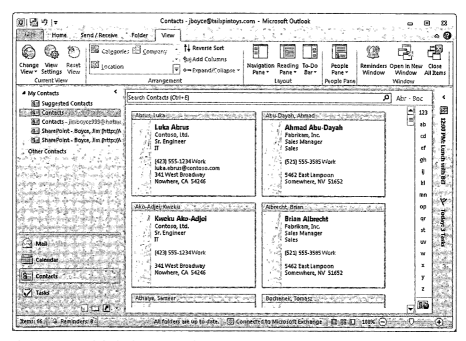

Figure 4-19 By default, the Contacts folder displays the Business Cards view.

For a detailed discussion of working with contacts, including the actions you can take with the contact form, see Chapter 18, "Creating and Managing Your Contacts."

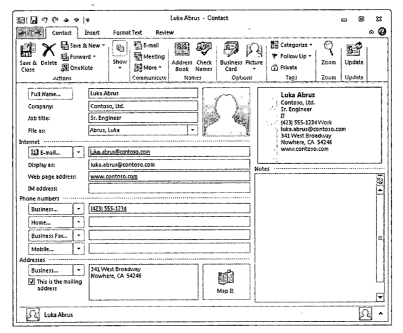

Figure 4-20 When you double-click a contact entry, you can view the contact form for that person.

Outlook 2010 offers several other ways to view the contents of your Contacts folder. Choose View, Current View, and then choose one of the following commands to change the view:

- Business Card   Shows the contact information as a virtual business card

- Card   Displays the name of each contact, along with address and telephone information

- Phone   Displays the contacts as a phone list organized by name

- List   Displays the contacts organized by company and name

In addition to these views, Outlook also offers some options in the Arrangement group on the View tab. You can choose between Categories, Company, and Location to group the contacts by those fields when a list view is displayed.

Adding contact entries to your Contacts folder is easy: Click New on the Home tab when the Contacts folder is open, or click New Items and choose Contact. Either action opens the contact form, in which you enter the contact's data.

Customizing the Contacts View

Like other views in other folders, the view in the Contacts folder can be customized to suit your needs and preferences. For example, you can adjust the view to display additional fields of information or to remove fields you don't need. You can sort the view based on specific contact criteria or group similar items together based on multiple criteria. For details about customizing the Contacts view, see Chapter 18.

Tasks

The Tasks folder contains your task list. The default Tasks view, shown in Figure 4-21, lists each task in a simple list with subject, due date, and status. Double-click an existing task to open the task form, which displays detailed information about the task, including due date, start date, status, notes, and so on, as shown in Figure 4-22. To add a new task to the list, double-click a blank list entry to open a new task form, where you can enter all the details about the task.

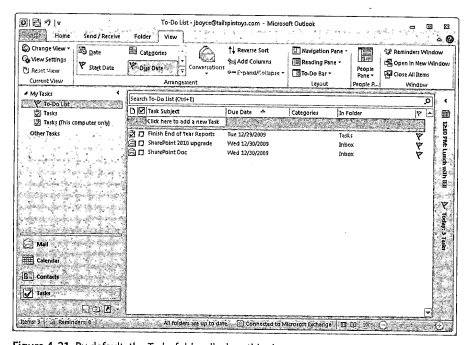

Figure 4-21 By default, the Tasks folder displays this view.

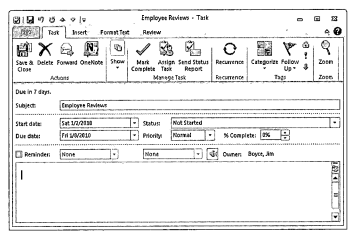

Figure 4-22 Use a task form to create a new task.

The task list shows tasks that you have assigned to others as well as those tasks assigned to you (by yourself or by others). These assignments can be one-time or recurring, and the list shows both in-progress and completed tasks. Additionally, any messages that you have flagged for follow-up appear in your task list.

Like other Outlook 2010 views, Tasks view provides a Reading pane that you can use to view details for a task without opening the task item. To display the Reading pane, Click the View tab, click Reading Pane, and then specify the location (either Right or Bottom).

Customizing the Tasks View

You can customize the view in the Tasks folder in a variety of ways—adding and removing columns, changing column names, and organizing tasks by category or other properties, to list a few. To customize the columns, click View Settings on the View tab, and then click Format Columns in the Advanced View Settings dialog box. The resulting dialog box allows you to select the format for each column, change the name, apply alignment, and so on. To change the order of columns in the view, simply drag the column headers into the desired positions, resizing as needed.

You can also organize your task list in various ways. You can click column headers to sort the columns in ascending or descending order, and you can group the columns based on a particular field or group of fields, just as you can in the Inbox and other Outlook 2010 folders.

You can also click View, Change View, and then choose one of the following commands to change the Tasks view:

- **Simple List**   Shows whether the task has been completed, the task name, the folder location of the task, categories, and the due date

- **Detailed**   Shows status, percent complete, dates modified or completed, and categories in addition to the information displayed in the Simple List view

- **Prioritized**   Organizes tasks by priority

- **Today**   Shows tasks due on the current day

- **Active**   Displays tasks that are active

- **Next Seven Days**   Displays tasks scheduled for the next seven days

- **Overdue**   Displays incomplete tasks with due dates that have passed

- **Assigned**   Shows the tasks assigned to specific people

- **Completed**   Shows only completed tasks

- **Server Tasks**   With Exchange Server accounts, helps you view assigned tasks

- **To-Do List**   Displays tasks in the To-Do List with a Reading pane

In addition to selecting these views, you can use the options in the Arrangement group on the View tab to organize tasks.

For more information about customizing the view in the Tasks folder, see the section "Working with Tasks in the Tasks Folder," on page 537.

Notes

With its Notes feature, Outlook 2010 helps you organize your thoughts and tasks. Each note can function as a stand-alone window, allowing you to view notes on your desktop outside Outlook 2010. The Notes pane provides a look into your Notes folder, where your notes are initially stored. From there, you can copy or move your notes to other locations (such as the desktop) or create shortcuts to them. By default, the initial Notes pane displays the notes as icons, with the first line of the note serving as the title under the note's icon, as shown in Figure 4-23.

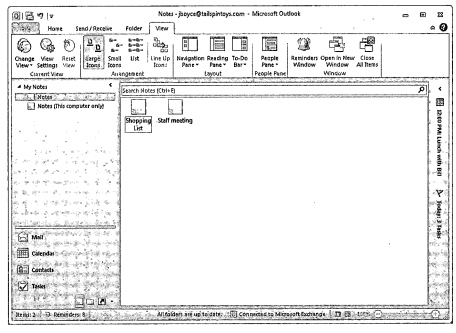

Figure 4-23 The standard Notes pane displays notes as icons.

As it does for other options, Outlook 2010 offers several other ways to view notes. You can click Change View on the View tab, and then choose one of the following:

- **Icon** Displays an icon for each note, with the first line of the note serving as the icon's description (the default view)

- **Notes List** Displays the notes as a line-by-line list

- **Last Seven Days** Resembles the Notes List view but restricts the display to only the past seven days and is based on the current date

You can also use the options in the Arrangement group of the View tab to display the notes using different sizes of icons.

You can show the Reading pane in the Notes folder, displaying the text of a note when you click it in the list. To choose a view, click Change View on the View tab of the ribbon and choose the desired view.

You can customize the views in the Notes folder the same way that you can in other folders. You can, for example, drag columns to rearrange them, resize columns, change column names and other properties, add other fields, and group notes based on various criteria.

For a detailed explanation of how to work with the Notes folder, see Chapter 23, "Notes and OneNote Integration."

As explained in Chapter 2, the Notes feature in Outlook can be useful, but for most people, it is probably only marginally so. OneNote offers a far wider breadth of features for taking notes, and if you haven't already done so, you should try OneNote to see what it can do. See Chapter 23 for more details on OneNote and its integration with Outlook.

Deleted Items

The Deleted Items folder contains Outlook 2010 items that you have deleted, and it can include all the Outlook 2010 item types (such as messages, contacts, and appointments). The Deleted Items folder offers a way for you to recover items you've deleted, because the items remain in the folder until you manually delete them from that location or allow Outlook 2010 to clean out the folder. When you delete an item from the Deleted Items folder, that item is deleted permanently.

You can configure Outlook 2010 to delete all items from the Deleted Items folder automatically when you exit Outlook 2010. To do so, click File, Options, and then click Advanced in the left pane. Select the Empty Deleted Items Folder When Exiting Outlook check box, and then click OK.

Choosing the Startup View

You might want to change the default Outlook 2010 view based on your type of work and the Outlook 2010 folders that you use most. Or you might want to use a particular view as the initial view because it presents the information you need right away each morning to start your workday.

You can designate any of the Outlook 2010 folders as your startup view. To do so, follow these steps:

1. In Outlook 2010, click File, Options.

2. Click Advanced in the left pane.

3. In the Outlook Start And Exit group, next to the Start Outlook In This Folder text box, click Browse, and then select the folder that you want to see by default when Outlook 2010 starts. Click the root branch (labeled with your email address) if you want to specify Outlook Today as the default view.

4. Click OK, and then click OK again to close the Outlook Options dialog box.

Using Other Outlook Features

In addition to the various folders and views described in this chapter, Outlook 2010 incorporates several other standard components in its interface. The following sections explain these features and how to use them effectively.

> **Note**
>
> This book assumes that you're familiar with your operating system and comfortable using menus. Therefore, neither the Outlook 2010 ribbon nor its individual tabs are discussed in this book, except for specific tabs and commands where applicable.

Using the Navigation Pane

The Navigation pane appears on the left in the Outlook 2010 window and contains shortcuts to the standard Outlook 2010 folders as well as shortcuts to folders you've created and other important data folders, as shown in Figure 4-24. Just click an icon in the Navigation pane to open that folder or item. The Navigation pane gives you quick access not only to Outlook 2010 folders but also to all your data.

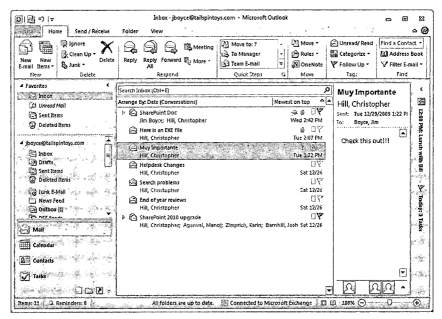

Figure 4-24 The Navigation pane provides quick access to all Outlook 2010 data and other frequently used resources and folders.

For a detailed discussion of the Navigation pane, including how to create your own groups and shortcuts, see the section "Customizing the Navigation Pane," on page 631.

For a detailed discussion of the Navigation pane, including how to create your own groups and shortcuts, see the section "Customizing the Navigation Pane," on page 631.

Tip

You can create new shortcuts in any of the existing Shortcuts groups in the Navigation pane, and you can also create your own groups.

Depending on your monitor's resolution and the number of shortcuts in each group, you might not be able to see all the icons in a group. If that's the case, you can use the scroll bar on the right edge of the Navigation pane to scroll through the icons in the selected group.

Using Objects in the Navigation Pane

Most of the time, you'll probably just click an icon in the Navigation pane to open its associated folder. However, you can also right-click a view button and use the resulting shortcut menu to perform various tasks with the selected object. For example, you might right-click the Calendar icon and then choose Open In New Window to open a second window showing the calendar's contents. To view a different folder, simply click the folder's button in the Navigation pane. The content of the upper portion of the Navigation pane changes according to the folder that you select. For example, the Navigation pane shows the Folder List if you click the Folder List button.

Controlling the Navigation Pane's Appearance

Outlook 2010 shows a selection of view buttons for standard folders in the Navigation pane. If you don't use certain folders very often, however, you might prefer to remove them from the Navigation pane to make room for other view buttons. For example, if you never use the Journal or Notes folder, you can remove those view buttons from the Navigation pane and use the Folder List to access those folders when needed.

To change the view buttons displayed in the Navigation pane, click Configure Buttons in the lower-right section of the Navigation pane (it's a small arrow button), and then choose Add Or Remove Buttons to open the shortcut menu shown in Figure 4-25. Click a folder in the list to either add it to or remove it from the Navigation pane. Those folders that are selected in the list appear in the pane.

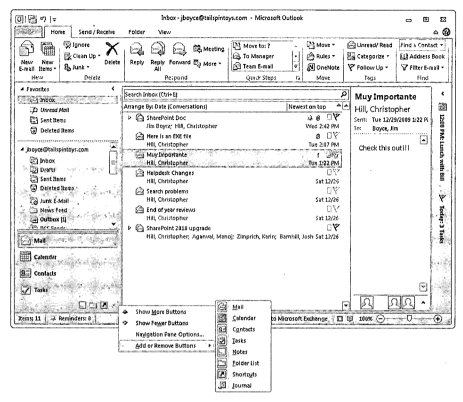

Figure 4-25 You can add standard view buttons or remove them from the Navigation pane.

If you need to add or remove more than one folder, click Configure Buttons, and then choose Navigation Pane Options to open the Navigation Pane Options dialog box. Select each folder that you want included in the Navigation pane, and then click OK.

> **Note**
>
> **Use the Move Up and Move Down buttons in the Navigation Pane Options dialog box to control the order of buttons in the Navigation pane.**

If you seldom use the Navigation pane, you can close it or minimize it to make room on the screen for the Folder List or other data. Simply click the View tab, click Navigation Pane, and then choose Off or Minimize to alter the display.

Using Multiple Outlook Windows

Although Outlook 2010 opens in a single window, it supports the use of multiple windows, which can be extremely useful. For example, you might want to keep your Inbox open while you browse through your schedule. Or perhaps you want to copy items from one folder to another by dragging them. Whatever the case, it's easy to use multiple windows in Outlook 2010.

When you right-click a folder in the Navigation pane, the shortcut menu for that folder contains the Open In New Window command. Choose this command to open the selected folder in a new window, keeping the existing folder open in the current window. You also can open a folder from the Folder List (discussed next) in a new window. Simply right-click a folder, and then choose Open In New Window to open that folder in a new window.

Using the Folder List

When you need to switch between folders, you'll probably use the Navigation pane most of the time. But the Navigation pane doesn't include shortcuts to all your folders by default, and adding those shortcuts can clutter the pane, especially if you have multiple data stores. Fortunately, Outlook 2010 provides another quick way to navigate your folders: the Folder List.

Click the Folder List button in the Navigation pane to display the Folder List, as shown in Figure 4-26. In the list, click the folder that you want to open.

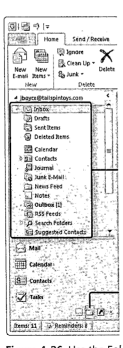

Figure 4-26 Use the Folder List to browse and select other folders.

Using the Status Bar

The status bar appears at the bottom of the Outlook 2010 window, as shown in Figure 4-27, and presents information about the current folder and selected items, such as the number of items in the folder. It can also include other status information, such as the progress of folder synchronization and connection status for Exchange Server.

Figure 4-27 The status bar provides useful information, such as the number of items in the selected folder or current connection status to the server.

You can customize the status bar to control what information appears in it. To do so, just right-click the status bar to display a pop-up menu with available items. Items that have a check by them appear on the status bar, and those without a check do not. Just put a check by the ones you want displayed (see Figure 4-28).

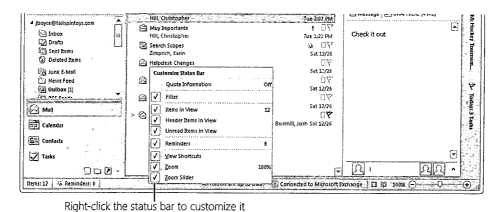

Right-click the status bar to customize it

Figure 4-28 You can customize the status bar.

Using the Reading Pane

In earlier sections of this chapter, you learned about the Reading pane, which allows you to preview Outlook 2010 items without opening them. For example, you can preview an email message in the Reading pane simply by clicking the message header. To turn the Reading pane on or off, click the View tab, click Reading Pane, and then choose Right, Bottom, or Off.

To some degree, the way that the Reading pane functions depends on how you configure it. For example, you can set up the Reading pane to mark messages as read after they've been previewed for a specified length of time. To configure the Reading pane, click File, Options, click Mail in the left pane of the Outlook Options dialog box, and then click Reading Pane. Select options based on the following list:

- **Mark Items As Read When Viewed In The Reading Pane**   Select this option to have messages marked as read when they've been previewed for the time specified by the following option.

- **Wait n Seconds Before Marking Item As Read**   Specify the number of seconds that a message must be displayed in the Reading pane before it is marked as read.

- **Mark Item As Read When Selection Changes**   Select this option to have the message in the Reading pane marked as read when you select another message.

- **Single Key Reading Using Spacebar**   Selecting this option allows you to use the Spacebar to move through your list of messages to preview them. Press Shift+Spacebar to move up the list. You also can use the Up Arrow and Down Arrow keys to move up and down the message list.

The Reading pane in Outlook 2010 offers some additional functionalities, which include the following:

- In a message, you can double-click an address in the Reading pane to view details for the address.

- The Reading pane header displays the message's attachments. You can double-click an attachment to open it, or right-click the attachment and choose other tasks on the shortcut menu (such as saving the attachment).

- The Reading pane displays Accept and Decline buttons so that you can accept or decline a meeting request in the Reading pane without opening the request.

- When a meeting invitation is selected, the Reading pane shows a snippet of your calendar with the proposed meeting and the adjacent items to help you determine if you can make the meeting or not (see Figure 4-29).

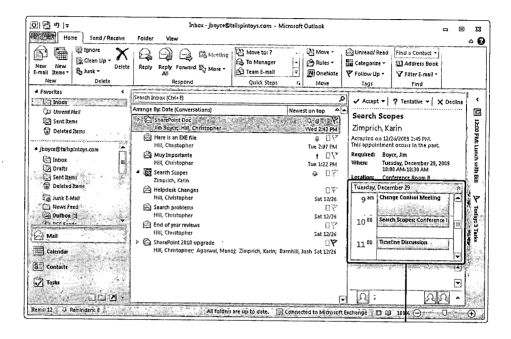

Figure 4-29 The Reading pane shows a preview of a proposed meeting on the calendar.

Using the InfoBar

The InfoBar is the banner near the top of an open email message, appointment, contact, or task. It tells you whether a message has been replied to or forwarded, along with the online status of a contact who is using instant messaging, and so on. The InfoBar in a message form, for example, displays the From, To, Cc, and other fields. In Outlook 2010, the InfoBar resides in the Reading pane, as shown in Figure 4-30.

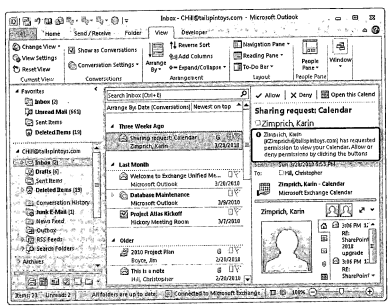

Figure 4-30 The InfoBar appears in the Reading pane as well as in message and appointment forms.

Some of the fields in the InfoBar simply display information, but others lead to more details. For example, you can double-click a name in the InfoBar to view the associated address and other contact information, or you can double-click attachments to open them. If the InfoBar displays a message that you replied to or that you forwarded, click that message and choose Find Related Messages to search for messages in the same conversation as the selected message.

Configuring Outlook Options

Because Outlook 2010 is a complex application with a broad range of capabilities, you have many options for controlling the way that it looks and functions. This portion of the chapter is designed to help you configure Outlook 2010 to perform as you require.

The following list describes the different pages in the Outlook Options dialog box, providing an overview of the features listed on that page and pointing out key new Outlook 2010 features. Because many of the options in this dialog box are best understood in the context of the feature they control, you'll find more detail about individual options in chapters that focus on a particular Outlook 2010 feature (messaging or scheduling, for example); be sure to consult the cross-references to the applicable chapters for more information.

To open the Options dialog box described here, start Outlook 2010, and then click File and choose Options. You'll find these pages on the dialog box (Figure 4-31 shows the General page):

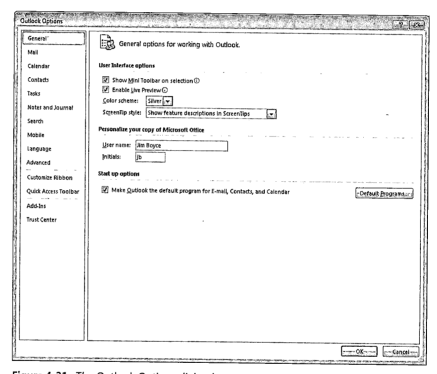

Figure 4-31. The Outlook Options dialog box.

NEW!

- **General**   Use this page to turn on or off the Mini Toolbar (which shows formatting options when you select text), enable Live Preview (which shows how a document will change when you place the mouse over a feature that would apply a change), set the color scheme for Outlook, and specify how ScreenTips behave. You can also personalize your copy of Office and set Outlook as the default program for email, contacts, and calendaring.

- **Mail**   This page contains options that control the default message format, editing options such as AutoCorrect, proofing (such as spell-checking), notifications when new emails arrive, conversation clean-up options, how Outlook handles replies and forwards, receipt tracking, and other mail-specific options. A new Outlook 2010 feature controlled from this page is the MailTips feature, which warns you about potential problems such as sending a message to too many people, sending a message that is too large for the recipients, and so on. To access these options, click MailTips Options to open the MailTips dialog box (see Figure 4-32).

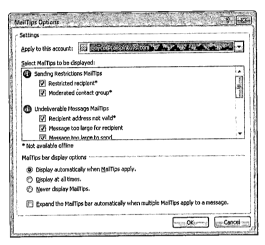

Figure 4-32. The MailTips Options dialog box.

- **Calendar**   Use these options to set the start and end times for your workday, set the start of the workweek, and set other general calendar options such as default reminder time and meeting invitation format. You can also add holidays, change free/busy options, set the color used on the calendar, set the default time zone, and set up an additional time zone. You can also configure Scheduling Assistant options and manage resource scheduling from this page.

- **Contacts**   On this page, change how contacts are saved and displayed, and set whether to display photos if available. Here's another new Outlook 2010 feature: The option Automatically Create Outlook Contacts For Recipients That Do Not Belong To An Outlook Address Book, if selected, causes new contacts to be added to the Suggested Contacts folder when you receive a message from or send a message to an address that does not exist in your Outlook Address Book. You'll see the Suggested Contacts folder listed in the Navigation pane when you open the folder list or open the Contacts folder.

- **Tasks** Use the options on this page to set a default reminder time for tasks, set task colors, set the Quick Click flag option, number of working hours per day and per week, and other general task options.

- **Notes And Journal** The options on this page control the default note size, color, and font, and enable you to access the Journal options, which control the items that are journaled automatically in Outlook.

- **Search** Use this page to specify how Outlook searches and displays search results, such as the highlight color. You can also access the Windows Search indexing options by clicking the Indexing Options button. This is the same as opening the Indexing Options item from the Control Panel.

- **Mobile** Use this page (see Figure 4-33) to set up calendar summaries and mobile reminders that are sent to your mobile device. You can also configure Outlook to forward items to your mobile phone when those items meet certain criteria, and set options for text messaging.

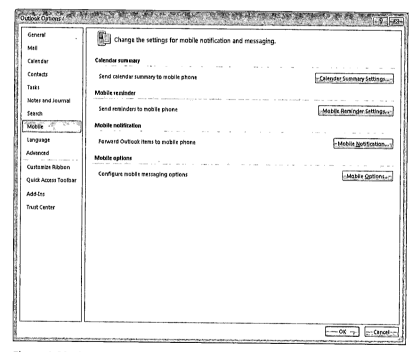

Figure 4-33. Set a variety of mobile notification and text messaging options from the Mobile page.

- **Language**   This page offers options that control which languages are used for proofing, grammar checking, sorting, and other language-specific tasks. You can also choose the display and Help languages from this page.

- **Advanced**   Use this page to set a variety of advanced options for Outlook that include the startup folder, whether to empty the Deleted Items folder when you exit Outlook, and settings that control when and how Outlook automatically archives your data. You can also control reminder options and how Outlook handles RSS feeds, set up send/receive groups, configure custom forms options, set dial-up connection settings, and configure international options.

  One Outlook 2010–specific feature on this page to note in the Other group on this page is the Allow Analysis Of Sent E-mails To Identify People You Commonly E-mail And Subjects You Commonly Discuss, And Upload This Information To The Default SharePoint Server. This option relates to the SharePoint Server Colleague Add-In. If this option is enabled, Outlook scans your sent email folder to look for names and keywords and periodically uploads that data to SharePoint. You can then use the Add Colleagues page on your SharePoint My Site to add colleagues and keywords based on those scans. The registry setting HKEY_CURRENT_USER\Software\Microsoft\ Office\14.0\Common\Portal\ColleagueImport\Enabled also determines whether this feature is enabled. A DWORD value of 0 turns it off and a value of 1 turns it on.

- **Customize Ribbon**   Use this page to customize the ribbon, adding commands you use frequently, removing those you seldom use, or turning off items altogether. For details on customizing the ribbon, see Chapter 26.

- **Quick Access Toolbar**   On this page, you can configure the Quick Access toolbar, which by default sits above the ribbon. See Chapter 26 for more details on customizing the Quick Access toolbar.

- **Add-Ins**   This page shows the add-ins installed for Outlook and organizes them by active, inactive, and disabled status. You can turn add-ins on or off by selecting an add-in category from the Manage drop-down list and clicking Go.

- **Trust Center**   The Trust Center Settings button on the Trust Center page opens the Trust Center dialog box, shown in Figure 4-34. This dialog box lets you configure a broad range of security-related settings for Outlook and is organized into the following pages:

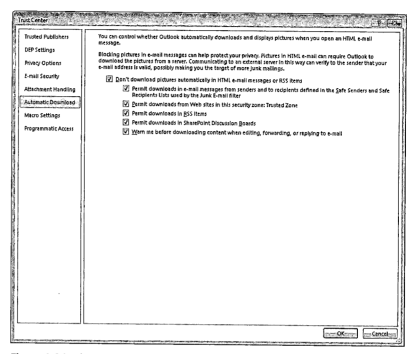

Figure 4-34. The Trust Center dialog box contains security-related settings.

- **Trusted Publishers**   Use this page to view certificates for trusted publishers. Certificates are used to sign add-ins digitally and allow Outlook to trust their execution.

- **DEP Settings**   Turn Data Execution Prevention (DEP) on or off with this page. DEP,
when turned on, prevents applications from using protected memory. Many viruses
and other security threats attack Windows through protected memory areas, so turning on DEP can help secure your computer against these threats.

- **Privacy Options**   Use this page to configure a handful of privacy-related options,
such as allowing Office to download troubleshooting data automatically for detecting and fixing potential problems. You can also configure translation and research
options from this page.

- **E-mail Security**   These options control encrypted email settings, certificates, enable
you to read all mail as plain text, and control scripting.

- **Attachment Handling**   Use these options to turn on Reply With Changes for
attachments (which adds additional properties to Office file attachments when
you send them), turn on or off Attachment Preview (which enables you to preview

attachments in the Reading pane in Outlook), and turn on or off individual file pre-view applications.

- **Automatic Downloads**   Use these options to control how Outlook handles pictures in HTML email or RSS items. Preventing image download can prevent spammers from validating your email address when you open a message containing an image.

- **Macro Settings**   Use these settings to specify which types of macros Outlook will allow to run.

- **Programmatic Access**   These options let you receive notifications when programs attempt to access your address book or send email automatically through Outlook. These options are disabled if you have a valid antivirus program.

Using Outlook Effectively

Other chapters in this book include sections that offer best-practice advice on using specific features, such as the calendar. This section of this chapter offers some best-practice advice overall on using Outlook 2010 effectively:

- **Integrate and take advantage of Outlook 2010**   If you have been using Outlook Express, Windows Mail, or another email client instead of Outlook 2010, switch to Outlook 2010. Outlook 2010 integrates many of the contact-management and track-ing features with email, making it an extremely useful productivity tool. In addition, Outlook 2010 offers some exceptional features for gathering and organizing email (such as search folders), making it an excellent choice for handling all your email needs.

- **Get organized**   Make extensive use of folders and categories to organize your mes-sages, contacts, appointments, and other Outlook 2010 data. The better you organize your data, the easier it will be to find and work with it, making you that much more efficient. Don't just throw stuff into your Outlook 2010 folders—take the time to manage your data effectively. In particular, make use of categories and search folders to help you manage your email, and use automatic formatting and color categories to organize your calendar.

- **Keep your Inbox cleared out**   Near the end of yourbes workday, allocate a certain amount of time to work through your Inbox and respond to each message. Reply to those you can and move them into appropriate folders for archiving. Those you can't respond to because they require follow-up should be flagged for follow-up. The fewer messages you have in your Inbox at the end of the day, the greater your sense of accomplishment when you leave the office.

- **Take advantage of the Navigation pane, Reading pane, and To-Do Bar**   These Outlook 2010 features can help you quickly navigate Outlook 2010 to find the information you need. In Outlook 2010, the capability to minimize the Navigation pane and To-Do Bar will give you a lot more window space in your Outlook 2010 folders.

For more best-practice advice on using specific Outlook 2010 features, look for the appropriate sections at the end of selected chapters throughout this book.

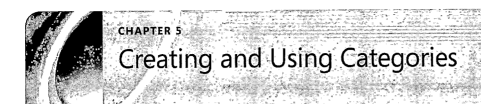

Creating and Using Categories

CHAPTER 5

O NE of the primary functions of Microsoft Outlook 2010 is to help you organize your data, whether that data is a collection of contacts, a task list, your schedule, or a month's worth of messages. To make this easier, you can use Outlook 2010 categories. A category is a combination of words or phrases and colors that you assign to Outlook 2010 items as a means of organizing them. For example, you might assign the category Personal to a message from a family member to differentiate that message from your work-related messages and then customize the Inbox view to exclude personal items. Outlook 2010 incorporates color with categories, making it easy to identify categories at a glance.

This chapter explains how categories work in Outlook 2010 and shows you how to work with color categories, add categories, assign categories to Outlook 2010 items, and use categories to arrange, display, and search through Outlook 2010 data.

Understanding Categories

If you've used a personal finance or checkbook program such as Microsoft Money or Intuit's Quicken, you're probably familiar with categories. In these programs, you can assign a category to each check, deposit, or other transaction and then view all transactions for a specific category, perhaps printing them in a report for tax purposes. For example, you might use categories to keep track of business expenses and separate them by certain criteria, such as reimbursement policy or tax deductions.

Outlook 2010 categories perform essentially the same function: you can assign categories to Outlook 2010 items and manipulate the data based on those categories. For example, you might use categories to assign Outlook 2010 items such as messages and tasks to a specific and I. You could then locate all items related to that project quickly. Alternatively, you might use categories to differentiate personal contacts from business contacts.

Whatever your need for organization, categories offer a handy and efficient way to achieve your goal.

> **Note**
>
> Outlook 2010 combines colors with categories, giving you the capability to see category assignments at a glance. As you'll learn later in this chapter, you can still use categories without colors, simply by assigning the color None to the category.

What can you do with categories? First, with integration of color with categories, you can tell instantly what category is assigned to a given item. For example, let's say you create a rule that assigns the Red category to all messages from a particular contact. You can then tell at a glance—without doing anything else—which messages are from that person. Or perhaps you assign the Red category to business messages and Green to personal. Whatever the case, color categories are a great means for visually identifying specific types of messages.

> **Tip**
>
> You can use automatic formatting to display items in certain colors when they meet criteria like sender, subject, and so on without assigning a category to the items. Alternatively, you can use rules to assign the categories automatically, which essentially gives you both automatic formatting and category options at the same time.

After you assign a category to each relevant Outlook 2010 item, you can sort, search, and organize your data according to the category. Figure 5-1, for example, shows the Advanced Find dialog box after a search for all Outlook 2010 items assigned to the category Toy Show. Figure 5-2 shows the Contacts folder organized by category, displaying all contacts who are involved in the toy show. The ability to search by category makes it easy to find all the items associated with a specific project, contract, issue, or general category.

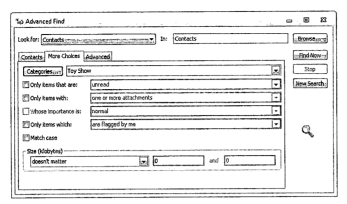

Figure 5-1 Use the Advanced Find dialog box to search for all items in a given category.

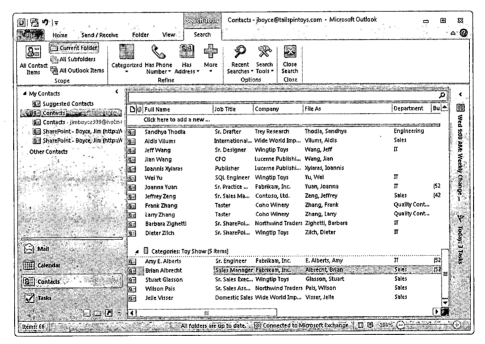

Figure 5-2 You can group contacts by category to list all contacts involved in a particular event or project.

> **Tip**
> You can perform a search for items based on their categories easily using the ribbon. Just click in the Search box, which causes the Search tab to appear in the ribbon. Then, click Categorized from the Refine group and choose the categories for which to search.

Categories are useful only if you apply them consistently. After you become disciplined in using categories and begin to assign them out of habit (or with rules), you'll wonder how you ever organized your day without them.

CAUTION

> The Master Category List in versions of Outlook prior to 2007 has been removed. Categories listed in the Master Category List but not assigned to any items are not imported when you upgrade to Outlook 2010.

Customizing Your Category List

Before you assign categories to Outlook 2010 items, you should go through the category list and add the categories that you need or tailor the existing categories to suit your needs. To determine which categories to add, spend some time thinking about how you intend to use them, including which colors you want to apply to specific categories. Although you can always add and modify categories later, creating the majority up front not only saves time but also helps you organize your thoughts and plan the use of categories more effectively.

Follow these steps when you're ready to create categories:

1. Open the Color Categories dialog box, shown in Figure 5-3, by selecting any item in Outlook 2010 and clicking Categorize, All Categories from the Home tab of the ribbon or by right-clicking an item and choosing Categorize, All Categories on the shortcut menu.

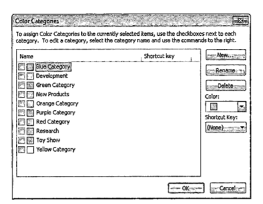

Figure 5-3. You can add a new category in the Color Categories dialog box.

2. Click New to open the Add New Category dialog box.

3. Type the new category name in the Name field, select a color in the Color drop-down list, optionally specify a shortcut key, and then click OK.

> **Tip**
> Select None in the Color drop-down list if you want a text-only category.

4. Repeat steps 2 and 3 to add other categories as desired, and then click OK to close the Color Categories dialog box.

> **Note**
> When you create a new category, Outlook 2010 automatically adds the category to the selected item. You must clear the category if you don't want it assigned to the selected item. For information about creating new categories while you are assigning categories to an item, see the next section, "Assigning Categories to Outlook Items."

The categories that you add to your category list depend entirely on the types of tasks that you perform with Outlook 2010, your type of business or organization, and your preferences. The following list suggests ways to categorize business-related data:

- Track items by project type or project name.

- Organize contacts by their type (for example, managers, assistants, technical experts, and financial advisors).

- Keep track of departmental assignments.

- Track different types of documents (for example, drafts, works in progress, and final versions).

- Track contacts by sales potential (for example, 30-day or 60-day).

Organize items by priority. The following list offers suggestions for categorizing personal data:

- Use color to identify critical or urgent issues.

- Organize personal contacts by type (friends, family, insurance agents, legal advisors, and medical contacts, for starters).

- Track items by area of interest.

- Organize items for hobbies.

- Track items related to vacation or other activities.

Assigning Categories to Outlook Items

Assigning categories to items is easy. You can assign multiple categories to each item if needed. For example, a particular contact might be involved in more than one project, so you might assign a category for each project to that contact. If you have a task that must be performed for multiple projects, you might assign those project categories to the task.

Outlook 2010 will display multiple colors for an item, depending on its type and location. For example, if you assign the Red, Blue, and Green categories to an email message, Outlook 2010 displays each of those three color indicators in the message header, as shown in Figure 5-4. You can resize the Categories column if you want Outlook 2010 to show indicators for all the assigned categories.

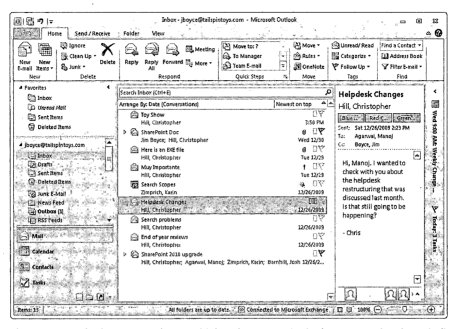

Figure 5-4 Outlook 2010 can show multiple color categories in the message header to indicate multiple categories.

In the Calendar view, Outlook 2010 displays the item using the last color you assigned and places as many color indicators as it can in the item label. So if you add the Blue, Green, and Red categories, Outlook 2010 colors the item as Red and puts Blue and Green indicators in the item for the Day and Week views. In the Month view, you see only the last color assigned.

To learn how to assign categories to existing items, see the next section, "Assigning Categories to Existing Outlook Items."

Follow these steps to assign categories to a new item:

1. Open the folder in which you want to create the item, and then click New.

2. Click Categorize in the Tags group on the ribbon. You'll find the Tags group on the first tab of the ribbon, but the tab name changes depending on the type of item that you are working with (Message, Appointment, Event, and so on).

3. Select a single category on the shortcut menu, or click All Categories, and in the Color Categories dialog box, select all the categories that pertain to the item. If you need to add a category, simply click New, type a name, and click OK.

4. Click OK to close the Color Categories dialog box and continue creating the item.

As you can see in step 3, you can create a category on the fly when you're assigning categories to an item. However, a drawback to creating categories on the fly is that you might not enter the category names consistently. As a result, you could end up with a category being given more than one name. As you might expect, Outlook 2010 treats category names literally, so any difference between two names, however minor, makes those categories different. Searching for one won't turn up items assigned to the other.

Assigning Categories to Existing Outlook Items

Often you will want to add categories to existing Outlook 2010 items. For example, you will likely want to categorize email messages after they arrive. The easiest way to assign a category to an existing item is to right-click the item, choose Categorize, and then choose a category from the shortcut menu, as shown in Figure 5-5. You can use this method for any of the Outlook 2010 items.

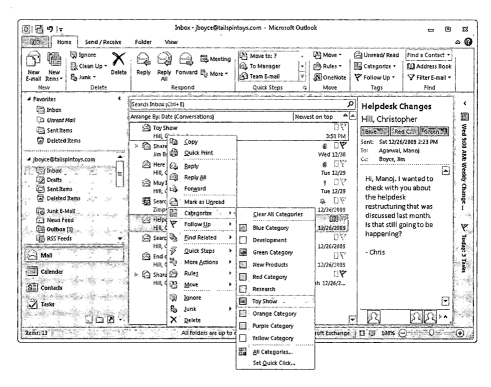

Figure 5-5 Right-click and choose a color category from the shortcut menu.

Assigning a Quick Click Category

Outlook 2010 offers the capability to assign a category quickly, with a single click. In message folders, with the Reading pane displayed on the right, you can click the Category column to assign a Quick Click category. You can also click the Category column on the To-Do Bar to assign a category to tasks in the same way.

Follow these steps to specify the Quick Click category:

1. Click Categorize in the Tags group on the ribbon, and then choose Set Quick Click to open the Set Quick Click dialog box, shown in Figure 5-6.

Figure 5-6. Use the Set Quick Click dialog box to specify the Quick Click category.

2. Select a category, and then click OK.

Assigning Categories Automatically

You can assign categories easily when you create an item, but you might prefer to simplify the process for items that will be assigned to the same category (or set of categories). For example, if you frequently create email messages that have specific category assignments, you could bypass the steps involved in adding the categories to each new message. You can accomplish this by using an email template.

For a detailed discussion of templates, see Chapter 24, "Using Templates."

You can use templates for other Outlook 2010 items as well. Simply create the template, assign categories to it as needed, and then save it with a name that will help you easily identify the category assignments or the function of the template. When you need to create a message with that specific set of category assignments, you can create it from the template rather than from scratch. Because the category assignments are stored in the template, new items created from the template are assigned those categories. Using templates to assign categories not only saves you the time involved in adding categories individually but also ensures that the category assignments are consistent. (For example, you won't misspell a name or forget to add a category.)

A more likely possibility is that you want to add categories to email messages when they arrive. You can create a rule to assign one or more categories to messages when they arrive or even when you send them. For example, let's say you subscribe to six newsletters and you want Outlook 2010 to highlight them in the Inbox with the Green category. A great way to do that is to assign the color category to the messages based on the recipient address or other unique characteristics of the messages.

To learn how to create and manage rules in Outlook 2010, see Chapter 11, "Processing Messages Automatically."

Modifying Categories and Category Assignments

At some point, you'll want to re-categorize Outlook 2010 items—that is, you'll want to add, remove, or modify their category assignments. For example, when one project ends and another begins, some of your contacts will move to a different project, and you'll want to change the categories assigned to the contact items. Perhaps you've added some new categories to organize your data further and want to assign those categories to existing items, or perhaps you made a mistake when you created an item or assigned categories to it, and now you need to make changes. Whatever the case, changing categories and category assignments is easy.

Changing Existing Categories

For one reason or another, you might need to change a category name. You might have misspelled the category when you created it, or you might want to change the wording a little. For example, you might delete the category Foes and create a new one named Friends to replace it (assuming that your friends are not really foes). You can also change existing categories in Outlook 2010. When you change a category, all items assigned to that category are updated.

For example, assume that you have created a category named Dallas Toy Show and made the category red. You open the Inbox and assign the category to several messages. Then you open the calendar and assign the category to a few meetings. A week later, you discover that the toy show is moving to Seattle. So you open the Color Categories dialog box, rename the category Seattle Toy Show, and change the color to blue. When you look in the Inbox, all the messages with that assigned category now show the new name and color. Likewise, the appointments in the calendar also show the new name and color.

If you need to change a category globally rather than add one, see the section "Changing Category Assignments of Multiple Items at One Time," on page 125.

Earlier in this chapter, you learned how to create new categories. Changing a category is much like adding a new one.

Follow these steps to change a category:

1. In Outlook 2010, select any item, and then choose Edit, Categorize, All Categories.

2. In the Color Categories dialog box, click a category to select it.

3. Click Rename, and then type a new name for the category.

4. If you want, select a new color in the Color drop-down list.

5. Click OK to close the Color Categories dialog box.

Changing Category Assignments

You can assign categories to an item at any time, adding and removing the categories you want. To change the categories assigned to a specific item, follow these steps:

1. In Outlook 2010, locate the item for which you want to change the category assignment.

2. Select the item and then click Categorize in the Tags group on the ribbon, or right-click the item and choose Categorize on the shortcut menu.

3. Select a new category in the drop-down list, or choose All Categories to open the Color Categories dialog box, and then assign or remove multiple categories.

Changing Category Assignments of Multiple Items at One Time

In some cases, you'll want to change the category assignments of several items at one time. For example, assume that you've assigned the category Seattle Toy Show to 50 messages in your Inbox. (You really should do a better job of cleaning out your Inbox!) Now you want to clear the categories on all those messages. You could change the messages one at a time, or you could hold down Ctrl, select each message, and then change the category. But for a larger number of items, there is an easier way—the trick is to use a view organized by category. To do this, perform the following steps:

1. Open the folder containing the items whose categories you want to change.

2. Click the View tab, click Change View, and choose List.

3. In the List view, click the Categories tab to organize the view by category.

4. Locate the items under the category that you want to change.

5. If the category that you want to assign to the items has not been assigned yet to any items, assign the category to one item. That item should now show up in the view under its category.

6. Click on the category you are changing, and drag it to the target category.

An important point to understand when using this method to change categories is that Outlook 2010 assigns the target category (the one on which you drop the items) exclusively to the items. For example, assume that you have several items with Red, Blue, and Green category assignments. You drag those items to the Yellow category. All the items now have only the Yellow category. The other categories are removed.

If you want to assign categories to a group of items, you have a couple of different methods to use. If the number of items is relatively small, hold down the Ctrl key, select each item, and then right-click an item and choose Categorize, followed by a category selection. Or choose All Categories to assign multiple new categories.

> **Note**
>
> A list view usually works best when you need to select multiple items.

If you need to change a lot of items, first organize the view by category (to do this, click the View tab on the ribbon, click Change View, choose List, and click the Categories column). Then right-click the category whose items you want to change, choose Categorize, and then choose a new category (or choose All Categories to modify multiple categories). Outlook 2010 displays a warning message informing you that the action will be applied to all items in the selected category. Click OK to continue with the change.

Organizing Data with Categories

Now that you've created your personal category list and faithfully assigned categories to all your data in Outlook 2010, how do you put those categories to work for you? Searching for items with given categories is a good example of how you can use categories to organize and sort your data: by specifying those categories in the Advanced Find dialog box, you can compile a list of items to which those categories have been assigned.

You also can sort items by category. To do so, follow these steps:

1. Open the folder containing the items that you want to sort. If the Categories field isn't displayed, right-click the column bar, and then choose Field Chooser.

2. Drag the Categories field to the column bar, and then close the Field Chooser dialog box.

3. Right-click the Categories column, and then choose Group By This Field.

> **Tip**
>
> To clear groupings, right-click the Categories column in the Group By box, and choose Don't Group By This Field.

Viewing Selected Categories Only

In many situations, it's beneficial to be able to restrict a view to show only selected categories. For example, perhaps you want to view all messages that have the Toy Show and Travel Required categories. Whatever the case, you can use a couple of methods to view only items with specific category assignments.

First, you can use a custom, filtered view to filter only those items that fit your criteria. Follow these steps to customize a view to show selected categories:

1. Open the Outlook 2010 folder that contains the items you want to view.

2. On the View tab of the ribbon, click View Settings in the Current View group.

3. In the Advanced View Settings dialog box, click Filter.

4. In the Filter dialog box, click the More Choices tab, as shown in Figure 5-7.

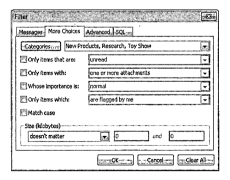

Figure 5-7. Use the More Choices tab in the Filter dialog box to create a custom view.

5. On the More Choices tab, click Categories, select the categories that you want to view, and then click OK.

6. Click OK in the Filter dialog box, and then click OK in the Customize View dialog box to view the filtered view.

See Chapter 26, "Creating Custom Views and Print Styles," to learn more about working with custom views.

Another way to view items with only selected categories, provided you are working with a mail folder, is a search folder. You can create a new search folder that shows only messages in the desired categories. Follow these steps to create the search folder:

1. Right-click Search Folders in the folder list (Navigation Pane), and then choose New Search Folder. Or click the arrow next to New on the Standard toolbar, and then choose Search Folder.

2. In the New Search Folder dialog box, shown in Figure 5-8, scroll to the bottom of the list, select Create A Custom Search Folder, and then click Choose.

Figure 5-8. Create a custom search folder in the New Search Folder dialog box.

3. In the Custom Search Folder dialog box, shown in Figure 5-9, type a name for the search folder in the Name field.

Figure 5-9. Specify properties in the Custom Search Folder dialog box.

4. Click Criteria to open the Search Folder Criteria dialog box, and then click More Choices.

5. Click Categories, and then select the categories to include in the search folder.

6. Click OK twice to return to the Custom Search Folder dialog box.

7. Click Browse, select the folders to be included in the search, and then click OK.

8. Click OK in the Custom Search Folder dialog box, and then click OK to close the New Search Folder dialog box.

See Chapter 10, "Finding and Organizing Messages," to learn more about creating and using search folders.

Sharing a Category List

If you work in a department, or if you share similar tasks and responsibilities with others, it's helpful to be able to share the same set of categories with those other users. Doing so helps to ensure that everyone is using the same categories, an important point when you're sharing items or receiving items from others that have categories assigned to them. For example, assume that your department is working on a handful of projects. Having everyone use the same project category names helps you organize your Outlook 2010 items and ensures that searches or sorts based on a given project display all items related to the project, including those you've received from others.

Sharing Categories with a Registry File

Outlook 2010 stores your category list in the Calendar folder as a hidden Outlook 2010 item, not in a file. This means that you can't simply share a file to share your categories. Instead, you can create a registry file to share categories.

CAUTION

An incorrect modification to the registry can prevent Outlook 2010 from running or could even prevent Microsoft Windows from starting. Be careful when editing the registry.

These steps outline the registry method, which copies categories into the registry:

1. Open Notepad, and then add the following text to the file:

```
Windows Registry Editor Version 5.00

[HKEY_CURRENT_USER\Software\Microsoft\Office\14.0\Outlook\Preferences]
"NewCategories"="Toy Show;New Products;Research"
```

2. In the text string, replace "Toy Show;New Products;Research" with your own category names, separating each category from the next with a semicolon.

3. Save the file with a .reg file name extension, and then close Notepad.

At this point, you have a registry file that other Outlook 2010 users can use to import the category list into their systems. Place the .reg file on a network share where the other users can access it, or share it on a CD, a universal serial bus (USB) drive, or other media. Then have the other users simply double-click the file to add the categories to their registry.

Sharing Categories with Email

Another (and perhaps safer) way to share categories is through email. By default, Outlook 2010 strips categories out of incoming messages so that they are not added automatically to your category list. Outlook 2010 uses a rule to enforce this behavior. If you turn off the rule, categories arrive with incoming messages. However, only the category text arrives; the color is set to None for these categories, but you can modify the categories to add your own colors.

Follow these steps to turn off the rule:

1. With the Mail folder open, click Rules on the Home tab, and then click Manage Rules And Alerts.

2. In the Rules And Alerts dialog box, clear the Clear Categories On Mail rule.

3. Click OK.

> **Note**
> In Microsoft Exchange Server 2007 and later, Clear Categories is enabled by default and is controlled by the server administrator, so the Clear Categories On Mail rule does not appear in the Rules And Alerts dialog box for Exchange Server accounts. See the Exchange Server Help documentation for the Set-TransportConfig command to learn how to enable and disable Clear Categories for Exchange Server 2007 and later.

With the rule turned off on the recipients' systems, you can now create a message, assign to it all the categories that you want to share, and then send the message. Follow these steps to add the categories to the outgoing message:

1. Start a new message.

2. In the message form, click the small arrow in the Tags area on the Message tab.

3. In the Properties dialog box, click Categories, and then assign categories to the message as desired.

4. Close the Message Options dialog box, and then send the message.

> **Note**
> You can use two registry settings to control whether Outlook 2010 will strip out categories for outgoing and incoming messages. These settings reside in HKEY_CURRENT_USER\Software\Microsoft\Office\14.0\Outlook\Preferences (although the settings do not exist by default). The setting AcceptCategories controls incoming messages, and the setting SendPersonalCategories controls outgoing messages.

Using Categories Effectively

The addition of color categories in Outlook 2010 makes categories even more useful and extends the ways that you can use categories to manage your schedule, messages, and other items in Outlook 2010. Like most Outlook 2010 features, categories are not useful in and of themselves—it's how you use them that makes them useful. Here are several tips for using categories effectively:

- **Create your categories first**   By creating your category list up front before you start assigning categories, you force yourself to take the time to think about what categories you need and how you will use them. What makes sense for someone else might not fit your needs, and vice versa. This doesn't mean that you can't add categories after the fact or change the way that you use categories, but some planning up front will help ensure that you get the most out of categorization.

- **Use categories in combination with folders to organize messages** Categories offer an excellent means for you to organize your Outlook 2010 data. Some people use folders to organize their messages; others use categories exclusively to manage their messages, keeping everything in the Inbox but assigning categories so that they can identify messages quickly. The best approach falls in between these two options, with a combination of folders and categories. Use categories to classify messages, but also use folders to organize those messages. For example, you might create a folder named Toy Show to store all messages relating to the upcoming toy show and then use categories to further classify messages in that folder.

- **Use search folders in combination with categories** After you have categorized your messages, you can use search folders to locate all messages with specified categories quickly. Search folders give you the benefit of potentially searching all your message folders for specific items, enabling you to locate all items with a specific category quickly, regardless of where they are stored. Take some time to consider which search folders will best suit your needs, and then create them.

- **Rely on colors to help you visually identify items** Although you can create categories with no color, color will help you tell at a glance that a given message, appointment, or other item fits a specific category. For example, you might color all your important meetings in red, personal appointments in green, and optional appointments or meetings in yellow. The ability to tell at a glance what an item is will help improve your productivity and effectiveness.

- **Assign color categories to messages using rules** Although you can certainly assign colors to messages manually, you should also take advantage of rules to assign categories for you automatically. For example, you might categorize messages from specific senders so that you can identify them easily in your Inbox, or use categories to identify messages from mailing lists, friends, and so on.

- **Identify your most commonly used category** Determine which category you use the most, and define that category as your Quick Click category. You can then assign that category with a single click of the mouse.

PART 2

Email and Other Messaging

A N email program isn't very useful without the capability to store addresses. Microsoft Outlook 2010, like other email–enabled applications, has this storage capability. In fact, Outlook 2010 offers multiple address books that not only can help make sending messages easy and efficient but also let you keep track of contact information for other purposes, such as postal mail, phone lists, and so on.

This chapter explores how Outlook 2010 stores addresses and explains how Outlook 2010 interacts with Microsoft Exchange Server (which has its own address lists) to provide addressing services. You'll learn how to store addresses in the Outlook 2010 Contacts folder and use them to address messages, meeting requests, appointments, and more. You'll also learn how to create distribution lists to broadcast messages and other items to groups of users and how to hide the details of the distribution list from recipients. The chapter concludes with a look at how you can share your address books with others.

> **Note**
> Although this chapter discusses the Contacts folder in the context of address lists, it doesn't cover this folder in detail.

For a detailed discussion of using and managing the Contacts folder, see Chapter 18, "Creating and Managing Your Contacts."

Understanding Address Books

As you begin working with addresses in Outlook 2010, you'll find that you can store them in multiple locations. For example, if you're using an Exchange Server account, you have a couple of locations from which to select addresses. Understanding where these address books reside is an important first step in putting them to work for you. The following sections describe the various address books in Outlook 2010 and how you can use them.

Outlook 2010 Address Book

On all installations, including those with no email accounts, Outlook 2010 creates a default Outlook Address Book (OAB). This address book consolidates all your Outlook 2010 Contacts folders. With a new installation of Outlook 2010, the OAB shows only one location for storing addresses: the default Contacts folder. As you add other Contacts folders, those additional folders appear in the OAB, as shown in Figure 6-1. As you'll learn in the section "Removing Contacts Folders from the OAB" later in this chapter, you can configure additional Contacts folders so that they don't appear in the OAB.

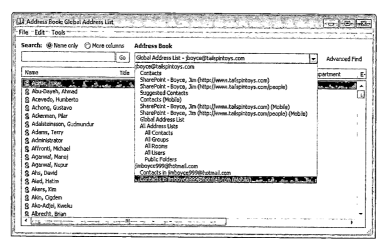

Figure 6-1 The OAB shows all Contacts folders for your profile.

For detailed information on creating and using additional Contacts folders, see the section "Creating Other Contacts Folders" on page 439.

The OAB functions as a virtual address book collection instead of as an address book because Outlook 2010 doesn't store the OAB as a file separate from your data store. Instead, the OAB provides a view into your Contacts folders and other contact sources.

> **Note**
>
> Earlier versions of Office Outlook prior to 2007 enabled users to store addresses in Personal Address Books (PABs), which were kept in separate files from the personal data store. Although PABs are not available in Outlook 2010, you can import them into a Contacts folder, which is visible in the OAB.

Global Address List (GAL)

When you use a profile that contains an Exchange Server account, you'll find one other address list in addition to the OAB: the Global Address List (GAL). This address list resides on the computer running Exchange Server and presents the list of mailboxes on the server as well as other address items created on the server, including distribution groups and external addresses (see Figure 6-2). However, users can't create address information in the GAL; only the Exchange Server system administrator can do this.

> **Note**
>
> An Exchange Server environment can and often does include more than one server. For the purposes of discussion in this book, we use the singular term server to refer to the collection of computers running Exchange Server that make up your Exchange Server environment.

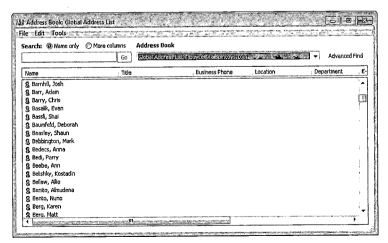

Figure 6-2 The Global Address List shows addresses on the computer running Exchange Server.

LDAP (Internet Directory Services)

Some email addresses are not available in the OAB or GAL but are available using the Light-weight Directory Access Protocol (LDAP). This requires network connectivity to the LDAP server. LDAP simply provides a mechanism for Outlook to query and obtain contact information from one or more servers that host LDAP data stores.

Details on configuration are found in Chapter 17, "Using LDAP Directory Services."

Other Address Lists

In addition to the OAB, GAL, and LDAP, you might see other address sources when you look for addresses in Outlook 2010. For example, in an organization with a large address list, the Exchange Server system administrator might create additional address lists to filter the view to show only a selection, such as contacts with last names starting with the letter A or contacts external to the organization. You might also see a list named All Address Lists. This list, which comes from Exchange Server, can be modified by the Exchange Server administrator to include additional address lists. The list can also include Public Folders (see Figure 6-3), which can store shared contacts. In addition, the list by default includes All Contacts, All Groups, All Rooms, and All Users, which sort addresses by type.

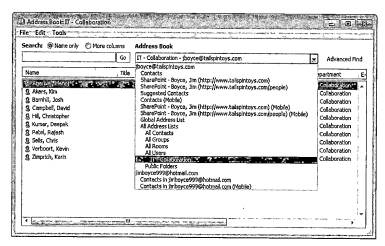

Figure 6-3 Additional address lists can display filtered lists of contacts.

Configuring Address Books and Addressing Options

Outlook 2010 offers a handful of settings that you can use to configure the way your address books display contacts and address information. You also can add other address books and choose which address book Outlook 2010 uses by default for opening and storing addresses and processing messages.

Setting the Contacts Display Option for the OAB

You can set only one option for the OAB. This setting controls the order in which Outlook 2010 displays names from the OAB: either First Last or using the File As field (Last Name, First Name).

Follow these steps to set this display option:

1. If Outlook 2010 is open, click File, Account Settings, and Account Settings, and then select the Address Books tab. If Outlook 2010 is not open, open the Mail item from the Control Panel, click E-Mail Accounts, and then select the Address Books tab.

2. Select Outlook Address Book and click Change to display the Microsoft Office Outlook Address Book dialog box, shown in Figure 6-4.

Figure 6-4 Select the display option for Outlook Address Book entries in the Microsoft Outlook Address Book dialog box.

3. In the Show Names By box, select the display format that you prefer. Click Close, and then click Close again.

Removing Contacts Folders from the OAB

In most cases, you'll want all your Contacts folders to appear in the OAB. If you have several Contacts folders, however, you might prefer to limit how many folders appear in the OAB, or you might simply want to restrict the folders to ensure that specific addresses are used.

You can set the folder's properties to determine whether it appears in the OAB by following these steps:

1. Open Outlook 2010 and open the folders list (or click the Contacts button in the Navigation pane). Then, right-click the Contacts folder in question and choose Properties.

2. Click the Outlook Address Book tab and clear the Show This Folder As An E-Mail Address Book option to prevent the folder from appearing in the OAB.

3. Change the folder name, if necessary, and then click OK.

> **Note**
> You can't remove the default Contacts folder from the OAB, nor can you remove the Hotmail address book if you are using the Outlook Connector for Hotmail.

Setting Other Addressing Options

You can configure other addressing options to determine which address book Outlook 2010 displays by default for selecting addresses, which address book is used by default for storing new addresses, and the order in which address books are processed when Outlook 2010 checks names for sending messages. The following sections explain these options in detail.

Selecting the Default Address Book for Lookup

To suit your needs or preferences, you can have Outlook 2010 display a different address list by default. For example, for profiles that include Exchange Server accounts, Outlook 2010 displays the GAL by default. If you use the GAL only infrequently and primarily use your Contacts folders for addressing, you might prefer to have Outlook 2010 show the OAB as the default address list instead of the GAL, or you might want to display a filtered address list other than the GAL on the server.

Follow these steps to specify the default address list:

1. In Outlook 2010, click Address Book in the Find group on the Home tab of the Ribbon. Outlook 2010 displays the Address Book dialog box.

2. Choose Tools, Options.

3. In the Addressing dialog box, select the default address list from the When Opening The Address Book, Show This Address List First drop-down list (see Figure 6-5).

Figure 6-5 You can specify the default address list in the Addressing dialog box.

4. Click OK.

Creating Address Entries in a Specific Address Book

Although you can't add addresses in the GAL or other server address books, you can store them in other, local address books. You can create addresses in the Address Book, and when you do so, Outlook 2010 suggests storing the entry in the address book that you have chosen as the default. If you want to store a particular address in a different address book, start by opening the Address Book as described in the previous section. Click File, New Entry to open the New Entry dialog box. Click the Put This Entry In The option and select the address book from the drop-down list (see Figure 6-6). Fill in the resulting Contact form and click Save & Close.

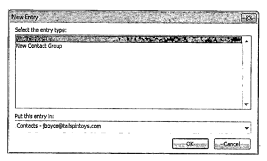

Figure 6-6 Use the New Entry dialog box to determine where to store a new address when you create it from the Address Book.

> **Note**
> Your local Contacts folder is the default location for storing new address book entries unless you set a different one as the default.

Specifying How Names Are Checked

When you create a message, you can specify the recipient's name instead of specifying the address. Instead of typing jim.boyce@tailspintoys.com, for example, you might type Jim Boyce and let Outlook 2010 convert the name to an email address for you. This saves you the time of opening the address book to look for the entry if you know the name under which it's stored. To have Outlook check the address, simply press Ctrl+K or click Check Names in the Names group on the ribbon.

Outlook 2010 checks the address books to determine the correct address based on the name you entered. Outlook 2010 checks names from multiple address books if they are defined in the current profile. For example, Outlook 2010 might process the address through the GAL first, then through your OAB, and then through the LDAP (assuming that all three are in the profile). If Outlook 2010 finds a match, it replaces the name in the message with the appropriate address. If it doesn't find a match or finds more than one, it displays the Check Names dialog box, shown in Figure 6-7, in which you can select the correct address, create a new one, or open the address book to display more names and then select an address.

Figure 6-7. The Check Names dialog box helps you resolve address problems before you send a message.

Why change the order in which Outlook 2010 checks your address books? If most of your addresses are stored in an address book other than the one Outlook 2010 is currently checking first, changing the order can speed up name checking, particularly if the address book contains numerous entries.

Here's how to change the address book order:

1. In Outlook 2010, open the Address Book window from the Find group on the ribbon and choose Tools, Options.

2. Choose Custom, click an address book, and then click the up and down arrow buttons to rearrange the address book order in the list.

3. Click OK to close the dialog box.

Creating Address Book Entries

To create a contact quickly while you're composing a message, type the email address in the To, Cc, or Bcc field, and then press Tab. The email address becomes underlined after a short delay. Right-click the email address and select Add To Outlook Contacts (see Figure 6-8). You can also create new contacts, contact groups, and other types of entries from any navigation pane. To do this, select the drop-down arrow next to the New Items button on the Home tab of the ribbon and choose the type of item to create.

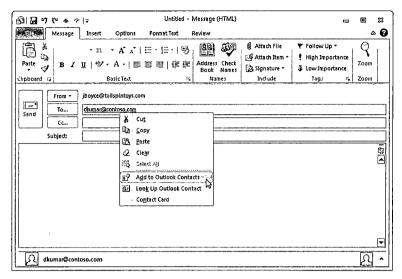

Figure 6-8 Right-clicking an email address gives you extra options.

Modifying Addresses

You can modify any addresses stored in your own address books, as well as in the address books of other users for which you have the appropriate access. You can modify an address while working with an email message or while working directly in the address book. If you're using a message form, click To, Cc, or Bcc. Right-click the address you want to change and click Properties. If you're working in the address book instead, just right-click the address and choose Properties. Outlook 2010 displays the same form you used to create the contact. Make the changes you want and click OK.

Removing Addresses

Removing a contact from the OAB is much easier than creating one. Open the OAB, select the address you want to delete, and press Delete.

Finding People in the Address Book

If your address book contains numerous addresses, as might be the case in a very large organization, it can be a chore to locate an address if you don't use it often. Outlook 2010 provides a search capability in the address book to overcome that problem, making it relatively easy to locate addresses based on several criteria.

> **Note**
> You can simply click in the text box at the top of the Address Book and type a name.
> Outlook 2010 locates the first name that matches the text you type. If you prefer to see
> only those items that match the text for which you are searching, you can use the Find
> dialog box, as described in the following steps.

Follow these steps to locate an address in any address book:

1. Click the Address Book button on the ribbon to open the address book.

2. In the Address Book drop-down list, select the address book you want to search.

3. Click Advanced Find to display the Find dialog box shown in Figure 6-9 (for Exchange
   Server address lists) or Figure 6-10 (for the OAB).

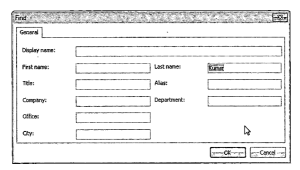

Figure 6-9 Use the Find dialog box to locate people in the Exchange Server GAL.

Figure 6-10 The Find dialog box offers only a single search field for OAB searches.

4. If you're searching an address list on the computer running Exchange Server, decide which criteria you want to use and enter data in the fields to define the search. If you're searching an OAB, specify the text to search for, which must be contained in the contact's name.

5. Click OK to perform the search.

When you click OK, Outlook 2010 performs a search in the selected address book based on your search criteria and displays the results in the Address Book window. You can revert to the full address book list by selecting the address book from the Address Book drop-down list. Select Search Results from the Address Book drop-down list to view the results of the last search.

INSIDE OUT   Using a directory service

In addition to searching your address books, you also can search a directory service for information about contacts. A directory service is a server that answers queries about data (typically contact information) stored on the server. For detailed information on setting up and using directory services in Outlook 2010, see the section "Configuring a Directory Service Account in Outlook," on page 423.

Using AutoComplete for Addresses

If you have used previous versions of Outlook, you are probably familiar with Outlook's nickname cache, which stored the addresses that you type in the address fields so that you would not have to type them again the next time you wanted to use them. Instead, you simply typed a few characters and Outlook suggested email addresses based on what you typed. In these previous versions of Outlook, these addresses were stored in a nickname file within your user profile.

Outlook 2010 still automatically keeps track of addresses that you enter in the address fields, but it does away with the nickname cache file and instead stores them in the Suggested Contacts folder in Outlook. When you type an address in the To, Cc, or Bcc fields, Outlook 2010 adds the address to the folder, which looks and functions much like your regular Outlook Contacts folder.

When you begin typing in any of these address fields, Outlook 2010 begins matching the typed characters against the entries in the Suggested Contacts folder. If it finds a match, it automatically completes the address. If there is more than one match in the folder, Outlook 2010 displays a drop-down list that contains the names for all the matching entries (see

Figure 6-11). Use the arrow keys or mouse to select a name from the list and then press Enter or Tab to add the address to the field.

> **Note**
>
> AutoComplete doesn't check to see whether a particular contact has more than one email address. Instead, it uses whatever address it finds in the Suggested Contacts folder. If Outlook 2010 has cached one address, but you prefer that it cache a different one, delete the existing cache entry (as explained in the next section). Then, address a new message to the contact using the desired email address to cache that address. Or, as the following section explains, you can simply create a contact entry in the Suggested Contacts folder.

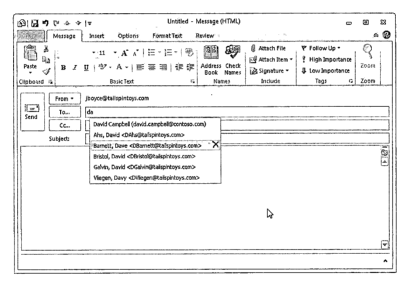

Figure 6-11 Select a name from the Suggested Contacts list offered by Outlook 2010.

You can turn AutoComplete on or off to suit your needs by following these steps:

1. Click File, choose Options, and click Mail in the left pane of the Outlook Options dialog box.

2. Scroll down to the Send Messages group of settings.

3. Select or clear the Use Auto-Complete List To Suggest Names When Typing In The To, Cc, And Bcc Lines check box to turn AutoComplete on or off, respectively.

> **Tip**
> You can move your Suggested Contacts folder file from one computer to another by simply exporting the items and then importing them. You can also back it up so you can restore it in the event your computer crashes.

See the section "Backing Up and Restoring Data," on page 769, for details.

Deleting or Adding Entries in the Suggested Contacts Folder

One common reason to delete a contact item from the Suggested Contacts folder is that you either don't use it very often or want to use a different email address for that contact.

It's easy to delete a name from the Suggested Contacts folder. One of the most direct ways is simply to open the Suggested Contacts folder, locate the item, and delete it. You can also get to it indirectly through the message form, which is often quicker than opening the folder and hunting for the item. To do this, perform the following steps:

1. Start a new email message and type the first few letters of the name.

2. When Outlook 2010 displays the shortcut menu with the matching entries, select the one you want to delete and then press Delete.

3. Repeat this process for any other cached addresses you want to delete.

As described in the previous section, you can add items to the Suggested Contacts folder simply by adding a new email address to one of the address fields on a message form and then sending the message. But because the Outlook 2010 Suggested Contacts folder acts just like your other Contacts folders, you can create items directly in the folder. Just click Contacts in the Navigation pane, and then click Suggested Contacts in the list of contact folders. Click New Contact in the ribbon, fill in as much information as you like (or just add the email address), and click Save & Close.

Deleting the Entire Contents of the Suggested Contacts Folder

On occasion, you might want to clear out your Suggested Contacts folder and let Outlook start fresh. Perhaps you have several hundred items in the folder or so many duplicates that you are getting too many off-target suggestions. You have two options for deleting all the items from the Suggested Contacts folder. One is simply to open the folder, press Ctrl+A to select all items in the folder, and then press Delete or click Delete in the ribbon. If you change your mind right after deleting something, immediately press Ctrl+Z to get it back.

You can also clear out the folder from the Outlook Options dialog box by doing the following:

1. Click File, Options to open the Outlook Options dialog box, then click Mail in the left pane.

2. Scroll down to the Send Messages group and click Empty Auto-Complete List.

Using Contact Groups (Distribution Lists)

If you often send messages to groups of people, adding all their addresses to a message one at a time can be a real chore, particularly if you're sending the message to many recipients. Contact groups in Outlook 2010 help simplify the process, enabling you to send a message to a single address and have it broadcast to all recipients in the group. Instead of addressing a message to each individual user in the sales department, for example, you could address it to the sales contact group. Outlook 2010 (or Exchange Server) takes care of sending the message to all the members of the group.

> **Tip**
> **Previous versions of Outlook refer to contact groups as distribution lists. The terms contact group and distribution list are used synonymously in this book except where noted.**

You can create contact groups in the OAB. You can't create contact groups in the GAL or other Exchange Server address lists—only the Exchange Server administrator can create the distribution lists on the server. However, you can modify distribution lists on the computer running Exchange Server if you're designated as the owner of the list.

Creating Contact Groups

Setting up a contact group in your OAB is a relatively simple procedure. You can create a contact group using addresses from multiple address books, which means, for example, that you might include addresses from the GAL on the computer running Exchange Server as well as personal addresses stored in your Contacts folder. You can also include addresses of different types (for example, Exchange Server addresses, Internet addresses, and X.400 addresses). In general, it's easiest to set up a contact group if all the addresses to be included already exist, but you can enter addresses on the fly if needed.

Follow these steps to create a contact group:

1. Open the address book.

2. Choose File, New Entry or right-click in any area of the address list field and click New Entry.

3. From the drop-down list, select the address book in which you want to store the distribution list.

4. In the Select The Entry Type list, select New Contact Group, and then click OK to display the Contact Group dialog box, as shown in Figure 6-12.

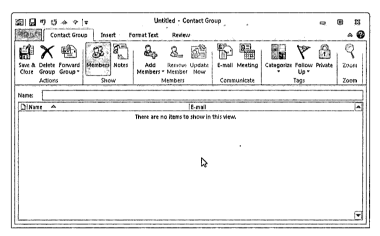

Figure 6-12 Use the Contact Group dialog box to create a contact group.

5. In the Name box, specify a name for the group. This is the contact group name that will appear in your address book.

6. Click Add Members, and then, if the contact already exists, choose From Outlook Contacts to add addresses from your Contacts folder, or choose From Address Book to add from other locations in the OAB (such as the Exchange Server GAL). In either case, the Select Members dialog box opens (see Figure 6-13).

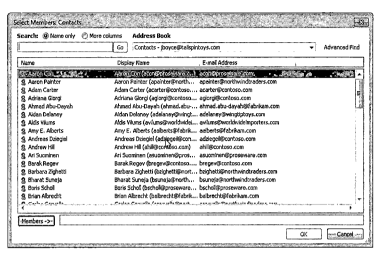

Figure 6-13 Add members to the distribution list using the Select Members dialog box.

7. If the contact does not already exist, click Add Members on the ribbon and choose New E-Mail Contact to open the Add New Member dialog box. Enter the person's name and email address and, if desired, choose a sending format for the recipient (such as plain text only). If you want Outlook to add the new contact to your Contacts folder, leave the Add to Contacts check box selected. Click OK when you finish adding members to the list.

8. Set other options as needed for the distribution list—for example, you can assign categories to the list, mark it as private, or add notes to the group.

9. Click Save & Close in the Contact Group dialog box.

> **Tip**
>
> Select the Advanced Find option in the Select Members dialog box to search all your address books for members. Enter a name or partial name to display all address book matches to find the desired contact.

Contact groups appear in the address book with a group icon and a boldface name to differentiate them from individual addresses (see Figure 6-14).

Figure 6-14 Outlook 2010 differentiates between addresses and contract groups in the address book.

INSIDE OUT   Address types identified

Outlook 2010 differentiates addresses in the Select Names dialog box as well as the Address Book. When you address an email message, you can tell which address is a fax number and which is an email address because Outlook displays those items separately in the list, even though they are stored in the same contact item. You can also easily differentiate personal addresses from work addresses in both the Select Names and Address Book dialog boxes.

Note

In a Contacts folder, contact groups look just like addresses, although Outlook 2010 displays a contact group in the address list with a group icon and with the contact group name in bold. The contact group also shows less information than a contact in the various Contacts folder views.

Modifying a Contact Group

Over time, you will add or remove names from your contact groups. To modify the contents of a group, locate the contact group in the address book or in your Contacts folder, open the group, and then use the Select Members button to modify the list. You can also remove members from the group by selecting the member and then clicking the Remove Member button on the ribbon, or by pressing Delete on your keyboard.

Renaming a Contact Group

You can change the name of a contact group any time after you create it to reflect changes in the way you use the list, to correct spelling, or for any other reason. To rename a contact group, locate the list in the address book, open it, and then change the name in the Name box. Click Save & Close to apply the change.

Deleting a Contact Group

You can delete a contact group the same way you delete an address. Locate the contact group in the address book or Contacts folder, select it, and then click the Delete button on the ribbon or press Delete. Alternatively, you can right-click the group and choose Delete from its shortcut menu.

> **Note**
> Deleting a contact group doesn't delete the addresses associated with the group.

Hiding Addresses When Using a Contact Group

If you include a contact group in the To or Cc field of a message, all the recipients of your message—whether members of the group or not—can see the addresses of individuals in the group. Outlook 2010 doesn't retain the group name in the address field of the message but instead replaces it with the actual addresses from the group.

In some cases, you might not want to have their addresses made public, even to other members of the group. In these situations, add the contact group to the Bcc (blind carbon copy) field instead of the To or Cc field. The Bcc field sends copies of the email to all addresses and contact groups but keeps the addresses hidden from the other recipients.

Contact Groups for Multiple Address Fields

Regardless of where you create a contact group, you can't allocate some addresses in the group to the To field and other addresses to the Cc or Bcc field. You can, however, place the contact group address in either the Cc or Bcc field, if needed.

If you often need to separate addresses from contact groups into different address fields, you can use a couple of techniques to simplify the process. First, consider splitting the contact groups into two or three separate groups. This approach works well if the To, Cc, and Bcc fields generally receive the same addresses each time. A second approach is to create a template with the addresses already filled in, as follows:

1. Start a new mail message.

2. To view the Bcc field, click the Options tab on the ribbon and then click Bcc.

3. Fill in the addresses in the appropriate fields as needed.

4. Click File and choose Save As.

5. In the Save As dialog box, choose Outlook Template from the Save As Type drop-down list.

6. Specify a name and location for the template and click Save.

When you need to send a message using the template, browse to the folder in which the template is stored and double-click the file to open the message template. Add any additional addresses, text, or attachments; then send the message as usual.

Using Distribution Lists with Exchange Server

You can use distribution lists with Exchange Server—which are set up by the Exchange Server administrator—in the same way that you use local contact groups to simplify broadcasting messages to multiple recipients. (As mentioned earlier, you can't create your own contact groups or distribution lists in the GAL or other Exchange Server address lists from Outlook 2010, although you can modify such a list if you are designated as the list owner.)

You can use a server-side distribution list in the same way that you use a local contact group. Select the list from the appropriate address list on the server. The list name is converted to addresses when you send the message, just as a local contact group is.

Adding a Server-Side Distribution List to Contacts

If you prefer working through your local address books instead of the server address lists, you might want to add a server-side distribution list to your local Contacts folder. You can do so easily through the address book or the list's dialog box. Open the address book, select the distribution list, and then choose File, Add To Contacts.

> **Tip**
>
> If you have the list's dialog box open, click Add To Contacts on the General tab. Outlook 2010 then adds the list to your Contacts folder.

When Outlook 2010 displays the distribution list, you can then modify the group, assign categories, send a meeting request or email, mark it as private, or even use the Proof button to run a spell-check or use the thesaurus (see Figure 6-15). Make any necessary changes to the distribution list and then click Save & Close.

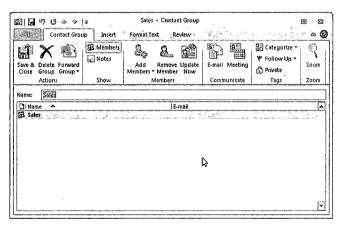

Figure 6-15 You can select various options for distribution lists you store in the Contacts folder.

Modifying a Server-Side Distribution List

If you are an owner of a server-side distribution list, you can modify its members and other properties. For example, perhaps you manage a team of people and the team has a distribution list in Exchange Server. A new person joins your team, and you want to add that person to the list. To do so, open the address book and double-click the distribution list to open it (see Figure 6-16). You can add or remove members by clicking Modify Members.

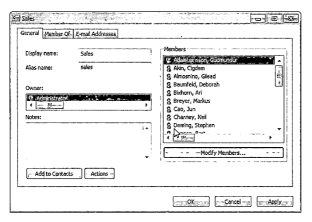

Figure 6-16 You can modify members of server-side distribution lists that you own.

Adding Addresses to the Address Book Automatically

When you receive a message from a sender whose address you want to save in your local Contacts folder, you can add the address manually. As it has for previous versions, however, Outlook 2010 also provides an easier method. With the message open, right-click the sender's address on the InfoBar and choose Add To Outlook Contacts.

Outlook 2010 offers a new method for adding contacts from incoming email, however, in the form of the Suggested Contacts folder. As new messages arrive, Outlook checks to see if the sender already exists in your Contacts folder. If not, Outlook adds the address to the Suggested Contacts folder. From there, you can drag the contact item to your regular Contacts folder or use copy and paste to copy it from one folder to another. Outlook also adds the addresses of people to whom you have addressed email.

Using the Mobile Address Book (MAB)

Like Outlook 2007, Outlook 2010 includes the Mobile Address Book (MAB), which is added automatically to your profile.

See the section "Using Outlook Mobile Service Accounts," on page 1005, for more details on Mobile Service accounts.

Like the OAB, the MAB does not actually store addresses. Instead, it searches for and displays existing addresses that have phone numbers in the Mobile contact field (see Figure 6-17). Because the MAB searches for and displays these contacts automatically, you don't have to do anything to add them to the MAB.

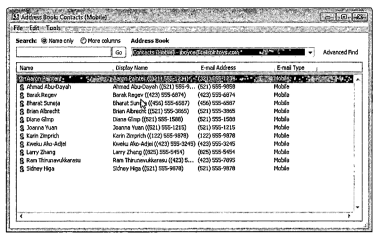

Figure 6-17 The MAB displays contacts that have entries in the Mobile contact field.

You can use the MAB as a means to look up mobile numbers for your contacts quickly. Just open the OAB and select Contacts (Mobile) in the Address Book drop-down list.

To learn how to work with the MAB in conjunction with an Outlook Mobile Service account, see the section "Using Outlook Mobile Service Accounts," on page 1005.

> **Note**
> Deleting an entry from the MAB deletes only the number in the Mobile field of the associated contact item; it does not delete the contact itself

CHAPTER 7

Using Internet Mail Accounts

TODAY, it seems as though everyone is using Internet email. So it's a good bet that you'll want to use Microsoft Outlook 2010 to send and receive messages through at least one Internet email account. For the purposes of this chapter, the term Internet email account refers to any email account for which you use POP3, Internet Message Access Protocol (IMAP), or Hypertext Transfer Protocol (HTTP).

This chapter focuses on setting up Outlook 2010 to access Internet mail servers and accounts. The chapter also covers topics related to sending and receiving Internet email. You'll learn how to create Internet email accounts, use multiple accounts, and work with email accounts for services such as Microsoft Hotmail. You'll also learn how to ensure that your messages are available from different locations, what to do if your email service won't accept outgoing mail from your dial-up location, and how to view full message headers in Internet email.

> **Note**
>
> This chapter assumes that your system is already set up to connect to the Internet, either on a broadband connection, such as a local area network (LAN), Digital Subscriber Line (DSL), or cable modem, or by a dial-up connection. Whatever the situation, your Internet service provider (ISP) or network administrator has likely set up the connection for you. This chapter instead focuses on configuring Outlook 2010 to use the existing connection and setting up specific types of accounts.

For help in creating email accounts and assigning the dial-up connection, see the section "Configuring Accounts and Services," on page 49.

Using Internet POP3 Email Accounts

Most Internet-based email servers use Simple Mail Transfer Protocol (SMTP) and POP3 to allow subscribers to send and receive messages across the Internet. (A few exceptions use IMAP; still other services, such as Hotmail and Yahoo!, use HTTP. Some, like Gmail, give you an option of which protocol to use. These other protocols are covered later in this chapter.) If you have an account with a local ISP or other service provider that offers POP3 accounts, or if your office server is a non–Microsoft Exchange Server system that supports only POP3, you can add an Internet email account to Outlook 2010 to access that server.

INSIDE OUT Configure multiple accounts in one profile

You can configure multiple email accounts in a single Outlook 2010 profile, giving you access to multiple servers to send and receive messages. For additional information, see the section "Using Multiple Accounts," on page 174.

Follow these steps to add an Internet email account to Outlook 2010:

1. With Outlook 2010 open, click File, Add Account.

2. To use the automatic discovery feature to obtain your server configuration information automatically from your existing email server, on the Add New Account page, shown in Figure 7-1, specify the following information:

   - **Your Name**   Specify your name as you want it to appear in the From box of messages you send.

   - **E-Mail Address**   Enter your email address in the form <user>@<domain. tld>, where <user> is your user account name and <domain.tld> is the name of your email domain.

   - **Password/Retype Password**   Type your password in the Password field, and then confirm the password in the Retype Password field.

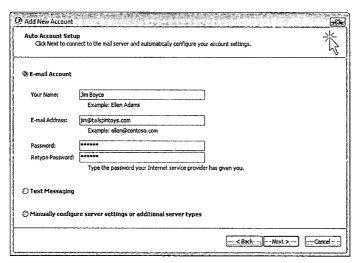

Figure 7-1 Use the Add New Account page to configure the email server settings automatically.

3. Enter your name, email address, and password (twice) for your email account, and then click Next. Outlook 2010 will try to connect to your email server and obtain configuration information via an encrypted connection. If Outlook is able to identify your account settings, the process is complete and you can skip the remaining steps.

4. If your email server doesn't support encrypted connections, this attempt will fail, and you will be prompted to try an unencrypted connection.

5. If this attempt doesn't complete, you will be prompted to verify the email address and click Retry.

6. If this attempt doesn't complete, the Problem Connecting To Server dialog box is displayed, indicating that you will need to configure the settings manually—the Manually Configure Server Settings check box will be selected automatically. Click Next to continue.

7. In the Choose Service dialog box, select Internet E-Mail, and then click Next.

8. On the Internet E-Mail Settings page, shown in Figure 7-2, configure the following settings:

- **Your Name**   Specify your name as you want it to appear in the From box of messages that others receive from you.

- **E-Mail Address**   Specify the email address for your account in the form <account>@<domain>—for example, chill@tailspintoys.com.

- **Account Type**   In the Server Information area, select the Account Type (in this case, POP3) of the email server.

- **Incoming Mail Server**   Specify the IP address or Domain Name System (DNS) name of the mail server that processes your incoming mail. This is the server where your POP3 mailbox is located and from which your incoming mail is downloaded. Often, your mail server will use the host name mail and your mail server's domain name. So an example of a mail server DNS name might be mail.tailspintoys.com. However, this isn't a given rule, so check with your ISP or network administrator for the correct mail server host name.

- **Outgoing Mail Server (SMTP)**   Specify the IP address or DNS name of the mail server that you use to send outgoing mail. In many cases, this is the same server as the one specified for incoming mail, but it can be different. Some organizations and many ISPs separate incoming and outgoing mail services onto different servers for load balancing, security, or other reasons.

> **Note**
> Many mail servers will not allow outgoing mail unless you authenticate on the server. See the section "Configuring Outgoing Server Settings for Internet Accounts," on page 167, for details.

- **User Name**   Specify the user account on the server that you must use to log on to your mailbox to retrieve your messages. In some cases, you should not include the domain portion of your email address. For example, if your address is chill@tailspintoys.com, your user name is chill. However, some mail servers require the full email address as the user name to log on.

- **Password**   Specify the password for the user account entered in the User Name box.

- **Remember Password**   Select this option to have Outlook 2010 maintain the password for this account in your local password cache, eliminating the need for you to enter the password each time you want to retrieve your mail. Clear this check box to prevent other users from downloading your mail while you are away from your computer. If the check box is cleared, Outlook 2010 prompts you for the password for each session.

- **Require Logon Using Secure Passwordbac Authentication (SPA)**   Select this option if your server uses SPA to authenticate your access to the server.

- **New Outlook Data File.** Choose this option to have Outlook 2010 create a new .pst file to contain your data for the new account.

- **Existing Outlook Data File.** Choose this option if you want to use an existing .pst file to store mail and other items for this account.

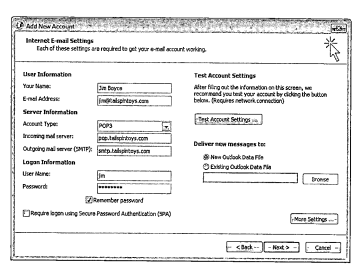

Figure 7-2 Use the Internet E-Mail Settings page to configure the account settings.

9. Click More Settings to display the Internet E-Mail Settings dialog box, shown in Figure 7-3. You can configure these settings based on the information in the following sections.

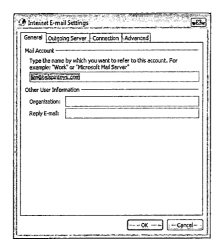

Figure 7-3 Use the General tab to specify the account name, organization, and reply email details.

Configuring General Settings for Internet Accounts

Use the General tab in the Internet E-Mail Settings dialog box (shown in Figure 7-3) to change the account name that is displayed in Outlook 2010 and to specify organization and reply address information as follows:

- **Mail Account** Specify the name of the account as you want it to appear in the Outlook 2010 account list. This name has no bearing on the server name or your account name. Use the name to differentiate one account from another—for example, you might have various accounts named Gmail, Work, and Personal.

- **Organization** Specify the group or organization name that you want to associate with the account.

- **Reply E-Mail** Specify an email address that you want others to use when replying to messages that you send with this account. For example, you might redirect replies to another mail server address if you are in the process of changing ISPs or mail servers. Enter the address in its full form—chill@tailspintoys.com, for example. Leave this option blank if you want users to reply to the email address that you specified in the E-Mail Address box for the account.

Configuring Outgoing Server Settings for Internet Accounts

Use the Outgoing Server tab, shown in Figure 7-4, to configure a handful of settings for the SMTP server that handles the account's outgoing messages. Although in most cases you won't need to modify these settings, you will have to do so if your server requires you to authenticate to send outgoing messages. Some ISPs use authentication as a means of allowing mail relay from their clients outside their local subnets. This allows authorized users to relay mail and prevents unauthorized relay or unauthorized users from sending spam through the server.

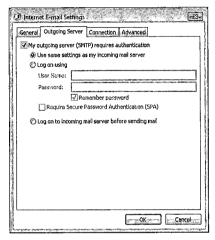

Figure 7-4 Use the Outgoing Server tab to configure authentication and other options for your SMTP server.

The Outgoing Server tab contains the following options:

- **My Outgoing Server (SMTP) Requires Authentication** Select this option if the SMTP mail server that processes your outgoing mail requires authentication. Connections that don't provide valid credentials are rejected. Selecting this option makes several other options on the tab available.

- **Use Same Settings As My Incoming Mail Server** Select this option if the SMTP server credentials are the same as your POP3 (incoming) server credentials.

- **Log On Using** Select this option if the SMTP server requires a different set of credentials from those required by your POP3 server. You should specify a valid account name on the SMTP server in the User Name box as well as a password for that account. In general, you will have to change this setting only if your SMTP and POP3 servers are separate physical servers.

- **Remember Password**   Select this check box to have Outlook 2010 save your password from session to session. Clear the check box if you want Outlook 2010 to prompt you for a password each time.

- **Require Secure Password Authentication (SPA)**   Select this check box if your server uses SPA to authenticate your access to the server.

- **Log On To Incoming Mail Server Before Sending Mail**   Select this option to have Outlook 2010 log on to the POP3 server before sending outgoing messages. Use this option if the outgoing and incoming mail servers are the same server and if the server is configured to require authentication to send messages.

Configuring Connection Settings for Internet Accounts

Use the Connection tab, shown in Figure 7-5, to specify how Outlook 2010 should connect to the mail server for this Internet account. You can connect using the LAN (which includes DSL and cable modem broadband connections), a dial-up connection, or a third-party dialer such as the one included with Windows Internet Explorer.

- **Connect Using My Local Area Network (LAN)**   Select the LAN option if your computer is hard-wired to the Internet (LAN, DSL, cable modem, or other persistent connection).

- **Connect Via Modem When Outlook Is Offline**   If you use a shared dial-up connection to access the Internet, select this check box if you want Outlook 2010 to attempt a LAN connection first, followed by a dial-up connection if the first attempt fails (for example, when your notebook PC is disconnected from the LAN but a dial-up connection is available).

- **Connect Using My Phone Line**   Select this option if you are using a dial-up connection as your default mode of connecting to the Internet or other network hosting your mail server. Select this option to use an existing dial-up networking connection or to create a new dial-up connection. Select the connection from the drop-down list, and then click Properties if you need to modify the dial-up connection. Click Add if you need to add a dial-up connection.

- **Connect Using Internet Explorer's Or A 3rd Party Dialer**   Select this option if you want Internet Explorer or another phone dialer application to dial your connection to the network hosting your mail server. If you want to connect to the Internet or to your remote network using the dialer that is included with Internet Explorer or a dialer that is included with a third-party dial-up client, select this option.

- **Use The Following Dial-Up Networking Connection**   Select the modem profile to use when dialing your ISP connection.

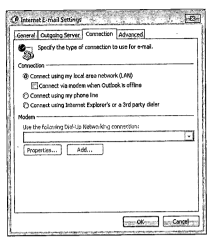

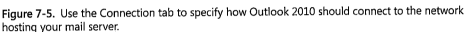

Figure 7-5. Use the Connection tab to specify how Outlook 2010 should connect to the network hosting your mail server.

Configuring Advanced Settings for Internet Accounts

Although you won't normally need to configure settings on the Advanced tab for an Internet account, the settings can be useful in some situations. You can use the following options on the Advanced tab, shown in Figure 7-6, to specify the SMTP and POP3 ports for the server, along with time-outs and these other settings:

- **Incoming Server (POP3)**   Specify the Transmission Control Protocol (TCP) port used by the POP3 server. The default port is 110. Specifying a nonstandard port works only if the server is listening for POP3 traffic on the specified port.

- **Outgoing Server (SMTP)**   Specify the TCP port used by the SMTP server for outgoing mail. The default port is 25. Specifying a nonstandard port works only if the server is listening for SMTP traffic on the specified port.

- **This Server Requires An Encrypted Connection (SSL)**   Choose this option if your mail server requires Secure Sockets Layer (SSL) to connect to the server. SSL provides an encrypted connection between your computer and the server for added security.

- **Use Defaults**   Click this button to restore the default port settings for POP3 and SMTP.

- **Use The Following Type Of Encrypted Connection**   If your server requires an encrypted connection, use this drop-down list to select the correct type of encryption method—either SSL, TLS, Auto, or None. Select SSL if the server requires the use of a

Secure Sockets Layer (SSL) connection, TLS if it requires Transport Layer Security (TLS), and Auto if you want Outlook 2010 to negotiate encryption automatically with the mail server. With rare exceptions, public POP3 and SMTP mail servers do not require SSL connections.

- **Server Timeouts** Use this control to change the period of time that Outlook 2010 will wait for a connection to the server.

- **Leave A Copy Of Messages On The Server** Select this check box to retain a copy of all messages on the server, downloading a copy of the message to Outlook 2010. This is a useful feature if you want to access the same POP3 account from different computers and want to be able to access your messages from each one. Clear this check box if you want Outlook 2010 to download your messages and then delete them from the server. Some servers impose a storage limit, making it impractical to leave all your messages on the server.

- **Remove From Server After n Days** Select this check box to have Outlook 2010 delete messages from the server a specified number of days after they are down-loaded to your system.

- **Remove From Server When Deleted From 'Deleted Items'** Select this option to have Outlook 2010 delete messages from the server when you delete the down-loaded copies from your local Deleted Items folder.

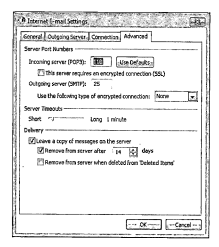

Figure 7-6 Use the Advanced tab to specify nonstandard TCP ports for the server.

Using IMAP Accounts

IMAP is becoming more common on Internet-based email servers because it offers several advantages over POP3. Outlook 2010 support for IMAP means that you can use Outlook 2010 to send and receive messages through IMAP servers as well as through Exchange Server, POP3, and the other mail server types that Outlook 2010 supports.

For more information about IMAP and its differences from POP3, see the section "IMAP," on page 33.

Configuring an IMAP account is a lot like configuring a POP3 account. The only real difference is that you select IMAP as the account type rather than POP3 when you add the account. You can refer to the preceding section on creating POP3 accounts, "Using Internet POP3 Email Accounts," for a description of the procedure to follow when adding an IMAP account. The one setting you might want to review or change for an IMAP account as opposed to a POP3 account is the root folder path. This setting is located on the Advanced tab of the account's Internet E-Mail Settings dialog box. To access this setting, open this dialog box, click More Settings, and then click Advanced. Specify the path to the specific folder in your mailbox folder structure that you want to use as the root for your mailbox. If you aren't sure what path to enter, leave this option blank to use the default path provided by the account.

Controlling Where Outlook Stores IMAP Messages

When you create an IMAP account in an Outlook 2010 profile, Outlook 2010 doesn't prompt you to specify the storage location for the IMAP folders. Instead, Outlook 2010 automatically creates a .pst file in which to store the messages. The folder branch for the account appears in Outlook 2010 with the email address of the IMAP account as the branch name by default, as shown in Figure 7-7. Each IMAP account in a profile uses a different .pst file, so all your IMAP accounts are separate from one another and each appears under its own branch in the folders list.

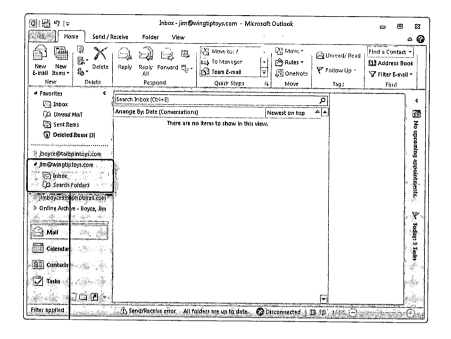

Figure 7-7 An IMAP account uses its own .pst file and appears as a separate folder branch.

How accounts are treated depends on the types of accounts you add to the profile. The following list summarizes the possibilities:

- **IMAP as the first or only account in the profile**   Outlook 2010 automatically creates a .pst file to contain the IMAP folder set and a second .pst file (which, for clarity, we'll call a global .pst file) to contain your other Outlook 2010 data such as contacts and calendar information.

- **Multiple IMAP accounts in the profile**   Each IMAP account uses a separate .pst file created by Outlook 2010. Outlook 2010 also adds a separate global .pst file to contain your other Outlook 2010 data.

- **IMAP first, followed by non-IMAP accounts**   The non-IMAP accounts default to storing their data in the global .pst that is created when you add the IMAP account. The global .pst is defined as the location where new mail is delivered. You can change the location after you set up the accounts, if you prefer. For example, if you add an Exchange Server account, you'll probably want to change the profile's properties to deliver mail to your Exchange Server mailbox instead of to the global .pst file. IMAP mail is unaffected by the setting and is still delivered to the IMAP account's .pst file.

- **Non-IMAP accounts followed by IMAP accounts**   The existing accounts maintain their default store location as defined by the settings in the profile. Added IMAP accounts each receive their own .pst file.

Using Outlook for Hotmail and Windows Live Accounts

With the addition of the Outlook Connector for Hotmail, you can access your Hotmail and Windows Live accounts through Outlook 2010 instead of using a web browser to send and receive messages. Using Outlook 2010 gives you the ability to compose and reply to messages offline and also gives you the advantages of Outlook 2010 composition, filtering, and other features that you might not otherwise have when managing your mail with a web browser.

> **Tip**
> The Outlook Connector for Outlook 2010 does not require a paid Hotmail or Windows Live account.

Installing and Configuring the Outlook Connector for Hotmail

The Outlook Connector for Hotmail is not included with Office; instead, it is available as a separate download from *http://office.microsoft.com/en-us/outlook/HA102225181033.aspx*. Installation is easy. Just visit the site, download the connector Setup file to your computer, and run it.

After you have added the Outlook Connector, adding a Hotmail or Windows Live account is almost automatic. When you open Outlook with a profile that does not already contain a Hotmail or Windows Live account, Outlook displays a dialog box to ask if you want to add a Hotmail account. Click Yes to display the Windows Live Hotmail Settings dialog box shown in Figure 7-8 (shown with the Advanced options visible).

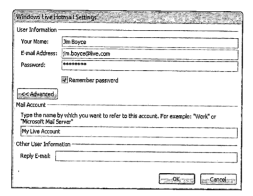

Figure 7-8 Use the Windows Live Hotmail Settings dialog box to add a Hotmail or Windows Live account to Outlook.

Enter these settings in the dialog box:

- **Your Name**   Enter your first and last name, or whatever name you want associated with the account.

- **E-Mail Address**   Enter your Hotmail or Windows Live email address.

- **Password**   Enter the password for the account.

- **Remember Password**   Check this box to have Outlook remember your password so you don't have to type it each time you connect to send or receive mail. However, note that with this setting, anyone who can access your computer can check your email. Get in the habit of locking your computer when you are away from it.

- **Mail Account**   Enter the name by which you want this account to appear in the Navigation pane in Outlook. If you leave this field blank, Outlook uses your email address as the title for the account.

- **Reply Address**   Enter a reply address if you want to use one that is different from your Hotmail or Windows Live address. Normally, you will leave this field blank.

You can also add a Hotmail/Windows Live account to your profile yourself (such as if you want to add multiple Hotmail/Windows Live accounts to a single profile, or if you previously had one in the profile but deleted it). Follow these steps to configure a Hotmail or Windows Live account in Outlook 2010 manually:

1. In Outlook 2010, click File and choose Account Settings, Account Settings.

2. On the E-Mail tab, click New, choose the Other option, click Microsoft Outlook Hotmail Connector, and then click Next.

3. The Windows Live Hotmail Settings dialog box is displayed (as shown in Figure 7-8). Enter information in the fields as described previously and click OK.

> **Tip**
> When you access your mail with the Outlook Connector, Outlook leaves a copy of your mail on the server. You do not need to configure this behavior.

Using Outlook with Gmail Accounts

Google not only supports web-based access to Gmail accounts, but it also supports both POP and IMAP. For that reason, you can configure Outlook to use either POP3 or IMAP to access your Gmail account. We've already explained earlier in this chapter how to set up POP3 and IMAP accounts, so the configuration steps in Outlook are simply a matter of adding the account to your profile and entering the right server settings. To get those settings, log onto your Gmail account from a web browser and click Help, then click either the POP or IMAP links under Other Ways To Access Gmail. You'll find the server names, ports, and other information there that you'll need to configure Outlook for Gmail. You can also access these configuration instructions from the Gmail Settings pages, as described next.

In addition to configuring Outlook, you must also enable either POP3 or IMAP in your Gmail account. To do so, log onto Gmail with a web browser, click the Settings link, and then click the Forwarding and POP/IMAP link. Here, you'll find links to the configuration information that you need in Outlook. Click the option to enable either IMAP or POP3 as appropriate. Then, configure the account settings in Outlook and test them from Outlook.

Synchronizing Outlook and Google Apps

If you use Google Apps, Google appsyou would probably like tighter integration between Outlook and Google Apps. Fortunately, you can get that integration through the Google Apps Sync for Microsoft Outlook, available as a download from Google's web site at *http://www.google.com/apps/intl/en/business/outlook_sync.html.* The Google Apps Sync add-on enables you to use Outlook to manage all your Google Apps mail, calendar events, and contacts from within Outlook. The add-on keeps the data synchronized between the Google cloud and Outlook, which means you can access the data either from Outlook or from a web browser, and that data will be the same regardless.

> **Note**
> Google Apps Sync requires either a paid or an education account.

To download and begin using the Google Apps Sync for Microsoft Outlook add-in, log onto Gmail with your web browser and click the Help link. You'll find a link to the Google Apps Sync for Microsoft Outlook information page under the Other Ways To Access Gmail section.

Using Multiple Accounts

Although many people still have only one email account, it's becoming much more common to have several. For example, you might have an email account for work, a personal POP3 account with your ISP, and a Hotmail or Gmail account. Outlook 2010 accommodates multiple accounts with ease, all in the same profile, which means that you don't need to switch profiles as you use different accounts.

Setting up for multiple accounts is easy—just add the accounts to your profile as needed. However, working with multiple accounts in a single profile carries a few considerations, as explained here.

Sending Messages Using a Specific Account

When you send a message, Outlook 2010 will use the default account unless you choose a different one before sending the message, as shown in Figure 7-9. This can sometimes be a problem when you have multiple accounts in your profile. For example, you might want to send a personal message through your personal POP3 account, but if your Exchange Server account is designated as the default, your personal message will go through your office mail server. This might violate company policies or expose your personal messages to review by a system administrator. In addition, the reply address comes from the account

that Outlook 2010 uses to send the message, which means that replies will come back to that account. You might want to check your POP3 mail from home, for example, but you find that replies have been directed to your office account because the original messages were sent under that account.

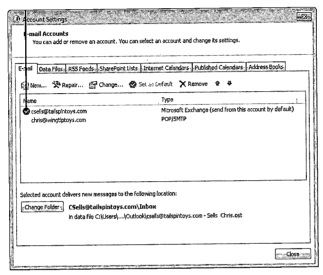

Figure 7-9 Outlook 2010 uses one of your email accounts as the default account for outgoing messages.

Sending messages with a specific account is simple in Outlook 2010. When you compose the message, click From in the message form, as shown in Figure 7-10, and then select the account that you want Outlook 2010 to use to send the current message. Outlook 2010 then uses the reply address and other settings for the selected account for that message.

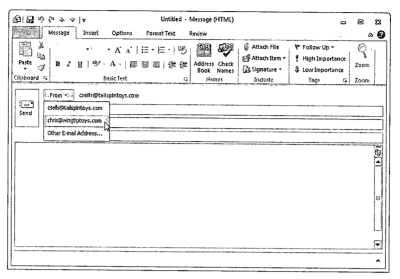

Figure 7-10 Select the account from which you want to send the message by using the Account button in the message form.

Another handy new feature in Outlook 2010 is the capability to send an email with a different reply-to address without changing any account settings. For example, assume you have a Windows Live Hotmail account but don't have the account included in your Outlook profile. However, you want to send a message to someone from Outlook and have the reply come back to your Hotmail account. To do that, start a new message, and in the Message form, click From and then click Other E-Mail Address to open the Send from Other E-Mail Address dialog box (see Figure 7-11). In the From box, type the email address you want replies sent to (in this example, your Hotmail account). From the Send Using drop-down list, choose the account to use to send out the email, and then click OK. Compose the message as you normally would, then click Send. In most cases (see the following paragraph) the email's address when it arrives in the recipient's mailbox will show that the message was sent on behalf of the specified address.

Figure 7-11 You can send using a reply address whose account is not in your Outlook profile.

This feature is particularly useful for users of Exchange Server who have Send On Behalf permission for another user. You can use this feature to send a message on behalf of another Exchange Server mailbox without adding that mailbox to your profile. If you don't have Send On Behalf permission, you'll receive a nondelivery receipt (NDR) telling you that you can't send the message. For other types of accounts, the capability to send on behalf of another email address depends on the mail server. For example, if you send through your Hotmail account, Hotmail will not honor the other send-on-behalf email address but instead will show the message as coming from your Hotmail address. Take the time to check your mail server before relying on this feature.

Keeping a Copy of Your Mail on the Server

If you want to be able to retrieve your mail from different computers, you might want to keep a copy of your messages on the mail server. This makes all messages available no matter where you are or which computer you use to retrieve them. For example, if your computer at the office is configured to retrieve messages from your POP3 account every hour and you don't leave a copy of the messages on the server, you'll be able to see only the last hour's worth of messages if you connect from a different computer.

IMAP stores messages on the server by default. POP3 accounts, however, work differently. By default, Outlook 2010 retrieves the messages from the POP3 server and deletes them from the server. If you want the messages to remain on the server, you need to configure Outlook 2010 specifically to do so. Here's how:

1. In Outlook 2010, choose File and choose Account Settings, Account Settings. Alternatively, start the Mail item in Control Panel, and then click E-Mail Accounts.

2. Select the POP3 account, and then click Change.

3. Click More Settings, and then click the Advanced tab.

4. Select Leave A Copy Of Messages On The Server, and then use the other two options in the Delivery group if you want Outlook 2010 to remove the messages after a specific time or after they have been deleted from your local Deleted Items folder.

5. Click OK, click Next, and then click Finish.

> **INSIDE OUT** Synchronization with IMAP
>
> Accessing a POP3 account from more than one computer can cause some real synchronization headaches. Rather than configuring the POP3 email client to leave messages on the POP3 email server so that you can access the messages from other computers, switch to using IMAP instead of POP3 if the server supports IMAP. The messages remain on the server by default, eliminating the need for you to worry about synchronization at all.

Viewing Full Message Headers

Internet messages include routing information in their headers that specifies the sending address and server, the route the message took to get to you, and other data. In most cases, the header offers more information than you need, particularly if all you're interested in is the body of the message. However, if you're trying to troubleshoot a mail problem or identify a sender who is spamming you, the headers can be useful.

> **INSIDE OUT** Track down spammers
>
> You can't always assume that the information in a message header is accurate. Spammers often spoof or impersonate another user or server—or relay mail through another server—to hide the true origin of the message. The header helps you identify where the mail came from so that you can inform the server's administrator that the server is being used to relay spam. To notify the administrator, you can send a message to postmaster@<domain>, where <domain> is the relaying mail server's domain, such as postmaster@tailspintoys.com. Most ISPs also make available an abuse mailbox, such as abuse@gmail.com.

To view the full message header, open the message, click File, and then click Properties to display the Properties dialog box, shown in Figure 7-12. The message header appears in the Internet Headers box. You can select the text and press Ctrl+C to copy the text to the Clipboard for inclusion in a note or other message.

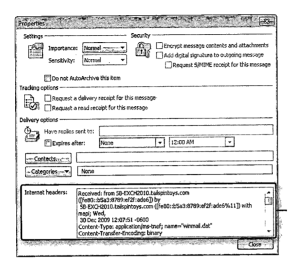

Figure 7-12 View the full message header in the Properties dialog box.

You can take several steps to reduce the amount of unsolicited email you receive. See Chapter 12, "Managing Junk Email," for details about blocking spam and filtering messages.

CHAPTER 8
Sending and Receiving Messages

O F all the features in Microsoft Outlook 2010, messaging is probably the most frequently used. Even if you use Outlook 2010 primarily for contact management or scheduling, chances are good that you also rely heavily on the Outlook 2010 email and other messaging capabilities. Because many of the Outlook 2010 key features make extensive use of messaging for workgroup collaboration and scheduling, understanding messaging is critical to using the program effectively.

This chapter provides an in-depth look at a wide range of topics related to sending and receiving messages with Outlook 2010. You'll learn the fundamentals—working with message forms, addressing, replying, and forwarding—but you'll also explore other, more advanced topics. For example, this chapter explains how to control when your messages are sent, how to save a copy of sent messages in specific folders, and how to work with attachments.

Working with Messages

This section of the chapter offers a primer to bring you up to speed on the Outlook 2010 basic messaging capabilities. It focuses on topics that relate to all types of email accounts. The we will is the place to start learning about Outlook 2010, so launch the program and open the Inbox folder. The next section explains how to work with message forms.

> **Note**
>
> If you haven't added email accounts to your profile, see the appropriate chapter for details. Chapter 7, "Using Internet Mail Accounts," explains how to configure POP3 (including Gmail accounts), Internet Message Access Protocol (IMAP), and Hotmail accounts; Chapter 39, "Configuring the Exchange Server Client," explains how to configure the Microsoft Exchange Server client.

Opening a Standard Message Form

You can begin a new message in Outlook 2010 by using any one of these methods:

- With any mail folder open, choose New E-mail from the New group on the Home tab of the ribbon.

- Click the New Items button and choose E-mail Message.

- With any mail folder open (such as the Inbox), press Ctrl+N.

Outlook 2010 uses a native email editor that is based on Microsoft Word 2010. When you begin a new message, Outlook 2010 displays the Untitled Message form, shown in Figure 8-1.

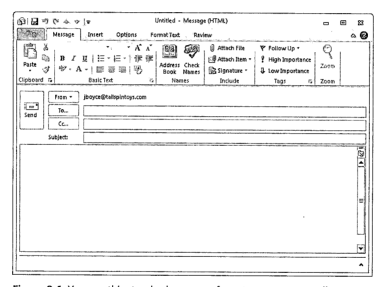

Figure 8-1 You use this standard message form to compose email messages.

Addressing Messages

The Outlook 2010 address books make it easy to address messages. When you want to send a message to someone whose address is stored in your Contacts folder or an address list on the server, you can click in the To box on the message form and type the recipient's name—you don't have to type the entire address. When you send the message, Outlook 2010 checks the name, locates the correct address, and adds it to the message. If multiple addresses match the name you specify, Outlook 2010 shows all the matches and prompts

you to select the appropriate one. If you want to send a message to someone whose address isn't in any of your address books, you need to type the full address in the To box.

For more information about Outlook 2010 address books, see Chapter 6, "Managing Address Books and Distribution Lists."

> ## Note
>
> Outlook 2010 can check the names and addresses of message recipients before you send the message. To perform this action, enter the names in the To box and either click the Check Names button on the ribbon or press Ctrl+K.

To open the address book (see Figure 8-2), click an Address Book button (To, Cc, or Bcc) beside an address box on the message form. Outlook 2010 opens the Select Names dialog box, which you can use to address the message.

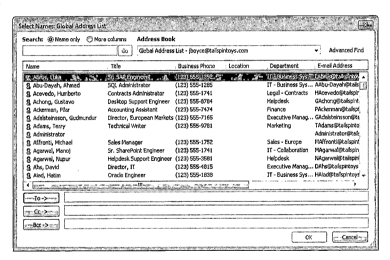

Figure 8-2 In the Select Names dialog box, you can select addresses from the address book.

Follow these steps to select addresses in this dialog box and add them to your message:

1. In the Address Book drop-down list, select the address list you want to view.

2. Select a name from the list, and click To, Cc, or Bcc to add the selected address to the specified address box.

3. Continue this process to add more recipients if necessary. Click OK when you're satisfied with the list.

> **Note**
>
> You can include multiple recipients in each address box on the message form. If you're typing the addresses yourself, separate them with a semicolon.

Including Carbon Copies and Blind Carbon Copies

You can direct a single message to multiple recipients by including multiple addresses in the To box on the message form or by using the Cc (Carbon Copy) and Bcc (Blind Carbon Copy) boxes. The Cc box appears by default on message forms, but the Bcc box does not. To display the Bcc box, on the Options tab on the ribbon, in the Show Fields group, choose Bcc. You use the Cc and Bcc boxes the same way you use the To box: Type a name or address in the box, or click the Address Book icon beside the box to open the address book.

> # INSIDE OUT   Hide addresses when necessary
>
> The names contained in the To and Cc boxes of your message are visible to all recipients of the message. If you're using a contact group or server-side distribution list, Outlook 2010 converts the names on the list to individual addresses, exposing those addresses to the recipients. If you want to hide the names of one or more recipients, or you don't want distribution lists exposed, place those names in the Bcc box.

Copying Someone on All Messages

In some situations, you might want every outgoing message to be copied to a particular person. For example, maybe you manage a small staff and want all employees' outgoing messages copied to you. Or perhaps you want to send a copy of all your outgoing messages to yourself at a separate email account.

Rules that you create with the Outlook 2010 Rules Wizard can process outgoing messages as well as incoming ones. One way to ensure that a recipient is copied on all outgoing messages is to add a rule that automatically adds the recipient to the message's Cc field. Follow these steps to do so:

1. On the Home tab on the ribbon, click Rules in the Move group and choose Manage Rules and Alerts to begin creating the rule.

2. Click New Rule, in the Start From A Blank Rule group, select Apply Rule On Messages I Send, and then click Next.

3. Click Next again without choosing any conditions to cause the rule to be used for all messages. Click Yes in the warning dialog box to confirm that you want the rule applied to all messages.

4. Select the action Cc The Message To People Or Public Group; then click the underlined link in the Rule Description box and select the addresses where you want to send the carbon copies. These addresses can be from any of your address lists in the Address Book, or you can type in specific addresses.

5. Click Next, set exceptions as needed, and then click Next.

6. Supply a Name for the rule, verify that the Turn On This Rule check box is selected, and ensure that you are satisfied with the rule settings; then click Finish. Click OK to close the Rules And Alerts dialog box.

For more details about working with message rules, see Chapter 11, "Processing Messages Automatically."

> **Note**
> Outlook might display a dialog box informing you that the rule you are creating is client-side only. For information on client-side rules, see the section "Creating and Using Rules" on page 302.

Unfortunately, Outlook 2010 doesn't offer a Bcc action for the rule. The add-on Always BCC for Outlook 2010, available at www.sperrysoftware.com/Outlook/Always-BCC.asp, enables you to add a Bcc recipient automatically. It is designed to work with the Outlook E-Mail Security Update for Outlook 2000 and the same features built into Outlook 2002 and later.

Using Templates and Custom Forms for Addressing

A rule is handy for copying all using, messages—or only certain messages—to one or more people, as explained in the preceding section. Contact groups and server-side distribution lists are handy for addressing a message to a group of people without entering the address for each person.

If you regularly send the same message to the same people but want to specify some on the To field, others in the Cc field, and still others in the Bcc field, contract groups and rules won't do the trick. Instead, you can use a template or a custom form to send the message. You create the form or template ahead of time with the addresses in the desired fields; you then open that item, complete it, and send it on its way. Use the following steps to create and use a template for this purpose:

1. In Outlook 2010, start a new message.

2. Enter the email or distribution list addresses as needed in the To, Cc, and Bcc fields.

3. Enter any other information that remains the same each time you send the message, such as subject or boilerplate text in the body of the message.

4. Click File and then click Save As.

5. Choose Outlook Template from the Save As Type drop-down list.

6. Enter a name in the File Name field, and if you want to use a location other than your Templates folder, choose a path for the template.

7. Click Save to save the template.

8. Close the message form and click No if prompted to save changes.

9. When it's time to create the message, click New Items on the Home tab of the ribbon, choose More Items, and select Choose Form to open the Choose Form dialog box (see Figure 8-3).

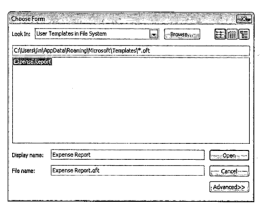

Figure 8-3 Open the template from the Choose Form dialog box.

10. Choose User Templates In File System from the Look In drop-down list, choose the template that you created in step 7, and click Open.

11. Add any other recipients of message content and click Send to send the message.

> **Note**
>
> If you use the default Template folder for your templates, you don't have to browse for them when you choose the User Templates In File System option.

See Chapter 24, "Using Templates," for more information on using templates in Outlook 2010, and Chapter 27, "Designing and Using Forms," for details on creating and using custom forms.

Specifying Message Priority and Sensitivity

By default, new messages have their priority set to Normal. You might want to change the priority to High for important or time-sensitive messages, or to Low for non–work mail or other messages that have relatively less importance. Outlook 2010 displays an icon in the Importance column of the recipient's Inbox to indicate High or Low priority. (For messages with Normal priority, no icon is displayed.)

The easiest way to set message priority is by using the Message tab on the Ribbon in the message form. In the Tags group, click the High Importance button (which has an exclamation point icon) to specify High priority. Click the Low Importance button (which has a down arrow icon) to specify Low priority. To set the priority back to Normal, click the selected priority again to remove the highlight around the button (see Figure 8-4).

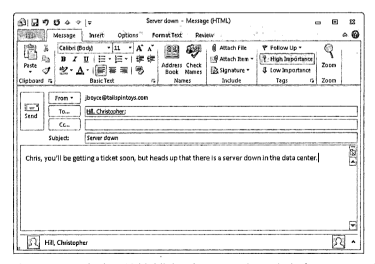

Figure 8-4 Outlook 2010 highlights the appropriate priority button to provide a visual indicator of the message's priority.

You also can specify a message's sensitivity by choosing a Normal (the default), Personal, Private, or Confidential sensitivity level. Setting sensitivity adds a tag to the message that displays the sensitivity level that you selected. This helps the recipient see at a glance how you want the message to be treated. To set sensitivity, on the Options tab on the ribbon, click the small Message Options button in the lower-right corner of the More Options group and select the sensitivity level from the Sensitivity drop-down list.

Saving a Message to Send Later

Although you can create some messages in a matter of seconds, others can take consider-ably longer—particularly if you're using formatting or special features, or if you're compos-ing a lengthy message. If you're interrupted while composing a message or if you simply want to leave the message to finish later, you can save the message in your Drafts folder. Later, when you have time, you can reopen the message, complete it, and send it. Click File and choose Save in the message form to have Outlook 2010 save the message to the Drafts folder (see Figure 8-5). When you're ready to work on the message again, open the Drafts folder and double-click the message to open it.

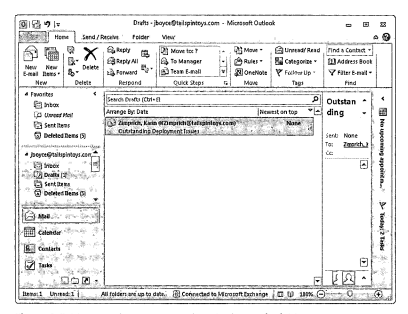

Figure 8-5 Messages in progress are kept in the Drafts folder.

> **Note**
> You also can click File and choose Save As to save a message as a Hypertext Markup Language (HTML) document (or in another document format) outside your Outlook 2010 folders.

Setting Sending Options

You can configure various options that affect how Outlook 2010 sends email messages. To set these options, in the main Outlook window, click File, Options and then click Mail in the left pane (see Figure 8-6). Scroll down to find the Send Messages group of settings.

For details on specifying which account is used to send a message, see the section "Sending Messages Using a Specific Account," on page 174.

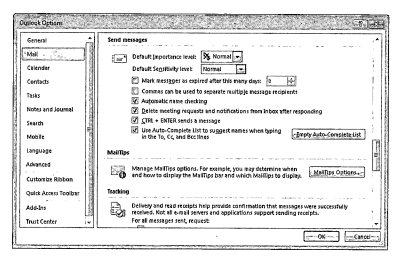

Figure 8-6 You can choose options for sending messages in the Mail page of the Outlook Options dialog box.

You can modify the following settings in the Send Messages group:

- **Default Importance Level**   This option sets the default importance or priority level for all new messages. When you compose a message, you can override this setting by clicking the High Importance button or the Low Importance button on the ribbon in the message form, or by clicking Message Options on the Options tab of the message form's ribbon and setting the priority in the Properties dialog box. The default setting is Normal.

- **Default Sensitivity Level**   This option sets the default sensitivity level for all new messages. When you compose a message, you can override this setting by clicking Message Options on the ribbon and setting the sensitivity level in the Properties dialog box. The default setting is Normal.

- **Mark Messages As Expired After This Many Days**   This option causes the messages to expire after the specified number of days. The message appears in striketh-rough in the recipient's mailbox at that time. (This setting does not necessarily work with every email client.)

- **Commas Can Be Used To Separate Multiple Message Recipients**   If this check box is selected, you can use commas as well as semicolons in the To, Cc, and Bcc boxes of a message form to separate addresses.

- **Automatic Name Checking**   Select this check box to have Outlook 2010 attempt to match names to email addresses. Verified addresses are underlined, and those for which Outlook 2010 finds multiple matches are underscored by a red wavy line. When multiple matches exist and you've used a particular address before, Outlook 2010 underscores the name with a green dashed line to indicate that other choices are available.

- **Delete Meeting Requests And Notifications From Inbox After Responding**   Select this check box to have Outlook 2010 delete a meeting request from your Inbox when you respond to the request. If you accept the meeting, Outlook 2010 enters the meeting in your calendar. Clear this check box if you want to retain the meeting request in your Inbox.

- **Use Auto-Complete List To Suggest Names When Typing In The To, Cc, And Bcc Lines**   When this check box is selected, Outlook 2010 completes addresses as you type them in the To, Cc, and Bcc lines of the message form. Clear this check box to turn off this automatic completion. See Chapter 6 for more information on the address nickname cache and how to work with it.

- **Ctrl+Enter Sends A Message**   When this check box is selected, Outlook 2010 accepts Ctrl+Enter as the equivalent of clicking the Send button when composing a message.

Other options in the Outlook Options dialog box are explained in other parts of this book, including in the following sections.

Controlling When Messages Are Sent

To specify when Outlook 2010 should send messages, click File, Options, and click Advanced in the left pane to locate the Send Immediately When Connected option in the Send And Receive group. With this option selected, Outlook 2010 sends messages as soon as you click Send (provided that Outlook 2010 is online). If Outlook 2010 is offline, the messages go into the Outbox until you process them with a send/receive operation (which is also what happens if you do not select this option).

Requesting Delivery and Read Receipts

You can request a delivery receipt or a read receipt for any message. Both types of receipts are messages that are delivered back to you after you send your message. A delivery receipt indicates the date and time your message was delivered to the recipient's mailbox. A read receipt indicates the date and time the recipient opened the message.

Specifying that you want a delivery receipt or read receipt for a message doesn't guarantee that you'll get one. The recipient's mail server or mail client might not support delivery and read receipts. The recipient might have configured the email client to reject requests for receipts automatically, or the recipient might answer No when prompted to send a receipt. If you receive a receipt, it's a good indication that the message was delivered or read. If you don't receive a receipt, however, don't assume that the message wasn't delivered or read. A message receipt serves only as a positive notification, not a negative one.

To request receipts for a message you're composing, click the Options tab on the Message ribbon. You'll find the delivery and read receipt options in the Tracking group (see Figure 8-7).

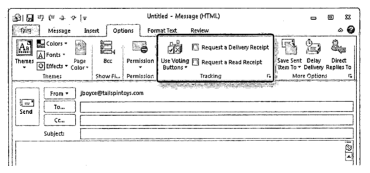

Figure 8-7 Use options in the Tracking group on the ribbon to request a delivery receipt, a read receipt, or both.

Using Message Tracking and Receipts Options

You can set options to determine how Outlook 2010 handles delivery and read receipts by default. In the main Outlook window, click File, Options, and click Mail in the left pane. Scroll down to the Tracking group, shown in Figure 8-8, in which you'll find the options discussed in this section.

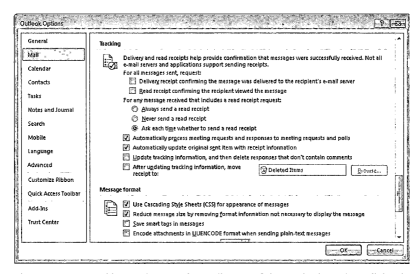

Figure 8-8 Set tracking options on the Mail page of the Outlook Options dialog box.

The following options control how Outlook 2010 requests read receipts and how the receipts are processed after they are received:

- **Automatically Process Meeting Requests And Responses To Meeting Requests And Polls**   Select this check box to have Outlook 2010 process all message receipt requests and responses when they arrive.

- **After Updating Tracking Information, Move Receipt To**   Select this check box to have Outlook 2010 move receipts from the Inbox to the specified folder.

- **Read Receipt Confirming The Recipient Viewed The Message**   Select this check box to have Outlook 2010 request a read receipt for each message you send. When you compose a message, you can override this setting; to do so, click the Options button in the Options group of the Message ribbon.

- **Delivery Receipt Confirming The Message Was Delivered To The Recipient's E-mail Server**   Select this check box to have Outlook 2010 request a delivery receipt for each message you send.

These three options in the Tracking group let you control how Outlook 2010 responds to requests from others for read receipts on messages that you receive and apply to Internet mail accounts only:

- **Always Send A Read Receipt**   When this option is selected, Outlook 2010 always sends a read receipt to any senders who request one. Outlook 2010 generates the read receipt when you open the message.

- **Never Send A Read Receipt**   Select this option to prevent Outlook 2010 from sending read receipts to senders who request them. Outlook 2010 will not prompt you regarding receipts.

- **Ask Each Time Whether To Send A Read Receipt**   Selecting this option enables you to control, on a message-by-message basis, whether Outlook 2010 sends read receipts. When you open a message for which the sender has requested a read receipt, Outlook 2010 prompts you to authorize the receipt. If you click Yes, Outlook 2010 generates and sends the receipt. If you click No, Outlook 2010 doesn't create or send a receipt.

> **Note**
> If selected, the Update Tracking Information, And Then Delete Responses That Don't Contain Comments check box causes Outlook 2010 to process voting and meeting requests and then delete them if they contain no comments.

See the section "Voting in Outlook," on page 962, to learn more about voting. See Chapter 19, "Scheduling Appointments," to learn about the Calendar and scheduling meetings.

Sending a Message for Review

If you compose a message from Word 2010 (that is, if you started Word 2010 outside Outlook 2010), you have the ability to send the message as a document for review. You might use this feature if you're collaborating on a document with others or incorporating their comments into the final draft. Recipients can review the document and add comments, which they send back to you. They also can incorporate the changes directly into the document, which enables them to take advantage of the Word 2010 revision marks (Track Changes) feature.

Before you can send a document for review, you must first add the Send For Review button to the Word 2010 Quick Access Toolbar. To do this, open the document in Word 2010, right-click the Quick Access Toolbar, and choose Customize Quick Access Toolbar. In the Word Options dialog box, select Commands Not In The Ribbon in the Choose Commands

From drop-down list. Select Send For Review and click Add; then click OK. In the document, make sure you have saved the document, click the Send For Review button, and then address and send the email message as usual.

For more detailed information on sending documents for review, see *Microsoft Word 2010 Inside Out*, by Katherine Murray (O'Reilly, 2010).

Replying to Messages

When you reply to a message, Outlook 2010 sends your reply to the person who sent you the message. Replying to a message is simple: select the message in the Inbox, and then click the Reply button on the Home tab on the ribbon; right-click the message and choose Reply; or press Ctrl+R. Outlook 2010 opens a message form and, depending on how you have configured Outlook 2010 for replies, can also include the original message content in various formats.

If the message to which you're replying was originally sent to multiple recipients, and you want to send your reply to all of them, click Reply To All; right-click and choose Reply To All; or press Ctrl+Shift+R.

For more information about message replies, see the section "Using Other Reply and Forwarding Options" on page 195.

> **Note**
>
> When you use Reply All, Outlook 2010 places all the addresses in the To box. If you don't want the recipients list to be visible, use the Bcc box to send blind carbon copies. To do this, click Reply All, highlight the addresses in the To box, and cut them. Then click in the Bcc box and paste the addresses there.

Forwarding Messages

In addition to replying to a message, you can forward the message to one or more recipients. To forward a message, select the message header in the message folder (the Inbox or another one), and then click Forward in the Respond group on the Home tab of the ribbon or press Ctrl+F. Outlook 2010 opens a new message form and either incorporates the original message in the body of the current one or attaches it to the new message.

If you forward a single message, Outlook 2010 forwards the original message in the body of your new message by default, and you can add your own comments. If you prefer, however, you can configure Outlook 2010 to forward messages as attachments instead of including them in the body of your messages.

> **Note**
> If you select multiple messages and click Forward, Outlook 2010 sends the messages as attachments instead of including them in the body of your message.

If you want to forward a single message as an attachment without reconfiguring the default behavior of Outlook, you can do so easily. Just click the message to select it, click the More Respond Options button in the Respond group of the Home tab, and then choose Forward As Attachment.

Using Other Reply and Forwarding Options

You can change how Outlook 2010 handles and formats message replies and forwarded messages. These options are found in the Replies And Forwards group on the Mail page of the Outlook Options dialog box, shown in Figure 8-9.

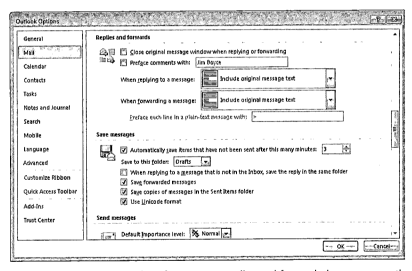

Figure 8-9 You can set options for message replies and forwarded messages on the Mail page of the Outlook Options dialog box.

To open this dialog box, click File, Options; then click Mail. You can then view or set the following options in the Replies And Forwards group that affect replies and forwards:

- **Close Original Message Windows When Replying Or Forwarding**   Select this check box to have Outlook 2010 close the message form when you click Reply or Forward. Clear this check box to have Outlook 2010 leave the message form open. If you frequently forward the same message with different comments to different recipients, it's useful to have Outlook 2010 leave the message open so that you don't have to open it again to perform the next forward.

- **When Replying To A Message**   Use this drop-down list to specify how Outlook 2010 handles the original message text when you reply to a message. You can choose to have Outlook 2010 generate a clean reply without the current message text, include the text without changes, or include but indent the text, for example. Note that you can either include the original message text in the body of your reply or add it to the message as an attachment.

- **When Forwarding A Message**   Use this drop-down list to specify how Outlook 2010 handles the original message text when you forward a message. You can, for example, include the message in the body of the forwarded message or add it as an attachment.

- **Preface Each Line In A Plain-Text Message With**   If you select the Prefix Each Line Of The Original Message option in the When Replying To A Message drop-down list or the When Forwarding A Message drop-down list, you can use this box to specify the character that Outlook 2010 uses to preface each line of the original message in the body of the reply or forwarded message. The default is an angle bracket (>) and a space, but you can use one or more characters of your choice.

- **Preface Comments With**   Select this check box and enter a name or other text in the associated box. Outlook 2010 will add the specified text to mark your typed comments in the body of a message that you are replying to or forwarding.

For more details on replying to and forwarding messages, see the sections "Replying to Messages" and "Forwarding Messages" earlier in this chapter.

Deleting Messages

When you delete messages from any folder other than the Deleted Items folder, the messages are moved to the Deleted Items folder. You can then recover the messages by moving them to other folders, if needed. When Outlook 2010 deletes messages from the Deleted Items folder, however, those messages are deleted from Outlook 2010 permanently.

You can set Outlook 2010 to delete all messages from the Deleted Items folder automatically whenever you exit the program, which helps keep the size of your message store manageable. However, it also means that unless you recover a deleted message before you exit Outlook 2010, that message is irretrievably lost. If you seldom have to recover deleted files, this might not be a problem for you.

To change what happens to items in the Deleted Items folder when you exit Outlook 2010, click File, Options, and then click Advanced in the left pane. Select or clear Empty Deleted Items Folders When Exiting Outlook, and then click OK.

Undeleting Messages

Exchange Server mailboxes have a retention period, defined by the Exchange Server administrator, which causes deleted items to be retained for a certain period of time after you have deleted them permanently from your Deleted Items folder. To recover a deleted item, in the Navigation pane, click any folder in your Exchange Server mailbox, and then click the Folder tab on the ribbon. Click Recover Deleted Items from the Clean Up group to open the Recover Deleted Items dialog box (see Figure 8-10). Click the item that you want to recover and click Recover Selected Items.

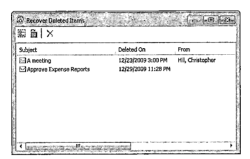

Figure 8-10 You can undelete items from an Exchange Server mailbox if they have not aged past the retention period.

Unfortunately, there is no way to recover permanently deleted items from non–Exchange Server accounts.

Controlling Synchronization and Send/Receive Times

Outlook 2010 uses send and receive groups (or send/receive groups) to control when messages are sent and received for specific email accounts. You can also use send/receive groups to define the types of items that Outlook 2010 synchronizes. Synchronization is the process in which Outlook 2010 synchronizes the local copy of your folders with your Exchange Server message store. For example, assume that while you were working offline, you created several new email messages and scheduled a few events. You connect to the computer running Exchange Server and perform a synchronization. Outlook 2010 uploads to your computer the changes you made locally and also downloads changes from the server to your local store, such as downloading messages that have been delivered to your Inbox on the server.

Send/receive groups enable you to be flexible in controlling which functions Outlook 2010 performs for synchronization. For example, you can set up a send/receive group for your Exchange Server account that synchronizes only your Inbox, not your other folders, for those times when you simply want to perform a quick check of your mail.

Send/receive groups also are handy for helping you manage different types of accounts. For example, if you integrate your personal and work email into a single profile, you can use send/receive groups to control when each type of mail is processed. You might create one send/receive group for your personal accounts and another for your work accounts. You can also use send/receive groups to limit network traffic to certain times of the day. For example, if your organization limits Internet connectivity to specific times, you could use send/receive groups to schedule your Internet accounts to synchronize during the allowed times.

Think of send/receive groups as a way to collect various accounts into groups and assign to each group specific send/receive and synchronization behavior. You can create multiple send/receive groups, and you can include the same account in multiple groups if needed.

Setting Up Send/Receive Groups

To set up or modify send/receive groups in Outlook 2010, click the Send/Receive tab on the ribbon, click Send/Receive Groups, and then click Define Send/Receive Groups. Outlook 2010 displays the Send/Receive Groups dialog box, shown in Figure 8-11. By default, Outlook 2010 sets up one group named All Accounts and configures it to send and receive when online and offline. You can modify or remove that group, add others, and configure other send/receive behavior in the Send/Receive Groups dialog box.

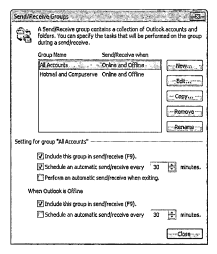

Figure 8-11 You can specify send/receive actions in the Send/Receive Groups dialog box.

When you select a group from the Group Name list, Outlook 2010 displays the following associated settings in the Setting For Group area of the dialog box:

- **Include This Group In Send/Receive (F9)**   Select this check box to have Outlook 2010 process accounts in the selected group when you click Send/Receive on the message form toolbar or press F9. Outlook 2010 provides this option for both online and offline behavior.

- **Schedule An Automatic Send/Receive Every n Minutes**   Select this check box to have Outlook 2010 check the accounts in the selected group every n minutes (the default is 30 minutes). Outlook 2010 provides this option for both online and offline behavior.

- **Perform An Automatic Send/Receive When Exiting**   Select this check box to have Outlook 2010 process the accounts in the selected group when you exit Outlook 2010 from an online session.

Creating New Groups

Although you could modify the All Accounts group to process only selected accounts, it's better to create other groups as needed and leave All Accounts as is for those times when you want to process all your email accounts together.

Follow these steps to create a new group:

1. In Outlook 2010, click the Send/Receive tab on the ribbon, click Send/Receive Groups, Define Send/Receive Groups.

2. Click New, type the name of the group as you want it to appear on the Send/Receive submenu, and click OK. Outlook 2010 displays the Send/Receive Settings dialog box, shown in Figure 8-12.

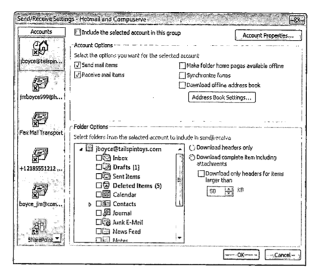

Figure 8-12 You can configure account processing in the Send/Receive Settings dialog box.

3. In the Accounts bar on the left, click the account you want to configure. By default, all accounts in the group are excluded from synchronization, as indicated by the red X on the account icon.

4. Select the Include The Selected Account In This Group check box to activate the remaining options in the dialog box and to have the account included when you process messages for the selected group.

5. In the Select Folders From The Selected Account To Include In Send/Receive list, select the check box beside each folder that you want Outlook 2010 to synchronize when processing this group.

6. Select other settings, using the following list as a guide:

   - **Send Mail Items**   Select this check box to have Outlook 2010 send outgoing mail for this account when a send/receive action occurs for the group.

   - **Receive Mail Items**   Select this check box to have Outlook 2010 retrieve incoming mail for this account when a send/receive action occurs for the group.

   - **Make Folder Home Pages Available Offline**   This check box has Outlook 2010 cache folder home pages offline so that they are available to you any time.

- **Synchronize Forms**   Select this check box to have Outlook 2010 synchronize changes to forms that have been made locally as well as changes that have been made on the server.

- **Download Offline Address Book**   When this check box is selected, Outlook 2010 updates the offline address book when a send/receive action occurs for the group.

- **Get Folder Unread Count**   For IMAP accounts only; you can select this option to have Outlook 2010 get the number of unread messages from the server.

7. If you need to apply filters or message size limits, do so. Otherwise, click OK, and then click Close to close the Send/Receive Groups dialog box.

For information on how to apply message size limits, see the section "Limiting Message Size," on this page.

Other options for the send/receive group are explained in the following sections.

Modifying Existing Groups

You can modify existing send/receive groups in much the same way you create new ones. Click the Send/Receive tab on the ribbon, click Send/Receive Groups, Define Send/Receive Groups. Select the group you want to modify and click Edit. The settings that you can modify are the same as those discussed in the preceding section.

Limiting Message Size

You can also use the Send/Receive Settings dialog box to specify a limit on message size for messages downloaded from the Inbox of the selected account. This provides an easy way to control large messages that arrive in your mailbox. Instead of downloading messages that are larger than the specified limit, Outlook 2010 downloads only the headers. You can then mark the messages for download or deletion, or simply double-click the message to download and open it.

Note

Specifying a message size limit in the Send/Receive Settings dialog box doesn't affect the size of messages that you can receive on the server. It simply directs Outlook 2010 to process them differently.

Follow these steps to specify a message size limit for an account:

1. Open the Send/Receive Groups dialog box as described previously.

2. Select a group to modify and click Edit.

3. From the Accounts bar, select the account containing the folder for which you want to set a message size limit.

4. Select a folder, as shown in Figure 8-13 (not available for POP3 accounts).

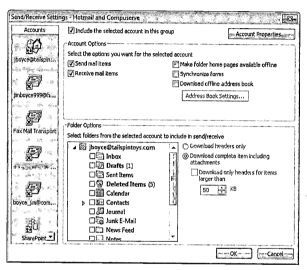

Figure 8-13 Select a folder and then set its parameters in the Send/Receive Settings dialog box.

5. Specify the criteria that you want to use to limit message download, based on the following option list, and click OK:

- **Download Headers Only**   Download only the message header, not the message body or attachments.

- **Download Complete Item Including Attachments**   Download the entire message, including body and attachments.

- **Download Only Headers For Items Larger Than**   Download only headers for messages over the specified size.

For details on processing headers for POP3 accounts, see the section "Working with Message Headers" on page 401.

Scheduling Send/Receive Synchronization

You can schedule synchronization for each send/receive group separately, giving you quite a bit of control over when Outlook 2010 processes your Inbox, Outbox, and other folders for synchronization. You can configure Outlook 2010 to process each send/receive group on a periodic basis and to process specific groups when you exit Outlook 2010. For example, you might schedule the All Accounts group to synchronize only when you exit Outlook 2010, even if you scheduled a handful of other groups to process messages more frequently during the day. Because you can create as many groups as needed and can place the same account in multiple groups, you have a good deal of flexibility in determining when each account is processed.

> ### Simplify with Cached Exchange Mode
> If you use an Exchange Server account, configure the account to use Cached Exchange Mode (keep a local copy of the mailbox) and avoid the issue of synchronization altogether. With Cached Exchange Mode enabled, Outlook 2010 handles synchronization on the fly, adjusting to online or offline status as needed.

For a discussion of Cached Exchange Mode, see Chapter 41, "Working Offline and Remotely."

Configuring Send/Receive Schedules

Follow these steps to configure synchronization for each send/receive group:

1. Open the Send/Receive Settings dialog box.

2. In the Send/Receive Groups dialog box, select the group for which you want to modify the schedule.

3. In the Setting For Group area, select Schedule An Automatic Send/Receive Every n Minutes, and then specify the number of minutes that should elapse between send/receive events for the selected group. Set this option for both online and offline behavior.

4. If you want the group to be processed when you exit Outlook 2010, select Perform An Automatic Send/Receive When Exiting.

You can use a combination of scheduled and manually initiated send/receive events to process messages and accounts. For example, you can specify in the Send/Receive Group dialog box that a given group (such as All Accounts) must be included when you click Send/Receive or press F9 and then configure other accounts to process as scheduled. Thus, some accounts might process only when you manually initiate the send/receive event, and others might process only by automatic execution. In addition, you can provide an overlap so that a specific account processes manually as well as by schedule—simply include the account in multiple groups with the appropriate settings for each group.

Disabling Scheduled Send/Receive Processing

On occasion, you might want to disable scheduled send/receive events altogether. For example, assume that you're working offline and don't have a connection through which you can check your accounts. In that situation, you can turn off scheduled send/receive processing until a connection can be reestablished.

To disable scheduled send/receive processing, click Send/Receive Groups on the ribbon and choose Disable Scheduled Send/Receive. Select this command again to enable the scheduled processing.

Configuring Other Messaging Options

This section of the chapter provides an explanation of additional options in Outlook 2010 that control messaging features and tasks. You can specify how you want to be notified when new mail arrives, configure how Outlook 2010 connects for email accounts that use dial-up networking, and control the formatting of Internet and international email messages.

Setting Up Notification of New Mail

You might not spend a lot of time in Outlook 2010 during the day if you're busy working with other applications. However, you might want Outlook 2010 to notify you when you receive new messages. Outlook 2010 offers severalfeatures Desktop Alert features to provide you with notification of the arrival of new messages. These options and additional notification options are located in the Message Arrival group on the Mail page of the Outlook Options dialog box (see Figure 8-14):

- Play A Sound   Select this option to have Outlook 2010 play a sound when a new message arrives. By using the Change System Sounds option in Control Panel, you can change the New Mail Notification sound to use a .wav file of your choosing.

- Briefly Change The Mouse Pointer   Select this option to have Outlook 2010 briefly change the pointer to a mail symbol when a new message arrives.

- Show An Envelope Icon In The Taskbar   Select this option to have Outlook 2010 place an envelope icon in the system tray when new mail arrives. You can double-click the envelope icon to open your mail. The icon disappears from the tray after you have read the messages.

- Display A Desktop Alert   Enable this option to have Outlook 2010 display a pop-up window on the desktop when a new message arrives.

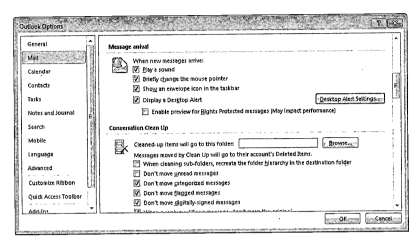

Figure 8-14 Specify notification settings in the Message Arrival group.

Tip

Outlook 2010 can display a desktop alert for new messages that arrive for any account, not just for the default Inbox.

If you enable this last option, click Desktop Alert Settings to display the Desktop Alert Settings dialog box (see Figure 8-15). In this dialog box, you specify the length of time the alert remains on the desktop and the alert's transparency value. Click Preview to preview the alert.

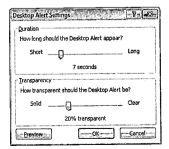

Figure 8-15 Configure alert settings with the Desktop Alert Settings dialog box.

Using Message Alerts

If you enable the Display A
, Outlook 2010 displays the alert for each new message. If you receive a lot of mail during the day, that's more than you need. Instead, you probably want Outlook 2010 to alert you only when you receive certain messages, such as those from people in your Contacts folder, from a specific sender, or with certain words in the subject. So instead of enabling this option globally, you might prefer to create a rule that causes the alert to be displayed when the rule fires.

There are two rule actions that you can use to generate alerts:

- Display A Desktop Alert   This action causes Outlook 2010 to display a desktop alert when the rule fires. The alert persists on the desktop for the period of time you have set for the alert on the Mail page of the Outlook Options dialog box.

- Display A Specific Message In The New Item Alert Window   With this action, you can specify a message that appears in the New Item Alerts window (see Figure 8-16). The window persists on the desktop until you close it.

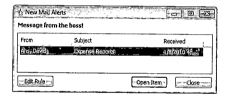

Figure 8-16 The New Item Alerts window displays text you specify.

Which action you use depends on whether you want a custom message to appear for the alert and whether you want the alert to persist until you close it or appear and then go away. To create an alert rule using one (or both) of these actions, create the rule as you would any other and select the alert action that you want to use.

> **Note**
> To create a rule that displays a New Item Alert, you can use the rule template Display Mail From Someone in the New Item Alert Window.

For more details about working with message rules, see Chapter 11.

If you create an alert rule that uses the Display A Desktop Alert action, it's likely that you will not want Outlook 2010 to display an alert for all messages. Open the Mail page of the Outlook Options dialog box as described previously, and then clear the Display A Desktop Alert option. If you use the Display A Specific Message In The New Item Alert Window rule, you might want to leave desktop alerts enabled, which causes Outlook 2010 to display a desktop alert for all messages and to display the New Item Alerts window for those messages that fire the rule.

> **Tip**
>
> If enabled, the Enable Preview For Rights Protected Messages option in the Message Arrival group causes Outlook to display a preview of rights-protected content (that is, content that is restricted in some way, such as preventing printing or forwarding).

Using Mobile Alerts

Chapter 43, "Making Outlook Mobile," discusses mobile features in detail, but mobile alerts bear mention in this section. To open the Rules And Alerts dialog box, click the Home tab, click Rules, and choose Manage Rules And Alerts. Click New Rule, and note that in the Stay Up To Date group, there is a rule template that will send an alert to your mobile device when you receive messages from a specified person. You can use this rule template to generate a mobile alert for any type of mail account, although you must add a contact for yourself in the Contacts folder and make sure to include your mobile number in the Mobile field. You can then select yourself as the recipient for the alert in the rule.

Users of Exchange Server have a different option for generating mobile alerts. To see these options, click File, Account Settings, and Manage Mobile Notifications. Outlook opens a web browser to connect to Exchange Server. Log in, click the Phone link in the left pane, click Text Messaging, and then use the links on the page to set calendar and email notification settings. For more details on using this feature, see Chapter 43.

Managing Messages and Attachments

Using the Outlook 2010 email features effectively requires more than understanding how to send and receive messages. This section of the chapter helps you get your messages and attachments under control.

Saving Messages Automatically

You can configure Outlook 2010 to save messages automatically in several ways—for example, saving the current message periodically or saving a copy of forwarded messages. You'll find the following options on the Mail page of the Outlook Options dialog box (see Figure 8-17):

- **Automatically Save Items That Have Not Been Sent After This Many Minutes** Use this check box to have Outlook 2010 save unsent messages in the Drafts folder. Outlook 2010 by default saves unsent messages to the Drafts folder every three minutes. Clear this check box if you don't want unsent messages saved in this folder.

- **Save To This Folder** Specify the folder in which you want Outlook 2010 to save unsent items. The default location is the Drafts folder.

- **When Replying To A Message That Is Not In The Inbox, Save The Reply In The Same Folder** With this check box selected, Outlook 2010 saves a copy of sent items to the Sent Items folder if the message originates from the Inbox (new message, reply, or forward). If the message originates from a folder other than the Inbox—such as a reply to a message stored in a different folder—Outlook 2010 saves the reply in the same folder as the original. If this option is cleared, Outlook 2010 saves all sent items in the Sent Items folder.

> **Note**
>
> You can also use rules to control where Outlook 2010 places messages. For more information on creating and using rules, see Chapter 11.

- **Save Forwarded Messages** Select this check box to save a copy of all messages that you forward. Messages are saved in either the Sent Items folder or the originating folder, depending on how you set the previous option.

- **Save Copies of Messages In The Sent Items Folder** Select this option to have Outlook save a copy of all new messages and replies that you send in the Sent Items folder (see the following section).

- **Use Unicode Format** Select this option to have Outlook store the saved messages in Unicode format.

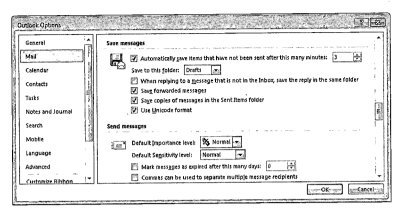

Figure 8-17 In the Mail page of the Outlook Options dialog box, you can choose whether Outlook 2010 automatically saves unsent messages.

Retaining a Copy of Sent Messages

Keeping track of the messages you send can often be critical, particularly in a work setting. Fortunately, with Outlook 2010, you can automatically retain a copy of each message you send, providing a record of when and to whom you sent the message.

By default, Outlook 2010 stores a copy of each sent message in the Sent Items folder. You can open this folder and sort the items to locate messages based on any message criteria. You can view, forward, move, and otherwise manage the contents of Sent Items just as you can with other folders.

If you allow Outlook 2010 to save a copy of messages in the Sent Items folder, over time the sheer volume of messages can overwhelm your system. You should therefore implement a means—whether manual or automatic—to archive or clear out the contents of the Sent Items folder. With the manual method, all you need to do is move or delete messages from the folder as your needs dictate.

If you want to automate the archival process, you can do so; for details on how to archive messages from any folder automatically, see the section "Managing Data" on page 756.

You'll find the Save Copies Of Messages In The Sent Items Folder option on the Mail page of the Outlook Options dialog box, as described in the previous section. Select this option to have Outlook store copies of sent items in that folder.

INSIDE OUT   Overriding default message-saving settings

If you need to change the Outlook 2010 behavior for a single message, you can override the setting. To choose the folder in which you want to save a message, with the message form open, on the Options tab, in the More Options group, click Save Sent Item To, click Other Folder, and then select the folder in which Outlook 2010 should save the message. If you normally save sent messages but do not want to keep a copy of this message, choose Do Not Save from the menu.

Working with Attachments

It's a sure bet that some of the messages you receive include attachments such as documents, pictures, or applications. Outlook 2010 has an attachment preview feature, which enables you to preview many types of files that you receive in email. In general, you can work with these attachments in Outlook 2010 without saving them separately to disk, although you can do so if needed.

Previewing Attachments

Attachment preview is a feature of Outlook 2010 that enables you to view the contents of files sent to you in email. You can preview some attachments in the Reading pane. Outlook 2010 comes with previewers for a variety of file types, including Office 2010 applications, web pages, and Microsoft Windows Media Player, as well as images and text files. Some vendors also make additional file previewers available for download at their websites.

To preview a file attachment, follow these steps:

1. In Outlook 2010, with the message selected, click the attachment in the Reading pane.

2. If the attachment type has a preview handler registered, Outlook 2010 displays a preview of the attachment (see Figure 8-18). If there is no preview handler for the attachment file type, Outlook 2010 displays a message indicating this. To view a file for which there is no previewer installed, save the file to disk and open it with the appropriate application.

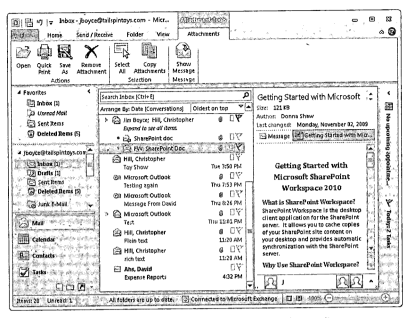

Figure 8-18 Outlook 2010 can preview an attachment in the Reading pane.

There are limitations on attachment preview, including the following:

- You can preview attachments in HTML and plain text messages, but not those in rich text messages (because of the way the attachments are embedded in rich text messages).

- For security reasons, active content (such as macros, scripts, and ActiveX controls) in the attached files is disabled.

You can configure how attachment previews are handled using the Trust Center. To choose attachment-previewing options, follow these steps:

1. With Outlook 2010 open, click File, Options, Trust Center, and click Trust Center Settings.

2. In Trust Center, select Attachment Handling.

3. To enable sending replies with edited attachments, select Add Properties To Attachments To Enable Reply With Changes.

4. If you do not want to be able to preview attachments, select Turn Off Attachment Preview.

5. To manage individual previewers, click Attachment And Document Previewers to open the File Previewing Options dialog box (see Figure 8-19). Select all the previewers that you want enabled and clear the check box of any previewer you want to disable. Click OK.

6. When you are satisfied with the attachment previewing configuration, click OK to close the Trust Center.

Figure 8-19 Enable or disable individual previewers.

Viewing Attachments

You might want to view an attachment in the application in which it was created, perhaps to display content that is disabled by the previewer. There are three ways to open a file in the external application directly from Outlook 2010:

- Right-click the attachment, either in the Reading pane or the open message, and choose Open.

- Double-click the attachment, either in the Reading pane or the open message.

- In either case, if the attachment is an Office document that originated outside your network (and the associated application is installed), Outlook 2010 opens the document using Protected View, discussed in Chapter 2. Protected View uses a rights-limited sandbox instance of the application to reduce the potential for virus infection from the attachment. Editing and other features are disabled, but you can view the document. To edit the document, click the Enable Editing button on the application's InfoBar (see Figure 8-20). If the document came from inside your network, such as from another mailbox in your same Exchange Server environment, it does not use Protected View, but simply opens the document for editing (or in read-only mode, depending on the document).

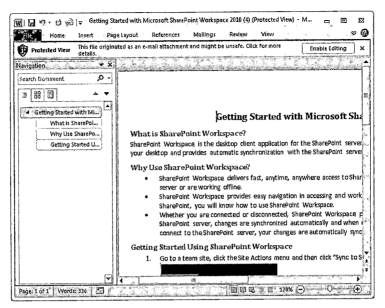

Figure 8-20 Outlook 2010 opens Office documents in Protected View if those documents originated outside your network (such as from the Internet).

For non-Office applications, Outlook either simply opens the document in its associated application or displays the Open With dialog box (see Figure 8-21), depending on how your computer is configured.

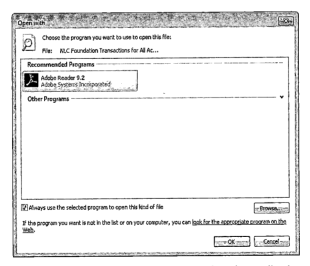

Figure 8-21 Outlook 2010 prompts to select the application to use for opening an attachment.

Saving Attachments to a Disk

In many instances, it's necessary to save attachments to a disk. For example, you might receive a self-extracting executable containing a program that you need to install. In that case, the best option is to save the file to disk and install it from there.

CAUTION

It's important to have antivirus protection installed on your computer to protect against viruses from a variety of potential sources, including email attachments. Saving an attachment to disk before opening it enables the antivirus application on your computer to scan the file before you open it. Make sure your antivirus solution is configured to scan files as soon as they are added to disk when they are accessed so you don't have to manually scan them each time.

You can save attachments using either of these methods:

- If you're using the Reading pane, right-click the attachment in the message and choose Save As.

- Click File, Save Attachments if you want to save one or more attachments or if the Reading pane is not available. You can also do this by right-clicking an attachment and choosing Save All Attachments. This option is handy when you want to save all attachments.

Saving Messages to a File

Although Outlook 2010 maintains your messages in your stored folders, occasionally you might need to save a message to a file. For example, you might want to archive a single message or a selection of messages outside Outlook 2010 or save a message to include as an attachment in another document. You can save a single message to a file or combine several messages into a single file.

To save one or more messages, open the Outlook 2010 folder in which the messages reside, and then select the message headers. Click File, Save As; then specify the path, file name, and file format. Click Save to save the message.

When you save a single message, Outlook 2010 gives you the option of saving it in one of the following formats:

- **Text Only**   Save the message as a text file, losing any formatting in the original message.

- **Outlook Template**   Save the message as an Outlook 2010 template that you can use to create other messages.

- **Outlook Message Format**   Save the message in MSG format, retaining all formatting and attachments within the message file.

- **Outlook Message Format–Unicode**   Save the message in MSG format with the Unicode character set.

- **HTML**   Save the message in HTML format, storing the images in a folder that you can view with a web browser.

- **MHT Files**   Save the message in MIME HTML (MHT) format as a single file with all its resources (such as images).

When you save a selection of messages, you can store the messages only in a text file, and Outlook 2010 combines the body of the selected messages in that text file. You can then concatenate the various messages (that is, join them sequentially) into a single text file. You might use this capability, for example, to create a message thread from a selection of messages.

Moving and Copying Messages Between Folders

Managing your messages often includes moving them to other folders. For example, if you're working on multiple projects, you might want to store the messages related to each specific project in the folder created for that project. The easiest method for moving a message between folders is to drag the message from its current location to the new location. If you want to copy a message instead of moving it, right-click the message, drag it to the folder, and then choose Copy.

If you can't see both the source and destination folders in the folder list, or if you prefer not to drag the message, you can use a different method of moving or copying. Select the message in the source folder, click Move on the Home tab of the ribbon, and choose Other Folder. Outlook 2010 displays a dialog box in which you select the destination folder (see Figure 8-22). Select the folder and click OK.

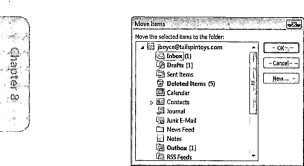

Figure 8-22 Use the Move Items dialog box to choose a destination folder.

Outlook keeps track of the last 10 folders to which you moved messages and displays that list on the ribbon when you click Move (see Figure 8-21). You can simply choose a folder from the list to move the message or messages to that folder.

> **Tip**
>
> If you find yourself working with a handful of folders frequently, add them to your Favorites in the Navigation pane. That way, you can simply drag the item to the folder in the Favorites group. To add a folder to Favorites, right-click the folder in the Navigation pane and choose Show In Favorites.

> **Note**
>
> You can use the shortcut menu to move a message to a specified folder by right-clicking the message and choosing Move, Other Folder from the resulting context menu.

You can copy messages to other folders using the ribbon in much the same way that you move them. Just click the message or messages, then click Move on the ribbon and choose Copy To Folder. Choose the folder and click OK.

A s email has become a more important part of many people's day, the content of email messages has gotten more complex. Whereas text was once adequate, an email message is now likely to contain just about anything: a table, clip art, a photograph, or a link to a website. Similarly, the overall look of an email message has evolved with the use of text formatting and stationery. Microsoft Outlook 2010 has a native email editor based on Microsoft Word 2010 that helps you get your message across clearly and easily.

In this chapter, you'll discover how to add more than just plain text to your messages by working with graphics, hyperlinks, files, attachments, and electronic business cards. As this chapter explains, you can also spruce up your messages by using themes or stationery, which allows you to apply a customized look to your messages. Outlook 2010 provides a choice of themes and stationery, or you can create your own. You'll also learn how to attach a text signature or an electronic business card automatically to each message you send.

Formatting Text in Messages

The majority of your messages might consist of unformatted text, but you can use formatted text and other elements to create rich text and multimedia messages. For example, you might want to use character or paragraph formatting for emphasis, add graphics, or insert hyperlinks to websites or other resources. The following sections explain how to accomplish these tasks.

Formatting text in messages is easy, particularly if you're comfortable with Word. Even if you're not, you should have little trouble adding some snap to your messages with character, paragraph, and other formatting.

Outlook 2010 uses a native email editor, based on Word 2010, with a rich palette of tools for you to use in creating and formatting messages. For example, you can apply paragraph formatting to indent some paragraphs but not others, create bulleted and numbered lists, and apply special color and font formatting. These options are simple to use. Understanding the underlying format in which your messages are sent, however, requires a little more exploration. Outlook 2010 supports three formats for email messages:

- **HTML format**   Lets you create multimedia messages that can be viewed directly in a web browser or an email client that supports Hypertext Markup Language (HTML).

- **Rich Text Format**   Lets you add paragraph and character formatting and embed graphics and other nontext media into your message. By default, Rich Text Format (RTF) messages are converted to HTML when sent to an Internet address, but you can configure Outlook to convert them to plain text instead or leave them in RTF.

> **Note**
> You can specify how Outlook 2010 handles rich text messages sent to the Internet by clicking File, Options. On the Mail page, scroll down to find the Message Format group of options. From the drop-down list labeled When Sending Messages In Rich Text Format To Internet Recipients, select the format that you prefer in the drop-down list. You can choose to have Outlook 2010 send messages as HTML, plain text, or rich text.

- **Plain text format**   Doesn't allow any special formatting, but it offers the broadest client support—every email client can read plain text messages.

By default, Outlook 2010 uses HTML as the format for sending messages. HTML format lets you create multimedia messages that can be viewed directly in a web browser and an email client. Depending on the capabilities of the recipient's email client, however, you might need to use a different format. Most current email clients today support HTML.

> **Note**
> Using HTML format for messages doesn't mean that you need to understand HTML to create a multimedia message. Outlook 2010 takes care of creating the underlying HTML code for you.

INSIDE OUT   Composing HTML Messages Outside of Outlook

Outlook provides lots of features for composing rich text messages in HTML format, including tables, graphics, and much more. In some situations, however, you might find it easier to use a different application to create very complex HTML messages, but still need to send them in Outlook. In this case, use an HTML editor to create and format the message, then simply copy the content from the HTML editor into a new, blank message in Outlook.

The Ribbon on the new message form provides many options for formatting messages. To choose the format for the current message, on the Format Text tab, in the Format group, select Plain Text, HTML, or Rich Text. To set the default message format for all new messages, click File, Options, and Mail, and then select the desired format from the Compose Message In This Format drop-down list (see Figure 9-1).

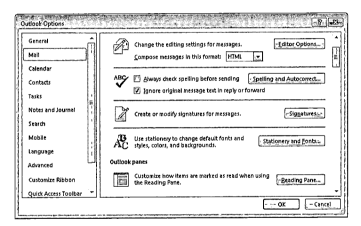

Figure 9-1 Use the Mail page to set the default message format.

On the Mail page of the Outlook Options dialog box, you can click Stationery And Fonts to display the Signatures And Stationery dialog box, shown in Figure 9-2. Use the options in this dialog box to control which fonts Outlook 2010 uses for specific tasks, such as composing new messages, replying to or forwarding a message, and composing or reading plain text messages. You can specify the font as well as the font size, color, and other font characteristics. You can also select Pick A New Color When Replying Or Forwarding to have Outlook 2010 choose a color that has not yet been used in that message for text that you add to a message when replying or forwarding it. This is useful when you are replying inline to someone else's message and want your text to be easily distinguishable.

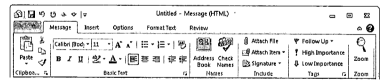

Figure 9-2 Use the Signatures And Stationery dialog box to control the appearance of fonts in Outlook 2010 for specific tasks.

For more information about stationery, see the section "Customizing the Appearance of Your Messages," on page 260.

Outlook 2010 has a number of text formatting controls that are distributed over a number of groups on multiple tabs. The most commonly used formatting commands are on the Message tab, in the Basic Text group, for convenient access, as shown in Figure 9-3. You can specify the font face, size, color, style (bold, italic, or underline), and highlight. Settings for bulleted or numbered lists are also available in this group.

Figure 9-3 Use the Basic Text group on the Message tab for common text formatting options.

INSIDE OUT   The appearance of the Ribbon changes

The exact appearance of the Ribbon varies depending on the width of the message window. A command might have an icon with a text label in full screen, appear as just an icon when the window is narrower, and then disappear altogether when the window is narrower still! If a particular command is not immediately apparent, you should resize the window to see whether the command becomes visible.

When you select some text in your message, a transparent mini-toolbar pops up next to your mouse pointer, as shown in Figure 9-4. If you move the mouse pointer over the toolbar, it becomes opaque, and you can choose formatting options to apply to the highlighted text.

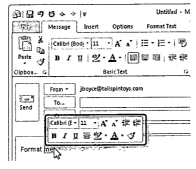

Figure 9-4 The mini-toolbar gives you immediate access to the most commonly used text formatting options.

Extensive text formatting capabilities are provided on the Format Text tab, shown in Figure 9-5, which has font and paragraph formatting as well as style-related options. In addition to the options found in the Basic Text group on the Message tab, you can apply character formatting such as strikethrough, subscript, and superscript. Finer paragraph control is provided with options such as line spacing, borders, and background shading. More complex multilevel lists are also available on this tab. In addition, you can sort text using the Sort option in the Paragraph group.

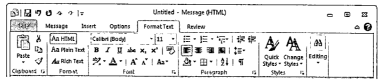

Figure 9-5 The Format Text tab has a wide range of text formatting options.

Several special text options like WordArt, drop caps, and text boxes are available on the Insert tab, in the Text group, as shown in Figure 9-6. You can also insert Quick Parts (pre-written sections of text), text boxes, or the date and time (with optional automatic update).

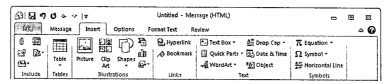

Figure 9-6 The Insert tab has text options that provide special effects.

Themes are configured on the Options tab, in the Themes group, as shown in Figure 9-7, where you can select a theme or change individual parts of your current theme.

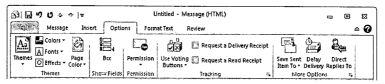

Figure 9-7 Use the Options tab to choose and configure a theme.

Formatting Lists

Outlook 2010 provides three types of lists: bulleted, numbered, and multilevel. Although each type of list looks different, the basic procedures used to create them are the same. Each type of list has a library of preconfigured styles, and you can define your own list styles if you want. All three types of lists are available in the Paragraph group on the Format Text tab; bulleted and numbered lists are also found on the Message tab, in the Basic Text group.

To format a bulleted list, follow these steps:

1. With the message open, select the text that you want formatted as a list.

2. On the Format Text tab, in the Paragraph group, select Bullets. To select a different style for the list, click the arrow next to Bullets, and then select a style from the library.

3. If you want to change the text to a different level, click Multilevel List, select Change List Level, and then choose the new level from the menu. Alternatively, simply press Tab with the cursor in the paragraph.

4. To create a new style for the list, click the arrow beside the Bullet button, and then select Define New Bullet to display the Define New Bullet dialog box, shown in Figure 9-8. Click Symbol, Picture, or Font, select the new bullet character in the resulting dialog box, and then click OK. Click OK again to close the Define New Bullet dialog box.

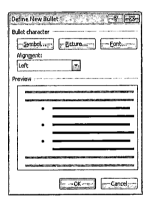

Figure 9-8 Choose the new bullet style in the Define New Bullet dialog box.

Numbered lists are created in much the same way as bulleted lists, letting you choose the number style (roman, Arabic, and so on) and related options. Multilevel lists have many additional options that you can configure, as shown in Figure 9-9, allowing you to create highly customized lists if needed.

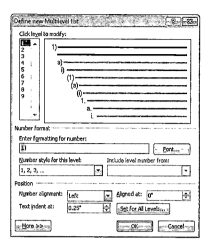

Figure 9-9 You can modify many options for multilevel lists in the Define New Multilevel List dialog box.

Options on the Format Text Tab

You can access only a portion of the text formatting options in the Basic Text group on the Message tab. A number of other options are available on the Format Text tab, including the following:

- **Character Formatting** Additional character styles include strikethrough, subscript, and superscript.

- **Shading** This option lets you apply a color to the background of the selected text.

- **Borders And Shading** You can choose options for adding borders, gridlines, and shading to selected paragraphs.

- **Line Spacing** You can set the spacing between lines and paragraphs. You can also open the Paragraph dialog box, which has settings for indentation, line breaks, and page breaks, as well as control over text flow that occurs over page breaks (widow/orphan control, keeping lines together, and so on).

- **Sort** Orders the selected paragraphs based on the criteria that you specify in the Sort Text dialog box.

- **Show/Hide** You can toggle the display of normally hidden formatting characters such as paragraph marks.

Working with Styles

Outlook 2010 lets you choose from a gallery of styles to format text easily using a number of predefined looks. Each theme has its own complete set of font styles, created based on the colors and fonts that you specify for the theme. You can also define your own custom style sets if you prefer to use styles that are not defined by the current theme. A *style set* is a working set of font styles used for messages: normal, heading, title, and so on.

The Quick Styles gallery, shown in Figure 9-10, displays the most commonly used styles, giving you an easy way to format the text in your message. When you define custom styles, they are also displayed in the Quick Styles gallery.

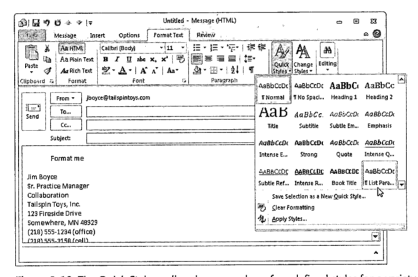

Figure 9-10 The Quick Styles gallery has a number of predefined styles for a variety of uses.

Styles shown in the Quick Styles gallery include:

- Normal

- List Paragraph

- Strong (bold)

- Headings (levels 1 and 2)

- Titles (title, subtitle, and book title)

- Emphasis (several italicized styles)

- Quotes (regular and bold)

- References (regular and bold)

To apply a style using the Quick Styles gallery, follow these steps:

1. With a message open, select the text that you want to format.

2. On the Format Text tab, in the Styles group, click Quick Styles to display the Quick Styles gallery.

> **Note**
> If the Ribbon is wide enough, a selection of Quick Styles will be displayed instead of the Quick Styles button. In this case, click More to view the Quick Styles gallery.

3. Point to a style that you are considering to see a Live Preview of the style applied to the selected text. In Figure 9-10, the text has been selected, and Live Preview has applied the List Paragraph Quick Style. Select the style that you want to apply.

You can create new styles that will be available in the Quick Styles gallery. To create a new Quick Style, first format some text as you want the new style to appear. Next, on the Format Text tab, in the Styles group, click Quick Styles, and then click Save Selection As A New Quick Style. The Create New Style From Formatting dialog box is displayed, in which you can give the style a name. You can also click Modify to change the style if you want.

To remove a style from the Quick Styles gallery, right-click the Quick Style in the gallery, and then choose Remove From Quick Styles gallery. The deletion is immediate, without a confirmation message box, but it can be undone using the Undo command (note that you must use it immediately, though—if you move on, it will be too late).

To display the complete list of styles, on the Format Text tab, in the Styles group, click the Styles button at the lower-right corner of the group to open the Styles dialog box. You can format your message in the same way as with Quick Styles, by selecting some text and then choosing the style to apply from the Styles dialog box.

New styles can be created, and the formatting of text in messages can be examined, by using the Style Inspector from the Styles window. The complete set of styles can be configured by clicking Manage Styles and using the Manage Styles dialog box. (There are approximately 300 styles available!) To configure options for the Styles window, click Options.

> **Note**
>
> When you change the theme, custom fonts are not changed unless they use a theme color—in which case, the color is updated. Resetting font styles is done by reapplying a style set.

You can change the fonts and colors used to determine the current Quick Styles. To change these options, on the Format Text tab, in the Styles group, click Change Styles, and then select one of the following options:

- **Style Set**   This setting specifies the font used for the Quick Styles. You can choose from several options or create your own style set from the existing message (saved as a Word 2010 template).

- **Colors**   You can select a set of theme colors to use for the font color set or create a custom set of theme colors.

- **Fonts**   This option lets you pick a font set from an existing theme or create your own font set by selecting a body font and a heading font.

- **Paragraph Spacing**   Choose from a selection of predefined paragraph spacing settings or create your own with settings for line spacing and spacing before and after paragraphs.

- **Set As Default**   Choosing this option sets the current configuration (theme, style set, and any customized settings except background) as the default for new messages.

Using Style Sets

A style set consists of a number of font styles, initially created from the theme settings, but customizable after that. Style sets can be created, saved, and applied independent of theme-related font changes and will override theme settings.

To work with style sets, with a new message open, on the Format Text tab, in the Styles group, click Change Styles, and then click Style Set. You can then choose from the following actions:

- To apply a style set, select the style set from the menu.

- To set the font styles back to the new message default, choose Reset To Quick Styles From Template.

- To set the font styles back to the Outlook 2010 default font styles, choose Reset Document Quick Styles.

- To create a new style set, select Save As Quick Style Set. The Save Quick Style Set dialog box will be displayed, allowing you to name the style set.

Creating a Custom Style Set

To customize font styles, follow these steps:

1. Type some text, and then format it as you want the updated style text to appear. (In this example, we will change the Title style.) Select the text, and on the Format Text tab, in the Styles group, click Quick Styles.

2. In the Quick Styles gallery, right-click Title, and then choose Update Title To Match Selection.

3. Repeat for each font style you want to define.

4. When you have finished customizing the font styles, delete all the text in your message. (This leaves the styles you created intact but creates the new message without unwanted text content.)

5. To save the style set that you created, on the Format Text tab, in the Styles group, click Change Styles, Style Set, and Save As Quick Style Set.

6. In the Save Quick Style Set dialog box, specify a file name for the style set, and then click Save. The style set is saved as a Word 2010 template file.

Using Tables

Using Outlook 2010, you can add a variety of tables to your email messages easily. You can use a Word 2010 table for textual information or a Microsoft Excel 2010 spreadsheet with its support for mathematical operations. You can apply a style to your table easily by selecting it from the visual gallery of built-in and custom styles.

Inserting a Table in a Message

You can add a table to your email quickly with one of several methods provided by Outlook 2010. To insert a table in a message, follow these steps:

1. With a message open, position the insertion point where you want the table to appear. (You can nest tables by setting the insertion point inside a table cell.)

2. On the Insert tab, in the Tables group, click Table to display the Insert Table menu. You can create a table using one of the following methods:

- . To draw a table, use the mini-table grid on the Insert Table menu. As you move your mouse over the table grid on the menu, you get a preview of the table in the body of your message, as shown in Figure 9-11. Click the lower-right cell of the desired table grid to insert it in the message.

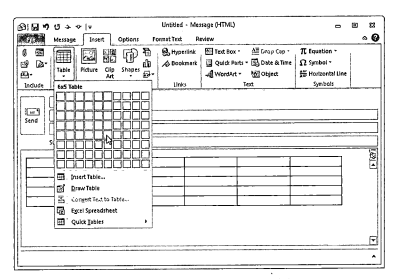

Figure 9-11 You can preview a table before you insert it in your message.

- Select Insert Table on the Insert Table menu to open the Insert Table dialog box, shown in Figure 9-12, and specify the table size and AutoFit behavior. Selecting the Remember Dimensions For New Tables check box makes these settings the default for new tables.

Figure 9-12 You choose the settings for a new table in the Insert Table dialog box.

- Selecting Draw Table lets you draw a single table cell in the message window. If needed, you can then split the cell or add cells to the table. When you finish editing the table, you can double-click anywhere else in your message to return to editing the text.

- Selecting Excel Spreadsheet creates an Excel 2010 table in the message and displays the Excel 2010 commands on the Ribbon. When you finish editing the spreadsheet, you can click anywhere else in your message to return to editing the text.

- Selecting Quick Tables displays a gallery that lets you select a previously saved table design. Outlook 2010 does not have any Quick Tables by default, so this option is usable only after you have created some Quick Tables of your own.

For information about creating Quick Tables, see the section "Working with Quick Tables," on page 232.

Working with Tables

When you select a table in an email message, the Ribbon displays two additional Table Tools tabs. The Design tab lets you control visual style effects and configure settings such as header rows. The Layout tab has commands that let you add and remove table cells and work with cell properties.

INSIDE OUT   Limitations on styling Excel 2010 spreadsheets

Although Excel 2010 tables provide a lot of additional functionality, you are limited in your ability to do page layout on an Excel 2010 object in your message. Neither of the Table Tools tabs (Design and Layout), which contain commands used to apply styles to tables, are available when an Excel 2010 object is selected. If you want to use the tools in Outlook 2010 to format your tables, you can create an Excel spreadsheet with your data and then copy the completed information to an appropriately sized Outlook 2010 table. You can then apply the Outlook 2010 built-in styling effects to the table.

On the Design tab, shown in Figure 9-13, specify the table style, colors, borders, and options, such as whether a header row is used, as described here:

- **Table Style Options**   You can apply specific effects to individual rows and columns, such as Header Row, Total Row, First Column, or Last Column. You can also choose to have rows, columns, or both banded in alternating colors for readability.

- **Table Styles**   You can select a visual table style from the built-in gallery, modify the current style, or create a new table style. Shading and Borders effects can be applied to a selection of cells.

- **Draw Borders**   This group contains commands to format the Line Style, Line Weight, and Pen Color. You can also draw a new table or erase existing table cells and content. You can also click the dialog box launcher to display the Borders And Shading dialog box and configure these options.

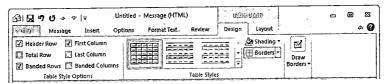

Figure 9-13 You can apply a variety of style options to a table by using the Design tab commands.

You can use the commands on the Layout tab, shown in Figure 9-14, to insert and delete cells and configure how the data is displayed inside table cells.

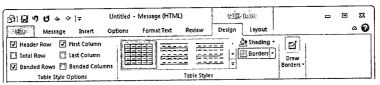

Figure 9-14 Use the Layout tab to manage cells and format the information they contain.

The Layout tab contains these command groups:

- **Table**   You can select all or part of the table, view gridlines (or turn them off), and display the Table Properties dialog box.

- **Rows & Columns** Rows and columns can be inserted and deleted using these commands. Clicking the Insert Cells dialog box launcher lets you specify the direction to shift existing cells when inserting new ones.

- **Merge** These commands let you merge cells, split cells, or split the table into multiple tables.

- **Cell Size** You can specify the size of individual cells, distribute rows or cells evenly, or choose AutoFit. Click the dialog box launcher to display the Table Properties dialog box, and then set the size, alignment, text wrapping options, and margins for the cell.

- **Alignment** You can choose from nine preset alignment options (Align Top Left, Align Top Right, Align Center, Align Bottom Right, and so on) for the selected table text. Text can be written from left to right, top to bottom, or bottom to top using the Text Direction command. Cell margins for the entire table can be set here as well.

- **Data** You can sort the table information, convert the table to text, or insert a formula using those commands. To have the header row repeat on tables that span multiple pages, select the header row in the table, and then click Repeat Header Rows.

Working with Quick Tables

The Quick Tables gallery is your personal gallery of tables that you can insert quickly into your messages. This can be simply an empty table formatted exactly the way that you want, or a complete table with not only a custom look but data as well. Once you have customized the appearance of a table, you can save it as a Quick Table so that you can re-create the format and style of frequently used tables easily.

To create a Quick Table, follow these steps:

1. Insert a table into a message, format it, and then enter any content that you want to be contained in your Quick Table (headings, for example).

2. Select the table (or part of it), and on the Insert tab, in the Table group, click Table, choose Quick Tables, and then click Save Selection To Quick Tables Gallery.

3. In the Create New Building Block dialog box, give the table a name, and then click OK. The Quick Table is now listed in the Quick Tables gallery for easy use. If you want the table to appear in a different gallery, such as Text Box or Quick Parts, select the gallery name from the Gallery drop-down list. (Some galleries are available only in the Building Blocks Organizer, shown in Figure 9-15.) You can assign a category to the table in the Category drop-down list. (This category is visible only in the Building Blocks Organizer.) The Options drop-down list selections have no effect on Quick Tables.

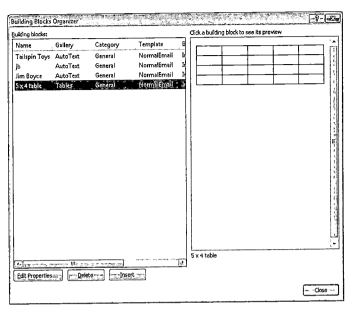

Figure 9-15 Use the Building Blocks Organizer to remove a Quick Table.

To remove a Quick Table from the gallery, on the Insert tab, click Table, Quick Tables, right-click the table, and then choose Organize And Delete to open the Building Blocks Organizer, shown in Figure 9-15. Select the table you want to remove, click Delete, click Yes, and then click Close.

INSIDE OUT   Add the Building Blocks Organizer to the Quick Access Toolbar

You can manage the entire range of building blocks, such as Quick Tables, Quick Parts, Text Boxes, and so on, in the Building Blocks Organizer. It is also the only way to insert Quick Tables that have been added to custom galleries. If you use the Building Blocks Organizer often, you might want to add an icon to the Quick Access Toolbar to give you quicker access. To add the Building Blocks Organizer to the Quick Access Toolbar, follow these steps:

1. With a new message open, right-click the Quick Access toolbar and choose Customize Quick Access Toolbar.

2. In the Choose Commands From drop-down list, select Commands Not In The Ribbon. Select Building Blocks Organizer, click Add, and then click OK.

Using Special Text Features

Outlook 2010 includes a number of text options and text objects that you can insert into your email messages. If you repeatedly type the same text in multiple messages, for example, you can save the text for reuse. You can apply decorative text effects such as drop caps and WordArt as well. These options are available on the Insert tab, in the Text group.

Quick Parts

Quick Parts are chunks of reusable content (text, graphics, and so on) that you can insert into a message with a click of your mouse. You can create a Quick Part for anything that you commonly have to enter into a message such as contact information, directions and a map, and so on.

To save a Quick Part, follow these steps:

1. Create a message with the content that you want to reuse, and then select the content.

2. On the Insert tab, in the Text group, click Quick Parts, and then select Save Selection To Quick Part Gallery. You can select a gallery in the Gallery drop-down list. (Remember that some galleries are available only in the Building Blocks Organizer.) You can assign a category to the table in the Category drop-down list. By default, a Quick Part is inserted in its own paragraph; if you want to insert the Quick Part without inserting a line break first, select Content Only from the Options drop-down list.

Once you have saved the Quick Part, using it is easy. To use the Quick Part, on the Insert tab, in the Text group, click Quick Parts, and then select the Quick Part from the gallery.

Drop Cap

You can use a drop cap to create a special look at the beginning of a paragraph. When you select a drop cap, Outlook 2010 creates a small text box and inserts a single, specially formatted character. (This character is still treated like part of the paragraph, not as a separate text box.) To create a drop cap, follow these steps:

1. Open the message, and then position the insertion point in the paragraph that should get the drop cap.

2. On the Insert tab, in the Text group, click Drop Cap, as shown in Figure 9-16.

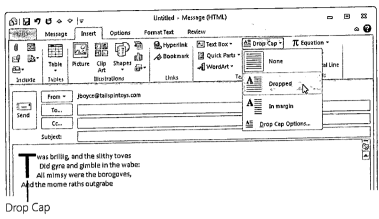

Drop Cap

Figure 9-16 You can add drop caps to your messages quickly.

3. Select Dropped or In Margin to create a drop cap. To format the drop cap, choose Drop Cap Options.

4. In the Drop Cap dialog box, you can specify the position, font, number of lines to drop, and distance from text. When you have finished, click OK.

Date & Time

To insert the date and time in the message, follow these steps:

1. With a message open, on the Insert tab, in the Text group, click Date & Time.

2. In the Date & Time dialog box, select the format you want in the Available Formats list. Select the Update Automatically check box if you want the time to be updated to the current time automatically, and then click OK.

Some of the options in the Text group operate more like objects than text. Options such as WordArt are inserted by creating an object; a tab is then added to the Ribbon for related WordArt commands. In contrast with normal text, you can move such objects to any location in the message (in the same way that you can position a graphic) for layout purposes.

Text Box

Use a text box to insert text inside a box at any location in the message. To create a text box, follow these steps:

1. With a message open, on the Insert tab, in the Text group, click Text Box, and then select Draw Text Box.

2. The Drawing Tools Format tab will be displayed, as shown in Figure 9-17, allowing you to style the box (shape, shadows, colors, and so on) and specify layout options (text wrapping, layering, and grouping).

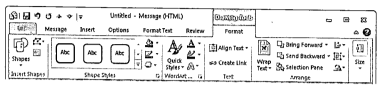

Figure 9-17 Use the Drawing Tools Format tab to apply styles to a text box.

3. Enter your text in the text box. This text can be formatted in the usual ways using the tools on the Format Text tab.

4. To move the text box, you can drag it with the mouse or select it and use the arrow keys on the keyboard to move it.

5. To rotate the text box, click on the rotate handle at the top of the box and move the mouse left or right.

WordArt

WordArt is highly formatted text inside a text box. The text typically has three-dimensional (3-D) shading, special edge bevels, curved paths, or other complex features. Figure 9-18 shows some examples of WordArt, along with the Drawing Tools Format tab, which you can use to modify the WordArt layout. To create WordArt, follow these steps:

1. With a message open, on the Insert tab, in the Text group, click WordArt.

2. Select a beginning style for your WordArt from the gallery.

3. Outlook inserts a text box with some sample text in the box using the selected style. Type your text in the text box.

To format your WordArt, click the WordArt object to display the Drawing Tools Format tab, shown in Figure 9-18, and then apply the desired effects to your WordArt. When you have finished, click outside the WordArt box to return to editing the rest of your message.

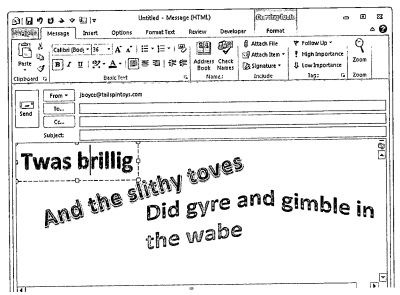

Figure 9-18 Format WordArt objects such as these using the commands on the Drawing Tools Format tab.

Object

The last option in the Text group of the Insert tab is Object, which lets you insert an object in your message. You can use an existing object or create a new one. To insert an object, with a message open, on the Insert tab, in the Text group, click Object. In the Object dialog box, select the object type or file name, and then click OK.

Including Illustrations in Messages

Outlook 2010 provides a variety of illustration types that you can use to enhance your email. You can add pictures, clip art, shapes, charts, and SmartArt. You control page layout, so you can place illustrations in any location in your message and then format them in a number of ways, including adding borders, shadows, and 3-D effects. (Exact options vary between illustration types.) You can wrap your text around illustrations in several styles and even layer text and graphics on top of each other, using transparency effects to make everything visible.

Each type of illustration has one or more groups of commands specific to it, providing the controls needed for that kind of illustration. They also share a number of groups of commands on the Ribbon and operate in much the same way. We will examine the process of inserting a picture in some detail in the next section, describing the common commands. Following that, we will highlight the differences between the other types of illustration.

Your ability to insert graphics in a message depends in part on which message format you use. With the new Outlook 2010 editor, you can insert embedded graphics when using HTML (the default) or RTF, with minor differences in layout options. You can't insert embedded graphics in a message that uses plain text format.

INSIDE OUT   Attach graphics files to plain text messages

Although you can't insert embedded graphics in a plain text message, you can attach a graphic (or other) file to plain text email. To attach a graphic to a plain text message, follow these steps:

1. In the message form, on the Insert tab, in the Include group, click Attach File.

2. In the Insert File dialog box, locate the file that you want to attach, and then click Insert.

Inserting a Picture from a File

Follow these steps to insert a picture in a message:

1. On the Insert tab, in the Illustrations group, click Picture to display the Insert Picture dialog box.

2. In the Insert Picture dialog box, select the graphics file to insert in the message, and then click Insert. (To insert a link to the image, click the arrow next to Insert, and then select Link To File or Insert And Link.)

3. In the message, when the picture is selected, Outlook 2010 displays the Picture Tools Format tab with tools used to format the picture, as shown in Figure 9-19.

Figure 9-19 You can adjust the appearance of the picture, as well as format how the picture is displayed in the email message.

To adjust the appearance of the picture, under Picture Tools, click the Format tab, and then, in the Adjust group, use the appropriate tools, as follows:

- **Remove Background**   Use a mask to remove parts of the picture, such as the extra scenery around a group of people.

- **Corrections**   You can increase or decrease the brightness or contrast, or sharpen or soften the image, by selecting a thumbnail on the menu.

- **Color**   You can apply different color saturations and color tone to the picture, as well as recolor using various accent colors.

- **Artistic Effects**   Apply one of several artistic effects such as chalk, pencil, and other effects to the picture.

- **Compress Pictures**   Outlook 2010 can compress the images in your email messages to minimize message size. When you select Compress Picture, you are given the option of compressing one picture or all the images in the message. In the Compress Pictures dialog box, you can set the automatic compression option, choose whether to delete cropped areas of images, and determine the picture quality.

- **Change Picture**   This option lets you replace the current image while keeping the object formatting and size settings intact.

- **Reset Picture**   You can reset the picture to the original image, discarding all changes that you have made.

4. You can customize how the picture appears in the message by using the options in the Picture Styles group, as described here:

- **Quick Styles**   You can choose from a number of framing and perspective options to set the overall look of the picture.

- **Picture Border**   You can add an optional border around the graphic, with a specified pixel width and pattern, and using the colors from your theme or custom colors. To configure additional border settings, choose More Lines on the Weight menu to display the Format Picture dialog box, shown in Figure 9-20, and then configure the Line Style settings.

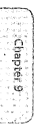

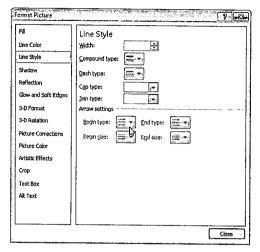

Figure 9-20 You can customize many aspects of the picture border in the Format Picture dialog box.

- **Picture Effects**   You can apply a number of effects to a picture to produce just the look you want for your message. The available effects are Shadow, Reflection, Glow, Soft Edges, Bevel, and 3-D Rotation. The Preset option has some preconfigured effects from which you can choose.

- **Picture Layout**   Changes the selected picture to a SmartArt graphic to apply SmartArt properties to the graphic and make it easy to manipulate and format the graphic using SmartArt shapes and properties.

5. You can specify how you want the image aligned in the message and how text will flow with the graphic using the options in the Arrange group. The commands operate as described here:

- **Bring Forward/Send Backward**   These options specify which layer the picture is in.

- **Wrap Text**   You can choose how the text wraps relative to the picture, selecting from having the image in line with text, behind text, or in front of text, or having the text only at the top and bottom of the picture or wrapped around a square. To drag a picture to a new location in the message, you must first select it and then choose either Behind Text or In Front Of Text.

- **Selection Pane**   Click to open the Selection And Visibility pane, where you can select pictures in the email.

- **Align**   You can line up multiple pictures (or other objects) by selecting them (using Shift-click) and then clicking Align. You can choose to align the edges or centers of the selected objects.

- **Group**   This command is unavailable when you are working with pictures.

- **Rotate**   You can change the orientation of the picture by selecting Rotate Right 90°, Rotate Left 90°, Flip Vertical, or Flip Horizontal. To have finer control over image orientation, choose More Rotation Options on the Rotate menu to open the Size dialog box, and then set the exact degree of rotation. (You can also resize and crop images in the Size dialog box.)

6. The picture can be resized and cropped with the settings in the Size group. To crop the image, select Crop, and then drag the cropping handles on the image. To resize the image, enter the new size in the Shape Height and Shape Width fields. (If Outlook 2010 is configured to constrain the aspect ratio of pictures, you need to enter only one of these options, not both.)

7. If you want to set Alternate Text (which is displayed in place of the picture for recipients whose email clients don't show graphics), right-click the picture, and then choose Format Picture on the shortcut menu. In the Format Picture dialog box, select Alt Text in the left pane. Enter your text in the Title box, and then click Close.

8. To add a hyperlink to the picture, right-click the picture, and then choose Hyperlink on the shortcut menu. (For detailed instructions on working with hyperlinks, see the section "Working with Hyperlinks," on page 250.)

Some, but not all, of the formatting and graphical effects are cumulative, and you might have to experiment to get exactly the effect you want.

INSIDE OUT   Find previous versions of your picture files

Outlook 2010 can search for previous versions of a picture file when you are inserting it into a message. Windows Vista and Windows 7 create these previous versions in one of two ways: when Windows creates a restore point or when you use the Back Up Wizard. (See the Windows Help Center for more information about creating previous versions of files.) If you have previous versions of your picture files, you can have Outlook 2010 search for them in the Insert Picture dialog box by clicking the arrow next to Insert and selecting Show Previous Versions. Outlook 2010 will display all previous versions of that image.

Inserting Clip Art

Inserting a clip art image opens the Clip Art task pane, which lets you search for the clip art image that you want to use. You can enter search terms and specify the collections to search, as well as limit the file types that are returned in the results. Once the clip art has been inserted, under Picture Tools, on the Format tab, use the commands as described in the preceding section.

Inserting Shapes

Outlook 2010 includes a library of shapes (previously called AutoShapes) from which you can select just the right one to illustrate your words. Shape types include lines, basic shapes (square, cylinder, and so on), arrows, flowchart objects, callouts, stars, and banners.

To insert a shape into a message, follow these steps:

1. With a message open, on the Insert tab, in the Illustrations group, select Shapes.

2. Choose a shape from the Shapes gallery.

3. Click and drag across the message where you want to create the shape.

4. With the shape selected, the Drawing Tools Format tab will be displayed, as shown in Figure 9-21.

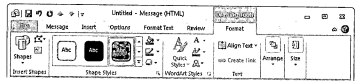

Figure 9-21 You can work with shapes using the commands on the Drawing Tools Format tab.

This tab provides you with these options for formatting the shape:

- **Insert Shapes** You can select a shape to create, edit a shape, or edit text with the commands in this group.

- **Shape Styles** This group provides a Quick Styles gallery of frame and fill effects, shape fill, shape outline, and shape changing effects. You can also apply a range of special effects such as shadows, reflection, and 3-D rotation.

- **Text**   Use these controls to align text in a text box and create a link between two text boxes so that text flows between them (see Figure 9-22).

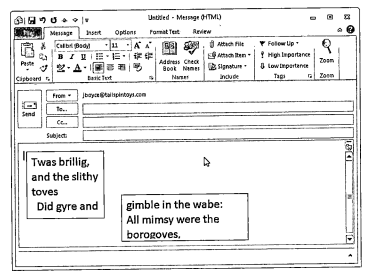

Figure 9-22 You can link text boxes so that the text flows between them.

- **Arrange**   This group controls how the shape is aligned in the message and how text flows with the graphic. You can move the shape to the front or back layer, control text wrapping, align multiple shapes, group shapes together, and control rotation of the shape.

- **Size**   This group lets you set the shape height and shape width.

INSIDE OUT   Insert a new drawing

To insert a blank drawing, with a message open, on the Insert tab, in the Illustrations group, click Shapes, and then click New Drawing Canvas. This will insert a blank drawing object in your message, in which you can draw using the Outlook 2010 built-in drawing tools.

Inserting a Chart

When you choose a chart as the illustration type to insert, the Insert Chart dialog box opens, allowing you to select the type of chart that you want to use. When you click OK, an Excel 2010 workbook is opened with a small amount of data entered. After you have entered your data, simply close the Excel window to update the chart and return to Outlook 2010. On the Ribbon, under Chart Tools, there are three tabs with quite a few commands allowing you fine control over the appearance of your chart, as described in the following sections.

Chart Tools Design Tab

The Chart Tools Design tab contains groups of commands that let you choose the type, style, and layout of the chart as well as the data it contains, as shown in Figure 9-23.

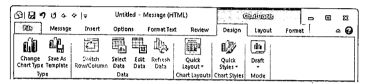

Figure 9-23 You can control the style and data for your chart using the Chart Tools Design tab.

The Design tab has these groups:

- **Type**   You can select the chart type (pie, bar, area, and so on) and save the current chart as a template.

- **Data**   This group has commands that let you manipulate your data in Excel 2010.

- **Chart Layouts**   You can choose from the Quick Layout gallery using various arrangements of the chart, legend, title, and other text.

- **Chart Styles**   This group consists of a Quick Styles gallery with a selection of colors, outlines, and effects.

- **Mode**   Choose between Draft Mode and Normal Mode for the current chart, and optionally apply a mode to all charts.

Chart Tools Layout Tab

The Chart Tools Layout tab, shown in Figure 9-24, has groups of commands that control the appearance of many aspects of the chart such as grid, labels, and background.

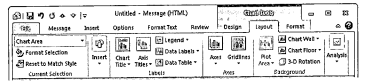

Figure 9-24 You can control the display of data and labels and add analysis tools to charts with the commands on the Chart Tools Layout tab.

The Layout tab contains these groups of commands:

- **Current Selection**   You can select a chart element and format the selection.

- **Insert**   You can insert a picture or shape or draw a text box inside your chart.

- **Labels**   These commands let you turn titles, legends, and data labels on and off. You can also format the style and placement of these labels.

- **Axes**   The Axes command controls the display of the horizontal and vertical axes; the Gridlines command does the same for the chart gridlines.

- **Background**   You can turn on the display of a background color on the Plot Area, Chart Floor, and Chart Wall and also control the 3-D rotation of the chart.

- **Analysis**   The commands in the Analysis group can add additional data to your charts. Each analysis option works with only certain types of charts. You can select a Trendline (most chart types), Drop Lines (area and line charts), High-Low Lines (two-dimensional line chart), Up/Down bars (line chart), and Error Bars with Standard Error, Percentage, or Standard Deviation (most chart types).

Chart Tools Format Tab

The Chart Tools Format tab, shown in Figure 9-25, provides you with the tools that you need to customize the appearance of your charts. You can control colors, styles, and effects and the page layout of your chart using these commands.

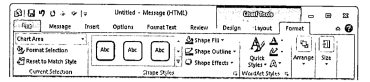

Figure 9-25 You can customize the appearance of your chart with the commands on the Chart Tools Format tab.

The Format tab contains these groups:

- **Current Selection**   You can select a chart element and format the selection with this group.

- **Shape Styles**   This group provides a Quick Styles gallery with frame and fill effects, shape fill, shape outline, and shape effects options.

- **WordArt Styles**   These commands control the text used in text labels, axes, titles, and legends. (WordArt commands are available only if a suitable chart component is selected.)

- **Arrange**   This group contains the text wrapping, layering, and alignment commands. (This group is not available if your message is in RTF format.)

- **Size**   This group specifies the shape height and shape width.

Inserting SmartArt

SmartArt is a type of reusable object designed as a means of displaying complex information in an easy-to-understand graphical format. Outlook 2010 includes a gallery of SmartArt graphics in formats that represent things such as a list, a hierarchy (like an organizational chart), a process (like a flowchart), or a relationship (such as a Venn diagram).

To insert a SmartArt graphic into a message, follow these steps:

1. With a message open, on the Insert tab, in the Illustrations group, select SmartArt.

2. In the Choose A SmartArt Graphic dialog box, shown in Figure 9-26, select a SmartArt graphic, and then click OK.

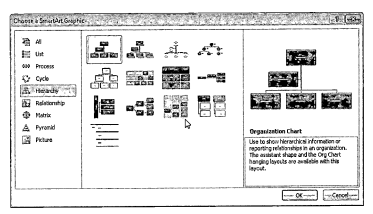

Figure 9-26 You can select the style of SmartArt graphic you want in the Choose A Smart-Art Graphic dialog box.

Once the SmartArt graphic is inserted in the message, you can add text and format the graphic. The two SmartArt Tools tabs are described in the following sections.

SmartArt Tools Design Tab

The SmartArt Tools Design tab, shown in Figure 9-27, contains groups of commands that let you work with the SmartArt content, adding and customizing shapes and changing layout and styles.

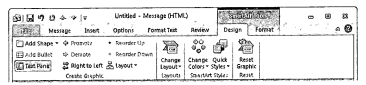

Figure 9-27 You can work with the graphics components and layout of SmartArt using the SmartArt Tools Design tab.

The groups available on the Design tab are:

- **Create Graphic**   You can add a shape, bullet, or text pane to the SmartArt graphic and manipulate the text layout inside the SmartArt shapes with this set of controls.

- **Layouts**   This group lets you change the SmartArt type either from the gallery or in the Choose A SmartArt Graphic dialog box.

- **SmartArt Styles**   You can change the colors used in the SmartArt and the effects used in the SmartArt style.

- **Reset**   The Reset Graphic command lets you quickly remove all custom formatting from the selected object.

SmartArt Tools Format Tab

The SmartArt Tools Format tab, shown in Figure 9-28, has the commands that you need to style the SmartArt and control its placement in the message.

Figure 9-28 You can change the appearance of the SmartArt text, frame, and background using the SmartArt Tools Format tab.

The groups available on the Format tab are:

- **Shapes**   You can choose the shapes to use as SmartArt elements and then resize those shapes.

- **Shape Styles**   This group provides frame and fill effects, shape fill, shape outline, and shape changing effects.

- **WordArt Styles**   You can format the text used in SmartArt objects, selecting a style from the gallery, Text Fill, Text Outline, and Text Effects. Each of these options has additional menu selections for fine-grained control over text format.

- **Arrange**   This group contains the text wrapping, layering, and alignment commands.

- **Size**   This group lets you specify the shape height and shape width.

Using Symbols in a Message

A few other options are available on the Insert tab for you to use in your email messages. You can also insert math equations, symbols (such as © or ™), and horizontal lines used for visual separation.

Inserting an Equation

To insert an equation in a message, follow these steps:

1. On the Insert tab, in the Symbols group, click Equation to create an empty equation box in your message.

2. Use the commands on the Equation Tools Design tab, shown in Figure 9-29, to create the equation, as follows:

   - **Tools**   You can specify how the equation is displayed: Linear is one-dimensional for easy editing, whereas Professional is two-dimensional for display. (These two commands are unavailable until you have entered some data in the equation.) You can enter plain text by clicking Normal Text. Clicking Equation displays the Equation gallery and lets you save new equations to it. Click the dialog box launcher to view the Equation Options dialog box.

   - **Symbols**   To add a symbol to the equation, click the symbol. (Click the More arrow to display the entire gallery.)

   - **Structures**   You can insert a number of mathematical structures into your equation easily by selecting a structure from the Structures group. You can choose a structure from these sets: Fraction, Script, Radical, Integral, Large Operator, Bracket, Function, Accent, Limit And Log, Operator, and Matrix. Each set has a number of selections, including many commonly used options.

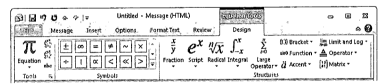

Figure 9-29 You can use the Equation Tools Design tab to complete your equation.

Inserting a Symbol

On the Insert tab, in the Symbols group, click Symbol. Select the symbol from the display of commonly used symbols, or click More Symbols to open the Symbol dialog box. In the Symbol dialog box, select the symbol, click Insert, and then click Close. (You can insert multiple symbols by clicking Insert after selecting one, then selecting the next symbol and clicking Insert again, and so on.)

Inserting a Horizontal Line

On the Insert tab, in the Symbols group, click Horizontal Line. Outlook 2010 will insert a line at the insertion point location. To format the line, right-click it, and then choose Format Horizontal Line. In the Format Horizontal Line dialog box, shown in Figure 9-30, you can set the size, color, and alignment of the line. (Outlook 2010 uses the most recent settings in this dialog box when you create new lines.)

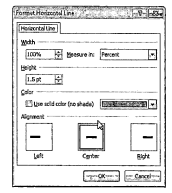

Figure 9-30 You can set the properties of horizontal lines in the Format Horizontal Line dialog box.

Working with Hyperlinks

You can insert hyperlinks to websites, email addresses, network shares, and other items in a message easily. When you type certain kinds of text in a message, Outlook 2010 automatically converts the text to a hyperlink, requiring no special action from you. For example, if you type an email address, an Internet Uniform Resource Locator (URL), or a Universal Naming Convention (UNC) path to a share, Outlook 2010 converts the text to a hyperlink. To indicate the hyperlink, Outlook 2010 underlines it and changes the font color.

When the recipient of your message clicks the hyperlink, the resulting action depends on the type of hyperlink. With an Internet URL, for example, the recipient can go to the specified website. With a UNC path, the remote share opens when the recipient clicks the hyperlink. This is a great way to point the recipient to a shared resource on your computer or another computer on the network.

INSIDE OUT   Follow a hyperlink

You can't follow (open) a hyperlink in a message that you're composing by just clicking the hyperlink. This action is restricted to allow you to click the hyperlink text and edit it. To follow a hyperlink in a message that you're composing, hold down the Ctrl key and click the hyperlink.

Inserting Hyperlinks

You have another option for inserting a hyperlink in a message:

1. Position the insertion point where you want to insert the hyperlink.

2. On the Insert tab, in the Links group, click Hyperlink to display the Insert Hyperlink dialog box, shown in Figure 9-31. (If you select text to use for the link, that text is inserted automatically in the Text To Display box.)

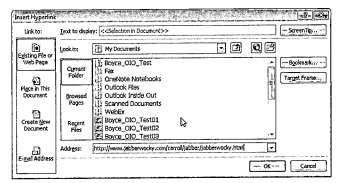

Figure 9-31 Use the Insert Hyperlink dialog box to insert a hyperlink and configure link settings.

The options displayed in the Insert Hyperlink dialog box vary according to the type of hyperlink you're inserting, as explained in the following sections.

Inserting Hyperlinks to Files or Web Pages

To insert a hyperlink to a file or web page, select Existing File Or Web Page in the Link To bar. Then provide the following information in the Insert Hyperlink dialog box:

- **Text To Display**   In this box, type the text that will serve as the hyperlink in the message. Outlook 2010 underlines this text and changes its color to indicate the hyperlink.

- **Look In**   In this area, choose the location that contains the data to which you want to link. You can choose from these options:

- **Current Folder**   If you are linking to a file, select Current Folder, and then use this drop-down list to locate and select the file on the local computer or on the network.

- **Browsed Pages**   To insert a hyperlink to a page that you've recently viewed in your web browser, click Browsed Pages. The document list in the dialog box changes to show a list of recently browsed pages from Windows Internet Explorer.

- **Recent Files**   If you want to insert a hyperlink to a file that you've used recently, click Recent Files to view a list of most recently used files in the document list of the dialog box.

- **Address**   Type the local path, the Internet URL, or the UNC path to the file or web-site in this box.

- **ScreenTip**   Click this button to define an optional ScreenTip that appears when the recipient's mouse pointer pauses over the hyperlink (when viewed in Internet Explorer version 4.0 or later).

INSIDE OUT   View custom ScreenTips

Even though you can add custom ScreenTips using Outlook 2010, they cannot be seen in email messages. Custom Screen Tips actually require Internet Explorer (version 4.0 or later). To see the ScreenTips that you add in Outlook 2010, you have to use Outlook Web Access (OWA) with Microsoft Exchange Server or first save the email message as an HTML file and then view it in Internet Explorer.

- **Bookmark**   Click this button to select an existing bookmark in the specified document. When the recipient clicks the hyperlink, the document opens at the bookmark location.

- **Target Frame**   Click this button to specify the browser frame in which you want the hyperlink to appear. For example, choose New Window if you want the hyperlink to open in a new window on the recipient's computer.

TROUBLESHOOTING

Recipients of your messages can't access linked files

If you're setting up a hyperlink to a local file, bear in mind that the recipient probably won't be able to access the file using the file's local path. For example, linking to C:\ Docs\Policies.doc would cause the recipient's system to try to open that path on his or her own system. You can use this method to point the recipient to a document on his or her own computer. However, if you want to point the recipient to a document on your computer, you must either specify a UNC path to the document or specify a URL (which requires that your computer function as a web server).

The form of the UNC path you specify depends on the operating system of the recipient. In Microsoft Windows 2000 and later versions, you can specify a deep UNC path, such as \\<server>\<share>\<subfolder>\<sub-subfolder>\<document>. doc, where <server> is the name of the computer sharing the resource, <share> is the share name, <subfolder> is the name of a folder in the path to the file, and <document> is the name of the document to open. Microsoft Windows 95, Microsoft Windows 98, Microsoft Windows Me, and Microsoft Windows NT are limited to \\<server>\<share>\<document>. For the deep hyperlink to work properly, however, the recipient must be using Windows 2000 or later.

Inserting a Hyperlink to a Place in the Current Message

If you click Place In This Document in the Link To bar, the Insert Hyperlink dialog box changes, as shown in Figure 9-32. The Select A Place In This Document area shows the available locations in the open document: headings, bookmarks, and the top of the document. Select the location to which you want to link, provide other information as necessary (the text to display in the hyperlink, for example, or perhaps a ScreenTip), and then click OK.

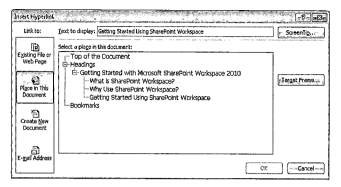

Figure 9-32 You can link easily to a location in the current document.

> **Note**
> This method is commonly used when you have opened a document in Word 2010 and are inserting a hyperlink in that document rather than in a separate email message.

Inserting a Hyperlink to a New Document

If you select Create New Document in the Link To bar of the Insert Hyperlink dialog box, you can specify the path to a new document and choose to either edit the document now or insert the hyperlink for later editing. You'll most often use this method for inserting hyperlinks in a Word 2010 document rather than in an email message.

Inserting a Hyperlink to an Email Address

If you select E-Mail Address in the Link To bar, you can insert an email address as a hyperlink in a message easily. When recipients click the hyperlink, their email programs will open a new email message addressed to the person you have specified in the hyperlink. Although you can simply type the email address in the message and let Outlook 2010 convert it to a *mailto:* link, you might prefer to use the Insert Hyperlink dialog box instead. As Figure 9-33 shows, you can use this dialog box to enter an email address or select from a list of email addresses that you have recently used on your system and to specify the subject for the message.

> **Tip**
> The main reason to use the Insert Hyperlink dialog box to insert an email link is to enable you to specify the subject of the message automatically.

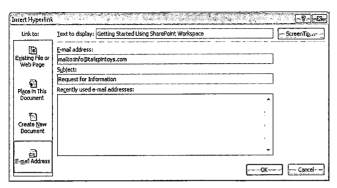

Figure 9-33 You can insert a *mailto:* hyperlink in your email message.

You can use the hyperlink's context menu to select, edit, and open the hyperlink, as well as copy it to the Clipboard. Just right-click the hyperlink and choose the appropriate option from the context menu.

Removing a Hyperlink

To remove a hyperlink, right-click the hyperlink, and then choose Remove Hyperlink on the context menu. Outlook 2010 retains the underlying text but removes the hyperlink.

Inserting Bookmarks

A *bookmark* is an internal reference used to locate a specific place in a document and link to it by name. When you insert a bookmark in Outlook 2010, it is then available in the Insert Hyperlink dialog box as a linkable location. This is particularly useful if you have a lengthy email message, or one with sections or illustrations that you want the reader to be able to find quickly. To insert a bookmark in a message, follow these steps:

1. With a message open, select the text (or picture, chart, and so on) that you want the bookmark to reference. On the Insert tab, in the Links group, click Bookmark.

2. In the Bookmark dialog box, shown in Figure 9-34, enter a name in the Bookmark Name box, click Add, and then click OK.

Figure 9-34 You can manage bookmarks using the Bookmark dialog box.

To remove a bookmark, on the Insert tab, in the Links group, click Bookmark. Select the bookmark that you want to remove, click Delete, and then click Close.

Including Other Items in a Message

You might also want to include things such as files and other Outlook 2010 items in your mail messages at times. Outlook 2010 makes it easy for you to insert a calendar, a business card, or another item in your email message.

Attaching Files

To attach a file to a message, follow these steps:

1. Position your insertion point where you want to insert the file, and on the Insert tab, in the Include group, select Attach File to open the Insert File dialog box.

2. Locate and select the file to insert, and then click Insert.

Alternatively, you can click the paper clip icon on the toolbar to insert a file as an attachment, or you can simply drag the file into the message window.

Inserting Files in the Body of a Message

Occasionally, you'll want to insert a file in the body of a message rather than attaching it to the message. For example, you might want to include a text file, a Word 2010 document, or another document as part of the message. To insert a file in the body of the message, you can use the steps described in the preceding section for attaching a file, with one difference: in step 2, click the button next to Insert, and then click Insert As Text.

> **Note**
> You can't insert non-text items in the body of an HTML message using the Attach File command. If you need to insert a document within the body of the message, regardless of the type of document, format the message as rich text.

INSIDE OUT Use the Clipboard to insert a file

In some cases, you'll find it easier to use the Clipboard to insert a file in a message, particularly if the file is already open in another window. (Just select the file, and then copy and paste or cut and paste it into the message.) You can also use the Clipboard when you need to insert only a portion of a file, such as a few paragraphs from a document.

Including an Outlook 2010 Item

You might want to include other Outlook 2010 items, such as messages and tasks, in a message you are sending. To include another Outlook 2010 item, follow these steps:

1. While creating a message, on the Insert tab, in the Include group, click Outlook Item.

2. In the Insert Item dialog box, shown in Figure 9-35, locate and select the item or items that you want to include.

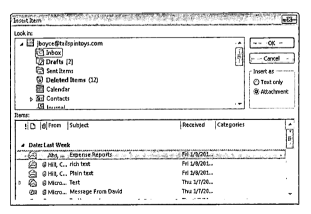

Figure 9-35 Select the Outlook 2010 items to include in a message in the Insert Item dialog box.

3. Select Attachment or Text Only, and then click OK.

> **Note**
>
> If the message is in RTF format, you also have the option to insert a shortcut to the item in the message.

Attaching a Business Card to a Message

With Outlook 2010, you can send a copy of a contact item in vCard format, a standard format for exchanging contact information. This allows the recipient to import the contact data into a contact management program, assuming that the recipient's program supports the vCard standard (as most do).

You can send a vCard by email from the Contacts folder without first opening a message. To do this, perform the following steps:

1. In Outlook 2010, open the Contacts folder, and then select the contact item that you want to send.

2. Click the Home tab, and in the Share group, click Forward Contact and choose As A Business Card. Outlook 2010 inserts the vCard into the message.

3. Complete the message as you normally would, and then click Send.

You can also include a business card in a message from the new message form. On the Insert tab, in the Include group, click Business Card. If the contact is displayed in the recently used contacts list on the menu, you can select the contact. Otherwise, choose Other Business Cards to open the Insert Business Card dialog box, and then select a name from the complete Contacts list.

> # INSIDE OUT Send data as an Outlook 2010 item
>
> If you know that the recipient uses Outlook 2010, in the Share group on the Home tab, click Forward Contact and choose As An Outlook Contact to send the contact data as an Outlook 2010 contact item. Outlook 2010 users can also use vCard attachments.

For more details on using and sharing vCards, see the section "Sharing Contacts," on page 464.

Including a Calendar

Outlook 2010 makes it easy for you to share part of your calendar with others by simply inserting a calendar in a message. You can choose the range of items to send from a single day to the entire calendar, or specify a range of dates. You also have control over what level of detail to include, whether your availability only, limited details (availability and subject only), or full details. You can also control the formatting and whether to include items marked private or attachments to items. To send a calendar in email, follow these steps:

1. While composing a message, on the Insert tab, in the Include group, click Calendar to open the Send A Calendar Via E-mail dialog box, as shown in Figure 9-36. Outlook will prompt you to switch to HTML if the message is currently plain text.

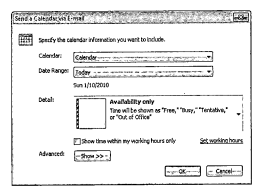

Figure 9-36 You can select the information that you want to include when sending a calendar via email.

2. Choose the Calendar, Date Range, and Detail level, and other parameters for the calendar. Click OK. Figure 9-37 shows a calendar inserted in a message.

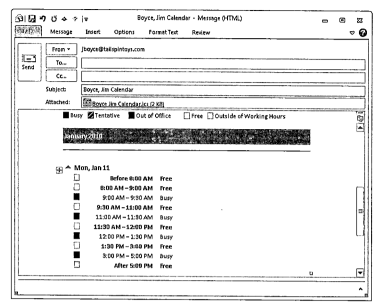

Figure 9-37 An example of a calendar inserted in a message.

See Chapter 35, "Sharing Calendars," for more information about sharing your calendar using Outlook 2010.

> **Note**
> We will discuss the use of signatures in the section "Using Signatures," on page 273.

Customizing the Appearance of Your Messages

By default, Outlook 2010 uses no background or special font characteristics for messages. However, it does support the use of themes and, to a lesser degree, stationery, so you can customize the look of your messages. Outlook 2010 has two types of themes as well as stationery, each of which functions a bit differently from the others. It helps to understand the differences between these options before you get started using them.

Understanding How Outlook Formats Messages

The appearance of an Outlook 2010 email message is the result of a complex behind-the-scenes interaction among a number of settings. A single message is likely to draw some of its formatting information from several different sources. While much of the process of determining how a given message looks is invisible to you, it helps to understand what goes into formatting an email message before you start working with these settings.

Office Themes

Themes apply a single, customizable look to your messages (and other elements of your business, since they can be shared across Office System 2010 applications) by combining several settings to create a specific look. Themes make it easy for you to create and implement a unified look and feel for all of your Office System documents.

A theme has a set of font faces, coordinated colors, and graphical effects that are combined to create a palette of styles that gives you a unified look for all the elements of your messages. Each portion of a theme can use built-in or custom settings that you create, giving you an endless number of combinations to work with. The components of a theme are:

- **Colors**   A set of colors that are applied consistently across all the graphical elements in your email. You can use built-in color sets or create your own.

- **Fonts**   Two fonts—one for body text and another for heading text—are used as the basis for the gallery of font styles used by that theme. Outlook 2010 has a number of built-in theme fonts, or you can create a custom set.

- **Effects**   An effect is a particular look for graphical objects created by using different values for lines, fills, and 3-D effects to create varying results. Effects are selected from a built-in gallery. You cannot create custom effects.

- **Page Color**   The page background can be a solid color, gradient, pattern, texture, or picture, or it can be left blank.

> **Note**
>
> Although you can save a theme that includes a background set by using the Page Color command, the background is not applied when you use that theme in Outlook 2010. To set a default background, you must use stationery or an older theme, or apply the background separately.

Office Themes are created in Outlook 2010, Word 2010, Excel 2010, and PowerPoint 2010. (Microsoft PowerPoint 2010 has the widest range of theme creation options.) In Outlook 2010, you create and apply these themes within an email message. Themes are stored as .thmx files under your user profile.

Older Themes

Outlook 2010 can also use themes from earlier versions of Outlook to apply a background (color or image), a set of colors, and a few styled items, such as fonts and bulleted lists. While you can set one of these themes to be the default for new Outlook 2010 messages in the Signatures And Stationery dialog box, you have to use Microsoft FrontPage 2003 to edit them. For most people, this limits the use of these themes to the built-in set. It's easier to create an Office Theme or stationery if you want the functionality that it supplies than to work with older themes. These themes are stored as a set of files (Office System theme file [.elm], setup file [.inf], and graphics files) in C:\Program Files\Common Files\Microsoft shared\THEMES14.

Stationery

Stationery creates a customized look for your email using a background image and font formatting. With most of the Office System document formatting moving to themes, stationery is mostly an older feature with only a background image and a few font styles, but it is the simplest way to get a background into new messages by default. Stationery is stored as HTML files in C:\Program Files\Common Files\Microsoft shared\Stationery, with supporting graphics in an associated folder. If you create or modify stationery using Word 2010, graphics and any other files that you use in the stationery are saved in a subfolder of the directory where you save the template.

> **Note**
>
> To use themes or stationery, you must use RTF or HTML format for the message.

Style Sets

Outlook 2010 creates a style set by applying the theme colors to the body and heading fonts to configure the actual font styles. You can customize the display of the fonts in a message and save it as a custom style set. Style sets are saved as Word 2010 templates.

Outlook 2010 combines these settings to configure the exact look of each message that you create. When you create a new message, the collective default settings for new messages that you have configured are applied, as described in Table 9-1. Backgrounds can come from older themes or stationery, while font and graphical styling information comes from the currently saved default settings (which is usually a theme). If you have customized font styles, those are loaded from the template that you created.

Table 9-1 Message Style Components

Component	Controlled By	To Set
Backgrounds	Stationery or older theme	Choose File, Options, and Mail, and then select Stationery And Fonts. On the Personal Stationery tab, under Theme Or Stationery To Use For New HTML Messages, choose Theme, and then select a theme.
Colors, fonts, and effects	Office Themes	When composing a message, on the Options tab, in the Themes group, click one of the Themes options.
Custom font styles	Style set	When composing a message, on the Format Text tab, in the Styles group, click Change Styles, and then choose Style Set.

Using Themes to Customize Your Messages

You can select a theme from the Themes gallery, shown in Figure 9-38, which displays built-in Office Themes and custom themes that you create.

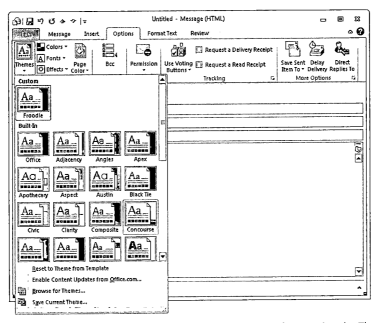

Figure 9-38 You can select a theme or save the current theme using the Themes command.

To select a theme, with a message open, on the Options tab, in the Themes group, click Theme, and then select a theme from the Themes gallery.

You can also choose Reset To Theme From Template, which causes new Outlook 2010 messages to use the Office Theme that is the default for new messages.

If you have additional themes saved locally, you can select Browse For Themes to find them on your hard disk or in a network location. You can also choose Save Current Theme to save the current theme as a custom theme.

INSIDE OUT   Find your custom themes quickly

Outlook 2010 saves custom themes that you create in the *<profile>*\AppData\Roaming\Microsoft\Templates\Document Themes folder, where *<profile>* is the location of your Windows profile. When you browse for additional themes, however, Outlook 2010 starts you in the *<profile>*\Documents folder. You need to change to the correct folder to see your themes. If you have saved a theme recently, you might be able to select the folder that contains the themes by clicking the Previous Locations arrow in the Choose Theme Or Themed Document dialog box. If not, select Save Current Theme on the Themes menu, select the path to the folder in the Address box, press Ctrl+C, and then click Cancel. You can then select Browse For Themes, paste the path into the Address Bar, and then press Enter to go to the correct location and find your themes quickly.

Colors

You can choose a set of colors to use for the text and other style options, or you can create a new set of custom colors. To select a color, with a message open, on the Options tab, in the Themes group, click Color. Select a set of theme colors in the Colors gallery, as shown in Figure 9-39.

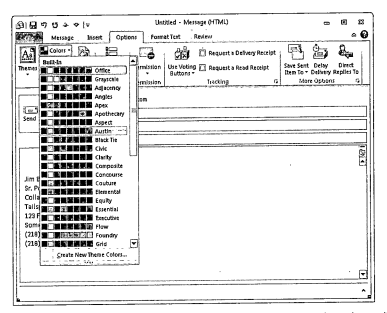

Figure 9-39 You can select a set of colors for your theme using the Colors gallery.

To create a new set of theme colors, follow these steps:

1. With a message open, on the Options tab, in the Themes group, click Color, and then click Create New Theme Colors.

2. In the Create New Theme Colors dialog box, shown in Figure 9-40, select the colors that you want, enter a name for the theme colors in the Name box, and then click Save. You can then select the theme colors from the Colors gallery.

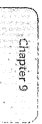

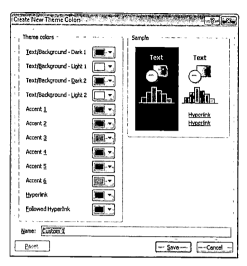

Figure 9-40 You can select a set of colors for your theme in the Create New Theme Colors dialog box.

Fonts

Themes use two font selections, in combination with colors and other settings, to create a range of Quick Styles for the fonts in your message. You choose a font for the headings and a font for the body text, and Outlook 2010 does the rest. You can control the font styles more precisely by saving stationery or saving a message form or using the options on the Ribbon, on the Format Text tab, in the Style group.

To select fonts, with a message open, on the Options tab, in the Themes group, click Fonts. Select a font pair from the Fonts gallery, as shown in Figure 9-41.

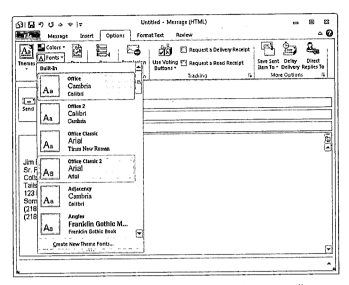

Figure 9-41 You can select the theme fonts in the Fonts gallery.

If you want to choose two specific fonts rather than a preset pair, follow these steps:

1. On the Fonts menu, choose Create New Theme Fonts.

2. In the Create New Theme Fonts dialog box, shown in Figure 9-42, select a heading font and a body font. Give the theme fonts a name, and then click Save.

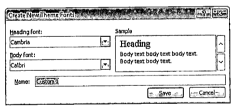

Figure 9-42 You can select one font for the body text of your messages and another for the headings in the Create New Theme Fonts dialog box.

Effects

Outlook 2010 themes use effects for creating a particular look in the graphical elements (such as SmartArt and charts) that you insert in your email. Effects vary in the weight of the lines they use and the opacity, glow, and texture of the surfaces on the objects that Outlook 2010 creates. The Effects gallery provides previews of the effects, but you should try out various effects on an email message with some graphical elements in it to see the various effects in action.

To select an effect for your messages, open a message, and on the Options tab, in the Themes group, click Effects, and then select an effect in the Effects gallery, shown in Figure 9-43.

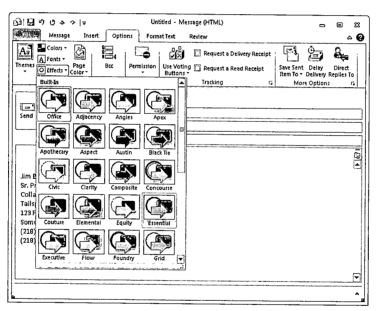

Figure 9-43 You can choose from a number of effects for the graphical elements of your messages.

Page Color

The Page Color option lets you select a background for the email message that you are composing. Outlook 2010 lets you choose from colors, gradients, textures, patterns, and pictures for your message background.

To select a page color, in Outlook 2010, with a new, blank email message open, on the Options tab, in the Themes group, select Page Color and do one of the following:

- To use a color that is displayed on the Page Colors menu, click the color. The Theme Colors area displays the theme colors on the top line and light-to-dark variations of each color in a vertical bar below the color. You can also choose a standard Video Graphics Array (VGA) color or no color.

- If you want to choose a different solid color, click More Colors to open the Colors dialog box. Select the color that you want to use, and then click OK.

- Select Fill Effects to use a gradient, texture, pattern, or picture as the message background. The Fill Effects dialog box has several tabs:

  - **Gradient**   The Gradient tab, shown in Figure 9-44, gives you several options to create a shaded background. Choose the number of colors to use, and then select the colors in the Color 1 and Color 2 drop-down lists. Choose a shading style, and then click a variant. The Sample area gives you a preview of the current settings. When you have finished, click OK.

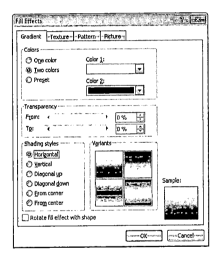

Figure 9-44 You can create your own shaded background on the Gradient tab in the Fill Effects dialog box.

  - **Texture**   Has a selection of small images that are tiled on the message background. Select a texture you like, or click Other Texture to select a different graphics file to use as the texture.

  - **Pattern**   Has a number of patterns to select from and lets you set the Foreground and Background colors to configure the final look of the pattern.

- **Picture**   Lets you choose a picture to use as the background by clicking Select Picture and locating the image you want to use.

INSIDE OUT   Use a background image automatically on new messages

Although you can add a background image to an email message using the Page Color command in the Theme group on the Options tab, a saved theme will not load the background image in an email message. You can use existing stationery, however, or a older theme, to apply a background image to your new email messages by default. The only way to choose your own background image for email messages is by creating new stationery, which allows you to apply a background and font styles to new messages.

Creating a Custom Theme

You can create a customized theme that you can share across your Office System documents. To create your own theme, follow these steps:

1. On the Options tab, in the Themes group, click Colors, and then select a set of colors to use.

2. On the Options tab, in the Themes group, click Fonts, and then select a pair of fonts to use.

3. On the Options tab, in the Themes group, click Effects, and then select a style of effects to use.

4. Once you are satisfied with the configuration of the theme, save it so that you can apply it easily later. To save the theme, on the Options tab, in the Themes group, click Themes, and then click Save Current Theme. Name the theme, and then click Save.

Note

Outlook 2010 saves custom themes to *<profile>*\AppData\Roaming\Microsoft\Templates\Document Themes.

When you load this theme, it will set the message colors, fonts, and effects but not the background settings. To save the background, you must create either stationery or a form. If you want to configure the theme settings as well as the background image, save a form.

If you want to specify only the background image and font styles that you manually format, create stationery.

Using Stationery to Customize Your Messages

With Outlook 2010 stationery, you use a set of characteristics that define the font style, color, and background image for messages. In effect, stationery can give your messages a certain look and feel, as shown in Figure 9-45. Stationery provides more limited customization than themes, and Outlook 2010 uses stationery very little. There are several built-in stationery options, although the only way to use them is to assign them as the default message format. In addition, you cannot create new stationery or customize existing stationery directly in Outlook 2010; you must use another program such as Word 2010.

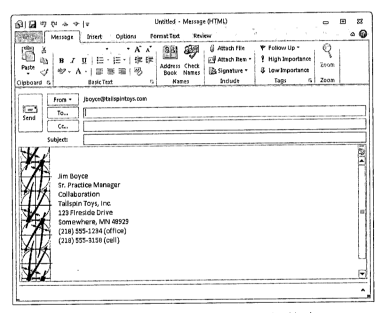

Figure 9-45 Stationery gives your messages a customized look.

You can assign a default stationery to be used in all your messages. To do so, follow these steps:

1. In Outlook 2010, click File, Options, and then select Mail in the left pane of the Outlook Options dialog box.

2. On the Mail page, click Stationery And Fonts to display the Signatures And Stationery dialog box.

3. On the Personal Stationery tab of the Signatures And Stationery dialog box, click Theme.

4. In the Theme Or Stationery dialog box, shown in Figure 9-46, choose the default stationery in the Choose A Theme list, and then click OK. If you have default stationery selected and no longer want your messages to use any stationery, follow the same procedure, but set the default stationery to No Theme.

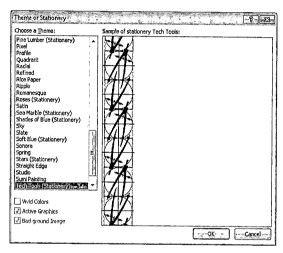

Figure 9-46 Use the Theme Or Stationery dialog box to preview and select stationery.

5. If you want to use fonts that are different from those in the stationery you just chose, in the Signatures And Stationery dialog box, in the Font drop-down list, under Theme Or Stationery For New HTML E-Mail Message, select either Use My Font When Replying And Forwarding Messages or Always Use My Fonts.

6. In the Signatures And Stationery dialog box, click the Font button for each font you want to customize, configure the options in the Font dialog box, and then click OK.

7. When you have finished setting the new message defaults, click OK to close the Signatures And Stationery dialog box.

> **INSIDE OUT**   **Create new stationery**
>
> You can create new stationery in Word 2010 to use with Outlook 2010. To do this, create a new document in Word 2010, select the picture that you want to use as a background, and then format any font style that you want to use with Outlook 2010. Save the file as HTML in the C:\Program Files\Common Files\Microsoft shared\Stationery folder. You can then choose this stationery as the default for new messages in the Signatures And Stationery dialog box.

Using Signatures

Outlook 2010 supports two types of signatures that you can add automatically (or manually) to outgoing messages: standard signatures and digital signatures. This chapter focuses on standard signatures, which can include text and graphics, depending on the mail format you choose.

To learn about digital signatures, which allow you to authenticate your identity and encrypt messages, see the section "Protecting Messages with Digital Signatures," on page 360.

Understanding Message Signatures

Outlook 2010 can add a signature automatically to your outgoing messages. You can specify different signatures for new messages and for replies or forwards. Signatures can include both text and graphics, as well as vCard attachments. Both rich text and HTML formats support inserting business cards and graphics in messages. If your signature contains graphics and you start a new message using plain text format, the graphics are removed, although any text defined by the signature remains. When you start a message using plain text format, business cards are attached, but they are not included in the body of the message.

Why use signatures? Many people use a signature to include their contact information in each message. Still others use a signature to include a favorite quote or other information in the message. In many cases, companies have a policy that all outgoing messages contain a legal disclaimer at the bottom of the message, and they can implement these disclaimers through signatures. Regardless of the type of information you want to include, creating and using signatures is easy.

INSIDE OUT Use multiple signatures

You can create a unique signature for each email account, and use one signature for new messages and a different one when you reply to or forward a message. When you send a message, Outlook 2010 appends the appropriate signature to the outgoing message.

Defining Signatures

If you want to include a graphic in a signature, check before you start to ensure that you already have that graphic on your computer or that it's available on the network.

Follow these steps to create a signature:

1. In Outlook 2010, click File, Options, and then select the Mail page.

2. Click Signatures to open the Signatures And Stationery dialog box, and then, on the E-mail Signature tab, click New.

3. In the New Signature dialog box, specify a name for the signature as it will appear in Outlook 2010, and then click OK.

4. In the Signatures And Stationery dialog box, click the signature that you just created in the Select Signature To Edit list.

5. In the Edit Signature area, type the text that you want to include in the signature, and then use the toolbar to format the text, as shown in Figure 9-47.

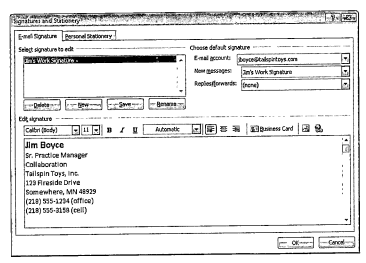

Figure 9-47 Format the text of your signature in the Edit Signature area of the Signatures And Stationery dialog box.

- To attach a vCard from an Outlook 2010 contact item, click Business Card. In the Insert Business Card dialog box, select the contact item, and then click OK.

- To insert a picture, click the Picture icon. In the Insert Picture dialog box, select the picture, and then click Insert.

- To insert a hyperlink, click the Hyperlink icon. In the Insert Hyperlink dialog box, select the location to link to, type the text to display (if needed), and then click Insert.

6. When you have finished with the signature, click Save.

7. Create other signatures if desired, and then click OK to close the Signatures And Stationery dialog box.

Adding Signatures to Messages

The signature that Outlook 2010 adds to new messages and the signature it adds to replies and forwards don't have to be the same. To set up different signatures for these different kinds of messages, click File, Options, select the Mail page, and then click Signatures.

In the Choose Default Signature area, select an account in the E-Mail Account drop-down list. Select a signature in the New Messages drop-down list and, if desired, one in the Replies/Forwards drop-down list.

INSIDE OUT   Specify the default message format

Keep in mind that the signature data that Outlook 2010 adds to the message depends on the message format specified on the Options tab. Set the message format to HTML or rich text if you want to create or edit signatures that contain graphics.

Other than letting you specify the signature for new messages or for replies and forwards, Outlook 2010 does not give you a way to control which signature is attached to a given message. For example, if you want to use different signatures for personal and business messages, you must switch signatures manually. However, Outlook 2010 does store signature options separately for each account, so you can control signatures to some degree just by sending messages through a specific account.

You can change the signature when composing a message. On the Insert tab, in the Include group, click Signature, and then select the signature on the menu. If you want a new signature, choose Signatures on the menu to open the Signatures And Stationery dialog box, and then create a new signature to use.

INSIDE OUT   Outlook 2010 uses only one signature per message

Outlook 2010 erases the current signature when you choose a new one on the Signatures menu in a message. If you are used to adding snippets of content to your messages using signatures with Outlook 2003 or 2007, you can use Quick Parts to accomplish this (and more). More information about Quick Parts is available in the section "Using Special Text Features," on page 234.

Backing Up Your Signatures

You should back up your signatures when you finish creating them and after you add a significant number of new ones. Signatures are stored in <*profile*>\AppData\Roaming\Microsoft\Signatures as a set of files (text, HTML, and rich text) and a corresponding folder of files containing pictures, Extensible Markup Language (XML) files, and theme data.

There is no provision for backing up your signatures inside Outlook 2010. To back up your signatures, you should back up the contents of <*profile*>\AppData\Roaming\Microsoft\Signatures.

Using the Proofing and Research Tools

From the old standby spelling and grammar check to research and translation tools, Outlook 2010 has a number of tools to help you get your message across clearly. You can perform searches across a wide variety of sources, from electronic reference books such as Microsoft Encarta to websites. A number of research options are installed by default, and you can add more to customize your searches. The default research options include reference books such as Encarta and thesauruses in multiple languages; general-purpose research websites, including Encarta Encyclopedia and MSN Research and Business; and financial websites such as MSN Money Stock Quotes and Thomson Gale Company Profiles.

INSIDE OUT   Switch research modes

Once you have opened the Research pane by selecting Research, Thesaurus, or Translate, you can switch among the three research modes by selecting different data sources to search in the drop-down list. Selecting a thesaurus from the Reference Books list is the same as clicking Thesaurus in the Proofing group.

On the Review tab, in the Proofing group, you'll find these two options:

- **Spelling & Grammar**   Performs a spelling and grammar check in accordance with the current configuration.

- **Research**   This option performs a search across the sources you select. You can choose categories to search (for example, All Reference Books) or individual data sources (for example, Encarta).

See the section "Configuring Research Options," later in this chapter, for details on customizing the services used for searches.

- **Thesaurus**   You can select English, French, or Spanish as the thesaurus language in the drop-down list.

- **Word Count**   Click to display the statistics for the message, including number of words, lines, paragraphs, pages, and characters. You can choose to include the contents of footnotes, endnotes, and text boxes in the statistics.

- **Translate** The translation features in Outlook 2010 let you translate small amounts of text between a number of common languages. Outlook gives you three options for translation: Send the text to an online site for translation, show a translation in the Research pane using local and online resources, or display a small translation window when you pause the pointer on a word. The following three items describe these features:

  - **Translate Item** Send the selected text to the Windows Live Translator website and view the translation in the resulting web page (see Figure 9-48).

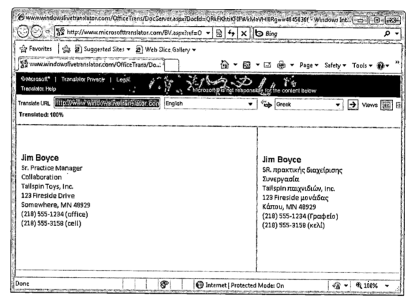

Figure 9-48 A selection of text can be translated into Greek using the Windows Live Translator website.

  - **Translate Selected Text** Show in the Research pane a translation of the selected text (see Figure 9-49).

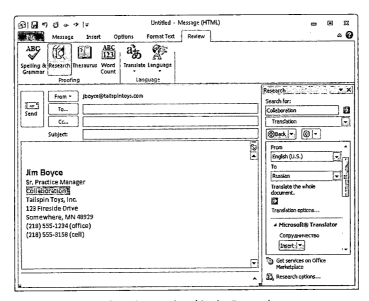

Figure 9-49 A word can be translated in the Research pane.

- **Mini Translator**   Selecting this option causes Outlook 2010 to display a ScreenTip with a brief translation of a word when you point to the word with the mouse, as shown in Figure 9-50.

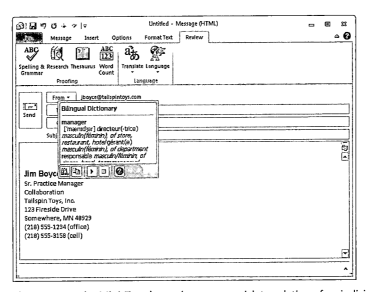

Figure 9-50. The Mini-Translator gives you a quick translation of an individual word.

- **Choose Translation Language**   Click this option to specify the language for the Translate Item and Mini Translator options. To set the translation languages for the Research pane, choose languages using the From and To drop-down lists.

Set the Proofing Language

When Outlook proofs your message for spelling and grammar, it does so using a specific language. For example, checking spelling of a French email using the English language would probably result in most of the words being marked as incorrectly spelled. For that reason, you need to specify the proofing language that you want Outlook to use. To do so, on the Review tab, click Language, Set Proofing Language. In the resulting Language dialog box, choose the language used by the majority of the message. You can use the Detect Language Automatically option to allow Outlook to detect the language automatically for any given word or phrase. If Outlook is having problems proofing a selection of text because it is incorrectly identifying the language, select the text, click Language, Set Proofing Language, choose a specific language from the list, and click OK.

Configuring Research Options

The list of services that Outlook 2010 uses when doing various forms of research can be customized to meet your individual needs. To configure the reference books and research sites that Outlook 2010 searches, on the Message tab, in the Proofing group, click Research. In the Research pane, select Research Options. You can select from the following options:

- **Services**   Activate services and resources that are installed by selecting the check box in the Services list. To deactivate a service, clear its check box.

- **Add Services**   To add more services, select Add Services, and then select the provider in the Advertised Services list. To add a new provider, enter the location of the service in the Address box.

- **Update/Remove**   To manage installed services, select Update/Remove to display the Update Or Remove Services dialog box. To update a service, select it in the Currently Installed Services, Grouped By Provider list, and then click Update to reinstall the provider for that service. To remove a service, select the provider in the list, and then click Remove. (You cannot remove installed options such as dictionaries and thesauruses.) Click Close when you have finished updating services.

- **Parental Control**   If you want to provide filtered access to research services, click Parental Control to open the Parental Control dialog box. You can then choose Turn On Content Filtering To Make Services Block Offensive Results. You can also opt to Allow Users To Search Only The Services That Can Block Offensive Results. In addition, these settings can be protected with a password.

> **Note**
> You must be logged on with an account that has administrative permissions for parental controls to configure Parental Control settings.

> **Tip**
> The parental controls provided by Outlook are separate from the parental controls provided in Windows 7. With the Windows 7 options, you can set time limits for using the computer; control access to games based on rating, content, or title; and allow or block specific programs. You should also check out Family Safety at Windows Live (*http://www.home.live.com*) to learn how you can use it to limit searches, control web browsing and chat, view Internet activity reports, and much more.

Chapter 9

W ITHOUT some means of organizing and filtering email, most people would be inundated with messages, many of which are absolutely useless. Fortunately, the Microsoft Outlook 2010 junk email filters can take care of most of, if not all, the useless messages. For the rest, you can use several Outlook 2010 features to help you organize messages, locate specific messages, and otherwise get control of your Inbox and other folders.

This chapter shows you how to customize your message folder views, which will help you organize your messages. You'll also learn about the Outlook 2010 search folders, which give you a great way to locate messages based on conditions that you specify and to organize messages without adding other folders to your mailbox. This chapter also explains how to use categories and custom views to organize your messages.

Using Conversation View

Outlook 2010 adds some new features for working with message threads, also called *conversations*. A message conversation comprises the original message and all of the replies that result from the original message. Outlook 2010 offers a new Conversation view that organizes all the messages in a conversation into an expandable/collapsible branch (see Figure 10-1).

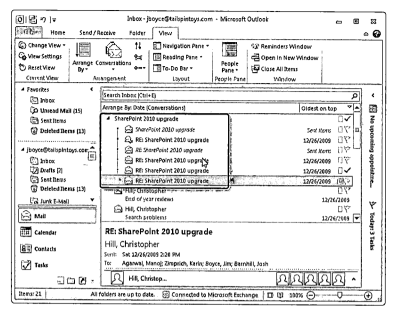

Figure 10-1 Use the Conversation view to show and manage related messages together.

The messages in a conversation need not be in the same folder. In fact, the Conversation view works much like a search folder (discussed later in this chapter) in that it locates and displays the related messages regardless of where they are located. So, for example, it shows your replies from the Sent Items folder, any replies in your Inbox, and any replies that you have filed in other folders.

If you are using a different view and want to switch to Conversation view, click the View tab on the Ribbon and click Date (Conversations) in the Arrangement group. You'll also find a handful of options under the Conversations group on the View ribbon that control the view. The first is a check box; the rest appear when you click Conversation Settings. These include:

- **Show Message In Conversations**   Select this option to turn on or off Conversation view.

- **Show Messages From Other Folders**   Select this option to have Outlook include related messages from other folders (such as Sent Items) in addition to those in the current folder.

- **Show Senders Above The Subjects**   List all senders for the conversation above the subject line.

- **Always Expand Conversations**   Select this option if you want Outlook to always expand conversations so you can see all the messages in them without having to expand them yourself.

- **Use Classic Indented View**   Select this option if you want the messages in the conversation to be indented to visually show the order in which you received them.

> **Tip**
> The Conversation view displays a dotted line that shows the relationship between messages in the conversation (which message replies to which other message). Click a message in the conversation to see its relationship.

Cleaning Up Conversations

Another benefit of the new conversation features of Outlook 2010 is the capability to delete messages with duplicated content automatically. For example, assume that you send a message to someone, who sends a reply. You reply to that message, and then receive another reply. So far, that's four messages. Each time there was a reply, the content of the original message and all the replies were duplicated. So, in reality, the last message contains not only the original message but all the replies. If all you need is the conversation and not the individual messages, why not just delete those first three messages and keep the fourth?

That's a simple scenario, but assume that you sent the message to 10 people, most replied to all at least once, and some messages bounced back and forth between people several times. At the end of the day, you have 30 messages on the same conversation, most of which are essentially duplicates of the others, but some have a little added content that the others don't have.

This is where the conversation cleanup in Outlook 2010 comes into play. It searches through the messages, finds the ones with duplicate content, and deletes them. The ones with unique content, it keeps. The result is that you have all the content from the conversation but have reduced the message count by a potentially significant amount, perhaps 50 percent or more. By default, when you run a cleanup, Outlook puts the duplicate messages in the Deleted Items folder of the account in which the messages are stored.

You have three different levels at which you can run a cleanup: selected conversation, all conversations in the folder, and all conversations in the folder and all subfolders. To clean up a single item, click the conversation and then, on the Home tab of the Ribbon, click the Clean Up button and choose Clean Up Conversation (see Figure 10-2). If you want to

clean up the whole folder, choose Clean Up Folder or Clean Up Folders and Subfolders, depending on whether you want to get the subfolders, too.

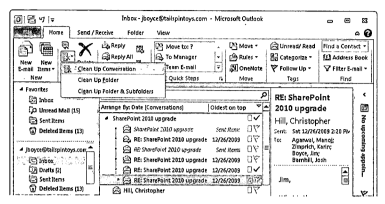

Figure 10-2 Choose Clean Up Conversation to clean up the selected conversation.

Setting Cleanup Options

As you might have guessed, you have a handful of options that control how conversation cleanup works. To set these options, click File, Options, Mail, and scroll down to the Conversation Clean Up group (see Figure 10-3).

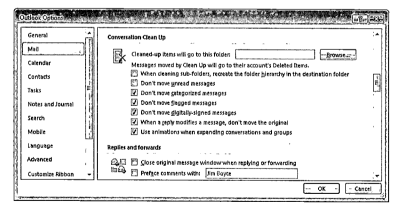

Figure 10-3 Set conversation cleanup options on the Mail page of the Outlook Options dialog box.

The options are generally self-explanatory. You can choose the folder in which to put the cleaned-up messages (by default, the Deleted Items folder), and also specify whether Outlook will move unread, categorized, flagged, or digitally signed messages. You can also direct Outlook not to move the original message if a reply to that message modifies the original.

> **Tip**
> Until you remove the messages permanently from the Deleted Items folder, you can recover just as you would any other deleted item. On a Microsoft Exchange Server mailbox, you can recover them up until the point at which the retention period defined by the Exchange Server administrator causes the messages to be purged from your mailbox.

Ignoring a Conversation

No doubt you've received messages that you didn't really need to be copied on, or that you simply don't care about. Or, maybe you've received one of those messages where some hapless soul has sent a message to 1,000 users. Some of those people reply to all, and pretty soon there are people replying to all telling everyone not to reply to all! Don't you wish you could ignore those messages? Well, you can in Outlook 2010.

Click a conversation to select it and then click Ignore Conversation in the Delete group on the Home tab of the Ribbon. After prompting you to confirm the action, Outlook moves all the current messages in the conversation to the Deleted Items folder (or other folder that you have designated in Outlook Options), and also automatically moves all future messages in that conversation there, as well.

Balancing Cleanup Against Retention

I confess that I am an email pack rat. I have every message from my Exchange Server mailbox for the past five years, the length of time I've been with my current employer. What isn't in my mailbox on the server is in one or more .pst files on my hard drive. Conversation cleanup is the middle ground between keeping all those messages or keeping none. You can keep the gist of all your email conversations without keeping every single message. That means potentially keeping your mailbox a more manageable size or having to archive less frequently. In either case, cleaning up the redundant messages reduces storage requirements on your server, your local computer, or both by reducing the sheer number of messages in your mail store.

If you have Exchange Server in your organization, you might already have an archiving solution in place like those from Mimosa Systems, EMC, or others. Generally, these solutions archive all messages that come into your mailbox, eliminating the need for you to archive items to a .pst on your local computer (and thereby avoiding the security risks associated with local .pst files). With an archiving solution in place, conversation cleanup makes even more sense, because all the messages in the conversation will be in your archive if you need them. Clean away!

Finding and Organizing Messages with Search Folders

The Outlook 2010 search folders are an extremely useful feature for finding and organizing messages. A *search folder* isn't really a folder but rather a special view that functions much like a separate folder. In effect, a search folder is a saved search. You specify conditions for the folder, such as all messages from a specific sender or all messages received in the last day, and Outlook 2010 displays in that search folder view those messages that meet the specified conditions.

In a way, a search folder is like a rule that moves messages to a special folder. However, although the messages seem to exist in the search folder, they continue to reside in their respective folders. For example, a search folder might show all messages in the Inbox and Sent Items folders that were sent by Jim Boyce. Even though these messages appear in the Jim Boyce search folder (for example), they are actually still located in the Inbox and Sent Items folders.

Using Search Folders

It isn't difficult at all to use a search folder. The Folder List includes a Search Folders branch, as shown in Figure 10-4, that lists all the search folder contents. Simply click a search folder in the Folder List to view the headers for the messages it contains.

Figure 10-4 Search folders appear under their own branch in the Folder List.

Customizing Search Folders

A new installation of Outlook 2010 includes four search folders by default, which you can use as is or customize to suit your needs:

- **Categorized Mail**   This search folder shows all messages that have categories assigned to them.

- **Fax**   If you are connected to an Exchange Server mailbox with unified messaging enabled, this search folder will enable you to see all received faxes in your mailbox.

- **Unread Mail**   This search folder shows all messages that are unread.

- **Voice Mail**   If you are connected to an Exchange Server mailbox with unified messaging enabled, this search folder shows all received voice-mail messages.

To customize an existing search folder, open the Folder List, right-click the folder, and then choose Customize This Search Folder to open the Customize dialog box, similar to the one shown in Figure 10-5.

Figure 10-5 Set the criteria or folders to include for a search folder in the Customize dialog box.

You can change the name of the search folder in the Name box in the Customize dialog box. To change the criteria for the search folder, click the Criteria button to display a dialog box that enables you to change your selection. The dialog box that appears depends on the criteria that you used when you created the folder. For example, if you are modifying a search folder that locates messages from a specific sender, Outlook 2010 displays the Select Names dialog box so that you can specify a different person (or additional people).

To change which folders are included in the search folder, click Browse in the Customize dialog box to open the Select Folder(s) dialog box. Select each folder that you want to include, or select the Personal Folders or Mailbox branch to include all folders in the mail store in the search. Select the Search Subfolders option to include all subfolders for a selected folder in the search. When you have finished selecting folders, click OK, and then click OK again to close the Customize dialog box.

Creating a New Search Folder

If the default search folders don't suit your needs, you can create your own search folder with the criteria and included subfolders that locate the messages you want. To create a search folder, right-click the Search Folders branch, and then choose New Search Folder to open the New Search Folder dialog box, shown in Figure 10-6.

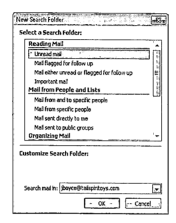

Figure 10-6 Create a new search folder with the New Search Folder dialog box.

The New Search Folder dialog box provides several predefined search folders, and you can create a custom search folder easily by choosing one from the list. If the search folder you select requires specifying additional criteria, click the Choose button to open a dialog box in which you specify the criteria. Then, in the New Search Folder dialog box, select an account in the Search Mail In drop-down list to search that account.

> **Note**
> The Choose button appears in the New Search Folder dialog box only if the selected search folder requires additional configuration, such as the sender's name.

If the predefined search folders won't do the trick, scroll to the bottom of the Select A Search Folder list, select Create A Custom Search Folder, and then click Choose to open the Custom Search Folder dialog box to specify a custom criterion for the search folder, a search folder name, and subfolders to include.

Finding Messages with Windows Search

If you are running Outlook 2010 on Windows 7 (or other version of Windows with Windows Search installed), you have some additional ways to search for messages outside of Outlook that can be very handy. To search for any item in Windows, whether in Outlook or not, click Start and start typing in the Search Programs And Files text box. As you type (assuming that indexing is enabled and has finished indexing the content on your computer), results appear above the text box that match your search. For example, Figure 10-7 shows a quick search for items related to Manoj Agarwal. In this example, Windows 7 found an Outlook profile, contacts, Really Simple Syndication (RSS) messages, and email.

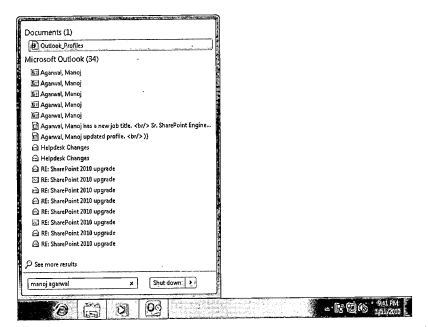

Figure 10-7 Windows 7 has returned several Outlook items related to Manoj Agarwal.

You can refine a search in Windows further by using keywords. For example, to find messages with "SharePoint" in the subject, type the following in the Search Programs And Files text box:

Subject:SharePoint

That will return results for messages containing SharePoint in the subject, but will also return other items, such as documents with SharePoint in the title. You can restrict your searches to Outlook items using a handful of keywords. Table 10-1 lists some useful, Outlook-related Windows search keywords to help you refine a search.

Table 10-1 Outlook-Related Windows Search Keywords

Description	Keyword	Example
Email sender	from	from:Manoj Agarwal
Has an attachment	attachment	has:attachment
Is an attachment	attachment	is:attachment
Size of an item	size	size:>2MB
Date of an item	date	date:>2/15/10<=3/15/10
Is an email	kind	kind:email
Is a contact	kind	kind:contact
Is a meeting	kind	kind:meetings
Restrict search to Outlook	store	store:mapi
Search by subject	subject	subject:sharepoint
Sent to someone	to	to:Manoj Agarwal
Copied to someone	cc	cc:Manoj Agarwal
Has a specified category	category	category:Toy Show
From a specified person	from	from:manoj agarwal
Received on a certain date	received	received:yesterday
Sent on a certain date	sent	sent:today
Sent to a specific address	toaddress, to	toaddress:magarwal@tailspintoys.com
The item has been read	isread	isread:false

> **Tip**
>
> Table 10-1 contains just some of the Outlook-related search terms that you can use to locate items. There are many others that are specific to the Outlook data types, including contacts, email messages, and calendar items. You'll find a complete description at *http://www.microsoft.com/windows/products/winfamily/desktopsearch/technicalresources/advquery.mspx.*

Keep in mind that you can limit your search to Outlook by using *store:mapi* in the search string. Also, you can use multiple search criteria to refine a search. For example, assume that you want to search only Outlook for email messages from Manoj Agarwal that have an attachment larger than 2 MB and were sent yesterday. Here's the search syntax to use:

store:mapi kind:email from:manoj agarwal hasattachment:true size:>2MB sent:yesterday

Flagging and Monitoring Messages and Contacts

Outlook 2010 allows you to *flag* a message to draw your attention to the message and display an optional reminder when the follow-up action is due. The flag appears in the message header, as shown in Figure 10-8.

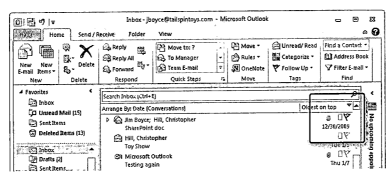

Figure 10-8 You can flag a message to highlight it or to include additional information.

Outlook 2003 offered six flag types, compared with just one in earlier versions. In Outlook 2010, as in Outlook 2007, colored flags are replaced by color categories, reducing follow-up flag colors to red and a few shades of pink. You can choose from one of five predefined flags or choose a custom flag. The predefined flags have date specifications of Today, Tomorrow, This Week, Next Week, and No Date. If you choose the custom flag option, you can specify any date you want. The predefined dates therefore give you a quick and easy way to assign a general follow-up date, while the custom option lets you specify a specific date.

See Chapter 5, "Creating and Using Categories," to learn more about color categories.

Flagging Received and Previously Sent Messages

You can flag messages that you've received from others, as well as those you've sent. This capability gives you a way to flag and follow up messages from your end. You can flag messages in any message folder, including the Sent Items folder.

INSIDE OUT   Add notes to received messages

You can use flags to add notes to messages you receive from others, giving yourself a quick reminder of pending tasks or other pertinent information. Outlook 2010 can generate a reminder for you concerning the flagged item. To set up Outlook 2010 to do so, right-click the message, choose Follow Up, Add Reminder, and then set a due date and time.

Follow these steps to flag a message you have received (or a message that resides in the Sent Items folder):

1. Locate the message that you want to flag.

2. Right-click the message, choose Follow Up, and then select a follow-up period from the cascading menu (Today, Tomorrow, and so on), or to specify a custom date, choose Custom.

3. If you chose Custom, enter the follow-up action text in the Flag To field or select an existing action from the drop-down list, and then specify a start date and an end date.

4. Click OK.

Flagging Outgoing Messages

With Outlook 2010, you can flag outgoing messages for follow-up for yourself, the recipient, or both. So, the capability to flag an outgoing message lets you set a reminder on the message to follow up on the message yourself. For example, you might send an email message to a coworker asking for information about a project. The follow-up flag could remind you in a week to follow up if you haven't had a response. You can also flag a message to generate a reminder on the recipient's computer.

Use the following steps to flag a message you send:

1. With the message form open prior to sending the message, on the Message tab on the Ribbon, in the Tags group, click Follow Up, and then click Add Reminder to open the Custom dialog box, shown in Figure 10-9.

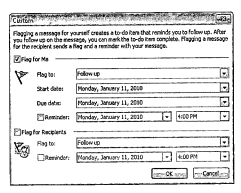

Figure 10-9 Select the flag text or type your own message in the Custom dialog box.

2. In the Flag To drop-down list, select the text you want to include with the flag, or type your own text in this box.

3. If you want to include a due date and a subsequent reminder, select the date in the Due Date drop-down list, which opens a calendar that you can use to select a date. Alternatively, you can enter a date, day, time, or other information as text in the Due Date box.

4. Click OK, and then send the message as you normally would.

Follow these steps to flag a message for follow-up on the recipient's computer:

1. Open a new message form, and then click Follow Up in the Options group on the Message tab.

2. Choose Add Reminder to open the Custom dialog box.

3. Select the Flag For Recipients option, and then select the follow-up action in the Flag To drop-down list.

4. Specify a reminder, and then click OK.

5. Complete the message, and then send it.

Viewing and Responding to Flagged Messages

A flag icon appears next to the message header for flagged messages in the message folder. If you have configured Outlook 2010 to display the Reading pane, the flag text appears in the InfoBar. The flag icons also help you to identify flagged messages regardless of whether the Reading pane is displayed. You can sort the view in the folder using the Flag column, listing all flagged messages together to make them easier to locate. To view the flag text when the Reading pane is turned off, simply open the message. The flag text appears in the message form's InfoBar.

Outlook 2010 has no special mechanism for processing flagged messages other than the reminders previously discussed. You simply call, email, or otherwise respond based on the flag message. To change the flag status, simply click the flag, or right-click a flagged message and then choose Mark Complete. To remove the flag from the message, right-click a flagged message, and then choose Clear Flag.

Flagging Contact Items

You can flag contact items as well as messages, marking them for follow-up or adding other notations to an item. For example, you might flag a contact item to remind yourself to call the person by a certain time or date or to send documents to the contact. A flag you add to a contact item isn't always readily apparent because the flag shows up as text, as shown in Figure 10-10. As you can for messages, you can use one of the Outlook 2010 predefined flags to mark a contact item, or you can specify your own flag text. Figure 10-11 shows that you can organize items by flag status.

> **Note**
> The flag field does not appear in Business Card view. In some of the other views, you can use the Field Chooser to add the Follow Up Flag field to the view.

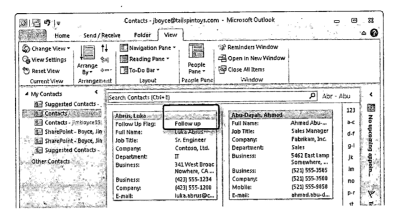

Figure 10-10 You can flag contacts as well as messages.

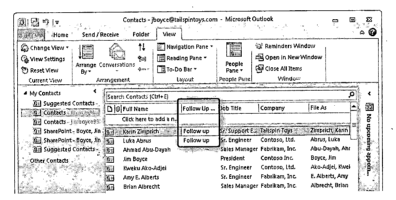

Figure 10-11 You can list items in the Contacts folder by flag.

Flagging a contact is easy—just right-click the contact, choose Follow Up, and then select a follow-up date. To assign a custom flag to a contact item, follow these steps:

1. Right-click the contact item, choose Follow Up, and then choose Custom.

2. In the Custom dialog box, select the flag type in the Flag To drop-down list, or type in your own text.

3. Specify the due date and time.

4. If desired, add a reminder, and then click OK.

Outlook 2010 does not use icons to represent flag status for contact items. You cannot format the Follow Up Flag column to display as anything other than text. To change the flag status for a contact item, right-click the item and then choose Mark Complete or Clear Flag.

Grouping Messages by Customizing the Folder View

To help you organize information, Outlook 2010 allows you to customize various message folder views. By default, Outlook 2010 displays only a small selection of columns for messages, including the From, Subject, Received, Size, Flag, Attachment, and Importance columns.

For details on how to add and remove columns from a folder view to show more or less information about your messages, see the section "Working with the Standard Outlook Views," on page 72.

You can sort messages easily using any of the column headers as your sort criterion. To view messages sorted alphabetically by sender, for example, click the column header of the From column (simple list views only). To sort messages by date received, click the column header of the Received column. Click the Attachment column header to view all messages with attachments.

In addition to managing your message view by controlling columns and sorting, you can *group* messages based on columns. Whereas sorting allows you to arrange messages in order using a single column as the sort criterion, grouping allows you to display the messages in groups based on one or more columns. For example, you might group messages based on sender, and then on date received, and finally on whether they have attachments. This method helps you locate messages more quickly than if you had to search through a message list sorted only by sender.

Grouping messages in a message folder is a relatively simple process:

1. In Outlook 2010, open the folder that you want to organize.

2. Right-click the column header, and then choose Group By This Field if you want to group based only on the selected field. Choose Group By Box if you want to group based on multiple columns.

Filtering a View Using Categories

As explained in Chapter 5, color categories in Outlook 2010 make it very easy to identify specific messages or types of messages. For example, you might categorize messages you receive from specific people so that you can see at a glance that a message is from a particular person without grouping on the From field.

In some situations, you might want to customize a view so that you see only messages that fall into certain categories. For example, assume that you have categorized messages for two projects, each with a unique category. Now you want to view all messages from both projects. The easiest way to do that is to filter the view so that it shows only messages with those two categories assigned to them. You can do that using a custom view or a search folder. Both of these methods are explained in the section "Viewing Selected Categories Only," on page 127.

Managing Email Effectively

Before we offer tips on effective email management, let's ask the question, "Why bother?" If you receive a large number of messages, the answer is probably staring you in the face—a chaotic Inbox full of messages. With a little bit of planning and effort, you can turn that Inbox into . . . well . . . an empty Inbox! When you leave the office at the end of the day with an empty Inbox, you'll be amazed at the sense of accomplishment you'll feel.

Here are some tips to help you get control of your mailbox:

- **Use Conversation view**   Take advantage of the new conversation features in Outlook 2010 to help you quickly organize messages by topic, clean up your Inbox, and ignore those inevitable message threads that are just not applicable or of interest to you.

- **Categorize, categorize, categorize**   Categorizing your messages offers several benefits. First, with color categories in Outlook 2010, assigning categories to messages will help you quickly identify specific types of messages. Second, you'll be able to search for messages by category with filtered views, search folders, and the search features built into Outlook 2010. You can assign categories manually or assign them automatically with rules. Whatever the case, the more diligent you are in assigning categories, the more useful they will be for finding messages and organizing your mailbox.

- **Organize with folders**   Although you could simply leave all messages in the Inbox, moving messages into other folders will unclutter your Inbox and help you locate messages when you need them. There is no right or wrong way to structure your message folders—use whatever structure and number of folders suits the way you work. What is important is that you organize in a way that suits you.

- **Organize with rules**   Use rules to move messages into other folders, assign categories, and otherwise process messages when they arrive in your Inbox. Rules enable you to organize your messages automatically, potentially saving you an enormous amount of time.

- **Let search folders organize for you**   Search folders are an extremely useful feature in Outlook 2010. With a search folder, you can organize messages based on almost any criteria without actually moving the messages from their current locations. Search folders take very little effort to set up and offer you the benefit of being able to search your entire mailbox for messages that fit the search criteria. You can bring together in one virtual folder all messages in your mail store that fit the search criteria.

F you receive a lot of messages, you might want to have the messages analyzed as they come in, to perform actions on them before you read them. For example, you can have all messages from a specific account sent to a specific folder. Perhaps you want messages that come from specific senders to be assigned high priority. Microsoft Outlook 2010 lets you manipulate your incoming messages to achieve the results that you want. This chapter shows you how to do this, starting with an overview of message rules and ending with a new feature in Outlook 2010, Quick Steps.

Understanding Message Rules

A *message rule* defines the actions that Outlook 2010 takes for a sent or received message if the message meets certain conditions specified by the rule. For example, you might create a rule that tells Outlook 2010 to move all messages from a specific sender or with a certain subject into a specified folder rather than leaving them in your default Inbox. Or you might want Outlook 2010 to place a copy of all outgoing high-priority messages in a special folder.

In Outlook 2010, you use one or more *conditions* for defining a message rule. These conditions can include the account from which the message was received, the message size, the sender or recipient, specific words in various fields or in the message itself, the priority assigned to the message, and a variety of other conditions. In addition, you can combine multiple actions to refine the rule and further control its function. For example, you might create a rule that moves all your incoming POP3 messages to a folder other than the Inbox and also deletes any messages that contain certain words in the Subject field. Although not a complete list, the following are some of the most common tasks you might perform with message rules:

- Organize messages based on sender, recipient, or subject.

- Copy or move messages from one folder to another.

- Flag messages.

- Delete messages automatically.

- Reply to, forward, or redirect messages to individuals or distribution lists.

- Respond to messages with a specific reply.

- Monitor message importance (priority).

- Print a message.

- Play a sound.

- Execute a script or start an application.

For details on how to generate automatic replies to messages, see the sections "Creating Automatic Responses with the Out Of Office Assistant," on page 345, and "Creating Automatic Responses with Custom Rules," on page 351.

Whatever your message processing requirements, Outlook 2010 probably offers a solution through a message rule, based on either a single condition or multiple conditions. You also can create multiple rules that work together to process your mail. As you begin to create and use message rules, keep in mind that you can define a rule to function either when a message is received or when it is sent. When you create a rule, you specify the event to which the rule applies.

Rather than focusing on defining rules for specific tasks, this chapter explains the general process of creating rules. With an understanding of this process, you should have no problem setting up rules for a variety of situations.

Creating and Using Rules

In Outlook 2010, you can create either *client-side* or *server-side* rules. Outlook 2010 stores client-side rules locally on your computer and uses them to process messages that come to your local folders, although you also can use client-side rules to process messages on computers running Microsoft Exchange Server. A client-side rule is needed when you're moving messages to a local folder instead of to a folder on the computer running Exchange Server. For example, if messages from a specific sender that arrive in your Exchange Server Inbox must be moved to one of your personal folders, the rule must function as a client-side rule because the computer running Exchange Server is not able to access your personal folders (and your computer might not even be turned on when the message arrives in your mailbox on the server).

Server-side rules reside on the computer running Exchange Server instead of on your local computer, and they can usually process messages in your Exchange Server mailbox whether or not you're logged on and running Outlook 2010. The Out Of Office Assistant is a good example of how server-side rules can be used. It processes messages that come into your Inbox on the server even when your computer is turned off and you're a thousand miles away. So long as Exchange Server is up and functioning, the server-side rules can perform their intended function.

When you create a rule, Outlook 2010 examines the rule's logic to determine whether it can function as a server-side rule or a client-side rule. If it can function as a server-side rule, Outlook 2010 stores the rule on the computer running Exchange Server and treats it as a server-side rule. If the rule must function as a client-side rule, Outlook 2010 stores it locally and appends *(client-only)* after the rule name to designate it as a client-side rule. Figure 11-1 shows two rules in Outlook 2010, one of which functions as a client-side rule and another that functions as a server-side rule.

> ## Note
> If you don't use an Exchange Server account, all rules that you create are client-side rules.

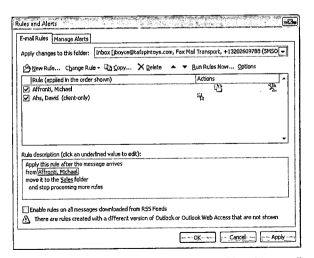

Figure 11-1 Outlook 2010 supports server-side rules as well as client-side rules.

TROUBLESHOOTING

Your server-side rules don't execute

Server-side rules, which process messages arriving in your Exchange Server Inbox, usually can execute when Outlook 2010 isn't running. In some cases, however, server-side rules can't function unless Outlook 2010 is running and you're connected to the server.

When a server-side rule is unable to process a message because Outlook 2010 is offline (or for other reasons), the computer running Exchange Server generates a deferred action message (DAM), which it uses to process the message when Outlook 2010 comes back online. When Outlook 2010 goes online, it receives the DAM, performs the action, and deletes the DAM.

For information about how to apply client-side rules to specific folders or to all accounts, see the section "Applying Rules to Specific Folders or All Folders," on page 312.

Creating New Rules from Existing Items

Outlook 2010 offers a handful of ways to create a rule. For example, you can click a message, and on the Home tab, click Rules in the Move group. Outlook offers options to create rules based on the sender or recipient, and the number of options varies depending on the message itself (see Figure 11-2). Click an option to open the Rules And Alerts dialog box, choose a folder, and click OK. Outlook will create a rule to move messages based on your selections.

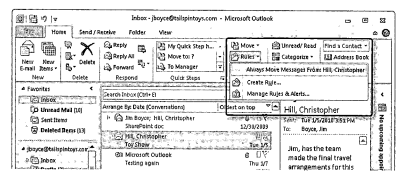

Figure 11-2 Use the options offered in the ribbon to create a rule based on the current message.

If you need to create a new rule for the currently selected message with different actions (such as creating a rule based on the subject of the message), click the message and, on the

Home tab, click Rules in the Move group and choose Create Rule. Outlook displays the Create Rule dialog box shown in Figure 11-3.

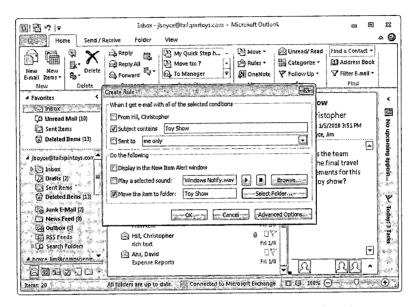

Figure 11-3 Use the Create Rule dialog box to create more complex rules.

The Create Rule dialog box offers properties based on the selected message, including sender, subject, and recipient. Choose the criteria for your rule using any combination of these three, then choose an action from the Do The Following group of controls. Click OK to create the rule. Outlook names the rule according to the criteria you selected, such as the sender's name and the subject.

Create New Rules Using the Rules Wizard

When you need more complex rules, need to perform tasks other than moving messages, or want to create a rule that is not based on a specific message, you can turn to the Rules Wizard. You can open the Rules Wizard in a couple of ways:

- To create a rule based on a selected message: With a message selected, on the Home tab, click Rules in the Move group, and then click Create Rule.

- To create a general rule, on the Home tab, click Rules in the Move group and then choose Manage Rules And Alerts. In the Rules And Alerts dialog box, click New Rule.

You'll first see the Rules And Alerts dialog box, shown in Figure 11-1. The E-Mail Rules tab contains all the existing rules that you have defined. Outlook 2010 applies the rules in the order in which they are listed, an important fact to consider when you're creating rules. You might use certain rules all the time but use others only at special times. Each rule includes a check box beside it. Select this check box when you want to use the rule; clear it when you want to disable the rule.

> **Note**
> You can't open the Rules And Alerts dialog box if you are working offline with an Exchange Server account.

For more information about determining the order in which message rules execute, see the section "Setting Rule Order," on page 315.

> **Tip**
> You can now create rules for your Windows Live Hotmail account, just as you can for other types of accounts. Note that using a Windows Live Hotmail account requires the Outlook Connector for Hotmail, discussed in detail in Chapter 7, "Using Internet Mail Accounts."

When you create a message rule using the Rules Wizard, you must first specify whether you want to create the rule from a predefined template or from scratch. Because the templates address common message processing tasks, using a template can save you a few steps. When you create a rule from scratch, you set up all the conditions for the rule as you create it. You can use many different conditions to define the actions the rule performs, all of which are available in the Rules Wizard. With or without a template, you have full control over the completed rule and can modify it to suit your needs. The Outlook 2010 templates are a great way to get started, however, if you're new to using Outlook 2010 or message rules.

Let's look first at the general procedure for creating rules and then at more specific steps. The general process is as follows:

1. Select the Inbox in which the rule will apply. For example, if you have an Exchange Server account and a Post Office Protocol (POP) account, you must choose the Inbox to which the rule will apply.

> **Note**
> The number of Inboxes offered in the Apply Changes To This Folder drop-down list on the E-mail Rules tab depends on the number of accounts in your Outlook profile and how they are configured to deliver mail. Accounts that use their own mail stores, such as Internet Message Access Protocol (IMAP) and Windows Live Hotmail accounts, will have their own entries in this drop-down list.

2. Specify when the rule applies—that is, when a message is received or when it is sent.

3. Specify the conditions that define which messages are processed—for example, account, sender, priority, or content.

4. Specify the action to take for messages that meet the specified conditions—for example, move, copy, or delete the message; change its priority; flag it for follow-up; or generate a reply.

5. Create other message rules to accomplish other tasks as needed, including possibly working in conjunction with other rules.

6. Set the order of rules as needed.

> **Note**
> When you specify multiple conditions for a rule, the rule combines these conditions in a logical AND operation—that is, the message must meet all the conditions to be considered subject to the rule. You also can create rules that use a logical OR operation, meaning that the message is subject to the rule if it meets any one of the conditions. For details, see the section "Creating Rules That Use OR Logic," on page 313.

The following steps guide you through the more specific process of creating a message rule:

1. On the Home tab, click Rules in the Move group and choose Manage Rules And Alerts to display the Rules And Alerts dialog box.

2. In the Apply Changes To This Folder drop-down list, select the folder to which you want to apply the rule. If you have only one Inbox, you don't need to make a selection.

Chapter 11

3. Click New Rule to display the wizard page shown in Figure 11-4.

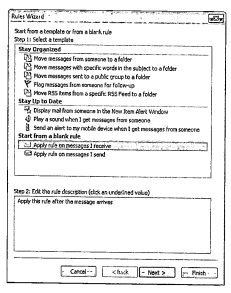

Figure 11-4 To create a rule, you can use a template or start from scratch.

4. If you want to use a template to create the rule, select the template from the list, and then click Next. To create a rule from scratch, choose Apply Rule On Messages I Receive or Apply Rule On Messages I Send, and then click Next.

5. In the Step 1: Select Condition(s) list in the top half of the wizard page shown in Figure 11-3, select the conditions that define the messages to which the rule should apply. For template-based rules, a condition is already selected, but you can change the condition and add others as necessary.

6. In the Step 2: Edit The Rule Description area of the wizard page (see Figure 11-5), click the underlined words that specify the data for the conditions. For example, if you're creating a rule to process messages from a specific account, click the word *specified*, which is underlined, and then select the account in the Account dialog box. Click OK, and then click Next.

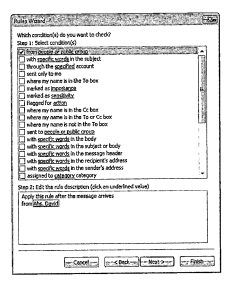

Figure 11-5 Select the conditions to define the messages to which the rule will apply.

7. In the Step 1: Select Action(s) area of the new wizard page, select the actions that you want Outlook 2010 to apply to messages that satisfy the specified conditions. For example, Figure 11-6 shows a rule that displays an alert for messages if they meet the rule condition.

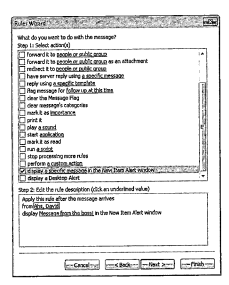

Figure 11-6 Select the actions that Outlook 2010 should take for messages that meet the rule's conditions.

8. In the Step 2: Edit The Rule Description area of the wizard page, click each underlined value needed to define the action, and then specify the data in the resulting dialog box. Click OK to close the dialog box, and then click Next.

9. In the Step 1: Select Exception(s) (If Necessary) area of the wizard page, select exceptions to the rule if needed, and specify the data for the exception conditions, as shown in Figure 11-7. Click Next.

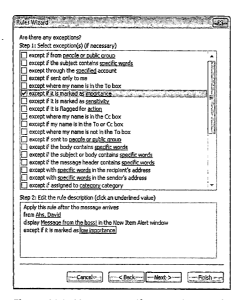

Figure 11-7 You can specify exceptions to the rule to fine-tune message processing.

10. On the final page of the Rules Wizard, shown in Figure 11-8, specify a name for the rule as you want it to appear in Outlook 2010.

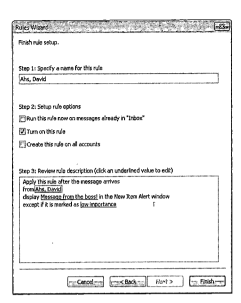

Figure 11-8 Configure a name and options for the rule.

11. Select options according to the following list, and then click Finish:

- **Run This Rule Now On Messages Already In "Inbox"**   Select this check box if you want Outlook 2010 to apply the rule to messages that you have already received and that currently reside in the Inbox folder in which the rule applies. For example, if you have created a rule to delete messages from a specific recipient, any existing messages from the recipient are deleted after you select this check box and click Finish to create the rule.

- **Turn On This Rule**   Select this check box to begin applying the rule that you have created.

- **Create This Rule On All Accounts**   Select this check box to apply the rule to all applicable folders. For example, if you have three folders listed in the Apply Changes To This Folder drop-down list at the top of the initial Rules Wizard page, selecting this check box causes Outlook 2010 to apply the rule to all three folders instead of only the selected folder.

For more details on using rules in various folders, see the following section, "Applying Rules to Specific Folders or All Folders."

> **Tip**
> To create a rule that operates on all messages, don't specify a condition that Outlook 2010 must check. Outlook 2010 prompts you to verify that you want the rule applied to all messages.

Applying Rules to Specific Folders or All Folders

When you first open the Rules And Alerts dialog box, it displays the rules that have already been defined for your profile, both client-side and server-side, as shown earlier in Figure 11-1. You might recall that you use the Apply Changes To This Folder drop-down list at the top of the dialog box to select the folder for which you want to create or modify a rule. The rules that appear in the list depend on the folder that you select, showing only the rules that apply to the selected folder.

To apply a rule to a specific folder, select that folder in the Apply Changes To This Folder drop-down list when you begin creating the rule. To apply a rule to all folders, select the Create This Rule On All Accounts option at the completion of the wizard (as explained in the preceding section).

Copying Rules to Other Folders

By default, Outlook 2010 doesn't create rules for all folders; instead, it creates the rule only for the selected folder. If you have created a rule for one folder but want to use it in a different folder, you can copy the rule to the other folder.

Follow these steps to do so:

1. Choose Tools, Rules And Alerts to open the Rules And Alerts dialog box.

> **Note**
> If necessary, choose the target folder from the Apply Changes To This folder list.

2. Select the rule that you want to copy, and then click Copy.

3. When you're prompted in the Copy Rules To dialog box, select the destination folder for the rule, and then click OK.

For details on sharing rules with other Outlook 2010 users, see the section "Sharing Rules with Others," on page 317.

Creating Rules That Use OR Logic

Up to now, you've explored relatively simple rules that function based on a single condition or on multiple AND conditions. In the latter case, the rule specifies multiple conditions and applies only to messages that meet all the conditions. If a rule is defined by three AND conditions, for example, Outlook 2010 uses it only on messages that meet condition 1, condition 2, and condition 3.

You also can create rules that follow OR logic. In this case, a rule specifies a single condition but multiple criteria for that condition. The rule will then act on any message that meets at least one of the criteria for the condition. For example, you might create a rule that deletes a message if the subject of the message contains any one of three words. If one of the conditions is met (that is, if the subject of a message contains at least one of the three words), Outlook 2010 deletes that message.

With Outlook 2010, you can create several rules that use OR logic within a single condition, but you can't create a single rule that uses OR logic on multiple conditions. For example, you might create a rule that deletes a message if the message contains the phrase "MLM," "Free Money," or "Guaranteed Results." However, you can't create a message rule that deletes the message if the subject of the message contains the words *Free Money* (condition 1), or if the message is from a specific sender (condition 2), or if the message is larger than a given size (condition 3). OR must operate within a single condition. When you create a rule with multiple conditions, Outlook 2010 always treats multiple conditions in the same rule using AND logic. You would have to create three separate rules to accommodate the latter example.

If you have a situation where you need to check for more than one piece of data in a single condition, you can do so easily enough; however, when you create the rule and define the condition, specify multiple items. For example, if you need a rule that processes messages based on three possible strings in the subject of the messages, click Specific Words in the rule description area of the Rules Wizard, where you specify rule conditions. In the Search Text dialog box, enter the strings separately. As you can see in Figure 11-9, the search list includes the word *or* to indicate that the rule applies if any one of the words appears in the subject.

Figure 11-9 Specify data separately to create a rule that uses OR logic.

Although you can't create a single rule with OR logic operating on multiple conditions in Outlook 2010, you can create rules that combine AND and OR logic. For example, you might create a rule that applied if the message arrived at a specific account and the subject contained the words *Free Money* or *Guaranteed Results*. Keep in mind that you must specify two conditions—not one—to build the rule. The first condition would check for the account, and the second would check for the words *Free Money* or *Guaranteed Results*.

Consider the following example:

1. On the Home tab, click Rules, Manage Rules And Alerts.

2. In the Rules And Alerts dialog box, click New Rule.

3. Click Apply Rule On Messages I Receive, and then click Next.

4. Select Through The Specified Account.

5. Select With Specific Words In The Subject.

6. At the bottom of the dialog box, click Specified, and then in the Account dialog box, select the email account and click OK.

7. Click Specific Words at the bottom of the dialog box to open the Search Text dialog box.

8. Type **Free Money**, and then click Add.

9. Type **Guaranteed Results**, click Add, and then click OK.

Look at the rule conditions in the Step 2 area of the dialog box. The rule indicates that it will act on messages that are from the specified account and that have the text *Free Money* or *Guaranteed Results* in the message.

Modifying Rules

You can modify a rule at any time after you create it. Modifying a rule is much like creating one. To modify a rule, on the Home tab, click Tools, Manage Rules And Alerts to open the Rules And Alerts dialog box. Select the rule that you want to modify, and then click Change Rule to display a menu of editing options. If you choose Edit Rule Settings on the menu, Outlook 2010 presents the same options you saw when you created the rule, and you can work with them the same way. Click Rename Rule to change the name of the rule, or click an action to add the selected action to the rule (retaining any existing actions).

Controlling Rules

Rules can be an effective tool for managing messages, but you also need to manage your rules to make them effective overall. For example, you need to consider the order in which rules run, control how and when rules run, and even disable or remove rules. The following sections explain how to control your rules.

Setting Rule Order

Outlook 2010 executes rules for incoming messages when they arrive in the Inbox, whether on the server or locally (depending on whether the rules are client-side or server-side). Outlook 2010 executes rules for outgoing messages when the messages arrive in the Sent Items folder.

As mentioned earlier, the order in which rules are listed in Outlook 2010 determines how Outlook 2010 applies them. In some situations, the sequence could be important. Perhaps you have one rule that moves high-priority messages to a separate folder and another rule that notifies you when high-priority messages arrive. For the latter rule to work properly, it needs to execute before the one that moves the messages, because the notification rule won't execute if the messages are no longer in the Inbox.

You can control the order of Outlook 2010 rules easily by taking the following steps:

1. On the Home tab, click Rules, Manage Rules And Alerts to open the Rules And Alerts dialog box.

2. Select a rule to be moved.

3. Use the Move Up and Move Down buttons to change the order in the list, as shown in Figure 11-10. Rules execute in the order listed, with the rule at the top executing first and the one at the bottom executing last.

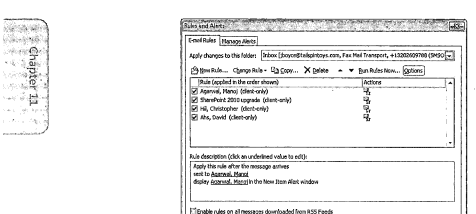

Figure 11-10 You can control execution order for rules by rearranging the rules list.

> **Note**
>
> An alert in Figure 11-10 indicates that there are additional rules created with a different version of Outlook or with Outlook Web Access (OWA) that are not shown in the list of rules. In this case, there is a server-side mobile alert rule that sends an alert to my mobile phone when a message arrives with importance set to High. The mobile alert rules do not appear in the Rules And Alerts dialog box.

Stopping Rules from Being Processed

In certain cases, you might want your message rules to stop being processed altogether. Perhaps someone has sent you a very large message that is causing your connection to time out or is taking a long time to download. You would like to create a rule to delete the message without downloading it, but you don't want any of your other rules to execute. In this case, you would place a new rule at the top of the list and define it so that the last action it takes is to stop processing any other rules. In effect, this allows you to bypass your other rules without going through the trouble of disabling them.

You can also use the Stop Processing More Rules action to control rule execution in other situations. To stop Outlook 2010 from executing other rules when a message meets a specific condition, include Stop Processing More Rules as the last action for the rule. You'll find this action in the What Do You Want To Do With The Message? list in the Rules Wizard.

Disabling and Removing Rules

In some cases, you might want to turn off message rules so that they don't execute. Perhaps you use a rule to do routine cleanup on your mail folders but don't want the rule to run automatically. Or perhaps you want to create a rule to use only once or twice but you would like to keep it in case you need it again later. In those cases, you can disable the rule. To do this, on the Home tab, click Rules, Manage Rules And Alerts, and then clear the check box for that rule in the list. Only those rules with check boxes that are selected will apply to incoming or outgoing messages.

If you don't plan to use a rule again, you can remove it by opening the Rules And Alerts dialog box, selecting the rule, and then clicking Delete.

Sharing Rules with Others

By default, Outlook 2010 stores server-side rules on the computer running Exchange Server and stores client-side rules on your local system. Regardless of where your message rules are stored, you can share them with others by exporting the rules to a file. You can then send the file as an email attachment or place it on a network share (or a local share) to allow other users to access it. You can also export the rules to create a backup of them for safekeeping or in case you need to move your Outlook 2010 rules to a new computer, as explained in the next section.

Follow these steps to export your message rules to a file:

1. On the Home tab, click Rules, Manage Rules And Alerts.

2. In the Rules And Alerts dialog box, click Options.

3. In the Options dialog box, shown in Figure 11-11, click Export Rules, and then select a path for the file in the resulting Save Exported Rules As dialog box (a standard file save dialog box).

Figure 11-11 Use the Options dialog box to import and export rules.

4. To save the rules using Outlook 2002, Outlook 2000, or Outlook 98 format, select the appropriate format in the Save As Type drop-down list. Otherwise, leave the selection at Rules Wizard Rules.

5. Click Save.

You can export your rules in any of four formats, depending on the version of Outlook used by the people with whom you want to share your rules. If you need to share with various users, export using the earliest version of Outlook. Later versions will be able to import the rules because they are forward-compatible.

> **Note**
> If you are sharing rules with someone else, at this point, you have a rules file that you can send to the other person. The following section explains how to restore rules, which is the process that the other person would use to import your rules.

Backing Up and Restoring Rules

Outlook 2010 stores server-side rules in your Exchange Server mailbox, so in principle, there is no reason to back up your server-side rules. We say "in principle" because that point of view assumes that the Exchange Server administrator is performing adequate backups of your mailbox so that you won't lose your messages or your rules. It's still a good idea to back up server-side rules just in case, using the method explained in the preceding section, "Sharing Rules with Others."

Outlook 2010 stores client-side rules in the default mail store—that is, the .pst file defined in your Outlook 2010 profile as the location for incoming mail. Storing the rules in the .pst file simplifies moving your rules to another computer because you are also likely to move your .pst file to the other computer to retain all your Outlook 2010 items. To make this process work, however, you need to add the .pst file to the second computer in a certain way.

Outlook 2010 checks the default mail store .pst file for the rules, but it doesn't check any other .pst files that you might have added to your profile. Therefore, if you added an email account to the profile and then added the .pst file from your old system, you won't see your rules.

One of the easiest methods for making sure things get set up correctly is to add the .pst file to your profile before you add the email account. Then when you add the account, Outlook 2010 uses the existing .pst file as the default store. The result is that your rules will be available without any additional manipulation.

Here's how to make that happen:

1. Open the Mail item in Control Panel.

2. In the Mail Setup dialog box, click Show Profiles.

3. Click Add, type a name for the profile, and then click OK.

4. Click Cancel. When asked whether you want to create a profile with no email accounts, click OK.

5. Click Properties to open the newly created profile.

6. Click Data Files to display the Data Files tab in the Account Settings dialog box.

7. Click Add, and then click OK in the New Outlook Data File dialog box.

8. In the Create Or Open Outlook Data File dialog box, browse to and select the .pst file that contains your rules, and then click OK.

9. Click OK in the Personal Folders dialog box.

10. In the Account Settings dialog box, click the newly added data file, and then click Set As Default.

11. Add your email accounts to the profile.

12. Click Close, click Close again, and then click OK to close the profile properties.

When you start Outlook 2010, you should now have access to the rules stored in the .pst file, plus all your existing Outlook 2010 items.

Using Rules to Move Messages Between Accounts

One common task that users often want to perform is to move messages between accounts. Assume that you have two accounts: an Exchange Server account for work and a POP3 account for personal messages. When certain messages come into your Exchange Server mailbox, you want them to be moved automatically to the .pst file for your other account. In this case, it's a simple matter to move the personal messages from the Exchange Server Inbox to the POP3 Inbox. Just create a rule that moves messages that meet the specified conditions to your POP3 Inbox.

> **Note**
> Before you run through these steps to create a rule for moving messages based on their account, create a folder to contain the messages.

Here's how to accomplish this:

1. On the Home tab, click Rules, Manage Rules And Alerts to open the Rules And Alerts dialog box.

2. Click New Rule, and in the Rules Wizard, select Apply Rule On Messages I Receive and then click Next.

3. Select Through The Specified Account. In the rule description area, click the underlined word *specified*, select your Exchange Server account, and then click OK.

4. Choose the other condition(s) that define the messages that you want moved between accounts, and click Next.

5. Select Move It To The Specified Folder, and then click the underlined word *specified* in the rule description area.

6. Select the folder in your .pst file to which the messages should be moved, and then click OK and Next.

7. Specify any exceptions to the rule, and then click Next again.

8. Specify a name for the rule and other options as needed, and then click Finish.

Running Rules Manually and in Specific Folders

Normally you use message rules to process messages when they arrive in your Inbox or are placed in the Sent Messages folder. However, you also can run rules manually at any time. Perhaps you have created a rule that you want to use periodically to clean out certain types of messages or move them to a specific folder. You don't want the rule to operate every time you check mail; instead, you want to execute it only when you think it's necessary. In this case, you can run the rule manually.

You might also want to run a rule manually when you need to run it in a folder other than the Inbox. For example, assume that you've deleted messages from a specific sender and now want to restore them, moving the messages from the Deleted Items folder back to your Inbox. In this situation, you could create the rule and then execute it manually in the Deleted Items folder.

It's easy to run a rule manually and in a specific folder by following these steps:

1. On the Home tab, click Rules, Manage Rules And Alerts.

2. Click Run Rules Now. Outlook 2010 displays the Run Rules Now dialog box.

3. Select the rule that you want to run in the list, as shown in Figure 11-12. By default, Outlook 2010 will run the rule in the Inbox unless you specify otherwise. Click Browse to browse for a different folder. If you also want to run the rule in subfolders of the selected folder, select the Include Subfolders check box.

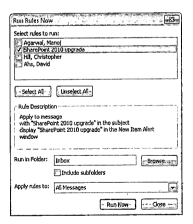

Figure 11-12 Use the Run Rules Now dialog box to run a rule manually in a specified folder.

4. In the Apply Rules To drop-down list, select the type of messages on which you want to run the rule (All Messages, Read Messages, or Unread Messages).

5. Click Run Now to execute the rule, or click Close to cancel.

Creating and Using Quick Steps

Quick Steps are a new feature in Outlook 2010 that you can use to process messages automatically in a way similar to the way rules work. In fact, if you've read through the rest of this chapter, Quick Steps should make a lot of sense to you. If you have worked with rules much, you'll also quickly come to appreciate how easy it is to create and use Quick Steps. Let's start with an explanation of what they are.

Quick Steps Overview

In a nutshell, Quick Steps are rules that you can apply to one or more messages whenever you need. Outlook 2010 includes several predefined Quick Steps, and you can also create your own. Unlike rules, however, Quick Steps don't have conditions. Instead, they contain one or more actions that are executed when you apply the Quick Step to one or more items.

For example, you might create a Quick Step to mark the selected message as read, send a predefined reply, set a category on the message, and then move it to a folder. Those actions are then performed on whatever message(s) you apply it to.

> **Note**
> Quick Steps are available only for email and other message types, like Really Simple Syndication (RSS) messages.

Using the Default Quick Steps

To see the list of available Quick Steps, open a message folder and, on the Home tab of the ribbon, click the More button in the Quick Steps group. The default Quick Steps are shown in the resulting menu (see Figure 11-11). You can also choose Manage Quick Steps to open the Manage Quick Steps dialog box (explored in the next section), which displays all the Quick Steps, including the following:

- **Move To Folder**   Moves the selected message(s) to a folder that you choose, then marks the messages as read.

- **To Manager**   Forwards the selected message to your manager. With Exchange Server accounts, Outlook automatically identifies your manager from the Manager field in Active Directory Domain Services (AD DS). If this field is incorrect, you can modify the Quick Step to specify the correct recipient address.

- **Team E-mail**   Creates a new email addressed to everyone who reports to you. As with the To Manager Quick Step, this one uses the Manager field in AD DS to determine who reports to you. You can modify the recipient list if needed.

- **Done**   Flags the message as complete, moves it to a folder that you choose, and marks the message as read.

- **Reply and Delete**   This Quick Step replies to the message and then deletes the original.

These default Quick Steps are not fully defined the first time you use them. The Move Quick Step, for example, prompts you to select a folder, specify the Inbox, or choose an option to always be prompted to select a folder. From that point on, the Quick Step retains those settings and you don't have to set them again (unless you want to modify the Quick Step). The name of the Move Quick Step changes to the name of the folder that you select (if you choose one rather than select the Inbox or have Outlook prompt you for a folder). Here's an example:

1. Open the Inbox, click a message, and, on the Home tab of the ribbon, click Move To: ?. Outlook displays the First Time Setup dialog box (see Figure 11-13).

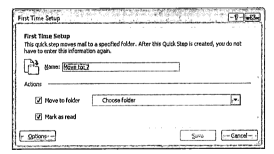

Figure 11-13 Configure the Quick Step using the First Time Setup dialog box.

2. In the Name text box, enter a new name for the Quick Step.

3. From the Move To Folder drop-down list, choose the desired destination for the message, or choose Always Ask For Folder if you want the Quick Step to prompt you to select the folder each time you use the Quick Step.

4. Click Save.

Your Quick Step is now customized, and the selected message(s) are moved and marked as read. If you want to reset the Quick Step to its default, on the Home tab, click the Manage Quick Steps button in the lower-right corner of the group. Then, click Reset To Defaults. This will reset all changes you have made to the Quick Steps, including deleting new Quick Steps that you have created.

CAUTION

> Click the Reset To Defaults button with care. You don't want to delete your custom Quick Steps accidentally.

Creating Your Own Quick Steps

As indicated in the previous section, you can modify the default Quick Steps, as well as create your own. Modifying the existing ones uses much the same process as creating a new one, so let's take a look at that process.

Creating Simple Quick Steps from Predefined Options

Outlook includes some partially defined Quick Steps to save a little time in creating your own. These include Quick Steps that perform the following actions on messages: move, categorize and move, flag and move, create new message, forward a message, and create a meeting request. To create one of these Quick Steps, click the Manage Quick Steps button in the Quick Steps group on the ribbon to open the Manage Quick Steps dialog box shown in Figure 11-14.

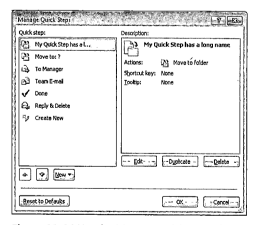

Figure 11-14 Use the Manage Quick Steps dialog box to create and manage Quick Steps.

Click New, and then choose one of the predefined Quick Step types. Outlook displays the First Time Setup dialog box, similar to the one shown in Figure 11-12. Specify a name, make your selections, and click Finish.

Creating Custom Quick Steps

You can also create custom Quick Steps that perform multiple actions that you specify. To create a new custom Quick Step, follow these steps:

1. On the Home tab, click the More button (if needed) in the Quick Steps group and choose Create New. Outlook displays the Edit Quick Step dialog box shown in Figure 11-15.

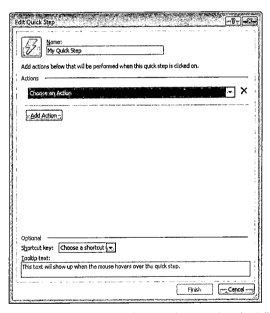

Figure 11-15 Create or edit a Quick Step using the Edit Quick Step dialog box.

2. In the Name field, type a name for the Quick Step. You can use a long name, but a short name will fit in the ribbon better.

3. From the drop-down list in the Actions group, choose the first action that you want the Quick Step to take.

4. If you want to add another action, click Add Action. Outlook adds another Choose An Action drop-down list to the Actions group. Choose the desired action, and then repeat the process to add any other actions as needed.

5. If you want to assign a shortcut key to the Quick Step so that you can start it from the keyboard, choose one from the Shortcut Key drop-down list.

6. If you want to add a tooltip that will appear when you pause the mouse over the Quick Step (to help you remember what it is for), type the text in the Tooltip Text field.

7. Click Finish.

Your new Quick Step should appear in the Quick Steps group on the ribbon. To use it, select one or more messages and then click the Quick Step on the ribbon.

Editing Quick Steps

Editing Quick Steps uses almost the same process as creating one. Click Manage Quick Steps in the Quick Steps group on the ribbon to open the Manage Quick Steps dialog box. Select the Quick Step you want to modify, and then click Edit. Outlook displays the Edit Quick Step dialog box, shown in Figure 11-14, which you can use to modify its settings as needed. Click Save when you are satisfied with your changes.

Copying Quick Steps

You can save some time creating a Quick Step by duplicating an existing one. Outlook copies all the settings to a new Quick Step, which you can customize as needed and save with a new name. To copy a Quick Step, click Manage Quick Steps on the ribbon, select the Quick Step that you want to copy, and click Duplicate. Outlook opens the Edit Quick Step dialog box with a copy of the Quick Step named Copy of *<original Quick Step name>*. Modify as needed and click Finish.

Using Quick Steps Effectively

Quick Steps make common actions available at the click of a button. There is no wrong or right way to use them, and people will have a different set of Quick Steps that they use most often, depending on how they use Outlook, whether they use it at work or home, and other factors. To get the most out of this handy new Outlook 2010 feature, take some time to think about the actions that you perform frequently in Outlook, and then create Quick Steps for those actions.

Here's a list of some common uses for Quick Steps to help stimulate your imagination:

- Move messages to a frequently used folder to organize your Inbox.

- Start a new message to your manager or to the people who work for you.

- Create a new meeting request to your team or manager.

- Categorize a message and move it to a folder.

- Set messages as read or unread.

- Flag a message for follow-up for a specific period of time.

- Create a task for yourself or assign a task based on the selected message.

- Create an appointment or meeting based on the selected message.

Managing Junk Email

IRED of wading through so much junk email? Anyone with an email account these days is hard-pressed to avoid unsolicited ads, invitations to multilevel marketing schemes, or unwanted adult content messages. Fortunately, Microsoft Outlook 2010 offers several features to help you deal with all the junk email coming through your Inbox.

Outlook 2010 improves on the junk email and adult content filters in earlier versions of Outlook to provide much better anti-junk-mail features. As in Outlook 2007, anti-phishing measures scan email for suspicious content and automatically disable it. The Junk E-Mail folder restricts certain email functionality, displaying email messages as plain text and preventing replies to messages contained in the folder, as well as blocking attachments and embedded links.

Outlook 2010 offers four levels of junk email protection, with Safe Senders and Safe Recipients lists to help you identify valid messages. It also provides a Blocked Senders list to help you identify email addresses and domains that send you junk email, which enables you to exclude those messages from your Inbox. Email can also be blocked based on the originating top-level domain or language encoding used.

How Outlook 2010 Junk Email Filtering Works

If you're familiar with the junk email filters in earlier versions of Outlook, you already know a little about how Outlook 2010 filters junk email. Before you start configuring Outlook 2010 to filter your junk email, you should have a better understanding of how it applies these filters.

As described earlier, Outlook 2010 provides four filter levels. To specify the filter level, click Junk in the Delete group of the ribbon's Home and click the Junk E-mail Options tab to display the Junk E-Mail Options dialog box, shown in Figure 12-1. The following sections explain the four filter levels.

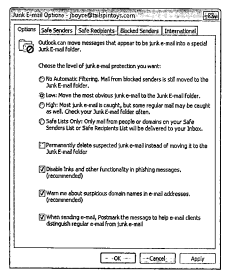

Figure 12-1 Use the Junk E-Mail Options dialog box to configure Outlook 2010 quickly to filter unwanted messages.

No Automatic Filtering

This option protects only against mail from individuals and domains in your Blocked Senders list, moving it to the Junk E-Mail folder. All other mail is delivered to your Inbox.

Low

This option functions essentially like the junk email and adult content filters in earlier versions of Outlook. Outlook 2010 uses a predefined filter to scan the body and subject of messages to identify likely spam.

You can't specify additional filter criteria for subject or content checking for this junk email filter, although you can create your own custom junk email rules to block messages using additional criteria.

High

This level uses the same filtering as the Low level, but it also uses additional message scanning logic to determine whether a message is spam. Outlook 2010 scans the message body and message header for likely indications that the message is spam. You do not have any control over this scanning, other than to enable it by choosing the High scanning level.

If you choose the High option, you should not enable the option to delete junk email messages rather than move them to the Junk E-Mail folder. Although Outlook 2010 will catch most spam, it will also generate false positives, blocking messages that you expect or want. You should review the Junk E-Mail folder periodically and mark any valid messages as not being junk email. Marking messages in this way is explained in the section "Marking and Unmarking Junk Email," on page 338.

Safe Lists Only

This level provides the most extreme message blocking. Only messages originating with senders in your Safe Senders and Safe Recipients lists are treated as valid messages, and all others are treated as junk email.

Although this protection level offers the highest chance of blocking all your junk mail, it also offers the highest chance of blocking wanted messages. To use this level effectively, you should allow Outlook 2010 to place messages in the Junk E-Mail folder and review the folder periodically for valid messages. When you find a valid message, add the sender to your Safe Senders list.

Understanding How Outlook 2010 Uses the Filter Lists

Outlook 2010 maintains three lists: Safe Senders, Safe Recipients, and Blocked Senders. Figure 12-2 shows a Blocked Senders list, which blocks all messages from these senders. Messages originating from an address or a domain on the list are filtered out. Entering a domain in the Blocked Senders list blocks all messages from that domain, regardless of the sender. Add *wingtiptoys.com* to the list, for example, and Outlook 2010 would block messages from *joe@wingtiptoys.com*, *jane@wingtiptoys.com*, and all other email addresses ending in *@wingtiptoys.com*.

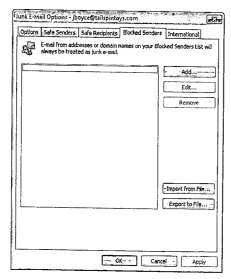

Figure 12-2 Use the Blocked Senders list to block messages by address or domain.

The Safe Senders and Safe Recipients lists identify senders and domains that Outlook 2010 should not filter, regardless of subject or content. Use the Safe Senders list to identify valid messages by their originating address. Use the Safe Recipients list to identify valid messages by their target address. For example, if you participate in a mailing list, messages for that list are sometimes addressed to a mailing list address rather than your own address, such as *list@wingtiptoys.com* rather than *jim@wingtiptoys.com*. Add the mailing list address to the Safe Recipients list to prevent Outlook 2010 from treating the mailing list messages as junk email.

You have two options for adding entries to each of the three filter lists: specify an email address, or specify a domain. As mentioned earlier, if you specify a domain, Outlook 2010 blocks all messages from that domain, regardless of sender. However, Outlook 2010 is rather selective in blocking. Specify *@wingtiptoys.com*, for example, and Outlook 2010 will block messages from *joe@wingtiptoys.com* and *jane@wingtiptoys.com* but will not block messages from *joe@sales.wingtiptoys.com*. You must specify the subdomain explicitly in a list to either accept or block that subdomain. For example, to block the subdomain *sales.wingtiptoys.com*, enter **sales.wingtiptoys.com** in the Blocked Senders list.

INSIDE OUT   Simplify management of filter lists

Outlook 2010 recognizes wildcard characters, so you can simply enter *.<domain> to block all messages from a domain and its subdomains. For example, use *.wingtiptoys. com to block *sales.wingtiptoys.com*, *support.wingtiptoys.com*, and all other subdomains of *wingtiptoys.com*. You can import and export a filter list, which enables you to move a list between computers or share the list with others. The filter list is simply a text file with a single email address on each line, making it easy to create and manage the list.

Outlook 2010 also lets you specify a set of top-level domains and language encodings to block as part of its junk email filtering. These options are set on the International tab by selecting the desired domains and encodings from the provided lists.

Deleting Instead of Moving Messages

Outlook 2010 by default moves junk email to the Junk E-Mail folder, which it creates in your mailbox. The Junk E-Mail folder gives you the capability to review your junk email messages before deleting them. If you prefer, you can configure Outlook 2010 to delete messages instead of placing them in the Junk E-Mail folder. As a general rule, you should configure Outlook 2010 to delete messages automatically only after you have spent a month using the Junk E-Mail folder, adding senders to your Safe Senders list and otherwise identifying to Outlook 2010 valid messages that have generated false positives.

How Outlook 2010 Phishing Protection Works

Phishing is an attempt to obtain personal information fraudulently by luring you to a website and asking you to disclose things like passwords, credit card numbers, and so on. This website is *spoofed*, or pretending to be a trusted site—sometimes remarkably well—when it is actually a fake set up to help steal your personal information. Phishing is often done by sending email that directs you to the spoofed site. With the widespread use of Hypertext Markup Language (HTML) email, it's easier to disguise the actual destination of a link, and accordingly, it is harder for you to detect the misdirection.

Fortunately, Outlook 2010 contains anti-phishing features to help protect you from suspicious websites and email addresses. Email messages are evaluated as they arrive, and messages that appear to be phishing are delivered to the Inbox, not the Junk E-Mail folder, but are otherwise treated much like junk email, with a number of functions disabled.

- **Disable Links And Other Functionality In Phishing Messages**   If Outlook 2010 determines that a message appears to be phishing, the message is delivered to the Inbox, but attachments and links in the message are blocked and the Reply and Reply All functions are disabled.

- **Warn Me About Suspicious Domain Names In E-Mail Addresses**   This option warns you when the sender's email domain uses certain characters in an attempt to masquerade as a well-known, legitimate business. Leaving this functionality enabled protects you against phishing attacks using spoofed email addresses.

> **Note**
> Phishing protection can be functional even when the No Automatic Filtering option is selected and other junk email protection options are disabled.

Enabling and Configuring Junk Email Filtering

To begin filtering out unwanted messages, start Outlook 2010 and follow these steps:

1. Open the Inbox folder and on the Home tab of the ribbon, click Junk and choose Junk E-mail Options to open the Junk E-Mail Options dialog box (shown in Figure 12-1).

2. Choose a level of protection on the Options tab, as explained earlier.

3. If you want to delete messages rather than move them to the Junk E-Mail folder, select the Permanently Delete Suspected Junk E-Mail Instead Of Moving It To The Junk E-Mail Folder check box.

4. Select the Disable Links And Other Functionality In Phishing Messages check box to protect against common phishing schemes.

5. If you want to be warned when a domain name appears to be spoofed, select Warn Me About Suspicious Domain Names In E-Mail Addresses.

6. Click OK to apply the filter changes.

To configure the lists that Outlook 2010 uses in filtering junk email, start Outlook 2010 and follow these steps:

1. Open the Junk E-Mail Options dialog box as described in the previous procedure.

2. Click the Safe Senders tab, and then click Add and enter the email address or domain of the sender that you want Outlook 2010 to deliver to your Inbox, regardless of content or subject. Click OK, and then repeat this for each sender that you want to add.

3. On the Safe Senders tab, select the Also Trust E-Mail From My Contacts check box if you want Outlook 2010 to always accept email from senders in your Contacts folder, regardless of content or subject. You can also choose to select the Automatically Add People I E-Mail To The Safe Senders List check box.

4. Click the Safe Recipients tab, and add the target addresses or domains for which Outlook 2010 should allow messages (used typically to accept email sent to a mailing list).

5. Click the Blocked Senders tab, and add the addresses or domains of junk email senders whose messages you want Outlook 2010 to explicitly block.

6. Click the International tab, and select the top-level domains and types of language encoding that Outlook 2010 should always block.

7. Click OK to apply the filter changes.

Controlling Automatic Downloads

Images and other online content present another potential hazard in email because you usually, at minimum, confirm that your email address is valid when you download this content. Content from unknown sources can also be malicious, containing Trojan horses, viruses, and so on.

The Trust Center, shown in Figure 12-3, lets you decide when Outlook 2010 should download external content in email messages, Really Simple Syndication (RSS) items, and Microsoft SharePoint discussion boards. The Safe Senders and Safe Recipients lists can be used to determine downloading settings, as can Security Zones.

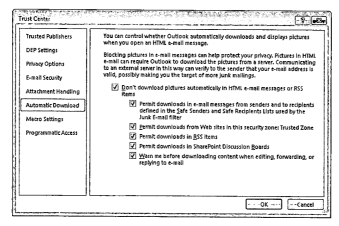

Figure 12-3 Configure Automatic Download options in the Trust Center.

The Automatic Download options are described in the following list:

- **Don't Download Pictures Automatically In HTML E-Mail Messages Or RSS Items** This setting prevents images from downloading to your computer automatically, except as directed by additional settings on this page. Blocking automatic image downloads protects you from spammers who use your connection to their server to verify your identity as well as from malicious content (a Trojan horse disguised as an image, for example).

- **Permit Downloads In E-Mail Messages From Senders And To Recipients Defined In The Safe Senders And Safe Recipients Lists Used By The Junk E-Mail Filter** You can tell Outlook 2010 to use the safe lists that you have created to determine which images it will download automatically. This lets you see images from those sources that you have already decided you trust while blocking other images.

- **Permit Downloads From Web Sites In This Security Zone: Trusted Zone** Content that resides on a website included in the Trusted Zone is downloaded automatically when this setting is enabled. This lets you receive images and other content from trusted sources, such as corporate servers or partners, based on a common list, reducing the amount of configuration needed.

- **Permit Downloads In RSS Items** Control over images downloading in RSS feeds is configured separately, allowing you to block images in RSS feeds without affecting email messages.

- **Permit Downloads In SharePoint Discussion Boards** You can configure whether to download content from SharePoint discussion boards separately, offering you greater control over the content that is downloaded to your computer.

- **Warn Me Before Downloading Content When Editing, Forwarding, Or Replying To E-Mail**   If this setting is enabled, Outlook 2010 will warn you before downloading content in messages that you are replying to, forwarding, or editing. If you choose not to download the images and continue with your actions, Outlook 2010 will remove the images from the message, and the recipient will not be able to retrieve them. This is an improvement over Outlook 2003, in which you could complete your operation only if you downloaded the images.

Configuring Automatic Downloading of External Content

To configure image downloading, start Outlook 2010, and then follow these steps:

1. Click File, Trust Center, and Trust Center Settings, and then select Automatic Download to view the options for handling image downloads (shown in Figure 12-3).

2. To stop Outlook 2010 from automatically downloading images, select the Don't Download Pictures Automatically In HTML E-Mail Messages Or RSS Items check box.

CAUTION

If this check box is not selected, all other options on this page will be unavailable, and all images will be displayed, creating potential security risks.

3. If you want to view images from sources that you trust, select the Permit Downloads In E-Mail Messages From Senders And To Recipients Defined In The Safe Senders And Safe Recipients Lists Used By The Junk E-Mail Filter check box.

4. To allow sites that you trust to download images, select Permit Downloads From Web Sites In This Security Zone: Trusted Zone.

5. If you want to view images in RSS feeds, select Permit Downloads In RSS Items.

6. To view images from SharePoint sites, select Permit Downloads In SharePoint Discussion Boards.

7. If you want Outlook 2010 to alert you that images are being downloaded when you take action on an email message, select Warn Me Before Downloading Content When Editing, Forwarding, Or Replying To E-Mail.

8. Apply the changes by clicking OK.

Marking and Unmarking Junk Email

The junk email filters in Outlook 2010 might not catch all the messages that you consider to be junk. You can mark and unmark messages as junk mail easily without opening the Junk E-Mail Options dialog box. When you receive a message that is junk but that Outlook 2010 does not place in the Junk E-Mail folder (or delete), right-click the message, choose Junk, and then choose the list to which you want the sender added. You also can add the sender to the Blocked Senders list (Block Sender) if you want.

If Outlook 2010 marks a message as junk mail and moves it to the Junk E-Mail folder but you don't want the message treated as junk mail, you can mark the message as not junk (essentially, unmark the message). Open the Junk E-Mail folder, right-click the message, and choose Junk, Not Junk. Outlook 2010 displays a Mark As Not Junk dialog box. If you click OK without taking any other action, Outlook 2010 moves the message back to the Inbox. Select the Always Trust E-Mail From option to also have the sender's email address added to the Safe Senders list. Any address that a message was sent to can also be added to the Safe Recipients List.

> **Note**
> If the message is from a sender inside your organization, you do not have the option of adding that sender to the Safe Senders List, either from the shortcut menu or from the Mark As Not Junk dialog box, because they are already categorized as safe senders.

Creating Other Junk Email Rules

Once you configure it and make adjustments for false positives, the filtering technology built into Outlook 2010 can be an effective tool for waging your daily fight against junk email. The filtering technology in Outlook 2010 isn't perfect, however, so you might need to handle junk email in other ways. One technique is to create your own rules to handle exceptions that the built-in filters can't adequately address.

You can create rules that look explicitly for keywords or phrases in the subject or body of a message or look for specific other criteria and then move those messages to the Junk E-Mail folder (or delete them). See Chapter 11, "Processing Messages Automatically," for details on creating and working with rules.

Reply or Unsubscribe?

Although you might be tempted to have Outlook 2010 automatically send a nasty reply to every piece of spam you receive, resist the urge. In many cases, the spammer's only way of knowing whether a recipient address is valid is when a reply comes back from that address. You make your address that much more desirable to spammers when you reply, because they then know that there's a person at the address. The best course of action is to delete the message without looking at it.

In the past, many spammers also used unsubscribe messages to identify valid addresses, which made unsubscribing to a particular spammer a hit-or-miss proposition. In some cases, the spammer would delete your address, and in others, it would simply add your address to the good email address list. With state and federal laws like CAN-SPAM and individuals and companies becoming more litigious, spammers more often than not heed unsubscribe requests. Just a few years ago, we would have recommended that you not bother unsubscribing to spam. Today, you will likely have at least a little better luck unsubscribing to spam without generating a flood of new messages. However, you should still approach the problem cautiously.

Other Spam Filtering Solutions

The spam blocking features in Outlook 2010 can help considerably in blocking unwanted messages, but there are other options that you should consider in addition to the Outlook 2010 filtering technologies.

Filtering in Exchange Server

If your company or organization uses Microsoft Exchange Server, you can perform some spam filtering tasks right at the server without adding third-party software. Exchange Server 2003 and later support domain filtering for virtual Simple Mail Transfer Protocol (SMTP) servers.

Exchange Server 2007 and 2010 offer some additional features not included in Exchange Server 2003, making it potentially more effective for blocking spam. One server in an organization is designated as the Edge Transport server and is responsible for mail flow and control between internal email servers and the Internet. By default, only unauthenticated, inbound email from the Internet is filtered, although internal email can also be filtered if desired.

Exchange Server 2007 and 2010 can filter email based on a number of different criteria, including:

- **Content**   Email messages are examined to see whether they have characteristics of spam and are checked against a safe list aggregated from the Safe Sender lists of Outlook 2007 and 2010 users within the organization.

- **Attachment**   Attachments can be filtered based on either the Multipurpose Internet Mail Extensions (MIME) type of the file or the file name. Administrators can choose to strip the attachment and deliver the message or reject the message, either with a failure message to the sender or silently.

- **Connection**   Email is evaluated based on the Internet Protocol (IP) address of the server that is attempting to send the message using a variety of safe and blocked lists to determine whether the message should be delivered.

- **Recipient**   The addresses that the email is sent to are compared to a local directory and an administrator-managed blocked list to determine what to do with the email.

- **Sender**   Like the Recipient filter, this filter uses a locally maintained blocked list to block certain addresses from sending email to the organization.

- **Sender ID**   The sending system's Domain Name System (DNS) server is queried to determine whether the IP address of the system that originated the message is autho-rized to send email from that domain. This verification process protects you against spoofed email addresses, a ploy commonly used by spammers and phishers alike.

- **Sender Reputation**   This feature collects information about email senders and evaluates incoming email based on a number of characteristics to assign a Spam Con-fidence Level (SCL) rating. This rating determines whether the message is delivered, and the rating is passed to other computers running Exchange Server when the mes-sage is sent to them.

If you are responsible for administering a computer running Exchange Server, you will find additional information in the Help files provided with Exchange Server.

Using Third-Party Filters

Several third-party antispam solutions are available that you can consider for your organi-zation. For example, Symantec's Mail Security for Microsoft Exchange Server provides con-tent scanning and filtering capabilities. Mail Security filters incoming messages for content, spyware, adware, and attachment file types (not just file name extensions).

Mail Security is available for Exchange Server, Domino, and SMTP servers. You'll find more information about Mail Security at *http://www.symantec.com/business/ mail-security-for-microsoft-exchange*.

Another product to consider is GFI Mail Essentials (*www.gfi.com/mes*). Mail Essentials provides several levels of content filtering with support for blocked lists, safe lists, and additional header checking options that enable it to detect and block spam based on a broad range of criteria.

These are just a few of the solutions available for filtering and managing messages. Many mail servers offer their own filtering capabilities, and many other products provide filtering services for existing mail servers.

One of the most prevalent spam filtering solutions is SpamAssassin, based on an open-source heuristic scanning application developed originally for UNIX-based servers. You can find information about open-source SpamAssassin at *spamassassin.apache.org*.

Managing Junk Email Effectively

Email is a critical tool for most people, but it can also be a frustration when you feel overwhelmed by junk email. By using the features provided in Outlook 2010 and taking a few additional steps, you can greatly reduce the amount of junk email that you receive and the corresponding risks:

- **Use the Outlook 2010 junk email filters and phishing protection**   The default option of Low on the Options tab in the Junk E-Mail Options dialog box provides some protection, but it might not be enough. You might want to raise the level to High and check your Junk E-Mail folder regularly to ensure that Outlook 2010 is not sending legitimate messages there. Use the International tab in the Junk E-Mail Options dialog box to block top-level domains from which you never want to receive messages or to block messages in specific languages.

- **Use the Safe Senders list and Blocked Senders list**   Building both your blocked and safe lists will make a considerable difference in how well Outlook 2010 can filter your email.

- **Update the Outlook 2010 junk email filters regularly**   Updates for Outlook 2010 can be obtained by clicking File, Help, and Check For Updates. You can also download updated filters from *office.microsoft.com/en-us/officeupdate/*.

- **Disable functionality that can confirm your identity inadvertently**   Features like read and delivery receipts and automatic acceptance of meeting requests can confirm your identity to a spammer. Outlook 2010 lets you configure receipt processing for Internet email differently from messages within your corporate network so that you can leave receipts on for your business contacts while disabling them for messages from outside the organization.

- **Guard your primary email address**   Many people have a secondary email address—often from a free public provider such as Windows Live Hotmail or Gmail—that they use when posting on message boards, newsgroups, and so on. Even so, you might want to change your email address when posting it in public by changing the @ to *AT* or inserting extra characters (such as *chrisHillREMOVE@wingtiptoys.com*). This can help prevent automated gathering of your address by spammers' robots.

- **Don't reply to spam**   Even a seemingly simple unsubscribe message confirms that your email address is valid, so unless you know the sender, just delete the message.

- **Don't automatically download images and other online content**   Spammers can verify your email address when you connect to the server to download the external content in a message. Online content is blocked by default, and it's a good idea to leave it that way. You can download content for an individual message by right-clicking the message box telling you that the content has been blocked and then selecting Download Pictures.

- **Don't forward chain email**   These messages clutter up inboxes, expose email addresses, and are all too often hoaxes. If you absolutely must forward a message, send it to only the few people who will definitely be interested, and use the BCC option for their email addresses.

- **Never provide personal information in email**   Even with a trusted correspondent, you should avoid sending critical data such as credit card or social security numbers in unencrypted email.

- **Don't provide personal information to links you get in email**   If you get email that appears to be from a company that you do business with, don't assume it actually is. Most email that provides a link and asks for personal data is spoofed in an attempt to get you to disclose this information. If you think the email might be valid, type the Uniform Resource Locator (URL) of the business into your browser rather than clicking the link in the email message to be sure you end up at the correct site.

- **Read each website's privacy policies**   Get in the habit of checking privacy policies before providing your email address to a website. Sure, this can take a minute or two, but it takes more than that to handle the spam that you will get if a site misuses or sells your email address. Most websites explain what they do with the information they collect; you might want to carefully consider whether to provide any information to those that do not.

- **Keep antivirus, spyware, and firewall protection up to date**   Outlook 2010 can help you avoid most junk email and the associated threats, but the most effective protection is a multilayered approach. You should also install firewall and antivirus software and make sure that it is kept up to date. You might also want to obtain utilities that protect against spyware and other malicious software.

Chapter 12

Responding to Messages Automatically

OST of the time, you probably answer your own messages, but no doubt, there are times when you would like Microsoft Outlook 2010 to reply to messages for you automatically. For example, when you are out of the office on vacation, you probably want people who send you messages to receive an automatic reply that you are out but will respond to them when you return.

There are other reasons to set up automatic replies. For example, maybe you are selling something from a website and want people to receive a price list when they send a message to one of your email accounts. Or perhaps you want to send a response when coworkers submit time sheets or other reports to you.

Whatever the case, Outlook 2010 offers several handy features to automate replies. Let's take a look at the easiest one to use—the Out Of Office Assistant.

Creating Automatic Responses with the Out Of Office Assistant

One of the key features in Outlook 2010 that makes it a great email client is the Out Of Office Assistant, which lets you automatically generate replies to incoming messages when you aren't in the office. For example, if you're going on vacation for a couple of weeks and won't be checking your email, you might want to have the Out Of Office Assistant send an automatic reply to let senders know that you'll respond to their messages when you get back; or you might do something similar when you are traveling for the day.

The Out Of Office Assistant is a Microsoft Exchange Server feature. To learn how to create automatic responses with custom rules for use with other email servers, see the section "Creating Automatic Responses with Custom Rules," later in this chapter.

Before you start learning about the Out Of Office Assistant, take a few minutes to consider a few other issues that relate to managing email when you're out of the office.

First, the Out Of Office Assistant is a server-side component for Exchange Server. This means that you can use it to process mail sent to your Exchange Server account but not your POP3, Internet Message Access Protocol (IMAP), or other email accounts unless those accounts deliver incoming messages to your Exchange Server Inbox. You can create rules to process your other accounts and simulate the function of the Out Of Office Assistant, but you must do this by creating custom rules.

Second, because the Out Of Office Assistant functions as a server-side component, it processes your messages even when Outlook 2010 isn't running (a likely situation if you're scuba diving off the Great Barrier Reef for a couple of weeks). To process your other accounts with custom Out Of Office rules, Outlook 2010 must be running and checking your messages periodically. If you have a direct Internet connection, you can configure the rules, configure your send/receive groups to allow Outlook 2010 to check messages for non–Exchange Server accounts periodically, and leave Outlook 2010 running. If you have a dial-up connection to these accounts, you'll have to also configure Outlook 2010 to dial when needed and disconnect after each send/receive operation.

Understanding Out Of Office Assistant Features

The features available in the Out Of Office Assistant depend on the version of Exchange Server that your account resides on. In Exchange Server 2003 and earlier, as soon as you turn on the Out Of Office Assistant, Exchange Server responds to received messages by replying with your specified Out Of Office reply. It continues to send Out Of Office replies until you turn off the Out Of Office Assistant. Exchange Server 2007 and 2010, on the other hand, let you specify the time period when you will be out. You don't have to turn on or turn off the assistant—just specify the start date and end date for the time you will be out of the office, and during that time, Exchange Server will respond with Out Of Office replies.

Another difference in Exchange Server 2007 and 2010 is the capability to specify different behavior for external and internal Out Of Office messages. For example, you might want to offer more information in the Out Of Office message that you send to coworkers, such as who will be handling issues while you are gone, but omit that information from replies sent to people outside your organization. You or your Exchange Server administrator can control how replies are sent to specific external domains. For example, your organization might want to allow Out Of Office replies to go to business partners in specific companies but not to other senders or specific domains, such as Microsoft Hotmail, Yahoo!, and so on. The Out Of Office Assistants in Exchange Server 2007 and 2010 can also be configured not to send replies to junk mail. In addition, you can now use fonts, colors, and formatting in your replies.

> **Note**
> Because the Out Of Office Assistant is a server-side feature, you can take advantage of the Out Of Office Assistant in Exchange Server 2007 and 2010 from other versions of Outlook in addition to Outlook 2010.

Using the Out Of Office Assistant is easy. Here's the process in a nutshell:

1. Specify the text that you want Outlook 2010 to use for automatic replies when you're out of the office.

2. If necessary, create custom rules for the computer running Exchange Server to use to process incoming messages during your absence.

   For information about custom Out Of Office rules, see the section "Creating Custom Out Of Office Rules," later in this chapter.

3. Turn on the Out Of Office Assistant, which causes the Out Of Office Assistant to start responding to incoming messages. Alternatively, if you are using an Exchange Server 2007 or 2010 account, you can specify the Out Of Office Assistant startup time, and Exchange Server will respond accordingly.

4. When you get back, turn off the Out Of Office Assistant so that it stops processing messages (unless you are using Exchange Server 2007 or later, where you can specify the end date for the Out of Office rule).

> **Note**
> When you start Outlook 2010, it checks to see whether the Out Of Office Assistant is turned on. If it is, Outlook 2010 displays a message below the ribbon indicating that Out of Office is turned on. After the Out Of Office Assistant is set up and functioning, messages that arrive in your Inbox receive an Out Of Office response with the message text that you've specified. Exchange Server keeps track of the send-to list and sends the Out Of Office response the first time that a message comes from a given sender. When subsequent messages from that sender are sent to your Inbox, an Out Of Office response is no longer sent. This procedure cuts down on the number of messages generated and keeps the senders from becoming annoyed by numerous Out Of Office replies.

> **Note**
>
> Exchange Server deletes the send-to list for Out Of Office responses when you turn off the Out Of Office Assistant from Outlook 2010.

Using the Out Of Office Assistant with Exchange Server 2003 and Earlier

Follow these steps to specify the text for automatic replies and to tell the computer running Exchange Server 2003 or earlier that you're out of the office:

1. In Outlook 2010, select the Exchange Server Inbox, and then File, Automatic Replies.

2. In the Automatic Replies dialog box, shown in Figure 13-1, type the body of your automatic message reply in the AutoReply box. While the Out Of Office Assistant is active, Exchange Server uses this message to reply to incoming messages.

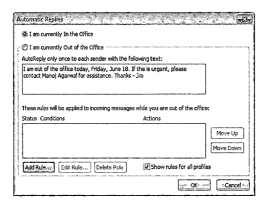

Figure 13-1. Use the Out Of Office Assistant dialog box to specify your automatic message reply.

3. Select I Am Currently Out Of The Office, and then click OK.

Using the Out Of Office Assistant for Exchange Server 2007 and 2010

Follow these steps to specify the text for automatic replies and to tell Exchange Server 2007 or earlier that you're out of the office:

1. In Outlook 2010, select the Exchange Server Inbox, and then click File, Automatic Replies.

2. In the Automatic Replies dialog box, shown in Figure 13-2, click Send Automatic Replies.

Figure 13-2. You can create custom rules to use with the Out Of Office Assistant.

3. Choose Only Send During This Time Range and then use the Start Time drop-down list to specify the starting date and time when you will be out of the office.

4. Use the End Time drop-down list to specify the date and time that you will return to the office.

5. Click in the Inside My Organization box, and then type your Out Of Office reply. If you want to enhance your message, use fonts and other options from the formatting tools on the Out Of Office toolbar.

6. Click the Outside My Organization tab, and then specify the message that you want sent to people outside your organization.

7. When you are satisfied with the message(s), click OK.

> **Note**
> If you want to turn off Out Of Office replies, click File, Automatic Replies, choose Do Not Send Automatic Replies, and click OK.

Creating Custom Out Of Office Rules

With the Out Of Office Assistant, you can create custom rules to use in addition to the basic automatic reply. To create a custom rule, open the Automatic Replies dialog box, click Rules, and then click Add Rule to display the Edit Rule dialog box, shown in Figure 13-3.

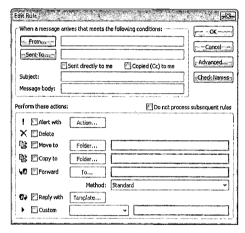

Figure 13-3 You can create custom rules to use with the Out Of Office Assistant.

The options in the Edit Rule dialog box are straightforward, particularly if you're experienced at creating rules. Specify the conditions that the incoming messages should meet, and then specify the action that Exchange Server should perform if a message meets those conditions.

If you need more help creating and using rules, see Chapter 11, "Processing Messages Automatically."

When you define the conditions, keep in mind that the Out Of Office Assistant conditions can be met by either full or partial matches. For example, you could type **yce** in the Sent To box, and the rule would apply if the address contained *Joyce, Boyce,* or *Cayce.* If you want the condition to be met only if the full string is found, enclose the text in quotation marks—for example, type **"Boyce"**.

Creating Automatic Responses with Custom Rules

The Out Of Office Assistant is great for generating automatic replies to messages that arrive in your Inbox when you're out of the office. However, the Out Of Office Assistant sends an Out Of Office response only the first time a message arrives from a given sender. Subsequent messages go into the Inbox without generating an automatic response.

In some cases, you might want Outlook 2010 to generate automatic replies to messages at any time or for other types of accounts that do not use Exchange Server. Perhaps you've set up an Internet email account to take inquiries about a product or service that you're selling. You can create a rule to send a specific reply automatically to messages that come in to that account. Alternatively, you might want people to be able to request information about specific products or topics by sending a message containing a certain keyword in the subject line. In that case, you can create a rule to generate a reply based on the subject of the message.

> **Note**
>
> In Web jargon, applications or rules that create automatic responses are often called *autoresponders*.

You create automatic responses such as these not by using the Out Of Office Assistant, but by creating custom Outlook 2010 rules with the Rules Wizard. As with other rules, you specify conditions that incoming messages must meet to receive a specific reply. For example, you might specify that an incoming message must contain the text *Framistats* in its subject to generate a reply that provides pricing on your line of gold-plated framistats. (Note that the text need not be case-sensitive.)

> **Note**
>
> You aren't limited to specifying conditions only for the subject of an incoming message. You can use any of the criteria supported by the Outlook 2010 rules to specify the conditions for an automatic response.

Setting Up the Reply

When you use a custom rule to create an automatic response, you don't define the reply text in the rule. Rather, you have two options: specifying a template on your local computer or setting up a specific message on the server. If you opt to use a template on your local computer, you create the message in Outlook 2010 and save it as a template file.

Follow these steps to create the template:

1. Begin a new message, and then enter the subject and body but leave the address boxes blank.

> **Note**
>
> Include an address in the Bcc field if you want a copy of all automatic responses sent to you or to another specific address.

2. Click File, and then choose Save As.

3. In the Save As dialog box, specify a path and name for the file, select Outlook Template (*.oft) in the Save As Type drop-down list, and then click Save.

Using a template from your local system causes the rule to function as a client-side rule. As a result, Outlook 2010 can use the rule to process accounts other than your Exchange Server account (such as a POP3 account), but Exchange Server can't generate automatic responses when Outlook 2010 isn't running or is offline.

TROUBLESHOOTING

Your autoresponse rule executes only once

When you create a rule using the Reply Using A Specific Template rule action, Outlook 2010 executes the rule only once for a given sender in each Outlook 2010 session. Outlook 2010 keeps track of the senders in a list and checks incoming messages against the list. For the first message from a given sender that matches the rule conditions, Outlook 2010 generates the response; for subsequent messages, Outlook 2010 doesn't generate the response. This prevents Outlook 2010 from sending repetitive responses to a person who sends you multiple messages that satisfy the rule conditions. Closing and restarting Outlook 2010 refreshes the sender list, and the next message from that sender that meets the criteria generates a response. The Out Of Office Assistant uses the same process—and this behavior is by design.

If you create a server-side rule that uses Have Server Reply Using A Specific Message, Exchange Server creates an autoresponse for all messages that meet the specified conditions, regardless of whether the message is the first from a particular sender.

Creating Automatic Responses from Local Templates

Follow these steps to create a client-side rule that responds to incoming messages with a reply from a template stored locally on your computer:

1. Compose the reply message and save it as a template (.oft) file.

2. Click the Home tab, click Rules, and choose Manage Rules And Alerts to open the Rules And Alerts dialog box.

3. Click New Rule.

4. Select Apply Rule On Messages I Receive, and then click Next.

5. Specify the conditions for the rule (such as Sent Only To Me or Where My Name Is In The To Box), and then click Next.

6. Select Reply Using A Specific Template, and then, in the rule description area, click the A Specific Template link.

7. In the Select A Reply Template dialog box, shown in Figure 13-4, select the template that you want to use for the reply, and then click Open.

> **Note**
> Use the Look In drop-down list to choose the location where the template is stored. You can open templates stored in Outlook or in the file system (including from a network file server).

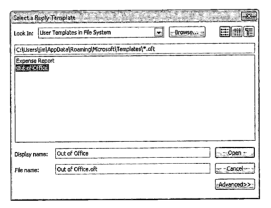

Figure 13-4. Select the message template to use as the reply.

8. Click Next, and then specify exceptions, if any, for the rule.

9. Click Next, specify final options for the rule, specify a name for the rule, and then click Finish.

> **Tip**
>
> By default, Outlook turns on the rule. You can clear the Turn On Rule check box prior to clicking Finish if you don't want the rule enabled right away.

Creating Automatic Responses from the Server

Follow these steps to create a server-side rule to generate automatic responses using a message stored on the server:

1. Click the Home tab, click Rules, and choose Manage Rules And Alerts to open the Rules And Alerts dialog box.

2. Click New Rule.

3. Select Apply Rule On Messages I Receive, and then click Next.

4. Specify the conditions for the rule, and then click Next.

5. Select Have Server Reply Using A Specific Message, and then, in the rule description area, click the A Specific Message link.

6. Create the message using the resulting message form, specifying the subject and text but no addresses (unless you want to copy the reply to a specific address), and then click Save & Close.

7. Click Next, and then specify exceptions, if any, for the rule.

8. Click Next, specify final options for the rule, and then click Finish.

CHAPTER 14

Securing Your System, Messages, and Identity

ICROSOFT Outlook 2010 includes features that can help protect your system from computer viruses and malicious programs, prevent others from using email to impersonate you, and prevent the interception of sensitive messages. Some of these features—such as the ability to block specific types of attachments—were first introduced in Outlook 2002. Other security features—such as the ability to block external images in HTML-based messages—were introduced in Outlook 2003. This feature enables Outlook to block Hypertext Markup Language (HTML) messages sent by spammers to identify valid recipient addresses. These messaging security features were extended and enhanced in Outlook 2007 and are also present in Outlook 2010.

This chapter begins with a look at the settings you can use to control HTML content. Because HTML messages can contain malicious scripts or even HTML code that can easily affect your system, the capability to handle these messages securely in Outlook 2010 is extremely important.

This chapter also discusses the use of both digital signatures and encryption. You can use a digital signature to authenticate your messages, proving to the recipient that a message indeed came from you, not from someone trying to impersonate you. Outlook 2010 enables you to encrypt outgoing messages to prevent them from being intercepted by unintended recipients; you can also read encrypted messages sent to you by others. In this chapter, you'll learn how to obtain and install certificates to send encrypted messages and how to share keys with others so that you can exchange encrypted messages.

Configuring HTML Message Handling

Spammers are always looking for new methods to identify valid email addresses. Knowing that a given address actually reaches someone is one step in helping spammers maintain their lists. If a particular address doesn't generate a response in some way, it's more likely to be removed from the list.

One way that spammers identify valid addresses is through the use of *web beacons*. Spammers often send HTML messages that contain links to external content, such as pictures or sound clips. When you display the message, your mail program retrieves the remote data to display it, and the remote server then validates your address. These external elements are the web beacons.

> **Note**
> Nonspammers also frequently include external content in messages to reduce the size of the message. So external content isn't a bad thing per se (depending on how it is used).

Since Outlook 2003, Outlook blocks external content from HTML messages by default, displaying a red X in the place of the missing content. The result is that these web beacons no longer work because the external content is not accessed when the message is displayed. Messages that fit criteria for the Safe Recipients and Safe Senders lists are treated as exceptions—the external content for these messages is not blocked.

> **Note**
> You can rest the mouse pointer on a blocked image to view the descriptive alternate text (if any) for the image.

When you preview an image in the Reading pane for which Outlook 2010 has blocked external content, Outlook 2010 displays a message in the InfoBar, indicating that the blocking occurred (see Figure 14-1). You can click the InfoBar and choose Download Pictures to view the external content. Outlook 2010 then downloads and displays the content in the Reading pane. The same is true if you open a message; Outlook 2010 displays a warning message, telling you that the content was blocked (see Figure 14-2). You can click the warning message and choose Download Pictures to download and view the content. Because Outlook 2010 blocks external content for messages in this way, you can take advantage of content blocking without using the Reading pane.

If you edit, forward, or reply to a message containing blocked content (from an open message or a message displayed in the Reading pane), Outlook 2010 displays a warning dialog box indicating that the external content will be downloaded if you continue. You can click OK to download the content and continue with the reply or forward, click No to tell Outlook 2010 to forward the content as text without downloading the content, or click Cancel to not open the message or download the content (see Figure 14-3). Thus, you can reply to or forward a message without downloading the external content.

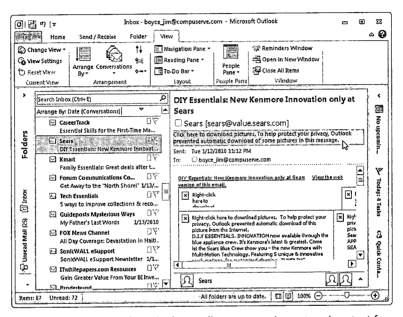

Figure 14-1 Click the InfoBar in the Reading pane to view external content for a selected message.

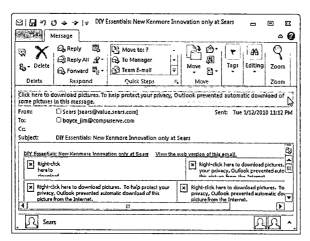

Figure 14-2 You can access blocked content when you open a message by clicking the InfoBar and selecting Download Pictures.

Figure 14-3 You can forward or reply to a message with blocked content without downloading the content.

Outlook 2010 provides a few options to control the way content blocking works. To configure these options, click File, Options, Trust Center, Trust Center Settings, and then click the Automatic Download page. Figure 14-4 shows the resulting Automatic Download settings page.

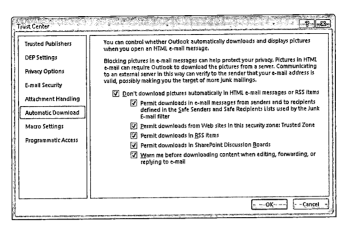

Figure 14-4 Configure content blocking with the Automatic Download settings page.

Configure content blocking using the following options:

- **Don't Download Pictures Automatically In HTML E-Mail Or RSS Items**   Select this check box to allow Outlook 2010 to block external picture content with the exception of messages that fit the Safe Senders and Safe Recipients lists. When selected, this check box enables the five check boxes below it to refine content blocking further.

- **Permit Downloads In E-mail Messages From Senders And To Recipients Defined In The Safe Senders And Safe Recipients List Used By The Junk E-Mail Filter**   Select this check box to allow Outlook to download content if the message is from a sender in your Safe Senders list or is addressed to a recipient in your Safe Recipients list.

- **Permit Downloads From Web Sites In This Security Zone: Trusted Zone**   Select this check box to allow external content from sites in the Trusted Sites zone in Windows Internet Explorer.

- **Permit Downloads In RSS Items**   Select this check box to allow external content included in Really Simple Syndication (RSS) feeds.

- **Permit Downloads In SharePoint Discussion Boards**   Select this check box to allow external content included in SharePoint Discussion Boards.

- **Warn Me Before Downloading Content When Editing, Forwarding, Or Replying To E-Mail**   Select this check box to receive a warning about external content when you edit, reply to, or forward a message for which external content has been blocked.

Chapter 14

To take advantage of the exceptions for external content, you must add the message's originating address to the Safe Senders list, add the recipient address to the Safe Recipients list, or add the remote domain to the Trusted Sites zone in Internet Options (in the Windows Security Center).

For more details on configuring the Safe Recipients and Safe Senders lists, see the section "Enabling and Configuring Junk Email Filtering," on page 334.

Protecting Messages with Digital Signatures

Outlook 2010 supports the use of *digital signatures* to sign messages and validate their authenticity. For example, you can sign a sensitive message digitally so that the recipient can know with relative certainty that the message came from you and that no one is impersonating you by using your email address. This section of the chapter explains digital certificates and signatures and how to use them in Outlook 2010.

Understanding Digital Certificates and Signatures

A *digital certificate* is the mechanism that makes digital signatures possible. Depending on its assigned purpose, you can use a digital certificate for a variety of tasks, including the following:

- Verifying your identity as the sender of an email message

- Encrypting data communications between computers—between a client and a server, for example

- Encrypting email messages to prevent easy interception

- Signing drivers and executable files to authenticate their origin

A digital certificate binds the identity of the certificate's owner to a pair of keys, one public and one private. At a minimum, a certificate contains the following information:

- The owner's public key

- The owner's name or alias

- A certificate expiration date

- A certificate serial number

- The name of the certificate issuer

- The digital signature of the issuer

The certificate can also include other identifying information, such as the owner's email address, postal address, country, or gender.

The two keys are the aspect of the certificate that enables authentication and encryption. The private key resides on your computer and is a large unique number. The certificate contains the public key, which you must give to recipients to whom you want to send authenticated or encrypted messages.

Think of it as having a "read content key" and a "create content key": one key (the private key) lets you create encrypted content, and the other key (the public key) lets others read the content encrypted with the private key.

Outlook 2010 uses slightly different methods for authenticating messages with digital signatures and for encrypting messages, as you'll see later in the chapter. Before you begin either task, however, you must first obtain a certificate.

Obtaining a Digital Certificate

Digital certificates are issued by certification authorities (CAs). In most cases, you obtain your email certificate from a public CA such as VeriSign or Thawte. However, systems based on Windows servers running Certificate Services can function as CAs, providing certificates to clients who request them. Check with your system administrator to determine whether your enterprise includes a CA. If it doesn't, you need to obtain your certificate from a public CA, usually at a minimal cost. Certificates are typically good for one year and must be renewed at the end of that period.

If you need to obtain your certificate from a public CA, point your web browser to the CA website, such as *www.verisign.com* or *www.thawte.com*. Follow the instructions provided by the site to obtain a certificate for signing and encrypting your email (see Figure 14-5, for example). The certificate might not be issued immediately; instead, the CA might send you an email message containing a Uniform Resource Locator (URL) that links to a page where you can retrieve the certificate. When you connect to that page, the CA installs the certificate on your system.

> **Note**
> Alternatively, in the Trust Center, click E-Mail Security, and then click on Get A Digital ID to display a page from the Microsoft website that includes links to several certificate authorities. Select a vendor under Available Digital IDs and click the link to its website to obtain a certificate.

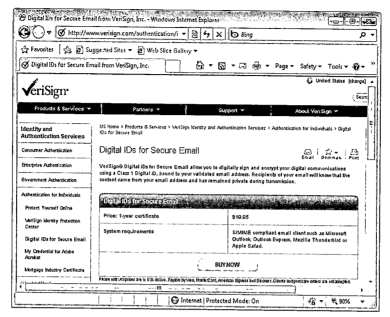

Figure 14-5 You can use the web to request a digital certificate from a public CA.

If you're obtaining a certificate from a CA on your network, the method that you use depends on whether the network includes an enterprise CA or a stand-alone CA.

If you're using Windows Vista or Windows 7 as a domain client on a network with an enterprise CA, follow these steps to request a certificate:

1. Click the Windows button, and then, in the Start Search box, type **MMC**. Click OK.

2. In the Microsoft Management Console (MMC), choose File, Add/Remove Snap-In.

3. In the Add Standalone Snap-In dialog box, select Certificates, and then click Add.

4. In the Certificates Snap-In dialog box, select My User Account, and then click Finish.

5. Click OK to return to the MMC.

6. Expand the Certificates–Current User branch.

7. Expand the Personal branch, right-click Certificates, and choose All Tasks, Request New Certificate. You can also right-click the Personal branch and choose All Tasks, Request New Certificate.

8. Follow the prompts provided by the Certificate Request Wizard and the enterprise CA to request your certificate. The certificate should install automatically.

To request a certificate from a stand-alone CA on your network (or if your computer is part of a workgroup), point your web browser to *http://<server>/certsrv*, where *<server>* is the name or Internet Protocol (IP) address of the CA. The CA provides a web page with a form that you must fill out to request the certificate (see Figure 14-6). Follow the CA prompts to request and obtain the certificate. The site includes a link that you can click to install the certificate.

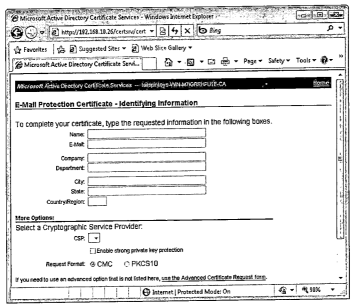

Figure 14-6 A Windows-based CA presents a web form that you can use to request a certificate.

Copying a Certificate to Another Computer

You can copy your certificate from one computer to another, which means that you can use it on more than one system. The process is simple: You first export (back up) your certificate to a file, and then you import the certificate into the other system. The following sections explain how to export and import certificates.

> # Note
>
> As you use the Certificate Import Wizard and the Certificate Export Wizard (discussed in the following sections), you might discover that they don't precisely match the descriptions presented here. Their appearance and operation might vary slightly, depending on the operating system you're running and the version of Internet Explorer you're using.

Backing Up Your Certificate

Whether you obtained your certificate from a public CA or from a CA on your network, you should back it up in case your system suffers a drive failure or if the certificate is lost or corrupted. You also should have a backup of the certificate so that you can export it to any other computers you use on a regular basis, such as a notebook computer or your home computer. In short, you need the certificate on every computer from which you plan to digitally sign or encrypt messages. To back up your certificate, you can use Outlook 2010, Internet Explorer, or the Certificates console. Each method offers the same capabilities; you can use any one of them.

Follow these steps to use Outlook 2010 to back up your certificate to a file:

1. In Outlook 2010, click File, Options, Trust Center, and Trust Center Settings, and then click E-Mail Security in the left pane.

2. Click Import/Export to display the Import/Export Digital ID dialog box, shown in Figure 14-7.

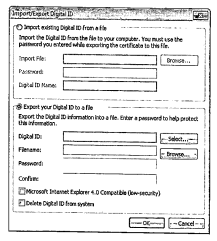

Figure 14-7 You can export certificates in the Import/Export Digital ID dialog box.

3. Select the Export Your Digital ID To A File option. Click Select, choose the certificate to be exported, and click OK.

4. Click Browse and specify the path and file name for the certificate file.

5. Enter and confirm a password.

6. If you plan to use the certificate on a system with Internet Explorer 4, select the Microsoft Internet Explorer 4.0 Compatible (Low-Security) check box. If you use Internet Explorer 5 or later, clear this check box.

7. If you want to remove this Digital ID from this computer, select the check box next to Delete Digital ID From System.

8. Click OK to export the file. The Exporting Your Private Exchange Key dialog box is displayed. Click OK to complete the export process.

If you want to use either Internet Explorer or the Certificates console to back up a certificate, use the Certificate Export Wizard, as follows:

1. If you're using Internet Explorer, begin by choosing Tools, Internet Options. Click the Content tab, and then click Certificates. In the Certificates dialog box, shown in Figure 14-8, select the certificate that you want to back up and click Export to start the wizard. If you're using the Certificates console, begin by opening the console and expanding Certificates–Current User/Personal/Certificates. Right-click the certificate that you want to export, and then choose All Tasks, Export to start the wizard.

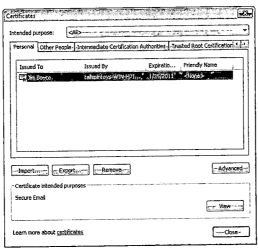

Figure 14-8 You can use the Certificates dialog box to export a certificate.

2. In the Certificate Export Wizard, click Next.

3. On the wizard page shown in Figure 14-9, select Yes, Export The Private Key; then click Next.

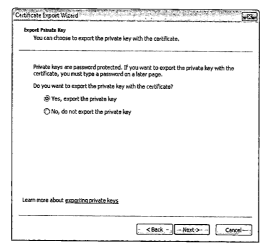

Figure 14-9 The wizard enables you to export the private key.

4. Select Personal Information Exchange; if other options are selected, clear them unless needed. (If you need to include all certificates in the certification path, remove the private key on export, or export all extended properties, and then select that option.) Click Next.

5. Specify and confirm a password to protect the private key and click Next.

6. Specify a path and file name for the certificate and click Next.

7. Review your selections and click Finish.

TROUBLESHOOTING

You can't export the private key

To use a certificate on a different computer, you must be able to export the private key. If the option to export the private key is unavailable when you run the Certificate Export Wizard, it means that the private key is marked as not exportable. Exportability is an option you choose when you request the certificate. If you request a certificate through a local CA, you must select the Advanced Request option to request a certificate with an exportable private key. If you imported the certificate from a file, you might not have selected the option to make the private key exportable during the import. If you still have the original certificate file, you can import it again—this time selecting the option that will enable you to export the private key.

Installing Your Certificate from a Backup

You can install (or reinstall) a certificate from a backup copy of the certificate file by using Outlook 2010, Internet Explorer, or the Certificates console. You must import the certificate to your computer from the backup file.

The following procedure assumes that you're installing the certificate using Outlook 2010:

1. Click File, Options, Trust Center, and Trust Center Settings, and then click E-Mail Security.

2. Click Import/Export to display the Import/Export Digital ID dialog box, shown in Figure 14-7.

3. In the Import Existing Digital ID From A File section, click Browse to locate the file containing the backup of the certificate.

4. In the Password box, type the password associated with the certificate file.

5. In the Digital ID Name box, type a name by which you want the certificate to be shown. Typically, you'll enter your name, mailbox name, or email address, but you can enter anything you want.

6. Click OK to import the certificate.

You can also import a certificate to your computer from a backup file using either Internet Explorer or the Certificates console, as explained here:

1. If you're using Internet Explorer, begin by choosing Tools, Internet Options. Click the Content tab, click Certificates, and then click Import to start the Certificate Import Wizard. If you're using the Certificates console, begin by opening the console. Right-click Certificates–Current User/Personal, and then click All Tasks, Import to start the wizard.

2. In the Certificate Import Wizard, click Next.

3. Browse and select the file to import, and then click Open. (If you don't see your certificate file, check the type of certificates shown in the Open dialog box by clicking the drop-down list to the right of the file name field.) After your certificate is selected in the File To Import dialog box, click Next.

4. If the certificate was stored with a password, you are prompted to enter the password. Provide the associated password and click Next.

5. Select the Automatically Select The Certificate Store Based On The Type Of Certificate option and click Next.

6. Click Finish.

Signing Messages

Now that you have a certificate on your system, you're ready to start digitally signing your outgoing messages so that recipients can verify your identity. When you send a digitally signed message, Outlook 2010 sends the original message and an encrypted copy of the message with your digital signature. The recipient's email application compares the two versions of the message to determine whether they are the same. If they are, no one has tampered with the message. The digital signature also enables the recipient to verify that the message is from you.

> **Note**
> Because signing your email requires Outlook 2010 to send two copies of the message (the unencrypted message and the encrypted copy), the signed email message is larger.

Understanding S/MIME and Clear-Text Options

Secure/Multipurpose Internet Mail Extensions (S/MIME), an Internet standard, is the mechanism in Outlook 2010 that enables you to digitally sign and encrypt messages. The email
client handles the encryption and decryption required for both functions.

Users with email clients that don't support S/MIME can't read digitally signed messages
unless you send the message as clear text (unencrypted). Without S/MIME support, the
recipient is also unable to verify the authenticity of the message or verify that the message
hasn't been altered. Without S/MIME, then, digital signatures are relatively useless. However, Outlook 2010 does offer you the option of sending a digitally signed message as clear
text to recipients who lack S/MIME support. If you need to send the same digitally signed
message to multiple recipients—some of whom have S/MIME-capable email clients and
some of whom do not—digitally signing the message allows those with S/MIME support to
authenticate it, and including the clear-text message allows the others to at least read it.

The following section explains how to send a digitally signed message, including how to
send the message in clear text for those recipients who require it.

Adding Your Digital Signature

Follow these steps to sign an outgoing message digitally:

1. Compose the message in Outlook 2010.

2. On the Options tab, in the More Options group, click the Message Options button (in
   the lower-right corner) to open the Message Options dialog box.

3. Click Security Settings to open the Security Properties dialog box, as shown in Figure
   14-10.

Figure 14-10 You can add a digital signature using the Security Properties dialog box.

4. Select Add Digital Signature To This Message, and then select other check boxes as indicated here:

- **Send This Message As Clear Text Signed**   Select this check box to include a clear-text copy of the message for recipients who don't have S/MIME-capable email applications. Clear this check box to prevent the message from being read by mail clients that don't support S/MIME.

- **Request S/MIME Receipt For This Message**   Select this check box to request a secure receipt to verify that the recipient has validated your digital signature. When the message has been received and saved, and your signature is verified (even if the recipient doesn't read the message), you receive a return receipt. No receipt is sent if your signature is not verified.

5. If necessary, select security settings in the Security Setting drop-down list. (If you have not yet configured your security options, you can do so by clicking Change Settings.)

For details on security option configuration, see the section "Creating and Using Security Profiles," on page 372.

6. Click OK to add the digital signature to the message.

> **Note**
>
> If you send a lot of digitally signed messages, you'll want to configure your security options to include a digital signature by default; see the following section for details. In addition, you might want to add a button to the toolbar to let you quickly sign the message without using a dialog box.

For details about how to add such a button to the toolbar, see the Inside Out sidebar "You need a faster way to sign a message digitally," on page 375.

Setting Global Security Options

To save time, you can configure your security settings to apply globally to all messages, changing settings only as needed for certain messages. In Outlook 2010, click File, Options, Trust Center, Trust Center Settings, and then click E-Mail Security. On the E-Mail Security page, shown in Figure 14-11, you can set security options using the following list as a guide.

- **Encrypt Contents And Attachments For Outgoing Messages** If most of the messages that you send need to be encrypted, select this check box to encrypt all outgoing messages by default. You can override encryption for a specific message by changing the message's properties when you compose it. Clear this check box if the majority of your outgoing messages do not need to be encrypted.

  For information about encryption, see the section "Encrypting Messages," on page 387.

- **Add Digital Signature To Outgoing Messages** If most of your messages need to be signed, select this check box to sign all outgoing messages digitally by default. Clear this check box if most of your messages do not need to be signed; you will be able to sign specific messages digitally as needed when you compose them.

- **Send Clear Text Signed Message When Sending Signed Messages** If you need to send digitally signed messages to recipients who do not have S/MIME capability, select this check box to send clear-text digitally signed messages by default. You can override this option for individual messages when you compose them. In most cases, you can clear this check box because most email clients support S/MIME.

- **Request S/MIME Receipt For All S/MIME-Signed Messages** Select this check box to request a secure receipt for all S/MIME messages by default. You can override the setting for individual messages when you compose them. A secure receipt indicates that your message has been received and the signature verified. No receipt is returned if the signature is not verified.

- **Settings** Select this option to configure more-advanced security settings and create additional security setting groups. For details, see the following section, "Creating and Using Security Profiles."

- **Publish To GAL** Click this button to publish your certificates to the Global Address List (GAL), making them available to other Microsoft Exchange Server users in your organization who might need to send you encrypted messages. This is an alternative to sending the other users a copy of your certificate.

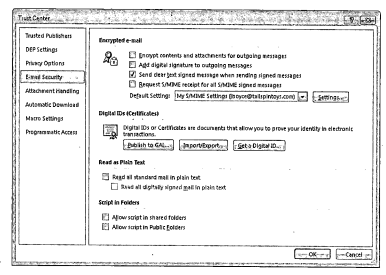

Figure 14-11 Use the E-Mail Security page of the Trust Center to configure options for digital signing and encryption.

Creating and Using Security Profiles

Although in most cases you need only one set of Outlook 2010 security settings, you can create and use multiple security profiles. For example, you might send most of your secure messages to other Exchange Server users and only occasionally send secure messages to Internet recipients. In that situation, you might maintain two sets of security settings: one that uses Exchange Server security and another that uses S/MIME, each with different certificates and hash algorithms (the method used to secure the data).

You can configure security profiles using the Change Security Settings dialog box, which you access through the Settings button on the E-Mail Security page of the Trust Center dialog box. One of your security profiles acts as the default, but you can select a different security profile any time it's needed.

Follow these steps to create and manage your security profiles:

1. In Outlook 2010, click File, Options, Trust Center, Trust Center Settings, and then click E-Mail Security.

2. Click Settings to display the Change Security Settings dialog box, shown in Figure 14-12. Set the options described in the following section as needed. If you are creating a new set of settings, start by clicking New prior to changing settings because selecting New clears all other setting values.

- **Security Settings Name**   Specify the name for the security profile that should appear in the Default Setting drop-down list on the Security tab.

- **Cryptographic Format**   In this drop-down list, select the secure message format for your messages. The default is S/MIME, but you also can select Exchange Server Security. Use S/MIME if you're sending secure messages to Internet recipients. You can use either S/MIME or Exchange Server Security when sending secure messages to recipients on your computer running Exchange Server.

- **Default Security Setting For This Cryptographic Message Format**   Select this check box to make the specified security settings the default settings for the message format you selected in the Cryptography Format drop-down list.

- **Default Security Setting For All Cryptographic Messages**   Select this check box to make the specified security settings the default settings for all secure messages for both S/MIME and Exchange Server security.

- **Security Labels**   Click to configure security labels, which display security information about a specific message and restrict which recipients can open, forward, or send that message.

- **New**   Click to create a new set of security settings.

- **Delete**   Click to delete the currently selected group of security settings.

- **Password**   Click to specify or change the password associated with the security settings.

- **Signing Certificate**   This read-only information indicates the certificate being used to sign your outgoing messages digitally. Click Choose if you want to choose a different certificate. Once you choose a signing certificate, all the fields in the Certificates and Algorithms are populated automatically.

  You assign the default signing and encryption certificates through the global security settings in Outlook 2010; for information, see the section "Setting Global Security Options," on page 370.

- **Hash Algorithm**   Use this drop-down list to change the hash algorithm used to encrypt messages. Hash algorithm options include MD5, SHA1, SHA256, SHA384, and SHA512. For more information on these hashing algorithms, see the following article:

"The .Net Developers Guide Cryptography Overview" (http://msdn.microsoft.com/en-us/library/92f9ye3s.aspx)

- **Encryption Certificate**   This read-only information indicates the certificate being used to encrypt your outgoing messages. Click Choose if you want to specify a different certificate.

- **Encryption Algorithm**   Use this drop-down list to change the encryption algorithm used to encrypt messages. The encryption algorithm is the mathematical method used to encrypt the data.

- **Send These Certificates With Signed Messages**   Select this check box to include your certificate with outgoing messages. Doing so allows recipients to send encrypted messages to you.

3. Click OK to close the Change Security Settings dialog box.

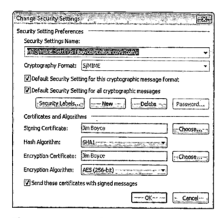

Figure 14-12 Configure your security profiles in the Change Security Settings dialog box.

4. In the Default Setting drop-down list on the E-Mail Security page, select the security profile you want to use by default and then click OK.

INSIDE OUT   You need a faster way to sign a message digitally

If you don't send a lot of digitally signed messages, you might not mind going through all the steps for getting to the Security Properties dialog box to sign a message that you compose. However, if you frequently send digitally signed messages but don't want to configure Outlook 2010 to sign all messages by default, all the clicking involved in signing the message can be onerous. To sign your messages digitally faster, consider adding a toolbar button that lets you toggle a digital signature with a single click by following these steps:

1.   Open the Inbox folder in Outlook 2010.

2.   Click New E-mail to display the message form for a new message.

3.   In the message form, choose the Customize Quick Access Toolbar drop-down list (at the end of the Quick Access Toolbar) and click More Commands.

4.   In the Choose Commands From drop-down list, select All Commands.

5.   In the All Commands list, shown in Figure 14-13, select Digitally Sign Message and click Add, then OK to close the dialog box. The Digitally Sign Message icon will be added to the end of the Quick Access Toolbar. If you later want to switch security profiles, you can select the profile that you want to use in the Default Setting drop-down list on the E-Mail Security page in the Trust Center dialog box.

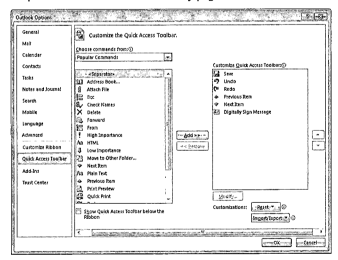

Figure 14-13. Use the Customize The Quick Access Toolbar to add the Digitally Sign Message command to the toolbar.

6.   Close the message form.

Now whenever you need to digitally sign or encrypt a message, you can click the appropriate button on the Quick Access Toolbar when you compose the message.

Reading Signed Messages

When you receive a digitally signed message, the Inbox displays a Secure Message icon in place of the standard envelope icon (see Figure 14-14) and shows a Signature button in the Reading pane. The message form also includes a Signature button (see Figure 14-15). You can click the Signature button in either the Reading pane or the form to display information about the certificate.

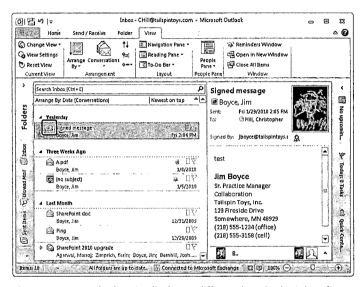

Figure 14-14 Outlook 2010 displays a different icon in the Inbox for secure messages.

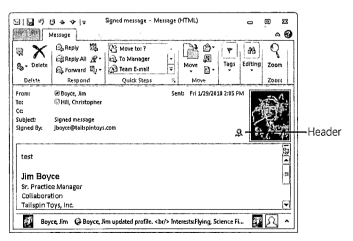

Figure 14-15 Click the Signature button on the message form to view information about the certificate.

Because Outlook 2010 supports S/MIME, you can view and read a digitally signed message without taking any special action. How Outlook 2010 treats the message, however, depends on the trust relationship of the associated certificate. If there are problems with the certificate, you'll see a message to that effect in the Reading pane header, as shown in Figure 14-16. You can click on the Digital Signature button to view more information about the certificate and optionally change its trust.

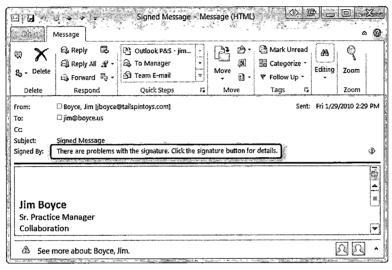

Figure 14-16 Outlook 2010 displays an error message if the digital signature of an incoming message is not trusted or there are other problems with the signature.

There is no danger per se in opening a message with an invalid certificate. However, you should verify that the message really came from the person listed as the sender and is not a forged message.

Changing Certificate Trust Relationships

To have Outlook 2010 authenticate a signed message and treat it as being from a trusted sender, you must add the certificate to your list of trusted certificates. An alternative is to configure Outlook 2010 to inherit trust for a certificate from the certificate's issuer. For example, assume that you have a CA in your enterprise. Instead of configuring each sender's certificate to be trusted explicitly, you can configure Outlook 2010 to inherit trust from the issuing CA—in other words, Outlook 2010 will trust implicitly all certificates issued by that CA.

Follow these steps to configure the trust relationship for a certificate:

1. In Outlook 2010, select the signed message. Click the Digital Signature button to view the Digital Signature dialog box (see Figure 14-17). The dialog box varies depending on whether the signature is valid (trusted) or invalid (not trusted).

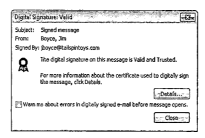

Figure 14-17 Use the Digital Signature dialog box to view status and properties of the certificate.

2. Click Details, and in the Message Security Properties dialog box, click the Signer line, and then click Edit Trust to display the Trust tab of the View Certificate dialog box, as shown in Figure 14-18.

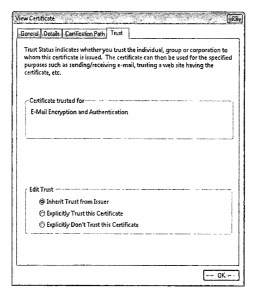

Figure 14-18 Use the Trust tab to configure the trust relationship for the certificate.

3. Select one of the following options:

- **Inherit Trust From Issuer**   Select this option to inherit the trust relationship from the issuing CA. For detailed information, see the following section, "Configuring CA Trust."

- **Explicitly Trust This Certificate**   Select this option to trust explicitly the certificate associated with the message if you are certain of the authenticity of the message and the validity of the sender's certificate.

- **Explicitly Don't Trust This Certificate**   Select this option to distrust explicitly the certificate associated with the message. Any other messages that you receive with the same certificate will generate an error message in Outlook 2010 when you attempt to view them.

4. Click OK, click Close to close the Message Security Properties dialog box, and click Close again to close the Digital Signature dialog box.

For information on viewing a certificate's other properties and configuring Outlook 2010 to validate certificates, see the section "Viewing and Validating a Digital Signature," on page 384.

Configuring CA Trust

Although you might not realize it, your computer system by default includes certificates from several public CAs (typically VeriSign, Thawte, Equifax, GTE, or several others), which were installed when you installed your operating system. By default, Outlook 2010 and other applications trust certificates issued by those CAs without requiring you to trust explicitly each certificate issued by the CA.

The easiest way to view these certificates is through Internet Explorer, as follows:

1. In Internet Explorer, choose Tools, Internet Options, and then click the Content tab. Alternatively, open the Internet Options item from the Control Panel.

2. Click Certificates to open the Certificates dialog box (see Figure 14-19). Click the Trusted Root Certification Authorities tab, which contains a list of the certificates.

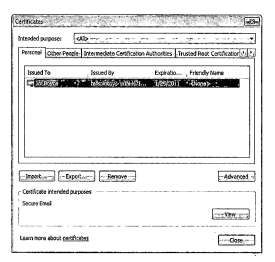

Figure 14-19 You can view a list of certificates in the Certificates dialog box in Internet Explorer.

If you have a personal certificate issued by a specific CA, the issuer's certificate is installed on your computer. Messages you receive that are signed with certificates issued by the same CA inherit trust from the issuer without requiring the installation of any additional certificates. If you have not yet obtained the CA certificate from your Enterprise CA, you need to add that CA's certificate to your system before certificates issued by that CA will be trusted.

Follow these steps to connect to a Windows-based enterprise CA to obtain the CA's certificate and install it on your system:

1. Point your web browser to *http://<*machine>*/certsrv*, where *<machine>* is the name or IP address of the CA.

2. After the page loads, select Download A CA Certificate, Certificate Chain, Or CRL.

3. Select Download CA Certificate, and then choose to Open (at this point, you could also save it to your computer if you want to save the certificate file for later use).

4. Click Install Certificate to install the CA's certificate on your system. This will start the Certificate Import Wizard. Click Next.

5. In the Certificate Store dialog box, select Automatically Select The Certificate Store Based Upon The Type Of Certificate. Click Next and then click Finish to add the CA certificate. You will be notified that the import was successful and will have to click OK twice to close the dialog boxes.

The procedure just outlined assumes that the CA administrator has not customized the certificate request pages for the CA. If the pages have been customized, the actual process you must follow could be slightly different from the one described here.

> **Note**
>
> If you prefer, you can download the CA certificate instead of installing it through the browser. Use this alternative when you need to install the CA certificate on more than one computer and must have the certificate as a file.

Configuring CA Trust for Multiple Computers

The process described in the preceding section is useful when configuring CA trust for a small number of computers, but it can be impractical with a large number of computers. In these situations, you can turn to Group Policy to configure CA trust in a wider area such as an organizational unit (OU), a domain, or an entire site.

You can create a certificate trust list (CTL), which is a signed list of root CA certificates that are considered trusted, and deploy that CTL through Group Policy. This solution requires that you be running the Active Directory Domain Services (AD DP) with desktop clients running Windows XP or later as domain members.

> **Tip**
>
> The steps in this section for creating and deploying a CTL are for Windows Server 2008. If you are running Windows Server 2003, open the AD Users and Computers console, and create a new Group Policy Object (GPO) or edit an existing GPO. In the Group Policy Editor, expand the branch User Configuration\Windows Settings\Security Settings\Public Key Policies\Enterprise Trust, right-click Enterprise Trust, and choose New, Certificate Trust List to start the Certificate Trust List Wizard.

Follow these steps on Windows Server 2008 to create and deploy the CTL:

1. Log on to a domain controller and open the Group Policy Management console.

2. Create a new GPO or edit an existing GPO at the necessary container in AD DS, such as an OU. Select the GPO and in the right pane, click More Actions, Edit.

3. In the Group Policy Management Editor, expand the branch User Configuration\ Policies\Windows Settings\Security Settings\Public Key Policies\Enterprise Trust.

4. Right-click Enterprise Trust and choose New, Certificate Trust List to start the Certificate Trust List Wizard.

5. Click Next, and then specify a name and valid duration for the CTL (both optional), as shown in Figure 14-20. Select one or more purposes for the CTL in the Designate Purposes list (in this example, choose Secure Email), and then click Next.

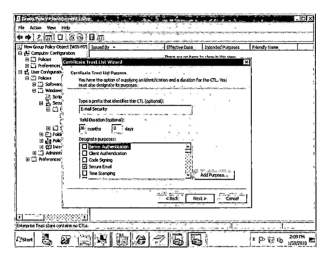

Figure 14-20 Select a purpose for the CTL and other properties, such as a friendly name for easy identification.

6. On the Certificates In The CTL page (see Figure 14-21), click Add From Store to add certificates to the list from the server's certificate store. Choose one or more certificates and click OK.

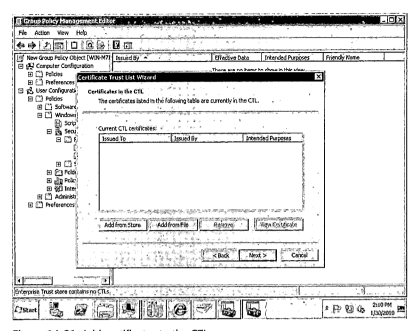

Figure 14-21 Add certificates to the CTL.

7. If the certificates are stored in an X.509 file, Microsoft Serialized Certificate Store, or PKCS #7 certificate file, click Add From File, select the file, and click Open.

8. Back on the Certificates In The CTL page, click Next. On the Signature Certificate page, select a certificate to sign the CTL. The certificate must be stored in the local computer certificate store instead of the user certificate store. Click Next after you select the certificate.

9. If you want, you can choose the Add A Timestamp To The Data option and specify a timestamp service URL if one is available. Otherwise, click Next.

10. If you want, enter a friendly name and description for the CTL to help identify it, click Next, and click Finish.

Viewing and Validating a Digital Signature

You can view the certificate associated with a signed message to obtain information about the issuer, the person to whom the certificate is issued, and other matters.

To do so, follow these steps:

1. Open the message and click the Digital Signature button in either the Reading pane or the message form; and then click Details to display the Message Security Properties dialog box, which provides information about the certificate's validity in the Description box.

2. Click Signer in the list to view additional signature information in the Description box, such as when the message was signed (see Figure 14-22).

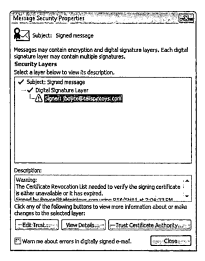

Figure 14-22 The Description box offers information about the validity of the certificate.

3. Click View Details to open the Signature dialog box, shown in Figure 14-23, which displays even more detail about the signature.

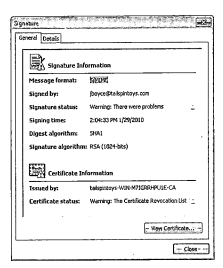

Figure 14-23 Use the Signature dialog box to view additional properties of the signature and to access the certificate.

4. On the General tab of the Signature dialog box, click View Certificate to display information about the certificate, including issuer, certification path, and trust mode.

5. Click OK, click Close to close the Message Security Properties dialog box, and click Close again to close the Digital Signature dialog box.

The CA uses a certificate revocation list (CRL) to indicate the validity of certificates. If you don't have a current CRL on your system, Outlook 2010 can treat the certificate as trusted, but it can't validate the certificate and will indicate this when you view the signature.

You can locate the path to the CRL by examining the certificate's properties as follows:

1. Click the Signature button for the message, either in the Reading pane or in the message form, and then click Details.

2. In the Message Security Properties dialog box, click Signer and then click View Details.

3. On the General tab of the Signature dialog box, click View Certificate and then click the Details tab (see Figure 14-24).

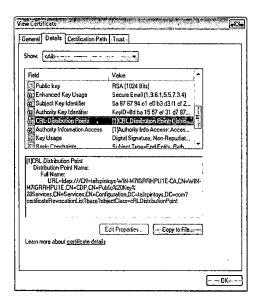

Figure 14-24 Use the Details tab to view the CRL path for the certificate.

4. Scroll through the list to find and select CRL Distribution Points.

5. Scroll through the list in the lower half of the dialog box to locate the URL for the CRL.

When you know the URL for the CRL, you can point your browser to the site to download and install the CRL. If a CA in your enterprise issued the certificate, you can obtain the CRL from the CA.

To obtain and install the CRL, follow these steps:

1. Point your browser to *http://<*machine*>/certsrv*, where *<machine>* is the name or IP address of the server.

2. Select the Retrieve The CA Certificate Or Certificate Revocation List option and click Next.

3. Click Download Latest Certificate Revocation List and save the file to disk.

4. After downloading the file, locate and right-click the file, and then choose Install CRL to install the current list.

Encrypting Messages

You can encrypt messages to prevent them from being read by unauthorized persons. Of course, it is true that with significant amounts of computing power and time, any encryption scheme can probably be broken. However, the chances of someone investing those resources in your email are pretty remote. So you can be assured that the email encryption that Outlook 2010 provides offers a relatively safe means of protecting sensitive messages against interception.

Before you can encrypt messages, you must have a certificate for that purpose installed on your computer. Typically, certificates issued for digital signing can also be used for encrypting email messages.

For detailed information on obtaining a personal certificate from a commercial CA or from an enterprise or stand-alone CA on your network, see the section "Obtaining a Digital Certificate," on page 361.

Getting Ready for Encryption

After you've obtained a certificate and installed it on your system, encrypting messages is a simple task. Getting to that point, however, depends in part on whether you're sending messages to an Exchange Server recipient on your network or to an Internet recipient.

Swapping Certificates

Before you can send an encrypted message to an Internet recipient, you must have a copy of the recipient's public key certificate. To read the message, the recipient must have a copy of your public key certificate, which means you first need to swap public certificates.

> **Note**
> When you are sending encrypted messages to an Exchange Server recipient, you don't need to swap certificates. Exchange Server takes care of the problem for you.

The easiest way to swap certificates is to send a digitally signed message to the recipient and have the recipient send you a signed message in return, as outlined here:

1. In Outlook 2010, click File, Options, Trust Center, Trust Center Settings, and then click the E-Mail Security link.

2. Click Settings to display the Change Security Settings dialog box.

3. Verify that you've selected S/MIME in the Cryptography Format drop-down list.

4. Select the Send These Certificates With Signed Messages option and click OK.

5. Click OK to close the Trust Center dialog box.

6. Compose the message and digitally sign it. Outlook 2010 will include the certificates with the message.

When you receive a signed message from someone with whom you're exchanging certificates, you must add the person to your Contacts folder to add the certificate by following these steps:

1. Open the message, right-click the sender's name, and then choose Add To Outlook Contacts. If the Reading pane is displayed, you can right-click the sender's name in the pane and choose Add To Outlook Contacts.

2. Outlook 2010 displays the Contact tab of the contact form (see Figure 14-25). Fill in additional information for the contact as needed.

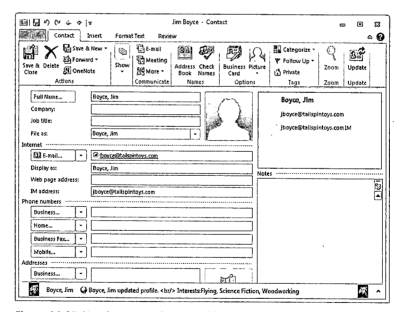

Figure 14-25 Use the contact form to add the sender's certificate to your system.

3. Click the Certificates button (in the Show group of the Contact tab). You should see the sender's certificate listed (see Figure 14-26), and you can view the certificate's properties by selecting it and clicking Properties. If no certificate is listed, contact the sender and ask for another digitally signed message.

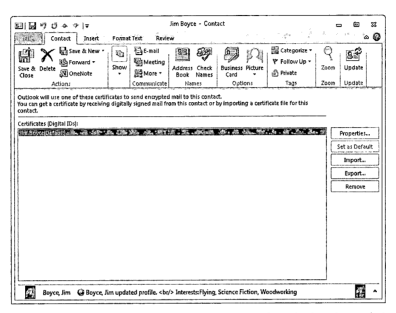

Figure 14-26 The Certificates button on the contact form displays the sender's certificate.

4. Click Save & Close to save the contact item and the certificate.

Obtaining a Recipient's Public Key from a Public CA

As an alternative to receiving a signed message with a certificate from another person, you might be able to obtain the person's certificate from the issuing CA. For example, if you know that the person has a certificate from VeriSign, you can download that individual's public key from the VeriSign website. Other public CAs offer similar services. To search for and download public keys from VeriSign (see Figure 14-27), connect to *https://digitalid. verisign.com/services/client/index.html*. Check the sites of other public CAs for similar links that enable you to download public keys from their servers.

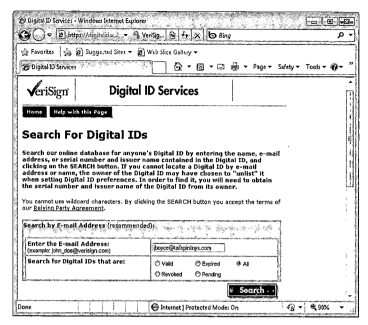

Figure 14-27 VeriSign, like other public CAs, provides a form you can use to search for and obtain public keys for certificate subscribers.

The process for downloading a public key varies by CA. In general, however, you enter the person's email address in a form to locate the certificate, and the form provides instructions for downloading the certificate. You should have no trouble obtaining the public key after you locate the certificate on the CA (there is a link to download the public key certificate from the CA to a file on your computer).

Save the public key to disk, and then follow these steps to install the key:

1. Open the Contacts folder in Outlook 2010.

2. Locate the contact for whom you downloaded the public key.

3. Open the contact item, and then click Certificates.

4. Click Import. Browse to and select the certificate file obtained from the CA and click Open.

5. Click Save & Close to save the contact changes.

Sending Encrypted Messages

When you have everything set up for sending and receiving encrypted messages, it's simple to send one. Just do the following:

1. Open Outlook 2010 and compose the message.

2. On the Options tab, click the Message Options button in the lower-right section of the More Options group to display the Message Options dialog box, and then click Security Settings.

3. Select Encrypt Message Contents And Attachments, and then click OK.

4. Click Close, and then send the message as you normally would.

5. If the message is protected by Exchange Server security, you can send it in one of three ways, depending on your system's security level:

   - If the security level is set to Medium (the default), Outlook 2010 displays a message informing you of your security setting. Click OK to send the message.

   - If the security level is set to Low, Outlook 2010 sends the message immediately, without any special action on your part.

   - If the security level is set to High, type your password to send the message.

> **Note**
> To make it easier to encrypt a message, you can add the Encrypt command to the Quick Access Toolbar in the message form. For details about the process involved in doing this, see the Inside Out sidebar "You need a faster way to sign a message digitally," on page 375.

Reading Encrypted Messages

When you receive an encrypted message, you can read it as you would read any other message, assuming that you have the sender's certificate. Double-click the message to open it. Note that Outlook 2010 uses an icon with a lock instead of the standard envelope icon to identify encrypted messages.

> **Note**
>
> You can't preview encrypted messages in the Reading pane. Also, the ability to read encrypted messages requires an S/MIME-capable mail client. Keep this in mind when sending encrypted messages to other users who might not have Outlook 2010 or another S/MIME-capable client.
>
> You can verify and modify the trust for a certificate when you read a message signed by that certificate. For information on viewing and changing the trust for a certificate, see the section "Changing Certificate Trust Relationships," on page 377.

Importing Certificates from Outlook Express

If you have used Microsoft Windows Mail or Microsoft Outlook Express to send and receive secure messages, your Windows Mail Contacts (or Outlook Express address book) contains the public keys of the recipients. You can import those certificates to use in Outlook 2010 if they are not already included in the Contacts folder. Unfortunately, Windows Mail and Outlook Express don't export the certificates when you export their address books; instead, you must export the certificates one at a time.

Follow these steps to move certificates from Windows Mail, Windows Live Mail, or Outlook Express to Outlook 2010:

1. Open Windows Mail and select Tools, Windows Contacts. If using Outlook Express, choose Tools, Address Book. For Windows Live Mail, choose Go, Contacts.

2. In Windows Contacts (for Windows Mail), the Address book (for Outlook Express), or Windows Live Contacts (Windows Live Mail) double-click the name of the person whose certificate you want to export.

3. Click the IDs tab in Windows Mail, or the Digital IDs tab in Outlook Express.

4. Select the certificate to export and click Export.

5. Save the certificate to a file. (Windows Mail and Outlook Express use the .cer file extension.)

6. Open Outlook 2010, open the Contacts folder, and open the contact item for the person who owns the certificate you're importing.

7. Click Certificates, click Import, select the file created in step 5, and click Open.

8. Save and close the contact form.

Protecting Data with Information Rights Management

In response to market demands for a system andwith which companies can protect proprietary and sensitive information, Microsoft has developed an umbrella of technologies called Information Rights Management (IRM). Outlook 2010 incorporates IRM, enabling you to send messages that prevent the recipient from forwarding, copying from, or printing the message. The recipient can view the message, but the features for accomplishing these other tasks are unavailable.

> **Note**
>
> IRM is an extension for the Microsoft Office system applications of Windows Rights Management. For information on using IRM with other Office applications, see *2010 Microsoft Office System Inside Out*, from Microsoft Press.

There are two paths to implementing IRM with the Office system. Microsoft offers an IRM service that, as of this writing, is free. This path requires that you have a Windows Live ID to send or view IRM-protected messages. You must log in to the service with your Windows Live ID credentials to download a certificate, which Outlook 2010 uses to verify your identity and enable the IRM features. The second path is to install Microsoft Windows Server 2003 running the Rights Management Service (RMS) on Windows Server 2003, or the Active Directory Rights Management Service on Windows Server 2008. With this path, users authenticate on the server with NTLM or Windows Live ID authentication and download their IRM certificates.

The first path provides simplicity because it does not require that organizations deploy an RMS server. The second path provides more flexibility because the RMS administrator can configure company-specific IRM policies, which are then available to users. For example, you might create a policy template requiring that only users within the company domain can open all email messages protected by the policy. You can create any number of templates to suit the company's data rights needs for the range of Office system applications and document types.

Not everyone who receives an IRM-protected message will be running Outlook 2003 or later, so Microsoft has developed the Rights Management Add-On for Internet Explorer, which enables these users to view the messages in Internet Explorer. Without this add-on, recipients cannot view IRM-protected messages. With the add-on, recipients can view the messages, but the capability to forward, copy, or print the message is disabled, just as it is in Outlook 2010.

> **Note**
>
> This chapter explains how to configure and use IRM in Outlook 2010 with the Microsoft IRM service. If you want to use RMS in Windows Server, you will find more information by searching *technet.microsoft.com* for "Active Directory Rights Management Services." RMS provides a much richer set of features and control than the free service offered by Microsoft, but it is beyond the scope of this book.

Using Microsoft's IRM Service

To configure Outlook 2010 to use the IRM service and send IRM-protected messages, follow these steps:

1. Open Outlook 2010 and start a new message. With the message form open, click File, Set Permissions, Do Not Forward.

2. If you do not have the IRM add-on installed, Outlook 2010 displays the dialog box shown in Figure 14-28. Choose Yes, I Want To Sign Up For This Free Service From Microsoft, and then click Next.

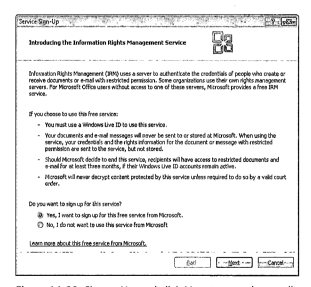

Figure 14-28 Choose Yes and click Next to start the enrollment process.

3. The wizard asks if you already have a Windows Live ID. If so, choose Yes and click Next to open a sign-in dialog box and enter your Windows Live credentials. If not, choose No and click Next; then follow the prompts to obtain a Windows Live ID.

4. After you obtain a Windows Live ID and log on, Outlook 2010 displays the page shown in Figure 14-29. Choose This Is A Private Computer to obtain a certificate that you can use on your own computer. Choose This Is A Public Or Shared Computer if you need a certificate only for a limited time, such as when you are working from a public computer. Then click Accept, Finish to complete the process.

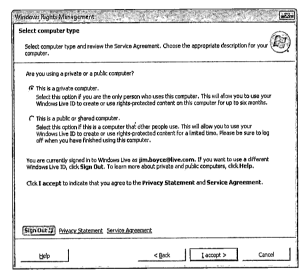

Figure 14-29 You can choose between a standard certificate and a temporary one.

> ## Note
> You can download a certificate for a given Microsoft Passport 25 times, or to 25 computers.

5. Outlook displays the Select User dialog box, which in this case will likely contain only one user (the one that you just created). Click OK.

6. Click the Message tab and note that the InfoBar in the form displays a Do Not Forward message, as shown in Figure 14-30, indicating that the message is protected by IRM.

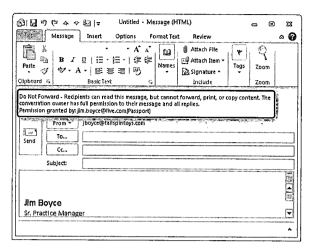

Figure 14-30 The InfoBar indicates when a message is protected by IRM.

7. Address the message and add the message body and attachments, if any, as you would for any other message, and then send the message.

Viewing IRM-Protected Messages

If you attempt to view an IRM-protected message without first obtaining a certificate, Outlook 2010 gives you the option of connecting to Microsoft's service to obtain one. After the certificate is installed, you can view the message, but Outlook 2010 indicates in the InfoBar (on both the Reading pane and message form) that the message is restricted (see Figure 14-31). The commands for forwarding, copying, and printing the message are disabled.

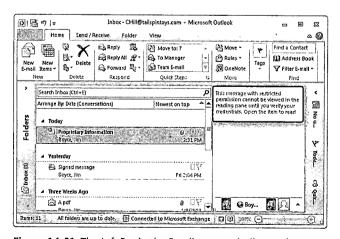

Figure 14-31 The InfoBar in the Reading pane indicates that a message is restricted.

Working with Multiple Accounts

It's possible that you use more than one Windows Live ID. If you have more than one Windows Live ID and need to choose between them when you send or view an IRM-protected message, open the message form for sending or viewing and click File, Set Permissions, Manage Credentials to open the Select User dialog box, as shown in Figure 14-32. Choose an account and click OK to use that account for the current message.

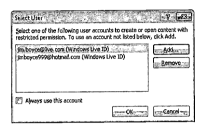

Figure 14-32 You can select from multiple accounts to restrict messages or view restricted messages.

If you have only one account configured on the computer and want to add another account, click Add to start the Service Sign-Up Wizard and download a certificate for another email address and corresponding Passport.

IKE earlier versions of Microsoft Outlook, Outlook 2010 includes a feature called *remote mail* that allows you to manage your email messages without downloading them from the server. Although you might not believe that you need yet another way to retrieve your messages, remote mail offers advantages that you'll come to appreciate over time.

Originally, remote mail was primarily a feature for Microsoft Exchange Server, but the Remote Mail feature for Exchange Server is removed in Outlook 2010 and replaced by the functionality in Cached Exchange Mode. However, non–Exchange Server accounts can take advantage of similar capabilities (which, for the sake of simplicity, this chapter refers to generically as *remote mail*). For example, you can download just message headers to review your messages before downloading the message bodies and attachments.

This chapter focuses specifically on using remote mail features in Outlook 2010. It explains how to set up your system to use remote mail for Internet Message Access Protocol (IMAP) and POP3 accounts, how to manage your messages through remote mail, and how to use alternatives to remote mail, such as send/receive groups.

Understanding Remote Mail Options

The primary advantage of using remote mail is the ability to work with the message headers of waiting messages without downloading the messages themselves. You can simply connect to the email server, download the headers for new messages, and disconnect. You can then take your time reviewing the message headers to decide which messages to download, which ones to delete without reading, and which ones to leave on the server to handle later. After you've made your decisions and marked the headers accordingly, you can connect again and download those messages you've marked to retrieve, either leaving the others on the server or deleting them.

Remote mail is extremely useful when you are pressed for time but have a message with a large attachment waiting on the server. You might want to retrieve only your most critical messages without spending the time or connect charges to download that message and its attachment. To accomplish this, you can connect with remote mail and select the messages that you want to download, leaving the one with the large attachment on the server until a less busy time when you can download it across the network or through a broadband Internet connection.

Remote mail is also useful when you discover a corrupt message in your mailbox, a message with a very large attachment, or a message that you suspect could be infected with a virus, and that message might otherwise prevent Outlook 2010 from downloading other messages. You can connect with remote mail, delete the offending message without downloading it, and then continue working normally.

> **Note**
> Remote mail works only for the Inbox with POP3 accounts; you can't use it to synchronize other folders. As explained later in this chapter, IMAP offers more flexibility.

Remote Mail in a Nutshell

The Remote Mail features in Outlook are much onethe same for POP3 and IMAP accounts. However, there are a few differences in the results. For example, for a POP3 account, after you download a message header, Outlook will not download the message automatically if the Reading pane is open and you click the message header. With an IMAP account, Outlook does download the message.

Another difference is that with a POP3 account, marking a message to download will cause the message to be downloaded to your computer and removed from the server. With IMAP accounts, the messages always remain on the server until you delete them. If you want to leave a copy of the message on the server for a POP3 account, mark the message to download a copy instead.

Finally, IMAP accounts offer additional capabilities for working with message headers that POP3 accounts do not, such as the capability to synchronize more than just the Inbox folder.

Working with Message Headers

The following sections explain the specific steps to follow as you perform various tasks with message headers through remote mail. You'll learn how to download the headers, how to mark them selectively, and how to process them.

Downloading Message Headers

When you want to process messages selectively, you first download the message headers and then decide what action you want to perform with each message based on its header. Downloading message headers for an account is easy. In Outlook 2010, click the Send/ Receive tab, click Send/Receive Groups, *<Account>* Only, Download Inbox Headers, where *<Account>* is the name of the account whose headers you want to download.

After you choose the Download Inbox Headers command, Outlook 2010 performs a send/ receive operation but downloads only message headers from the specified account. If you use a dialup connection, you can then disconnect from the server to review the headers and decide what to do with each message.

Outlook 2010 displays the downloaded message headers in the Inbox. Outlook 2010 displays an icon in the Header Status column to indicate that the message has not yet been downloaded, as shown in Figure 15-1. A message header that has not been marked for download shows a sheet of paper with the corner folded over. A message marked for download shows the same icon but with an arrow at the bottom.

Figure 15-1 Outlook 2010 places an icon in the Header Status column to indicate that the message itself has yet to be downloaded.

Marking and Unmarking Message Headers

After you download the headers, you can decide what to do with each message: retrieve it, download a copy, or delete it.

Marking to Retrieve a Message

To mark a message to be downloaded from the server to your local store, select the message header, click the Send/Receive tab, and choose Mark To Download. Alternatively, you can right-click the message header and choose Mark To Download.

> **Note**
> To select multiple message headers quickly, hold down the Ctrl or Shift key while you click the message headers.

Marking to Retrieve a Copy

In some cases, you might want to download a copy of a message but also leave the message on the server—for example, you might need to retrieve the same message from a different computer. To mark a message header to have Outlook 2010 retrieve a copy, select the message header, click the Send/Receive tab, click the arrow beside Mark to Download, and choose Mark To Download Message Copy. Outlook 2010 indicates in the Header Status column of the Inbox that the message is marked for download by changing the message icon accordingly, as shown in Figure 15-2.

Figure 15-2 This message is marked to have Outlook 2010 retrieve a copy.

> **Note**
> As explained earlier, it isn't necessary to download a copy from an IMAP account, as those servers continue to store a copy of the message on the server. Downloading a copy is applicable only to POP3.

> **Note**
> So that you can identify the pending action easily, Outlook 2010 displays different icons in the Header Status column of the Inbox for messages marked to download and messages marked to download a copy.

Marking to Delete a Message

You also can mark messages to be deleted from the server without downloading. You might do this for junk mail or messages with large attachments that you don't need and don't want choking your download session.

To mark a message for deletion, select the message header, right-click it, and choose Delete or press the Delete key. Outlook 2010 strikes through the message header and changes the download icon to indicate that the message will be deleted the next time you process messages, as shown in Figure 15-3.

Figure 15-3 A strikethrough indicates that the message will be deleted without downloading.

Unmarking a Message

As you work with message headers, you'll occasionally change your mind after you've marked a message. In that case, you can unmark the message. Select the message header, right-click it, and then choose Unmark To Download. Alternatively, you can click the Send/Receive tab and click Unmark To Download.

You also can unmark all message headers, clearing all pending actions. To do so, click the Send/Receive tab, click the arrow beside Unmark To Download, and choose Unmark All to Download.

Processing Marked Headers

After you've reviewed and marked the message headers, you can process the messages to apply the actions that you've chosen. When you do so, for example, messages marked for download are downloaded to your system, and messages marked for deletion are deleted from the server.

To process all marked messages, click the Send/Receive tab and then click Process Marked Headers. Outlook 2010 connects and performs the specified actions.

Selective Downloading for IMAP Accounts

IMAP accounts offer some features for selective processing that are not available with POP3 accounts, primarily the capability to download headers from multiple folders (not just the Inbox, as with a POP3 account). Outlook gives you the option of downloading message headers from all your subscribed folders.

To configure these settings, click the Send/Receive tab on the ribbon, click Send/Receive Groups, and choose Define Send/Receive Groups. Select the send/receive group that you want to modify for your IMAP account and click Edit. Select the IMAP account in the accounts list, and then note that Outlook gives you the option of selecting multiple folders for download (see Figure 15-4).

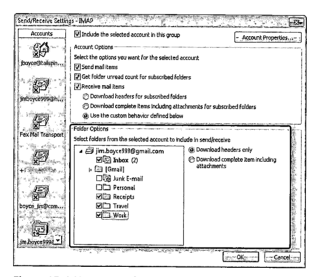

Figure 15-4 You can configure Outlook to download headers for multiple folders in your IMAP mailbox.

You can configure the send/receive group to download headers for all subscribed folders, download the complete item and attachments for subscribed folders, or choose the custom option and specify a selection of folders.

Selective Downloading for POP3 Using Send/Receive Groups

Using send/receive groups in Outlook 2010 gives you additional options for selective message processing with POP3 accounts. You can configure a POP3 account in a send/receive group to download only headers, for example, or to download only those messages smaller than a specified size while retrieving only headers for larger messages. If you prefer to process your POP3 account selectively—perhaps because you connect over a dial-up connection, or because you want to delete unwanted messages before they arrive in your Inbox, or because you need to control which messages are downloaded—you can use a send/receive group to process the account.

For details on setting up send/receive groups, see the section "Controlling Synchronization and Send/Receive Times," on page 197.

Let's assume that your profile includes two POP3 accounts: your main work account and a personal account. You want to download complete items for your work account, but download only headers for your personal account. The solution is to configure a send/receive group accordingly.

> **Note**
> You can't use send/receive groups for selective processing with Hotmail accounts.

You can configure multiple send/receive groups, using different settings for each (although some settings, such as Exchange Server filters, apply to all send/receive groups to which the folder belongs). For example, you might configure your POP3 accounts in the All Accounts send/receive group to download message bodies and attachments, but create a second send/receive group named POP3 Remote, which processes only message headers for your POP3 accounts when that group is executed.

Retrieving Only Message Headers

After you decide which combination of send/receive groups makes the most sense for you, follow these steps to configure a POP3 account to retrieve only message headers and then process the headers:

1. In Outlook 2010, click the Send/Receive tab, click Send/Receive Groups, and choose Define Send/Receive Groups.

2. Select the existing send/receive group in which you want to configure POP3 accounts for headers only (or create a group for that purpose), and then click Edit.

3. In the Accounts list in the Send/Receive Settings dialog box, shown in Figure 15-5, click the POP3 account.

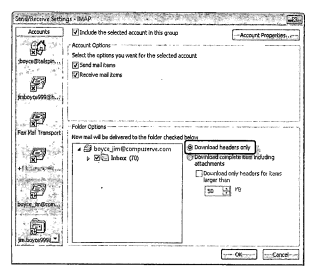

Figure 15-5 You can configure a POP3 account to download only headers.

4. If you are creating a new group, select the Include The Selected Account In This Group check box.

5. Select the Download Headers Only option.

6. If you don't want the group to send messages from the selected POP3 account, clear the Send Mail Items check box.

7. Click OK, and then close the Send/Receive Groups dialog box.

8. Click Send/Receive, Send/Receive Groups, and then select the group to be processed according to the settings that you specified in the preceding steps. Outlook 2010 then downloads message headers.

9. Review and mark the downloaded message headers, and then click Process Marked Headers on the Send/Receive tab to process the messages.

Retrieving Based on Message Size

You can configure a POP3 account in a send/receive group to specify a message size limit. Messages that meet or are below the specified size limit are downloaded in their entirety, complete with attachments. For messages larger than the specified size, only headers are downloaded. This is an easy way to restrict the volume of incoming POP3 mail and keep large messages from choking a low-bandwidth connection such as a dial-up connection.

Follow these steps to configure a POP3 account in a send/receive group to download headers only for messages over a specified size:

1. In Outlook 2010, click the Send/Receive tab, and then click Send/Receive Groups, Define Send/Receive Groups.

2. Select or create the send/receive group, and then click Edit.

3. Select the POP3 account in the Accounts list in the Send/Receive Settings dialog box, and then select the Download Complete Item Including Attachments option.

4. Select Download Only Headers For Items Larger Than *n* KB, as shown in Figure 15-6.

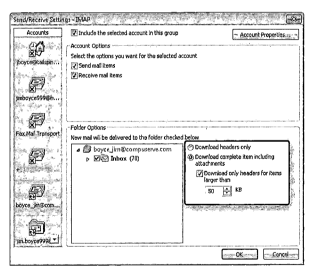

Figure 15-6 You can specify a message size limit to control connect time and mail volume.

5. Enter a value to define the message size limit, and then click OK.

6. Click Close to close the Send/Receive Groups dialog box.

Keeping Messages on the Server

Often you'll want to keep a copy of your messages on the server and download a copy. For example, you might be checking your messages from the office but want to be able to retrieve them from home or from your notebook computer. Or perhaps you're using remote mail to process a few important messages and want to leave copies on the server for safekeeping. You can configure the account to leave a copy of all messages on the server, allowing you to retrieve the messages again from another system.

When you configure a POP3 account to retain messages on the server, you also can specify that the messages must be removed after they've been on the server for a designated period of time. Alternatively, you could have Outlook 2010 delete the messages from the server when you delete them from your Deleted Items folder, which prevents the messages from being downloaded again from the server after you've deleted your local copies.

Here's how to configure these options for POP3 accounts:

1. In Outlook 2010, click File, Account Settings, and Account Settings.

2. Select the E-Mail tab.

3. Select the POP3 account, and then choose Change.

4. Click More Settings, and then click the Advanced tab, shown in Figure 15-7.

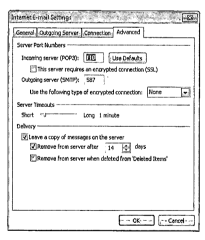

Figure 15-7 Use the Advanced tab to configure the account to leave messages on the server.

5. Select the Leave A Copy Of Messages On The Server check box, and then select one of the two associated check boxes (or both) if needed. Click OK.

6. Click Next, and then click Finish.

CHAPTER 16

Using RSS Feeds

ICROSOFT Outlook 2010, like Outlook 2007 before it, supports Really Simple Syndication (RSS)—a feature that gives the ability to integrate external information provided by content publishers (such as news websites) into a folder in Outlook 2010. The information is transmitted in a particular Extensible Markup Language (XML) format (described as an *RSS feed*). To use this information, you configure Outlook 2010 to subscribe to the RSS feeds that provide the stories or information that you want. These stories (or other RSS-provided information) are stored in a feed-specific folder under the RSS Feeds folder in Outlook 2010.

Understanding RSS

RSS is essentially an XML-based means to format news stories and other dynamically changing Web content so that RSS-aware software applications can access and retrieve this content automatically. Many web browsers, such as Windows Internet Explorer, have a built-in RSS-aware component (sometimes called a *news aggregator* or a *news reader*) that can connect to RSS feed locations and retrieve RSS-formatted content. Using such a feed in Outlook 2010 is easy, because you simply paste in the Uniform Resource Locator (URL) to the RSS feed that you want to retrieve, and Outlook 2010 takes care of the rest.

RSS is also referred to as *web content syndication*, where users subscribe to the content that they want from news sites (and other websites providing dynamic information). In this case, a subscription is not like signing up for a newsletter, where you have to provide an email address for the information to be sent to. Rather, to subscribe to RSS feeds, you only have to locate the URL for the specific feed that you want and configure your RSS reader (in this case, Outlook 2010) to connect to that URL. The RSS reader will retrieve the information (news articles, or other dynamic content) automatically from the site.

> **Note**
> Some RSS feeds might require you to log in to an account with a user name and password to retrieve the RSS feed.

Configuring RSS

Setting up RSS feeds in Outlook 2010 is very easy to do—simply decide which sites you want to get RSS feeds from, determine the appropriate URL for the RSS feed from that site, and provide that URL to Outlook 2010. Each website creates its own URL format for delivering RSS content. Consider the following examples of RSS feed URLs:

- **MSDN Web site**   *msdn.microsoft.com/rss.xml*

- **Seattle Times**   *seattletimes.nwsource.com/rss/home.xml*

- **Google News**   *news.google.com/nwshp?hl=en&tab=wn&q=&output=rss*

- **CNN Top Stories**   *rss.cnn.com/rss/cnn_topstories.rss*

Adding RSS Feeds to Outlook

To add a new RSS feed from a site to your Outlook 2010 RSS Feeds folder, you will first have to determine the appropriate URL for the site or for the specific feed from the site (as many sites have more than one RSS feed). Typically, RSS feeds are indicated by an RSS feed icon on the page.

To add a new RSS feed to Outlook 2010, do the following:

1. Right-click the RSS Feeds folder in the Navigation pane, and then select Add A New RSS Feed, as shown in Figure 16-1.

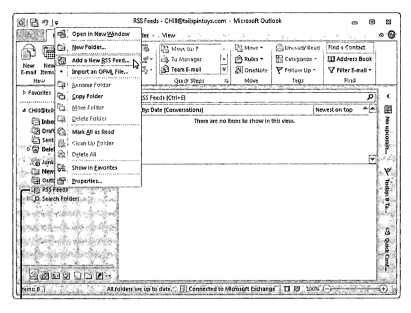

Figure 16-1 Right-click the RSS Feeds folder to begin adding a new feed.

2. The New RSS Feed dialog box is displayed, as shown in Figure 16-2. This is the location to type (or paste) the URL of the RSS feed that you want to add. In this example, the URL for the MSDN Web site RSS feed is used. Click Add to add the URL of the new RSS feed.

Figure 16-2 Enter the URL of the new RSS feed that you want to add.

3. You are then asked to confirm whether to add this URL as a new RSS feed and warned that you should add RSS feeds only from sources that you trust, as shown in Figure 16-3. Clicking Yes adds the RSS feed using default values.

Figure 16-3 A verification is requested, with an Advanced option for additional control over the RSS feed.

4. Click Advanced to access further control over the RSS feed. Once the site is accessed, the RSS Feed Options dialog box is displayed, as shown in Figure 16-4, enabling you to change the following aspects of the RSS feed:

   - **General**   The General area displays the name of the feed (as shown in Outlook 2010), the Channel Name, the Location (the URL entered to access the RSS feed), and the Description provided by the RSS feed source. The Feed Name box lets you change the name of the feed displayed in the Outlook 2010 RSS Feeds folder.

   - **Delivery Location**   The Delivery Location area displays the location within the Outlook 2010 mailbox as well as the path on the drive and the file name of the Outlook 2010 data file storing the folder. Clicking the Change Folder button in this area opens the New RSS Feed Delivery Location dialog box, which lets you create a new folder or select a new Outlook 2010 data file to store the RSS feeds in.

   - **Downloads**   The Downloads area includes two options specifying how Outlook 2010 deals with downloading RSS information (both are not selected by default): The Automatically Download Enclosures For This Feed option enables the automatic downloading of attachments connected to articles in this feed. The Download The Full Article As An .html Attachment To Each Item option instructs Outlook 2010 to handle the articles in this RSS feed automatically by downloading the complete articles as .html attachments.

   - **Update Limit**   The Update This Feed With The Publisher's Recommendation check box in the Update Limit area (selected by default) sets the timing of updates to the RSS feed to be controlled by the publisher, using the update time specified by the source of the RSS feed.

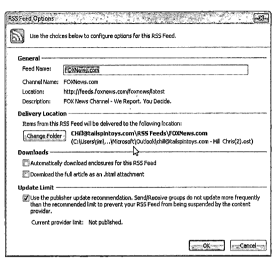

Figure 16-4 The RSS Feed Options dialog box lets you set the name, location, and update limit as well as control what is downloaded in the RSS feed.

5. After you have completed setting the options in the RSS Feed Options dialog box, click OK to return to the confirmation dialog box shown in Figure 16-3. Click Yes to confirm the addition of the RSS feed.

Using Your RSS Feeds

After the RSS feeds have been added, you can begin to use them to access the information provided in the feed. To get to the RSS-provided information, click the Folder icon at the bottom of the Navigation pane and then scroll down to the RSS Feeds folder. The feeds that you have configured will appear under the RSS Feeds folder, as shown in Figure 16-5, and will display the title of the feed and the number of unread articles in parentheses following the title.

Selecting the specific RSS feed that you are interested in will display the list of articles. Selecting a specific article will display the summary of the article in the Reading pane with links to the complete article. You can right-click the item and choose Download Content, Download Article. Outlook downloads the article, which then appears as a Hypertext Markup Language (HTML) attachment to the item (see Figure 16-6). Double-click the attachment to view the item in your browser. If you have already downloaded the item, right-click it and choose Download Content, Update Article to get an updated copy of the item.

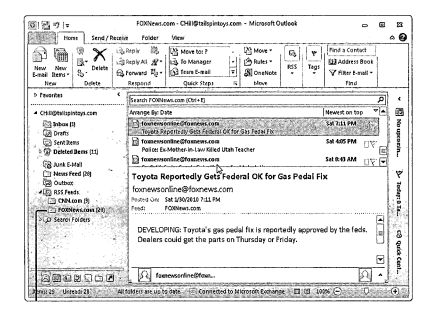

Figure 16-5 Selecting a particular RSS feed displays a list of downloaded articles from that site.

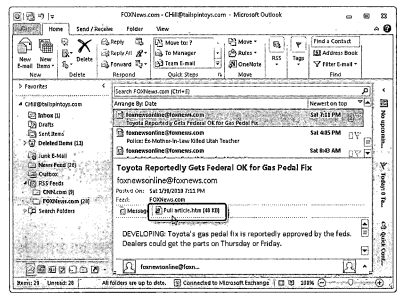

Figure 16-6 A downloaded item appears as an .html attachment to the item.

You can also click the View Article link in the item if you simply want to open a browser to display the item from its website.

You can perform common message-oriented actions on RSS feed messages. For example, you can forward them, mark them as read or unread, categorize them, apply Quick Steps to them, and so on, just as you can for other types of messages in a message folder.

Adding an OPML File to Outlook

Outline Processor Markup Language (OPML) is a popular means of exchanging lists of RSS feeds, enabling sites to provide a set of RSS feeds to subscribers in a single file. OPML is another XML-based format, one specifically designed to handle information structured as an outline, yet it also has been successfully used to handle lists of RSS feeds.

To add an OPML-based list of RSS feeds to Outlook 2010, follow these steps:

1. Right-click the RSS Feeds folder in the Navigation pane, and then choose Import An OPML File, as shown in Figure 16-7.

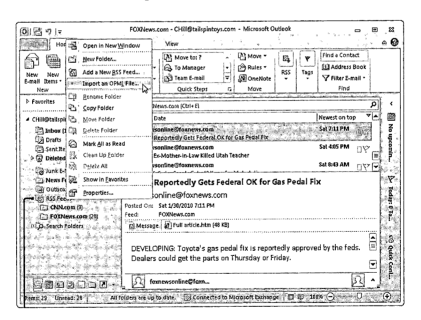

Figure 16-7 Importing a list of RSS feeds via an OPML file.

2. The Import An OPML File Wizard is displayed, as shown in Figure 16-8. Browse to the location on your computer or network that contains the OPML file with the list of RSS feeds, select the file, and then click OK.

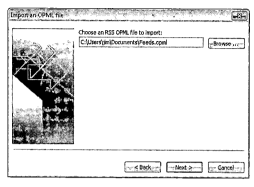

Figure 16-8 Select the OPML file containing the RSS feeds.

3. After selecting the OPML file, the Import An OPML File wizard displays a list of RSS feeds that the OPML file contains, as shown in Figure 16-9, and enables the selection of each RSS feed to be added to your Outlook 2010 RSS Feeds folder. Select each desired RSS feed in the list by clicking the check box next to the feed (or click the Select All button to select all of them). After you have selected all the RSS feeds that you want, click Next.

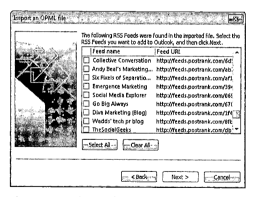

Figure 16-9 Choose the RSS feeds to import.

4. Click Finish to return to Outlook 2010, and then go to the RSS Feeds folder to review the new RSS feeds added through the OPML file.

Managing Your RSS Feeds

Once you have your RSS feeds set up, you might want to change aspects of how the RSS feeds are configured, such as changing the URL that the RSS feed is derived from, changing how it downloads enclosures, or changing how other users can access a particular RSS feed on your computer.

You can configure options for controlling RSS feeds in Outlook 2010 in several ways. To control how Outlook 2010 handles all RSS feeds, click File, Options, and then click Advanced to display the Advanced page of the Options dialog box, shown in Figure 16-10. On this page, you'll find the following two options that affect RSS feeds:

- **Synchronize RSS Feeds To The Common Feed List (CFL) In Windows**   If this option is enabled, feeds that you add in Outlook are synchronized to a common feed list (CFL) available to Internet Explorer 7 or later, as well as other programs that can use the CFL. Likewise, feeds that you add from IE are added to Outlook automatically.

- **Any RSS Feed Item That Is Updated Appears As New**   If an item has been updated, Outlook marks it as unread again.

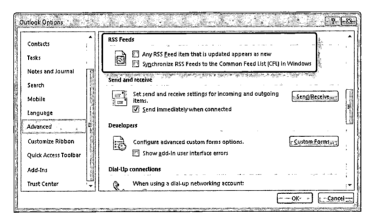

Figure 16-10 Configure the handling of RSS feed items and synchronization on the Advanced page of the Options dialog box.

To change the configuration of an RSS feed once it has been set up, click File, Account Settings, and then choose Account Settings. In the Account Settings dialog box, click the RSS Feeds tab, shown in Figure 16-11, select the RSS feed that you want to modify, and then click Change.

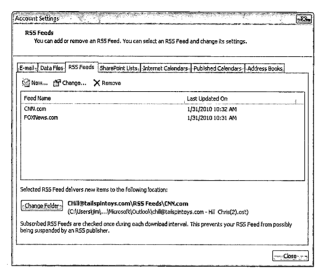

Figure 16-11 Select the RSS Feeds tab to change an RSS feed configuration.

The name of the RSS feed can be modified in the RSS Feed Options dialog box, shown in Figure 16-12, and the Channel Name, Location, and Description are displayed. You can change the mailbox folder as well as the mail storage file in which the RSS feed is contained by clicking Change Folder. The Downloads area includes controls for how RSS downloads are handled, including the Automatically Download Enclosures For This RSS Feed and the Download The Full Article As An .html Attachment To Each Item options. Although the Update Limit option to use the publisher's recommendation for update frequency is selected, this option can be disabled, allowing you to update the feed manually. For more information about configuring these options, see the section "Adding RSS Feeds to Outlook," on page 410.

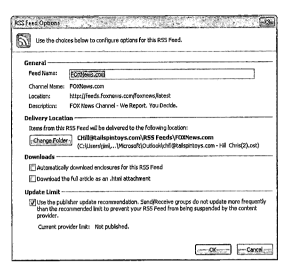

Figure 16-12 The RSS Feed Options dialog box lets you control the name, the storage location, and how the RSS download is managed.

You can also enable or disable downloads in RSS feeds in the Trust Center, on the Automatic Downloads page, where you can select or clear the Permit Downloads In RSS Items check box.

Setting RSS Properties

A core set of configuration controls for RSS feeds is available on the Properties dialog box accessible in the RSS Feeds folder (and all RSS folders created under it). To set these RSS configuration options, right-click the RSS Feeds folder (or the desired subfolder), and then choose Properties. Note that only a few of the tabs are applicable to RSS feeds, and those tabs are the ones described in this section.

The General tab, as shown in Figure 16-13, enables you to set the name of the RSS folder and the description, as well as whether to display the number of all items or just unread items. In addition, you can configure the form used in posting to the RSS folder, and display the folder size (on both the local computer and the server). Clicking Clear Offline Items removes the data from the offline data store.

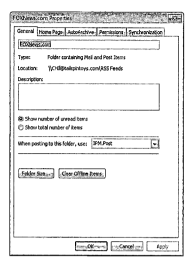

Figure 16-13 The General tab of the RSS Feeds Properties dialog box enables setting RSS folder properties.

To control the archiving of RSS feeds, you select the AutoArchive tab in the RSS Feeds Properties dialog box, shown in Figure 16-14, and then configure the archiving settings to your preference. The default is not to archive the RSS items, but you can configure the Archive This Folder Using These Settings option to set the time limit (the point at which Outlook 2010 cleans out items older than the set period). After you have set the archive time limit, you can configure where archived items are moved.

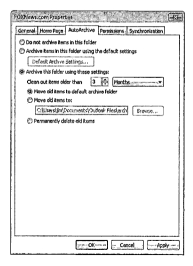

Figure 16-14 Set the archive option, time limit, and archive location for this RSS feed.

The Synchronization tab lets you set the synchronization filter for the RSS feed. Click Filter to display the Filter dialog box, and then select the filter criteria to apply to the offline copy of the RSS items associated with this folder.

Creating Rules for RSS Feeds

Outlook includes a couple of rule conditions that you can use to create rules for your RSS feeds. For example, even though the messages for a given RSS feed arrive in their own folder by default, you might want those messages moved to a different folder; or perhaps you are watching a particular topic and want items related to that topic to pop into your Inbox, where you will see them right away.

You create a rule for RSS items in the same way that you create them for other message items, such as searching for text in the body or subject. There are two RSS-specific conditions you can use as well:

- **From RSS Feeds With The Specified Text In The Title**   Use this condition to process RSS items that come from a specific feed, searching for the feed name in the title.

- **From Any RSS Feed**   Use this condition to process all RSS feed items.

For other RSS processing, use the conditions that you would normally use for message items. For example, if you want to track a specific topic, use the With Specific Words In The Subject Or Body condition, and then specify the topic word or phrase in the rule's condition. Then, provide the applicable action, such as moving the item to your Inbox.

Lᵢₓₕₜᵥₑᵢₘₜ IGHTWEIGHT Directory Access Protocol (LDAP) is a standard method for querying directory services. For example, you can query LDAP servers for the address, phone number, or other information associated with an entry in the directory. Windows Server uses LDAP as the primary mechanism for accessing Active Directory Domain Services (AD DS).

This chapter explores LDAP and explains how to configure LDAP directory service accounts in Microsoft Outlook 2010.

Overview of LDAP Services

LDAP was designed to require less overhead and fewer resources than its predecessor, Directory Access Protocol (DAP), which was developed for X.500, a standards-based directory service. LDAP is a standards-based protocol that allows clients to query data in a directory service over a Transmission Control Protocol (TCP) connection. AD DS, Novell eDirectory, IBM WebSphere, and directory services on the Internet such as Bigfoot, Info-Space, and Yahoo! all employ LDAP to implement searches of their databases.

You will find much more information about LDAP at *technet.microsoft.com* if you perform a search for "LDAP" or "Lightweight Directory Access Protocol."

Configuring a Directory Service Account in Outlook

In addition to supporting email accounts, Outlook 2010 also allows you to add LDAP-based directory service accounts that enable you to query for subscriber information in the remote server's directory. The LDAP server might be internal to your organization, hosted by another company, or one of several LDAP directories located on the Internet. With an LDAP account in your profile, you can look up names, addresses, and other information stored in the directory.

To set up and configure an LDAP account in Outlook 2010, follow these steps:

1. Open the Mail item in Control Panel and click E-mail Accounts. Alternatively, if Outlook 2010 is already started, click File, Account Settings, and Account Settings.

2. Select the Address Books tab, and then click New.

3. Select Internet Directory Service (LDAP), and then click Next.

4. On the Directory Service (LDAP) Settings page of the Add New E-Mail Account wizard, shown in Figure 17-1, type the server name or the Internet Protocol (IP) address in the Server Name box.

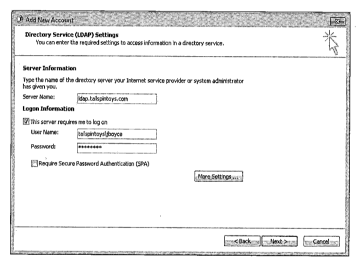

Figure 17-1 Specify the server name, and supply logon credentials if the server requires authentication.

5. If the server requires authentication, select the This Server Requires Me To Log On check box. Specify the logon credentials in the User Name and Password boxes. If you're authenticating on a Windows Server domain controller, include the domain by entering <domain>\<user> in the User Name box, where *<domain>* is the domain name and *<user>* is the user account.

INSIDE OUT   Add the domain for LDAP authentication

Failing to include the domain in the authentication string will result in the authentication error message "Failed to connect to <server> due to invalid authentication." If you clear the This Server Requires Me To Log On check box and the server requires authentication, you'll receive the error message "No entries were found. You may need to supply authentication information in order to be able to access the directory." Clear this check box only if the server allows anonymous LDAP queries.

6. Click More Settings to open the Microsoft LDAP Directory dialog box, shown in Figure 17-2.

Figure 17-2 Change the display name, port, and other properties as needed.

7. Change the name in the Display Name box to the name that you want Outlook 2010 to display in the address book for the directory service.

8. In the Port box, type the port number required by the LDAP server. The default port is 389, although you can use 3268 for most searches in an AD DS global catalog (GC).

INSIDE OUT   Use two ports

Port 3268 is the default port for the AD DS GC. Certain types of data are available through one specific port, whereas other types of data are accessed through the other. For example, read-only copies of data from other domains are available only through the GC port. For that reason, you might create two directory services, one for each port.

9. You can select the Use Secure Sockets Layer (SSL) check box to connect to the LDAP server through SSL. This option works only if the server allows an SSL connection. If using SSL, the default port is 636 (or 3269 for the GC).

10. In the Microsoft LDAP Directory dialog box, click the Search tab, shown in Figure 17-3.

Figure 17-3 Use the Search tab to configure the time-out, number of hits to return, and the search base.

11. Specify the search time-out and the maximum number of entries you want returned in a search. In the Search Base box, either select Use Default (the Users container) or type the root for your search in the directory. If you're searching AD DS, for example, you might enter **dc=**<domain>**,dc=**<suffix>, where <domain> is your domain name (without the domain suffix). Specify the domain suffix (net, com, org, or us, for example) as the last data item. (See the following section, "Setting the Search Base," for more details.) To be able to browse the directory, select the Enable Browsing (Requires Server Support) check box. The AD DS domain controller must allow browsing for this feature to work.

12. Click OK to close the dialog box, and then click Next and click Finish to complete the account setup.

> **Note**
>
> Queries to AD DS using SSL should be directed to port 636. GC queries using SSL should be directed to port 3269.

You can use the directory service accounts created in Outlook 2010 to perform LDAP queries from within Outlook 2010.

Setting the Search Base

The search base for an LDAP query specifies the container in the directory service where the query will be performed. You can set the search base to target more closely the information that you're trying to find, but to do so, you must understand what the search base really is. (For AD DS queries, you can generally use the Default search base to locate users.)

Each entry in the directory has a Distinguished Name (DN), which is a fully qualified name that identifies that specific object. Relative Distinguished Names (RDNs) are concatenated to form the DN, which uniquely identifies the object in the directory. RDNs include the following:

- **cn=**   Common name
- **ou=**   Organizational unit
- **o=**   Organization
- **c=**   Country
- **dc=**   Domain

> **Note**
>
> AD DS drops the *c=* attribute and adds the *dc=* attribute.

For example, assume that you want to search the Users container in the domain tailspin-toys.com. The search base would be as follows:

cn=users,dc=tailspintoys,dc=com

Notice that the domain is represented by two *dc* attributes. If the domain that you are searching is microsoft.com, you would use *dc=microsoft,dc=com* instead.

In some cases, the part of the directory you want to search will be in a specific organizational unit (OU), or you might be setting up multiple LDAP accounts in Outlook 2010, each configured to search a specific OU. For example, perhaps your company has Sales, Marketing, Support, External Contacts, and a handful of other OUs, and you want to configure an LDAP query for each one. One solution is to add an LDAP service for each and configure the search base accordingly. For example, let's say we're configuring an LDAP service account to query the Support OU in the tailspintoys.com domain. The search base would be as follows: *ou=support,dc=tailspintoys,dc=com*.

Keep the following points in mind when deciding on a search base:

- Specifying no search bases causes Outlook 2010 to retrieve objects from the entire directory.

- Specifying a search base sets the branch of the directory to search in the directory tree.

If you decide to include a search base, determine the common name for the object or OU, and then add the domain. You can't specify just the *ou* or *cn* attribute without the domain, but you can specify the domain by itself to perform a top-down search of the domain.

> **Note**
> If you need to search different branches of the directory tree, you can add multiple LDAP service accounts to your profile, each with the appropriate search base. Alternatively, add only one LDAP service account and then simply change its search base when you need to query a different branch.

TROUBLESHOOTING

Your LDAP query returns this error message: "There are no entries in the directory service that match your search criteria"

Sooner or later, you'll attempt to query an LDAP server that you know contains at least one item meeting your search criteria, but you'll receive an error message telling you that no entries in the directory service match your criteria. One possible cause of this problem is that the search option specified at the LDAP server might be preventing the query from completing successfully. For example, you might be issuing an "any" query, but the server is configured to treat such queries as initial queries.

You might also receive this error message if you've incorrectly set the LDAP directory service account properties—for example, you might have configured the account to use port 389 when the server requires SSL. Check your directory service account settings to ensure that you have specified the proper server name or address, port, and search base.

Using LDAP to Find People

You can perform LDAP queries in Outlook 2010 by using directory service accounts you add to Outlook 2010. Follow these steps to perform an LDAP query with an LDAP server in Outlook 2010:

1. In Outlook 2010, click Address Book on the Home tab of the ribbon to open the Address Book window.

2. In the Outlook Address Book, select the directory service in the Address Book drop-down list. Depending on how the directory service account is configured (whether or not Enable Browsing is enabled), Outlook 2010 might display the contents of the directory immediately in the Address Book. When browsing is enabled, Outlook can access directory information and display it in the Address Book automatically. For information about how to enable browsing, see the section "Configuring a Directory Service Account in Outlook," on page 423, and Figure 17-3. If Enable Browsing is not selected, no names will be listed. Type your search keywords and click Go to perform a search.

3. To search using specific criteria, click the Advanced Find link or choose Tools, Find. Either action opens the Find dialog box, shown in Figure 17-4.

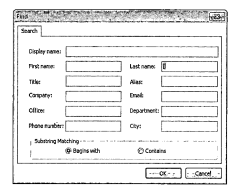

Figure 17-4 Use the Find dialog box to specify the criteria for the LDAP query.

4. Specify the criteria for the search, and then click OK. If objects meeting the search criteria exist within the LDAP directory, the results will show a list of all matching objects.

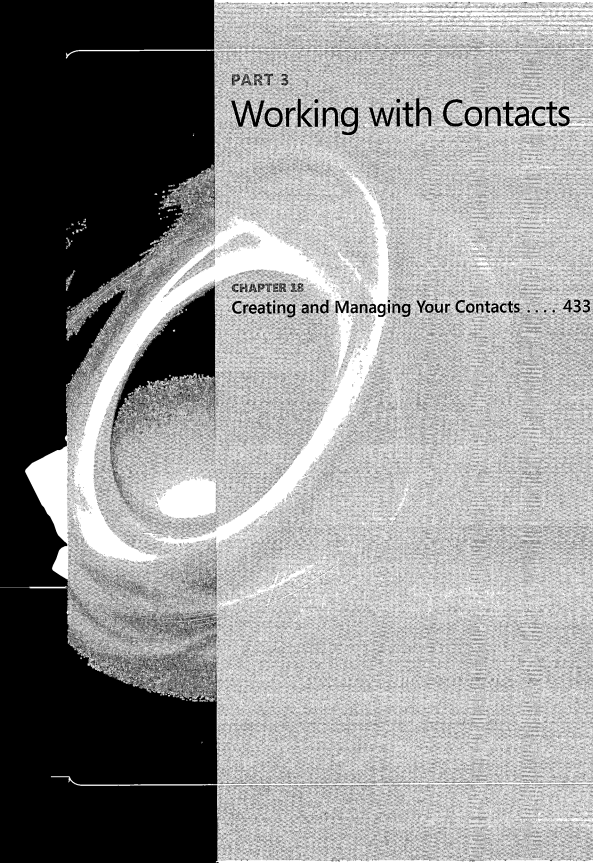

PART 3

Working with Contacts

T HE Contacts folder in Microsoft Outlook 2010 is an electronic tool that can organize and store the thousands of details you need to know to communicate with
people, businesses, and organizations. You can use the Contacts folder to store email
addresses, street addresses, multiple phone numbers, and any other information that relates
to a contact, such as a birthday or an anniversary date.

From a contact entry in your list of contacts, you can click a button or choose a command
to have Outlook 2010 address a meeting request, an email message, a letter, or a task
request to the contact. If you have a modem, Voice over Internet Protocol (VoIP) phone,
Office Communicator, or other online conferencing application, you can have Outlook 2010
dial the contact's phone number. You can link any Outlook 2010 item or Microsoft Office
2010 system document to a contact to help you track activities associated with the contact.

Outlook 2010 allows you to customize the view in the Contacts folder to review and print
your contact information. You can sort, group, or filter your contacts list to better manage
the information or to quickly find entries.

Outlook 2010 integrates well with Microsoft Windows SharePoint Services (WSS) and
Microsoft SharePoint Server, both of which provide the means for users to share documents, contacts, messages, and other items through a web-based interface. You can export
contacts from Outlook 2010 to a SharePoint site, or vice versa.

Outlook 2010 also supports the use of vCards, the Internet standard for creating and sharing virtual business cards. You can save a contact entry as a vCard and send it in an email
message. You can also add a vCard to your email signature.

This chapter discusses contact management in Outlook 2010. The Outlook 2010 Contacts feature provides powerful tools to help you manage, organize, and find important contact information.

Working with the Contacts Folder

The Contacts folder is one of the Outlook 2010 default folders. This folder stores information such as name, physical address, phone number, and email address for each contact. You can use the Contacts folder to address email messages, place phone calls, distribute bulk mailings through mail merge (in Microsoft Word 2010), and perform many other communication tasks quickly. The Contacts folder, however, is not the same as your address book. Your Outlook Address Book (OAB) lets you access the Contacts folder for addressing messages, but the Address Book also lets you access addresses stored in other address lists.

For detailed information about working with address books in Outlook 2010, see Chapter 6, "Managing Address Books and Distribution Lists."

You can open the Contacts folder either by clicking the Contacts button in the Navigation pane or by opening the Folder List and clicking Contacts. When you open the folder, you'll see its default view, Business Cards, which displays contact entries as virtual business cards that show name, address, phone number, and a handful of other items for each contact, as shown in Figure 18-1. Outlook 2010 provides several predefined views for the Contacts folder that offer different ways to display and sort the contacts list.

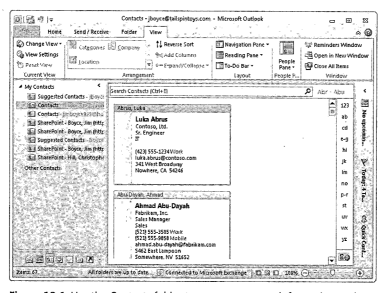

Figure 18-1 Use the Contacts folder to manage contact information such as address, phone number, and fax number for your business associates and friends.

For details about the available views in the Contacts folder and how to work with them, see the section "Viewing Contacts," on page 452.

> **Note**
> You can use the alphabet index on the right in the folder window to jump quickly to a specific area in the Contacts folder. For example, click LM to jump to the list of contacts whose names begin with L or M.

When you double-click an entry in the Contacts folder, Outlook 2010 opens a contact form similar to the one shown in Figure 18-2. This multitabbed form lets you view and modify a wealth of information about the person. You also can initiate actions related to the contact. For example, you can click the More button in the Communicate group on the Contact tab on the ribbon and then choose Call to dial the contact's phone number. You'll learn more about these tasks throughout the remainder of this chapter. The following section explains how to create a contact entry and also introduces the tabs on the ribbon to help you understand the types of information that you can store.

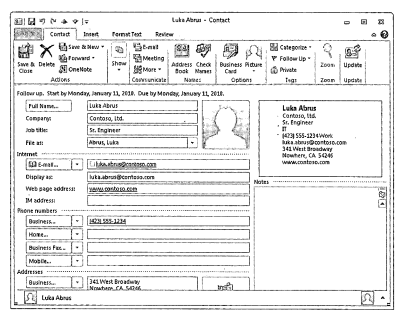

Figure 18-2 The General page of a contact form shows address, phone number, and other information about the contact.

Creating a Contact Entry

To create a contact entry, you can start from scratch, or you can base the new entry on a similar existing entry—for example, the entry for a contact from the same company.

You can open a contact form and create a new entry in any of the following ways:

- Click New Contact on the Home tab on the ribbon with the Contacts folder open.

- Right-click a blank area in the Contacts folder (not a contact entry), and then choose New Contact.

- With the Contacts folder open, press Ctrl+N.

- In any other folder view (such as Messages), click the arrow next to the New Items button on the ribbon, and then choose Contact.

When the contact form opens, type the contact's name in the Full Name box and enter the information that you want to include for the contact, switching between General and Details views (using the Show button) as needed. To save the entry, click Save & Close. To save this entry and continue to add contacts, click Save And New. To copy the company information to another new contact, click Save And New and then choose Contact From The Same Company.

Filling in the information on the contact form is straightforward. You might find a few of the features especially useful. For example, the File As drop-down list allows you to specify how you want the contact to be listed in the Contacts folder. You can choose to list the contact in either Last Name, First Name format or First Name, Last Name format; to list the contact by company name rather than personal name; or to use a combination of contact name and company name.

You can also store more phone numbers in the contact entry than the four that are displayed on the form. When you click the down arrow next to a phone number entry, as shown in Figure 18-3, you see a list of possible phone numbers from which you can select a number to view or modify; the checked items on the list are those that currently contain information. When you select a number, Outlook 2010 shows it on the form.

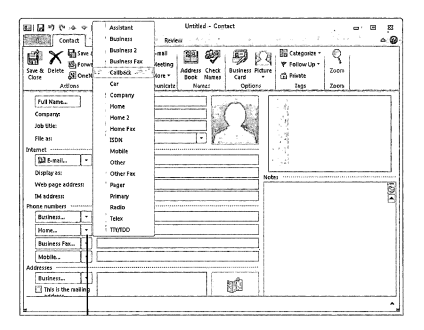

Figure 18-3 You can store multiple phone numbers for a contact, but only four appear on the form at one time.

In addition to storing multiple phone numbers for a contact, you also can store multiple physical addresses. Click the down arrow next to the Address button on the form to select a business, home, or other address. (By default, the button is labeled Business.) The E-Mail box can also store multiple addresses; click the down arrow to choose one of three email addresses for the individual. For example, you might list both business and personal addresses for the contact. The Details page of the contact form, shown in Figure 18-4, lets you add other information, such as the contact's department, office number, birthday, and anniversary. To view Details, click Show on the Contact tab of the ribbon and choose Details. Internet Free/Busy is a feature of Outlook 2010 that allows you to see when others are free or busy so that you can schedule meetings efficiently. Outlook 2010 users have the option to publish their free/busy information to a user-specified Uniform Resource Locator (URL) file server, which you can enter in the Address box.

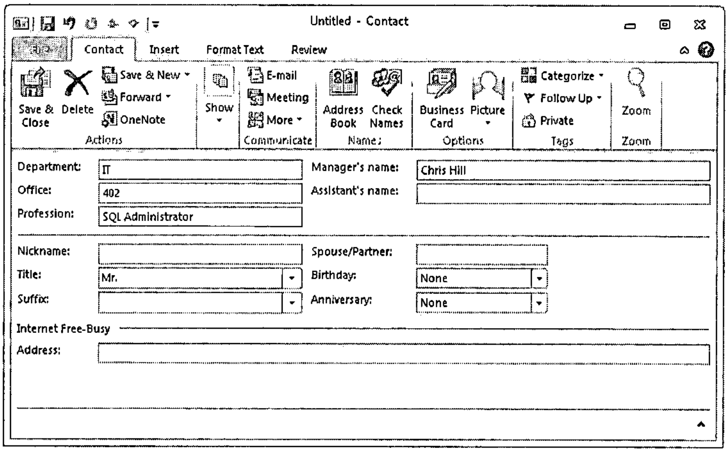

Figure 18-4 The Details page stores additional information—both business and personal—about the contact.

The Activities page of the contact form is useful for locating email messages, logged phone calls, and other items or activities associated with a specific contact. For information about using the Activities page, see the section "Associating a Contact with Other Items and Documents," on page 441.

INSIDE OUT   Add contacts quickly

When you use one of the table views (such as Phone List) to display your Contacts folder, you'll see a row at the top of the list labeled Click Here To Add A New Contact. This is a handy way to enter a contact's name and phone number quickly—simply type the information directly in the row, and Outlook 2010 adds the contact entry to the folder.

Creating Contact Entries from the Same Company

If you have several contacts who work for the same company, you can use an existing contact entry to create a new entry. Simply select the existing entry in Business Cards or Address Cards view, click New Items, and then choose Contact From Same Company. Outlook 2010 opens a new contact form with all the company information (name, address, and phone numbers) supplied—all you have to do is fill in the personal details for that individual.

> **Note**
>
> You can also use a template to create multiple contact entries that share common data such as company affiliation. For information about working with templates in Outlook 2010, see Chapter 24, "Using Templates."

Creating a Contact Entry from an Email Message

When you receive an email message from someone you'd like to add to your contacts list, you can create a contact entry directly from the message. In the From box of the message form or in the InfoBar in the Reading pane, right-click the name, and then choose Add To Outlook Contacts from the shortcut menu. Outlook 2010 opens a new contact form with the sender's name and email address already entered. Add any other necessary data for the contact, and then click Save & Close to create the entry.

Copying an Existing Contact Entry

In some cases, you might want to create a copy of a contact entry. For example, although you can keep both personal and business data in a single entry, you might want to store the data separately. You can save time by copying the existing entry rather than creating a new one from scratch.

To copy a contact entry in the Contacts folder, right-click and drag the entry to an empty spot in the folder, and then choose Copy. Outlook 2010 displays the Duplicate Contact Detected dialog box. Click Add New Contact, and then click Add to create a new entry containing all the same information as the original. You also can copy contact information to another folder. Open the folder where the contact entry is stored, and then locate the destination folder in the Navigation pane or in the Folder List. Right-click and drag the contact entry to the destination folder, and then choose Copy on the shortcut menu.

Creating Other Contacts Folders

In addition to providing its default Contacts folder, Outlook 2010 allows you to use multiple contacts folders to organize your contacts easily. For example, you might use a shared contacts folder jointly with members of your workgroup for business contacts and keep your personal contacts in a separate folder; or you might prefer to keep contact information that you use infrequently in a separate folder to reduce the clutter in your main Contacts folder. The process of creating a contact entry in any contacts folder is the same regardless of the folder's location—whether it is part of your Microsoft Exchange Server account or in a personal folder (.pst) file, for example.

To create a new folder for storing contacts, follow these steps:

1. Right-click Contacts in the Folder List and choose New Folder to open the Create New Folder dialog box, shown in Figure 18-5.

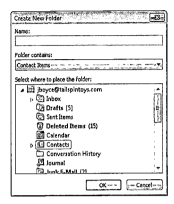

Figure 18-5 Use the Create New Folder dialog box to create new Outlook 2010 folders.

2. In the Name box, type a name for the folder. This is the folder name that will be displayed in Outlook 2010 (in the Navigation pane and in the Folder List, for example).

3. Select Contact Items in the Folder Contains drop-down list.

4. In the Select Where To Place The Folder list, select the location for the new folder.

5. Click OK.

When you create a new contacts folder using this method, Outlook 2010 sets up the folder using default properties for permissions, rules, descriptions, forms, and views.

Working with Contacts

You can do much more with your Outlook 2010 contacts list than just view address and phone information. Outlook 2010 provides a set of tools that make it easy to phone, write, email, or communicate with contacts in other ways. This section explains these tools.

Associating a Contact with Other Items and Documents

As you work with contacts, it's useful to have email messages, appointments, tasks, documents, or other items related to the contact at your fingertips. You can relate items to a contact by inserting one Outlook 2010 item in another. For example, if you create a task to call several of your contacts, you can use the Outlook Item button on the Insert tab to insert those contacts in the task. To do this, do the following:

1. With the task open, click Outlook Item on the Insert tab.

2. Select the contacts in the resulting Insert Item dialog box, shown in Figure 18-6.

3. Click OK to insert the item.

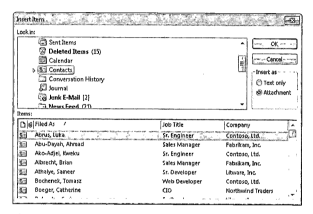

Figure 18-6 Use the Insert Item dialog box to associate contacts with a task.

For details on setting up tasks, see the section "Working with Tasks in the Tasks Folder," on page 537.

Email messages that you send to a contact are associated to that contact and appear on the Activities page of the contact form automatically. On the Contact tab of the ribbon of any contact form, clicking the Activities button in the Show group displays all the items associated with that contact, as shown in Figure 18-7. Outlook 2010 searches for links to items in the main Outlook 2010 folders, including Contacts, email (Inbox and other message folders), Journal, Notes, Tasks, and Calendar.

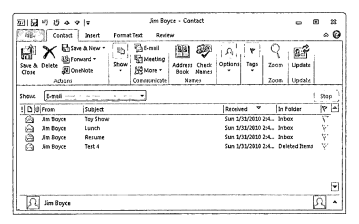

Figure 18-7 The Activities page shows all items linked to the contact.

What good is the Activities page? It's extremely useful for finding items associated with a specific contact. For example, you could sort the Inbox by sender to locate an email message from a particular person, or you could use the Activities page of his or her contact form to achieve the same result. You could also view a list of the tasks assigned to an individual by checking the Activities page. Although you can view these associations in other folders, the Activities page not only offers an easier way to view the links but also lets you see all linked items, not just specific types of items.

Associating Contacts and Documents

In many cases, you might want to insert one or more documents in a contact. For example, assume that you manage contracts for several individuals or companies. You can insert a contract document into the contact that is covered by the contract to make it easier to open the document from the contact form. With this association, you don't need to remember the document name if you know the name of the contact with whom it is associated.

Follow these steps to insert a document in a contact:

1. Open the Contacts folder, open the contact item, and then click the Insert tab.

2. Click Attach File.

3. Locate the files that you want to associate with the contact, and then click Insert.

4. The file now appears in the Notes area of the contact details.

5. Click the Contact tab, and then click Save & Close to create the link.

When you want to open the document, simply open the contact form and click the link in the Notes section.

In the preceding example, you actually inserted the document in the contact item. An alternative is to insert a hyperlink to the document in the contact item. The advantage to this method is that you are not duplicating the document—it remains in its original location on the disk. When you need to open the document, you can click the hyperlink in the contact item. Alternatively, you can open the document from its location on the disk. Another benefit of linking rather than embedding is that if the source document changes, you'll see the up-to-date copy when you open it from inside the contact item in Outlook. If you embed the document in the contact item instead, any changes to the original are not reflected in the copy stored in Outlook.

Linking a document in a contact is easy. In step 3 of the preceding procedure, rather than click Insert, click the down arrow next to the Insert button, and then select Insert As Hyperlink.

Removing a Link

Occasionally, you'll want to remove a link between a contact and another item. For example, perhaps you've accidentally linked the wrong document to a contact.

To remove a link from a contact to an item, follow these steps:

1. Open the contact item, and then, on the Contact tab, in the Show group, click General.

2. In the Note section of the contact form, select the item that you want to delete and press the Delete key.

> **Note**
> Although you can remove the contact association in a task, doing so removes the task from the contact's Activities page only if the task is assigned to someone other than the linked contact. If the contact owns the task, the task continues to be listed on the Activities page even after the task is marked as completed.

Assigning Categories to Contacts

A *category* is a keyword or a phrase that helps you keep track of items so that you can find, sort, filter, or group them easily. Use categories to keep track of different types of items that are related but stored in different folders. For example, you can keep track of all the meetings, contacts, and messages for a specific project when you create a category named after the project and then assign items to it.

Categories also give you a way to keep track of contacts without putting them in separate folders. For example, you can keep business and personal contacts in the same contacts folder and use the Business and Personal categories to sort the two sets of contacts into separate groups.

One quick way to assign categories to a contact is to right-click the contact item, choose Categorize, and then click a category. If the category you want doesn't appear in the category list, choose All Categories on the shortcut menu. Then, in the Color Categories dialog box, you can select the check boxes next to the categories that you want to assign to the contact. Alternatively, you can open the contact item, click the Categorize button on the contact form, and select a category, or click All Categories to open the Color Categories dialog box. This dialog box is useful not only for assigning categories but also for reviewing the categories that you've already assigned to an item.

For more information about how to assign a category to a contact; how to use categories to sort, filter, and group contact items; and how to create your own categories, see Chapter 5, "Creating and Using Categories."

Resolving Duplicate Contacts

If you create a contact entry using the same name or email address as an entry that already exists in your Contacts folder, Outlook 2010 displays the Duplicate Contact Detected dialog box, in which you can choose to either add the new contact entry or update your existing entry with the new information, as shown in Figure 18-8.

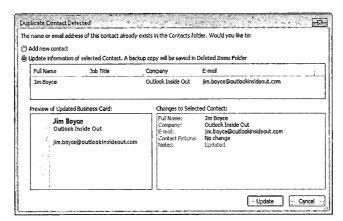

Figure 18-8 Use the Duplicate Contact Detected dialog box to tell Outlook 2010 how to handle a duplicate contact.

If you select the first option, Outlook 2010 adds the new contact to your Contacts folder, and you'll now have two entries listed under the same name or email address. In that case, you'll probably want to add some information to the contact forms—perhaps company affiliation or a middle initial—to distinguish the two entries.

If you select the second option, to update the existing entry with information from the new one, Outlook 2010 compares the fields containing data in both entries and copies the data from the new entry into any fields that have conflicting data. For example, if you have a contact named Chris Ashton whose phone number is 555-5655, and you create a new contact entry for Chris Ashton with a new phone number, Outlook 2010 copies the new number into the existing entry and leaves the other fields the same.

In case you need to revert to the information in the original contact entry, a copy of the original entry is stored in your Deleted Items folder whenever Outlook 2010 copies new data.

> **Note**
>
> If you are adding many contacts, Outlook 2010 can save the information faster if you do not require the program to detect duplicates. To turn off duplicate detection, click File, Options. Click Contacts, and then clear the Check For Duplicates When Saving New Contacts check box.

Phoning a Contact

If you have a modem, VoIP phone, or voice conferencing software (such as Office Communicator), you can use Outlook 2010 to dial any phone number that you specify, including phone numbers for contacts in your contacts list.

To make a phone call to a contact using Outlook 2010, follow these steps:

1. Open the Contacts folder.

2. Click a contact item, click More in the Communicate group on the Home tab, choose Call, and then choose a number to open the New Call dialog box with the contact's phone number already entered, as shown in Figure 18-9. If the contact form is open, in the Communicate group of the ribbon, click the More button and then choose Call.

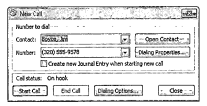

Figure 18-9 Select the number to call and other options in the New Call dialog box.

- If you want Outlook 2010 to use a phone number associated with a different contact, type the contact's name in the Contact box, and then press Tab or click in the Number box. Alternatively, you can simply type the phone number in the Number box.

- If the contact entry for the person you're calling already includes phone numbers, select the phone number in the Number box. If the contact entry doesn't specify a phone number, type the number in the Number box.

3. To keep a record of the call in the journal, select the Create New Journal Entry When Starting New Call check box. If you select this check box, a journal entry opens with the timer running after you start the call. You can type notes in the text box of the journal entry while you talk.

4. Click Start Call.

5. Pick up the phone handset, and click Talk to begin the call.

6. If you created a journal entry for the call, click Pause Timer to stop the clock when you've finished the call, and then click Save & Close.

7. Click End Call, and then hang up the phone.

INSIDE OUT   Keep track of phone calls

If you want to time a call and type notes in Outlook 2010 while you talk, you can create a journal entry for the call as you dial. The journal entry form contains a timer that you can start and stop and also provides space to type notes. For example, you might want to use this option if you bill clients for time spent on phone conversations. For more information about using the journal for phone calls, see Chapter 22, "Tracking Documents and Activities with the Journal."

> **Note**
> If you omit the country code and area code from a phone number, the automatic phone dialer uses settings from the Dialing Properties dialog box, which you can access through the Phone And Modem Options icon in the Control Panel or by clicking Dialing Properties in the New Call dialog box. If you include letters in the phone number, the automatic phone dialer does not recognize them.

Sending an Email Message to a Contact

If you're working in the Contacts folder, you can send an email message to one of your contacts without switching to the Inbox folder. This is a handy feature that can save a lot of time in an average workday.

Here's how to send a message from the Contacts folder:

1. In the Contacts folder, select the contact item, and then click E-mail in the Communicate group on the Home tab. Alternatively, right-click the contact, click Create, and then click E-mail.

2. In the Subject box, type the subject of the message.

3. In the message body, type the message.

4. Click Send.

Connecting to a Contact's Website

It seems everyone has a website these days, whether it's a company's site or a collection of family photos. If you have the URL for a contact's web page recorded in the contact entry, you can connect to that site directly from Outlook 2010. This is particularly handy for linking to business sites from a company contact entry—for example, you might create a link to the company's support or sales page. Associating websites with contacts is often more meaningful than simply storing a URL in your Favorites folder.

With the contact item open, you can connect to the contact's website by clicking the URL in the Web Page Address field.

Scheduling Appointments and Meetings with Contacts

Many Outlook 2010 users believe that the Calendar folder is the only place you can schedule a new appointment or meeting easily, but that's not the case. You can schedule an appointment or a meeting in any Outlook 2010 folder. The Contacts folder, however, is a logical place to create new appointments and meetings because those events are often associated with one or more contacts stored in the Contacts folder.

Scheduling a Meeting with a Contact

Meetings differ from appointments in that they are collaborative efforts that involve the schedules of all the attendees. When you set up a meeting, Outlook 2010 creates and sends meeting requests to the individuals you want to invite. You can create meeting requests for any number of contacts through the Contacts folder, saving the time of switching folders.

To send a meeting request to one or more of your contacts from the Contacts folder, follow these steps:

1. Open the Contacts folder, and then select the contact entries for those people you want to invite to the meeting. (To select multiple entries, hold down the Ctrl key and click the entries.)

2. Click Meeting in the Communicate group of the Home tab on the ribbon.

3. In the Subject box, type a description of the proposed meeting.

4. In the Location box, type the location.

5. Enter the proposed start and end times for the meeting.

6. Select any other options that you want.

7. Click Send.

For details about setting up meetings and sending meeting requests, see Chapter 20, "Scheduling Meetings and Resources."

Assigning a Task to a Contact

The Tasks folder in Outlook 2010 offers a handy way to keep track of your work and the work that you delegate to others. For example, if you manage a group of people, you probably use the Tasks folder to assign tasks to the people who work for you. However, if you need to assign a job to one of your contacts, you can do this directly from the Contacts folder. Doing so adds the contact's name to the Contacts box in the task request.

Follow these steps to assign a task to a contact:

1. In the Contacts folder, select the contact, click More in the Communicate group on the Home tab of the ribbon, and choose Assign Task.

2. Outlook 2010 opens a new task form with the contact's email address added in the To field. Enter other information as needed, such as start and stop dates for the task.

3. Click Send to send the task request.

Flagging a Contact for Follow-Up

You can flag a contact item for follow-up to have Outlook 2010 remind you to call or email the contact. For example, suppose that you want to make a note to yourself to call a colleague at 10:00 A.M. tomorrow to ask about the status of a project. You could create a note in the Notes folder, create a task, or add an appointment to your schedule, but an easy way to create the reminder is to add a follow-up flag to the contact entry in the Contacts folder. Outlook 2010 adds the follow-up flag as text to the Card view, but there is no other visual indicator that contacts are flagged. However, you can click the To-Do Bar and see the contacts' names in the Task List with a follow-up flag, as shown in Figure 18-10.

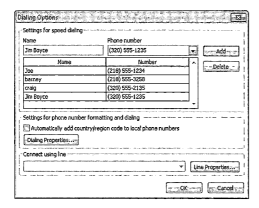

Figure 18-10 The contact appears with a follow-up flag in the Task List.

If you specify a particular date and time for follow-up when you add the flag, Outlook 2010 generates a reminder at the appointed time. Adding a reminder helps ensure that you don't forget to follow up with the contact at the appropriate time.

Follow these steps to flag a contact for follow-up:

1. In the Contacts folder, select the contact that you want to flag, and then in the Tags group on the Home tab on the ribbon, and click Follow Up. Alternatively, right-click the contact, and then choose Follow Up.

2. If one of the default follow-up time options suits you, click it. If not, click Custom to open the Custom dialog box.

3. In the Flag To box of the Custom dialog box, shown in Figure 18-11, select the flag text that you want Outlook 2010 to use or type your own flag text.

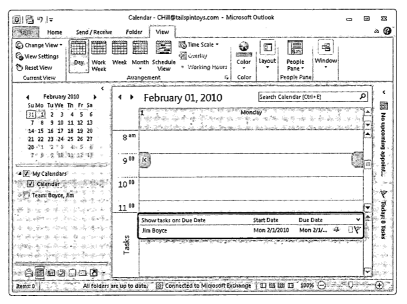

Figure 18-11 Use the Custom dialog box to specify the flag text and set an optional reminder.

4. Select a start date in the Start Date drop-down list, and then select a due date in the Due Date drop-down list.

5. If you want a reminder, click the Reminder option, select a date, and then specify a time.

6. Click OK. Outlook 2010 adds the flag text to the contact item and adds an entry to your task list.

When you have completed your follow-up action, you can remove the flag from the contact item (clear the flag) or mark the follow-up as completed. If you clear the flag, Outlook 2010 removes it from the contact item and the task list. If you prefer to have the flag remain, you can mark the follow-up as completed. In this case, the follow-up text remains, but the contact form includes a message indicating that the follow-up was accomplished (and the date). When you flag a contact as complete, the item disappears from the Task List.

Use one of the following methods to mark a follow-up flag as completed:

- Select the flagged contact item, click Follow Up on the Home tab, and then click Mark Complete.

- Right-click the contact item, click Follow Up, and then click Mark Complete.

Use one of the following methods to clear a flag, which removes it from the contact item:

- Select the contact item, click Follow Up, and then click Clear Flag.

- Right-click the contact item in the Contacts folder, click Follow Up, and then click Clear Flag.

Finding Contacts

If you store only a small list of contacts, finding a particular contact is usually not a problem. As the number of contacts grows, however, it becomes more and more difficult to locate information, especially if you aren't sure about a name. For example, you might remember that a person works for a certain company but can't recall the person's name. Outlook 2010 provides features to help you quickly and easily locate contact information.

Perhaps the easiest method of locating a contact, if you know the name, is to type the name in the Search Contacts box and then press Enter. Outlook 2010 locates the contact and filters the view to display it. If more than one contact matches the data you've entered, Outlook 2010 displays all of them, as shown in Figure 18-12.

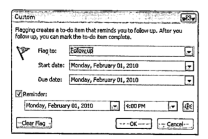

Figure 18-12 Click in the Search box to search for contacts.

The options on the Search tab can help you refine your search. For example, you can search by email address, phone number, category, and more. Use the Scope group to specify where to search, whether in the current folder, all subfolders, or all of Outlook.

Finally, if you need to perform an advanced search, click Search Tools and choose Advanced Find to open the Advanced Find dialog box, shown in Figure 18-13. You can use this dialog box to perform more complex searches based on multiple conditions, such as searching for both name and company.

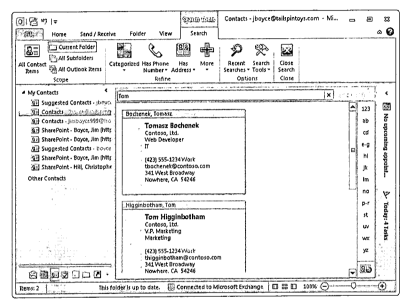

Figure 18-13 Use the Advanced Find dialog box to perform more complex searches using multiple conditions.

For a detailed discussion of how to perform both simple and complex searches in Outlook 2010, see Chapter 32, "Finding and Organizing Outlook Data."

Viewing Contacts

Outlook 2010 provides predefined views for reviewing your contacts list in the Contacts folder. For example, Card view displays names and addresses of contacts in blocks that look like address labels. This view is a convenient way to look up a contact's mailing address. In Phone view, Outlook 2010 displays contact entries in table rows with details such as phone, job title, and department name in columns. This view is helpful for quickly finding a contact's phone number or job title. You can customize the various standard views to control the amount of detail or to help you organize and analyze information.

Using Standard Views in the Contacts Folder

The Contacts folder offers several standard formats for viewing contacts. To change views, select a view in the Navigation pane or click View, Current View, and then select the view that you want to use. Two of the standard formats are card views, and the rest are table views, as described in the following list:

- **Business Cards**   This view shows the contacts in a business card format.

- **Card**   This view displays contact entries as individual cards with name, one mailing address, and business and home phone numbers.

- **Phone**   This table view displays a list with the contact's name, the company name, business phone number, business fax number, home phone number, mobile phone number, categories, and a check box to enable or disable journaling for the contact.

- **List**   This view displays the items as a general list.

> ### Note
> You can resize address cards easily by dragging the vertical separator between columns, which changes the width of all card columns.

Customizing Contacts View

The methods of customizing the view in Outlook 2010 folders are generally the same for all folders. This section examines some specific ways that you might customize the Contacts folder to make it easier to locate and work with contacts. For example, you might use a specific color for contacts who work for a particular company. You can also change the fonts used for the card headings and body, specify card width and height, and automatically format contact entries based on rules.

Chapter 26, "Creating Custom Views and Print Styles," covers additional ways to customize views.

Filtering Contacts View

You can filter the view in the Contacts folder to show only those contacts that meet the conditions that you specify in the filter. For example, you can use a filter to view only those contacts who work for a particular company or who live in a particular city.

Follow these steps to set up a view filter in the Contacts folder:

1. Open the Contacts folder, select the view you want to change, and then click View Settings on the View tab.

2. Click Filter in the Advanced View Settings dialog box.

3. In the Filter dialog box, specify the conditions for the filter. If you don't see the items that you need to specify for the condition, use the Field drop-down list on the Advanced tab to select the necessary field.

4. Click OK to close the Filter dialog box, and then click OK in the Advanced View Settings dialog box to apply the filter.

When you want to view the entire contents of the folder again, you can remove the filter using the procedure detailed here:

1. Select the view and click View Settings in the View tab on the ribbon.

2. Click Filter.

3. In the Filter dialog box, click Clear All, and then click OK.

4. Click OK to close the Advanced View Settings dialog box.

> **Note**
> If you want to reset the view to its default properties, click Reset Current View in the Advanced View Settings dialog box.

Configuring Fonts and Card Dimensions

You can change the font used for card headings and the card body text. You can also change the font style, size, and script, but not the color.

Follow these steps to change the font for card headings and body text:

1. Display the view that you want to modify and then click View Settings in the View tab on the ribbon.

2. In the Advanced View Settings dialog box, click Other Settings to display the Format Card View dialog box, shown in Figure 18-14.

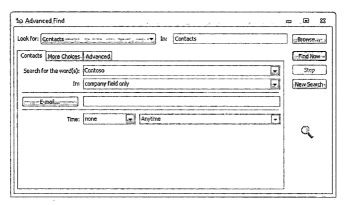

Figure 18-14 Use the Format Card View dialog box to specify the font for card headings and body text.

3. Click Font in the Card Headings or Card Fields area of the dialog box to open a standard Font dialog box in which you can select font characteristics.

4. Make your font selections, and then click OK.

5. Specify options according to the following list, and then click OK:

   - **Allow In-Cell Editing**   Selecting this check box allows you to modify contact data by clicking a field in the view without opening the contact form.

   - **Show Empty Fields**   Select this check box if you want to show all fields for all contacts, even if the fields are empty. Clear this check box to simplify the view of your Contacts folder. Note that when this check box is selected, Outlook 2010 displays all fields defined for the view, not all contact fields.

   - **Card Width**   Set the card width (in number of characters) using this option.

   - **Multi-Line Field Height**   Use this option to specify the number of lines that you want to display on the card for multiline fields.

6. Click OK to close the Advanced View Settings dialog box.

Using Automatic Formatting

Outlook 2010 performs some limited automatic formatting of data in the Contacts folder. For example, it uses bold for contact group items, regular font for unread contacts, and red for overdue contacts (contact entries with an overdue follow-up flag). You can make changes to these automatic formatting rules, and you can even create your own rules. For example, you might want to display overdue contacts in blue rather than in red, or you might want to use a particular color for all contacts who work for a certain company.

Follow these steps to modify the formatting for an existing rule or to create a new rule:

1. Open the Contacts folder and display the view that you want to modify, and then click View Settings.

2. Click Conditional Formatting in the Advanced View Settings dialog box to display the Conditional Formatting dialog box, shown in Figure 18-15.

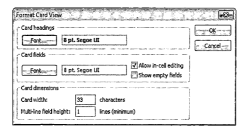

Figure 18-15 Use the Conditional Formatting dialog box to create custom rules that control how Outlook 2010 displays contacts.

3. If you want to modify an existing rule, select the rule, and then click Font to change the font characteristics or click Condition to modify the condition for the rule. If you are changing the condition, skip to step 6. Otherwise, skip to step 7.

> **Note**
> You can modify a rule condition only for rules that you have created. You cannot change the condition for the three predefined rules.

4. Click Add if you want to add a new rule. Outlook 2010 creates a new rule named Untitled.

5. Type a new name in the Name field, click Font and specify font characteristics, and then click Condition to open the Filter dialog box, shown in Figure 18-16.

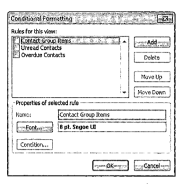

Figure 18-16 You can specify complex conditions using the Filter dialog box.

6. Specify the criteria to define the rule condition. For example, click Advanced, click Field, click Frequently Used Fields, and click Company. Then select Contains in the Condition drop-down list and type a company name in the Value box. This will format all contacts from the specified company automatically using the font properties you specify in the next step.
Click OK to close the Filter dialog box, click Font in the Conditional Formatting dialog box, specify the font properties, and then click OK.

7. Close the Conditional Formatting and Advanced View Settings dialog boxes to view the effects of the new rule.

> **Note**
> Automatic formatting rules follow the hierarchy in the list shown in the Automatic Formatting dialog box. Use the Move Up and Move Down buttons to change the order of rules in the lists and thereby change the order in which they are applied.

Filtering Contacts with Categories

Categorizing contacts allows you to organize your contacts into groups that you create. For example, categories provide an easy way to distinguish all your personal contacts from business contacts. Categorizing also gives you the ability to group people from different companies who are all involved in the same project. Outlook 2010 provides an easy way for you to categorize your contacts, using color coding to distinguish the categories from each other. You can also define custom labels for categories so that you can identify the category by both color and label.

You can define your categories either by using a color category for the first time or by using the Color Categories dialog box. Outlook 2010 offers a couple of ways to open the Color Categories dialog box:

- Click the Categorize button in the Tags group on the Home tab on the ribbon, and then click All Categories.

- Right-click any contact item, and then choose Categorize, All Categories.

> **Note**
>
> When you use a color category for the first time, Outlook 2010 displays a Rename Category dialog box that lets you change the text associated with the category.

To create a new category and assign a color to it, follow these steps:

1. In the Color Categories dialog box, click New.

2. Type an appropriate name for the category, and then select a color in the drop-down color palette.

3. Click OK.

> **Note**
>
> For quick category assignment, assign a unique shortcut key to each of the categories that you use most often. You can assign the shortcut key through the Color Categories dialog box.

You should now see the category that you just created in your category list. To assign these categories to your contacts, follow these steps:

1. In the Contacts folder, right-click any item in the contacts list.

2. Click Categorize on the shortcut menu.

3. Select the category that you just added.

Now that you have categorized your contacts, it's time to view them. To do this, open any list view that includes the Categories column, right-click the Categories column, and choose Group By This Field.

For more information about categories, see Chapter 5, "Creating and Using Categories."

Printing Contacts

As an experienced user of Windows, you probably need little if any explanation of how to print. So rather than focusing on basic printing commands, this section offers some insight into why you might print from the Contacts folder and what your options are when you do print.

Why print? If you're like most people, you probably try to work from your computer as much as possible and reduce the amount of paper that you generate. The completely paperless office is still a distant goal for most people, however, and there will be times when you want to print your contacts list. For example, you might need to take a copy of your contacts with you on a business trip, but you don't have a notebook computer. A hard copy of your contacts is the solution to this problem.

Outlook 2010 supports several predefined styles that allow you to print contact information using various formats, including preprinted sheets for several popular day planners. You can print a single contact entry, a selection of entries, or all entries. To print a selection (one or more), first select the contact entries to print by holding down the Ctrl key and clicking each one. If you want to print all contacts, first select all the contacts. Then choose File, Print to open the Print page, shown in Figure 18-17.

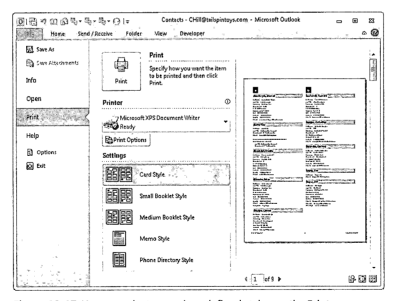

Figure 18-17 You can select several predefined styles on the Print page.

In the Settings area of the Print page, you can select one of five print styles (depending on the contact view that you selected before clicking File, Print), each of which results in a different printed layout. You can use the styles as listed, modify them, or create new styles. To modify an existing style, double-click the style to open the Page Setup dialog box, which resembles the one shown in Figure 18-18.

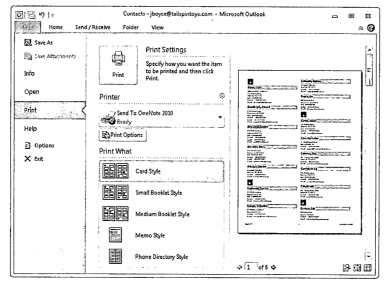

Figure 18-18 Modify a print style in the Page Setup dialog box.

Use the Format tab of this dialog box to specify fonts and shading and to set options such as printing a contact index on the side of each page, adding headings for each letter, and setting the number of columns. Use the Paper tab to select the type of paper, such as a pre-printed sheet for your day planner, as well as to set up margins, paper source, and orientation. Use the Header/Footer tab to add a header, a footer, or both to the printout.

For a detailed discussion of printing in Outlook 2010, see the section "Printing in Outlook," on page 668.

Custom Contact Printing with Word

Although Outlook 2010 provides several features for printing, your capability to customize the way that the printed documents look is rather limited. You can overcome this limitation by using Word 2010 rather than Outlook 2010 to print contacts. You have considerable control over how a Word 2010 document looks and is printed, making Word 2010 an excellent tool for custom printing. You can copy data from Outlook 2010 to Word 2010 manually, but it's much more efficient to use a macro to automate the process and make custom contact printing a one-click process. Because the process requires macros and macros haven't yet been covered in detail, refer to the section, "Custom Printing with Scripts and Word," on page 676, which explains how to print contacts using Word 2010. It also includes sample macro code that you can tailor to your specific needs.

Working with Contact Groups

A contact group (also called a *distribution list*) is a collection of contacts. It provides an easy way to send messages to a group of people. For example, if you frequently send messages to the marketing team, you can create a contact group named Marketing Team that contains the names of all members of this team. A message sent to this contact group goes to all recipients who belong to the group. Outlook 2010 converts the address list to individual addresses, so recipients see their own names and the names of all other recipients in the To box of the message instead of seeing the name of the contact group. You can use contact groups in messages, task requests, and meeting requests.

INSIDE OUT   Use nested contact groups

Contact groups can contain other contact groups as well as individual addresses. For example, you might create a contact group for each of seven departments and then create one contact group containing those seven others. You could use this second group when you need to send messages to all seven departments.

You can create contact groups in your Contacts folder using your contacts list. You can store addresses from any available source, such as the Global Address List (GAL), a contacts list, and so on. In general, you should create your contact groups in the location where you store the majority of your addresses.

Creating a Personal Contact Group

Follow these steps to create a new contact group in the Contacts folder:

1. Open the Contacts folder and click New Contact Group to open a contact group form, as shown in Figure 18-19.

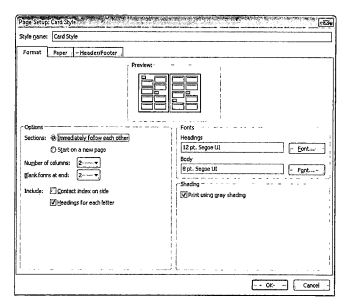

Figure 18-19 Add members to and remove members from a contact group on the contact group form.

2. Type the name for your contact group in the Name box. This is the list name that will appear in your Contacts folder. If you're creating a contact group for the marketing department, for example, use the name "Marketing."

3. In the Members group, click Add Members and then choose From Address Book to open the Select Members dialog box, shown in Figure 18-20.

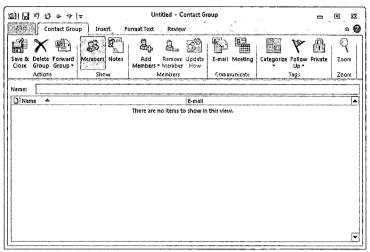

Figure 18-20 Use the Select Members dialog box to select addresses to include in the list.

4. In the Address Book drop-down list, select the location from which you want to select addresses (for example, the GAL or the Contacts folder).

5. In the Search box, type a name that you want to include, which locates the name in the list, or select the name from the Name list, and then click Members.

6. Repeat steps 4 and 5 to add all addressees to the list, and then click OK when you've finished.

7. If you want to add a longer description of the contact group, click Notes and type the text.

8. Click Save & Close. The new contact group is added to your contacts list.

You probably realized that Outlook offers a couple of other options for adding members to a group. When you click Add Members, Outlook offers two additional options: From Outlook Contacts and New E-mail Contact. Choose the former if you want to add members from your Contacts folder. Choose the latter if you simply want to add an email address to the group.

Adding or Deleting Names in a Contact Group

You can add and delete names in a contact group easily. For example, perhaps your department has added a few new employees and you need to add their addresses to the department contact group.

Follow these steps to add or remove names in a contact group:

1. In your Contacts folder, open the contact group to display the contact group form.

2. Perform one or more of the following actions as desired:

    *   To add an address from an address book or a contacts folder, click Add Members, and then choose either From Outlook Contacts or From Address Book.

    *   To add an address that is not in a contacts folder or an address book, click Add Members, New E-mail Contact.

    *   To delete a name, click the name, and then click Remove Member.

3. Click Save & Close.

INSIDE OUT   Fine-tune contact groups

You can assign categories to a contact group, mark it as private, or add notes to it by using the contact group form. You can also update addresses in a contact group if their source addresses have changed. For example, if you've changed a colleague's email address in the contact entry and now want to update the corresponding address in the contact group, you can open the contact group, select the address, and click Update Now on the contact group form.

Sharing Contacts

Outlook 2010 lets you share contacts with others by sending vCards through email or by sharing your Contacts folder. The former method lets you share contacts with people who don't use Outlook 2010 or who don't have access to your network or to your computer running Exchange Server. The latter method—sharing your Contacts folder—is a good solution when you need to provide access to contacts for others on your network. This section explains how to share contacts through vCards, offers a brief overview of sharing the Contacts folder, and explains how to share contacts from a public folder.

> **Note**
>
> You can use WSS or SharePoint Server to share contacts and even integrate those
> contacts within Outlook 2010. See Chapter 38, "Collaboration with Outlook and Share-
> Point," to learn how to work with and share contacts from a SharePoint site.

Sharing Your Contacts Folders

If you're running Outlook 2010 with Exchange Server, you can assign permissions to a
folder stored in your Exchange Server mailbox to give other users access to that folder.
You can grant permissions on a group basis or a per-user basis. Outlook 2010 provides
two groups by default—Anonymous and Default—that you can use to assign permissions
on a global basis. You also can add individual users to the permissions list and use contact
groups to assign permissions.

Follow these steps to set permissions on your Contacts folder to allow other users access to
your contacts:

1. Open the Folder List, right-click the Contacts folder, and then choose Share, Folder
   Permissions to display the Contacts Properties dialog box for the folder (see Figure
   18-21).

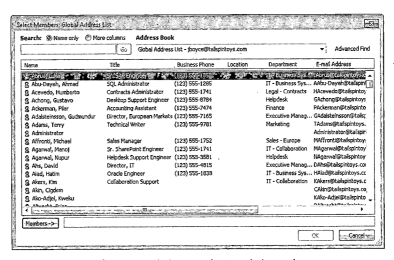

Figure 18-21 Configure permissions on the Permissions tab.

2. Click Add to display the Add Users dialog box.

3. Select the person for whom you want to configure permissions, and then click Add. Click OK to return to the Permissions tab.

4. In the Name box, select the name of the person that you just added.

5. In the Permission Level drop-down list, select a permissions level according to the tasks that the user should be able to perform with your Contacts folder. When you select a permissions level, Outlook 2010 selects one or more individual permissions in the Permissions area. You also can select or clear individual permissions as needed.

6. Click OK to save the permission changes.

You can grant several permissions for a folder, and you can assign them in any combination you need. See the section "Sharing Your Calendar," on page 849, to learn more about sharing permissions for Outlook folders.

For a complete explanation of permissions and folder sharing, see the section "Granting Access to Folders," on page 842.

Sharing Contacts with vCards

A vCard presents contact information as an electronic business card that can be sent through email. vCards are based on an open standard, allowing any application that supports vCards to share contact information. In addition to sending a vCard as an attachment, you can include it with your message signature.

When you receive a message with a vCard attached, a paper clip icon appears in the Reading pane to indicate the attached vCard. Use one of the following methods to add the data in the vCard as a contact entry:

- In the Reading pane, click the file name that appears.

- If you've opened the message, right-click the business card icon in the message, and then choose Open.

After you can view the information sent in the vCard, click Save & Close to add the information to your contacts list.

> **Note**
> You can drag a vCard from a message to your Contacts folder to add the contact information.

Creating a vCard from a Contact Entry

As mentioned earlier, one way to send contact information to someone else is to attach the contact entry to a message as a vCard. You can use this method to share your own contact information or to share one or more other contact entries with another person.

Follow these steps to attach a vCard to a message:

1. In the Contacts folder, select the contact item that you want to send as a vCard.

2. On the Home tab, click Forward Contact and choose As A Business Card. Outlook 2010 opens a new message form with the contact entry attached as a vCard.

3. Specify an address, complete the message as you would any other, and then click Send to send it.

Including a vCard with Your Signature

The second method of sharing a contact is useful when you want to share your own contact information. Rather than attaching it to a message, you can have Outlook 2010 send it along with your message signature, which ensures that the vCard is sent with all outgoing messages.

> **Note**
>
> You can attach text (such as a favorite quote) and graphics to each outgoing message as part of your signature. For complete details on using signatures with Outlook 2010, see the section "Using Signatures," on page 273.

Follow these steps to add your contact information as a vCard to your message signature:

1. Create your own contact entry if you have not already done so.

2. Click File, Options.

3. Click Mail, Signatures.

4. Click New.

5. Enter a name for your signature (such as vCard).

6. Click Business Card.

7. Browse to your own business card, and then click OK.

8. In the Signatures And Stationery dialog box, shown in Figure 18-22, add other information as needed.

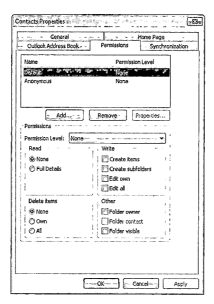

Figure 18-22 Use the Signatures And Stationery dialog box to add text, graphics, and a vCard to your outgoing messages automatically.

9. Click OK twice.

From now on, your contact information will be attached to outgoing messages.

> **Tip**
>
> To prevent signatures from being added to your outgoing messages, click File, Options, click Mail, Signatures, and then select None in the New Messages drop-down list.

Saving a Contact Entry as a vCard

In addition to sending vCards as email attachments, Outlook 2010 allows you to save a contact entry to a file as a vCard. You might do this if you want to link to vCards on a website so that others can download the vCards directly rather than receiving a message with the vCards attached. Alternatively, perhaps you want to save a large number of contacts as vCards and send them to someone in a .zip file or on a CD.

Follow these steps to save a contact item as a vCard file:

1. Open the contact item that you want to save as a vCard.

2. Click File, Save As. In the Save As type drop-down list, select vCard Files (*.vcf).

3. Type a name in the File Name box, and then click Save.

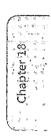

Saving a vCard Attachment in Your Contacts Folder

When you receive a message containing a vCard attachment, you'll probably want to save the vCard as a contact item in your Contacts folder. Follow these steps to do so:

1. Open the message containing the attached vCard.

2. Double-click the attached vCard to open it.

3. In the open contact form, click Save & Close. The information in the vCard is saved in your Contacts folder by default.

Setting Contact Options

Outlook 2010 provides several options that control how it stores and displays contacts. To view these options, click File, Options, and then click Contacts in the left pane. On the Contacts page of the Outlook Options dialog box, shown in Figure 18-23, you can configure the following options:

- **Default "Full Name" Order**   This option specifies how Outlook 2010 creates the Full Name field when you click Full Name in the new contact form and enter the contact's first, middle, and last names, along with suffix and title.

- **Default "File As" Order**   This option specifies the name that Outlook 2010 uses in the card title. Outlook 2010 uses the information that you specify for first, middle, and last name, as well as company, to create the card title based on how this option is set.

- **Check For Duplicates When Saving New Contacts**   Select this check box if you want Outlook 2010 to check for duplicate contacts when you create new contacts.

- **Show Contacts Linked To The Current Item**   When contacts are linked to other Outlook items, show those contacts when viewing the item.

- **Show An Additional Index**   Use this option to display a second index at the right edge of the Contacts folder in a different language.

- **Display Online Status Next To Name**   Show online presence information for the contact.

- **Show User Photographs When Available**   Show photos for those users who have a photo associated in Outlook or through the Outlook Social Connector.

- **Automatically Create Outlook Contacts For Recipients That Do Not Belong To An Outlook Address Book**   Use this option to create contacts in the Suggested Contacts folder automatically when you send and receive messages to or from contacts not already in one of the Contacts folders.

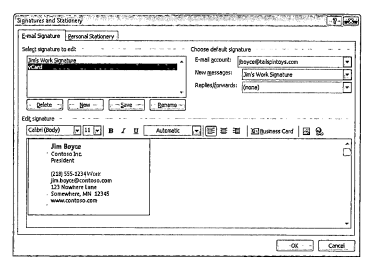

Figure 18-23 Configure options for contacts in the Contact Options dialog box.

Using Contacts Effectively

Contacts can be a very powerful tool in Outlook 2010. As with any Outlook 2010 feature, you can use them in different ways to suit your needs, and how you use them might not be the most effective way for someone else. However, there are some things you can do to make contacts more useful:

- **Be complete**   The more information that you can include for each contact, the more useful your contacts will be. For example, fill in as many of the phone number fields as you can; this will give you more options when using Outlook 2010 to dial a contact.

- **Use categories to your advantage**   Assigning categories to your contacts will help you organize them more effectively—for example, keeping your personal contacts separated from your business contacts.

- **Enter the company name for your business contacts**   Entering the company name in the contact will enable you to group your contacts by company, making it easier not only to locate contacts but also to modify contacts globally when a company change occurs (such as a phone number or company name change).

- **Work from the contact**   If you work in the Contacts folder a lot, keep in mind that you can initiate certain actions from the Contacts folder, such as issuing a new meeting request, assigning a task, creating a new journal entry, or calling the contact. This can save you the trouble of switching to a different folder to initiate these actions.

- **Don't forget the picture**   The capability to add a picture can be very useful. For example, if your organization is growing rapidly or is already large, providing pictures in contacts for employees can help your staff get to know everyone.

PART 4

Managing Your Time and Tasks

CHAPTER 19

Scheduling Appointments

F OR most of us, a calendar is a basic tool for organizing our lives, both at work and at home. With the calendar in Microsoft Outlook 2010, you can schedule regular appointments, all-day and multiday events, and meetings. You can view your schedule almost any way you want. In addition, you can share your calendar with others, which is a big help when scheduling organizational activities.

This chapter first describes the calendar and explains how to work with the basic Calendar folder view. Then you'll learn how to schedule and work with appointments and events. You'll also learn about the more advanced view options for the calendar and about how to share your calendar and free/busy information and view different time zones.

Both this chapter and the next focus on the features available in the Office Outlook 2010 Calendar folder. This chapter covers appointments and events; Chapter 20, "Scheduling Meetings and Resources," discusses how to handle meetings and resources.

Calendar Basics

The Outlook 2010 Calendar folder provides a central location for storing vast amounts of information about your schedule. Figure 19-1 shows a basic one-day view of a calendar. You see this view when you click the Calendar icon in the Navigation pane to open the folder and then click Day on the Home tab of the ribbon. This example calendar contains no appointments yet, and no tasks are listed in the Daily Task List.

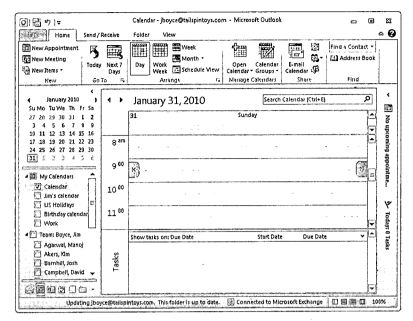

Figure 19-1 The Day view of the Outlook 2010 calendar.

Understanding Calendar Items

The Outlook 2010 calendar can contain three types of items: appointments, events, and meetings.

- An appointment, which is the default calendar item, involves only your schedule and time and does not require other attendees or resources. The calendar shows appointments in the time slots corresponding to their start and end times.

- When an appointment lasts longer than 24 hours, it becomes an event. An event is not marked on the calendar in a time slot, but rather in a banner at the top of the day on which it occurs.

- An appointment becomes a meeting when you invite other people, which requires coordinating their schedules, or when you must schedule resources. Meetings can be in-person meetings established through Outlook 2010 meeting requests. (Meetings can also be set up online using Microsoft Office Live Meeting, which is a separate application.) In this chapter and in Chapter 20, we'll look at meeting requests in Outlook 2010.

For in-depth information about meetings initiated in Outlook 2010, see Chapter 20, "Scheduling Meetings and Resources."

You can create an appointment in any of these ways:

- Click New Appointment on the Home tab.

- When any other Outlook 2010 folder is open, click the arrow next to New Items on the toolbar, and then choose Appointment.

- Click a time slot on the calendar (or drag to select a time range), and simply type the subject of the appointment in the time slot.

For detailed information about creating appointments and using the appointment form, see the section "Working with One-Time Appointments," on page 483.

Using the Time Bar

When you choose a calendar display of 7 or fewer days, the Time Bar appears, displaying 30-minute time increments by default. Figure 19-2 shows the Time Bar set to 30-minute increments, with a selection of appointments on the calendar, the shortest of which is 30 minutes.

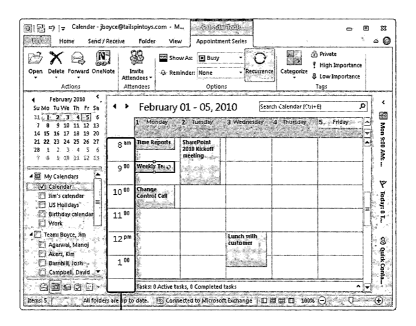

Figure 19-2 By default, the Time Bar is set to display 30-minute increments.

You can set the Time Bar to display different time increments. To do so, begin by right-clicking the Time Bar to display the shortcut menu shown in Figure 19-3.

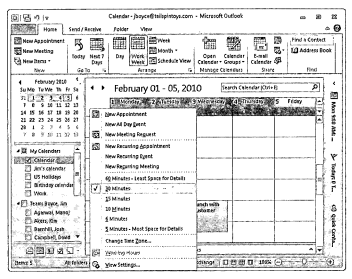

Figure 19-3 Use the Time Bar shortcut menu to change the time increment.

If you want to change the time scale to 10 minutes, select 10 Minutes; subsequently, the 30-minute appointment takes up three time intervals instead of one, as shown in Figure 19-4.

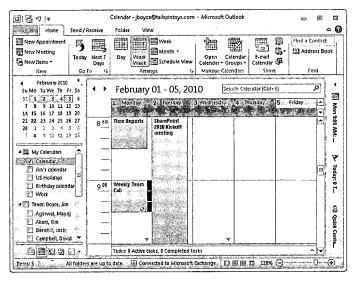

Figure 19-4 The Time Bar has been changed to display 10-minute increments.

To choose a 60-minute interval, right-click the Time Bar, and then select 60 Minutes; Figure 19-5 shows the result. Note that the scheduled time of the appointment is displayed as a ScreenTip when you place the mouse pointer over the appointment subject on the calendar.

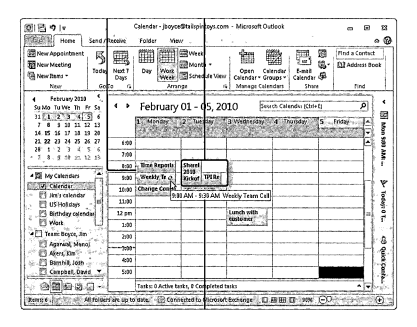

Figure 19-5 The Time Bar is set to 60-minute intervals and the time is displayed when you place the mouse pointer over the appointment.

Outlook 2010 places appointments side by side on the calendar when they are scheduled in the same time interval (as shown in Figure 19-5). In addition, a notch at the left edge of an item indicates that it does not consume the entire time slot.

Using the Date Navigator

The Date Navigator is shown as a small calendar at the top of the Navigation pane. It has several important uses. For example, you can use it to select the day to view on the calendar—in effect, jumping from one date to another. When you click a day in the Date Navigator, Outlook 2010 displays that day according to how you have set the view (by using the Day, Work Week, or Week tab):

- In Day view, the selected day is displayed.

- In Work Week view (including five days by default—configurable by clicking File, Options, and finally Calendar), Outlook 2010 displays the week containing the day that you clicked in the Date Navigator.

- In Week view (including seven days), the calendar displays the complete week containing the date you click.

> **Note**
>
> When the To-Do Bar is displayed (and not minimized), the Date Navigator appears at the top of the To-Do Bar. When you close or minimize the To-Do Bar, the Date Navigator moves to the top of the Navigation pane.

By clicking the right and left arrows next to the month names in the Date Navigator, you can scroll forward and backward through the months.

For more information about the Day, Work Week, Week, and Month views, see the section "Setting the Number of Days Displayed" on page 482.

Another use of the Date Navigator is to denote days that contain scheduled items. Those days appear in bold type; days with no scheduled items appear as regular text. This allows you to assess your monthly schedule at a glance.

Last, you can use the Date Navigator to view multiple days on the calendar. In the Date Navigator, simply drag across the range of days you want to view; those days will all appear on the calendar. For example, Figure 19-6 shows what happens when you drag across three days in the Date Navigator. You can also view multiple consecutive days by clicking the first day and then holding down the Shift key and clicking the last day. To view multiple non-consecutive days, click the first day that you want to view and then hold down the Ctrl key and click each day that you want to add to the view.

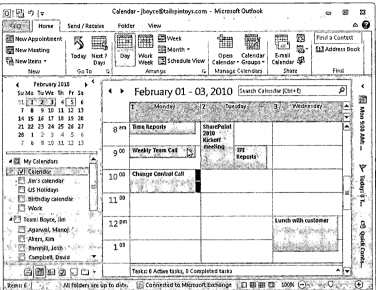

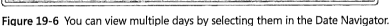

Figure 19-6 You can view multiple days by selecting them in the Date Navigator.

Using the To-Do Bar

The To-Do Bar replaces the Taskpad in previous versions of Outlook and offers an easy way of working with tasks from the Calendar folder. The To-Do Bar is not turned on by default, but it can be enabled using the To-Do Bar button in the Layout group on the View tab. The To-Do Bar displays existing tasks from the Tasks folder and also allows you to add new tasks. Adding a new task is as simple as clicking in the Task List area of the To-Do Bar and typing the task subject. Double-click the task item to open the task form if you'd like to add more details. When you create a task in the To-Do Bar, Outlook 2010 automatically adds it to the Tasks folder.

One of the main advantages of having the To-Do Bar in the Calendar folder is that it enables you to assess your schedule and fit in tasks where appropriate. When you drag a task from the Task List to the calendar, an appointment is added. When you double-click the appointment, the appointment form appears, with the task information filled in. You need only set the schedule information for the appointment and save it to the calendar (as explained in the section "Working with One-Time Appointments," on page 483).

Setting the Number of Days Displayed

You can set the number of days displayed in the calendar in several ways. One way is to use the Date Navigator, as discussed earlier. The easiest way, however, is to use the appropriate button in the Arrangement group of the View tab. To select the number of days to view, click the Day, Work Week, or Week button. You can click the Month button and choose between three levels of detail for the Month view.

When the calendar displays 7 or fewer days, the time bar shows the time of day. Figure 19-7 shows the calendar with five days displayed.

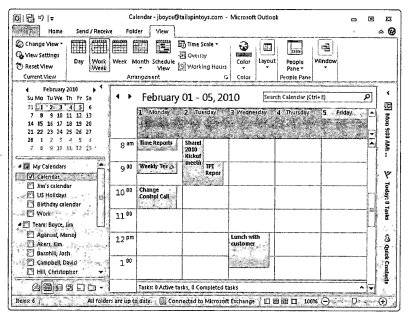

Figure 19-7 The calendar display changes depending on the number of days you are viewing.

When you select more than seven days in the Date Navigator, the times are replaced by dates, as shown in Figure 19-8. The Date Navigator and the To-Do Bar can also appear in Month view, as shown in Figure 19-8.

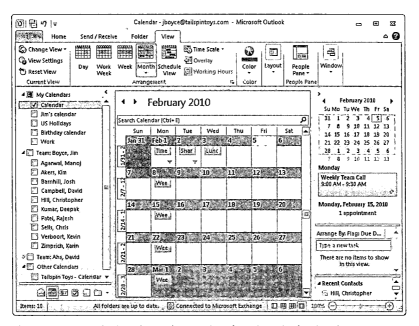

Figure 19-8 Month view shows dates rather than times in the time bar.

Selecting a Date

You can select a date in two ways. The first is by using the Date Navigator, as described earlier. The second way is to click the Today button on the Home tab on the ribbon; this action takes you to the current day using whatever view is currently shown.

Working with One-Time Appointments

The most basic calendar item is the one-time appointment. You can create a one-time appointment in several ways:

- If the Calendar folder is not open, click New Items on the Home tab on the ribbon, and then choose Appointment. The appointment defaults to the next full 30 minutes.

- If the Calendar folder is open, select a time in the calendar and then click New Appointment on the ribbon, or alternatively, right-click the calendar and choose New Appointment. The appointment is scheduled for the time selected in the calendar.

- Right-click a date in Month view, and then choose New Appointment. The appointment defaults to your specified start-of-workday time and runs for 30 minutes.

When you take any of these actions, Outlook 2010 opens the appointment form, shown in Figure 19-9, where you can specify information for the new item.

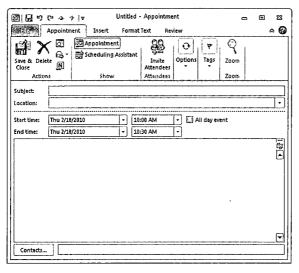

Figure 19-9 Use the appointment form to create a new appointment.

INSIDE OUT   Create an appointment quickly

To create an appointment quickly, you can click a blank time slot on the calendar and type the subject of the appointment. When you use this method, however, Outlook 2010 doesn't open a new appointment form automatically. To add details to the appointment, you must double-click the new appointment to open the form. Note that if you click a blank date in Month view and type a subject, Outlook 2010 creates an all-day event rather than an appointment.

Specifying the Subject and Location

Type the subject of an appointment in the Subject box at the top of the appointment form. Make the subject as descriptive as possible because it will appear on the calendar.

If you want, you can type a location for the appointment in the Location box. To view a list of all previously typed locations, click the Location drop-down arrow; you can select a location in this list. Outlook 2010 will display the location that you specify next to the appointment subject in Calendar view (and in parentheses next to the subject in ScreenTips when you place the mouse pointer over the scheduled appointment).

Specifying Start and End Times

You set the start and end times of the appointment by typing the date and time in the Start Time and End Time boxes or by clicking the drop-down arrows beside each box. If you click a drop-down arrow for a date, a calendar appears. Click a drop-down arrow for time, and a list of potential start and end times in 30-minute increments appears. The End Time drop-down list shows how long the appointment will be for each given end time. You can also click in these fields and type a value. For example, you might use this method when you want to create a 15-minute appointment when Outlook 2010 is set to use a 30-minute default appointment duration. If you select an appointment time that conflicts with another appointment, a bar above the Subject line will display the message "Conflicts with another appointment."

Setting a Reminder

You can set a reminder for an appointment by clicking the Reminder arrow in the Options group on the Appointment tab. In the Reminder drop-down list, you can specify when the reminder should appear; the default is 15 minutes before the appointment. By default, a reminder both plays a sound and displays a reminder window, as shown in Figure 19-10. If you don't want the reminder to play a sound, or if you want to use a different sound, click the Sound option at the bottom of the Reminder drop-down list to change the settings.

> ## Note
> To change the default behavior of appointment reminders, click File, Options, and then Calendar. In the Calendar Options area of the page, you can select (or clear) the default reminder and set the default reminder time.

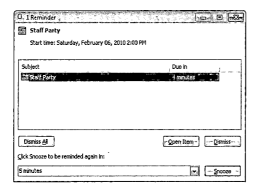

Figure 19-10 You can dismiss a reminder by clicking Dismiss or postpone it by clicking Snooze.

Classifying an Appointment

Outlook 2010 uses color and patterns to indicate free/busy information for appointments. In the calendar itself, Outlook 2010 does not show an indicator next to appointments marked Busy. It uses the following bars at the left edge of the appointment to indicate status:

- Free (white)

- Tentative (shaded with diagonal lines)

- Out Of Office (shaded dark purple)

> ## Note
> When you are scheduling a meeting or viewing a group schedule, Outlook 2010 shows busy time using a blue bar.

The indicator (a small bar to the left of the appointment) appears on your local calendar and is also displayed when other users view the free/busy times for that calendar. By default, the time occupied by an appointment is classified as Busy. To reclassify an appointment, select the indicator in the Show As drop-down list in the Options group, as shown in Figure 19-11.

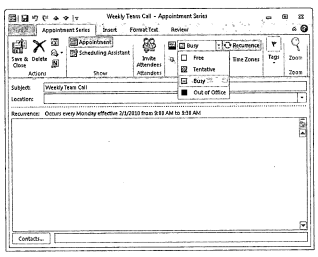

Figure 19-11 Use this drop-down list to select a classification for your appointment, which specifies how the appointment is displayed on your calendar.

Adding a Note

Sometimes an appointment requires more detail. You might need to remind yourself about documents that you need to bring to the appointment, or perhaps you need to write down directions to an unfamiliar location. When that's the case, you can add a note by typing your text in the large text area of the form, as shown in Figure 19-12.

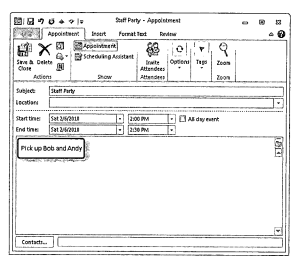

Figure 19-12 You can write a note on the appointment form.

Categorizing an Appointment

Assigning a category to an appointment is simply another method of organizing your information. Outlook 2010 provides a number of default categories associated with colors, and you can customize the names for each category. The color association enables you to identify the categories of appointments more easily within your calendar. You can create additional categories as desired and associate each with a specific color. Outlook 2010 allows you to categorize your appointments so that you can then filter or sort them before viewing. In this way, you can get an overview of all Outlook 2010 items based on a particular category. For example, you could view all appointments, meetings, messages, contacts, and tasks that have been assigned the same category—perhaps all the items related to a specific work project or objective.

For more information about working with categories in Outlook 2010, see Chapter 5, "Creating and Using Categories."

To assign a category to an appointment, click Categorize in the Tags group of the appointment tab. To assign a single category to the appointment, simply select the category in the drop-down list, as shown in Figure 19-13. To select multiple categories, modify existing categories, or create new categories, select the All Categories option at the bottom of the drop-down list.

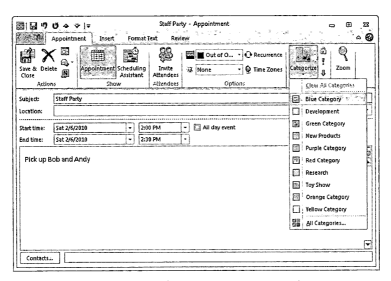

Figure 19-13 You can assign color categories to your appointment.

When you select All Categories, the Color Categories dialog box is displayed, as shown in Figure 19-14, enabling you to manage the categories. In this dialog box, you can select one or more categories and then click OK to assign them to the appointment. You can also rename or delete any of the existing categories and change the color association, as well as assigning a shortcut key for each category.

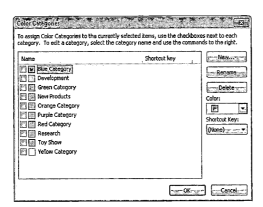

Figure 19-14 You can assign multiple categories to your appointment and configure a category label, color, and shortcut key.

Saving an Appointment

You can save an appointment in several ways. The most basic method is to click the Save & Close button on the ribbon. This saves the appointment in the Calendar folder and closes the appointment form. If you want to save the appointment but keep the form open, click the Save button on the Quick Access Toolbar (or click File and then Save).

A more complex way to save appointments allows them to be transferred to other users (who might or might not use Outlook 2010) and opened in other applications. To save your appointments in any of a number of file formats, click File, and then choose Save As to display the Save As dialog box, shown in Figure 19-15.

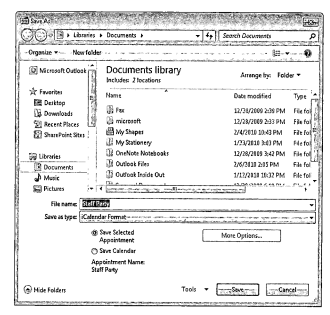

Figure 19-15 You can save your appointment in any of several formats so that the appointment can be opened with another application. You can also save the calendar or any date range portion of it.

The following formats are available:

- Rich Text Format and Text Only   These formats save the appointment in a file that text editors can read. Figure 19-16 shows an example of an appointment saved in Rich Text Format (RTF) and then opened in WordPad.

Note

You can create a new appointment from an Outlook 2010 Template file by clicking New Items, Choose Form, and then selecting User Templates In File System in the Look In list.

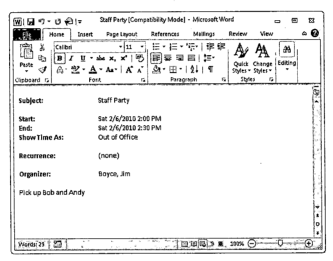

Figure 19-16 An appointment saved in Rich Text Format or Text Only can be displayed in any application that supports those file types.

- **Outlook Template**   This format allows you to save an appointment and use it later to create new appointments.

- **Outlook Message Format and Outlook Message Format – Unicode**   Saving an appointment in one of these formats is almost the same as saving an appointment to the calendar, except that the appointment is saved in a file in case you want to archive the file or move it to another installation of Outlook 2010. You can view the file in Outlook 2010, and the data appears as it would if you had opened the item from the calendar.

- **iCalendar Format and vCalendar Format**   These formats are used to share schedule items with people who use applications other than Outlook 2010. iCalendar is a newer version of the standard (maintained by the Internet Mail Consortium) and should be used if possible.

Changing an Appointment to an Event

To change an appointment to an event, select the All Day Event check box on the appointment form. When an appointment is converted to an event, the start and end times are removed and only the start and end dates are left because events by definition last all day. The event appears in the banner area of the calendar.

Working with One-Time Events

An event is an appointment that lasts for one or more entire days. You can create an event by right-clicking the calendar and then choosing New All Day Event. Unlike appointments, events are not shown in time slots on the calendar. Instead, events are displayed as banners at the top of the calendar day. Figure 19-17 shows the calendar with a scheduled event—in this case, a trade show.

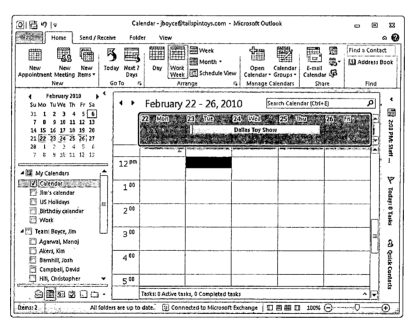

Figure 19-17 Outlook 2010 displays events as banners on the calendar.

INSIDE OUT   **Create an event quickly**

A simple way to add an event is to click the banner area of the calendar and start typing the subject of the event. When you add an event this way, the event is automatically set to last for only the selected day. Alternatively, in Month view, click a date and then type the subject to create a one-time event on that date. To add details and change the duration of the event, you must use the event form.

Using the Event Form

You can use an event form in much the same way you use an appointment form, with a few exceptions:

- You can set the start and end times only as dates, not times. (If you select times, the form changes from an event form to an appointment form, and the All Day Event check box is cleared.)

- The default reminder is set to 18 hours.

- The time is shown by default as Free, as opposed to Busy.

The event form and the appointment form look the same except that the All Day Event check box is selected on the event form. You can open an event form by right-clicking the time in Calendar view and then choosing New All Day Event.

To create an event using the event form, type the subject, specify the start and end dates, add any optional information, and then click Save & Close in the Actions group. Figure 19-18 shows the event form for a trade show event.

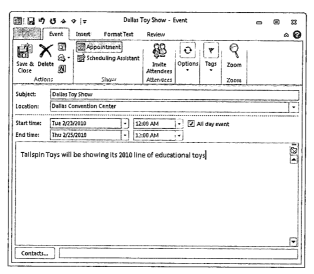

Figure 19-18 Use the event form to specify the details of an event to be added to your calendar.

Changing an Event to an Appointment

To change an event to an appointment, clear the All Day Event check box on the event form. The boxes for start and end times are re-enabled, and the event will now be displayed in time slots on the calendar, not in the banner area.

Creating a Recurring Appointment or Event

When you create a recurring appointment or a recurring event, Outlook 2010 automatically displays the recurrences in the calendar. A recurring appointment could be something as simple as a reminder to feed your fish every day or pay your mortgage every month. You can create a recurring calendar item by right-clicking the calendar and then choosing New Recurring Appointment or New Recurring Event. Alternatively, you can open a normal (non-recurring) item and then click the Recurrence button in the Options group. Either method displays the Appointment Recurrence dialog box, shown in Figure 19-19.

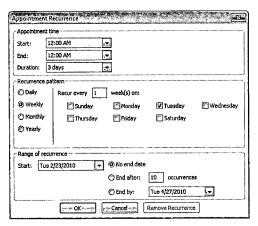

Figure 19-19 You can specify criteria that direct Outlook 2010 to display an appointment or event multiple times in the calendar.

In the Appointment Time area, you set the appointment time and duration. If you're creating the recurrence from an existing nonrecurring appointment, the time of that appointment is listed by default.

The Recurrence Pattern area changes depending on whether you select the Daily, Weekly, Monthly, or Yearly option, as follows:

- **Daily**   Specify the number of days or every weekday.

- **Weekly**   Specify the number of weeks and the day (or days) of the week.

- **Monthly**   Specify the number of months as well as the day of the month (such as the 27th) or the day and week of the month (such as the fourth Wednesday). Use the The Last Day Of Every 1 Month(s) option, rather than specifying the 31st, if you want the item to recur on the last day of each month (because not every month has 31 days).

- **Yearly**   Specify the date (such as December 27) or the day and week of the month (such as the fourth Wednesday of each December).

At the bottom of the Appointment Recurrence dialog box is the Range Of Recurrence area. By default, the start date is the current day, and the recurrence is set to No End Date. You can choose to have the appointment recur a specified number of times and then stop, or you can set it to recur until a specified date and then stop—either method has the same effect. For example, to set a recurring appointment that starts on the first Monday of a month and continues for four Mondays in that month, you could either set it to occur four times or set it to occur until the last day of the month.

Modifying an Appointment or Event

There are many reasons you might need to change a scheduled appointment or event—an event could be rescheduled, an appointment could be moved to a better time, or the topical focus could be added to or changed. In each case, you will need to modify the existing appointment or event, updating information or changing the date or time.

Changing an Appointment or Event

Modifying an existing appointment or event is easy. First, open the appointment or event by locating it in the calendar and then either double-clicking or right-clicking it and choosing Open. Make the necessary changes in the form, and then click Save & Close on the ribbon. The updated appointment or event is saved in the Calendar folder.

Deleting an Appointment or Event

You can delete an appointment or event in several ways. To send the item to the Deleted Items folder, right-click the item and choose Delete, or select the item and press the Delete key. To permanently delete the item, hold down Shift while choosing Delete or pressing the Delete key.

CAUTION

You cannot recover an item that has been deleted using the Shift key unless you are using Microsoft Exchange Server and your administrator has configured the server for a retention period.

Using Categories and Colors

You can use color as a tool to identify appointments and events. In Outlook 2003, the assignment of colors and categories was separate from that of other categories, but in Outlook 2007 these were combined, and that carries over to Outlook 2010. The easiest way to assign color to an appointment is to use the Categorize drop-down list on the appointment form. You can also direct Outlook 2010 to assign color labels automatically via the Automatic Formatting option in Outlook 2010.

Assigning Color Categories to an Appointment Manually

The Categorize drop-down list on the appointment form shows the different color labels (associated with categories) that you can assign to an appointment as a visual cue to indicate the topic of the appointment. Categories can also reflect appointment importance or requirements. Simply select a color in the drop-down list when you fill in the appointment form. In Figure 19-20, the appointment shown is a business one, and it will be displayed on the calendar in the specified color. To set colors independent of categories, use the conditional formatting rules described in the next section.

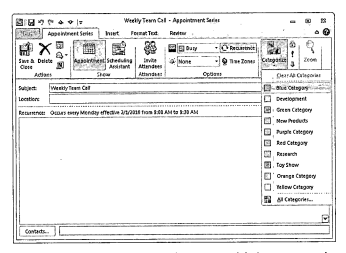

Figure 19-20 You can assign a color category label to your appointment.

You can assign a category to an appointment without associating a color with it, by defining a category and selecting None for the color. Categories without colors will not provide the visual cue that enables you to identify the nature of an appointment quickly, but they still are useful—for example, when you filter your Calendar view by category.

> **Note**
> Manual color category settings always override automatic settings, even when the category color setting is set to None.

Assigning Color to an Appointment Automatically

To have Outlook 2010 automatically assign a color label to an appointment, you can create conditional formatting rules.

To assign color automatically, do the following:

1. Click the View tab and click View Settings to display the Advanced View Settings dialog box. Then click Conditional Formatting.

2. Click Add to add a new rule.

3. Type a name and assign a label to the new rule. Figure 19-21 shows a rule to color all Important appointments automatically with red.

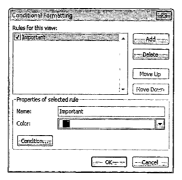

Figure 19-21 This new rule automatically assigns the red color to all appointments with high importance.

4. Click Condition to open the Filter dialog box, shown in Figure 19-22, where you specify the condition for the rule.

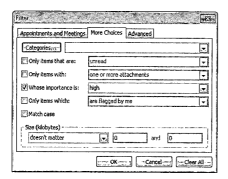

Figure 19-22 The Filter dialog box lets you set a filter that defines the condition on which the automatic color rule works.

For details about using filters, see the section "Customizing the Current Calendar View" on this page.

5. In this dialog box, assign a condition to the rule. For example, you might search for a word or phrase in all appointments, such as searching for the words Phone Conference in the Subject and Notes fields, and marking these appointments using the Red color category if Phone Conference is found.

> ### Note
> The More Choices and Advanced tabs in the Filter dialog box enable you to select other criteria, such as categories, read status, attachments, size, or matching fields.

6. Click OK to assign the condition to the new rule.

7. Click OK twice, once to close the Conditional Formatting dialog box and again to close the Advanced View Settings dialog box.

Printing Calendar Items

You can print calendar items in two ways. The simplest method is to right-click the item and then choose Quick Print from the shortcut menu. This method prints the item using the default settings.

The other way to print an item is to first open it by double-clicking it. You can then click File, Print to display the Print dialog box.

You can make selections in the Print dialog box to change the target printer, the number of copies, and the print style, if necessary. The print style defines how the printed item will look. Click Print Options, Page Setup to change the options for the selected style. In the Page Setup dialog box, use the Format tab to set fonts and shading; the Paper tab to change the paper size, orientation, and margin settings; and the Header/Footer tab to add information to be printed at the top and bottom of the page.

Customizing the Current Calendar View

In addition to setting the number of days displayed, configuring the Time Bar, and color-coding your appointments, you can customize the standard view of the Calendar folder in other ways. You can redefine fields, set up filters that define which items are displayed on your calendar, and control fonts and other view settings. To configure the view, click View

Settings on the View tab on the ribbon to open the Advanced View Settings dialog box, shown in Figure 19-23.

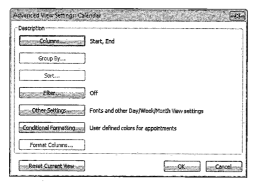

Figure 19-23 Use the Advanced View Settings dialog box to change view settings.

INSIDE OUT **Customize additional views**

You can also customize views other than the current one. To do so, click Change View, Manage Views. Select the view in the Manage All Views dialog box, and then click Modify. This displays the Advanced View Settings dialog box, where you can change the options for the selected view.

Redefining Fields

Only two of the fields used for calendar items can be redefined: the Start and End fields. The values in these fields determine an item's precise location on the calendar—that is, where the item is displayed. By default, the value contained in the Start field is the start time of the appointment and the value contained in the End field is the end time of the appointment, which means that the item is displayed on the calendar in the time interval defined by the item's Start and End values.

To redefine either the Start or the End value, click Columns in the Advanced View Settings dialog box to open the Date/Time Fields dialog box. In the Available Date/Time Fields list, select the field that you want to use for the Start field, and then click Start. Click the End button to change the End field. For example, if you redefine the Start field to Recurrence Range Start and the End field to Recurrence Range End, all recurring calendar items will be displayed as a single item that starts on the date of the first occurrence and ends on the

date of the last occurrence. This can be handy if you want to view the entire recurrence range for a given item graphically.

Filtering Calendar Items

You can filter calendar items based on their content, their assigned category, or other criteria. By filtering the current view, you can determine which calendar items are displayed on your calendar—for example, all items related to one of your work projects, all items that involve a specific coworker, or items with a particular importance level.

To filter calendar items, follow these steps:

1. On the View tab on the ribbon, click View Settings to open the Advanced View Settings dialog box.

2. Click Filter to open the Filter dialog box.

3. If the Appointments And Meetings tab isn't displayed, as shown in Figure 19-24, click it to bring it to the front.

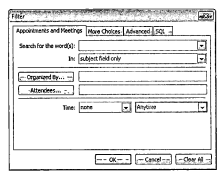

Figure 19-24 You can filter calendar items based on a specified word or phrase.

4. In the Search For The Word(s) box, type the word or phrase you want to use as the filter.

5. In the In drop-down list, select which areas of the calendar item to search—for example, you might have Outlook 2010 look only in the Subject field of your appointments.

6. Click OK. Outlook 2010 displays on your calendar only those calendar items that contain the specified word or phrase.

To set additional criteria, you can use the three other tabs in the Filter dialog box—More Choices, Advanced, and SQL—as follows:

- **More Choices** On this tab, you can click Categories to select any number of categories. After you click OK, only calendar items belonging to the selected categories are displayed on the calendar. Using the check boxes on the More Choices tab, you can filter items based on whether they are read or unread, whether they have attachments, their flag status, or their importance setting. The final check box on the tab enables or disables case matching for the word or phrase specified on the Appointments And Meetings tab. You can also filter items depending on size.

- **Advanced** This tab allows an even wider range of filter criteria. You can specify any field, adding a condition such as Contains or Is Not Empty or a value for conditions that require one. Clicking Add To List adds the criteria to the list of filters.

- **SQL** This tab has two purposes. In most cases, it displays the Structured Query Language (SQL) code for the filter, based on the filter criteria you select on the other three tabs. If the Edit These Criteria Directly check box is selected, however, you can manually type the SQL code for filtering calendar items directly on the SQL tab. This flexibility allows you to fine-tune your filters with a great degree of precision.

Controlling Fonts and Other View Settings

You can use the Advanced View Settings dialog box (previously shown in Figure 19-23) to make additional changes to the current view. In the Advanced View Settings dialog box, click Other Settings to display the Format Day/Week/Month View dialog box, shown in Figure 19-25.

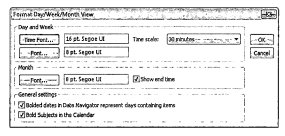

Figure 19-25 You can use the Format Day/Week/Month View dialog box to set font preferences for the Calendar folder as well as other options.

In the Format Day/Week/Month View dialog box, you can do the following:

- Set the fonts used in Calendar view.

- Set the calendar's time increments by selecting an option in the Time Scale drop-down list. This sets the amount of time represented by each interval in the Time Bar.

- Specify whether days with scheduled items should appear in bold in the Date Navigator.

- Specify whether Subjects in the calendar should appear in bold.

Creating a Custom View

Up to now, we have looked only at the customization of existing views, but you can also create completely new views and copy and modify views. If your current view is one that you use often but nevertheless must change frequently to filter calendar items or modify fields, you might find it easier to create a new view.

To create a view or to see a list of already defined views, on the View tab, click Change View, Manage Views to open the Manage All Views dialog box, shown in Figure 19-26.

> **Note**
>
> To work with the Outlook 2010 calendar views, you must open the Calendar folder.

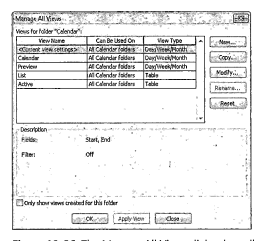

Figure 19-26 The Manage All Views dialog box allows you to see and work with the currently defined views as well as create new ones.

Creating a New View

To create a view, follow these steps:

1. Click New in the Manage All Views dialog box to open the Create A New View dialog box, shown in Figure 19-27.

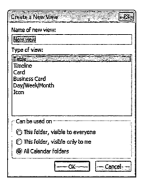

Figure 19-27 You can use the Create A New View dialog box to specify a name, a view type, the folder to which the view applies, and who is allowed to see the view.

2. Name the new view, and then select a view type. In the Can Be Used On area, specify the folder to which the view applies and who is allowed to see the view. You can select one of the following options:

   - This Folder, Visible To Everyone Limits the view to the current folder and makes it available to any user.

   - This Folder, Visible Only To Me Limits the view to the current folder, but makes it available only to the current user.

   - All Calendar Folders Allows the view to be used in any Calendar folder by any user.

3. Click OK to create the new view. The Customize View dialog box appears, in which you can set the options for the new view.

INSIDE OUT   Change the availability of an existing view

The Modify option in the Manage All Views dialog box does not let you change the availability of an existing view. To change the availability of an existing view or who is allowed to see a view, first copy the view and assign a name to the copy. (See the next section for more information about copying views.) Then select a new option in the Can Be Used On area. Last, delete the original view and rename the new view using the name of the deleted view.

For information about setting view options in the Customize View dialog box, see the section "Customizing the Current Calendar View," on page 499.

Copying a View

If you want to modify an existing view but also want to keep the original, you can make a copy of the view. To copy a view, select it in the Manage All Views dialog box, and then click Copy. In the Copy View dialog box, you can specify the name of the new view, the folder to which the view will apply, and who is allowed to see the view. Click OK to create the copy, which is added to the list in the Manage All Views dialog box and the list on the Change View menu on the View tab.

Using Overlay Mode to View Multiple Calendars in One

There are times when you need to view and compare multiple schedules to identify related items, such as workflow dependencies within a project, as well as to find and alleviate scheduling conflicts. For example, you might want to view your personal calendar in contrast to your departmental calendar to compare scheduling and task overlaps, or perhaps you want to view calendars for multiple team members to identify a free slot for a meeting. Outlook 2010 enables you to view multiple calendars in overlay mode, as shown in Figure 19-28.

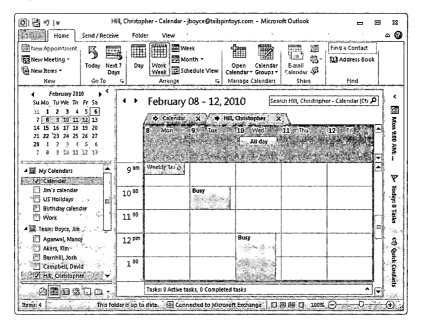

Figure 19-28 You can overlay multiple calendars to view related or conflicting schedules.

To view multiple calendars in overlay mode:

1. Select multiple calendars by selecting the check boxes next to the calendars in the Navigation pane.

2. Right-click one of the calendars in the Navigation pane, and then choose Overlay.

> **Note**
> You can click the left arrow icon at the left edge of the calendar's name tab to overlay the calendar with the leftmost calendar. Click the right arrow icon to move the selected calendar out of overlay mode.

Backing Up Your Schedule

To back up items in your Calendar folder, you must export the data to a personal folder (.pst) file. To do so, follow these steps:

1. Click File, Open, and then Import to start the Import And Export Wizard.

2. Click Export To A File, as shown in Figure 19-29, and then click Next.

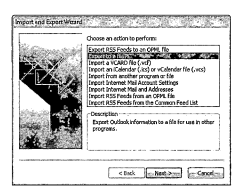

Figure 19-29 To back up calendar items, start the Import And Export Wizard, and then select Export To A File.

3. On the Export To A File page, shown in Figure 19-30, select Outlook Data File (.pst), and then click Next.

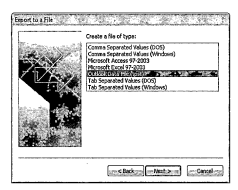

Figure 19-30 Calendar items should be backed up to a .pst file.

4. In the Export Personal Folders dialog box, select the folder to export (the Calendar folder in the example shown in Figure 19-31). If you select the Include Subfolders check box, any subfolders of the selected folder are exported as well.

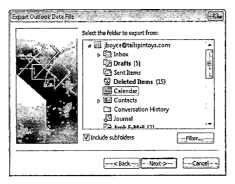

Figure 19-31 You use the Export Outlook Data File dialog box to specify the folder to export to a file.

5. Enter a name for the .pst file in the text box, or click Browse to select an existing .pst file.

6. Click Filter to open the Filter dialog box, in which you can specify the items to be exported. You can use the Filter dialog box if you want to export only specific items from your Calendar folder. If you choose not to use the Filter dialog box, all items will be exported. Click Next to continue.

For details about using the Filter dialog box, see the section "Filtering Calendar Items," on page 501.

7. Specify the exported file and the export options. The export options control how Outlook 2010 handles items that have duplicates in the target file. You can choose to overwrite duplicates, create duplicates in the file, or not export duplicate items.

8. Click Finish. If you did not select an existing .pst file, the Create Outlook Data File dialog box, shown in Figure 19-32, appears.

Figure 19-32 Type a password and verify the password before creating the .pst file.

9. Type password (optional) and click OK to create the file.

To restore data backed up to the .pst file, follow these steps:

1. Click File, Open, and then Import to start the Import And Export Wizard.

2. Select Import From Another Program Or File, and then click Next.

3. Select Outlook Data File (.pst), and then click Next.

4. On the Import Personal Folders page, specify the backup file and how Outlook 2010 should handle duplicate items. You can choose to overwrite duplicates, create duplicate items, or not import duplicates. Then click Next. If you assigned a password to the backup file, you will be prompted to enter it at this point.

5. Select the folder within the .pst file to be imported (the Calendar folder in this case), decide whether to include subfolders, and select the target folder. (By default, the target folder is the folder with the same name in the current mailbox, as shown in Figure 19-33.) You can also click Filter to specify in the Filter dialog box which items are to be imported.

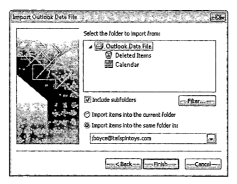

Figure 19-33 When you're importing items, you must select the folder to be imported from the .pst file, whether to include subfolders, and the target folder.

6. Click Finish to complete the import process.

Managing Time Zones

Outlook 2010 gives you a great deal of flexibility when it comes to time zones on your calendar. You can change time zones easily and even add a second time zone to the calendar. If you work for a corporation that has multiple offices in different time zones, being able to reference your calendar with various zones quickly can make scheduling simpler.

Changing the Time Zone

To work with time zones, use the Time Zone dialog box, shown in Figure 19-34. To open this dialog box, right-click the Time Bar and choose Change Time Zone. (Alternatively, click File, Options, and then Calendar.)

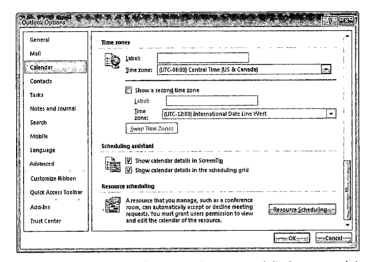

Figure 19-34 You can set the current time zone and display a second time zone.

In the Time Zone group, you can specify a label for the current time zone, which is displayed above the Time Bar on your calendar. You can also set the time zone that you want to use by selecting it in the Time Zone drop-down list, and you can also choose a second time zone to show.

> **Note**
> Changing the time zone in the Time Zone dialog box has the same effect as changing the time zone by using the Date And Time dialog box through Control Panel (Classic View).

When you change the time zone, the time of your appointments adjusts as well. Your appointments stay at their scheduled time in the original time zone but move to the appropriate time in the new time zone. For example, an appointment scheduled for 10:00 A.M. in the Central Time zone will move to 8:00 A.M. if the time zone is changed to Pacific Time. Appointments are scheduled in absolute time, regardless of the time zone.

Using Two Time Zones

To add a second time zone to your calendar, follow these steps:

1. In the Time Zones group, select the Show A Second Time Zone check box.

2. Assign a label to the second time zone. This step is not necessary, but it can help to avoid confusion later on. (If your first time zone does not already have a label, adding one now will allow you to distinguish between the two easily.)

3. In the second Time Zone drop-down list, select the second time zone.

4. Click Swap Time Zones to swap the current time zone with the second time zone. This feature is useful if you travel between corporate offices in different time zones.

Figure 19-35 shows the calendar after these changes have been applied.

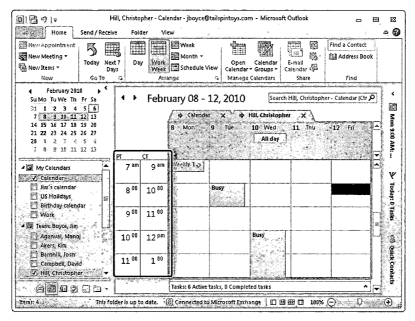

Figure 19-35 The calendar displays both time zones in the Time Bar under their respective labels.

Managing Your Calendar Effectively

Your Outlook 2010 calendar can help you track your appointments and events and facilitate your collaboration with coworkers, vendors, and clients. To maximize the value of the Outlook 2010 calendar, you will want to provide as much detail in the information that you enter as you can. In addition to simply marking the dates and times of scheduled appointments and events, the calendar information will serve as a quick reference to key points in your workflow, projects, and goals. In addition, the interface features (such as Categories and Conditional Formatting) can provide valuable visual and cognitive cues to the nature and importance of your calendar information, as follows:

- **Use color categories for quick identification.** Outlook 2010 has combined color and category labeling of appointments and events and allows you to define the name of each category and the color associated with it. By defining a set of categories that fits the categories of events, appointments, and information you will be storing in your calendar, you can make it easy to mark (and later identify) the nature and significance of items in your calendar at a glance. These user-defined color categories can provide you with visual cues that help you identify calendar items, tasks, and email that are related—such as a departmental project or role-based recurring activities. The color categories in Outlook 2010 are contained in your default data file; thus for users of Exchange Server, your color categories are available regardless of which computer you log on from.

- **Use conditional formatting to format items based on user-selectable criteria.** In addition to color categories, you can use conditional formatting to assign a color to appointments, events, and so on in your calendar based on criteria that you define. This can be particularly useful in that you can provide specific words, phrases, or other criteria that Outlook 2010 will use to automatically tag the appointment or event with a specific color. You can use conditional formatting, for example, to find the phrase Phone Conference in the Subject or Notes field of appointments and automatically color all those items in your calendar (with a color you select) to provide you with visual cues that the item involves a phone conference.

  For specific information about how to assign colors automatically, see the section "Assigning Color to an Appointment Automatically," on page 498.

- **Delegate calendar update responsibilities.**   In managing your calendar, scheduling appointments and events, and communicating your schedule information effectively, you can use the abilities to delegate access and degrees of editing and authoring control to team members, assistants, and key people involved in ongoing projects.

> **Note**
> To delegate control over your calendar (or other functions of Outlook 2010), you and the person you are delegating to must both be using Exchange Server for your mail servers.

  For network environments using Exchange Server, however, the ability to delegate differential levels of control can be a useful way to turn schedule management into a cooperative effort. Even without providing other users with the ability to send email messages as you, you can nevertheless enable them to read your schedule, create new items or subfolders, edit and delete their own additions to your schedule, and even edit all calendar content. When you are working closely with an associate or a team member on a mutual project, that person could add schedule items on your behalf that address his or her area (documentation, code development, marketing) of responsibility.

- **Share your calendar information.**   In addition to those environments where you can delegate access to read information from and write information to your calendar directly, in all cases you can post your calendar information to the external or internal web servers so that management, team, and project members can view your schedule information. In some cases, you might want to publish only the free/busy portion of your schedule information—for example, when publishing your schedule on the Internet. But when publishing your schedule to internal corporate web servers, you will want to provide access to more detail so that coworkers and managers stay up to date. The calendar-sharing options let you specify the date range and level of detail published, determine access (everyone or just those you invite), and select calendar update frequency. You can also share your calendar via email with the selected group of email recipients for whom your calendar is relevant. This option also lets you choose the date range and level of detail sent so that you can control how much of your calendar information you are providing.

  For detailed information about sharing calendars, see Chapter 35, "Sharing Calendars."

- **Use views to manage your calendar.** The various views of your calendar provide a built-in way for you to quickly assess your schedule—simply switching between the Day, Week, and Month tabs reminds you of your scheduled activities. Using the built-in views enables you to see your schedule laid out as a timeline (which you can view on a daily, weekly, or monthly basis). Other default views enable you to see all your scheduled items as a list that you can sort by date, type of appointment or event, subject, category, and a range of other criteria. Using these views can help you quickly find events and appointments of current topical interest and provide reminders of upcoming scheduled obligations. When specific view and filter criteria are particularly useful for you, creating a custom view using these criteria will provide you with an instant ability to see your schedule information in that format.

- **Use Overlays to Compare Calendars.** For everyone in a work environment, the scheduling of appointments and events has interdependencies with coworkers, teams, project groups, and departments. To avoid scheduling conflicts, it can be very helpful to align your schedule with schedules from other people or groups you are working with. Using Outlook 2010 to bring in additional calendars (from coworkers or groups) and review them in overlay mode greatly facilitates the comparing of schedules.

Bᴇꜰᴏʀᴇ the introduction of workgroup software such as Microsoft Exchange Server and Microsoft Outlook 2010, scheduling a meeting could be a difficult task. Now all it takes is a few simple steps to avoid those endless email exchanges trying to find a suitable meeting time for all invitees. Outlook 2010 provides you with a single place to schedule both people and resources for meetings. You can take advantage of these features whether or not you use Exchange Server.

Chapter 19, "Scheduling Appointments," tells you all about scheduling appointments. Meetings and appointments are similar, of course: both types of items appear on your calendar, and you can create, view, and store them in your Calendar folder in Outlook 2010. An appointment, however, involves only your schedule and time, whereas a meeting involves inviting others and coordinating their schedules. Another difference is that a meeting often requires you to schedule resources, such as a conference room or an overhead projector.

You can schedule meetings with other Outlook 2010 users as well as those who use any email or collaboration application that supports the vCalendar or iCalendar standard. (For more information, see the section "iCalendar, vCalendar, and vCard," on page 36.) This chapter takes you through the process of scheduling meetings and lining up resources.

Sending a Meeting Request

To schedule a meeting, you begin by selecting your calendar in Outlook 2010 and sending a meeting request. Click New Meeting on the Home tab on the ribbon, or click New Items and choose Meeting. The meeting form opens, as shown in Figure 20-1.

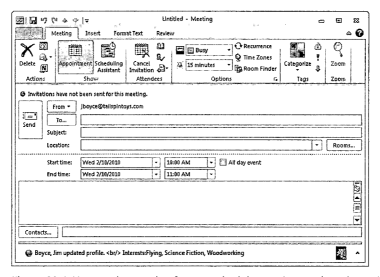

Figure 20-1 You use the meeting form to schedule meetings and send meeting requests.

A meeting request is like an appointment item, but with a few additional details, and you can work with it in much the same way you work with an appointment. This chapter describes only the parts of a meeting request that differ from an appointment.

For details about creating and working with appointments in the Calendar folder in Outlook 2010, see Chapter 19.

Scheduling a Meeting

To invite people to your meeting, start by selecting their names on the Meeting tab. You can type each name in the To box, separating the names with a semicolon. When you enter the names manually, Outlook 2010 considers each person a required attendee. Alternatively, you can click To to open the Select Attendees And Resources dialog box, shown in Figure 20-2. In this dialog box, select a name in the Name list, and then click Required or Optional to designate whether that person's attendance is critical. (This choice will be reflected in the meeting request that you send to these individuals.) After you have finished adding names, click OK to close the dialog box.

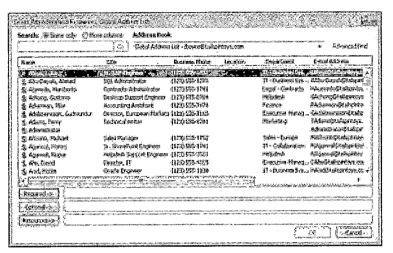

Figure 20-2 In the Select Attendees And Resources dialog box, you can add the names of the individuals you're inviting to your meeting.

> **Note**
>
> When using a non–Exchange Server account, the Show group on the Meeting tab of the ribbon contains a Scheduling button that opens the Scheduling page. With an Exchange Server account, the button is labeled Scheduling Assistant, and when clicked, the button opens the Scheduling Assistant. The two are nearly identical, but there are minor differences, such as the lack of the AutoPick feature in the Scheduling Assistant. See the section, "Scheduling a Meeting with the Scheduling Assistant," on page 521, for more details.

Clicking Scheduling on the Meeting tab displays the Scheduling page, shown in Figure 20-3. You can click in the Click Here To Add A Name box in the All Attendees column and type a name or an email address. Alternatively, you can click Add Attendees to open the Address Book and choose attendees.

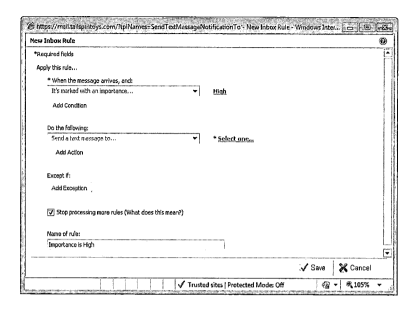

Figure 20-3 You can use the Scheduling page to add meeting attendees and view their schedules.

INSIDE OUT   Select the correct address list

Can't find the attendee you're looking for, and you know that attendee is in the address book? Make sure that the correct address list is selected in the Address Book drop-down list. By default, the Global Address List (GAL), which shows all names from your Exchange Server organization, is selected (if you're running Outlook 2010 with Exchange Server). It is possible to change the default address list, however, and yours could be set to something else.

After you have added the names of the individuals you want to invite, the Scheduling page on the meeting form displays free/busy information for all the people you selected (unless Outlook is unable to retrieve the free/busy information, as indicated in the example in Figure 20-3).

The icons you see beside each name have the meanings indicated in Table 20-1:

Table 20-1   Table Title to come

Icon	Description
⊙	The magnifying glass icon indicates the meeting organizer.
⬆	The arrow icon indicates a required attendee.
ⓘ	The icon containing the letter *i* indicates an optional attendee.
⌂	The building icon indicates a scheduled resource.

INSIDE OUT   Specify free/busy server location

Outlook 2010 queries the free/busy time of each attendee based on the settings you have configured for that purpose. As you'll see in Chapter 35, "Sharing Calendars," you can configure Outlook 2010 to check Microsoft Office Online, another globally specified free/busy server, and individual servers specified with each contact. These all work in conjunction with Exchange Server, if it is present.

After you have identified a time slot that fits everyone's schedules, you can schedule the meeting for a particular time slot using the Meeting Start Time and Meeting End Time drop-down lists.

If you want Outlook 2010 to fit the meeting into the next available time slot, click AutoPick Next. By default, AutoPick selects the next time slot in which all attendees and at least one resource are free.

Note
The AutoPick feature is not available in the Scheduling Assistant for Exchange Server accounts (discussed in a later section of this chapter).

INSIDE OUT   Configure the AutoPick feature

To change the default actions of AutoPick, click Options on the Scheduling page, and then make your choices on the AutoPick menu. You can set AutoPick to select the next time slot in which all attendees and all resources are free, the next time slot in which all attendees and at least one resource are free (the default), a time slot in which only required attendees are free, or a time slot in which required attendees and at least one resource are free.

You can specify whether the display of free/busy information on the Scheduling page should show only working hours (the default) or the entire day. To define working hours for your calendar, click File, Options, and then click Calendar. To set displayed hours for a meeting, click the Options button on the Scheduling page and set or clear the Show Only My Working Hours option. Working hours are a way of displaying your time in the Calendar folder and controlling which hours are displayed on the Scheduling page. In m. cases, including nonworking hours on the Scheduling page would become unmanageable.

After you have selected all the attendees, found an available time slot, and filled in all the necessary details on the message form, click Send on the form to send the meeting request to the attendees.

Scheduling a Meeting from an Email (Reply With Meeting)

Often, emails are the real source for meeting requests. For example, you might receive an email from someone asking for information about a project or task. Outlook 2010 makes it easy to reply to that message with a meeting request. To reply to a message using a meeting request, select the message in the Inbox or other message folder and click Reply With Meeting in the Respond group on the Home tab on the ribbon. Outlook displays a new meeting request form, automatically adds the message sender and recipient(s) to the meeting request, and adds the message contents to the notes section of the meeting invitation. Complete the invitation properties as you normally would and then click Send.

Scheduling a Meeting from the Contacts Folder

If it's more convenient, you can initiate meeting requests from the Contacts folder instead of the Calendar folder. Select one or more contacts in the Contacts folder and click Meeting on the Home tab on the ribbon; or right-click the contact entry for the person you want to invite to a meeting, and then choose Create, Meeting. The meeting form opens with the contact's name in the To box. From here, you can select more attendees and enter meeting details such as subject and location.

If the contact entry contains an address for an Internet free/busy server (found on the Details page of the contact entry, in the Address box of the Internet Free/Busy area), you can download the contact's free/busy information by clicking Options in the Scheduling Assistant and then selecting Refresh Free/Busy. You can also download the contact's free/busy information from Microsoft Office Online, if the contact uses that service, or from another free/busy server if one is specified in the Free/Busy Options dialog box. (This will be explained in detail in Chapter 35.)

For details about Microsoft Office Online, see the section "Managing Your Shared Calendar Information," on page 853.

Changing a Meeting

To change any part of a meeting request, including attendees, times, or other information, first double-click the meeting item in the Calendar folder to open it, and then make your changes. Click the Save icon on the Quick Access Toolbar to save the changes to the Calendar folder, or click Send Update to send an updated meeting request to the attendees. If you make changes that affect the other attendees, such as adding or removing attendees or changing the time or location, you should click Send Update so that the attendees get the new information.

Scheduling a Meeting with the Scheduling Assistant

When you are using Outlook 2010 with Exchange Server, you have an enhanced tool for scheduling meetings called Scheduling Assistant. In most ways, scheduling a meeting with Scheduling Assistant is the same as scheduling a meeting with other types of accounts. This section of the chapter focuses on the different options available in the Scheduling Assistant.

To schedule a meeting, you begin by sending a meeting request. Click New Meeting on the Home tab on the ribbon, or click New and choose Meeting. The meeting form opens, similar to the one shown previously in Figure 20-1. Select the attendees either on the Appointment page by clicking To and using the Select Attendees And Resources dialog box, or on the Scheduling Assistant page by clicking in the Click Here To Add A Name box and typing the name or address.

When you request a meeting (only in Exchange Server 2010), you can select one or more rooms to reserve for the meeting by clicking the Rooms button to the right of the Location box (as shown in Figure 20-4). When you click Rooms, the Select Rooms dialog box is displayed, as shown in Figure 20-5. To select a room, click the room (or hold down the Ctrl key and click to select multiple rooms), click the Rooms button at the bottom of the dialog box to add the rooms to your meeting request, and then click OK.

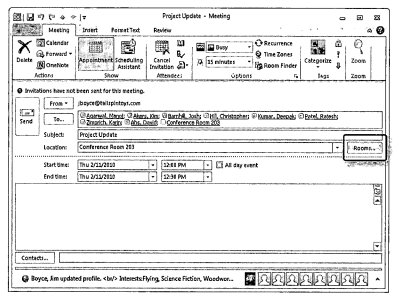

Figure 20-4 Click Rooms to select a room for the meeting.

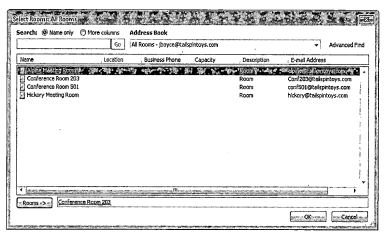

Figure 20-5 The Select Rooms dialog box lets you add one or more rooms to the meeting request.

As Figure 20-6 shows, the Scheduling Assistant page is slightly different from the Scheduling page for non–Exchange Server accounts. For example, the AutoPick option is not available, but the Add Rooms button is available. In addition, the Room Finder pane appears, enabling you to locate an available room for the meeting. Click the Room Finder button in the Options group of the Meeting tab to show or hide the Room Finder.

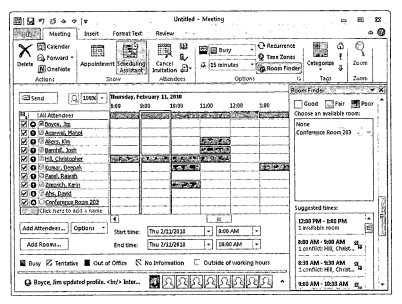

Figure 20-6   Use the Room Finder to locate a room for your meeting.

Responding to a Meeting Request

When you click Send on a meeting form, a meeting request email message is sent to the invited attendees. This message allows the attendees to accept, tentatively accept, or reject the meeting invitation; propose a new time for the meeting; and include a message in the reply.

Receiving a Request for a Meeting

The attendees you've invited to your meeting will receive a meeting request message similar to the one shown in Figure 20-7. The message includes a preview of the calendar, showing the requested meeting and any adjacent and conflicting calendar items.

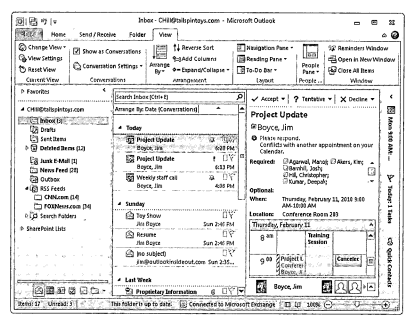

Figure 20-7 A meeting request received by an invited attendee.

An invited attendee has four options when replying to a meeting request:

- Accept the meeting outright.

- Accept the meeting tentatively.

- Decline the meeting.

- Propose a new time for the meeting.

When an attendee chooses to accept, tentatively accept, or decline a meeting request, he or she is presented with three options: send the response now (which sends the default response), edit the response before sending (which allows the attendee to send a message with the response), or do not send a response. Each of these options is available in the meeting message header, as shown in Figure 20-8 (the Propose New Time option is

not shown here, but it is available if the Reading pane is wide enough). For example, if you want to accept a meeting invitation but add some notes to your response, click Accept and choose Edit The Response Before Sending. You can then type some notes in the response and click Send to send it.

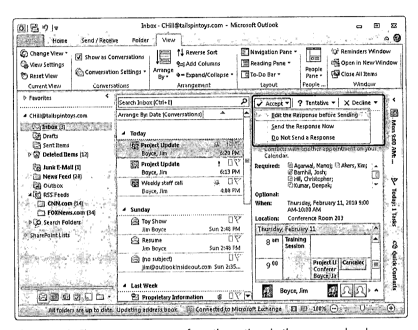

Figure 20-8 Choose your response from the options in the message header.

You can also propose a new meeting time for a meeting invitation that you have received. Click Propose New Time, and then choose Tentative And Propose New Time or Decline And Propose New Time (see Figure 20-9), depending on whether you want to accept or decline the invitation. The Propose New Time dialog box that appears is essentially the same as the Scheduling page of the meeting form (see Figure 20-10). From here, the attendee can select a new time for the meeting and propose it to the meeting organizer by clicking Propose Time.

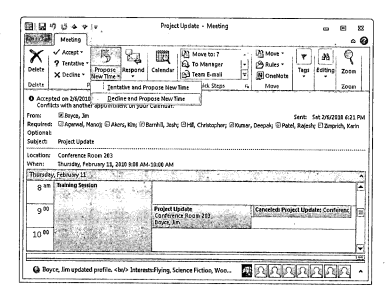

Figure 20-9 You can propose a new time for a meeting.

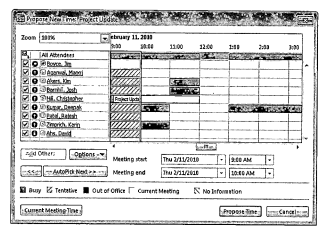

Figure 20-10 Choose a new time for the meeting and click Propose Time.

TROUBLESHOOTING

You've lost a meeting request

When you respond to a meeting request in email, the original request message is automatically deleted from your Inbox. Outlook 2010 automatically adds the meeting information to your Calendar folder when you receive the email message. If you respond to the meeting request from your calendar, however, the email message is not deleted from your Inbox.

If you need to retrieve any of the data in the email message, check your Deleted Items folder for the meeting request itself and your Calendar folder for the meeting information.

To have Outlook 2010 keep meeting request messages in your Inbox even after you've responded, follow these steps:

1. Click File, Options, and then click Mail.

2. Scroll down to locate the Send Messages group of settings.

3. Clear the Delete Meeting Request And Notifications From Inbox After Responding check box.

Receiving a Response to Your Request

When an invited attendee responds to a meeting request, a message is returned to you, the meeting organizer. This message contains the response, including any message the attendee chose to include. In the meeting request response shown in Figure 20-11, the attendee has accepted the meeting and included a message. Notice that the response also lists the attendees who have accepted, tentatively accepted, and declined up to this point.

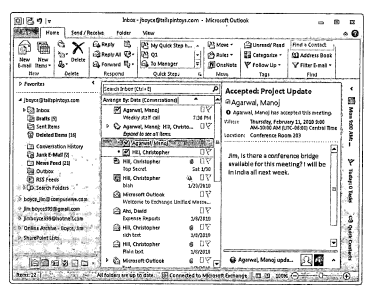

Figure 20-11 A response to a meeting request shows the acceptance status of the request and any message from the attendee.

Figure 20-12 shows a response in which the attendee has selected the Propose A New Time option on a meeting request.

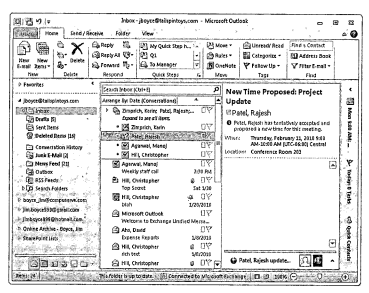

Figure 20-12 When an invited attendee proposes a new time for the meeting, the response to the meeting organizer looks like this.

When you receive a response proposing a new meeting time, you have two choices after you open the response:

- Click Accept Proposal to accept the new time and open the meeting form. Verify any changes, and then click Send Update to send the new proposed time to the attendees.

- Click View All Proposals to open the Scheduling page of the meeting form, which displays a list of all proposed new times for the meeting suggested by any of the attendees, as shown in Figure 20-13. You can select a new time from the list of proposed times and then click Send to send the new proposed time to the meeting attendees.

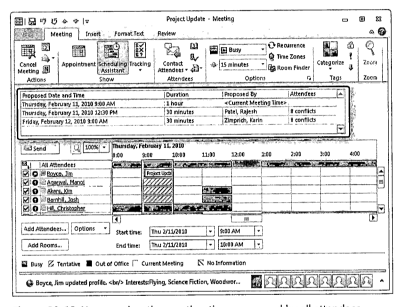

Figure 20-13 You can view the meeting times proposed by all attendees.

Checking Attendees

After you send a meeting request, you can check which attendees have accepted or declined by opening the meeting form in the Calendar folder and clicking the form's Tracking button in the Show group on the Meeting tab, as shown in Figure 20-14. (The Tracking button is not displayed on the initial meeting form; Outlook 2010 adds it after the meeting request has been sent.) The Tracking button shows each invited attendee and indicates whether their attendance is required or optional and the status of their response. The meeting organizer is the only person who can view the status of attendees.

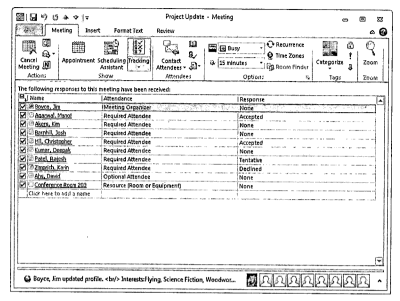

Figure 20-14 Only the person who scheduled the meeting can view the status of the attendees.

Scheduling Resources

To plan and carry out a meeting successfully, you'll usually need to schedule resources as well as people. *Resources* are items (such as computers and projectors) or locations (such as a meeting room) that are required for a meeting. You select resources in much the same way you select attendees.

The ability to schedule resources is typically most useful when you need to set up a meeting, but you might find other occasions when this capability comes in handy. For example, you might want to schedule laptop computers for employees to take home for the weekend or schedule digital cameras to take to building sites.

Setting Up Resources for Scheduling

You schedule a resource by sending a meeting request, adding the resource as a third type of attendee. (The other two types of attendees are Required and Optional, as previously mentioned; see the section "Checking Attendees," on page 529.) Because a resource is scheduled as a type of attendee, it must have a mailbox and a method of accepting or rejecting meeting requests. When you use Outlook 2010 and Exchange Server, a resource is almost identical to any other Exchange Server user except that it is configured to allow another user (the resource administrator) full access to its mailbox. In Exchange Server 2007 or 2010, unlike user mailbox accounts, all resource mailbox accounts are disabled automatically (yet are still accessible as resources from within Outlook 2010).

The first step in setting up a resource for scheduling is to create (or have your system administrator create) a mailbox and an account for the resource. In many cases, resource account names are preceded by a symbol, such as # or &, so that the names, when alphabetized, appear as a group at the top or bottom of the GAL.

How resources are assigned on the mail server running Exchange Server depends on which version of Exchange Server you are using. When you set up resource accounts on a server running Exchange Server 2003, you have to go into Active Directory Users And Computers (within the domain in which the server running Exchange Server is operating) and create and configure user accounts and the subsequent mailboxes. You then have to modify the Mailbox Rights and assign Full Mailbox Access to the resource administrator. The resource administrator has to create a new profile and use the profile to access the mailbox and configure (using the Scheduling Resources option) the Automatically Accept Meeting Requests And Process Cancellations option, which allows the resource scheduling to work. To avoid schedule conflicts, it's also necessary to select Automatically Decline Conflicting Meeting Requests.

When you are using Exchange Server 2007 or 2010, you can schedule both room and equipment resources. Instead of using the Active Directory Users And Computers console to add users and their mail accounts, you use the Exchange Management Console. To add a user account and mailbox to Exchange Server 2010, you browse to the Recipients Configuration container and then select the New Mailbox link. The New Mailbox dialog box provides four options for mailbox creation:

- **User Mailbox**   In this option, the User mailbox is associated with a user account, enabling the user to send, receive, and store email messages, calendar items, tasks, and other Outlook 2010 items.

- **Room Mailbox**   In this option, the Room mailbox is reserved as a resource-type mailbox, and the associated account in Active Directory Domain Services (AD DS) is disabled.

- **Equipment Mailbox**   In this option, the Equipment mailbox is also reserved as a resource-type mailbox, and the associated account in AD DS is disabled.

- **Linked Mailbox**   In this option, the Linked mailbox is employed for users that will access the mailbox from a separate trusted forest.

To assign resources for use in Outlook 2010, you add a new mailbox, select the resource type (either Room or Equipment), and then complete the required information (which is essentially the same information that you would provide for any user account—name, logon name, password, and alias). After you have created a Room mailbox, for instance, when you click the Rooms button in an Outlook 2010 meeting form, all the rooms associated with Room mailboxes will be displayed. Equipment resources (as well as rooms) are displayed in the Select Attendees And Resources list and can be included in the meeting request by selecting the desired equipment and clicking Resources.

Using the Configured Resources

To schedule a resource after you have configured it, create a meeting request and fill in the details. When you add attendees to the meeting request using the Select Attendees And Resources dialog box, select the resource you want to add from the list and then click Resources, as shown in Figure 20-15. Resources are added to the Resources box instead of to the Required or Optional box. When you have finished adding resources, click OK. Then complete and send the meeting request as you normally would.

For details about creating and sending meeting requests, see the section "Sending a Meeting Request," on page 516.

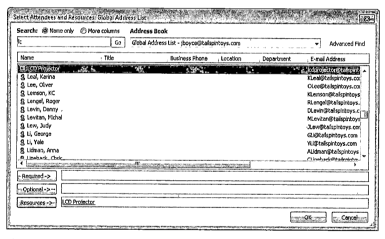

Figure 20-15 Add a resource by selecting it from the list and clicking Resources.

With Exchange Server 2007 and later, a resource's free/busy time appears in the Scheduling Assistant just like the free/busy time for a user. Therefore, you can tell at a glance when a resource is available, enabling you to schedule the meeting around the resource or the room's availability.

If the resource's mailbox is configured to use the Exchange Server Resource Booking Attendant, you will receive an automatic response to your meeting request from the Attendant,

as shown in Figure 20-16. If the resource is managed manually, you will receive a response from the resource's delegate.

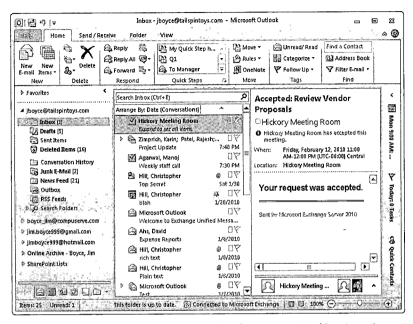

Figure 20-16 This response was generated by the Resource Booking Attendant.

In addition, depending on how the resource mailbox is configured, you might also be able to submit out-of-policy requests to the resource, such as booking a room outside its normally available hours. In these instances, a resource delegate will receive the request and process it.

Viewing a Room Calendar

The fact that rooms are treated as special mailboxes in Exchange Server made it possible for the Outlook development team to build in some special features for working with rooms. You've already seen that you can select a room with the Scheduling Assistant and view its availability in your meeting invitation before you send it. In addition, you can view room calendars within Outlook and, if needed, overlay them on your own calendar or over other peoples' calendars.

To view a room calendar, first open your Calendar folder. Then, in the Manage Calendars group on the Home tab on the ribbon, click Open Calendar and choose From Room List. Outlook displays the Select Name dialog box (shown in Figure 20-5), where you can choose the room whose calendar you want to view. Select one or more rooms, click Rooms, and then click OK. Outlook displays the room's calendar alongside your own, as in Figure 20-17.

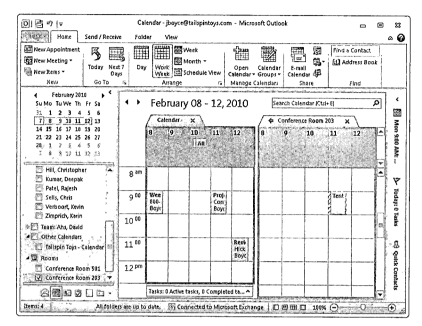

Figure 20-17 You can view room calendars alongside your own calendar.

The capability to view room free/busy information in Outlook means that you can determine ahead of time what rooms are most likely to be available before you even start booking your meeting. For example, if you want to book a meeting for your team, overlay all your team calendars with your own, and then open the desired room calendar and overlay that as well. You'll be able to tell at a glance what times match both your team's collective schedule and the room's.

Managing Meetings Effectively

Meetings are an essential part of working in a corporate business environment. While necessary, they are not always the most effective use of your time. Using the scheduling tools in Outlook 2010 can help you expedite the scheduling of meetings, remind you in advance of upcoming meetings, and help you complete your meetings on time. Using the Outlook 2010 meeting scheduling capability can help improve the quality of your meetings as well. By planning the meeting and notifying all participants of the agenda (in the content of the meeting request), you give them (and yourself) time to prepare notes, documents, and other presentation materials ahead of time. This also allows participants an opportunity to present questions, concerns, and additions to the agenda prior to the meeting, thus ensuring a more comprehensive meeting that isn't distracted by unforeseen complications. You should also keep in mind the specific characteristics of the people invited to each meeting, anticipate aspects (people who show up late, are too verbose, or are distracted easily) that can impair meeting efficiency, and plan your meeting strategy to avoid such issues.

Find the Best Time for the Meeting

When you schedule a meeting in your Outlook 2010 calendar, you can use Outlook 2010 to review the free/busy time on the schedules of the other people you invite to the meeting, thus enabling you to pick times that are available for all attendees when you initially schedule the meeting. To view free/busy information when scheduling a meeting (adding a new meeting request), click Scheduling in the Show group on the Meeting tab. After you have added all attendees, their free/busy information will be retrieved and displayed in a timeline, showing the status of the schedules for each period in the timeline. In addition, resources (such as reserved rooms) will be displayed, showing you which times are available to use the resources. You can refresh the free/busy information by clicking Options and then selecting Refresh Free/Busy. You can also use AutoPick to select a meeting time. Outlook 2010 will select the next available meeting time based on your AutoPick criteria, such as All People, One Resource to pick the first time when all the attendees are free and one resource (such as a conference room) is available. The AutoPick criteria can be set on the Options, AutoPick menu, which lets you specify whether to require all or some attendees and whether one or more resources have to be available.

Use Scheduling Assistant to Help Schedule Meetings

If you have Outlook 2010 set up as a client to Exchange Server, the scheduling functionality is expanded—the Location box on the Appointment page on the Meeting tab has a Rooms button that facilitates meeting room selection, and the Scheduling Assistant page provides further capability to review free/busy information and find available meeting times. In addition to the Free/Busy grid displaying the available times for a meeting, the Suggested Times pane (on the right) shows the Date Navigator, with color-coded dates for possible meeting days (the darker the color, the lower the possibility of scheduling a meeting with the selected attendees). Below the Date Navigator is the selected Duration setting for the meeting, followed by a list of suggested times and showing how many of the requested attendees are free to attend.

Using these features, you can reliably schedule meetings where all people and resources are available, without a flurry of back-and-forth emails to determine availability for a particular date and time.

Set a Sufficient Reminder to Enable You to Make Meetings on Time

Using the Outlook 2010 reminders can facilitate your getting to your meetings on time. You can assess your own work pattern and determine the best default time for Outlook 2010 to remind you of upcoming meetings. Click File, Options to open the Options dialog box, where you can set the default reminder time in the Calendar area to alert you at the best time prior to the meeting. You can also set reminders for specific meetings to provide an additional reminder (perhaps closer to the start of the meeting) by selecting the reminder time in the Options group on the Appointment page for each meeting.

Microsoft Outlook 2010 offers a broad selection of tools to help you manage your workday, including techniques for handling email; a way to manage appointments, meetings, and events; a handy method of creating quick notes; and a journal for tracking projects, calls, and other items. All these tools are often related to creating and completing tasks. For example, writing this book was a long string of tasks to be completed: drawing up the outline, writing each chapter, and reviewing edits, for starters.

In your job, your tasks during the average day are no doubt different. Perhaps they include completing contracts, making sales calls, writing or reviewing documents, completing reports, developing websites, or developing program code. Some tasks take only a little time to complete, whereas others can take days, weeks, or even months.

Outlook 2010 provides the means not only to track your own tasks but also to manage those tasks you need to assign to others. This feature is a much more efficient and effective way to manage tasks than using a notebook, sticky notes, or just your memory. You can set reminders and sort tasks according to category, priority, or status to help you view and manage them.

This chapter examines the Tasks folder and its related features. In addition to learning how to manage your own tasks, you'll also learn to assign tasks to and manage tasks assigned to others.

Working with Tasks in the Tasks Folder

Outlook 2010 provides several ways for you to create and manage tasks. You can create one-time tasks or recurring tasks, set up reminders for tasks, and assign tasks to others. In this section, you'll see how to create tasks for yourself and how to use Outlook 2010 to manage those tasks effectively.

The default view in the Tasks folder is the To-Do List, shown in Figure 21-1, which organizes the tasks by Due Date. Depending on the amount of space available in the view, Outlook 2010 shows additional columns in the To-Do List view, such as Start Date, Reminder Time, Due Date, the folder in which the tasks are located, and Categories.

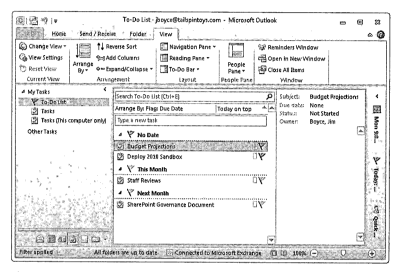

Figure 21-1 Outlook 2010 uses a simple To-Do list as the default Tasks folder view.

The columns in the To-Do List include:

- **Icon**   The Icon column indicates the type of task. For example, it can indicate either that the task is yours or that it's assigned to another person. The clipboard icon with a check mark indicates that the task is your own. An arrow pointing to a small person symbol indicates that the task is assigned to someone else. In addition, the icon can also be an envelope, indicating a message item for follow-up.

- **Task Subject**   You can enter any text in the Subject column, but generally, this text should describe the task to be performed. You can also add notes to each task to identify further the purpose or goal of the task.

- **Start Date**   This column indicates the start date for the task.

- **Reminder Time**   This column shows the reminder for the task.

- **Due Date**   This column indicates the due date for the task and by default shows the day and date. You can specify different date formats if you want.

- **In Folder**   This column shows the folder in which the task is located.

- **Categories**   This column shows the categories, if any, assigned to the task.

- **Flag Status**   This column shows the task's current flag status, and you can use the column to mark the task as complete or right-click to choose other options.

For details on customizing the Tasks folder view, see the section "Viewing and Customizing the Tasks Folder," on page 556. For additional information about features in Outlook 2010 that can help you use and manage views, see the section "Using Other Outlook Features," on page 100.

Most details appear in the Reading pane. You can also view all the details of a task by double-clicking the task item. Doing so opens the task form, the format of which varies depending on whether the task is yours or is assigned to someone else. Figure 21-2 shows the form for a task that belongs to you. Figure 21-3 shows the Task page of a form for a task assigned to someone else.

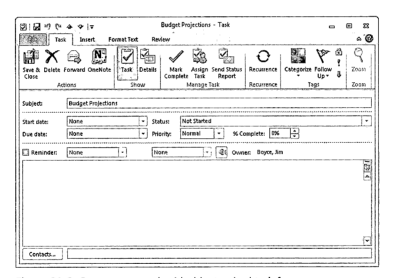

Figure 21-2 Create a new task with this standard task form.

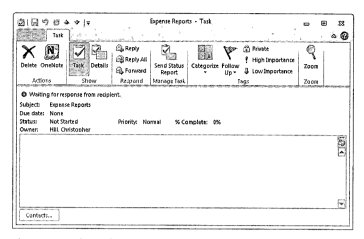

Figure 21-3 This task is assigned to someone else.

The Details page of the task form, shown in Figure 21-4, shows additional information about the task, such as date completed, total work required, actual work performed, and related background information.

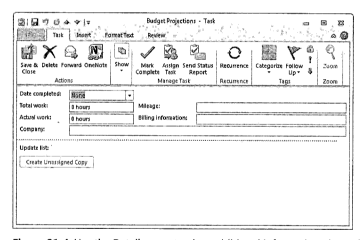

Figure 21-4 Use the Details page to view additional information about the task.

Tip

Press Ctrl+Tab to switch between pages in any multi-paged dialog box or form, including the task form.

> **Browsing Tasks Quickly**
>
> Although you can open tasks by double-clicking them in the Tasks folder, you might prefer to cycle through your tasks right in the task form. For example, when you want to review several tasks, opening and closing them from the task list one after another is a waste of effort. Instead, you can use the Next Item and Previous Item buttons on the form's Quick Access Toolbar to display tasks in forward or reverse order (relative to the listed order in the Tasks folder). The list doesn't cycle from end to beginning or beginning to end, however, so clicking a button when you're at either of those points in the list closes the task form.

Creating a Task

Creating a task is mechanically much the same as creating any item in Outlook 2010. Use any of the following methods to create a new task:

- Between the column header bar and the first task in the list is a new task entry line labeled Click Here To Add A New Task. In the To-Do Bar, the box is labeled Type A New Task. Click the line and start typing if you want to specify only the subject for the task, without initially adding details or selecting options. You can open the task at any time afterward to add other information.

- Double-click in an empty area of the task list.

- Right-click in an empty area of the task list, and then choose New Task.

- With the Tasks folder open, click New Task on the Home tab on the ribbon.

- With any Outlook 2010 folder open, click New Items, and then choose Task. This allows you to create a new task when another folder, such as the Inbox or the Calendar folder, is displayed.

The options on the task form are straightforward. Simply select the options that you want and set the task properties (such as start date and due date). Opening the Due Date or Start Date drop-down list displays a calendar that you can use to specify the month and date for the task. If no specific date is required for the task, you can leave the default value None selected. If you currently have a date selected and want to set the date to None, select None from the drop-down list.

INSIDE OUT   Specify total work and actual work

As you'll learn a little later in this section, you can specify values for Total Work and Actual Work on the Details page of the task form. Total Work indicates the total number of hours (days, weeks, and so on) required for the task; Actual Work lets you record the amount of work performed to date on the task. Unfortunately, the % Complete value on the Task page is not tied to either of these numbers. Thus, if Total Work is set to 40 hours and Actual Work is set to 20 hours, the % Complete box doesn't show 50 percent complete. Instead, you must specify the value for % Complete manually.

Note

The % Complete value is tied to the Status field on the Task page. If you set % Complete to 100, Outlook 2010 sets the status to Completed. If you set % Complete to 0, Outlook 2010 sets the status to Not Started. Any value between 0 and 100 results in a status of In Progress. Selecting a value in the Status drop-down list has a similar effect on % Complete. Select Not Started, for example, and Outlook 2010 sets the % Complete value to 0.

In addition to entering information such as the percentage of work that's completed, the priority, and the status, you can also set a reminder for the task. As it does for other Outlook 2010 items, such as appointments, Outlook 2010 can display a reminder window and play a sound as a reminder to start or complete the task. You can set only one reminder per task, so it's up to you to decide when you want Outlook 2010 to remind you about the task. Click the speaker button on the task form to select the audio file that you want Outlook 2010 to use for the reminder.

One key task setting is the Owner setting. When you create a task, you own that task initially. Only the owner can modify a task. Task ownership is relevant only to assigned tasks—that is, tasks that you assign to others to perform.

For details about task ownership, see the section "Assigning Tasks to Others," on page 547.

Other information that you can specify on the Task tab of the task form's ribbon includes categories and the private or nonprivate status of the task. The ability to assign categories to tasks can help you organize your tasks. You can assign multiple categories to each task as needed and view the Tasks folder sorted by category. For example, you might assign project categories to tasks to help you sort the tasks according to project, allowing you to focus on the tasks for a specific project.

For details on working with categories, see the section "Assigning Categories to Outlook Items," on page 120.

The private or nonprivate status of a task allows you to control whether others who have delegate access to your folders can see a specific task. Tasks marked as private aren't visible unless you explicitly grant permission to the delegate to view private items. To control the visibility of private items, click File, Account Settings, and then Delegate Access. Double-click a delegate, and in the Delegate Permissions dialog box, shown in Figure 21-5, select or clear the Delegate Can See My Private Items check box. Repeat the process for any other delegates as needed.

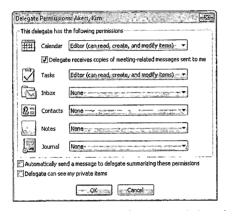

Figure 21-5 Use the Delegate Permissions dialog box to control the visibility of private items.

> **Note**
> The Delegates option is available only if you're using Microsoft Exchange Server.

The Details page of the task form (shown in Figure 21-4) allows you to specify additional information about the task. To view the Details page, click Details in the Show group of the ribbon. The options on the Details page include the following:

- **Date Completed**   Use this calendar to record the date that the task is completed. This is the actual completion date, not the projected completion date.

- **Total Work**   Specify the total amount of work required for the task. You can enter a value in minutes, hours, days, or weeks by entering a value followed by the unit, such as 3 days.

- **Actual Work**   Record the total amount of work performed on the task to date. You can enter the data using the same units as in the Total Work box.

- **Company**   List any companies associated with the task, such as suppliers, customers, or clients.

- **Mileage**   Record mileage associated with the task if mileage is reimbursable or a tax-deductible expense.

- **Billing Information**   Record information related to billing for the task, such as rate, person to bill, and billing address.

- **Update List**   This option applies to tasks assigned to others. It shows the person who originally sent the task request and the names of all others who received the task request, reassigned the task to someone else, or elected to keep an updated copy of the task on their task list. When you send a task status message, Outlook 2010 adds these people as recipients of the status message.

- **Create Unassigned Copy**   Use this button to create a copy of an assigned task that you can send to another person.

For details on working with the update list, assigned tasks, and unassigned copies, see the section "Assigning Tasks to Others," on page 547.

TROUBLESHOOTING

Others can't see your tasks

For others to see your tasks, you must share your Tasks folder. If you're using Exchange Server as your mail server, you can also allow others to see your tasks by granting them delegate access to your Tasks folder. The two methods are similar, with one major difference: Granting delegate access to others allows them to send messages on your behalf. Sharing a folder simply gives others access to it without granting send-on-behalf-of permission.

To share your Tasks folder without granting send-on-behalf-of permission, right-click the Tasks folder icon in the Folder List in the Navigation pane, and then choose Properties. Click the Permissions tab, and then add or remove users and permissions as needed.

For additional details on sharing folders and setting permissions, see the section "Granting Access to Folders," on page 842. To learn how to set up delegate access to your folders, see Chapter 34.

Creating a Recurring Task

Earlier in this chapter, you learned several ways to create a task that occurs once. You can also use Outlook 2010 to create recurring tasks. For example, you might create a recurring task for reports that you have to submit on a weekly, monthly, or quarterly basis. Perhaps you perform backup operations once a week and want Outlook 2010 to remind you to do this.

You create a recurring task much the same way you create a single-instance task, except that when the task form is open, you click the Recurrence button on the Task tab of the ribbon to display the Task Recurrence dialog box, shown in Figure 21-6.

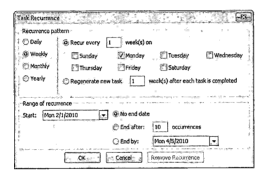

Figure 21-6 Create recurring tasks by using the Task Recurrence dialog box.

You can select daily, weekly, monthly, or yearly recurrence. Selecting one of these four options in the dialog box changes the options available in the dialog box, allowing you to select the recurrence pattern. For example, select Weekly, and then select the days of the week on which you want the task to occur.

When you create a recurring task, one of the decisions you must make is whether you want the task to recur at a specified period regardless of the task's completion status. You can also choose to regenerate a new task after the existing task is completed. For example, you can create a task that recurs every Friday. The task will recur whether or not you marked the previous instance as completed. If you need to complete the previous task before the next task is generated, however, you should configure the recurrence so that the new task is created only after the previous one is completed. For example, perhaps you run a series of reports, but each relies on the previous report being completed. In this situation, you would probably want to set up the task to regenerate only after the preceding one was completed.

The Regenerate New Task option in the Task Recurrence dialog box allows you to configure the recurrence so that the new task is generated a specified period of time after the previous task is completed. Select the Regenerate New Task option, and then specify the period of time that should pass after completion of the task before the task is regenerated.

Other options for a recurring task are the same as those for a one-time task. Specify subject, details, contacts, categories, and other information as needed. Remember to set up a reminder for the task if you want Outlook 2010 to remind you before the task's assigned completion time.

Adding a Reminder

You can add a reminder to a task when you create the task or after you create it. As with reminders for appointments, you specify the date and time for the reminder as well as an optional sound that Outlook 2010 can play along with the reminder.

To add a reminder, follow these steps:

1. Open the task, and then select Reminder on the Task page.

2. Use the calendar in the drop-down list next to the Reminder check box to select the date, and then select a time for the reminder. You can select a time in half-hour increments in the drop-down list or specify your own value by typing it in the box.

3. Click the speaker button to open the Reminder Sound dialog box, in which you select a WAV file to assign to the reminder.

4. Click OK, and then close the task form.

> **Note**
> Outlook 2010 uses a default time of 8:00 A.M. for the reminder. You can change this default value by clicking File, Options, and Tasks, and then setting the Default Reminder Time option.

Setting a Task Estimate

When you create a task, you might also want to estimate the time that it will take to complete the task. You can enter this estimate in the Total Work box on the Details page of the task form. As the task progresses, you can change the Total Work value to reflect your changing estimate or leave it at the original value to track time overruns and underruns for the task. For example, assume that you propose a 40-hour task to a client. As you work

through the task, you continue to update the Actual Work box to reflect the number of hours you've worked on the task. You reach 40 hours of work on the task and haven't completed it. You then have to make a decision: Do you update the Total Work value to show a new estimate for completion and bill the client accordingly, or do you leave it as is and absorb the cost overrun?

Unfortunately, the Total Work and Actual Work fields are simple, nonreactive data fields. Outlook 2010 provides no interaction between the two to determine an actual % Complete value for the task. For that reason—and because Outlook 2010 can't calculate job costs based on charge rates and the amount of work completed—Outlook 2010 by itself generally isn't a complete job tracking or billing application. You should investigate third-party applications to perform that task or develop your own applications using the Microsoft Office 2010 system as a development platform.

Marking a Task as Completed

Logically, the goal for most tasks is completion. At some point, therefore, you'll want to mark tasks as completed. When you mark a task as completed, Outlook 2010 strikes through the task in the task list to provide a visual cue that the task has been finished. The easiest way to mark a task as completed is to place a check in the Complete column, which by default is the first column from the left in the Detailed view. Alternatively, click the Mark Complete button on the ribbon. You can also mark a task as completed on the Task page, simply by selecting Completed in the Status drop-down list or setting the % Complete box to 100.

Outlook 2010 by default sorts the task list by completion status. If you've changed the list to sort based on a different column, simply click that column header. For example, clicking the Complete column header sorts the task list by completion status. If you want to view only completed tasks, click Change View on the View tab on the ribbon and choose Completed. Viewing only incomplete tasks is just as easy: click Change View and choose Active.

For additional details on customizing the Tasks folder view, see the section "Viewing and Customizing the Tasks Folder," on page 556.

Assigning Tasks to Others

In addition to creating tasks for yourself in Outlook 2010, you can assign tasks to others. For example, you might manage a staff of several people and frequently need to assign them projects or certain tasks in a project. The main benefit of using Outlook 2010 to assign those tasks is that you can receive status reports on assigned tasks and view these status reports in your Tasks folder. Outlook 2010 automates the process of sending task requests and processing responses to those requests. You'll learn more about assigning tasks in the sections that follow. First, however, you need to understand task ownership.

About Task Ownership

When you create a task, you initially own that task. Only a task's owner can make changes to the task. This means that you can modify the properties (the percent complete, the status, the start date, and so on) of all tasks that you create and own. When you assign a task to someone else and that person accepts the task, the assignee becomes the owner of the task. You can then view the task's properties, but you can no longer change them. Similarly, you become the owner of tasks assigned to you when you accept them, and you can then make changes to those tasks.

A task's *Owner* property is a read-only value, which appears in the Owner box on the Task page. You can click the value, but you can't change it directly. The only way to change owners is to assign the task and have the assignee accept it.

Making or Accepting an Assignment

Assigning a task to someone else is a simple process. In general, you create the task, add details, and specify options for the task. Then you tell Outlook 2010 to whom you want to assign the task, and Outlook 2010 takes care of generating the task request and sending it to the assignee.

Follow these steps to assign a task to someone else:

1. In Outlook 2010, open the Tasks folder, and create a new task.

2. Add information and set options for the task such as start date, due date, status, and priority.

3. On the Task tab, in the Manage Task group, click Assign Task. Outlook 2010 changes the form to include additional options, as shown in Figure 21-7.

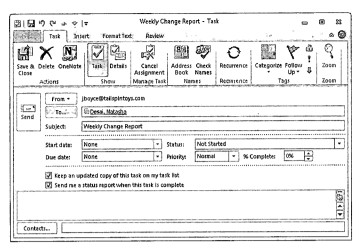

Figure 21-7 Outlook 2010 offers additional options when you assign a task to someone else.

4. In the To box, enter the address of the person to whom you're assigning the task, or click To to browse the Address Book for the person's address.

5. Outlook 2010 automatically selects the following two check boxes. Set them as you want, and then click Send to send the task request to the assignee.

- **Keep An Updated Copy Of This Task On My Task List**   Select this check box if you want to keep a copy of the task in your own task list. You'll receive updates when the assignee makes changes to the task, such as a change in the % Complete status. If you clear this check box, you won't receive updates, nor will the task appear in your task list.

- **Send Me A Status Report When This Task Is Complete**   Select this check box if you want to receive a status report on completion. The status report comes in the form of an email message that Outlook 2010 generates automatically on the assignee's system when the assignee marks the task as completed.

For information about task updates and status reports, see the section "Tracking the Progress of a Task," on page 554.

> **Note**
> Click Cancel Assignment on the ribbon to cancel an assignment and restore the original task form.

When you click Send, Outlook 2010 creates a task request message and sends it to the assignee. If you open the task, you'll see a status message indicating that Outlook 2010 is waiting for a response from the assignee, as shown in Figure 21-8. This message changes after you receive a response and indicates whether the assignee accepted the task.

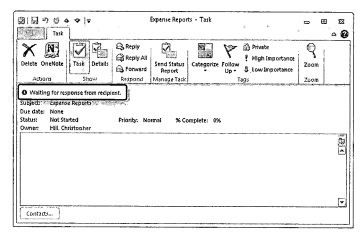

Figure 21-8 Outlook 2010 indicates that it is waiting for a response to a task request for a selected task.

When you receive a task request from someone who wants to assign a task to you, the message includes buttons that allow you to accept or decline the task. Figure 21-9 shows the buttons on the InfoBar when the Reading pane is displayed.

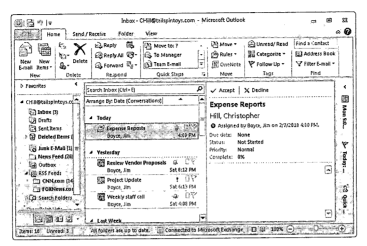

Figure 21-9 You can accept or decline a task request easily by clicking the Accept or Decline button on the InfoBar in the Reading pane.

You can click either Accept or Decline to respond to the request. If the Reading pane isn't visible, you can open the message and then click Accept or Decline in the Respond group on the message form's ribbon. When you do so, Outlook 2010 displays either an Accepting Task or a Declining Task dialog box, giving you the option of sending the accept or decline message as is or editing it. For example, you might want to add a note to the message that you'll have to change the due date for the task or that you need additional information about the task. Select Edit The Response Before Sending in the dialog box if you want to add your own comments; select Send The Response Now if you don't want to add comments. Then click OK to generate the message. The next time that you synchronize your Outbox with the server, the message will be sent.

You have one more option in addition to accepting or declining a task request that's waiting for your response—you can assign the task to someone else. For example, assume that you manage a small group of people. Your supervisor assigns a task to you, and you want to assign it to one of the people under you. When you receive the task request, open it, click Assign Task, and then select the person to whom you want to assign the task. Outlook 2010 creates a task request and sends it to the assignee. When the assignee accepts the task, his or her copy of Outlook 2010 sends an acceptance notice to you and adds both the originator's address and your address to the update list on the Details page of the task form. This means that changes to the task by the assignee are updated to your copy of the task and to the originator's copy.

TROUBLESHOOTING

Task requests keep disappearing

After you accept or decline a task, Outlook 2010 automatically deletes the task request from your Inbox. Unlike meeting requests, task requests are always deleted—Outlook 2010 doesn't provide an option that allows you to control this behavior. Outlook 2010 does, however, keep a copy of the task request in the Sent Items folder. Outlook 2010 also deletes task update messages after you read them. These messages are generated automatically when someone modifies an assigned task. Outlook 2010 sends the task update message to the people listed in the update list on the Details page of the task form. Although you can move these update messages out of the Deleted Items folder manually, Outlook 2010 provides no way to prevent them from being deleted.

When a response to a task assignment reaches you, Outlook 2010 doesn't act automatically on the response. For example, if someone accepts a task that you assigned, Outlook 2010 doesn't consider the task accepted until you open the response. Until that point, the Info-Bar in the Reading pane still indicates that Outlook 2010 is waiting for a response. When you open the response, the InfoBar in the message form indicates whether the task has been accepted or declined, depending on the assignee's action. Outlook 2010 deletes the response when you close the message. You have no options for controlling this behavior—Outlook 2010 always deletes the response.

If an assignee declines your task request, you can assign the task to someone else (or reassign it to the same individual) easily. Open the response, and click Assign Task on the form's toolbar just as you would when assigning a new task.

Reclaiming Ownership of a Declined Task

Your tasks won't always be accepted—you're bound to receive a rejection now and then. When you do, you have two choices: assign the task to someone else, or reclaim ownership so that you can modify or complete the task yourself. To reclaim a task, open the message containing the declined task request, and then click Return To Task List on the Task tab of the ribbon.

> **Note**
>
> When you assign a task, the assignee becomes the temporary owner until he or she accepts or rejects the task. Reclaiming the task restores your ownership so that you can modify the task.

Assigning Tasks to Multiple People

In some situations, you'll no doubt want to assign a task to more than one person. As a department manager, for example, you might need to assign a project to all the people in your department, or at least to a small group. Outlook 2010 is somewhat limited in task management: It can't track task status when you assign a task to more than one person. You can certainly assign the task, but you won't receive status reports.

What's the solution? You must change the way that you assign tasks, if only slightly. Rather than assigning the whole project as a single task, for example, break the project into separate tasks and assign each one individually, or break a specific task into multiple tasks. Use a similar name for each task to help you recognize that each one is really part of the same task. For example, you might use the names Quarterly Report: Joe and Quarterly Report: Jane to assign the preparation of a quarterly report to both Joe and Jane.

INSIDE OUT   Working around limitations

Although the Outlook 2010 task management features are certainly useful, a more comprehensive set of tools for distributing and managing tasks within a project would be a great addition to the program. For example, the ability to subdivide a task automatically would be helpful, as would the ability to assign a task to multiple people and still receive updates without having to subdivide the task. You can, however, work around this by adjusting the way that you assign and manage tasks.

Assigning Multiple Tasks Through an Assistant or a Group Leader

If you manage more than one group, task assignment becomes a little more complex because you probably have more than one group or department leader under you. Ideally, you would assign a task to a group leader, and the group leader would then delegate portions of the task to members of his or her group. How you accomplish that delegation depends on whether you want to receive status updates directly from group members or only from the group leader.

If you want to receive updates from group members, divide the overall task into sub-tasks and assign them to the group leader. The leader can then assign the tasks as needed to individuals in the group. Task updates are then sent to both you and the group leader. If you prefer to receive updates only from the group leader, create a single all-encompassing task and assign it to the group leader, who can then divide the project into individual tasks to assign to group members as needed.

Tracking the Progress of a Task

When you assign a task, you can choose to keep an updated copy of the task in your task list. This copy allows you to track the status of the task. As the assignee adds or changes task information—such as changing the Total Work value—that assignee's copy of Outlook 2010 generates an update and sends it to the addresses listed in the task's update list (on the Details page of the task form). Typically, the update list includes only one name—the name of the person who assigned the task. If the task was delegated (passed from one person to another), the update list shows all persons in the assignment chain.

Note

If you assign a task to multiple people, Outlook 2010 can no longer track task status. This limitation is one reason to subdivide a task, as explained in the preceding section.

As mentioned, Outlook 2010 sends task status messages to the update list addresses when an assignee makes changes to a task. When you receive a status message, Outlook 2010 updates your copy of the task when you read the status message. Outlook 2010 then deletes the status message, with one exception: When the assignee marks the task as

completed, Outlook 2010 sends a Task Completed message to the update list addresses. When you receive and read the message, Outlook 2010 marks your copy of the task as completed but does not delete the Task Completed message. Figure 21-10 shows a Task Completed message.

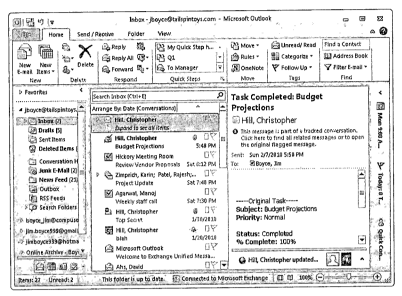

Figure 21-10 Outlook 2010 generates a Task Completed message when an assignee marks a task as completed.

Sending a Task Status Report

As you work on an assigned task, you'll probably want to send status updates to the person who assigned the task to you. Sending task status reports is more than easy—it's automatic. Outlook 2010 generates the updates each time you modify the task, such as when you change the % Complete value.

You can also send an update manually, which is useful when you want to send an update without actually modifying the task. To send an update, open the task and then click the Send Status Report button in the Manage Task group of the Task tab. Outlook opens a new email message with the properties for the task in the body of the message, including Status, % Complete, and Actual Work. You can add your own notes and then click Send to send the message.

Creating an Unassigned Copy of an Assigned Task

Outlook 2010 allows you to create an unassigned copy of a task that you have assigned to someone else. This unassigned copy goes into your task list with you as the owner. You can then work on the task yourself or assign it to someone else. For example, suppose that you assigned a task to someone but you want to work on it too. You can create a copy and then work on the copy, changing its dates, completion status, and other information as you go.

Creating an unassigned copy has one drawback, however: You will no longer receive updates for the assigned task. This makes it more difficult to track the other person's progress on the assigned task.

Follow these steps to create an unassigned copy of a task:

1. In Outlook 2010, open the Tasks folder, and then click the assigned task.

2. Click the Tasks tab on the ribbon, click Details, and then click Create Unassigned Copy.

3. Outlook 2010 displays a warning that creating the copy will prevent you from receiving updates to the assigned task. Click OK to create the copy or Cancel to cancel the process.

4. Outlook 2010 replaces the existing task with a new one. The new task has the same name except that the word *copy* is appended to the name in the Subject box. Make changes as needed to the task, and then choose Save & Close to save the changes.

Viewing and Customizing the Tasks Folder

As mentioned at the beginning of this chapter, Outlook 2010 uses the To-Do List view as the default Tasks folder view. Several other predefined views are also available, including those described in the following list. To use any of these views, click the View tab, click Change View, and then select the view you want.

- **Simple List**   Shows the task subject, the due date, categories, folder, and whether the task is completed

- **Detailed**   Shows the same information as a simple list, along with status, date completed, and modified date

- **Active**   Shows tasks that are active (incomplete)

- **Next Seven Days**   Shows tasks for the next seven days

- **Overdue**   Shows incomplete tasks with due dates that have passed

- **Assigned**   Shows tasks assigned to specific people

- **Completed Tasks**   Shows only completed tasks

- **Today**   Shows tasks due today

- **Server Tasks**   Shows tasks stored on a server running Microsoft SharePoint

- **To-Do List**   Shows the To-Do List

Outlook 2010 provides several ways to customize the view of the Tasks folder. These meth-ods are the same as those for other Outlook 2010 folders. For details on sorting, grouping by various columns, adding and removing columns, and customizing the folder view in other ways, see the section "Inbox," on page 73.

For information about using filters to locate and display specific tasks, such as those with cer-tain dates, or other properties, see the section "Using Advanced Find," on page 799.

ng the customizing methods described in Chapter 4, "Working In and ook," you might also want to change the way Outlook 2010 displays cer-Tasks folder. For example, you could change the font or character size for es or change the color that Outlook 2010 uses to display overdue tasks The following sections explain how to make these types of changes in the

Fonts and Table View Settings

Outlook 2010 by default uses an 8-point Segoe UI font for column headings, rows, and AutoPreview text. You can select a different font or different font characteristics (point size, italic, color, and so on). You also can change the style and color for the gridlines in list views and specify whether to show the Reading pane.

Follow these steps to customize your view settings:

1. Click View Settings on the View tab on the ribbon, or right-click the column header bar and then choose View Settings.

2. In the Advanced View Settings dialog box, click Other Settings to display the Other Settings dialog box, shown in Figure 21-11.

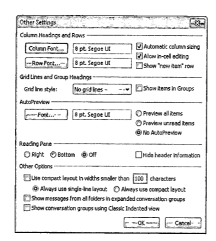

Figure 21-11 Configure font properties for the Tasks folder in the Other Settings dialog box.

3. Click Column Font or Row Font in the Column Headings And Rows area of the dialog box, or click Font in the AutoPreview area to open a standard Font dialog box that you can use to configure font, size, and other settings for the specified text.

> **Note**
>
> You can change color only for the AutoPreview text. Row and column text is displayed in a fixed color.

4. Use the options in the Grid Lines And Group Headings area to specify the line type and color that you want Outlook 2010 to use for list views.

5. Set the other options, using the following list as a guide:

- **Automatic Column Sizing** Sizes columns automatically and fits them to the display's width. Clear this check box to specify your own column width (by dragging each column's header), and use a scroll bar to view columns that don't fit the display.

- **Allow In-Cell Editing**   Allows you to click in a cell and modify the contents. If this check box is cleared, you must open the task to make changes.

- **Show "New Item" Row**   Displays a row at the top of the list for adding new tasks. The New Item row appears only if the Allow In-Cell Editing option is selected.

- **Show Items in Groups**   Group items together (such as by date).

- **Preview All Items**   Turns on AutoPreview and causes Outlook 2010 to display the first three lines of the contents of all items.

- **Preview Unread Items**   Turns on AutoPreview and causes Outlook 2010 to display the first three lines of the contents of unread items only.

- **No AutoPreview**   Displays only the headings for items and does not display AutoPreview text.

- **Reading Pane**   The options in this area control the location of the Reading pane. Click Off to hide the Reading pane. You also can choose View, Reading Pane to select the location or turn the Reading pane on or off.

- **Hide Header Information**   Choose this option to not show header information in the Reading pane.

- **Other Options**   These options control a handful of settings that determine view layout.

6. Click OK to close the Other Settings dialog box, and then click OK to close the Customize View dialog box.

Using Conditional Formatting

Outlook 2010 can perform conditional text formatting in the Tasks folder just as it can for other folders. For example, Outlook 2010 displays overdue tasks in red and uses gray strikethroughs for completed and read tasks. Outlook 2010 has five predefined conditional formatting rules, and you can create additional rules if you want to set up additional conditional formatting. For example, you might create a rule to show in red all tasks that haven't been started and are due within the next seven days.

To create conditional formatting rules, click View Settings, Conditional Formatting to display the Conditional Formatting dialog box, shown in Figure 21-12.

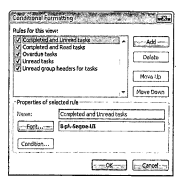

Figure 21-12 Modify or create custom automatic formatting rules in the Conditional Formatting dialog box.

Follow these steps to create a new rule:

1. In the Conditional Formatting dialog box, click Add. This creates a new rule named Untitled.

2. Type a title for the rule, and then click Font. Use the resulting Font dialog box to specify the font characteristics that you want Outlook 2010 to use for tasks that meet the rule's conditions. Click OK to close the Font dialog box.

3. Click Condition to open the Filter dialog box, shown in Figure 21-13. Specify the criteria for the condition. For example, select Due in the Time drop-down list, and then select In The Next 7 Days. This specifies that you want Outlook 2010 to use the font selections from step 2 to format any tasks that are due within the next seven days.

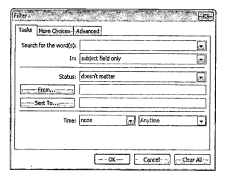

Figure 21-13 Use the Filter dialog box to specify conditions for the formatting rule.

4. Use the More Choices and Advanced tabs to set other conditions as needed, and then click OK.

5. Add other rules as needed. Click OK to close the Conditional Formatting dialog box, and then click OK to close the Advanced View Settings dialog box.

You can create fairly complex rules using the Filter dialog box, which can help you organize and identify specific types of tasks. Also note that you can change the order of the rules in the Automatic Formatting dialog box by using the Move Up and Move Down buttons. Outlook 2010 applies the rules in order from top to bottom, so it's possible for one rule to override another.

Setting General Task Options

Outlook 2010 provides a few options that control the appearance of items in the Tasks folder, reminders, and other task-related elements. To set these options, click File, Options, and Tasks. On the Tasks page of the Options dialog box, you'll find the following options:

- **Default Reminder Time**   Specifies the default reminder time for tasks. This option is set to 8:00 A.M. by default, but you can change the time if you want—perhaps you'd prefer to see reminders at 10:00 A.M. instead. Keep in mind that this setting is the default that Outlook 2010 uses for task reminders when you create a task, but you can change the reminder time for individual tasks as needed.

- **Overdue Task Color**   Select the color that you want Outlook 2010 to use to display overdue tasks.

- **Completed Task Color**   Select the color that you want Outlook 2010 to use to display completed tasks.

- **Keep My Task List Updated With Copies Of Tasks I Assign To Other People**   Select this option to have Outlook 2010 keep a copy of assigned tasks in your Tasks folder and update their status when assignees make changes to the tasks.

- **Send Status Reports When I Complete An Assigned Task**   Select this option to have Outlook 2010 send status reports to you when you complete a task that was assigned to you.

- **Set Reminders On Tasks With Due Dates**   Select this option to have Outlook 2010 set a reminder on tasks with due dates. Outlook 2010 bases the timer on the task's due date and the reminder time specified in the Options dialog box.

- **Task Working Hours Per Day**   Use this option to set the number of hours in your workday.

- **Task Working Hours Per Week**   Use this option to set the number of hours in the workweek.

Working with Tasks in Other Ways

Outlook 2010 provides a few other ways to work with tasks in addition to the Tasks folder. The following sections explain how to set up and track tasks in the task list area of the To-Do Bar, in the Daily Task List, and in Outlook Today view.

Working with Tasks in the To-Do Bar

The To-Do Bar is an interface feature that you can show or hide in Outlook 2010, and the task list is a component of the To-Do Bar. Figure 21-14 shows the To-Do Bar with the task list at the bottom.

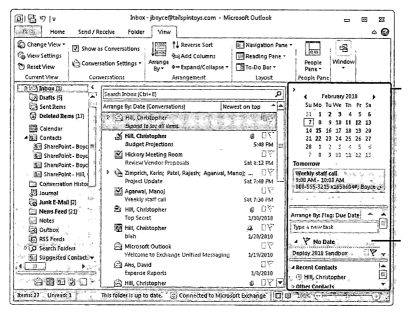

Figure 21-14 The task list appears at the bottom of the To-Do Bar.

By default, Outlook 2010 shows only subject, category color indicator, a reminder bell (if the task has a reminder set), and flag status for each task in the task list, but as you expand the width of the To-Do Bar, other columns appear. You can add and remove columns as needed. To do so, right-click the column header bar above the task list, and then choose View Settings. In the Advanced View Settings dialog box, click Columns to open the Show Columns dialog box, where you can specify the columns to include in the view and their order.

You can modify tasks directly in the task list just as you can in the Tasks folder, depending on the view settings that you've specified. For example, if you've turned on in-cell editing, you can make changes to a task simply by clicking it and typing the needed changes. You can mark a task as completed, change the Actual Work value, change the due date, and so on: The task list is, in this respect, no different from the Tasks folder. The primary benefit of the task list is that it allows you to work with your tasks in a single window along with the other tools in the view.

INSIDE OUT   Show and hide the task list

To show or hide the task list in the To-Do Bar, choose To-Do Bar from the Layout group of the View tab, and then choose Task List from the menu.

You can use the same methods that you use to create tasks in the Tasks folder to create a new task in the task list. Right-click in the empty area of the task list, and then choose New Task or New Task Request, depending on whether you're creating the task for yourself or assigning it to someone else. If both the Show New Item Row option and in-cell editing are enabled, you can click the Type A New Task row between the first task in the list and the column header to create a new task. Alternatively, you can click the arrow next to the New button on the Standard toolbar and then choose Task to create a new task.

Changing the Task List View

Outlook 2010 offers six views for the task list, and you can create custom views as well. To change the view, right-click in an empty area of the task list, choose Arrange By, and then select a view. You can also click on a column header in the task list and choose a view.

Working with Tasks in Outlook Today

Chapter 4 explains how Outlook Today gives you quick access to a useful selection of data. Outlook Today view is shown in Figure 21-15. The Calendar area displays meetings and events scheduled for the current day (and for subsequent days, if space allows). The Messages area indicates the number of unread messages in your Inbox, messages in the Drafts folder, and unsent messages in the Outbox. The Tasks area lists your tasks.

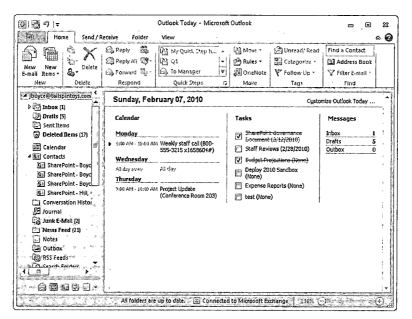

Figure 21-15 Outlook Today offers quick access to a range of information.

For more information about using Outlook Today, see the section "Working with the Standard Outlook Views," on page 72.

You can't create a task by clicking in the Tasks area of Outlook Today, but you can click the New Items button on the Home tab on the ribbon and then choose Task to create a new task. To modify a task, click the task's name in the list to open the task form. Mark a task as completed by selecting the check box next to its name.

Using the Daily Task List

Outlook 2010 adds a new way to manage tasks through the Daily Task List, which optionally appears at the bottom of the calendar, as shown in Figure 21-16. The Daily Task List shows the list of tasks that are due on the selected day. You can work with the tasks in the Daily Task List much as you can with the tasks in the To-Do Bar.

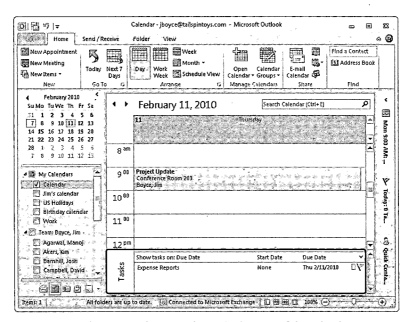

Figure 21-16 The Daily Task List resides at the bottom of the calendar.

When the Daily Task List is displayed, you can click the Minimize button at the far-right edge of the Daily Task List column bar to minimize it. Likewise, when the Daily Task List is minimized, click the Restore button to display it.

Managing Tasks Effectively

Tasks are one of the Outlook 2010 features that many people overlook, spending their time instead primarily in the Inbox, Contacts, and Calendar folders. Nevertheless, tasks can be extremely useful and a powerful productivity and workflow tool. If you haven't used tasks before, spend the time to become familiar with them. When you are comfortable using tasks, the following tips will help you make the most of them:

- **Really use them**   Tasks won't do you much good if you just put a few on your task list and then don't really use them. Instead, use tasks in Outlook 2010 for all of your daily, weekly, and monthly tasks. Make sure to set progress status as you go along and mark tasks as complete when you complete them.

- **Use task assignment**   Outlook 2010 tasks can be a great tool for helping you orga-nize your day and get your job done. Task assignment extends that benefit across your team or workgroup. Get your group in the habit of using tasks, and then start using task assignment across the group to manage tasks.

- **Use realistic due dates**   Setting realistic due dates for your tasks and working on the tasks accordingly will help you integrate tasks into your daily work schedule. The keys to being successful using Outlook 2010 tasks are to be diligent about how you use them and to integrate them into your workday and workflow.

- **Use reminders**   By assigning reminders to your tasks, you'll be able to keep track of when the tasks are coming due. Assign a reminder period that is sufficiently long to enable you to complete the task by its due date.

- **Keep the tasks at hand**   Use the task list in the To-Do Bar and the Daily Task List in the Calendar folder to keep your tasks visible at all times so that you can work with them easily and see their status.

R EMEMBERING everything that you've done during the course of a busy day—email mes-sages sent, phone calls made, appointments set up—can be difficult. However, the Journal feature in Microsoft Outlook 2010, which records your daily activities, can help you keep track of it all. In addition to tracking Outlook 2010 items such as email messages and appointments automatically, you can use the journal to monitor every Microsoft Office 2010 system document that you create or modify. You can also manually record an activity that occurs away from your computer—a phone conversation, for example, or a handwritten letter that you mailed or received.

The Journal folder provides a single place to track all your work and your daily interactions. For example, you can use the journal to list all items related to a specific contact: email messages sent and received, meetings attended, and tasks assigned. You can track all the hours you've spent on activities related to a particular project, or you can use the journal to retrieve detailed information based on when you performed an action—for example, if you know that you worked on a Microsoft Excel 2010 document last Tuesday but can't remem-ber the path to the file, you can look up the document quickly if you've configured the journal to record work automatically on Excel 2010 files.

This chapter shows you how to record your work in the journal both automatically and manually. You'll also learn how to view and print your journal in standard and customized views.

Understanding the Outlook Journal

The Journal folder, shown in Figure 22-1, provides you with tools to track and record daily activities. Although other components of Outlook 2010 provide similar note-keeping capabilities, only the journal provides a full (and optionally automatic) means to date and timestamp an activity, log the entry type (for example, a phone call or a meeting request), and even track the time spent on an activity for billing purposes.

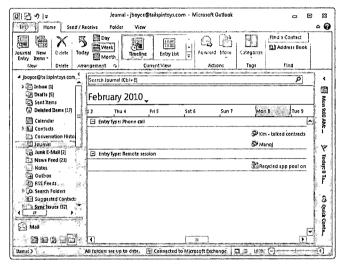

Figure 22-1 Use the journal as an electronic diary of events, phone calls, tasks, and other daily items.

Outlook 2010 records entries in your Journal folder based on when an action occurs. For example, a Microsoft Word 2010 document is recorded on the journal timeline when you create or modify the document. You can organize journal entries on the timeline into logical groups—such as email messages, meetings, phone calls, or any items related to a specific project. You also can assign categories to journal items and organize the folder view by category. For example, you could assign a project name as a category to all journal items associated with that project, which would allow you to group journal entries by project easily.

You can open a journal entry form, as shown in Figure 22-2, and review details about an activity, or you can use the journal entry as a shortcut to go directly to the Outlook 2010 item or the file referred to in the journal entry.

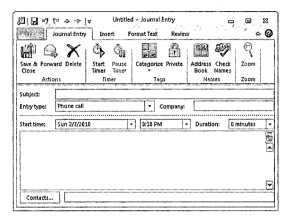

Figure 22-2 The journal entry form contains many fields to help you organize, store, and find your journal entries.

The Outlook 2010 journal is an electronic diary. Everything that you normally write in your calendar or day planner (what you did, when you did it, and all the details that you want to remember) you can record in the journal.

To open the Journal folder, click the Journal icon in the Navigation pane. Figure 22-1 shows the journal Timeline view, which you see the first time that you open the journal. Figure 22-3 shows Entry List view, another way of organizing your Journal folder.

For information about the views available to organize your Journal folder, see the section "Viewing the Journal," on page 586.

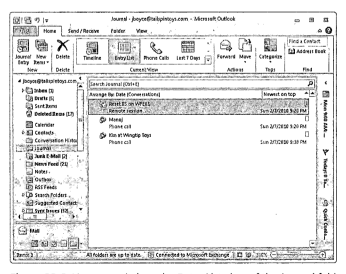

Figure 22-3 You can switch to the Entry List view of the Journal folder.

Using Automatic Journaling

You can have Outlook 2010 create automatic journal entries for a wide range of items, including email messages (both sent and received), task requests, and files that you create or open in other Office system applications. In fact, you can use automatic journaling to record activities based on any contact, Office system document, or Outlook 2010 item that you select.

For example, suppose that you routinely exchange important email messages with a business associate, and you want to track all exchanges for reference. Incoming messages from this associate arrive in your Inbox. You read them, reply to them, and then archive the incoming messages to another folder. Now, however, your associate's messages are stored in one folder and your replies are in another. (By default, replies are stored in the Outlook 2010 Sent Items folder.) Configuring the journal to track all your email exchanges with your associate automatically places a record of all messages relating to this contact (both received and sent) in one convenient location. Instead of hunting for your response to your associate's question from two weeks ago, you can open the journal and find the entry associated with the message. Double-click the link embedded in the journal entry, and Outlook 2010 takes you to the message containing your response. Figure 22-4 shows a journal entry automatically added from an email message.

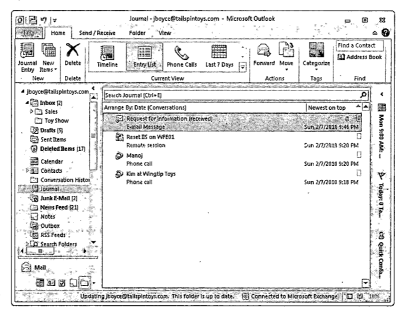

Figure 22-4 The journal can note automatically when you send or receive email messages to or from specific contacts.

Chapter 22

INSIDE OUT   Organize messages using search folders

Search folders are another useful tool for organizing messages. You might set up a search folder that lists all the messages to or from a specific contact to help you quickly find those messages. See Chapter 10, "Finding and Organizing Messages," for a complete discussion of search folders.

INSIDE OUT   Find email items quickly

To find email items in the journal more quickly, select Entry List view, and then click the Contact column to sort the view according to contact. This helps you see all journal items associated with a specific contact, including those items created automatically from email messages.

As another example, let's say you deal with several different types of Word documents in a day, such as contracts, quotes, or other documents. Turning on automatic document tracking for this application could provide some interesting insight into how your workday is allocated and which documents are the most demanding. The same holds true for other Office system applications that you use frequently.

If you use document tracking in such a scenario, however, you should be aware of the distinction between how Outlook 2010 tracks a document and how Word 2010 itself records editing time. In Word 2010, you can click File and then view the Total Editing Time property on the Backstage view. Outlook 2010 tracks the time that a document is open, whereas Word 2010 tracks the time spent physically editing a document (that is, pressing keys). The Outlook 2010 journal automatically records the entire span of time a document is open, even if you are away from your desk tending to other matters.

If a record of the actual time spent working on a document is important to you (whether you're mulling a paragraph, reading a lengthy section, or editing or entering new text), the journal offers a more realistic record. However, if you fail to close the document when you move on to other things, you'll end up adding time to the document's journal entry that wasn't really spent on the document. It's best to use a combination of the Word 2010 Total Editing Time field and the Outlook 2010 journal's tracking to get a realistic picture of how you spend your time.

Overall, the best choice is usually to use automatic tracking for your critical contacts and for specific applications that benefit from an automatic audit trail. You can place other items in the journal manually as required.

> **Note**
>
> After you set it up, the journal's automatic tracking is always on. A piece of Outlook 2010 code runs in the background and monitors the Office system applications that you've selected to track—even if Outlook 2010 itself is closed.

Another issue to consider in relation to journaling is latency. When you use automatic tracking for documents, you'll often notice a significant lag between the time that you close a document and the time that the entry appears (or is updated) in the journal. Also, keep in mind that if you've opened the document previously, the most recent tracking entry doesn't appear at the top of the list. By default, journal entries are ordered according to start date, which in this case would be the first time the document was opened or created, not the most recent time.

> **Note**
>
> Using automatic journaling can have a significantly negative impact on the performance of your applications because of the added overhead involved in journaling. This might not be apparent on your system, depending on its capabilities and the types of documents you use. However, if you see a significant decrease in performance after turning on automatic journaling and can't afford the performance drop, you'll need to stop automatic journaling and resort to adding journal entries manually.

Setting Journal Options

The journal has many options that allow you to control what is recorded, how it is recorded, and when it is recorded. To set journal options, click File, Options. On the Notes and Journal page, click Journal Options to open the Journal Options dialog box, shown in Figure 22-5. The choices that you make in this dialog box determine how your journal is set up and what it tracks.

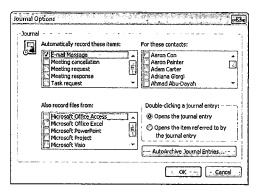

Figure 22-5 The Journal Options dialog box contains customization choices for the journal.

The following list summarizes the options in the Journal Options dialog box:

- **Automatically Record These Items**   Select from a list of Outlook 2010 items that can be tracked as journal entries. All options here involve three forms of messaging: regular email, meeting notifications, and task delegation. Item types selected in this list are tracked for the contacts that you specify in the For These Contacts list. Selecting an item to track without choosing an associated contact has no effect for that tracking option.

- **For These Contacts**   Here, you link items that you want to track with those contacts you want to track them for—task requests from your boss, for example. Outlook 2010 then automatically creates journal entries for the selected contacts and related items. Only contacts in your main Contacts folder can be selected for automatic journaling. You'll need to move (or copy) contact entries from subfolders to the main Contacts folder if you want to track items for them.

- **Also Record Files From**   Outlook 2010 creates an automatic journal entry every time an Office system application selected in this list creates or accesses a document. The selections available depend on which Office system applications are installed on your system. Documents from Microsoft Access, Microsoft Excel, Microsoft Power-Point, Microsoft Word, and Microsoft Project can be tracked.

CAUTION

When you set up automatic tracking for a particular document type (for example, Word 2010 documents), this setting applies to all documents that you create, open, close, or save with the selected application. Thus, automatic tracking can also create many journal entries filled with information you might not need to preserve. Make this selection with care.

- **Double-Clicking A Journal Entry** Double-clicking a journal entry can open either the entry itself or the item referred to by the entry, depending on your selection in this area of the dialog box. Use this option to specify which action you prefer as the default. You can later override this setting by right-clicking the journal entry in any journal view.

- **AutoArchive Journal Entries** Click to open the Journal Properties dialog box and configure archive settings for the Journal folder.

For details on archiving Outlook 2010 items, see Chapter 30, "Archiving, Backing Up, and Restoring Outlook Data."

Turning Off Automatic Journaling

You won't find a one-click solution when you want to turn off automatic journaling. To turn off this feature, you must open the Journal Options dialog box and clear all the check boxes in the Automatically Record These Items and Also Record Files From lists. It's not necessary to clear contacts selected in the For These Contacts list. Because automatic journaling consists of tracking specific Outlook 2010 events for a contact as well as when specific types of Office system files are accessed, breaking the link for items to track is enough.

TROUBLESHOOTING

Automatic journaling is causing delays

Automatic journaling can cause very long delays during manual or automatic save operations as well as when you exit the application. Although it might appear that the application has stopped responding, in fact it is simply saving the journal information. If your system stops responding during these procedures, check Outlook 2010 to see whether automatic journaling is turned on for the specific application involved. If so, wait a minute or two to give the application a chance to save your data, and then turn off automatic journaling if it has become too inconvenient to use. You can continue to add journal items manually for the application, if needed.

Recording Email Messages Automatically

Recording email to and from colleagues in the journal is a great way to keep track of discussions and decisions concerning a project, and it's easy to locate those messages later.

To record email messages exchanged with a specific contact, follow these steps:

1. In Outlook 2010, click File, Options, and then, on the Notes And Journal page, click Journal Options to open the Journal Options dialog box.

2. In the Automatically Record These Items list, select the E-Mail Message check box.

3. In the For These Contacts list, select the contact whose email you want to record.

4. Click OK twice to close both dialog boxes.

Recording Contact Information Automatically

You can configure your journal to keep track of your interactions with any one of your contacts automatically. If you're working with a colleague on a specific project, for example, you might want to monitor your progress by recording every email message, meeting, and task that involves this colleague.

To set up your journal to keep such a record based on the name of the contact, follow these steps:

1. In Outlook 2010, click File, Options, and then, on the Notes And Journal page, click Journal Options to open the Journal Options dialog box.

2. In the Automatically Record These Items list, select the types of Outlook 2010 items that you want to record in the journal.

3. In the For These Contacts list, select the relevant contact. (You can select more than one.)

4. Click OK twice to close both dialog boxes.

Recording Document Activity Automatically

Suppose that you create and maintain custom Excel 2010 workbooks for the different divisions in your corporate enterprise. In the course of a busy day, it's easy to forget to write down which files you worked on and for how long. There's a better way than keeping track on paper: you can have the journal automatically record every Office system file you open, including when and how long you had each file open. Outlook 2010 can monitor your files and create a journal entry for every document you open and work on from other Office system applications such as Microsoft Visio, Word, Excel, Access, PowerPoint, and Project.

> **Note**
> Although the journal can record work automatically only in these Office system programs, you can enter your work from other programs manually.

Follow these steps to record automatically files that you create or open:

1. In Outlook 2010, click File, Options, and then, on the Notes And Journal page, click Journal Options to open the Journal Options dialog box.

2. In the Also Record Files From list, select the programs for which you want to record files automatically in your journal. When you create, open, close, or save a document from any of the selected programs, the journal will record a new entry.

3. By default, double-clicking an icon on the journal timeline opens the journal entry. If you'd rather be able to open the associated file when you double-click the icon, select the Opens The Item Referred To By The Journal Entry option.

> **Note**
> Regardless of which option you choose to be the default in the Journal Options dialog box, you can always right-click an icon on the journal timeline and then choose either Open Journal Entry or Open Item Referred To on the shortcut menu.

4. Click OK twice to close both dialog boxes.

INSIDE OUT Add items manually

If you've set up automatic journaling for all entries created by an application (Excel 2010, for example), every document you create in that application generates a journal entry. If you right-click an entry and choose Open Item Referred To, Outlook 2010 opens the document that created the journal entry. However, this behavior can change. If you add a document item manually to the entry and the icon for that item appears before the original document's icon in the entry, Outlook 2010 opens the manually added document. In other words, Outlook 2010 always opens the first document referenced in the entry when you choose Open Item Referred To on the entry's shortcut menu. This can be confusing because the subject continues to reference the original document. In addition, the manually added document does not appear in the View Attachments list on the entry's shortcut menu unless you inserted it as a file instead of as a shortcut. So when you add entries manually, make sure to place the icon for the document added manually after the original document's icon and insert the document as a file.

INSIDE OUT How the journal handles changes to tracked items

Because journal entries contain links to your documents instead of copies of the actual documents, the entries might reference documents that no longer exist on your system. The journal has no way to record the deletion, moving, or renaming of files, so while the journal entries for the deleted objects still exist, the referenced objects don't open.

Similarly, the journal can't find email messages that have been moved from the Inbox to another folder. If you change the text on the subject line of a tracked email message, the journal entry keeps the old subject line, but it can still find and open the message.

Adding Journal Items Manually

Automatic journaling can be tremendously useful, but what if some of the work that you need to track is done in applications other than Office system applications? You can't record the files automatically in your journal, but you can record them manually. Alternatively, what if you want to track your work only in a specific Word 2010 file rather than in every Word 2010 document? Instead of turning on automatic recording for all Word 2010 files, you can record your work manually in only specified files.

Likewise, if you want to record a nonelectronic event in your journal—a chat at the water cooler, a box of chocolates sent to a client, or your approval of a printed proposal—you can add a journal entry manually. You can also use this method if you'd prefer to pick and choose which documents, messages, meetings, and task requests are entered in the journal rather than having Outlook 2010 routinely record all such items.

Recording Work in a File Manually

To keep a record of when and how long you worked in a file (along with any extraneous notes to yourself), follow these steps:

1. Locate the file that you want to work in. You can browse to the folder that contains the file using any technique you like.

2. Drag the file icon in the folder window to the Journal icon in the Navigation pane. It's easiest to drag the file if you resize both the Outlook 2010 window and the folder window so that you can clearly see both.

3. Click Start Timer to begin recording your working hours, as shown in Figure 22-6, and then double-click the file shortcut icon to open the file. At any time, you can enter notes to yourself in the area where the shortcut icon is located.

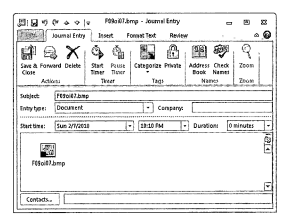

Figure 22-6 Click Start Timer to start recording time spent on a document.

4. When you finish working in the file, remember to stop the journal timer by clicking Pause Timer and then clicking Save & Close.

> **Note**
> If you need to take a temporary break in your work, click Pause Timer. When you return to work on the file, click Start Timer to continue recording your working hours.

Recording Outlook Items Manually

Recording an Outlook 2010 item such as a task in the journal is even easier than recording a file: Open the Outlook 2010 window where the item is listed and then drag the item to the Journal icon in the Navigation pane. For example, suppose that you want to record how much time you spend cleaning out your filing cabinets, a task that you've entered in the Tasks folder. Open the Tasks folder and then drag the task item to the Journal icon in the Navigation pane. Click Start Timer and go to work. Then click Pause Timer to take a break. When you finish, click Save & Close.

Recording Other Activities Manually

Any activity that you want to record can be entered in your journal. For example, you can monitor the time that you spend on the Internet (which can be considerable) as well as recording any web page addresses you want to save and other notes you need to jot down.

To do so, follow these steps:

1. Double-click a blank area in your Journal folder. A new journal entry form opens.

2. In the Subject box, type a description of your activity.

3. In the Entry Type box, select an appropriate entry type for the activity. You can't create your own entry type on this screen, but you can choose among several available types. For example, you could classify an Internet search as Remote Session. Type any notes, including hyperlinks, in the body of the journal item.

   For information about custom entry types, see the section "Creating and Using Custom Entry Types," on page 581.

4. Click Start Timer to begin recording your activity.

5. When you've finished with your activity, click Pause Timer to stop the timer, and then click Save & Close to close the journal entry.

Recording Phone Calls Manually

When you use automatic dialing to call a contact, you can time the phone call, type notes in Outlook 2010 while you talk, and create a journal entry for the call. This feature can come in handy if, for example, you bill clients for your time spent on phone conversations.

Follow these steps to keep a record of an outgoing call in the journal:

1. Open the Contacts folder and select the contact entry for the person that you want to call.

2. In the Communicate group on the Contact tab, click More, Journal Entry. Doing so opens the Journal Entry form with the Entry Type set to Phone Call (Figure 22-7).

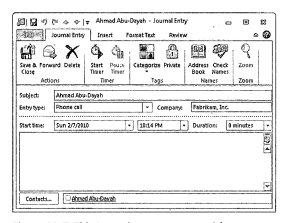

Figure 22-7 This Journal entry was started from a contact.

3. Start your call and click Start Timer. You can type notes in the body of the journal entry while you talk.

4. When you've finished with the call, click Pause Timer to stop the clock, and then click Save & Close.

You also can create journal entries for incoming calls, although Outlook 2010 currently offers no means of automatically creating journal entries when you pick up the phone and start talking. Instead, when you answer the call and realize that you want to track it, you can open the journal as you begin the conversation, start a new journal item, and click Start Timer. Make notes as needed, and click Pause Timer when you hang up. Add any necessary details to the journal entry form, and then click Save & Close to create the item.

INSIDE OUT   Use the journal as an inexpensive stopwatch

You can start a new journal item and use the timer to time any activity, assuming that you don't need to-the-second timing. Just stop the timer and close the form without saving it unless you actually want to save the information in the journal.

For information about setting up automatic phone dialing and making calls from the Contacts folder, see the section "Working with Contacts," on page 440.

Creating and Using Custom Entry Types

You can assign categories to all Outlook 2010 items to provide a means of sorting and organizing those items. The journal is no exception: Each journal item can have multiple categories assigned to it. Journal items, however, can also be classified by *entry type*, which defines the purpose of the journal item. In many respects, entry types are like categories, because you can use them to sort and search for journal items.

When you create a journal item manually, Outlook 2010 assumes that you're creating a phone call journal entry and automatically selects Phone Call as the entry type. However, you can select a different entry type in the Entry Type drop-down list. Figure 22-8 shows some of the available entry types.

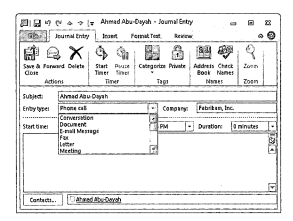

Figure 22-8 You can select entry types from a predefined list.

Unlike categories, which you can create on the fly, journal entry types are limited to those types found in the predefined list in Outlook 2010. Although the default entry types cover a lot of bases, they don't offer much flexibility. For example, you might want to use the journal to track your activity in an application that isn't included in the list, or you might need to keep track of trips to the doctor, school programs, or other events. Although you don't have the ability to add entry types directly when you create a journal entry, you can modify the registry to add journal entry types. You can use these user-defined entry types for journal items that you enter manually.

Here's how:

1. Open the Registry Editor by choosing Start, clicking in the Search box, typing **regedit**, and then pressing Enter. (In Microsoft Windows XP, click Run, type **regedit** in the Open box, press Enter, and then accept the UAC prompt.)

2. Open the key HKEY_CURRENT_USER\Software\Microsoft\Shared Tools\Outlook\ Journaling.

3. Right-click Journaling, and then choose New, Key.

4. Rename the key based on what the new entry type will be. For example, you might name the type **Volunteer Time**.

5. Right-click the key that you just created, and then choose New, String Value. Rename the string value **Description**.

6. Double-click the Description value that you just created, and then set its value to the text you want to appear in the Entry Types drop-down list, such as **Volunteer Time.**

7. Close the Registry Editor.

After you have edited the registry to add the new entry type, it appears on the journal entry form in the Entry Type drop-down list, as shown in Figure 22-9.

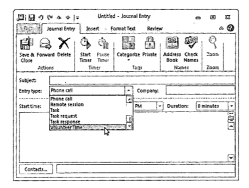

Figure 22-9 Your custom entry type appears in the drop-down list.

Changing Journal Entries

You can modify any details of a journal entry—for example, adding more notes to yourself, adding a contact's names or categories, or changing the duration of your activity. You can also move the entry to a different position on the journal timeline if you entered the wrong start date or time when you began recording the activity.

For information about timeline views in the Journal folder, see the section "Viewing the Journal," on page 586.

Modifying an Entry

Suppose that in the middle of your department budget meeting, you realize that you didn't stop the journal timer when you stopped working on a spreadsheet to come to the meeting. You know that you worked on the spreadsheet for about three hours, however, so you can change the journal entry to reflect your actual work time.

To change the duration or any other property of an existing journal entry, follow these steps:

1. Open the Journal folder, and double-click the entry to open it.

2. Select the information that you want to change and then enter the correct data. For example, to change an incorrect record of how long you spent on an activity, click in the Duration box, change the value, and press Enter.

3. Make other changes as needed in the journal entry form.

4. Click Save & Close.

Moving an Entry on the Timeline

Suppose that you belatedly created a journal entry for a phone call that you made yesterday and inadvertently entered the wrong date. When you later notice that the journal entry is in the wrong spot on the timeline, you can move the entry to the correct date.

Follow these steps to do so:

1. Open the Journal folder, and double-click the entry to open it.

2. In the Start Time box, type or select a date.

3. Click Save & Close. Outlook 2010 then moves the entry to the correct spot on the timeline.

Deleting an Entry

Deleting a single entry from your journal timeline is easy: Either click the entry's icon to select it and then press Delete, or right-click the entry's icon and choose Delete on the shortcut menu.

What if you've been recording your work automatically in Excel 2010 workbooks but have also been experimenting with Excel 2010, creating several test workbooks that you don't want to save or track? Now you have numerous useless entries cluttering up your Journal folder. You can delete them one at a time, but it's faster to switch to a table view of your entries, sort them so that all the useless entries are in one group, and delete them all at once.

For information about the various views in the Journal folder, including table views and time-line views, see the section "Viewing the Journal," on page 586.

Follow these steps to delete a group of entries:

1. On the Home tab on the ribbon, in the Current View group, select Entry List. The view switches to a table view of all your journal entries.

2. To sort the entries so that all the ones that you want to delete appear together, click the Entry Type column header. To sort specific entries by subject within a group of entry types, hold down the Shift key while you click the Subject column header.

> **Note**
> You can sort by as many as four fields using this method of holding down the Shift key while you click column headers. Clicking the Contact header or Cat-egories header will group the journal items by that category and clear the other sort settings. Once the list is grouped, you can sort on multiple categories as described earlier.

3. To select and delete multiple journal entries, press Shift or Ctrl while you select the entries that you want to delete, and then click the Delete button on the toolbar. (Alternatively, you can press the Delete key to delete selected entries or right-click any of the selected entries and choose Delete on the shortcut menu.)

4. When you finish deleting the journal entries that you don't want, you can select the view you were using previously on the Current View list in the Navigation pane.

Connecting Journal Activities to Individual Contacts

If you work on a project with a colleague, you can associate your journal entries for the project with that colleague's contact entry. All the journal entries that are associated with the contact will appear when you select Activities view on the contact form.

For example, Figure 22-10 shows a journal entry for a phone call to an associate. To connect a journal entry to a contact, click Contacts at the bottom of the journal entry form. In the resulting Select Contacts dialog box, click the names of the contacts with whom the journal entry should be associated, and then click OK. The selected names will appear in the Contacts box at the bottom of the journal entry form.

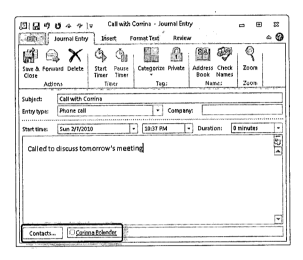

Figure 22-10 This journal entry shows a phone call entry associated with a contact.

So what does this do for you? When you open the contact entry for an associated contact and click Activities in the Show group on the Contact tab, as shown in Figure 22-11, you'll see a list of every Outlook 2010 item associated with that contact. You can open any of these items by double-clicking it. This is just one more way that Outlook 2010 keeps all your information interconnected.

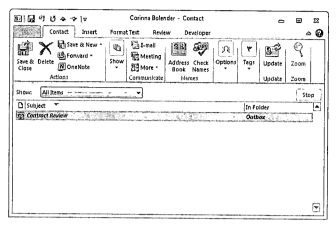

Figure 22-11 The Activities page shows all items associated with the selected contact.

Viewing the Journal

When you look at the Journal folder in a monthly timeline view, you get a good overall picture of your recorded activities, but you must point to an individual icon to identify the activity. (When you point to an icon, a subject label appears.) You can make a few changes to a journal timeline view—for example, you can choose to always display the subject labels for icons in a monthly view, or you can specify a more useful length for the labels. You can also show week numbers in the timeline heading, which is useful for planning in some industries.

Because the Outlook 2010 journal creates a record of your activities, the standard views available in the Journal folder differ considerably from the views in other types of Outlook 2010 folders. The following sections introduce you to each of the Journal folder views.

> ### Note
> You can choose whether to view a timeline in a journal view in day, week, or month increments by clicking the Day, Week, or Month button on the toolbar. These buttons are available only in the journal views that show a timeline and are not available in list views.

Using Timeline View

The default view for the Journal folder is Timeline view, shown in Figure 22-12. In this view, the journal entries are arranged in a timeline and are categorized by the entry type. To select Timeline view, click Timeline in the Current View group on the Home tab on the ribbon.

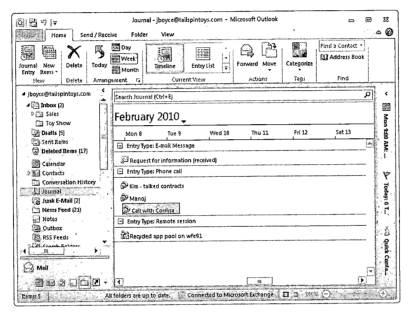

Figure 22-12 Timeline view is the default Journal folder view.

Each entry type is indicated in a title bar. You can click the small box on the left in the title bar to expand or contract the type. A plus sign (+) in the box means that the type is collapsed, whereas a minus sign (–) indicates that the type is expanded. You might need to use the vertical scroll bar to see the complete list. When you expand a type, you can view any journal entries for that type in the area below the title bar.

> **Note**
>
> If you're surprised to find no entries when you expand a particular entry type, that's because Outlook 2010 displays the entries as a timeline. If no entries for the selected entry type were created recently, you might need to use the horizontal scroll bar to find the most recent entries.

Timeline view is most useful if you want to find out which documents you worked on during a specific period. This view is not particularly useful for locating documents based on any other criteria. For example, you wouldn't want to use Timeline view to locate all documents relating to a particular contact.

Using Entry List View

Entry List view, shown in Figure 22-13, might be the most useful view of all. This view dispenses with the timeline and instead displays all journal entries in a table.

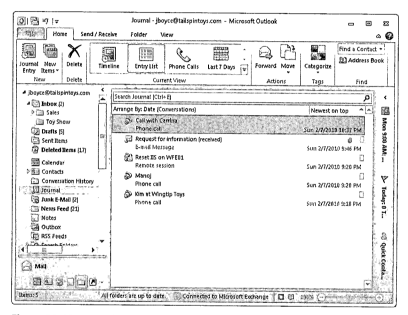

Figure 22-13 Entry List view displays journal entries in a table instead of on a timeline.

Because Entry List view does not use the timeline to display entries, it's much easier to view the list of entries—you don't have to use the horizontal scroll bar to locate the items. By default, this view is sorted in descending order based on the start date, but you can sort the list quickly using any of the column headers. Simply click a column header to sort the list; click the header a second time to reverse the sort order.

The paper clip icon in the second column of Entry List view indicates that an entry contains an item or shortcut such as document or email. Note that this column will not be displayed if the width of the window is too narrow.

Using Last Seven Days View

Last Seven Days view resembles Entry List view. This view is useful when you need to locate items that you've worked on recently—especially if you can't quite remember the file name, contact, or category.

When you look closely at Last Seven Days view, you might notice that something doesn't look quite right: The dates shown for the journal entries clearly span much more than a week. The explanation is that the dates shown are the start dates for the journal entries, not the dates when the items were last accessed. Outlook 2010 is displaying the journal entries that have been created, accessed, or modified within the past week. Each entry shown in this view was accessed in some way during the past week, although the original entries might have been created quite some time ago.

INSIDE OUT   Change the period of time shown in Last Seven Days view

You can customize Last Seven Days view to specify a different time period, such as the past month. To do so, click the View tab on the ribbon, click View Settings, click Filter in the Advanced View Settings dialog box, and then click the Advanced tab. Remove the existing Modified criteria and add your own that reference the desired time range.

Using Phone Calls View

Phone Calls view, shown in Figure 22-14, displays only journal items that are associated with phone calls. Tracking phone calls and viewing them in the Journal folder can be extremely helpful. You can, for example, monitor the time you spend on billable calls. Even if you don't bill for your time, you'll find that phone call journal entries make it easier to recall phone conversations.

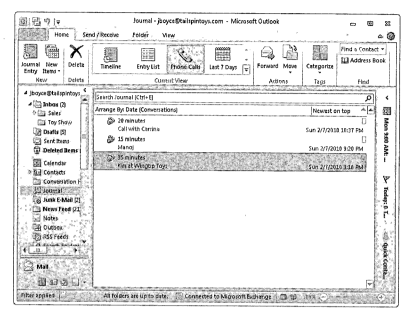

Figure 22-14 Use Phone Calls view to organize the Journal folder according to journal items associated with phone calls.

> **Note**
> Remember to link your phone call journal entries to the appropriate contacts so that it will be easier to find all entries relating to specific contacts.

Customizing Journal Views

All the standard views in the Journal folder are customizable in a variety of ways. The changes you make to these views are persistent, however, so proceed with care. If you end up mangling a standard view beyond repair, it can be restored to its default by using the Reset button in the Manage All Views dialog box, which you can open by clicking Change View on the View tab and choosing Manage Views.

For information about creating custom views in Outlook 2010, see Chapter 26, "Creating Custom Views and Print Styles."

Displaying Item Labels on the Monthly Timeline

Displaying the subject line of each journal item in a timeline view gives you additional information about those items without requiring you to point to each item with your mouse to display the ScreenTip-style label.

To display item labels on a monthly timeline, follow these steps:

1. In a timeline view, right-click in an empty area of the Journal folder, choose View Settings on the shortcut menu, and click Other Settings in the Advanced View Settings dialog box.

2. In the Format Timeline View dialog box, select the Show Label When Viewing By Month check box.

> **Note**
> By default, the label width is 80 characters, but if you find that your labels are too short or too long, return to this dialog box and change the number in the Maximum Label Width box. The label width applies to the labels in the day and week timeline, as well as the month timeline. To hide the display of week numbers as well, you can clear the Show Week Numbers check box.

3. Click OK to close the dialog box.

Showing Week Numbers

In some industries, it's important to know schedules based on weeks of the year. You can show week numbers in your timeline view by following these steps:

1. With the journal displayed in a timeline view, right-click in an empty area of the Journal folder, click View Settings, and then, in the Advanced View Settings dialog box, click Other Settings.

2. In the Format Timeline View dialog box, select the Show Week Numbers check box.

3. Click OK twice to close the dialog box. In a monthly timeline, week numbers replace dates. In week and day views, both the week number and dates are displayed in the timeline header.

Printing Journal Items

The options available when you print from the Journal folder depend on whether a timeline view or a table (list) view is currently open. In a table view, you can open and print individual items, print the entire list, or print only selected rows. Printing the table is useful if you want a snapshot of the journal for a specific period of time. You can print list views using either Table Style or Memo Style print styles (explained shortly).

> **Tip**
> You don't have to open an item to print it. Simply right-click the item, and then choose Print from the shortcut menu.

In a timeline view, you can print individual journal items or several items at a time (hold down the Ctrl key and click to select multiple items). You can print one or more items, each on an individual page, in Memo Style, and you can print attached files along with the journal entry details. To print the attached files, select the Print Attached Files check box in the Print dialog box.

For more information about printing views in Outlook 2010 and creating custom print styles, see Chapter 27, "Designing and Using Forms."

Table Style, shown in Figure 22-15, is available from any table view. It prints the selected view just as you see it in Outlook 2010: each item in a separate row, with the fields displayed as columns. Table Style has limited configuration options. Note that in Figure 22-15, all the Journal items were printed to an .xps file using Table Style.

Memo Style, shown in Figure 22-16, prints one item per page, with your name as the title and the details of the record after that. Memo Style is a simple and quick one-item-at-a-time print style. You can specify the title and field fonts, paper options, and the contents and fonts used by the header and footer.

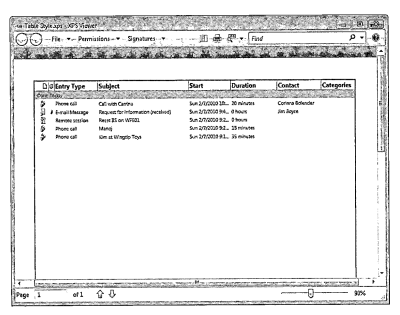

Figure 22-15   Table Style prints journal entries in a table.

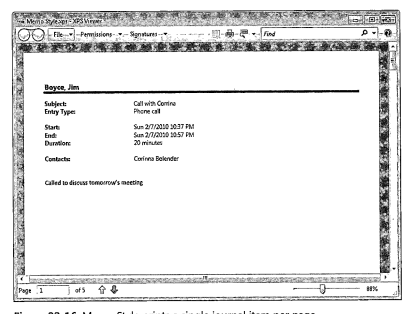

Figure 22-16   Memo Style prints a single journal item per page.

Printing from the Journal folder is not a particularly difficult task for anyone who has used and printed from any Windows-based application. However, you might be wondering how you can print just a selection of a table view. For example, you might need to print only the items that fall within a specific range or those associated with a particular contact.

Follow these steps to print a selection of a table view:

1. Open the table view.

2. Click columns as needed to sort the data to help you locate the items you want to print. For example, click the Start column header to locate items that fall within a certain time range, or click the Contact column header to locate items associated with a specific contact.

3. Select the first item in the range, hold down the Shift key, and then select the last item in the range.

4. Choose File, Print to open the Print dialog box.

5. Select Table Style in the Print Style area, and then click Print Options to open the Print dialog box.

6. Select the Only Selected Rows option.

7. Set other print options as needed, and then click Print.

Sharing Journal Information

Because the Outlook 2010 journal keeps track of activities using a timeline, you might find that it is one of the most useful of the Outlook 2010 folders to share. If you're working on a project with several people, a shared Outlook 2010 Journal folder might be just what you need to make certain everyone is on track.

If you and all the people with whom you want to share the Journal folder use Microsoft Exchange Server, you can share the Journal folder.

Follow these steps to share a personal Journal folder:

1. In Outlook 2010, open the Folder List.

2. Right-click the Journal folder, and then choose Share, Folder Permissions to open the Permissions tab of the Journal Properties dialog box, as shown in Figure 22-17.

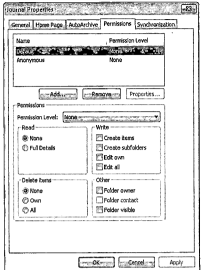

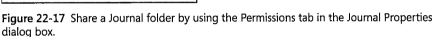

Figure 22-17 Share a Journal folder by using the Permissions tab in the Journal Properties dialog box.

3. Click Default, and then select the desired options in the Permissions area to specify the types of tasks that all users can perform if they have no explicit permissions set.

4. Click Add to open the Add Users dialog box, select a user (or more than one), click Add, and then click OK to return to the Permissions tab.

5. With the user selected in the Name list, select permissions in the Permissions area to specify the tasks that this user can perform. You can select a Permission Level and then customize the permissions as needed.

6. Click OK to apply the permissions.

For details about sharing folders, see the section "Granting Access to Folders," on page 842.

If you want to invite specific people to share your journal, you can send them an email message to let them know that you have granted them permission to view your journal. You can also request to share their journals as part of this message. The permissions that you set control the types of access that will be allowed. The recipients of the message can accept or decline the invitation to share your journal and also decide whether to share their journals with you.

To invite someone to share your journal, follow these steps:

1. In Outlook 2010, open the Folder List.

2. Right-click the Journal folder, and then choose Share, Share Journal to create a Sharing Invitation email message.

3. Select the recipients, and then click Send to send the message.

4. If the recipients share their journals with you, there will be an Open This Journal option on the Sharing tab of the ribbon. When you view another person's journal, a new group named People's Journals is created in the Navigation pane, and a link to the other journal is added to it.

Using the Journal Effectively

The journal can be a useful tool, helping you track how you spend your time over the course of the workday. This information, collected over time, can be used for a range of things such as reporting, billing, and staffing allocation. You can analyze your work activities to get a clearer picture of which projects and activities occupy your time and then use that data to optimize your time and productivity.

Make Using the Journal a Habit

The more information that a journal item contains, the more useful it is. Get in the habit of entering critical information when you create a journal item, especially contacts, categories, and the contents of other fields used for organization and retrieval of journal items. It takes only a minute to make notes or update the time spent on an activity while it's fresh in your mind, and by providing as much information as possible, you ensure that you have all the information you might need.

By using the journal regularly, you will also become more familiar with how it operates and what sort of data it is recording. Although the journal can accumulate a lot of information, both automatically and manually, it's unlikely that it will store exactly what you want right after you start using it. Taking a few minutes on a regular basis to fine-tune your journal settings will pay off when it comes time to analyze the accumulated data. If you find yourself deleting a specific sort of entry more often than not, stop automatically recording it.

Use the Journal's Automatic Recording Features

The journal offers automatic recording of certain Outlook 2010 activities and time spent editing Office system documents. Enabling automatic tracking of those items provides you with quite a bit of data with no additional effort. These options should be used judiciously, however, to ensure against collecting so much information that it becomes difficult to find the important items among the unneeded ones.

INSIDE OUT   Set up automatic journaling for a new contact

When you create a new contact entry in your Outlook 2010 Contacts folder, click All Fields on the Contact tab. In the Select From drop-down list, select Frequently Used Fields, and then set the Journal field to Yes. This is the same as selecting the contact in the Journal Options dialog box; the journal will then record the types of activities that you selected.

Use the Journal Only for Those Things You Need to Track

It might be tempting to turn on all the automatic recording options for the journal so that you collect the maximum possible amount of information. Although you can do this, you might discover that doing so introduces a lot of unnecessary journal items. Outlook 2010 automatically records email messages, journal items, notes, and upcoming tasks and appointments for each entry in the Contacts folder, so in general you don't need to record these items in the journal. You can view these items by opening the Contacts folder and selecting Activities in the Show group.

Note
If you want to export a file containing records of items like email messages and notes to work with in an Excel 2010 workbook or an and 2010 database, you must track these items using the journal. Although these activities can be viewed on the Activities page for a contact, you cannot export information to a file from there.

Similarly, you might want to be careful about automatically recording all work that you do in a certain type of document. If most of your work in Excel 2010 is on projects that you want to track with the journal, turning on automatic recording for Excel 2010 files is a good idea; you can delete the occasional unneeded journal item. If, on the other hand, most of your time in Word 2010 is spent on projects or tasks that don't need to be tracked, you should create journal items manually for those few Word 2010 documents that actually need them.

Add Addresses to Your Primary Contacts Folder

The automatic recording feature of the journal works only with the contents of your primary Contacts folder, not with the Exchange Server Global Address List (GAL) or any secondary Contacts folders. If you want to record automatically journal items associated with people whose email addresses are in a secondary Contacts folder or provided by the GAL, you must first add them to your primary Contacts folder.

To copy or move contacts between folders, open the Outlook 2010 Contacts folder, and then select the source folder in the My Contacts list in the Navigation pane. Right-click an entry and drag it to the destination Contacts folder (by default, the primary Contacts folder is the top one in the list), and then select Move or Copy.

Create Custom Entry Types to Meet Your Individual Needs

Although there are a number of entry types in the default journal configuration, there are likely to be additional entry types that you would find useful. You might want the ability to track things such as travel time or research as discrete entry types to make billing for those activities easier and more accurate. You should add custom entry types so that your journal reflects how you spend your time in greater detail. See the section "Creating and Using Custom Entry Types," on page 581, for detailed information about creating additional entry types.

Time Management Using the Journal

Once you have started to use the journal to track your activities, you can analyze your current time usage to find ways to increase your productivity. You are likely to discover some unexpected time leaks—things that consume an inordinate amount of your time. Identifying these time leaks is the first step in correcting them and getting better control over your work time.

By examining journal items in a variety of views, you can assess how much time a given project, client, or activity is currently taking. If you need more extensive analysis and reporting functionality, journal information can be exported to a file for use with external programs.

Using Views to Analyze Time Usage

Choosing the right view for the job will make it easier for you to understand and use the information collected by the journal. There are a number of predefined views available, allowing you to choose the view that makes it easiest to review a particular set of items.

The journal provides two types of views by default:

- **Timeline views**   Journal items are displayed on a timeline, which can be set to show a single day, a week, or a month at a time, with items grouped by Entry Type, Contact, or Category. Timeline views are particularly good for looking at the specific tasks that occupied a given period of time and can be used to assess time usage and predict time allocation needs.

- **List views**   These views display journal items in a simple tabular format, making them useful for reviewing a large amount of data quickly. Entry List view displays all journal items, Last Seven Days view limits the display to the past week, and Phone Calls view shows only that type of entry.

Using Custom Views of the Journal

Although the existing journal views provide a number of ways to look at your journal, you will probably want your own customized views of the information. To create a custom view, on the View tab, click Change View, Manage Views. In the Manage All Views dialog box, select New. Give the view a name, specify where the view can be used and to whom it will be visible, and then click OK. In the Advanced View Settings dialog box, configure the available options for your custom view, and then click OK.

For detailed information about creating custom views in Outlook 2010, see Chapter 26.

Exporting Journal Items to Other Programs

You might want to analyze the information contained in the journal using a database or a spreadsheet application, each of which offers certain capabilities not available in Outlook 2010. If you need to perform mathematical calculations on your journal data, for example, you can export the information to Excel 2010. For database style analysis and reporting, you can create an Access 2010 database from journal information.

To export your journal, follow these steps:

1. In Outlook 2010, click File, Open, and choose Import to open the Import And Export Wizard.

2. In the Choose An Action To Perform list, select Export To A File, and then click Next.

3. In the Create A File Of Type list, select the Microsoft Access or Microsoft Excel file format, and then click Next.

4. In the Select A Folder To Export From list, select the Journal folder, and then click Next.

5. Enter a name for the exported file, and then click Next.

At this point, you can either click Finish to create the exported file or select Map Custom Fields if you want to customize the field mappings for the exported data. If you select Map Custom Fields, the Map Custom Fields dialog box will open, as shown in Figure 22-18, allowing you to drag a value from Outlook 2010 to a field in the exported document. To change the name of a mapped field, click the Field name in the To box and type the new name. After you have completed mapping the fields, you can click Next and review individual journal entries to verify that the mapping is correct. When you are satisfied with the field mappings, click OK to return to the Export To A File dialog box, and then click Finish to create the file.

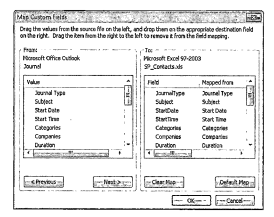

Figure 22-18 Connect journal fields to fields in the exported file in the Map Custom Fields dialog box.

F you're like most people, there's at least one note stuck to your monitor, lying on your desk, or tucked in a drawer, keeping some critical piece of information relatively safe until you need it again—safe, that is, until you lose the note. If you're looking for a better way to keep track of all the small bits of information you receive every day, you can use Microsoft Outlook 2010 to create electronic notes for quick to-do lists, phone numbers, shopping lists—you name it. Notes reside in the Notes folder by default, but you can copy or move notes to other Outlook 2010 folders, use them in documents, place them on the desktop, or place them in your other file system folders. This chapter examines notes and explores how to use them effectively in Outlook 2010 as well as how to integrate them in your other applications.

If your requirements are modest, the Notes folder in Outlook will likely serve your needs. However, notes in Outlook don't offer much in terms of capability beyond simple text-based notes. That's where Microsoft OneNote 2010 comes in. OneNote is an excellent tool for taking notes and working with other information in a notebook-like interface. This chapter also explores OneNote and explains how you can copy information easily between Outlook and OneNote.

Understanding Outlook Notes

You can use Outlook 2010 notes to keep track of any kind of text-based information. For example, you might make a note as a reminder to call someone, to pick up a few things from the store on the way home, or to jot down a phone number. Outlook 2010 notes are really just simple text files, which you can create and view in the Outlook 2010 Notes folder, as shown in Figure 23-1.

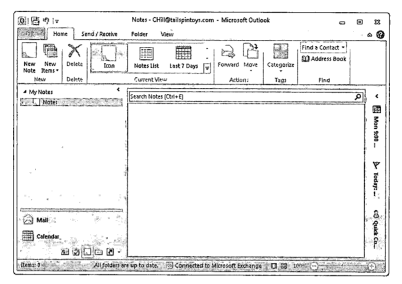

Figure 23-1 You can create and view your notes in the Notes folder.

When you create a new note, Outlook 2010 opens a window similar to the one shown in Figure 23-2. The Note window is essentially a text box. As you type, the text wraps, and the window scrolls to accommodate the text. At the bottom of the Note window, Outlook 2010 displays the modified date, which for a new note is the date and time that you created the note.

Figure 23-2 To create a new note, type in a Note window.

You don't have to save the note explicitly—just close the Note window, and Outlook 2010 adds the note that you've created to the Notes folder. You can copy or move a note to another Outlook 2010 folder or to a file system folder (such as your desktop), copy the text to the Clipboard for inclusion in another document, or save the note to a text file. The following sections explain not only how to perform these actions, but also how to use notes in other ways.

INSIDE OUT   Choose the best feature for the job

Although you can use notes in Outlook 2010 to keep track of just about any kind of information, a note is not always the best approach. Be sure you're not using the note in place of a more effective Outlook 2010 feature. For example, if you need to remind yourself to make a casual phone call at some time during the day, a note might suffice. However, if you need to set up an important conference call, it's better to create an appointment or a task and have Outlook 2010 provide a reminder at the appropriate time. Likewise, the Contacts folder is the best place to keep track of contact information, rather than recording it on scattered notes. Notes are great when you need speed and convenience, but when another Outlook 2010 feature is suitable, you should view a note as a stopgap. For example, you might create a note for a quick to-do list now and then add each item as a task in your Tasks folder later, when you have the time. As you become more familiar with notes, take a look at how you use them to make sure you're working effectively.

Configuring Note Options

Before you start creating notes, you might want to take a few minutes to configure the options that control the default appearance of notes.

To set these options, follow these steps:

1. Start Outlook 2010, and click File, Options.

2. Click Notes and Journal to display the dialog box shown in Figure 23-3.

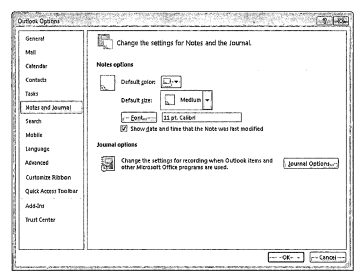

Figure 23-3 Use the Options dialog box to control the size and color of the Note window and the font used for notes.

3. Set the various options in this dialog box to configure the default color for notes (the color of the Note window), the default size of the window, and the font used for the note text, and then click OK.

You can change the window size of any individual note by dragging the border of the Note window. You also can change the color of an existing note at any time (as explained in the following section).

> **Tip**
> Because Outlook 2010 stores the date and time modified for each note, you should check to make sure that your system time is accurate before creating a note.

Working with Notes

Of all the features in Outlook 2010, notes are by far the easiest to use. The following sections explain how to create notes, change their color, copy them to other folders, and more.

Adding a Note

You create notes in the Notes folder. To open this folder, click the Notes icon at the bottom of the Navigation pane.

After you've opened the folder, follow these steps to create a note:

1. Right-click in the Notes folder and choose New Note on the shortcut menu, or simply double-click in the folder window. Either action opens a blank Note window.

2. Type your note directly in the window.

3. Click the Close button in the upper-right corner of the Note window to close and save the note.

If the current view is set to Icons, Outlook 2010 uses the first approximately 26 characters in the note as the title and displays the title under the icon for the note in the Notes folder.

Reading and Editing a Note

To read a note, you can double-click it to open the Note window or point to or click the icon for the note and read the text under the icon. Switching to Notes List view (on the View menu, choose Current View, Notes List) shows more contiguous content. To change the content of a note, open it as just described, and then edit it the same way that you would edit a text file. Keep in mind, however, that you have no formatting options, so your notes are limited to plain text. To save your changes, simply close the Note window.

After you have opened a note, a note icon appears in the upper-left corner of the Note window, which provides a menu of editing options, as follows:

- **Note**   Creates a new note

- **Save As**   Saves the current note as a new note

- **Delete**   Deletes the current note (without confirmation)

- **Forward**   Forwards the note as an attachment to a new email message

- **Cut**   Cuts the selected text in the current note

- **Copy**   Copies the selected text in the current note

- **Paste**   Pastes the cut or copied text in the current note

- **Categorize**   Enables you to assign categories to the note

- **Contacts** Lets you assign a contact to the note

- **Save & Close** Saves the note and closes the Note window

Forwarding a Note

Although you'll probably create notes mainly for your own use, you might need to forward a note to someone. For example, a colleague might request a phone number or other contact information that you've stored in a note. The easiest way to share the information is to forward the note as an email message. Because Outlook 2010 sends the note as an attachment, the recipient can easily copy the note to his or her own Notes folder, place it on the desktop, or use the Clipboard to copy the data to a new contact entry.

To forward a note, follow these steps:

1. Open the Notes folder, right-click the note, and choose Forward on the shortcut menu. Outlook 2010 opens a standard message form. If you are using Hypertext Markup Language (HTML) or plain text for the message, the note is shown as an attachment to the message, as shown in Figure 23-4. If you are sending a note in a rich text message, Outlook 2010 embeds the note as an icon in the body of the message.

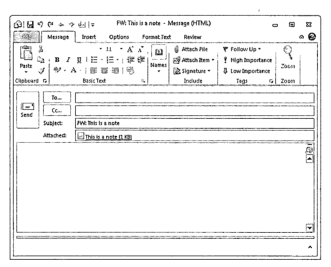

Figure 23-4. When you forward a note, Outlook 2010 attaches it to the message.

2. Complete and send the message as you would any other message.

You can send notes in email messages using other methods too—you're not limited to embedding the note in the message or attaching it. For example, if you click in the Folder List at the bottom of the Navigation pane, you can open the Notes folder and then use the right mouse button to drag the selected note to the Inbox. The resulting shortcut menu allows you to create a message with the note as text in the body of the message, as a shortcut, or as an attachment.

Adding a Note Sent to You

When someone else sends you a note in an email message, you can work with the note directly in the message. The note appears as an attachment to the message, as shown in Figure 23-5. You can open the message and double-click the note to open it in a Note window, but you'll probably prefer to copy the note to your own Notes folder.

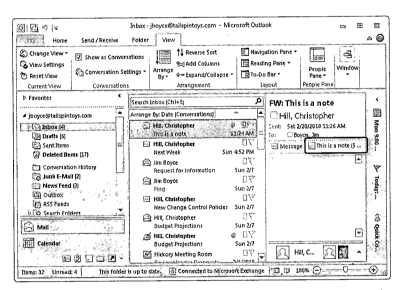

Figure 23-5 When a note is embedded in an email message, you can open the note by double-clicking it.

To copy a note you've received to your Notes folder, follow these steps:

1. Open the Navigation pane (if it is not already open), click the Folder List icon, and then scroll down so that the Notes folder is visible.

2. Open your Inbox, locate the note, and drag it to the Notes folder in the Navigation pane. If the Reading pane in the Inbox is open, you can drag the note from there; otherwise, open the message and drag the note.

Using a Note to Create a Task or an Appointment

If you've made a note about a task you must perform or an appointment you must keep, you can create an Outlook 2010 task or appointment directly from the note easily. To do so, drag the note to the Tasks icon or the Calendar icon in the Navigation pane, as appropriate. Alternatively, you can click the Folder List icon in the Navigation pane and then select the note and drag it to the Tasks folder or Calendar folder. Outlook 2010 opens a new task form or a new appointment form with the note contents as the subject and contents of the task or appointment.

Moving and Copying Notes

You can move and copy notes to other folders. How Outlook 2010 treats the note depends on the destination folder itself. For example, if you copy a note to another Notes folder, Outlook 2010 treats it as a note. But if you copy a note to the Calendar or Tasks folder, Outlook 2010 uses the note to create a new appointment or a new task.

If you use the right mouse button to drag a note to the Contacts icon (or Contacts folder, if the Folder List is open) in the Navigation pane, Outlook 2010 creates a new contact and gives you several options for how to handle the note text. Outlook 2010 can add the text to the contact, add it as an attachment, or add it as a shortcut, depending on your selection. You can also copy the note as a journal entry by using the right mouse button to drag it to the Journal icon in the Navigation pane. You can then choose to create the journal item with the note as an attachment or as a shortcut.

> **Tip**
> Copying a note within the Notes folder is easy. Just use the right mouse button to drag the note to a new location in the folder, release the mouse button, and choose Copy.

You can move or copy notes by dragging. To move a note to another Notes folder, drag the icon for the note to the destination folder. To copy a note instead of moving it, hold down the Ctrl key while dragging the note.

> **Note**
> Dragging a note to a non-notes folder always copies the note rather than moving it; the original note remains in the Notes folder.

Copying a Note to the Clipboard

If you want to use the text of a note in another application or another Outlook 2010 folder, you can copy the note text to the Clipboard. For example, you might copy a phone number from a note to a contact entry in the Contacts folder. To copy information from inside a note, open the note, select the desired text, and then press Ctrl+C. To copy the entire contents of a note from an email attachment to the Clipboard, right-click the note, and then choose Copy. If you're working with the note in the Notes folder, you can select the note and then choose Edit, Copy or press Ctrl+C. Start the application or open the form in which you want to use the note text, and then choose Edit, Paste or press Ctrl+V to paste the data from the Clipboard. By default, this process will copy the text of the note down to the end of the first paragraph (the first place you pressed Enter in the note). To copy the entire contents of a note, open the note and select all the text (or right-click and choose Select All), and then right-click and select Copy.

> **Note**
> If you copy a note from an email message and then paste the note into another message, Outlook 2010 copies the note as an embedded Object Linking and Embedding (OLE) object rather than as text.

Copying a Note to the Desktop or Another Folder

In addition to moving and copying notes inside Outlook 2010, you can move or copy notes to your desktop or to another file system folder. Outlook 2010 creates an .msg file (an Outlook 2010 message file) to contain the note when you copy or move it outside Outlook 2010. After you have copied or moved the note, you can double-click the file to open it.

To copy a note to the desktop or a file system folder, you need only drag it from the Notes folder to the desired destination. To move the note instead of copying it, hold down the Shift key while dragging.

> **Note**
> You can also move or copy a note from the desktop or a file system folder to your Notes folder. Just drag the note from its current location to the Notes folder.

Changing Note Color

By default, Outlook 2010 notes are yellow; however, you can change the default color in the Options dialog box. To change the default color of Notes, click File, Options, click Notes and Journal, and then select one of the five available colors (blue, green, pink, yellow, or white) in the Default Color drop-down list as your default.

You can change the color of an individual note at any time by changing its category and thus the color it is associated with (see the next section).

For information about the Notes Options dialog box, see "Configuring Note Options," on page 603.

Assigning Color Categories to Notes

You can assign categories to notes, just as you can to any other Outlook 2010 item. Categorizing helps you organize your notes, particularly if you choose to view your Notes folder by category. By default, notes are not assigned to any category. (When displayed by category, unless otherwise assigned to a specific category, the notes show up under None.) You can assign multiple categories to each note. For example, you might assign a project category to a note as well as an Urgent category.

You assign colors to notes in Outlook 2010 by selecting a category and thus the color associated with it. You can have a category with no color association and assign that category to a note, but this will effectively color the note white. You can have more than one category using the same color, so there is a bit of flexibility in color and category assignment. You might, for example, decide to color all your marketing communications green and thus set up a general Marketing category, a Sales Calls category, and a New Client Meetings category, all associated with the color green. In this way, you provide yourself with the visual cue (the color green) that the notes (appointments, meetings, email messages, and so on) colored green are related to marketing efforts, and yet you can still differentiate the nature of the item (general marketing, sales call, new client meeting, and so on) when you sort them by category.

For information about By Category view, see "Viewing Notes," on page 612.

To assign categories to a note, follow these steps:

1. Right-click the note and choose Categorize, or select the note and click Categorize on the Home tab on the ribbon.

2. On the Categorize menu, shown in Figure 23-6, choose the applicable category.

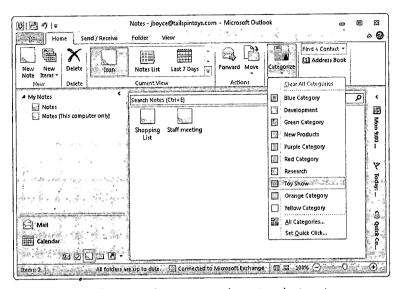

Figure 23-6 Use the Categorize menu to assign categories to notes.

3. If you don't see the categories you need, or if you want to select multiple categories for the note, click All Categories to display the Color Categories dialog box, click New to create the required category and to associate a color, and then click OK.

4. Click OK in the Color Categories dialog box to close the dialog box and assign the selected categories.

You can view the categories assigned to notes by using any one of several methods. For example, you can click Notes List in the Current View group of the Home tab, and then click the Categories column to view the Notes folder organized by category.

For detailed information about working with categories, see Chapter 5, "Creating and Using Categories."

Printing a Note

To print a note, select the note, and then choose File, Print. Alternatively, you can right-click the note and choose Quick Print on the note's shortcut menu. Outlook 2010 prints your name at the top of the page, followed by the date that the note was created or last modified, the categories assigned to the note (if any), and the body of the note text.

Date and Time Stamping Notes

Outlook 2010 stamps each note with the date and time that you created it and displays this information at the bottom of the Note window. This date and time remain until you modify the note by adding or removing text. Outlook 2010 then replaces the original date and time with the date and time you modified the text and stores this information with the note.

INSIDE OUT   Change a note's timestamp

Simply opening and reading a note does not change its timestamp. If you need to modify the note but retain the original timestamp, create a copy of the note and modify the copy. Drag the note to another location in the Notes folder to create the copy.

Deleting a Note

If you no longer need a note, you can delete it. Deleting a note moves it to the Deleted Items folder. What happens to it from there depends on how you have configured Outlook 2010 to process deleted items. If Outlook 2010 clears out the Deleted Items folder each time you exit the program, for example, the note is deleted permanently at that time. You can delete a note in any of the following ways:

- Right-click the note, and then choose Delete.

- Select the note, and then press the Delete key.

- Select the note, and then click Delete on the Home tab on the ribbon.

- Drag the note to the Deleted Items folder in the Navigation pane.

Viewing Notes

Outlook 2010 provides three predefined views for the Notes folder. To switch to a different view, simply click the desired view in the Current View group on the Home tab on the ribbon. You can use any of the following predefined views:

- **Icons**   This default view displays an icon for each note with the first line of the note text serving as the icon's description.

- **Notes List**   This view displays the notes as a line-by-line list showing the entire contents of the note (with AutoPreview on).

- **Last Seven Days**   This view is similar to Notes List view and displays the entire contents of the notes (with AutoPreview on), but only those notes created or modified within the past seven days, based on the current date.

You can use the Reading pane with the Notes folder (click the View tab, click Reading Pane, and then choose Right or Bottom) to display the text of a note when you click the note.

You can customize any of the views in the Notes folder the same way you customize the standard views in other folders. You can, for example, drag columns to rearrange them, resize columns, change column names and other properties, add other fields, and group notes based on various criteria.

For details about creating your own custom views, see Chapter 26, "Creating Custom Views and Print Styles."

Creating New Notes Folders

You can create a new folder for notes in Outlook 2010 easily in a couple of ways. If you click the Folder List icon at the bottom of the Navigation pane, you can then right-click the Notes folder and choose New Folder. When you provide a name for the new folder, it is added below the current Notes folder.

Overview of OneNote

By now, if you have used Outlook notes much, you have no doubt come to the conclusion that while useful, their usefulness is somewhat limited. If you need to keep track of lots of notes, include graphics in them, or do anything other than keep simple text notes, Outlook isn't the right tool. If this is your situation, it's quite likely that OneNote *is* the right tool for you. Figure 23-7 shows the OneNote program window with two notebooks, Personal and Work.

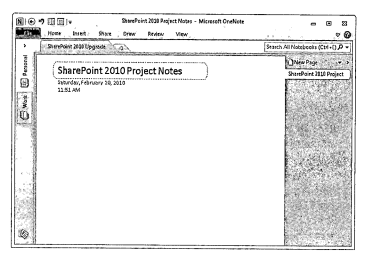

Figure 23-7 The OneNote window with two notebooks.

Using OneNote is really very easy. This section of the chapter isn't designed to cover all aspects of OneNote, but rather just to give you an overview of what it can do.

Start by creating a new notebook as follows:

1. Click File, New to display the New Notebook page (see Figure 23-8).

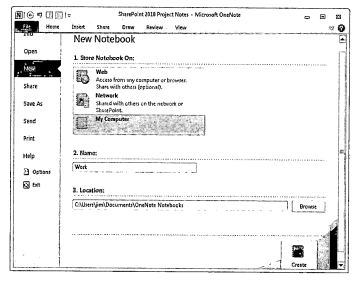

Figure 23-8 Create a new notebook named "Work."

2. Click My Computer, and then click in the Name text box.

3. Type a name for your new notebook, such as **Work**.

4. If needed, click Browse to choose a location for the notebook, or leave the default selection as is.

5. Click Create Notebook.

When you create a new notebook, OneNote automatically creates a new section in the notebook. Sections are indicated by tabs at the top of the window, and sections help you separate and organize your notes in OneNote. You can move between sections simply by clicking the tabs. For example, the current section in Figure 23-7 is named SharePoint 2010 Upgrade.

Each OneNote section can contain multiple pages and subpages. You navigate through the pages using the page tabs at the right of the window, as shown in Figure 23-9. Simply click New Page to create a new page in the current section.

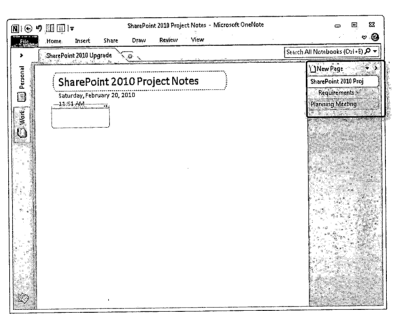

Figure 23-9 Use pages and subpages to organize your notes further.

At this point, you have a notebook and some pages to experiment with. As you work with OneNote, you'll come to appreciate the fact that you can not only add text to your notes, but also easily add drawing shapes, audio and video clips (such as recorded meetings), equations, symbols, pictures, tables, and much, much more. For now, however, let's take a look at how you can add Outlook items to OneNote.

Copying Items from Outlook to OneNote

After you become comfortable using OneNote to track your notes from projects, meetings, etc., you'll no doubt want to include data from Outlook in your notes. For example, perhaps you want to copy some emails about a particular project to the section or page in OneNote that is associated with that project; or maybe you have a page with notes from a meeting and you want to insert the meeting item into OneNote so the meeting time and attendee list is in your OneNote notes. Whatever the case, it's easy to insert Outlook items in One-Note. The following example uses a meeting as an example:

1. In Outlook, create a new meeting invitation and add an agenda and other information as needed, and then send the meeting invitation.

2. Right-click the meeting in the calendar and choose OneNote (see Figure 23-10).

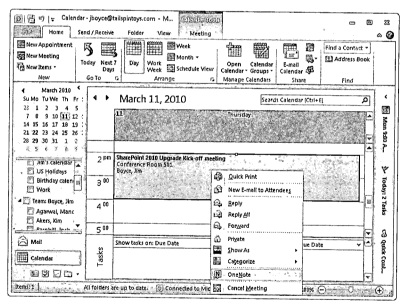

Figure 23-10 Right-click a meeting and choose OneNote to copy it to OneNote.

3. In the Selection Location in OneNote dialog box (see Figure 23-11), choose the section where you want the meeting.

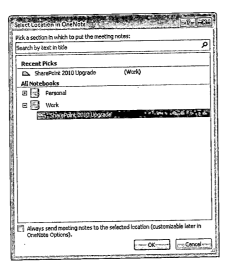

Figure 23-11 Choose the section in which to place the meeting.

As Figure 23-12 shows, the meeting is copied into OneNote as a new page. The page name comes from the meeting subject. The details for the meeting appear in a table on the page, and the Link to Outlook Item link below the items lets you quickly open the Outlook item from OneNote.

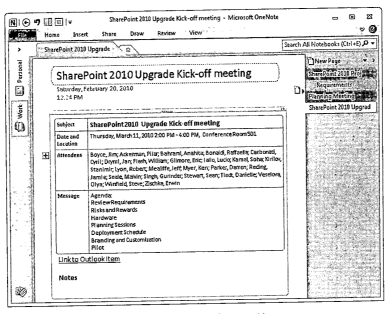

Figure 23-12 An Outlook meeting is copied to OneNote.

You are not limited to copying meeting items from Outlook to OneNote. You can also copy email, contact, and task items to OneNote. If you don't see a OneNote button in the Outlook ribbon when you select an item, just right-click the item and choose OneNote to copy it to OneNote.

PART 5

Customizing Outlook

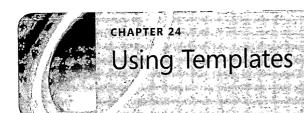

I F you use Microsoft Word frequently, you're probably familiar with templates. These useful tools can help you quickly and easily create documents that share standard elements—for example, boilerplate text, special font and paragraph formatting, and paragraph styles.

You can also use templates in Microsoft Outlook 2010 to streamline a variety of tasks. There is nothing magical about these templates; they are simply Outlook 2010 items that you use to create other Outlook 2010 items. For example, you might create an email template for preparing a weekly status report that you send to your staff or management. Perhaps you use email messages to submit expense reports and would like to use a template to simplify the process.

This chapter not only discusses email templates but also explores the use of templates for other Outlook 2010 items. For example, you'll learn how to use templates to create appointments, contact entries, task requests, and journal entries. The chapter also suggests some ways of sharing templates with others.

Working with Email Templates

An email template is really nothing more than a standard email message that you have saved as a template. Here are some suggested uses for email templates:

- Create an expense report form.

- Send product information to potential clients.

- Create status reports for ongoing projects.

- Send messages to specific groups of recipients.

- Create a form for information requests or product registration.

When you need to send similar messages frequently, creating a message template can save you quite a bit of time, particularly if the message contains a great deal of frequently used text, graphics, or form elements. You also reduce potential errors by reusing the same message each time rather than creating multiple messages from scratch. You can use the template to provide the bulk of the message, filling in any additional information required in each particular instance.

Creating an Email Template

Creating an email template is as easy as creating an email message. You can start by opening a new message form, just as you would if you were sending a new message to a single recipient or group.

To create an email template from scratch, follow these steps:

1. With the Inbox folder open, click the New E-mail button on the toolbar to open a new mail message form. Enter the boilerplate text and any information that you want to include every time you send a message based on this template. For example, you can specify the subject, address, other headings, bullets, lists, and tables.

2. Click File, and then click Save As in the message form.

3. In the Save As dialog box, shown in Figure 24-1, specify a name for the file. Select Outlook Template in the Save As Type drop-down list. Outlook 2010 adds an .oft file name extension to the file name. You can specify a path if you want to save the file in a different location.

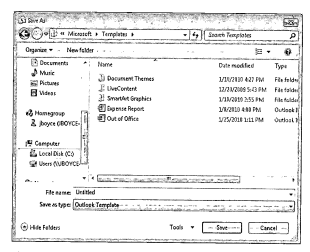

Figure 24-1 Save your newly created template as an .oft file.

Outlook 2010 opens your My Documents folder with the file type corresponding to the current item (HTML, Rich Text Format, or Text Only). The default location for user templates, however, depends on your operating system. In Microsoft Windows XP, the location is the *<profile>*\Application Data\Microsoft\Templates folder, and in Windows Vista and Windows 7, it is the *<profile>*\AppData\Roaming\Microsoft\ Templates folder, where *<profile>* is your user profile folder (which is Documents And Settings*<user>* on most systems running Windows XP systems, but is Users*<user>* on systems running Windows Vista and Windows 7). When you select Outlook Template as the file type, Outlook 2010 automatically switches to your Templates folder.

4. Click Save to save the template. Close the message form, and then click No when asked whether you want to save the changes.

You can create as many email templates as you need, storing them on your local hard disk or on a network server. Placing templates on a network server allows other Outlook users to use them as well.

Using an Email Template

After you create an email template, it's a simple matter to use the template to create a message by following these steps:

1. In Outlook 2010, click New Items on the Home tab on the ribbon, and then click More Items, Choose Form. Outlook 2010 opens the Choose Form dialog box, as shown in Figure 24-2.

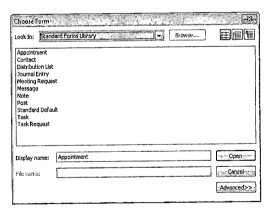

Figure 24-2 Select the template in the Choose Form dialog box.

2. In the Look In drop-down list (which is set to Standard Forms Library by default), select the location where the template is stored. In this example, the template is stored in the user default template folder. To use this template, select User Templates In File System.

3. Select the template from the list, and then click Open to display a message form based on the template data.

4. Fill in the message form to include any additional or modified information, and then send the message as you would any other.

Using a Template with a Contact Group

You can easily send messages to recipients in a contact group without using a template: Simply start a new message, select the contact group from the Address Book, and send the message. If the messages you send to the members of the list are different each time you use the list, you don't need a template. However, if the messages contain much the same information time after time, they're good candidates for templates. For example, you might need to submit weekly reports to a group of administrators or managers, send task lists to people who work for you, or broadcast regular updates about products or services.

You create a template for a contact group the same way that you create any other email template. The only difference is that you store the list of recipients within the template. To do so, simply select the contact group in the appropriate address box when you create the template. If you don't want the various members of the group to see the addresses of other members on the list, be sure to insert the distribution group in the Bcc box rather than in the To or Cc box.

For more information about working with contact groups, see Chapter 6, "Managing Address Books and Distribution Lists."

Using Other Outlook Template Types

Email messages are not the only Outlook 2010 item that you can create from a template. In fact, you can create a template for any type of Outlook 2010 item. This section of the chapter explores some common situations in which you might use specific types of templates.

Appointments and Meetings

You might find it useful to create templates for setting up certain types of appointments and meetings. If you prefer to use a set of appointment properties that differ from the Outlook 2010 default properties, you can use a template that contains your preferred settings and then create each new appointment or meeting from that template. For example, if you have regular meetings with the same group of people, you can set up a template in which those individuals are already selected on the Scheduling page so that you don't have to assemble the list each time you schedule a meeting. Perhaps you prefer to have Outlook 2010 issue a reminder an hour before each appointment rather than the default of 15 minutes.

You can create templates for appointments and meetings the same way you create email templates. Open a new appointment form or meeting request, and then fill in all the data that will be standard each time you use the template. Then click File, Save As, and save the file as an Outlook Template. When you want to use the template, click New Items, More Items, and Choose Form, and then follow the steps outlined in "Using an Email Template," on page 623.

For more information about using appointment forms and their settings, see Chapter 19, "Scheduling Appointments." For details about meeting requests, see Chapter 20, "Scheduling Meetings and Resources."

Contacts

In your Contacts folder, you're likely to add contact entries for people who work in or belong to the same organization, business, department, or other entity. These contacts might share the same company name, address, or primary phone number. In such a case, why not create a template to save yourself the trouble of entering the information for each contact entry separately (and potentially getting it wrong)? Or, for example, you might use the same conferencing Uniform Resource Locator (URL) for all your online meetings hosted by Microsoft Office Live Meeting. Why not create a template that specifies the URL, eliminating the chore of setting it each time you create a new contact?

As with other templates, you create a contact template by opening a new contact form and filling in the standard data. Then click File, Save As, and save the contact as an Outlook Template.

For more information about creating contact entries and working in the Contacts folder, see Chapter 18, "Creating and Managing Your Contacts."

INSIDE OUT Create contacts from the same company

You can create contact entries that share common company information by selecting a contact item and clicking New Items, Contact From Same Company. However, this might not give you the results you need in all cases. For example, the Contact From Same Company command uses the same address, company name, main business phone number, business fax number, and web page address for the new contact as for the selected one. If you also want to use the same directory server, categories, notes, or other properties for the new contacts, it's best to create a contact entry, save it as a template, and then create other contact entries from the template.

Tasks and Task Requests

If you perform the same task frequently, you can create a basic task as a template and then modify it as needed for each occurrence of the task. You also can create a task template with a specific set of properties and then use it to create various tasks. For example, you could create all your tasks with the status specified as In Progress rather than the default Not Started; or perhaps you need to create many tasks with the same set of categories assigned to them.

In addition to creating task items from templates, you might also want to use templates to create task requests. A task request template is handy if you manage a group of people to whom you need to assign similar or identical tasks. Set up a template that incorporates the common elements, and then create each task request from the template, filling in or modifying the unique elements and addressing the request to the specific person assigned to the task.

You use the same methods described earlier for email templates to create and open templates for tasks and task requests.

For more information about creating tasks and task requests, see Chapter 21, "Managing Your Tasks."

Journal Entries

You can use the Outlook 2010 journal to keep track of activities such as phone calls, remote sessions, or other actions that you want to record. Why use journal templates? Any time you find yourself adding a manual journal entry for the same type of activity with the same or similar properties, consider creating a template for the action. Perhaps you frequently record journal entries for phone calls to a particular individual, account, or company that contain the same phone number or company name or log the same duration. Rather than creating a journal entry from scratch each time, create a template and use the template instead.

For more information about working with the Outlook 2010 journal, see Chapter 22, "Tracking Documents and Activities with the Journal."

Editing Templates

Outlook 2010 stores templates as .oft files when you save them to disk. You can modify any template to make changes as needed.

To modify a template, follow these steps:

1. Click New Items, More Items, and Choose Form.

2. Outlook 2010 displays the Choose Form dialog box (shown in Figure 24-2). In the Look In drop-down list, select the location where the template is stored.

3. Select the template, and then click Open.

4. Make changes as needed, and then choose Save & Close (or click File and then click Save) to save the changes.

> **Note**
> To find templates that you've created so that you can edit them, choose User Templates In File System from the Look In drop-down list in the Choose Form dialog box, and then browse to the folder where you saved the template.

Sharing Templates

In some situations, you might find it useful to share templates with other users. For example, assume that you're responsible for managing several people who all submit the same type of report to you on a regular basis through email. In that situation, you might create an email template with the appropriate boilerplate information and your address in the To box and then have the staff use that template to generate the reports. This ensures that everyone is providing comparable information. In addition, whenever you need a different set of data from these employees, you need only modify the template or create a new one from it.

The easiest way to find the location where Outlook 2010 stores your templates is to save a template, or at least go through the motions of saving it. Open a form, click File, Save As, and then select Outlook Templates. Outlook 2010 displays the path to the folder.

Why do you need to know where Outlook 2010 stores your templates? To share a template, you need to share the template file. This means placing the template in a shared network folder, sharing your template folder, or sending the template file to other users (the least desirable option). For any of these options, you need to know the location of the template file that you want to share. After you locate the file, you can share the folder that contains it, copy the template to a network share, or forward it to other users as an attachment.

INSIDE OUT   Share a template using a network share

Probably the best option for sharing a template is to create a network share and place the template in that share. Configure permissions for the share so that you have full control and other users have read-only access to the folder. This allows you to make changes to the template while allowing others to use but not modify it. If other users need to create and manage templates in the same folder, give all users the permissions necessary to create and modify files in the folder and then use file-level NTFS file system permissions for individual template files to control which users can modify them.

Using Templates Effectively

The ability to use templates for Outlook 2010 email, meetings, appointments, tasks, and even journal entries provides you with the means to implement shortcuts in creating new items. Consider how much of your work involves repeatedly sending out email messages, meeting requests, and so on that are essentially the same information structure even though the details differ from day to day. Here are some guidelines to using templates:

- **Look at items you use repeatedly and create templates for them.** Imagine if every time you found yourself creating meetings, tasks, or email messages that contained common, repeated elements, instead of simply creating yet another individual meeting invitation (with your latest agenda and required materials), you created a template with only the common elements (meeting topic, agenda list, required materials, and meeting goals). Within a short time, you would have a catalog of templates available that corresponded to your specific Outlook 2010 items. Then when you needed to schedule such a meeting, you could use the template to shortcut the process of producing the meeting request. Examples of this could include the following:

    - Meeting templates for team meetings, general department meetings, budget meetings, and project meetings (a different one for each project)

    - Email templates for regular team notices (work schedules, weekly meetings, team building, and so on), submitting travel or expense reports, project-related updates (a different one for each project), responding to information requests, and client/customer communications (a different one for each client)

    - Appointment templates for phone conferences, job interviews, client interviews, and offsite sales presentations

    - Task templates for weekly reports, weekly and monthly to-do lists, project tasks (a different template for each project), and quarterly and annual reports

    Your own uses of templates will exceed and differ from those in the preceding list, and yet you can see how the use of templates can speed up many Outlook 2010 operations that you perform repeatedly.

- **Share your templates with others in your organization.** Each organization has many people who perform similar (if not the same) activities, tasks, and operations. Thus, it is likely that templates that you create to facilitate your own work will also be useful to your coworkers. Every team in your organization, for example, has (at least structurally) similar weekly/monthly status reports, and many employees have the same annual/semiannual review reporting requirements. As you create templates to ease your workflow, assess and identify the other people or groups within your organization that could benefit from each template (or a closely related derivation).

- **Store templates where they are easily accessible.** After you have created templates that are useful to other people in your organization, you need to store the templates in a location that is accessible to everyone who could use them. The default location for templates on your system is not the best place to share them from because your system might not be online at all times that others need access to the templates. You also might have templates in the default folder that you don't actually want to share.

It is more useful to create a folder on a commonly accessible file server or Distributed File System (DFS) share and copy all the templates that you want to share to this location. On this file share, you can set sharing permissions to allow other users appropriate permissions. For example, if any other users should be able to add or modify templates, you can grant Change permission to the Everyone group (or the Domain Users group); however, if no one should be able to modify or add templates, you can set share permissions to Read. You can also use NTFS file system permissions to further control access and the ability to add, modify, or delete the templates on a per-template basis. Once the share has been created, the templates have been uploaded, and the appropriate share-level and file-level permissions have been applied, you should send email messages to the relevant groups and users to inform them of the template location, access, and restrictions.

Customizing the Outlook Interface

MICROSOFT Outlook 2010 has an easy-to-use yet powerful interface that serves most users well right out of the box. However, you probably perform certain tasks that are not readily available through the standard Outlook 2010 interface. For example, perhaps you have a handful of macros you use often and want quick access to them.

As all Microsoft Office 2010 system applications do, Outlook 2010 provides a way to tailor the interface to your needs. You can customize the Navigation pane to add your own shortcuts, customize the To-Do Bar, customize the Outlook Today view and other standard views, customize the ribbon and Quick Access toolbar, and customize the way Outlook 2010 displays your folders.

This chapter focuses on the various ways that you can fine-tune Outlook 2010 to the way you work. Some of the changes covered are minor; others are more significant. All of them can enhance your experience with Outlook 2010 and make it a more useful tool for bringing efficiency to your workday.

Customizing the Navigation Pane

Most people browse through Outlook 2010 folders using the Navigation pane. This section explains how you can customize the Navigation pane to suit your preferences.

A Quick Tour of the Navigation Pane

The Navigation pane, which appears on the left side of the Outlook 2010 window, was introduced in Outlook 2003 and replaces the Outlook Bar, which was a staple of the Outlook interface prior to Outlook 2003. The Navigation pane gives you quick access to all your Outlook 2010 folders. Outlook 2010 gives you the capability to minimize the Navigation pane to gain more window space for the current folder view but still open the Navigation pane quickly when you need it.

The Navigation pane contains buttons that serve as shortcuts to your Outlook 2010 folders, as shown in Figure 25-1. The Navigation pane also includes shortcuts to a few common items, including the Outlook Today view and the Microsoft Office Online website. You can access these shortcuts by clicking the Shortcuts icon at the bottom of the Navigation pane.

Click to minimize

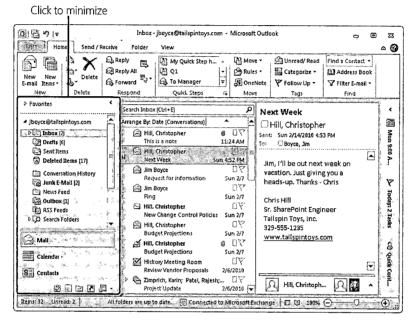

Figure 25-1 The Navigation pane provides shortcuts to Outlook 2010 folders and other objects.

You can make several changes to the Navigation pane, including adding and removing groups, adding and removing shortcuts, and changing the appearance of its icons. The following sections explain these changes.

> **Note**
>
> You can change the width of the Navigation pane by dragging its border.

Showing and Hiding the Navigation Pane

If you use the Navigation pane often, you'll probably want it to remain open all the time, but if you work with a particular Outlook 2010 folder most of the time, you might prefer to have the additional space for your favorite folder view or the Reading pane. In Outlook 2010, you have the capability to minimize the Navigation pane to gain more window space but easily restore it when you need it, as shown in Figure 25-2. To minimize the Navigation pane, click the View tab, click Navigation Pane, and then choose Minimize. Alternatively, simply click the left-facing arrow near the upper-right corner of the Navigation pane, as indicated in Figure 25-1. When the Navigation pane is minimized, you'll find an Expand The Navigation Pane button in the upper-right corner of the Navigation pane, as shown in Figure 25-2. Just click this button to expand the Navigation pane.

Click to
restore

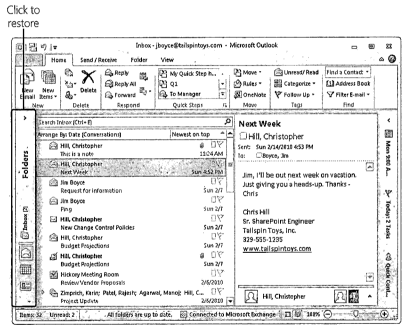

Figure 25-2 The Navigation pane has a minimized state.

Outlook 2010 also allows you to turn on or turn off the Navigation pane as needed. Click View, Navigation Pane, and then choose Off to turn it off.

Changing the Number of Buttons on the Navigation Pane

Outlook 2010 can display up to eight buttons in the bottom portion of the Navigation pane, and these include a button for each of the standard Outlook 2010 folders, the Folder List, and Shortcuts. The number of buttons displayed depends on the size of the Outlook 2010 window and how many buttons you choose to show. If you need more space for the Folder List, for example, you can simply drag the bar above the Mail button to resize the lower portion of the Navigation pane, which changes the number of buttons shown. You can show or hide buttons by clicking the arrow at the bottom of the Navigation pane and choosing Show More Buttons or Show Fewer Buttons, as shown in Figure 25-3.

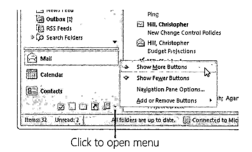

Click to open menu

Figure 25-3 Use this menu to show or hide buttons.

Outlook 2010 does not show all the available buttons in the Navigation pane by default. For example, the Journal button doesn't appear by default in the Navigation pane. To add or remove buttons, click Configure Buttons at the bottom of the Navigation pane, click Add Or Remove Buttons, and then select the button that you want to add or remove.

> **Note**
>
> If you want to add or remove more than one folder, right-click a folder button in the Navigation pane, and then choose Navigation Pane Options to open a dialog box that you can use to add and remove buttons for the folders.

Adding a Shortcut to an Outlook Folder or a Public Folder

The Navigation pane includes buttons for each of the built-in Outlook 2010 folders, and the Folder List provides quick access to all other Outlook 2010 folders and public folders (which are available only with Microsoft Exchange Server). You can add shortcuts to any folder easily by following these steps:

1. Click the Shortcuts button at the bottom of the Navigation pane to open the Shortcuts pane.

2. Right-click Shortcuts in the Navigation pane and choose New Shortcut to open the Add To Navigation Pane dialog box, shown in Figure 25-4.

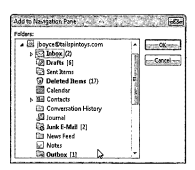

Figure 25-4 Select the folder for which you want to add a shortcut.

3. Select a folder in the list, and then click OK. Outlook 2010 adds the shortcut to the Shortcuts group.

4. Drag the shortcut to a different group, if desired.

Adding a File Folder or Document to the Navigation Pane

You can create shortcuts to file system folders or Outlook 2010 folders and add them to existing Navigation pane groups or to new groups that you create. For example, if you use a particular document folder often, you might want to add that folder to one of your Navigation pane shortcut groups.

The process is similar, regardless of the type of shortcut you're adding. Follow these steps:

1. In Outlook 2010, open the group in which you want to create the shortcut.

2. Click the Shortcuts button in the Navigation pane to open the Shortcuts pane.

3. In Microsoft Windows, open the folder containing the folder or file for which you want to create a shortcut, and then position the folder and the Outlook 2010 window so that you can see both, as shown in Figure 25-5.

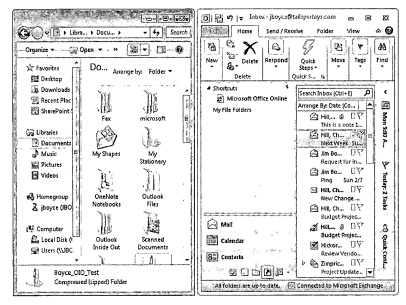

Figure 25-5 Drag a shortcut, folder, or document from Windows to the Navigation pane to create a shortcut.

4. Drag the folder or document from the folder window to the shortcut group name where you want to add it. Place it on the group header itself, not within the group.

INSIDE OUT   Create shortcuts to network shares that you use often

You can specify Universal Naming Convention (UNC) paths in addition to mapped drives. A UNC path takes the form \\<*server*>\<*share*>, where <*server*> is the computer sharing the folder and <*share*> is the folder's share name. You can specify longer UNC paths, such as \\<*server*>\Documents\Contracts\Completed. To use network shortcuts in Outlook 2010, first create the shortcut on the desktop and then drag it to a shortcut group in the Navigation pane.

Adding a Web Site to the Navigation Pane

You can add shortcuts to websites to the Navigation pane. This lets you quickly open a site from Outlook 2010 to do research, check stock quotes, view news, and so on. The website opens within the Outlook window.

To add a website shortcut to the Navigation pane, first create the shortcut on the desktop or in another folder. Open the Navigation pane shortcut group in which you want to place the shortcut, and then simply drag the existing shortcut to the Navigation pane and place it on the group header (such as Favorite Web Sites). You can also copy shortcuts from your Favorites menu easily. Open your web browser, open the Favorites menu, and then right-click the favorite and choose Copy. Right-click the desktop and choose Paste. Then drag the shortcut from the desktop to the shortcut group in the Navigation pane.

INSIDE OUT   Create new web shortcuts

You can create new web shortcuts on the desktop or in a file system folder (such as My Documents) by right-clicking the location and choosing New, Shortcut. On the first page of the Create Shortcut Wizard, type the Uniform Resource Locator (URL) to the web page, File Transfer Protocol (FTP) site, or other Internet resource. Use http:// as the URL prefix for web pages, use ftp:// for FTP sites, and use https:// for sites that use Secure Sockets Layer (SSL) for security.

Removing a Shortcut from the Navigation Pane

If you decide that you no longer want a particular shortcut in the Navigation pane, you can remove it easily. Simply right-click the shortcut and then choose Delete Shortcut. Click Yes to remove the shortcut or No to cancel the action.

Renaming a Shortcut in the Navigation Pane

In some cases, you'll want to change the name that Outlook 2010 assigns to a shortcut in the Navigation pane. For example, when you add a website shortcut, its name is the URL, which typically doesn't fit very well in the Navigation pane. Perhaps you simply want to change the shortcut's name to something more descriptive and easier to remember.

To change the shortcut name, right-click the shortcut, and then choose Rename Shortcut. Type the new name, and then press Enter.

Working with Groups in the Navigation Pane

Outlook 2010 creates one group named Shortcuts, in the Navigation pane by default. You can also add your own groups, remove groups, and rename them. This section explains these tasks.

Adding a Group to the Navigation Pane

At some point, you might want to add your own groups of shortcuts to the Navigation pane to help you reorganize existing shortcuts or organize new shortcuts. For example, you might want to create a group to contain all your web shortcuts.

Adding a new group is easy. Right-click the Shortcuts button in the Navigation pane, and then click New Shortcut Group. Outlook 2010 adds a new group named New Group and highlights the group name so that you can change it, as shown in Figure 25-6. Type the group name, and then press Enter. Then begin adding shortcuts or moving shortcuts to the group from your other groups.

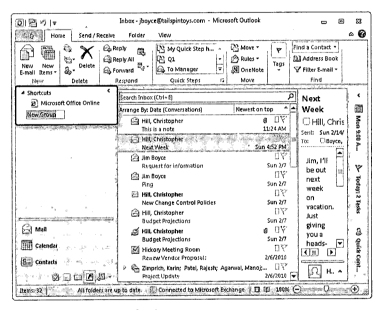

Figure 25-6 Type a name for the new group.

Renaming a Group in the Navigation Pane

You can rename a group as easily as you rename a shortcut. Start Outlook 2010, right-click the group name in the Navigation pane, and then choose Rename Group. Type a new name for the group, and then press Enter.

Removing a Group from the Navigation Pane

If you decide that you want to remove a group from the Navigation pane, you can do so at any time. Simply right-click the group name in the Navigation pane and then choose Delete Group. Click Yes to remove the group or No to cancel the action.

> **Note**
>
> If the group that you remove contains shortcuts that you've copied from other locations (such as the desktop), removing the group does not affect those shortcuts. Only the group is removed from the Navigation pane; the shortcuts remain in their other locations. Shortcuts that exist only in that group, however, are deleted.

Customizing the To-Do Bar

The To-Do Bar combines the Date Navigator, appointments, the task list, and the Quick Contacts list. The To-Do Bar sits at the right side of the Outlook 2010 window, as shown in Figure 25-7. As with the Navigation pane, you can minimize the To-Do Bar to make more window space available for your Outlook 2010 folders or for the Reading pane but still access the To-Do Bar quickly when you need it.

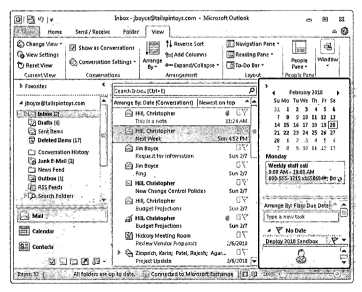

Figure 25-7 The To-Do Bar combines the Date Navigator, appointments, the task list, and the Office Communicator Quick Contacts list.

> **Note**
>
> To display the To-Do Bar, click View, To-Do Bar, and then choose Normal.

You can control which of these items appears in the To-Do Bar. To customize the To-Do Bar, choose To-Do Bar on the View tab, and then select or clear the Date Navigator, Appointments, Task List, and Quick Contacts options. To control other options for the To-Do Bar, click the View tab, click To-Do Bar, and then choose Options. In the resulting To-Do Bar Options dialog box, shown in Figure 25-8, you can specify the number of month rows in the Date Navigator and the number of appointments shown in the Appointments area.

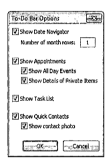

Figure 25-8 Set options for the To-Do Bar in the To-Do Bar Options dialog box.

Customizing the Ribbon

While the ribbon existed in only some parts of Outlook 2007, the ribbon is now pervasive in Outlook 2010. As you might expect, you have quite a bit of control over what appears in the Outlook ribbon. You can change the name of some items in the ribbon and even create your own tabs and option groups.

You manage the ribbon through the Outlook Options dialog box, as shown in Figure 25-9. To open these options, right-click the ribbon and choose Customize The Ribbon; or click File, choose Options, and then click Customize Ribbon in the left pane.

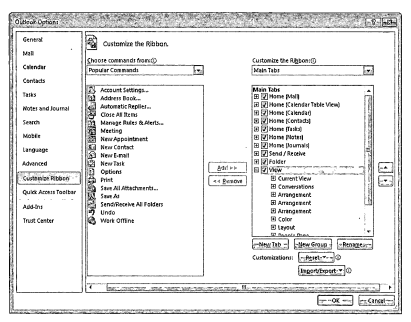

Figure 25-9 Use the Outlook Options dialog box to customize the ribbon.

> **Tip**
>
> You can minimize the ribbon to gain more space for the rest of the Outlook interface when you aren't using the ribbon. Just click the Minimize The Ribbon button (an up-facing arrow next to the Help button). The button changes to a down-facing arrow. Click the button to restore the ribbon.

Modifying Existing Items and Tabs

As mentioned previously, you can make changes to existing items in the ribbon. Depending on the item, you might be able to remove it from the ribbon altogether. However, most of the items that appear in the ribbon by default cannot be removed. For example, in the Customize Ribbon page of the Outlook Options dialog box, expand the Home (Mail) group, expand Tags, and click the Follow Up branch. Note that the Remove button is dimmed, indicating that you can't remove this particular item. If the Remove button is not dimmed when you click an item, you can remove that item from the ribbon. Also, note that you can remove the default groups but not individual items in them. For example, you can remove the Tags group from the Home tab altogether, but you can't remove the Follow Up item individually.

If some of the group names in the ribbon don't make sense to you, or you feel you have a better, more descriptive name, you can rename the group. Just expand the list in the Outlook Options dialog box, click the group name, and then click Rename. Type a new name and click OK. (Note that some groups cannot be renamed.)

Adding New Items

It's easy to add other items to the existing ribbon tabs, making those commands and options that you use most frequently readily available. You can't add new items to the default groups included with Outlook, but you can create your own groups to contain the items. Here's how:

1. Start by right-clicking the ribbon and choosing Customize The Ribbon to open the Customize The Ribbon page of the Outlook Options dialog box.

2. From the tabs list at the right of the dialog box, select the tab that you want to modify.

3. Click New Group to add a new group named New Group (Custom).

4. With the new group selected, click Rename, enter a name for the new group, and click OK.

5. Next, in the Choose Commands From drop-down list identified in Figure 25-10, choose the types of commands that you want to add. For example, choose All Commands to show a list of all available commands.

6. Scroll through the list of commands and find the one that you want to add.

7. With the custom group selected in the right-hand list, click Add to add the item to the group.

Choose a command
category

Choose a custom
group

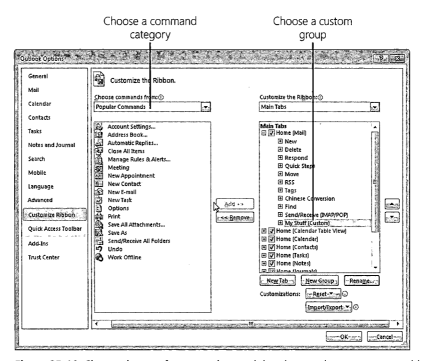

Figure 25-10 Choose the set of commands containing the one that you want to add.

Creating Your Own Ribbon Tabs

While you might want to add some of your own groups to the existing ribbon tabs, more than likely you will want to add your own tabs and then add the commands that you use most often to the custom tabs. This is a great way to keep your customizations separate from the default tab sets.

Creating a new tab is easy. Just click New Tab on the Customize The Ribbon page of the Outlook Options dialog box. Outlook adds a new tab named New Tab (Custom). Select the newly created tab and click Rename to give it a more descriptive name of your choice. Figure 25-11 shows a new tab called Jim's Stuff added to the ribbon, with just the default New Group and no commands or options.

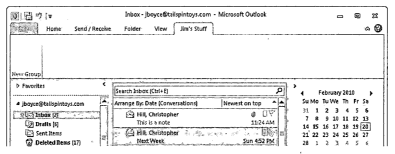

Figure 25-11 A custom tab added to the ribbon.

At this point, your new tab is a blank canvas. You can add groups as you see fit and add commands, macros, and so on to those groups. It doesn't matter if you already have a particular command on another tab. You can add it to your custom tab to make it readily available, along with all the other commands and options you use frequently. Use the process described previously in this chapter to add new groups and add items to the groups.

The next step is to organize the groups on your custom tab, placing individual items in the desired order as well as putting the groups themselves in the desired order. Here's how to rearrange items:

1. Right-click the ribbon and choose Customize The Ribbon to open the Customize The Ribbon page of the Outlook Options dialog box.

2. In the right half of the dialog box, expand the group whose items you want to rearrange.

3. To rearrange the items in a group, click the item you want to move. Use the Move Up and Move Down buttons indicated in Figure 25-12 to move the item up or down.

4. To rearrange the groups themselves, expand the tab containing the groups that you want to rearrange, and then use the Move Up and Move Down buttons to rearrange them.

5. To rearrange the order of the tabs on the ribbon, select a tab from the list and use the Move Up and Move Down buttons to rearrange as desired.

6. Click OK when you are satisfied with the new ribbon arrangement.

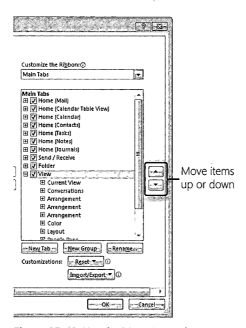

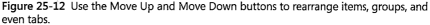

Move items
up or down

Figure 25-12 Use the Move Up and Move Down buttons to rearrange items, groups, and even tabs.

Sharing Your Customized Ribbon

If you have spent a lot of time customizing your ribbon and you want to share it with others who have the same general needs, you can export the customizations to a file so they can import it into their own copy of Outlook 2010. To export your ribbon customizations to a file, click File, Options, and click Customize Ribbon in the left pane. Click Import/Export and choose Export All Customizations. In the File Save dialog box, enter a name for the customization file and click Save. Then place the file on a network share or Microsoft SharePoint site, email it, or otherwise provide it to the others who you want to have the same customizations. They can then click Import/Export on the Customize Ribbon page of the Outlook Options dialog box, choose Import Customization File, and import the file into Outlook.

Resetting Customizations

If you decide you don't like the changes you've made to the ribbon, right-click the ribbon and choose Customize The Ribbon, and then click Reset. Choose Reset Only Selected Ribbon Tab to reset only the currently selected ribbon tab; or choose Reset All Customizations to return the ribbon to its default state.

Customizing the Quick Access Toolbar

The Quick Access toolbar appears by default above the ribbon in the Outlook interface. It is a thin toolbar with small icons that you can customize to put frequently used commands close at hand (see Figure 25-13).

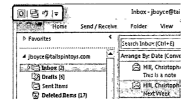

Figure 25-13 Use the Quick Access toolbar to access frequently used commands.

By default, the Quick Access toolbar only contains a very few items. However, you can add other items to the Quick Access toolbar easily. In fact, Outlook provides a menu of prese-lected items that you can add. To add items from this list, click the Customize Quick Access Toolbar button at the right edge of the Quick Access toolbar to open the menu shown in Figure 25-14. Choose an item from the menu to either add or remove it from the Quick Access toolbar.

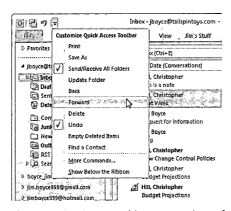

Figure 25-14 You can add or remove items from the Quick Access toolbar easily.

Tip

You can move the Quick Access toolbar under the ribbon if you prefer. Click the Cus-tomize Quick Access Toolbar button at the right edge of the toolbar and choose Show Below The Ribbon.

To add commands not shown in the menu, click the Customize Quick Access Toolbar button and choose More Commands from the menu. Outlook displays the Quick Access Toolbar page of the Outlook Options dialog box, shown in Figure 25-15.

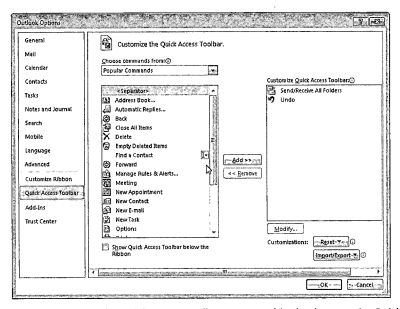

Figure 25-15 Use the Quick Access Toolbar page to add other items to the Quick Access toolbar.

Adding items to the Quick Access toolbar is easy. Just select an item and click Add. Click an item and click Remove to remove it from the toolbar. Use the Move Up and Move Down buttons to arrange items on the toolbar to your liking. Then click OK to save the changes.

> **Tip**
>
> As you can with the ribbon customizations, you can export your Quick Access toolbar customizations to a file that can be used by others to import those customizations into their own copy of Outlook. Use the Import/Export button on the Quick Access Toolbar page of the Outlook Options dialog box to export or import a customized Quick Access toolbar.

Customizing the Outlook Today View

Outlook 2010 uses the Outlook Today view as its default view. Outlook Today combines your most commonly used Outlook 2010 data into a single view, summarizing your schedule, tasks, and key email folders for the current day, as shown in Figure 25-16. You can work with the view as is or modify it to suit your needs. This section explores how to customize the Outlook Today view.

For a basic description of how to use the Outlook Today view, see the next section, "Configuring Outlook Today."

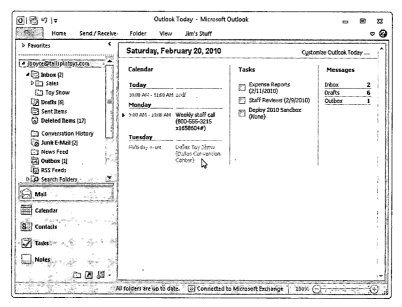

Figure 25-16 Outlook Today summarizes your current day.

Although Outlook Today presents useful information, it might not show all the information you want or need to really keep track of your workday. You can customize the Outlook Today view to show additional information and use Hypertext Markup Language (HTML) to present a truly customized interface. The following sections explain how.

Configuring Outlook Today

You can configure several options that control how this view looks, as well as the data that it displays. To configure the view, click the Customize Outlook Today link in Outlook Today view (in the upper-right corner of the view in all styles except Winter, where it appears in the lower-right area). The Customize Outlook Today page shown in Figure 25-17 appears.

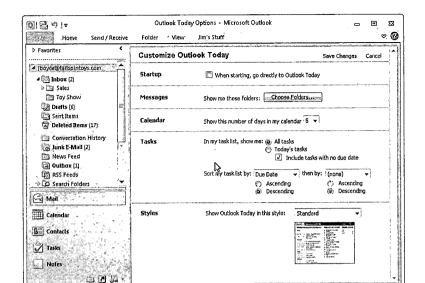

Figure 25-17 Use the settings shown here to configure the Outlook Today view.

The following sections explain the changes you can make to the Outlook Today view on this page. When you're satisfied with the changes, click Save Changes in the Customize Outlook Today title bar, or click Cancel to close the page without applying the changes.

Specifying the Startup View

If you select the When Starting, Go Directly To Outlook Today check box, Outlook 2010 opens the Outlook Today view when you first start the program.

You also can specify the startup folder by using Outlook 2010 options, as explained here:

1. Click File, Options.

2. Click Advanced.

3. Beside the Start Outlook In This Folder box, click Browse.

4. Select the top level of your mailbox, indicated by the email address of the account.

5. Click OK twice to close the dialog boxes.

The Startup In This Folder drop-down list specifies the folder that Outlook 2010 will use by default when you start Outlook 2010. Choosing Outlook Today in the list has the same effect as selecting When Starting, Go Directly To Outlook Today in the Customize Outlook Today page.

> **Note**
> If Outlook Today is configured as the default view and you clear the When Starting, Go Directly To Outlook Today check box without specifying a different startup folder in the Options dialog box, Outlook 2010 makes your Inbox the startup folder by default.

Specifying Folders to Show

The Outlook Today view shows the Drafts, Inbox, and Outbox folders. If you seldom use the Drafts folder, you might prefer to remove it from Outlook Today; or perhaps you want to add other folders to the view, such as Tasks and Contacts, to give you a quick way to open those folders without using the Navigation pane.

To configure the folders that Outlook Today displays, click Choose Folders on the Customize Outlook Today page to open the Select Folder dialog box, shown in Figure 25-18. Select each folder that you want to display, and then click OK.

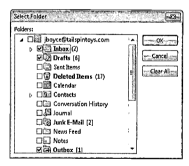

Figure 25-18 Use the Select Folder dialog box to choose the folders that you want Outlook Today to display.

Setting Calendar Options

The Calendar portion of the Outlook Today view displays a certain number of days from your calendar based on the current date. You can specify the number of days displayed by using the Show This Number Of Days In My Calendar option. Select a number from 1 to 7.

Setting Task Options

The Tasks area of the Customize Outlook Today page lets you configure how Outlook Today displays your tasks. The following list summarizes these options:

- **All Tasks**   Shows all tasks regardless of the status or completion deadline.

- **Today's Tasks**   Shows overdue tasks and incomplete tasks that are due today.

- **Include Tasks With No Due Date**   Shows tasks to which you've assigned no due date.

- **Sort My Task List By criteria Then By criteria**   Sort your task list according to the task's importance, due date, creation time, and start date. You can specify two sort conditions and also choose between ascending or descending sort order for both conditions.

Using Styles

By default, Outlook Today displays its information using three columns on a white background. Outlook 2010 provides additional styles that you can select to change the overall appearance of the Outlook Today view. Use the Show Outlook Today In This Style drop-down list to select a style. The Customize Outlook Today page shows a sample of the style after you select it.

E ARLIER chapters in this book discussed the standard views that Microsoft Outlook 2010 provides for its many folders and data types. Those chapters also discussed customizing standard views by grouping and sorting items and by adding and removing columns, changing column order and properties, filtering the view, and so on.

In this chapter, you'll learn how to create custom views in Outlook 2010 to present the information you want in a format that suits your needs. Because generating a printed version of your data is often a byproduct of creating a view, this chapter also focuses on how to create custom print styles in Outlook 2010. For those situations in which the Outlook 2010 custom views and print styles won't give you the results you need, you can turn to scripts and Microsoft Word 2010 to accomplish custom printing tasks.

For more information about customizing existing views, see the section "Working with the Standard Outlook Views," on page 72. You'll also find information about specific views in the chapters that cover them. For example, for more information about working with and customizing views in the Contacts folder, see the section "Viewing Contacts," on page 452.

Creating and Using Custom Views

If the options for customizing existing Outlook 2010 views don't provide the information view that you need, you can create your own views. You have two options for doing this: modifying an existing view or creating a new view from scratch.

Basing a New View on an Existing View

You can create a new, custom view from an existing view if the existing one offers most of the view elements that you need. This is usually the easiest method because it requires the least amount of work.

Follow these steps to create a new, custom view from an existing view:

1. Open the folder for which you want to modify the view, and then select the view to display it.

2. On the View tab, click Change View and choose Save Current View As A New View to open the Copy View dialog box, shown in Figure 26-1.

Figure 26-1 Use the Copy View dialog box to create a new view.

3. In the Copy View dialog box, type a name in the Name Of New View box, and then select one of the following options:47

   - **This Folder, Visible To Everyone**   Makes the view available only in the folder from which it was created. Anyone with access to the specified folder can use the view.

   - **This Folder, Visible Only To Me**   Makes the view available only in the folder from which it was created. Only the person who created the view can use it.

   - **All Type Folders**   Makes the view available in all folders that match the specified folder type. For example, when you create a custom view based on the Inbox, this option becomes All Mail And Post Folders, and Outlook 2010 makes the view available from the Inbox, Outbox, Drafts, Sent Items, and other message folders. If you base the new view on the Contacts folder, this option becomes All Contact Folders and makes the view available from all contacts folders.

4. On the View tab, click View Settings to open the Advanced View Settings dialog box, as shown in Figure 26-2.

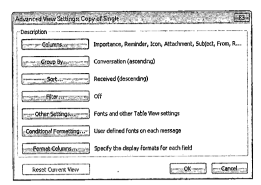

Figure 26-2 The Advanced View Settings dialog box lets you access the functions that you can use to define your custom view.

5. Use the options provided in the Advanced View Settings dialog box to customize the view.

   For details on all the options that you can configure in the Customize View dialog box, see the section "Customizing a View's Settings," on page 659.

6. After you've modified the settings as needed, click OK to close the Customize View dialog box and apply the view changes.

Creating a New View from Scratch

You can create an Outlook 2010 view from scratch if the view you want doesn't have much in common with any of the existing views. For example, perhaps you want to create an Inbox view that displays your messages as icons rather than headers, as shown in Figure 26-3. You can't modify a standard message view to display messages as icons, so you need to create the view from scratch.

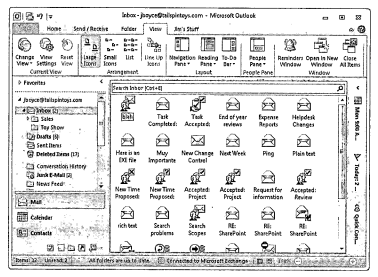

Figure 26-3 This Inbox view shows message icons rather than headers.

The process for creating a view from scratch is much like the process of modifying an exist-ing view. When you create a new view, however, you have additional options for specifying the view.

Follow these steps to create a view from scratch:

1. Open the folder or folder type for which you want to create a custom view.

2. Click the View tab and then click Change View, Manage Views to open the Manage All Views dialog box.

3. Click New to open the Create A New View dialog box, shown in Figure 26-4.

Figure 26-4 You can create several types of new views.

4. In the Name Of New View box, type a name for your new view.

5. In the Type Of View list, select the type of view you want to create, as follows:

- **Table** Presents information in tabular form, with one item per row and columns laid out according to your selections. The default Inbox view is an example of a table view.

- **Timeline** Displays items on a timeline based on the item's creation date (such as the received date for a message or the event date for a meeting). You might find this view type most useful for the Calendar folder.

- **Card** Displays information using cards, as in Address Cards view (the default view in the Contacts folder).

- **Business Card** Displays information using customizable, graphical business cards, similar to Detailed Address Cards view.

- **Day/Week/Month** Displays days in the left half of the window and monthly calendars in the right half. The actual view depends on the type of folder for which you create the view. Figure 26-5 shows a Day/Week/Month view created for the Inbox folder.

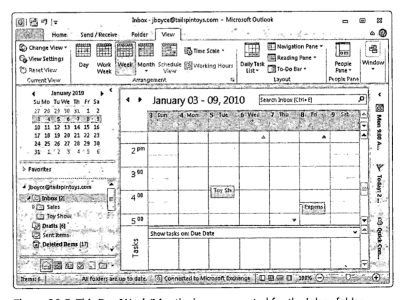

Figure 26-5 This Day/Week/Month view was created for the Inbox folder.

- **Icon** Displays the items as icons, much as a file system folder does.

6. In the Can Be Used On area, select an option as described in the preceding section, and then click OK. The Advanced View Settings dialog box opens.

7. Customize the view as needed, and then click OK.

8. Click Apply View to apply the view, or click Close to close the dialog box without applying the view.

For details on all the options you can configure in the Customize View dialog box, see the section "Customizing a View's Settings," on page 659.

Modifying, Renaming, or Deleting a View

You can easily modify, rename, and delete custom from aboutviews. For example, perhaps you want to apply a filter to a view in the Contacts folder to show only those contacts who work for a particular company. Maybe you want to have Outlook 2010 apply a certain label to appointments that have specified text in the subject.

To modify, rename, or delete a view, follow these steps:

1. Click the View tab, and click Change View, Manage Views to open the Manage All Views dialog box.

2. In the Views For Folder list, select the view that you want to change, and then do one of the following:

   • To modify the view, click Modify. Use the options in the Customize View dialog box to apply changes to the view (as explained in the following section).

   • To rename the view, click Rename, and then type the new name.

   • To delete the view, click Delete. The Reset button changes to Delete if you select a custom view.

3. Click Close.

Customizing a View's Settings

Outlook 2010 gives you considerable control over the appearance and contents of a view. When you define a new view or modify an existing view, you end up in the Advanced View Settings dialog box, shown in Figure 26-2. To open this dialog box, click the View tab and click View Settings in the Current View group.

The options available in the Advanced View Settings dialog box change according to the folder selected. For example, the options for the Contacts folder differ in some respects from the options for the Inbox. The same general concepts hold true for each type of folder, however. The following sections explain the various ways that you can use these dialog box options to customize a view.

Configuring Columns

In most cases, clicking Columns in the Advanced View Settings dialog box opens the Show Columns dialog box, similar to the one shown in Figure 26-6, in which you can select the columns that you want to include in the view. (Exceptions to this behavior are discussed later in the section.) For example, you might use the dialog box to add the Cc or Sensitivity column to the view.

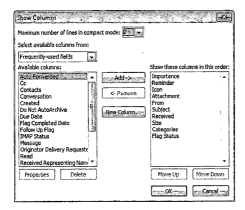

Figure 26-6 Use the Show Columns dialog box to add columns to or remove columns from the view.

Adding columns in the Show Columns dialog box is easy. The available columns (those not already in the view) appear in the list on the left, and the columns already displayed appear in the list on the right. Select a column in the Available Columns list, and then click Add to add it to the view. To remove a column from the view, select the field in the Show These Columns In This Order list, and then click Remove. Use the Move Up and Move Down buttons to rearrange the order in which the columns are displayed in the view.

TROUBLESHOOTING

You need to restore a view to its original settings

You've customized a view, and now you've decided that you need the old view back. (For the future, remember that you can copy an existing view. Rather than modifying an existing view, you can copy a view and then modify the copy. This way you'll still have the original view if you need it.)

It's easy to restore a standard view to its previous settings, however. Click View Settings on the View tab and then click Reset Current View. Click Yes when prompted to confirm the action.

Tip

You can rearrange the order in which columns are displayed in a table view by dragging the column header for a column to a new location on the column header bar.

Tip

You can click New Column in the Show Columns dialog box to create a custom column. For additional information about creating and using custom columns, see Chapter 27, "Designing and Using Forms."

In some cases, clicking Columns in the Advanced View Settings dialog box opens a Date/Time Fields dialog box similar to the one shown in Figure 26-7. This occurs when you're working with a view that shows time duration, such as Day/Week/Month view in the Calendar folder or By Type view in the Journal folder—in effect, nontable views that show time duration graphically.

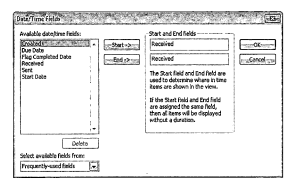

Figure 26-7 In the Date/Time Fields dialog box, specify the date fields used to show duration.

You use the Date/Time Fields dialog box to specify the fields that Outlook 2010 will use to show item duration in the view. The default settings vary but are typically either Start and End or Start Date and Due Date. As an example, you might use the Date/Time Fields dialog box to change the Task Timeline view in the Tasks folder to show the Date Completed field for the task's end rather than the Due Date field.

Grouping Data

Sometimes it's helpful to be able to group items in an Outlook 2010 folder based on specific data fields. For example, you might want to group tasks by owner so that you can see at a glance the tasks assigned to specific people. Perhaps you want to organize contacts by country or region. In these and similar cases, you can modify an existing view or create a new one to organize the view based on the most pertinent data. To group data in a view, click Group By in the Advanced View Settings dialog box to open the Group By dialog box, shown in Figure 26-8.

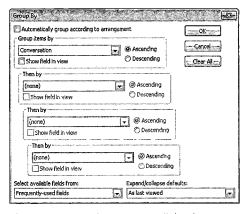

Figure 26-8 Use the Group By dialog box to specify criteria for grouping items in a view.

Follow these steps to group data in a view:

1. In the Group By dialog box, clear the Automatically Group According To Arrangement check box.

2. Select a field type in the Select Available Fields From drop-down list at the bottom of the dialog box. This selection controls the fields that appear in the Group Items By drop-down list.

3. Select a field in the Group Items By drop-down list, and then select either Ascending or Descending, depending on the sort order that you want to use. Select the Show Field In View check box to display the field in the view.

4. If you want to create subgroups under the main group, select a field in the Then By drop-down list. (The dialog box contains three such lists, providing three additional grouping levels.) For example, you might group tasks by Owner and then by Due Date.

5. After you've specified all the grouping levels that you need, use the Expand/Collapse Defaults drop-down list to specify how you want Outlook 2010 to treat the groups. Use the following list as a guide:

   - **As Last Viewed**   Collapses or expands the group according to its state in the previous session.

   - **All Expanded**   Expands all items in all groups.

   - **All Collapsed**   Collapses all items in all groups.

6. When you're satisfied with the group settings, click OK to close the Group By dialog box. Then click OK to close the Advanced View Settings dialog box.

Sorting Data

Sorting data in a view is different from grouping data. For example, you might group the Tasks folder by owner. Each group in the view then shows the tasks assigned to a particular person. You can then sort the data within the group as needed. For example, you might sort the tasks based first on due date and then on subject. Figure 26-9 shows the Tasks folder grouped by owner and sorted by due date.

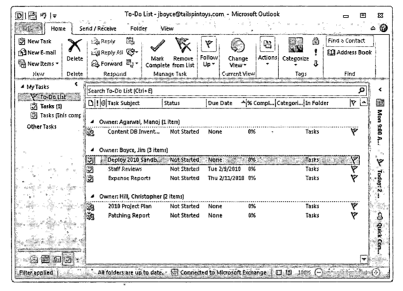

Figure 26-9 In this view, tasks are grouped by owner and then sorted by due date.

Sorting doesn't rely on grouping—you can sort a view whether or not it is grouped. For example, you might sort the Inbox based on the Received column to show messages in the order in which you received them.

INSIDE OUT   Sort table views quickly

You can sort a table view quickly by clicking the column header for the column by which you want to sort the view. Click the header again to change between ascending and descending sort order.

To create a sort order when you customize or define a view, click Sort in the Advanced View Settings dialog box to open the Sort dialog box, shown in Figure 26-10.

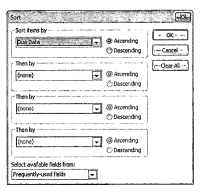

Figure 26-10 Configure a sort order for the view in the Sort dialog box.

To configure sorting in the Sort dialog box, follow these steps:

1. In the Select Available Fields From drop-down list, select the type of field that the sort should be based on.

2. In the Sort Items By drop-down list, select the specific field by which you want to sort the view.

3. Select Ascending or Descending, depending on the type of sort you need.

4. Use the Then By lists to specify additional sort levels, if necessary.

5. Click OK to close the Sort dialog box, and then click OK to close the Customize View dialog box.

Applying Filters to the View

In Outlook 2010, filtering a view is an extremely powerful feature that gives you considerable control over the data displayed in a given view. For example, you might have hundreds of messages in your Inbox and need to filter the view to show only those messages from a particular sender. You could simply sort the Inbox by the From field and scan the list of messages, but you might want to refine the search a little, perhaps viewing only messages from a specific sender that have an attachment and were sent within the previous week. Filters allow you to do just that.

To configure a filter, click Filter in the Advanced View Settings dialog box to open the Filter dialog box, shown in Figure 26-11. This multi-tabbed dialog box lets you specify multiple conditions to define which items will appear in the view.

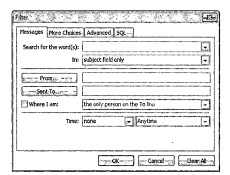

Figure 26-11 Use the Filter dialog box to specify multiple conditions that determine what data appears in the view.

Note that the first tab in the Filter dialog box varies according to the current folder type. For a contacts folder, for example, the first tab is labeled Contacts and offers options for creating filter conditions that apply to contacts. For a message folder, the first tab is labeled Messages and provides options for creating filter conditions specific to messages.

The various tabs in the Filter dialog box include a broad range of options that let you specify multiple conditions for the filter. You can use conditions from more than one tab. For example, you might enter words to search for and a sender on the Messages tab, select categories on the More Choices tab, and specify a particular field and value on the Advanced tab.

> **Tip**
>
> The Advanced tab of the Filter dialog box gives you access to all available fields and several criteria (Contains, Doesn't Contain, and Is Empty, for example), making it the place to go to configure conditions not available on the other tabs. To define filter criteria, select a field in the Field drop-down list, select an option in the Condition drop-down list, type a value, and then click Add. Use the SQL tab to perform Structured Query Language (SQL) queries to retrieve data from the folder to show in the custom view.

Configuring Fonts and Other General Settings

When you click Other Settings in the Advanced View Settings dialog box, Outlook 2010 opens a dialog box that lets you configure some general settings for the custom view. These options vary from one folder type to another—for example, the Contacts folder, the Inbox, and the Calendar folder all use different options. You can change such properties as the font used for column headers and row text, the grid style and shading for table views, and a handful of other general options.

Creating Rules for Conditional Formatting of Text

Click Conditional Formatting in the Advanced View Settings dialog box to display the Conditional Formatting dialog box, similar to the one shown in Figure 26-12. This dialog box lets you create rules that cause Outlook 2010 to format data in the view automatically based on the criteria that you specify. For example, you might create an automatic conditional formatting rule that has Outlook 2010 display in blue all tasks that you own and display all other tasks in black. Or perhaps you may create a rule to display in green all contacts from a specific company.

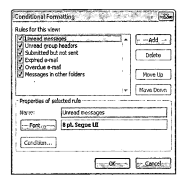

Figure 26-12 Use the Conditional Formatting dialog box to create rules that automatically format text in views based on the conditions that you specify.

As you're working in the Conditional Formatting dialog box, keep in mind that you can't create task-oriented rules, as you can with the Rules Wizard. For example, you can't create a rule in this dialog box that moves messages from one folder to another. The rules you create in the Conditional Formatting dialog box control only the appearance (color, font, and font styles) of data in the view.

For information about the Rules Wizard, see Chapter 11, "Processing Messages Automatically."

You can't modify the conditions for predefined rules, but you can specify the font characteristics to use for the rule. You can also create your own rules and change the order in which rules are applied to achieve the results you need.

To set up a one formatting rule for text, follow these steps:

1. Click Add in the Conditional Formatting dialog box to add a new rule named Untitled.

2. Click Font to open a standard Font dialog box, in which you specify the font, font style, and color that will apply to text that meets the rule's condition.

3. Close the Font dialog box, and then click Condition to open the Filter dialog box, shown in Figure 26-13. This dialog box offers three tabs that you can use to specify the condition for the rule. You can specify multiple conditions from multiple tabs, if needed.

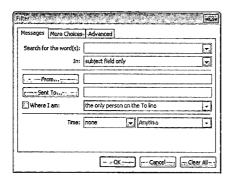

Figure 26-13 Specify conditions for the rule in the Filter dialog box.

4. Click OK when you're satisfied with the filter condition.

TROUBLESHOOTING

You need to restrict the available views

In some situations, you might want to restrict the available views to only the custom views you've created, hiding the standard views that Outlook 2010 provides. For example, perhaps you created a custom calendar view that you want all employees to use instead of the standard calendar views because your custom view includes additional information that the standard views don't contain. When you restrict the Outlook 2010 views to only custom views, the standard views no longer appear on the View menu.

You must configure each folder separately. For example, you might restrict the Calendar folder views without restricting the Inbox folder views. This would give users the ability to choose one of the standard Outlook 2010 views in the Inbox folder but would limit their choices to only custom views in the Calendar folder.

Follow these steps to restrict the views that Outlook 2010 provides on the View menu:

1. In Outlook 2010, select the folder for which you want to restrict views.

2. Click View, Change View, Manage Views to open the Manage All Views dialog box.

3. Select the Only Show Views Created For This Folder check box, and then click Close.

4. Repeat steps 2 and 3 to restrict other folders as necessary.

Note
The option to tell Outlook 2010 to use only custom views for a folder is not available in the Tasks folder.

Printing in Outlook

Many users work in Outlook 2010 and never print any of the items that they store in the program. For other users, however, the ability to print from Outlook 2010 is important. For example, if you use a hard-copy day planner rather than a notebook computer or a Personal Digital Assistant (PDA) to keep track of your daily schedule, you might prepare the schedule in Outlook 2010 and then print it for insertion in the day planner.

This section examines the options and methods for printing your Outlook 2010 data. It also explains how to customize the print styles provided by Outlook 2010 to create custom styles that better suit your preferences or needs.

Overview of Print Styles

Outlook 2010 offers several predefined print styles that you can use to print information from various Outlook 2010 folders. The most common print styles are Table and Memo, but there are others available, particularly for Calendar folders.

> **Note**
> Most views that have just Table and Memo styles available have only the Table style available if no item is selected.

INSIDE OUT   Printing a timeline

You can print only individual items when you're working with a timeline view. However, if you're scheduling a major project, a printout of a timeline view would be useful. If you need that capability, consider using Microsoft Project 2010 instead of Outlook 2010.

The easiest way to view a print style is simply to preview the style when you print. Click File, Print and then view the print styles on the Print page, as shown in Figure 26-14. Printing is discussed in more detail in the following section.

Printing from Outlook

Printing from Outlook 2010 is just as easy as printing from any other application. Simply select the view or item that you want to print, and then choose File, Print. Outlook 2010 displays a Print page similar to the one shown in Figure 26-14. The contents of the page vary according to the type of view from which you're printing.

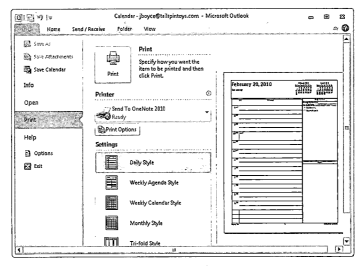

Figure 26-14 You can select an existing print style in the Print page.

From the Settings list, select a print style. For example, select Phone Directory Style for the Contacts folder to print a phone list, or select one of the two booklet styles to print contact entries for a day planner. If you need to fine-tune the print settings, click Print Options to display a Print dialog box similar to the one shown in Figure 26-15.

For additional details on printing contacts and using different print styles with the Contacts folder, see the section "Printing Contacts," on page 459.

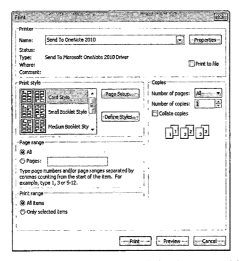

Figure 26-15 Use the Print dialog box to modify print options for the selected style.

Click Page Setup and use the Format tab of the Page Setup dialog box to specify the layout, fonts, and other general properties for the job. The options on the Format tab vary from one folder type to another. For example, you can use the Format tab to set the following options, some of which are specific to particular folder types:

- Whether Outlook 2010 keeps sections together or starts a new page for each section

- The number of columns per page

- The number of blank forms to print at the end of the job (such as blank contact forms)

- Whether Outlook 2010 prints a contact index on the page edge

- Whether letter headings for each alphabetic section of a contact list are included

- The font used for headings and for body text

- Whether Outlook 2010 adds gray shading to headings

- Whether the Daily Task List, To-Do Bar, or Notes areas are printed with a calendar

- Whether weekends are printed in a calendar view

- Whether Outlook 2010 prints one month of a calendar per page

Use the Paper tab, shown in Figure 26-16, to configure the page type, size, source, and other properties. For example, in the Type list on the Paper tab, you can select the type of day planner that you use so that Outlook 2010 prints using that style.

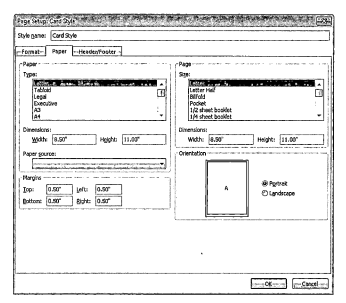

Figure 26-16 Use the Paper tab to configure the paper source, size, type, and other paper settings.

Use the Header/Footer tab, shown in Figure 26-17, to specify the items that you want printed in the header and the footer. This tab provides three boxes for the header and three for the footer. The left box specifies items that print on the left side of the page, the middle box specifies items that print in the middle of the page, and the right box specifies items that print on the right side of the page. You can enter text manually or use the buttons near the bottom to insert specific data such as page numbers, the user, the time, and other dynamic data.

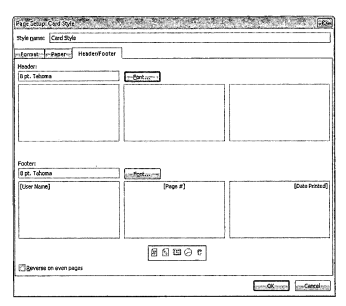

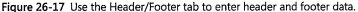

Figure 26-17 Use the Header/Footer tab to enter header and footer data.

After you select the page setup options, you can return to the Print page to preview the document. Click Print Options again; set the printer properties, the number of copies to print, and other general print settings, and then click Print to print or click Preview to pre-view the document.

Creating Custom Print Styles

Outlook 2010 provides a broad range of print styles, so it's likely that they will fit most of your needs. When these print styles don't quite offer what you need or want, however, you can create a custom print style.

> **Tip**
> If you find yourself using an existing print style but frequently making the same option changes before printing, modify the existing print style to create a custom print style.

You can either modify an existing print style or copy a style and then modify it to incorporate the changes that you need. If you always use the same modifications on a particular print style, you might prefer to simply modify that existing style rather than creating a new one. If you use the default style occasionally but modify its properties for most other print jobs, consider creating a custom print style based on the existing one so that both are available.

Follow these steps to modify or create a new print style:

1. Open the view for which you want to modify the print style or on which you want to base your custom print style.

2. Choose File, Print, Print Options, and finally Define Styles to open the Define Print Styles dialog box, shown in Figure 26-18.

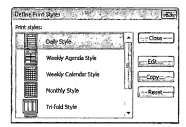

Figure 26-18 Use the Define Print Styles dialog box to modify and copy print styles.

3. If you want to create a new style, select an existing style, and then click Copy. Otherwise, select an existing style, and then click Edit. In either case, Outlook 2010 displays a Page Setup dialog box similar to the one shown in Figure 26-19.

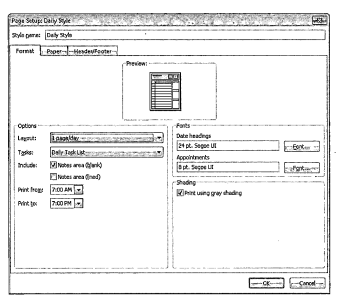

Figure 26-19 Use the Page Setup dialog box to specify properties for the print style.

4. Specify options as needed in the dialog box, and then click OK to apply the changes.

5. In the Define Print Styles dialog box, click Close.

When you want to print using a particular style, open the view from which you want to print and then choose File, Print. On the Print page, select the style in the Settings list, set other properties as necessary, and then click OK to print.

Deleting Print Styles

If you've created some custom print styles but no longer use them, or if you've been experimenting with print styles and have a few samples you want to delete, removing them is simple.

Follow these steps to remove a print style:

1. Choose File, Print, Print Options, and finally Define Styles to open the Define Print Styles dialog box.

2. Select the style you want to remove, and then click Delete.

3. When you have finished deleting print styles, click Close.

Resetting Print Styles

You can't delete the standard print styles provided in Outlook 2010, but you can restore them to their default state. For example, suppose that you made several changes to the default Small Booklet style for the Contacts folder. Now you want to restore the print style to its default settings, but you don't remember what they are. Fortunately, Outlook 2010 remembers them for you.

To reset a print style, follow these steps:

1. Choose File, Print, Print Options, and finally Define Styles to open the Define Print Styles dialog box.

2. Select the style you want to reset and then click Reset. Outlook 2010 prompts you to verify the action.

3. Click OK to reset the style or Cancel to cancel the operation.

4. Click Close.

Custom Printing with Scripts and Word

The existing print styles in Outlook 2010 and the capability to define custom styles accommodate the needs of most users. In some situations, however, these built-in printing features are not enough. With a little custom scripting and Word 2010, however, you can overcome these limitations.

Word 2010 offers almost unlimited print layout capabilities, making it a great tool for laying out almost any type of document. For example, assume that you're not satisfied with the way Outlook 2010 prints messages from mail folders. When you print a message, the recipient's name appears in large, bold type at the top of the page, as shown in Figure 26-20. You are likely printing your own messages, so you might want different information—such as the message subject—displayed on the first line.

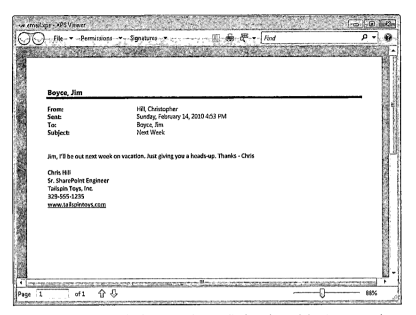

Figure 26-20 The standard message layout displays the recipient's name at the top of the page.

Although you can make minimal changes to the print layout, such as adding headers or footers, you can't do much in Outlook 2010 to change the way that most items are printed. You can, however, copy Outlook 2010 items to Word 2010, format the document as needed, and then print it from Word. You might think that moving the data from Outlook 2010 to Word 2010 is a time-consuming task, but you can make it happen in less than a second, provided you create a script to accomplish the task for you.

Using a Custom Contact Style

In this first example, assume that you want to create a specific layout for contacts that prints the contact name in bold, places the contact's picture in the upper-right corner, and then includes selected contact information such as address, phone, email, and other properties underneath. Figure 26-21 illustrates this custom print layout.

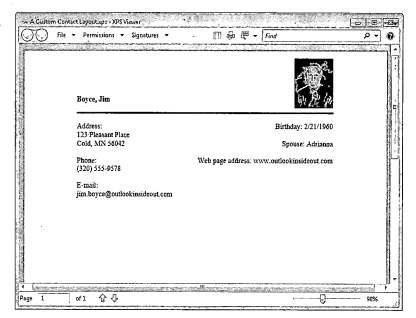

Figure 26-21 This custom contact layout presents selected information in a specific layout.

The first step in creating this custom contact style is to create the document layout in Word 2010.

In a nutshell, this means creating a document template that contains a text form field for each contact item that you want included on the printout and then following these steps:

1. In Word 2010, open a new document. If the Developer tab does not appear in the ribbon, click File, Options, and then Customize Ribbon. Place a check beside Developer in the list of ribbon tabs, and then click OK.

2. Enter labels for the Outlook 2010 fields. Then position the insertion point after the first label, and on the Developer tab, in the Controls group, select the Rich Text content control to insert a field to contain the data that will come from the Outlook 2010 contact.

3. Select the first text form field, and on the Insert tab, in the Links group, choose Bookmark. In the Bookmark dialog box, shown in Figure 26-22, type a name for the bookmark that identifies the field (such as **LastName**), and then click Add.

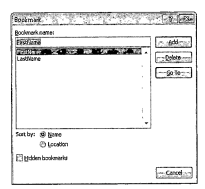

Figure 26-22 Add a bookmark for each text form field.

4. Select the remaining fields and add bookmarks for them, naming the bookmarks according to the information that the field will contain, such as FirstName, Email, Phone, and so on.

5. Select the Title field, format it using a larger font, and then add any other characteristics, such as bold type.

6. Draw a line separating the name and other information, if desired.

7. Click File, click Save As, Word Template, specify the path C:\myMail and the name CustomContactPrint.dotx, click Save, and then exit Word 2010.

You now have a template that is ready to be filled in by Outlook 2010. The next step is to create a macro in Outlook 2010 that copies the desired information from the current contact item to the form and then prints the form. The following sample macro accomplishes these tasks. However, this sample does not provide extensive error checking, so consider this a starting point for your own macro. For example, you might want to add code that verifies that the current item is a contact item, and if not, displays an error message and exits.

Getting Ready to Use Macros

Outlook 2010 has tighter security settings than earlier versions, so before you can run macros, you have to set the macro security level to allow unsigned macros to execute. You also have to configure Outlook 2010 to display the Developer tab on the ribbon so that you can access macro commands from an open Outlook 2010 item.

To configure macro security in Outlook 2010, click File, Options, Trust Center, and Trust Center Settings. In the Trust Center, click Macro Settings. Choose Notifications For All Macros, and then click OK. If you prefer not to have Outlook 2010 warn you when a macro is trying to execute, you can select Enable All Macros—but be careful, because this allows any macro to execute without your knowledge.

Click the Developer tab, click Macros, choose Macros, type **CustomContactPrint** in the Macro Name field, and then click Create. Enter the following code:

```
Sub CustomContactPrint()
    'Set up objects
    Dim strTemplate As String
    Dim objWord As Object
    Dim objDocs As Object
    Dim objApp As Application
    Dim objItem As Object
    Dim objAttach As Object
    Dim numAttach As Integer
    Dim objNS As NameSpace
    Dim mybklist As Object
    Dim x As Integer
    Dim pictureSaved As Boolean
    Dim myShape As Object
    'Dim ContactAddress
    'Create a Word document and current contact item object
    Set objApp = CreateObject("Outlook.Application")
    Set objNS = objApp.GetNamespace("MAPI")
    'Check to ensure Outlook item is selected
    If TypeName(objApp.ActiveInspector) = "Nothing" Then
        MsgBox "Contact not open. Exiting", vbOKOnly + vbInformation, "Outlook Inside
Out"
        Exit Sub
    End If
    Set objItem = objApp.ActiveInspector.CurrentItem
    Set objWord = CreateObject("Word.Application")
    strTemplate = "c:\myMail\CustomContactPrint.dotx"
    Set objDocs = objWord.Documents
```

```
objDocs.Add strTemplate
Set mybklist = objWord.activeDocument.Bookmarks
'Fill in the form
objWord.activeDocument.Bookmarks("LastName").Select
objWord.Selection.TypeText CStr(objItem.LastName)
objWord.activeDocument.Bookmarks("FirstName").Select
objWord.Selection.TypeText CStr(objItem.FirstName)
If objItem.HasPicture = True Then
    Set objAttach = objItem.Attachments
    numAttach = objAttach.Count
    For x = 1 To numAttach
        If objAttach.Item(x).DisplayName = "ContactPicture.jpg" Then
            objAttach.Item(x).SaveAsFile "C:\myMail\" & _
            objAttach.Item(x).DisplayName
            pictureSaved = True
        End If
    Next x
    If pictureSaved = True Then
        objWord.activeDocument.Bookmarks("Picture").Select
        Set myShape = objWord.activeDocument.Shapes.AddPicture("c:\myMail\Con-
tactPicture.jpg", False, True, 432, -25)
        objWord.activeDocument.Shapes(1).Left = 432 - objWord.activeDocument.
Shapes(1).Width
    End If
End If
objWord.activeDocument.Bookmarks("Address1").Select
objWord.Selection.TypeText CStr(objItem.BusinessAddressStreet)
objWord.activeDocument.Bookmarks("Address2").Select
objWord.Selection.TypeText CStr(objItem.BusinessAddressCity)
objWord.Selection.TypeText ", "
objWord.Selection.TypeText CStr(objItem.BusinessAddressState)
objWord.Selection.TypeText " "
objWord.Selection.TypeText CStr(objItem.BusinessAddressPostalCode)
objWord.activeDocument.Bookmarks("Birthday").Select
objWord.Selection.TypeText CStr(objItem.Birthday)
objWord.activeDocument.Bookmarks("Spouse").Select
objWord.Selection.TypeText CStr(objItem.Spouse)
objWord.activeDocument.Bookmarks("Phone1").Select
objWord.Selection.TypeText CStr(objItem.BusinessTelephoneNumber)
objWord.activeDocument.Bookmarks("WebPage").Select
objWord.Selection.TypeText CStr(objItem.BusinessHomePage)
objWord.activeDocument.Bookmarks("Email1").Select
objWord.Selection.TypeText CStr(objItem.Email1Address)
'Print and exit
objWord.PrintOut Background:=True

'Process other system events until printing is finished
While objWord.BackgroundPrintingStatus
    DoEvents
Wend
```

```
        objWord.Quit SaveChanges:=wdvbaDoNotSaveChanges
        Set objApp = Nothing
        Set objNS = Nothing
        Set objItem = Nothing
        Set objWord = Nothing
        Set objDocs = Nothing
        Set mybklist = Nothing
End Sub
```

If you examine this macro code, you'll see that it uses named bookmarks to locate the position in the document where each contact element will be inserted. Also, notice that the lines in the macro that insert specific contact items reference those items by their Outlook 2010 object model names, such as Email1Address, BusinessTelephoneNumber, BusinessHomePage, and so on. If you want to modify this macro to insert other contact items, you'll need to know the item names. To view contact item properties, click Visual Basic on the Developer tab in the Outlook ribbon, and then choose Help, Microsoft Visual Basic Help. Select Outlook Object Model Reference, and then click ContactItem Object. Click the Properties link, and then scroll through the list of properties to locate the one that you need.

This macro also determines whether the contact has a picture associated with it. If so, the macro cycles through the attachments to locate the picture (which is always named ContactPicture.jpg) and saves it to disk. The macro then inserts the picture in the Word 2010 document. Although ContactPicture.jpg is always the first attachment, regardless of the order in which items are attached or their names, this macro checks each attachment anyway to accommodate future changes in Outlook 2010 regarding picture attachments.

> **Note**
> The macro saves the picture file in the folder you created for the Word 2010 templates, C:\myMail\. You can change the macro code to save and load the picture from any path. You can also change the path location for the Word 2010 document template as needed.

To run the macro and print a contact in this format, in the Contacts folder, open the contact that you want to print. On the Developer tab, in the Code group, select Macros. (If you have not added the Developer tab to the ribbon, press Alt+F8.) Click the Macros button and choose the Project1.CustomContactPrint macro. The macro will run and print the open contact on the default printer.

Using a Custom Message Style

You can use a method similar to the one in the preceding section to print messages from Outlook 2010 using Word 2010. For example, assume that you want to print email messages with the subject in large, bold type at the top of the page and with other message content printed below that. Figure 26-23 shows a sample form in Word 2010. Use the same general steps detailed in the preceding section to create a Word 2010 template that contains the form text fields and bookmarks needed to hold the message items.

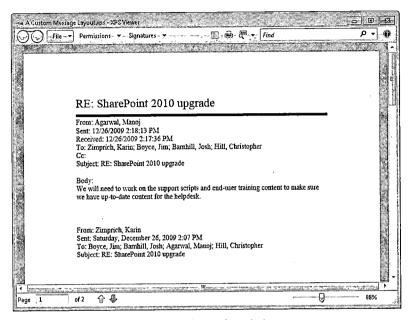

Figure 26-23 A sample form in Word 2010 for printing messages.

After you create the document template in Word 2010 and save it, open the Microsoft Visual Basic Editor and create the following macro:

```
Sub CustomMessagePrint()
    'Set up objects
    Dim strTemplate As String
    Dim objWord As Object
    Dim objDocs As Object
    Dim objApp As Application
    Dim objItem As Object
    Dim objNS As NameSpace
    Dim mybklist As Object
    'Create a Word document and current message item object
    Set objApp = CreateObject("Outlook.Application")
    Set objNS = objApp.GetNamespace("MAPI")
    'Check to ensure Outlook item is selected
    If TypeName(objApp.ActiveInspector) = "Nothing" Then
        MsgBox "Message not open. Exiting", vbOKOnly + vbInformation, "Outlook Inside
Out"
```

```
        Exit Sub
    End If
    Set objItem = objApp.ActiveInspector.CurrentItem
    Set objWord = CreateObject("Word.Application")
    strTemplate = "c:\myMail\prnmsg.dotx"
    Set objDocs = objWord.Documents
    objDocs.Add strTemplate
    Set mybklist = objWord.activeDocument.Bookmarks
    'Fill in the form
    objWord.activeDocument.Bookmarks("Title").Select
    objWord.Selection.TypeText CStr(objItem.Subject)
    objWord.activeDocument.Bookmarks("From").Select
    objWord.Selection.TypeText CStr(objItem.SenderName)
    objWord.activeDocument.Bookmarks("Sent").Select
    objWord.Selection.TypeText CStr(objItem.SentOn)
    objWord.activeDocument.Bookmarks("Received").Select
    objWord.Selection.TypeText CStr(objItem.ReceivedTime)
    objWord.activeDocument.Bookmarks("To").Select
    objWord.Selection.TypeText CStr(objItem.To)
    objWord.activeDocument.Bookmarks("Cc").Select
    objWord.Selection.TypeText CStr(objItem.CC)
    objWord.activeDocument.Bookmarks("Subject").Select
    objWord.Selection.TypeText CStr(objItem.Subject)
    objWord.activeDocument.Bookmarks("Body").Select
    objWord.Selection.TypeText CStr(objItem.Body)
    'Print and exit

    objWord.PrintOut Background:=True
    'Process other system events until printing is finished
    While objWord.BackgroundPrintingStatus
        DoEvents
    Wend
    objWord.Quit SaveChanges:=wdvbaDoNotSaveChanges
End Sub
```

As with the CustomContactPrint macro, you can customize this macro and document template to accommodate different or additional message fields as needed.

Custom Printing with Excel

Microsoft Excel 2010 is another solution to custom printing requirements, particularly for Outlook 2010 table views. For example, assume that you want to print all your Outlook 2010 contacts but you want to arrange them in a different order from what the Table style offers in Outlook 2010 and use different formatting for some of the columns. The solution is simple: Copy the contacts to Excel 2010, format and rearrange as needed, and print by following these steps:

1. Open the Outlook 2010 folder containing the items you want to print, and then choose a table view. This example uses the Phone view, as shown in Figure 26-24.

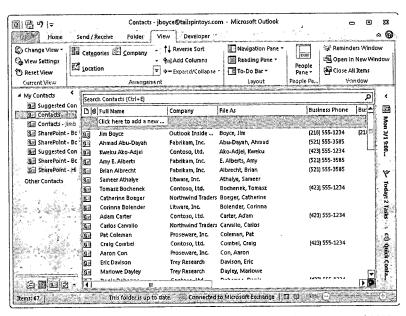

Figure 26-24 You can copy data from an Outlook 2010 table view to Excel 2010 easily.

2. Select the items that you want included in the printed document, and then press Ctrl+C or choose Edit, Copy to copy the items to the Clipboard.

3. Start Excel 2010, and then press Ctrl+V or choose Edit, Paste to paste the data into Excel 2010, as shown in Figure 26-25.

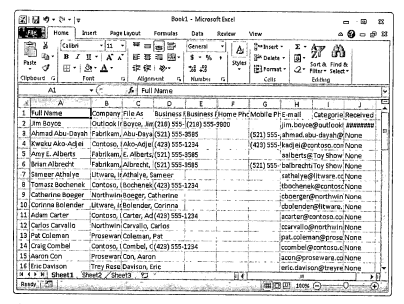

Figure 26-25 Copy data to Excel 2010, and then arrange, format, and print.

4. Rearrange columns, apply formatting, and otherwise adjust the layout as needed, and then print the worksheet.

VEN without any custom programming, Microsoft Outlook 2010 provides an excellent set of features. In fact, many organizations don't need anything beyond what Outlook 2010 offers right out of the box. Others, however, have special needs that Outlook 2010 does not address, perhaps because of the way these organizations do business or because of specific requirements in their particular industries. In such cases, you have ample opportunity to extend the functionality of Outlook 2010 through custom design and programming.

For example, you might need to add some fields to your message forms or your meeting request forms. Perhaps you need an easier way for users to perform mail merge operations with Microsoft Word 2010 and Outlook 2010 contacts lists. Maybe you simply want to fine-tune your forms to add your company logo, special instructions, or warnings for users.

Whatever your situation, you can easily make changes to the existing Outlook 2010 forms, or you can even design new ones. The changes you make can be simple or complex: You might add one or two fields to the standard contact form, or you might add a considerable amount of program code to allow Outlook 2010 to perform custom tasks or interact with other Microsoft Office 2010 system applications. This chapter starts you on the right path by explaining how Outlook 2010 uses forms and how you can customize them to suit your needs. If you aren't comfortable programming with Microsoft Visual Basic for Applications (VBA), don't worry—you can accomplish a lot with custom forms without ever writing a single line of program code.

Forms are such a normal part of everything we do on computers that we sometimes take them for granted. It's still true, however, that a lot of programs used all over the world can be accessed only with screens that provide monochrome text and puzzling menus with strange codes and submission sequences. With their versatility and ease of use, forms offer a revolutionary approach, and you can unlock their power with several mouse clicks and

some solid planning. This chapter discusses using Outlook 2010 forms as part of a software solution for individual computing needs. It also examines the types of forms that you can modify and create and how the forms are created, published, and stored.

With Outlook 2010, you can employ two basic strategies for form development. The first is to use or modify a standard form. The second is to create your own form from scratch. With either strategy, it's important to remember that you're programming events that are specifically associated with the item involved, not with the Outlook 2010 application generally. In other words, when you put code behind your form, you're dealing with events related to the item that's represented by the form. For example, if you were to design a form to create a custom email message, you'd probably program a common event named *Item_Send*, which occurs when the item (the message) is sent. You couldn't program the form to respond to an event that fires (that is, occurs or executes) when the item is specifically sent from the Outbox to another user's Inbox or when the user's view changes from one folder to another. This is because in form development, you can access only the events associated with the item in question.

Overview of Standard Forms, Item Types, and Message Classes

Outlook 2010 uses a combination of forms, item types, and message classes as its fundamental components. Although you don't need to understand much about any of these three components to use Outlook 2010, a developer must understand them reasonably well. Obviously, the more you know, the more powerful your Outlook 2010–based solution will be.

Outlook Forms

Outlook 2010 provides numerous predefined forms that you can use as the foundation of your form-based solution. These standard forms include the following:

- Appointment form

- Contact form

- Distribution List form

- Journal entry form

- Meeting request form

- Message form

- Note form

- Post form

- Standard Default form

- Task form

- Task request form

As this list of Outlook 2010 forms indicates, the basic item types available in a typical Outlook 2010 installation are each represented by a corresponding form. The Outlook 2010 forms in this list match the ones that you are used to working with on a daily basis, so you are not starting with a blank slate when you want to customize a form for your own use.

Each of these forms comes with built-in user interface elements and corresponding functionality. For example, the appointment form shown in Figure 27-1 has interface elements and functions that relate to setting appointments, such as generating reminders and controlling the calendar display. The contact form, in contrast, is designed to permit the addition or modification of contact information.

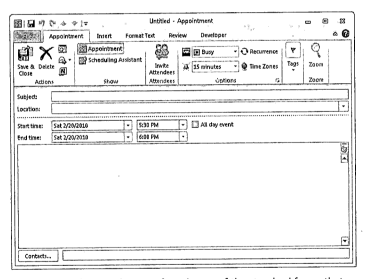

Figure 27-1 The appointment form is one of the standard forms that you can use in Outlook 2010.

Outlook Item Types

Several basic item types are part of an Outlook 2010 installation. Among the Office 2010 system VBA item types that you can use are the following ones specific to Outlook 2010:

- MailItem

- ContactItem

- TaskItem

- AppointmentItem

- PostItem

- NoteItem

> **Note**
>
> Other item types are built into Outlook 2010, including the JournalItem and DistListItem types. This book does not cover these additional types, but you can find information about them by consulting the Microsoft MSDN website (*http://msdn.microsoft.com*) and searching for these item types.

These item types represent built-in functionality. If you have ever used Outlook 2010 to create an email message or to add an appointment to your calendar, you have benefited from this functionality. Of particular importance is the fact that this functionality is accessible to you as you develop custom solutions with Outlook 2010. Outlook 2010 provides corresponding forms for each of these item types, and these standard forms are designed with behaviors that directly relate to the item types that they represent. You can extend the behaviors of these forms and use all the functions and properties of the item types, some of which are not exposed in the standard forms. In addition, you can reach beyond Outlook 2010 to incorporate the functionality of other Microsoft Office system applications such as Word 2010, Microsoft Excel 2010, Microsoft InfoPath 2010, Microsoft PowerPoint 2010, Microsoft Project 2010, Microsoft Visio 2010, and any application or control that exposes a programmatic Component Object Model (COM) interface.

Outlook Message Classes

Although forms and item types are the basic elements you need to understand to create a custom Outlook 2010 solution, it's helpful to know what a message class is and how it relates to Outlook 2010 form development. A message class represents to Outlook 2010 internally what an item type represents to a user or developer externally. In other words, when a user opens an email message from the Inbox, that message is a MailItem. Internally, however, Outlook 2010 calls it by a different name: IPM.Note. IPM (which stands for "inter-personal message") is a holdover from earlier generations of Microsoft's messaging systems. All messages in Outlook 2010 are representations of an IPM of some sort. An appointment calendar item, for example, is an IPM.Appointment. The list of default message classes includes the following:

- IPM.Note

- IPM.Contact

- IPM.DistList

- IPM.Appointment

- IPM.Task

- IPM.Post

- IPM.Activity

- IPM.Schedule.Meeting.Request

- IPM.StickyNote

- IPM.TaskRequest

Again, unless you're developing a fairly sophisticated collaborative solution, these message classes won't surface often. However, understanding what they mean to Outlook 2010 will help as you progress in your use of the program and in developing Outlook 2010 solutions.

Creating Custom Forms from Standard Forms

A standard form is a great point of departure for developing a custom solution. For example, have you ever sent an email message with an attached document to someone and forgotten to include the attachment? In a large company, this rather common error could amount to hundreds, if not thousands, of extra email messages being sent each day as users send follow-up messages containing the omitted attachments. If the attachment was a document needed for review, there is the potential for significant time loss as well. By adding a small script to the standard mail message form, you can avoid this problem. You can assess programmatically whether an attachment has actually been added to the email message and prompt the user to add one if needed.

To begin working with the standard forms, first verify that you have added the Developer tab to the ribbon. If not, right-click the ribbon and choose Customize The Ribbon. Place a check beside Developer in the left-hand list, and then click OK. Next, click the Developer tab in the ribbon, and then click Design A Form to display the Design Form dialog box, shown in Figure 27-2. You can simply select one of the standard forms listed in this dialog box and begin working with the form in design mode. Later sections in this chapter discuss how to save and publish the forms that you modify or create.

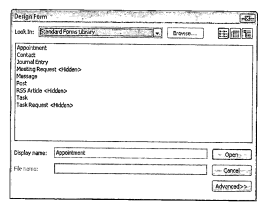

Figure 27-2 In the Design Form dialog box, you can choose the type of form that you want to create.

INSIDE OUT   Avoid scripts when opening forms for design purposes

When you choose to redesign an existing form, that form might have a script with event handlers that will fire when you open the form in design mode. Usually, however, you don't want to have code firing when you're trying to design a form. To keep this from happening, hold down the Shift key as you click the form to open it for design. The code will still be present and will run when you debug the form, but it will not run while you open, design, and save the form.

Compose vs. Read

One of the most basic processes in Outlook 2010 is sending and receiving messages and documents. Although this is a fairly simple process, it requires a close look. In nearly all cases, the form that a sender employs to compose an email message is not the exact form that the receiver of that message uses to read the message. For example, the recipient of an

email message can't modify the body of the message without replying to or forwarding the message. This is because the standard forms have Compose and Read areas.

Figure 27-3 shows a message being composed; Figure 27-4 shows the same message after it has been received.

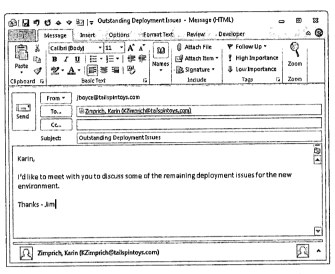

Figure 27-3 Compose a message using a standard message form.

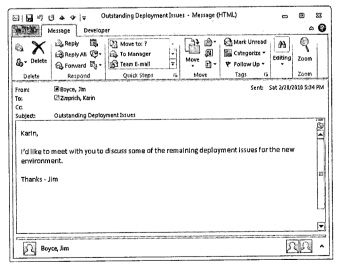

Figure 27-4 Here is the same message shown in Figure 27-3 after it has been received. Notice that some fields can no longer be modified.

Notice that some of the fields, such as Subject and To, can't be modified by the recipient in the Read version. It is, however, entirely possible to configure a form with identical Compose and Read areas. Whether this makes sense for your Outlook 2010 solution is up to you.

To work with a standard form, click Design A Form on the Developer tab to display the Design Form dialog box (shown in Figure 27-2), and then select a Message type form. When you're working with a standard form in design mode, you can switch between the Compose and Read pages by clicking the Page button in the Form group on the Developer tab and choosing Edit Compose Page or Edit Read Page. You can select these options by clicking Page, as shown in Figure 27-5, and then clicking the Edit Compose Page or Edit Read Page option.

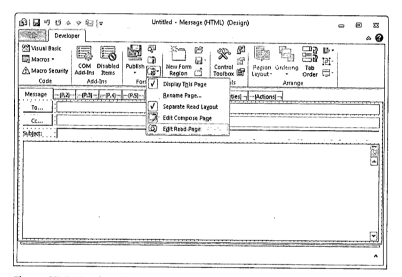

Figure 27-5 Use the Edit Compose Page and Edit Read Page options located in the Page menu to switch between compose and read views of the form.

In Figure 27-6, the Compose page of the standard message form is ready for editing. When you click Edit Read Page, the Read view of the form appears for editing, as shown in Figure 27-7.

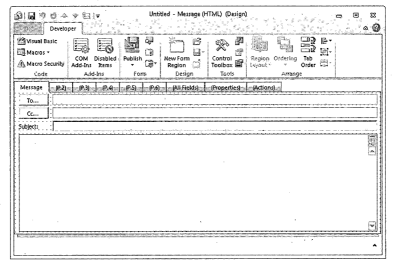

Figure 27-6 This standard Compose area is ready for editing.

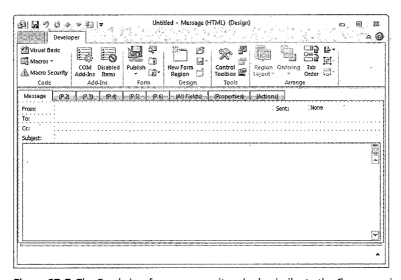

Figure 27-7 The Read view for a message item looks similar to the Compose view.

Because this is a standard form, a number of controls are already on the form. For example, the text box control for the body of the message is the largest element on the form. This control is bound to an Outlook 2010 field. The following section examines fields and what they mean to an Outlook 2010 solution; working with controls is discussed in the section "Adding and Arranging Controls," on page 699.

Outlook Fields

An Outlook 2010 field represents a discrete unit of information that is intelligible to Outlook 2010, such as the Bcc and To fields in an email message. You don't need to tell Outlook 2010 that email messages have these fields—they are already included in the standard form. Outlook 2010 provides a number of fields that you can use, and you can also add new fields. In theory, an unlimited number of fields are available, but the most common practice is to use a generous number of the built-in fields and a judicious number of new, user-defined properties. For now, this discussion focuses on the fields that are already available to you.

Because it provides so many built-in fields, Outlook 2010 groups them to make it easier to find the ones that you need. For example, some fields, such as To, From, Subject, Importance, Expires, Due By, Created, Size, and Attachment, are particular to email messages. Other fields, such as City, Children, and Birthday, are associated with Outlook 2010 contacts. You can, however, use fields from other forms to suit your needs on any form that you're designing—for example, Outlook 2010 doesn't prevent you from adding a Birthday field to an email form.

You can find more information about user-defined fields in the Outlook 2007 Developer Reference at *http://msdn.microsoft.com/en-us/library/bb208195.aspx*. Although this article was written for an earlier version of Outlook, the information in the article also applies to Outlook 2010.

When you work with a form, you can view the available fields in the Field Chooser, shown in Figure 27-8. To display the Field Chooser (if closed), click the Field Chooser button in the Tools group on the Developer tab; this button is a toggle that shows or hides the Field Chooser. In the Field Chooser, the fields are organized by categories and displayed in a list. You can choose a category in the drop-down list and then search in the body of the Field Chooser for the fields you need.

Figure 27-8 The Field Chooser allows you to view and choose the fields available for use.

Item Types and Fields

The scrollable list of fields shown in the Field Chooser in Figure 27-8 contains all the fields available for a form published in a certain folder. The standard item types come with a number of fields already defined. For example, a mail message comes with To, Subject, Body, and Sent fields already defined. Although you have the full range of fields available as you modify or create a form, you can speed your development time and decrease your effort by carefully selecting a standard form that most closely corresponds to the solution you're developing. This way, you can use as many built-in fields as possible. You'll learn how to represent these fields on your form using controls in the section "Adding and Arranging Controls," on page 699.

Creating Custom Forms from Scratch

Working with standard forms is great if you want to build a solution that is directly related to one of the Outlook 2010 item types. However, you might need an Outlook 2010 form that isn't based on an item type at all. For example, you might want to create a form that allows users to report their work hours or initiate a purchase order. Although you could base these examples on a standard form, they could just as easily require a completely new form that you need to create.

The good news is that creating a completely new form is easier than it sounds. In fact, Outlook 2010 doesn't really permit you to create forms completely from scratch, although you can certainly achieve the same effect. You have two ways to create a form that doesn't contain any built-in form elements:

- Modify a standard form by deleting all built-in interface elements from the form and adding your own.

- Modify a standard form by hiding the page that contains built-in interface elements and showing a new page that contains elements that you add.

You'll learn how to add pages to forms in the next section. First let's look at how to break down a standard form to a blank form by removing built-in interface controls.

Follow these steps to turn a standard post form (a form that is used to post a note into a folder) into a blank form:

1. Click the Developer tab.

2. Click Design A Form.

3. Select the Post form, and then click Open. The form opens in design mode, with the Message page selected.

4. Click each control (TextBox, Label, Button, and so on) on the Message page and delete it.

5. With the Message page still selected, click Page in the Form group, and then select Rename Page.

6. Type a new name in the dialog box and then click OK.

The form now looks similar to the form shown in Figure 27-7, although that one was based on the Message form and also has some changes. The figure shows a modified (blank) Compose area for this form, but you can also modify the Read area (via Edit Read Page). Of course, you'll also want to make these pages do something, but for now, you at least have a blank form to work with. To have this blank form available as a template, click File, File, and Save As, and then select Outlook Template from the Save As Type drop-down list.

Creating Multipage Forms

A multipage form allows you to fit a great deal of information on one form while also reducing confusion for the user. For example, you could create a form on which employees could both report their time for the week and report any expenses for which they need reimbursement. By using two pages, one form can serve both needs.

Any form can be a multipage form; all possible pages are already on the form that you create or modify. However, these pages are not visible automatically. If you look closely at the names on the page tabs shown previously in Figure 27-7, you'll see that except for the first name in the list, the name of each page is enclosed in parentheses, indicating that the page is not visible. To change the Visible property of a page, click its tab, click Page, Page, and then select Display This Page.

> **Note**
> You can make all pages visible, but you cannot make all pages invisible. If you try to do so, Outlook 2010 tells you that at least one page must be visible on the form.

The first (default) page of a form, which is initially visible, has Compose and Read capabilities already available, as mentioned earlier. The additional pages on a form, which are initially invisible, don't have these capabilities until you add them. To do so, select one of these pages, click Page, and then choose Separate Read Layout, which activates the Edit Compose Page and Edit Read Page buttons.

Adding and Arranging Controls

The real power of forms comes from the controls that you place on them. To construct a robust Outlook 2010 forms solution, you need to plan carefully what the form is supposed to do; what pieces of information it will display, modify, save, or send; which controls will display these information units; and how the controls will be laid out. You can put two types of controls on a form: a control that is bound to an Outlook 2010 field and a control that is not. This section looks first at field-bound controls. Field-bound controls are bound to specific control types, such as drop-down lists, text boxes, command buttons, labels, or check boxes.

To display a field on your form, follow these steps:

1. Display the Field Chooser, and then select a field category in the drop-down list.

2. In the scrollable list in the Field Chooser, select the field that you want, and then drag it onto the form.

3. Format the control as needed.

INSIDE OUT   Work with the users of the form

You can place any number of controls on a form, but it's a good idea to plan your form with an eye toward usability. Work closely with those individuals who will be using the form to ensure that it corresponds to their real needs. Find out how the users want the forms to be laid out, and listen to their suggestions about how the information should flow. No matter how much work you put into your solution, it won't be useful unless people actually use it.

You can resize, move, or rename a control, and you can change a number of its properties. To resize the control, select the control by clicking it, and position the mouse pointer over one of the control handles, which are represented by small boxes. When a small arrow appears, you can drag the handles in the appropriate direction to resize the control.

To move a control to a new location, simply drag it. Notice that the form's canvas is covered with a grid. Each point on the grid is a possible location for a corner or other relevant point on a control. You can choose to have controls snap to the grid points by right-clicking the grid and selecting Snap To Grid. You can define the distances between the points on this grid. This is important because the greater the scale of the grid (the greater the distance between points on the grid), the fewer places you can locate a control on your form. Conversely, the smaller the scale, the more you can refine the positioning of your controls.

To change the grid, follow these steps:

1. In the Arrange group, click Align.

2. Click Set Grid Size.

3. Type a value (in pixels) for the height and width spacing.

4. Click OK.

The smaller the number that you use for spacing, the smaller the scale. This means that more points on the grid will appear, and you can have more control over where your objects fit on the grid. The default is 8, but 3 is a good number to choose for greater positioning control.

INSIDE OUT   Limit controls on your forms

When you're using controls on forms, you can be tempted to make one form do too much. Although there's no precise limit for the number of controls that can be included on one form, the recommendation is using fewer than 300. However, my experience with custom forms development suggests that even 200 is excessive. You should try to keep the number of controls down to a few dozen or so when possible. Forms that try to do too much usually become confusing to users, and these forms often do not perform well. Keeping your forms focused and giving them a crisp design makes them easier to code and debug too. If you find that your form is overloaded, consider creating a COM add-in to allow a broader application context, or develop a stand-alone application that handles all your information needs.

Properties

Controls have a number of properties that you can view and modify. To find out what these properties are, right-click a control and then choose Properties on the shortcut menu to display the Properties dialog box. Figure 27-9 shows a Properties dialog box for a text box control.

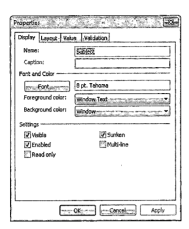

Figure 27-9 You can use the Properties dialog box to modify the properties of a control.

Display

The Display tab of a control's Properties dialog box (a text box example is shown in Figure 27-9) lists the most commonly used properties of the particular control. Changing the setting of a property in this dialog box enables the Apply button; clicking Apply or OK sets the value of that property for the selected control.

The default names of controls are rather generic, such as TextBox1 or CheckBox1. You'll want to change these to names that are more descriptive for your solution, such as txtFirstName or chkHasVacation.

You can learn more about naming conventions for controls by visiting the Microsoft MSDN website at *msdn.microsoft.com* and searching for "Visual Basic Coding Conventions Overview."

Layout

The Layout tab in the Properties dialog box lets you set the position of the field within the form. The position settings are set in pixels offset from the top and left side of the form. You can specify the height and width of the field as displayed in the form by setting the Height and Width values. You can also configure the field to resize itself automatically as the form size is being changed by selecting the Resize With Form check box in the Automatic Layout area, as shown in Figure 27-10.

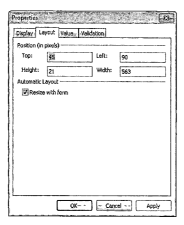

Figure 27-10 Use the Layout tab to set the position and size of a control.

Value

The Value tab in the Properties dialog box, shown in Figure 27-11, contains a number of settings that relate to the field value that the control represents. As mentioned, each control in the Field Chooser list is bound to an Outlook 2010 field. When you modify the properties of a control, you can change the field to which the control is bound.

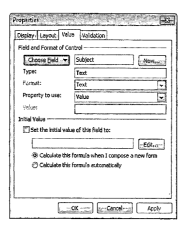

Figure 27-11 Use the options on the Value tab to set the field and format for a control.

To change the bound-field property, click Choose Field and then select the field to which you want to bind the control in the drop-down list. Make sure that the field value is bound to the correct property of your control. Normally, the field value is tied to the control's *Value* property; this is rarely changed. However, you can change this setting so that, for example, the value of a field is tied to your control's *Enabled* property. In this case, if the value of the field is *True*, the control is enabled; if the value is *False*, the control is not enabled.

You can also set the initial value of your control to display a default value. Select the Initial Value Of This Field To check box, and then type an initial value in the text box. This value doesn't have to be predetermined—you can have it correspond to a dynamic value, such as the current day or the concatenation of Subject field and the current date. To make the initial value more dynamic, click Edit to open the Initial Value For dialog box; an example is shown in Figure 27-12.

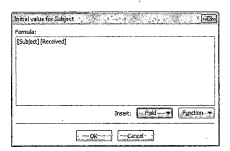

Figure 27-12 Use this dialog box to customize the initial value for a control.

In this dialog box, you establish a formula for the initial value of your control. For example, you can simply insert a built-in function, such as *Date( )*, for the formula.

To insert a built-in function—the *Date( )* function, in this example—follow these steps:

1. Click Function.

2. Click Date/Time, and then click Date( ).

3. The function appears in the Formula text box.

4. Click OK, and then click OK again to close the Properties dialog box.

When you run the form, the text box control will contain the current date as its initial value. Your users can always change the control's initial value unless you set the control to Read Only (on the Display tab).

Validation

The Validation tab in the Properties dialog box allows you to set certain properties that relate to how (or whether) the value of the control is validated. For example, if you create a form for a purchase order, you might want to ensure that users indicate the quantity

of parts that they want to order. The order processing staff will send you many thanks for requiring certain values before the purchase order gets to them because it reduces the amount of information traffic and busywork needed to process an order.

Suppose that you've added a control to your form that requires a value for a text box, and that value is required to be less than or equal to 10 characters. If the user fails to enter a valid value, Outlook 2010 will display a message that prompts the user to enter a correct value.

To set the properties on the Validation tab that will be necessary for this example, as shown in Figure 27-13, follow these steps:

1. Display the Properties dialog box, and then click the Validation tab.

2. Select the A Value Is Required For This Field check box.

3. Select the Validate This Field Before Closing The Form check box.

4. Click the Edit button located to the right of the Validation Formula text box.

5. Click Function.

6. Click Text, Len(string), and then click OK. The *Len(string)* function appears in the Validation Formula text box.

7. In the Validation Formula text box, type **<=10** after the function, and then click OK.

8. In the Display This Message If The Validation Fails text box, type the following text (including the quotation marks):

   "Please enter a value between 1 and 10 characters in length."

   Alternatively, you can click Edit, type the message without quotation marks, and then click OK.

9. Click OK to close the Properties dialog box.

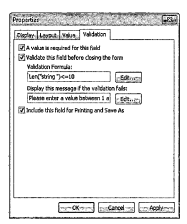

Figure 27-13 Use the Validation tab to require and verify the value entered in a control.

In the example exercise, when a user works with your form, the text box that requires validation must contain a value, and the value must be less than or equal to 10 characters. If
the value the user enters is 11 characters or more, Outlook 2010 will display a message box
containing the validation text that you provided when the user tries to send the form. The
user can then make the appropriate changes to the text box value and attempt to resend
the form.

Standard Controls

This chapter has thus far concentrated on controls that are bound to Outlook 2010 fields
and that appear in the Field Chooser. However, these aren't the only controls that you can
add to a form. This section takes a brief look at some of the standard controls that are available in Outlook 2010, as well as controls that come as part of the Office system.

Controls appear in a Control Toolbox, which is a small, resizable window made visible when
you click the button next to the Field Chooser button on the form. Figure 27-14 shows the
Toolbox.

Figure 27-14 The Control Toolbox allows you to add controls to your form.

As you hold the mouse pointer over the control icons in the Toolbox, the name of each control appears. To add one of these controls to your form, drag the control icon onto the form. You can then resize and reposition the control or set its properties, as discussed earlier.

> **Tip**
>
> **Refer to the Outlook Developer Reference at** *msdn.microsoft.com* **to learn more about the properties, methods, events, and possible uses of the standard controls.**

These standard controls are useful but limited. As your skills in developing Outlook 2010–based solutions progress, you'll find that you need functionality that transcends the abilities of the standard controls provided in the Toolbox. Fortunately, you can add other controls and make them accessible via the Toolbox window. For example, if you design a number of forms that need the Outlook Date Control to enable the user to pick a date, you can add that control to the Control Toolbox.

Follow these steps to add the Outlook Date control to the Toolbox:

1. Right-click an empty area of the Toolbox window.

2. Choose Custom Controls.

3. Scroll down the Available Controls list, and then click the box next to Microsoft Outlook Date Control.

4. Click OK. The control appears in the Custom Controls dialog box.

You can now add this control to a form and work with its specific properties and behaviors just as you did for the standard controls.

Custom controls can make your Outlook 2010 solution extremely robust and powerful. However, be aware that the control you're using might not exist on the computer of the person receiving the message. In other words, although you might have a particular control on your computer, the person who uses your form to compose a message or receives a message composed on your form might not have that control installed. For your solution to work, you need to ensure that the custom controls you use are distributed to and installed on other users' computers properly.

> **Note**
> Methods of distributing custom controls vary widely. Some controls come without an installing package, many use Microsoft Installer, and others use a third-party installation mechanism. You should read the documentation that accompanies your custom control or consult the manufacturer to determine the best method for distributing your control.

After creating your form, you can test it to see what it looks like when it is run. With the new form open, choose Run This Form in the Form group. This won't cause the form to close or disappear; instead, Outlook 2010 produces a new form based on the form that you've just created. The newly created form is an actual running form that you can send and read, and any included functions or scripts are also run when the form is opened.

Adding Graphics to Forms

Although developing solutions in Outlook 2010 can require much thought and effort, users might not necessarily share your enthusiasm and excitement about the forms that you've created. One way to increase acceptance and usability is to add some pleasing graphics to the forms. These graphics can come in a variety of formats, such as JPEG, GIF, WMF, EMF, and ICO.

One way to add a graphic to your form is to use the image control from the Control Toolbox. Initially, the control will appear as a gray square. You can resize it, just as you can resize any of the standard controls, although it's a good idea to place the picture in the control before you resize it. Set the picture source for the image control by using the Properties dialog box, shown in Figure 27-15. Double-click the Picture property, and then select the desired picture in the Load Picture dialog box.

Figure 27-15 Use the Properties dialog box to select a picture to insert into the image control.

Follow these steps to insert a picture in your control:

1. Right-click the image control that you placed on your form.

2. Click Advanced Properties.

3. In the list of properties, scroll down to the Picture property.

4. Select the Picture property and then click the ellipsis button (...) at the top of the form, or simply double-click the Picture property.

5. In the Load Picture dialog box, navigate to the picture that you want to appear in the image control, and then click Open.

6. Close the Advanced Properties dialog box, and then verify that the control now contains the picture you chose.

INSIDE OUT   Change your images at run time

As is the case with all the controls that you use on a custom form, you can change the values of many of their properties when the form is running. For example, you can create a form with an image that changes based on certain criteria. You can add code to your form that alters the setting of the control's *Picture* property and thus loads an image into the control that is different from the image you specified at design time.

Another way to make your forms more attractive and usable is to add an icon to buttons on the forms. You can configure the command button available in the Toolbox to display both a text caption and a graphic. For example, if your button sends a custom message to a recipient when clicked, you could add an envelope image to the button to convey the notion of sending a message. To have the button display an image, set the *Picture* property for the button just as you would for an image control. You can also set the *Picture* property for other controls, such as text boxes and labels.

In addition, you can display a custom icon in the form's title bar. Outlook 2010 always displays a default icon in the upper-left corner of a form that indicates whether it is a task form, an appointment form, and so on. You can change this icon by clicking the Properties tab of your form when you're working in design mode. Click Change Large Icon or Change Small Icon, and then navigate to the .ico file you want to use. The Large Icon setting tells Outlook 2010 which image to display when a user displays the properties of the form. The Small Icon setting specifies the title bar image and the image that is shown when the form is displayed in an Outlook 2010 folder.

Adding User-Defined Fields

There are times when the types of data that you need to share, gather, or track with forms exceed the Outlook 2010 default field definitions. You might want to have your contact form display the hire date and review date, for example, but these fields don't exist in the Outlook 2010 field list.

You can define new fields that contain information that is relevant to your use of Outlook 2010. These user-defined fields can be bound to a control in the same way that you bind a preexisting field to controls in Outlook 2010 forms.

When you want to implement a new field in a form, start by opening the Design Form dialog box. To create a new form field, you can either open the Field Chooser and click New or click the All Fields tab and then click New.

The New Column dialog box will prompt you for the field name, data type, and display format for the new field. In the Name box, type the name of the new field, such as **Hire Date**, and then select the data type for the field in the Type drop-down list—in this case, Date/ Time. In the Format drop-down list, select the display format for the date (or day, time, and date) layout that you want for the field.

The new field is added to the Select From drop-down list, and you can find the new field in the User Defined Fields In Inbox item. The field can be selected in the Field Chooser and on the All Fields tab. To use your new field, drag it onto your form. You will need to remember to add the field to both the Compose Page and the Read Page, and commonly you will want to set the properties of the field in the Read Page to read-only (on the Display tab).

Publishing and Sharing Forms

After you create your form and define its behaviors, properties, and settings, you'll want to make it available to users. First, however, you'll need to preserve your form in one of these two ways:

- Save the form as a file.

- Publish the form to a folder or other location.

Saving Forms

You can save a form by clicking File and then clicking Save As. In the Save As dialog box, select the file name and location. The form file is saved as an Outlook Template file (.oft).

Publishing Forms

Publishing a form is a lot like saving the form. When you finish your form, you can publish it to a specific folder location. You can publish it to your Inbox or another folder in your mailbox, a public folder, the Organizational Forms Library (with Microsoft Exchange Server), or your Personal Forms Library.

Follow these steps to publish a form to a folder or forms library:

1. Click Design A Form on the Developer tab.

2. In the Design Form dialog box, select the location (such as User Templates In File System) containing the form that you want to publish.

3. Select the form that you want to publish, and then click Open.

4. In the Form group, click Publish, and then click Publish Form As to open the Publish Form As dialog box. (The first time you use the Publish button, the Publish Form As dialog box will be displayed, but after a form has been saved once, the Publish button will simply save the existing form, overwriting the previous version.)

5. In the Look In drop-down list, select the folder or forms library where you want to publish the form. (The default is the Personal Forms Library.)

6. Type the display name and the form name.

7. Click Publish in the Publish Form As dialog box to save the form in the selected location.

INSIDE OUT Create a staging area for your forms

When you're creating a form, it's a good idea to keep the production version of the form separate from the development version. Create a staging folder where you publish the forms that you're working on. When you complete a form design, publish your form in this staging folder at regular intervals so that you don't lose the modifications you've made to the form. Only people designing and testing forms for your organization should have access to this folder.

After you publish a form, the folder in which you publish it contains the form itself and all the underlying information that another person's instance of Outlook 2010 needs to understand the form.

Choosing Forms

After you have created a custom form and saved or published it for common use, you will need to select the form to use it. Custom forms are normally stored in a location related to their expected use. Custom forms intended for common use, for example, are usually stored in an accessible network location. If you have a custom form intended for your own use, however, you would store it in the Personal Forms Library. Alternatively, if you want to use a form that you have saved to a folder on your local hard disk, you would store it using the User Templates In File System location.

In each of these cases, to locate your custom form, select the appropriate location in the Look In drop-down list of the Choose Form dialog box, shown in Figure 27-16.

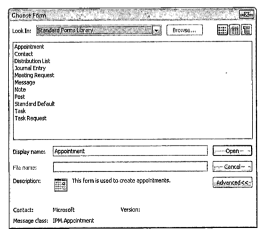

Figure 27-16 Select a custom form in the Choose Form dialog box by first selecting its location.

To use a custom form from these (or any other) locations, follow these steps:

1. Click Choose Form on the Developer tab.

2. In the Choose Form dialog box, select the location in which your custom form is stored (such as the Personal Forms Library).

3. Select the custom form that you want to use.

4. Click Open.

Using Forms Effectively

Each of the forms in Outlook 2010 serves the same purpose—to present information in a specific format. Outlook 2010 forms provide access to all Outlook 2010 items (messages, notes, meetings, tasks, journal entries, and so on) and enable you to create custom forms using any of the available fields. By creating custom forms that align with your workflow, you can ease the communication of information as well as the transfer of data important to your business.

In creating custom forms, you begin by selecting a default form that most closely resembles the form and function that you want for your new forms. You can then choose to add or delete fields on the default page and/or create additional pages containing fields to display or gather further information. Here are some pointers about using forms:

- **Know when not to create forms** Outlook 2010 form creation can give you the capability to customize email messages, meeting requests, and other Outlook 2010 items, but if existing forms provide the functionality you need, it is easier and more effective to use the existing forms. When you consider creating a new form, start by asking "Is the functionality I need already present in an existing form?" Consider that in addition to the time needed to create a custom form, there are distribution logistics (how you get the form to all who would need it), as well as training needed to enable people to effectively use the new form.

  When you are communicating to customers, vendors, and others outside your organization, you'll need to determine whether they are using Outlook 2010 with Rich Text Format (RTF) support enabled or some other email application. For Outlook 2010 forms to work, the recipient must also be using Outlook 2010 as an email client and must have RTF support.

- **Keep forms simple but comprehensive** Once you have decided that a new form is necessary, evaluate the information that you need the form to display, transmit, or gather, and then limit the form information to the minimum data required to fulfill your operational or organizational needs. You can create a custom form with multiple pages containing an exhaustive array of fields, yet the complexity of using such a form could easily outweigh any hoped-for benefits. Keep in mind that each custom form that you create is intended to facilitate the communication of information. The easier it is for people to use the custom form to exchange information, the more likely it is that people will use the form, and thus the more value it will have for your organization.

Consider a custom form created to enhance customer relationship management by including 15 fields of concise contact information, key project assessment, and a project status summary vs. a custom form that includes five pages containing 200 fields of exhaustive contact information, step-by-step project notes, milestones and timelines, equipment reserved, travel time, technical assessments, customer evaluation, and so on. The first option with 15 fields is much more likely to be used. When you actually have a need to gather 200 fields' worth of information, you'll want to consider subdividing the data into related sets and then creating separate forms for each set.

- **Use user-defined fields to store information not included by default in Outlook**   Although Outlook 2010 contains fields for the data it uses in contacts, email, meeting requests, tasks, and so on, there are invariably additional pieces of information that your organization could benefit by having included that are not part of the Outlook 2010 default field set. Consider additions to the meeting form that could be useful when you're scheduling meetings with coworkers. For example, to identify who will be leading the meeting, you could add a Presenter field to the custom meeting request form. Likewise, you might consider adding Food Preferences and Food Allergies fields to a custom appointment form for those appointments with clients or staff that involve dining out or food being brought into the event.

  You might want to add information in your contacts list that isn't shared, but that assists you in working with others or relating to their personal interests. You could, for example, create a custom contact form to enable you to track the specialized knowledge or favorite sports of each of the people in your contacts list. Then, for example, when you want to find a coworker who just happens to know how IPv6 actually works, you can search for "IPv6" and display the names of every person in your contacts list who is fluent in IPv6. (Searching for user-defined fields requires you to select the Query Builder and then add your custom form and fields to the query criteria.)

Mıcʀosoғт Outlook 2010 is a feature-rich product and, as such, has an option, a wizard, or a graphical tool for accomplishing nearly anything that you require from a personal information manager. If something does come up that the folks at Microsoft haven't planned for, however, you also have the option of customizing Outlook 2010 by using its built-in support for Microsoft Visual Basic code additions. Through the use of flexible Microsoft Visual Basic for Applications (VBA) scripting options and built-in security controls, you can simplify and automate common tasks.

In this chapter, you'll learn how to create and use a macro. This includes creating the macro, stepping through a macro to test it, and deleting macros you no longer need. In addition, you'll find out about implementing security options for macros.

See Chapter 11, "Processing Messages Automatically," for a discussion of Quick Steps, which enable you to process messages automatically.

Understanding Automation Options

Outlook 2010 has a number of built-in automation options that allow the application to perform certain tasks for you. For example, the Rules Wizard automatically moves, copies, and forwards email messages. The Out Of Office Assistant acts as an answering service when you're away.

For information about these examples of built-in automation options, see Chapter 11 and the section "Creating Automatic Responses with the Out Of Office Assistant," on page 345.

If a built-in option can accomplish the automated task that you require, it should be your first choice. By using a built-in option instead of a custom one, you minimize problems that can occur if you need to reinstall Outlook 2010 or use Outlook 2010 on multiple machines.

Using standardized options also guards against compatibility problems with upgrades to Outlook 2010.

If none of the automation options does the trick, however, you can accomplish just about any customization by using VBA. This chapter focuses on the use of VBA procedures known as *macros* to automate common tasks.

Understanding Macros

So just what is a macro? In general terms, a macro is a number of commands grouped together to execute a particular task. Macros are like small programs that operate within other programs. Macros have been around for a long time, and all Microsoft Office 2010 system products support them at some level. In Outlook 2010, macros are implemented as VBA procedures that are not linked to a particular form and are available from anywhere in Outlook 2010. In Outlook 2010, you manage macros by using commands in the Code area on the Developer tab. To display the Developer tab, right-click the ribbon and choose Customize The Ribbon. In the Outlook Options dialog box, place a check beside Developer in the tab list on the right and click OK.

Using Macros

Macros are most useful for tasks that must be performed repeatedly without change. Even so, because a macro contains Visual Basic code, it can be flexible and can respond to variables or user input. With the power of scripting, a macro can accomplish a task in the most efficient way in response to specific conditions.

CAUTION

Macros can be extremely powerful. This power can be a great asset for you, but it can also mean that any problems can become serious ones. Like many other things, macros can be dangerous when used improperly. Inexperienced programmers should take great care when writing and using macros in Outlook 2010.

The following are the three basic programming elements you can work with in an Outlook 2010 macro:

- **Object**   An object is a particular part of a program, such as a button, a menu item, or a text field. Objects make up any element of Outlook 2010 that you can see or work with. An object has properties, and how you set these properties determines how the object functions.

- **Property**   Any part of an object—its color, its width, and its value—is part of the set of attributes that make up its properties.

- **Method**   A method is a task that an object carries out, such as showing a form or reading file information. Methods can be modified based on user input or the value of certain properties.

In general, a VBA macro either determines or modifies the value of an object property or calls a method. Macros, then, are nothing more than simple programs that use VBA to access or modify Outlook 2010 information.

> **Note**
>
> Before you can work with macros, you might need to configure macro security settings. For information about configuring macro security, see the section "Setting Macro Security," on page 725.

> **Note**
>
> In Microsoft Excel 2010 and Microsoft Word 2010, you can simply record your mouse movements and keystrokes using the Macro Recorder, and the computer plays them back when you execute the macro. Outlook 2010 doesn't include a macro recorder, so you have to create macros by writing the macro code yourself. Therefore, users familiar with programming basics and VBA will have a head start in learning to create Outlook 2010 macros.

Creating a Macro from Scratch

The process for creating an Outlook 2010 macro is simple. The process for creating a *useful* macro, on the other hand, is more complex. In this chapter, we'll fall back on the most basic of functions, the "Hello World" message box macro. This macro creates a function that displays a message box containing the text *Hello World*. Clicking OK (the only button) closes the message box and ends the macro.

To create this macro, follow these steps:

1. Click the Developer tab, click Macros, and choose Macros to open the Macros dialog box.

2. In the Macro Name box, type a descriptive name for your new macro (no spaces are allowed). In Figure 28-1, the macro is titled *HelloWorldMsgBox*.

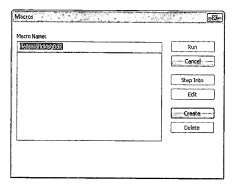

Figure 28-1 Enter the name for a new macro in the Macro Name box.

3. Click Create. Visual Basic starts, which allows you to add functionality to your macro. For those who are not programmers, creating VBA code might seem daunting, but simple tasks are actually quite easy to write code for. (Note that if you have macros, they will be displayed in this window, each in its own section of the project file.)

4. The first line of the macro starts with *Sub* and contains the macro name—in this case, *HelloWorldMsgBox*. On the next line, type the following, as shown in Figure 28-2:

MsgBox ("Hello World")

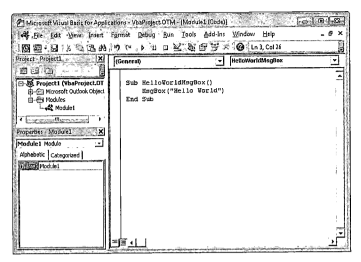

Figure 28-2 You add code between the first and last lines of a macro.

5. To test the code, choose Run, Run Sub/UserForm, or click the Run Sub/UserForm button on the toolbar. The message box shown in Figure 28-3 appears.

Figure 28-3 The Hello World message box appears when you run the macro.

> **Note**
> If you get a message saying macros are not enabled, you should check your macro security settings. To learn how to configure macro security, see the section "Setting Macro Security," on page 725.

6. Choose File, Save. (The file name, which cannot be changed here, is VbaProject.OTM.)

7. Close the Visual Basic Editor.

Running a Macro

After you save a macro, it is available for use. Click the Developer tab, click Macros, and then select the *Project1.HelloWorldMsgBox* macro. The message box appears, just as it did when you tested the macro in the Visual Basic Editor.

Although macros are available from the Developer tab, in some cases you might want to add a macro to the ribbon or Quick Access Toolbar to make it readily available when you need it. To add the macro to a tab in the Outlook 2010 ribbon, follow these steps:

1. Right-click the ribbon and choose Customize The Ribbon.

2. In the Choose Commands From list, select Macros. The *HelloWorldMsgBox* macro appears on the left, as shown in Figure 28-4.

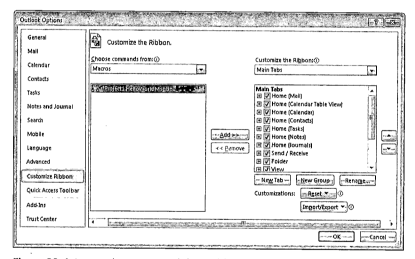

Figure 28-4 Locate the macro, and then add it to the desired tab.

3. Select a custom group in which to place the macro (you can't add the macro to any of the default groups).

4. Click Add to add *HelloWorldMsgBox* macro to the group. Clicking the button in the group will run the macro.

To add the macro to the Quick Access Toolbar, follow these steps:

1. Click Customize Quick Access Toolbar, and then choose More Commands to open the Editor Options dialog box.

2. In the Choose Commands From drop-down list, select Macros. The *HelloWorldMsgBox* macro appears in the list below, as shown in Figure 28-5.

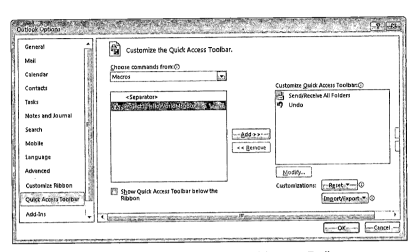

Figure 28-5 Add a button for the macro to the Quick Access Toolbar.

3. Click Add to add the *HelloWorldMsgBox* macro button to the Quick Access Toolbar.

4. Click OK to close the Outlook Options dialog box.

Editing a Macro

After you create a macro, you can edit it by returning to the Macros dialog box as follows:

1. Open the Macros dialog box from the Developer tab, and then, in the Macros dialog box, select the *HelloWorldMsgBox* macro and click Edit. The Visual Basic Editor starts and displays the selected macro.

2. Modify the macro so that it matches the following:

```
Sub HelloWorldMsgBox()
MsgBox ("Click OK to create a new message")
Set newMsg = Application.CreateItem(0)
    newMsg.Subject = "Sample Message from a Macro"
    newMsg.Body = "You can even add text automatically."
    newMsg.Display
End Sub
```

3. Verify that the changed macro works properly by clicking the Run Sub/UserForm button on the Microsoft Visual Basic toolbar. Instead of showing a simple message box as before, the macro should now present you with an email message window.

(This window might be hidden behind the Microsoft Visual Basic for Applications window.) The message should have information automatically filled in in the subject and body fields, as shown in Figure 28-6.

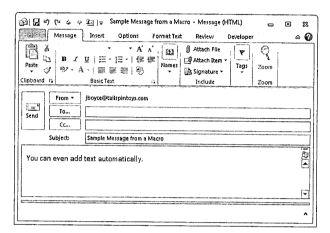

Figure 28-6 The modified macro displays an email message window.

4. Save the changes to your Visual Basic project, and then close the Microsoft Visual Basic for Applications window. Close the email message that you created.

5. When you return to the Macros dialog box, select the modified macro, and then click Run. You should see the same email message that you saw in Figure 28-6. Close the email message.

> **Note**
>
> When you edit a macro, you'll eventually want to save it and test the changes. To ensure that you can return to the original macro in case of trouble, first export the project so that you can retrieve it later. For more information about exporting, see the section "Sharing Macros with Others," on page 724.

Stepping Through a Macro

When you're creating a macro, it's often helpful to step through the code, which allows you to watch each line as it is being processed and see problems as they occur. To do this, open the *HelloWorldMsgBox* macro for editing (as described in the preceding section), and then press F8. Alternatively, open the Macros dialog box, select a macro, and then choose Step

Into. The first line of the macro is highlighted, and its code is processed. To process the next line, press F8 again.

Step through the rest of the macro using the F8 key. Notice that clicking OK merely closes the message box rather than creating the email message. This is because later steps are not followed automatically. The new email message is created only after you press F8 through the line of the subprocedure that displays it—in this case, the last line of the macro.

> ## Note
> You can step through a macro only when it is being edited. When macros are executed from within Outlook 2010, they automatically move through all procedures.

TROUBLESHOOTING

Your macro doesn't run properly

If you are having problems getting a macro to run properly, you can try several approaches to determine the source of the problem. The most common problem is incorrect syntax in your code. Finding errors in code can be a vexing job, but using the step-through process generally helps to find the line that is causing you problems.

If your syntax is correct, the problem might have to do with the way you're running the macro. Among the problems you should check for are the security settings on the macro and the security settings on the computer. Also, if the macro has been deleted but a toolbar button still remains, you might be trying to run a macro that no longer exists.

Deleting a Macro

Sometimes a macro outlives its usefulness. To delete a macro that you no longer need, click the Developer tab, click Macros, and choose Macros. In the Macros dialog box, select the macro that you want to remove, and then click Delete. When you're prompted to verify that you want to delete the macro permanently, click Yes to remove the macro from the list, making its code unavailable to Outlook 2010.

> **Note**
>
> If you have created a toolbar button for a macro that you subsequently delete, you must locate the button and remove it in a separate operation.

Sharing Macros with Others

If you're creating macros for use by a group of people, or even an entire organization, the macros must be installed separately for each user. Unfortunately, although the Macros dialog box has options for creating and deleting macros, it has no option for adding macros from other places. You can't share macros in the same way you can share files. Instead, sharing macros with other users is generally a two-step process: the user who creates the macro must export the macro code, and the other user must import the code. To share a macro, follow these steps:

1. On the Developer tab, click Visual Basic in the Code group.

2. In Microsoft Visual Basic, choose File, Export File to open the Export File dialog box, shown in Figure 28-7.

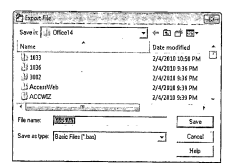

Figure 28-7 A macro file is exported so that it can be shared.

3. In the Save As Type box, save the project as a .bas file. (By doing so, you can then email the file to another user or make it available on the network.)

Once another user has access to the .bas file, that user can install the macro by following these steps:

1. On the Developer tab, click Visual Basic.

2. In the Visual Basic Editor, choose File, Import File.

3. Browse to the file, open it, and then save it.

The user can now access the macro through the Macros dialog box.

Setting Macro Security

Macros have several advantages, including their power, their flexibility, and their ability to run automatically, even without your knowledge. These advantages have a dark side, however, and poorly written or malicious macros can do significant damage to an Outlook 2010 message store. Because of the potential danger that macros pose, the Outlook 2010 Tools menu offers four security levels for Outlook 2010 macros:

- **Disable All Macros Without Notification**   Macros are totally disabled, and Outlook 2010 does not display any warning that a macro is attempting to run.

- **Notifications For Digitally Signed Macros; All Other Macros Disabled**   Your system can run only macros that are signed digitally. This means that some macros— even benign and potentially useful ones—are not available unless they are signed.

- **Notifications For All Macros**   You will be prompted as to whether you want to run any macros.

- **Enable All Macros (Not Recommended)**   Macros run automatically, regardless of their signature. This is the most dangerous setting.

For information about digital signatures, see the section "Protecting Messages with Digital Signatures," on page 360.

To view or change the security level, on the Developer tab, click Macro Security to open the Macro Settings page of the Trust Center, as shown in Figure 28-8. (You can also access the Trust Center by opening an Outlook 2010 item and, on the Developer tab, in the Code group, clicking Macro Security.) The default setting is Notifications For Digitally Signed Macros; All Other Macros Are Disabled, which is probably the best choice for most users.

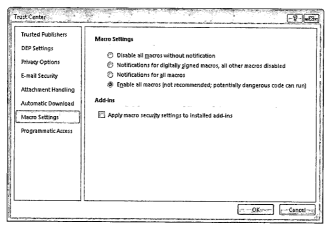

Figure 28-8 You can set the security level for macros in the Trust Center.

INSIDE OUT   Security and user-created macros

When you create your own macros, they are not controlled by the security settings. User-created macros do not need to be signed and will run regardless of the security setting that you have selected—even if you choose the Disable All Macros Without Notification option! This is nice for purposes of design and editing, but it assumes that you realize exactly what a macro will do. Moreover, it means that when you want to test macro security settings, you must run Outlook 2010 using a different user account.

Specifying Trusted Sources

To reduce the number of times you're prompted about whether to run a macro (if you've set the security level to Notifications For Digitally Signed Macros; All Other Macros Disabled) or to be able to run macros at all (if you've set the security level to Notifications For All Macros), you can specify a trusted source.

When a digitally signed macro runs, Outlook 2010 displays the certificate attached to the macro. In addition to choosing whether to run the macro, you're given the choice of adding the certificate holder (the organization or individual who created the macro) to your list of trusted sources. Once the holder of the certificate is trusted, any macros signed with that certificate run without prompting at the Notifications For Digitally Signed Macros; All Other Macros Disabled security setting. To view the list of trusted certificates or to remove a trusted source, click File, Options, Trust Center, and finally Trust Center Settings. Click

Trusted Publishers to view the sources. To remove a trusted source, select the source and then click Remove.

Signing Your Macros to Avoid Security Warnings

Macro security in Outlook 2010 gives you control over when macros can run, which helps prevent malicious code from affecting the system of someone using Outlook 2010. In Outlook 2010, when macro security is set to Notifications For Digitally Signed Macros; All Other Macros Disabled, only digitally signed macros from trusted sources can run. A setting of Notifications For All Macros causes Outlook 2010 to prompt you whether to enable and allow macros to run. A setting of Enable All Macros allows all macros to run, which poses significant risks from malicious code.

If you create your own macros, you probably would like to sign your macros digitally so that they will run on other people's computers without triggering Outlook 2010 macro security warnings. Outlook 2010, like all versions since Outlook 2000, provides the means to sign VBA projects.

To create a self-signing certificate, follow these steps:

1. Choose Start, All Programs, Microsoft Office, and Microsoft Office 2010 Tools, and then select Digital Certificate For VBA Projects.

2. Type a descriptive name for your certificate, such as **Outlook 2010 Code Signing Certificate**, in the Your Certificate's Name dialog box, and then click OK.

3. Click OK to confirm the creation of the certificate.

To sign a macro, follow these steps:

1. On the Developer tab, click Macros, Macros to open the Macros dialog box.

2. Select a macro, and then click Edit to open the Visual Basic Editor.

3. Choose Tools, Digital Signature to open the Digital Signature dialog box.

4. Click Choose, select your code-signing certificate, and then click OK. Click OK again, and then close the Visual Basic Editor.

On the computer that will be running the macro, verify that you have configured Outlook 2010 macro security for either the Notifications For Digitally Signed Macros; All Other Macros Disabled setting or the Notifications For All Macros setting, and then attempt to run a macro. When Outlook 2010 asks whether you want to trust the macro publisher, click Yes. Your custom macros should now run on that computer without triggering the Outlook 2010 security warnings.

PART 6

Managing and Securing Outlook

L IKE any system, Microsoft Outlook 2010 can become overloaded with messages, contact information, appointments, and other data. If you can't manage all this data, you'll be lost each time you try to find a particular item. Outlook 2010 helps you manage information by providing folders for storing your data. You also can create your own folders, move data between folders, and set folder properties.

This chapter focuses on managing your Outlook 2010 folders and their contents. You'll learn how to create new folders to store email messages, contact information, and other files. You'll also learn how to set up Outlook 2010 folders to use web views so that you can display web pages inside folders. In addition, you'll find out what it takes to archive your data when you want to archive data on the spot.

Understanding Outlook Folders

Outlook 2010 folders are used like the folders you use in Windows Explorer. You use Outlook 2010 folders to store items that you work with, such as email messages and attachments, contact entries, journal entries, tasks, appointments, and notes. Outlook 2010 includes default folders for each type of item—for example, the Calendar, Contacts, Journal, Inbox, RSS Feeds, and Tasks folders. Along with these item-type folders are other default folders, such as Deleted Items, Drafts, Junk E-Mail, Outbox, and Sent Items.

If you are not using a Microsoft Exchange Server account, these folders are all part of your personal folders (.pst) file, so they are private. If you are running Outlook 2010 with Exchange Server, others on your network to whom you've assigned rights can view and manage items stored in these folders.

> **Note**
>
> In addition to the folders listed here, in an Exchange Server environment, your Exchange Server administrator can set up public folders that appear in your Folder List but are stored on the computer running Exchange Server. You and others who have rights to these public folders will see a Public Folders icon in your Folder List. If you have the necessary rights, you can create and delete these public folders, store and manage items in them, and see content added to them by other users.

> **Tip**
>
> The Folder tab on the ribbon contains commands and options that you can use to manage folders and the items in those folders. The items that appear on the Folder tab depend on the selected folder. For example, the Clean Up Folder button only shows up on the Folder tab when you are viewing a mail folder. Likewise, the Share Calendar button only shows up on the Folder tab when you are viewing a calendar folder. Take some time to experiment with the Folder tab to learn what commands and options are available from it in each folder type.

Working with the Folder List

If you move between folders frequently, you might want to navigate by using a combination of the Navigation pane and the Folder List. The Navigation pane gives you quick access to the Outlook 2010 folders that the majority of people use most often. However, you might use different Outlook 2010 folders, or you might want to access certain file system folders from Outlook 2010. For example, suppose that you have an Exchange Server account but also use a set of personal folders to store personal messages and contacts or other data. Because Outlook 2010 doesn't automatically add shortcuts in the Navigation pane for your other folders, the best way to access these folders is usually through the Folder List, as shown in Figure 29-1.

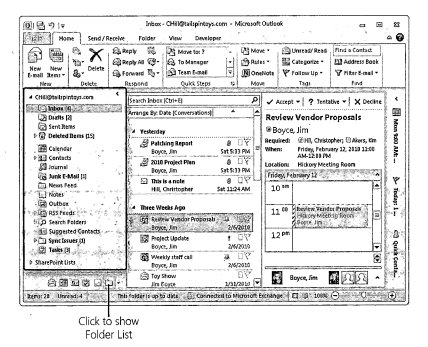

Click to show
Folder List

Figure 29-1 Use the Folder List to move between folders not listed in the Navigation pane, or to see which folders are included in a given store.

If the Navigation pane is not minimized, click the Folder List button at the bottom of the Navigation pane. The Navigation pane then displays the Folder List as shown in Figure 29-1. You can click folders in the list to view the contents of those folders.

If the Navigation pane is minimized, click the Configure Buttons button at the bottom of the minimized Navigation pane and choose Folder List. The Folder List will appear as a pop-up window, and after you click a folder in the list, the Folder List disappears again.

> **Note**
> You can right-click a folder in the Folder List to display the folder's shortcut menu, which gives you access to specific actions that you can perform on the folder. Many of these actions, such as opening and deleting folders, are explained in the following sections.

Using and Managing Folders

When you perform an action in Outlook 2010, you typically do so inside a folder. Outlook 2010 provides a handful of actions that you can perform with folders to change their behavior, location, appearance, and so on, as described in the following sections.

Using a Folder

When you're ready to work with information in Outlook 2010, you first go to the folder in which that information is stored. For example, to read a new email message downloaded to your Inbox folder, you must open the Inbox folder and then select the message to read. To open a folder, click its button in the Navigation pane or click the folder name in the Folder List.

When you open the folder, its contents are displayed in the main Outlook 2010 window. To see the contents of a particular folder item, you must open the item using one of these methods:

- Double-click the item in the main Outlook 2010 window.

- Right-click the item, and then choose Open.

- Click the item, and then press Enter.

- Click the item, and then press Ctrl+O.

Depending on the type of folder you open, the Reading pane might be available. The Reading pane displays the contents of the currently selected item without requiring you to open a separate window for the folder item. The Reading pane is handy because it provides a quick view and can help keep your desktop tidier. To display the Reading pane, click the View tab, click Reading Pane, and then select Right or Bottom.

By default, the Reading pane appears on the right in the main Outlook 2010 window, as shown in Figure 29-2. You can resize this pane by dragging the edge. To see an item in the Reading pane, simply select the item in the folder.

Follow these steps to create a folder:

1. Take one of the following actions to display the Create New Folder dialog box:

   - Right-click a folder in the Folder List, and then choose New Folder.

   - Press Ctrl+Shift+E.

   - Click the Folder tab on the ribbon and click New Folder.

2. In the Name box, type a name for the folder, as shown in Figure 29-3.

Figure 29-3 Use the Create New Folder dialog box to specify folder type, location, and other properties of a new folder.

3. From the Folder Contains drop-down list, choose the type of item you want to store in this new folder.

4. From the Select Where To Place The Folder list, select the location for the new folder. Selecting the Inbox, for example, places the new folder as a subfolder of the Inbox.

5. Click OK.

Adding a Folder Shortcut to the Navigation Pane

If you have a frequently used folder that isn't listed in the Navigation pane, you can create a shortcut to the folder in the Shortcuts area of the Navigation pane. To do so, follow these steps:

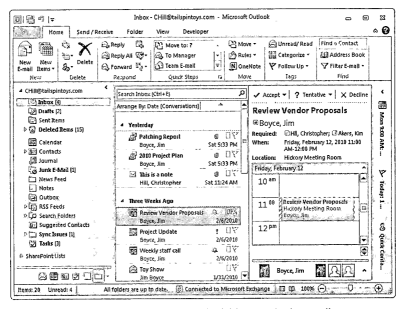

Figure 29-2 You can view the contents of a folder item in the Reading pane.

For more information about working with the Reading pane, see the section "Wo the Standard Outlook Views," on page 72.

> **Note**
>
> Only one item can be open in the Reading pane at any given time. If you wan additional items, you must double-click them to display them in separate win

Creating a Folder

As you know, Outlook 2010 provides a basic set of folders in which you can sto types of data, such as the Contacts folder for storing contact information. As y look 2010 more, you'll want to add other folders to organize your data. For ex might add other message folders to store particular kinds of messages.

Each Outlook 2010 folder you add has a specific *type* based on the type of dat For example, a mail folder differs from a contacts folder because the former st sages and the latter stores contact entries. Similarly, a calendar folder stores a and events, and a notes folder stores notes. When you add a folder, you speci type. You also specify the name of the folder and its location.

1. At the bottom of the Navigation pane, click Shortcuts.

2. In the Shortcuts pane, right-click the group where you want to add the shortcut and choose New Shortcut to display the Add To Navigation Pane dialog box, shown in Figure 29-4.

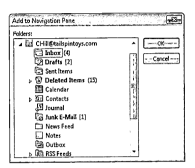

Figure 29-4 Add folders to the Shortcuts pane with the Add To Navigation Pane dialog box.

3. Select a folder in the list, and then click OK.

You can also create your own shortcut groups. To do this, right-click an existing group and choose New Shortcut Group. Outlook 2010 creates a new shortcut and highlights the name so that you can change it. Type a new name, and then press Enter. You can move shortcuts from one group to another easily, simply by dragging them.

> **Note**
>
> You can drag folders, documents, and web shortcuts to a group in the Shortcuts pane to create shortcuts to those items quickly. See the section "Customizing the Navigation Pane," on page 633, for more details on working with shortcuts.

When you want to remove a shortcut, right-click it, choose Delete Shortcut, and then click Yes.

TROUBLESHOOTING

A folder and contents remain when a shortcut is removed

When you remove a folder shortcut from the Navigation pane, you remove only the shortcut. You do not remove the folder from Outlook 2010, nor do you delete the folder's contents. For information about deleting a folder and its contents, see the section "Deleting a Folder," on page 746.

If you decide that a folder shortcut should be renamed, follow these steps:

1. Right-click the folder shortcut that you want to rename.

2. Choose Rename Shortcut.

3. Type a new name, and then press Enter.

> **Note**
>
> When you rename the folder shortcut, the folder name in the Folder List does not change; only the shortcut name changes.

Working with Favorite Email Folders

A handy feature in Outlook 2010 is the Favorites list in the Navigation pane for your email. When you click the Mail button in the Navigation pane, Outlook 2010 displays a Favorites list at the top of the Navigation pane. By default, this list includes four of the most commonly used mail folders: the Inbox, Unread Mail, Sent Items folders, and Deleted Items, as shown in Figure 29-5.

You can add folders to and remove folders from the Favorites list easily. To add an email folder to the Favorites list, right-click the folder and then choose Show In Favorites. To remove an email folder from the Favorites list, right-click the folder in the Folder List or in the Favorites list, and then choose Remove From Favorites. (This only removes the folder from the Favorites list; it does not delete the folder itself.)

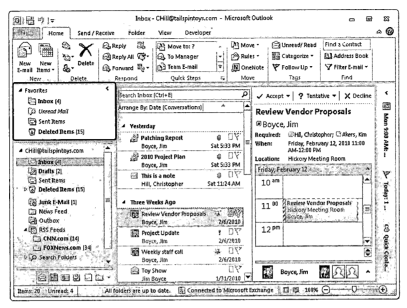

Figure 29-5 Use the Favorites list to open frequently used folders quickly.

You can also change the order of favorite folders in the list. Right-click the folder in the list and choose Move Up In List or Move Down In List, or simply drag the folder to the desired location in the list.

Working with Other Folder Groups

The other default Outlook folders (Calendar, Tasks, etc.) do not offer a Favorites list like the Mail folder. However, they offer a feature that is just as useful—folder groups. When you open the Calendar folder, for example, you'll see at least one folder group named My Calendars. If you are using an Exchange Server account, you'll also see a Team group that shows the calendars for the people who report to you, according to the Direct Reports field in your Active Directory Domain Services (AD DS) account. Figure 29-6 shows these two calendar folder groups.

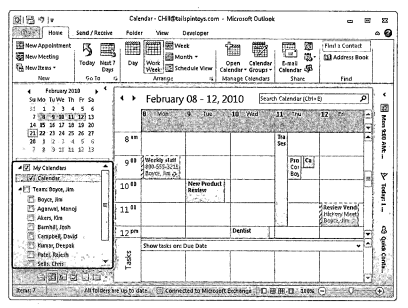

Figure 29-6 This profile shows two calendar folder groups.

The default folder groups included in Outlook 2010 for the default folders include My Calendars, My Contacts, My Tasks, My Notes, and My Journals. Each of these groups functions in the same way. For example, you can click the arrow beside the folder group to expand or collapse the group, showing or hiding its contents.

Creating Folder Groups

You can create your own folder groups to help organize the folders of that type. For example, if you have multiple Contact folders, you might add a couple of folder groups to separate your work and personal contacts, or separate Microsoft SharePoint contacts from your other contacts. Alternatively, you might add folder groups to organize the calendars for people from other departments.

Creating a folder group is easy. Open the folder where you want to add the group (such as the Calendar folder), right-click an existing folder group (such as My Calendars), and choose New *<Folder>* Group, where *<Folder>* is the folder type, such as Calendar. Outlook adds a new group with the name *New Group* and highlights the name so you can type a new one. Type the desired name for the group and press Enter.

Adding Folders to a Group

At this point, you can move folders easily from one group to another. Just click and drag a folder and place it on the group name. If the group already contains folders, you can drag the folder into the group and position it as you like. Figure 29-7 shows a couple of examples of folder groups being used to organize folders in the Navigation pane.

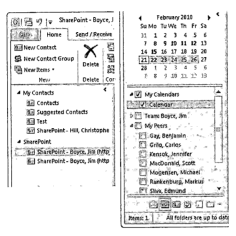

Figure 29-7 These folder groups are used to organize contact and calendar folders.

With one exception, Outlook folder groups let you organize the folders that are already a part of your Outlook data store. For example, you can't create contact folders on the fly to add to a contact folder group. Instead, you create the folder and then add it to the folder group.

The exception is calendar folders. When you work with a calendar folder group, you can add calendars from the Address Book (for other Exchange Server mailbox users), a room list (also for Exchange Server), or shared calendars (from the Internet or a calendar-sharing service). This makes it possible to group together calendars from multiple sources into one calendar group.

> **Tip**
> You can't modify the Team calendar group. It is built automatically from the Direct Reports list in AD DS.

To add a calendar to a calendar group, right-click the group to which you want to add the calendar and choose Add Calendar, followed by the location from which you want to add the calendar. For example, choose From Address Book to add one or more calendars of other Exchange Server users. Alternatively, choose Room List to add one or more calendars from the Exchange Server room list. After you add the calendar, it will show up in the group, as shown in Figure 29-7.

Remove Folders from a Group

Sooner or later, you'll want to remove a folder from a folder group, and this is a key difference to remember from the Favorites email folder list—when you delete a folder from a non-mail folder group, you delete the folder and its contents. For example, if you delete a contact folder, all the contacts in the folder, as well as the folder itself, are deleted. Outlook will prompt you to approve the deletion, and then it will place the items in the Deleted Items folder. You can recover them from there if necessary (until you clean out the folder, of course).

Renaming a Folder

Sometimes you need to change a folder's name, perhaps as a result of project modifications or a company name change. Unfortunately, you can't rename the default folders created by Outlook 2010. You can, however, change the names of folders that you create. To rename a folder, begin by performing one of these actions:

- Click the folder to select it, click the Folder tab on the ribbon, and click Rename Folder.

- Open the Folder List, right-click the folder, and then choose Rename.

- Select the folder, and then click the folder name to highlight it.

After taking one of these actions, simply type the new name and then press Enter to have the change take effect.

Another way to change a folder's name is through its Properties dialog box, as shown in Figure 29-8, which you can display by right-clicking the folder in the Folder List and choosing Properties. On the General tab, type a new name in the top box. Click OK to save the name and to return to the Folder List.

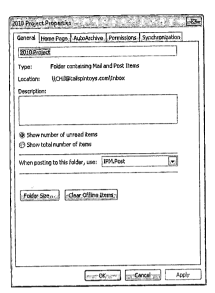

Figure 29-8 You can change a folder's name in its Properties dialog box.

> **Note**
> When you change a folder's name, shortcuts to the folder in the Navigation pane are updated to reflect the change.

Copying and Moving a Folder

Occasionally, you might need to move or copy a folder from one location to another. For example, suppose that you've created some message folders in your Inbox to organize messages, but now you want to move those folders to a folder other than the Inbox. Or maybe you want to copy the Contacts folder from your Exchange Server mailbox to a set of personal folders.

Moving or copying folders is easy. Open the Folder List, right-click the folder that you want to move or copy, and choose either Move or Copy from the shortcut menu. Outlook 2010 displays a Move Folder dialog box, as shown in Figure 29-9, or a Copy Folder dialog box. Select the folder in which you want to store the moved or copied folder and click OK, or choose New to create a new folder in which to store the moved or copied folder.

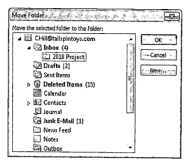

Figure 29-9 To move a folder, select its new location in the Move Folder dialog box.

Another way to move a folder is to drag it to a new location. You can copy a folder using a similar technique—just hold down the Ctrl key while dragging.

You can move one type of folder so that it becomes a subfolder of another type of folder. For example, suppose that you receive email messages containing contact information. You can store these messages in a folder named, say, Contact Info. You then can store the Contact Info folder as a subfolder of Contacts. The type of data that you can store in the subfolder is the type you originally established for that folder. (For example, when a mail-type folder becomes a subfolder of a contacts-type folder, neither folder changes its type.)

If you want to move or copy a folder to the root of the folder store, move or copy the folder to the topmost folder in the list (indicated in the Navigation pane by the email address for your account).

Deleting a Folder

You can delete an Outlook 2010 folder in the same way that you delete a folder in Windows Explorer or My Computer. When you delete an Outlook 2010 folder, it's removed from the Folder List and placed in the Deleted Items folder. This way, if you decide you want the folder back, you can retrieve it from the Deleted Items folder.

When you delete a folder, you delete the contents of the folder as well. The contents move with the folder to the Deleted Items folder and can be retrieved along with the folder later. (The items can be retrieved only until the Deleted Items folder is emptied.) You also can retrieve individual items from the Deleted Items folder, even if those items were deleted as part of a folder deletion. For example, if you delete a message folder named Project Alpha containing three messages, you can retrieve one, two, or all three messages individually without retrieving the Project Alpha folder. To retrieve a folder from the Deleted Items folder, click Deleted Items and then select the folder to retrieve. Move that folder from the Deleted Items folder to its original location or to another location.

Although you can't delete any of the default folders (the folders that Outlook 2010 provides), you can delete folders that you've added.

To do so, follow these steps:

1. Make sure that the folder doesn't contain any data that you need to keep or any data that you have not archived or backed up.

2. Open the Folder List, right-click the folder, and then choose Delete.

3. Click Yes to confirm the deletion or No to cancel.

INSIDE OUT   Delete items matching a specific date automatically

Outlook 2010 can remove items in a folder that match a specified date automatically. If Outlook 2010 is configured to empty the Deleted Items folder on a certain date or whenever you quit the program, however, you might lose important items that you accidentally or prematurely sent to that folder. To see the deletion date of a folder, right-click the folder, and then choose Properties. On the AutoArchive tab, if the Archive This Folder Using These Settings option is selected, look to see whether the Permanently Delete Old Items option is also selected. If it is, the time in the Clean Out Old Items Older Than option specifies how much time you have to retrieve an item from that folder. Don't assume that the folder you deleted last year will still be around today.

Setting Folder Properties

Folders have several properties that control the way they appear and function, as well as others that control archiving, administration, and other activities. To view or set these properties, click the Folder tab on the ribbon and then click Folder Properties; or open the Folder List, right-click the folder, and then choose Properties to open a Properties dialog box for the folder. The following sections explain the options on each of the tabs in the Properties dialog box.

Configuring General Folder Properties

You can use the General tab, shown in Figure 29-10, to locate information about a folder, name the folder, add a descriptive comment, and set other properties.

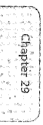

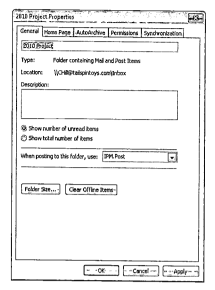

Figure 29-10 Use the General tab of a folder's Properties dialog box to view information about the folder and set a few general properties.

The options on the General tab are described in the following list:

- **Name** In the top box, specify the name for the folder as you want it to appear in Outlook 2010.

- **Type** This read-only property specifies the type of content that the folder contains.

- **Location** This read-only property specifies the location in the folder hierarchy for the selected folder.

- **Description** Use this box to type a description of the folder if you want. The description appears only in the folder's Properties dialog box.

- **Show Number Of Unread Items** Use this option with message folders to cause Outlook 2010 to display, in the Folder List and the Favorites list, the number of unread messages in the folder. Outlook 2010 displays the folder name in bold if the item contains unread messages and includes the number of unread items in parentheses to the right of the folder name.

- **Show Total Number Of Items** Use this option with all folder types to show the total number of items in the folder. Outlook 2010 shows the folder name in bold if it contains unread items and displays the total number of items to the right of the folder name. This option can be particularly useful with search folders to show the total number of items that match the search folder's criteria.

- **When Posting To This Folder, Use**   This drop-down list includes two selections. One is the default type of item that you can store in the folder, such as Contacts for a contacts folder. The other is Forms. If you select Forms from the list, Outlook 2010 opens the Choose Form dialog box, shown in Figure 29-11. Here, you can select the form that the folder should use for new items added to the folder. For example, you might want to use a custom appointment form for a calendar folder.

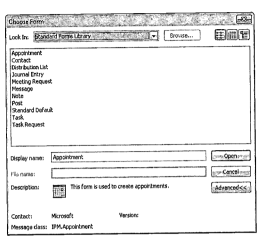

Figure 29-11 Specify the type of form to be used by the folder.

- **Folder Size**   Click this button to view information about the amount of space a folder and its subfolders use.

- **Clear Offline Items**   This button removes all items from your offline store.

TROUBLESHOOTING

Assigning a form to a folder fails

The option to select Forms in the When Posting To This Folder, Use drop-down list enables you to select a custom-designed form (of the correct type) to control entry of items into the folder. There is a constraint, however—what you select when you choose Forms and then select a form type from the Standard Forms Library or Personal Forms Library has to match the object type of the folder. If you create a new mail folder, for example, the form selected has to also be of the IPM.Post type. Likewise, if you create a calendar folder, the form selected has to be of the IPM.Appointment type. If the type doesn't match, you get an error message stating, "You cannot create an item of this type in this folder."

Configuring Home Page Properties for a Folder

The Home Page tab lets you assign a web page as the default home page for a folder, as shown in Figure 29-12. The Restore Defaults button resets the selections on the tab to the default values. Once a web page is assigned, however, the Offline Web Page Settings button is enabled, to check for updates and download the selected pages for offline viewing.

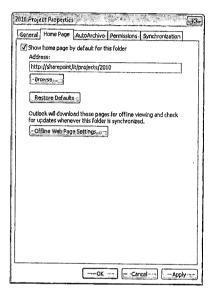

Figure 29-12 You can specify a web page to be used as a default home page by the folder.

Configuring AutoArchive Properties for a Folder

The AutoArchive feature of Outlook automatically archives items after a specified period, which can help you avoid having folders cluttered with old messages, tasks, and so on. You configure archival properties on the AutoArchive tab of a folder's Properties dialog box. For details, see the section "Configuring Automatic Archiving," on page 767.

Configuring Permissions for a Folder

You can control access to folders in Outlook 2010 by selecting the Permissions tab and specifying the users who will be granted access and the type of access they will be granted. The default permissions provide full control to the owner of the folder, as shown in Figure 29-13, and assign no permissions to access or modify content to the Default and Anonymous groups. To add users to the Permissions list, click Add, and then select the user to include in the list. Once a user has been added, select the user, and use the drop-down list next to Permission Level to set the general permission level (Owner, Publishing Editor, Editor, Publishing Author, Author, Non-Editing Author, Reviewer, Contributor, or None). You can refine the permission level further by selecting options in the Read, Write, Delete Items, and Other areas.

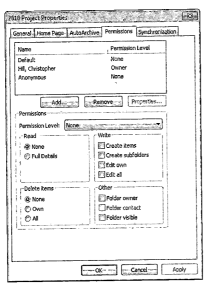

Figure 29-13 To control access to a folder, set permission levels for users accessing the folder.

Configuring Synchronization Properties for a Folder

The Synchronization tab lets you filter the content that is synchronized with a folder. To establish a filter, click Filter, and in the Filter dialog box, shown in Figure 29-14, configure the criteria that you want the filter to use when downloading new items. The Filter dialog box simply sets the filter criteria; it does not perform the synchronization. To synchronize folder content, click Send/Receive All Folders on the Send/Receive tab on the ribbon.

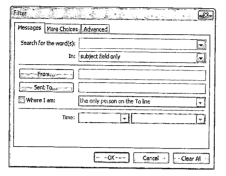

Figure 29-14 Set the criteria to filter the content that is downloaded when the folder is synchronized with the server.

Configuring Properties for a Contacts Folder

The Contacts folder has additional properties that you can control. When configuring properties for a Contacts folder, you can set the following address book options on the Outlook Address Book tab:

- **Show This Folder As An E-Mail Address Book**   Select this option to have Outlook 2010 display contacts in a way that lets you select email addresses from the Address Book dialog box. (This is selected automatically for the default Contacts folder.)

- **Name Of The Address Book**   Specify the address book name.

Using Home Pages with Folders

There is no question that the Internet is pervasive, and you probably spend at least some portion of your day either on public websites or in your company intranet or SharePoint sites. This section describes how you can access the Internet by specifying a web page as a home page for a folder.

Why Use Home Pages?

When you assign a web page as a home page for a folder, you make it convenient and easy to access intranet or Internet resources. The primary reason to use a web view in a folder is to access a website or an intranet resource without leaving Outlook 2010. As shown in Figure 29-15, you can open a folder that includes a web page as a home page and then access another page from there. You no longer have to start a separate web browser, such as Windows Internet Explorer, to open the web page.

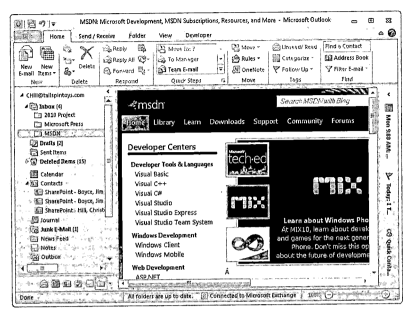

Figure 29-15 You can view a web page without leaving Outlook 2010.

> **Tip**
>
> Assigning a website to a folder isn't the only way to view web content from inside Outlook 2010. You can also add web shortcuts to the Shortcuts list. The site shows up within Outlook in the same way as shown in Figure 29-15.

Accessing websites from within Outlook might seem like an odd thing to you at first, but it can actually be a very useful feature. For example, assume that, like many office workers, you spend 60 percent or more of your day working in Outlook, but you also spend a lot of time in one or more SharePoint sites. Rather than leave Outlook, open Internet Explorer, and browse the SharePoint site outside Outlook, you can instead integrate your most frequently used SharePoint sites in Outlook, either through shortcuts or by setting a folder path. What's more, the capability to add websites in Outlook can help you organize the information you access on a regular basis, making it possible to access documents, shared contacts and calendars, and all your email and other Outlook items—all from a single program.

The one potential downside to viewing websites in Outlook is that you have no browser menu when viewing the site. This means that you can't resize the site in the Outlook window if it is too small or too large to fit well. If you start out with enough desktop space, however, you'll likely have no problems viewing sites in Outlook.

> **Tip**
>
> Some SharePoint lists can be integrated in Outlook in other ways. For example, you can connect shared calendars to Outlook so that they appear in your Calendar folder and can be overlaid with your other calendars (or even other SharePoint calendars). For more details on integrating SharePoint and Outlook, see Chapter 38, "Collaboration with Outlook and SharePoint."

Assigning a Web Page to a Folder

You can assign a web page to any folder in your Folder List.

To assign a web page, follow these steps:

1. Right-click a folder in the Folder List, and then choose Properties.

2. Click the Home Page tab, as shown in Figure 29-16.

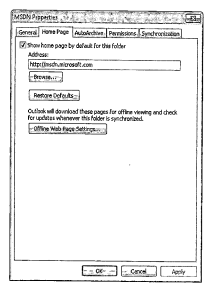

Figure 29-16 Specify a web page view for a folder using the Properties dialog box.

3. Set web page view properties as necessary, using the following options:

- **Show Home Page By Default For This Folder**   Select this check box if you want Outlook 2010 to display the web page rather than the existing default folder view.

- **Address**   Specify the Uniform Resource Locator (URL) of a local or remote Hypertext Markup Language (HTML) page or another Internet resource, such as a File Transfer Protocol (FTP) site. In this example, the following URL for the MSDN website is specified: *http://msdn.microsoft.com*.

- **Browse**   Click to browse for a URL.

- **Restore Defaults**   Click to restore the default settings (no web page).

4. For the folder that you want to assign a web page to, type the URL (Internet or local address) for the web page that you want to display. You also can click Browse and then select a web page in the Find Web Files dialog box. Click OK after selecting a page to return to the Home Page tab.

5. Click OK.

Removing a Web Page from a Folder

After a while, you might tire of using a web view in a folder, or the web page might become obsolete. At that point, you'll want to get rid of it.

To remove a web page from a folder, follow these steps:

1. Right-click the folder in the Folder List, and then choose Properties.

2. Click the Home Page tab.

3. Clear the Show Home Page By Default For This Folder check box.

4. Click OK.

Using a Folder's Home Page

Each time that you open a folder with a home page view, Outlook 2010 displays the specified web page according to the Home Page options you selected. If the web page includes hyperlinks, you can click them to navigate to other pages or sites.

> ## INSIDE OUT Create shortcuts to web pages
>
> You can create shortcuts to web pages by clicking the Shortcuts icon at the bottom of the Navigation pane to open the Shortcut pane and then dragging a URL link (from Internet Explorer or another browser) to the Shortcut pane. An alternative to creating shortcuts is to create Outlook 2010 folders and then assign them a home page. This method has the advantage of making the pages available from the Folder List—just click the folder in the Folder List to navigate to the associated web page or FTP folder.

Using Multiple Personal Folders

If you don't use Outlook 2010 with Exchange Server, you use personal folders for storing your Outlook 2010 information and data. Your Outlook data items are stored in a local .pst file. (With Exchange Server, your messages, calendar, and other items are stored centrally on the server, although you can use .pst files in conjunction with an Exchange Server account.)

You can create multiple personal folders to help you organize your data. For example, you can store email messages associated with a project or a client in one folder and store other messages and items in a more general folder. Another useful way to set up multiple .pst files is to use one for archiving. This can help you back up your data more consistently, and Outlook 2010 can prompt you at different intervals to ensure that your archive is up to date.

> **Note**
> As Outlook 2010 copies items to the archive file, it removes them from their original location. As a result, the archiving of Outlook 2010 items is essentially a "move" process.

You can also use a .pst file to share information with other users on your network. The users must have read/write permissions to open the file.

After you create a .pst file, it appears in the Folder List automatically. You can add it to a Shortcuts group in the Navigation pane just as you can with any other folders. You then can access the .pst file simply by clicking its shortcut.

For information about adding a folder shortcut, see the section "Adding a Folder Shortcut to the Navigation Pane," on page 739.

Adding a Personal Folder

A personal folder can have any name you give it. By default, the names take the form My Outlook Data File(1).pst, My Outlook Data File(2).pst, and so on. At the top of the Folder List, you can see the name of the active personal folder, which by default shows your email address as the name.

To add a personal folder, follow these steps:

1. Click File, Account Settings, and Account Settings, click the Data Files tab, and then click Add to open the New Outlook Data File dialog box.

2. Select Outlook Data File if you will not be using the .pst file with an earlier version of Outlook. Choose Outlook 97-2002 Data File if you need to use the .pst file with an earlier version of Outlook.

3. Click OK. The Create Or Open Outlook Data File dialog box appears as shown in Figure 29-17.

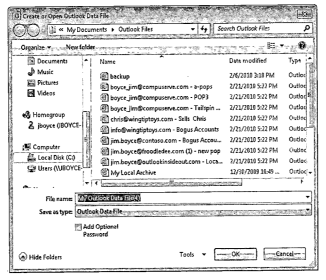

Figure 29-17 Use the Create or Open Outlook Data File dialog box to create a new .pst file.

4. In the File Name box, type a name for the new personal folders file. This is the name that will appear in the Navigation pane.

5. If you want to protect your .pst file further, place a check in the Add Optional Password check box.

6. Click OK.

7. If you chose the option to password-protect the file, Outlook prompts for a password. Enter and confirm the password in the resulting dialog box and click OK.

> **Note**
>
> **If you want to limit who can access your .pst file, you should not save your Outlook 2010 password in the password list.**

8. The new personal folders item appears in the Data Files list. Click Close in the Account Settings dialog box, and the new personal folder (named in step 4) is accessible in the Folder List.

Removing a Personal Folder

If you no longer need a set of personal folders (contained in a .pst file), you can remove the file from your Outlook profile. Removing a set of personal folders from your profile does not delete the .pst file—it remains intact, and you can add it back to the profile or add it to a different profile, if needed.

When you are ready to remove a .pst file, follow these steps to remove it:

1. In the Navigation pane, right-click the set of folders that you want to remove.

2. Choose Close.

Managing Data

As you use Outlook 2010, you'll find that folders will become full of messages, appointments, and other items. One way to manage this data is to copy or move it to other folders so that the data is organized according to how you work. In addition, you need to make sure that your data is backed up and archived properly in case you accidentally delete data or a system failure occurs.

In this section, you'll learn how to copy and move data to folders.

Copying and Moving Data to Other Folders

Occasionally, you might need to move or copy data from one location to another. For example, perhaps you've received an email message from a client connected with a project that you're managing. Instead of keeping that message in the Inbox folder, where it might get lost with all the other messages that you receive every day, you can move it to a folder devoted to that particular project.

To move data to another folder, follow these steps:

1. Select the Outlook item that you want to move.

2. In the Home tab on the ribbon, click Move, Other Folder to open the Move Items dialog box, shown in Figure 29-18.

> **Tip**
>
> Press Ctrl+Z if you need to move the item back to its original location. This command is effective only immediately after you've performed the move, before you do anything else.

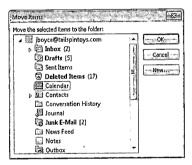

Figure 29-18 Use the Move Items dialog box to move data to a different location.

3. Select an existing folder, or click New to create a folder in which to store the moved data.

4. Click OK. The data is moved to the selected location.

Another way to move data is to select it in the folder and drag it to a new location. Similarly, you can copy data by holding down the Ctrl key while you drag. Alternatively, you can right-click an item, drag it to a new location, and then release the right mouse button and select either Move or Copy.

Storing Items in the Root of Your Mail Store

If you move an item to the root of the mail store by choosing the top branch in the Folder List (indicated by the email address of the account), Outlook 2010 dutifully moves the item to the root of your mail store. If the destination was a secondary set of personal folders, you can view the items simply by clicking the top branch in the Folder List.

However, Outlook 2010 displays the Outlook Today view when you click the top branch in the Folder List, effectively hiding any items stored there. You can perform a search to locate and display the items, but an easier method is to simply turn off the Outlook Today view temporarily (or permanently, if you never use it).

To do this, in the Navigation pane, right-click the root of your mail store and choose Data File Properties. Click the Home Page tab, clear the Show Home Page By Default For This Folder check box, and then click OK. You can now view and work with the items that are located in the root of your mail store. To restore the Outlook Today view, select the Show Home Page By Default For This Folder check box.

> **Note**
> An Outlook data file is essentially a type of database file, and as items are removed, the space that they use is not necessarily reclaimed. To reduce the file size, you must use the Compact command. To do this, click File, Account Settings, and Account Settings, click the Data Files tab, and then select your .pst file. Choose Settings, and then click Compact Now in the Outlook Data File dialog box. (Outlook also automatically compacts the file periodically.)

Archiving, Backing Up, and Restoring Outlook Data

O VER time, your Microsoft Outlook 2010 data store can become overloaded with messages, contact information, appointments, and other data. If you can't manage all this data, you'll be lost each time you try to find a particular item. What's more, the more data in your data store, the larger your .pst file (if you're using one) or your Microsoft Exchange Server mailbox. Many companies impose mailbox size limits to help manage disk use on the servers, so the size of your mailbox can become a problem.

This chapter focuses on managing your Outlook 2010 folders and their contents. You'll learn how to archive your data, both manually and automatically, using AutoArchive. You'll also learn how to back up your data and recover it when needed.

Archiving Your Outlook Data

Sooner or later, you will likely want to move some of your Outlook 2010 items to a separate location because you no longer need them but don't want to delete them. For example, perhaps you want to keep copies of all the messages in your Sent Items folder so that you can refer to them later if needed, but you don't want them to stay in Sent Items. In these situations, you can use the Outlook 2010 AutoArchive feature to move out those old items.

The Outlook 2010 AutoArchive feature archives data automatically according to settings that you configure for each folder or all your folders. There is no right or wrong timeframe for AutoArchive; for some people, a month is appropriate, and for others, weekly. It's mainly a factor of how much email you send and receive, although the other items in your mailbox also contribute to the overall space used. For example, because of the volume of email I receive in my "day job" mailbox, I have to archive about twice a month or run afoul of my 200 MB mailbox limit.

> # Tip
>
> If your company uses Exchange Server, a better solution to users archiving their
> mailbox to a local .pst (which has negative security and backup implications) is to
> use a server-side archiving solution. Exchange Server 2010 includes an online archive
> option, which moves messages to a user's archive mailbox on the server based on
> retention criteria that you set. Or, you can choose a solution such as those from Barra-
> cuda, Mimosa Systems, GFI, and others. These archiving solutions not only help users
> keep their mailboxes trimmed down, but also can eliminate duplicate attachments,
> reduce storage requirements for Exchange Server, and facilitate discovery.

To set up a folder to archive automatically using the default AutoArchive settings, follow
these steps:

1. Right-click a folder in the Folder List, choose Properties, and then, in the Properties
   dialog box, click the AutoArchive tab.

2. Select Archive Items In This Folder Using The Default Settings, as shown in Figure
   30-1.

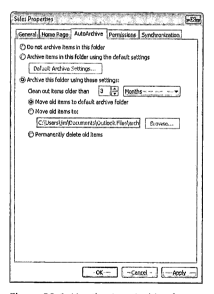

Figure 30-1 Use the AutoArchive feature to archive the data in your folders.

3. Click OK.

4. Repeat these steps for each folder that you want to archive.

By default, Outlook 2010 starts AutoArchive every 14 days and archives your data in the selected folder to the Archive.pst personal folders file.

 For information about changing the default AutoArchive settings, see the section "Configuring Automatic Archiving," on page 765.

You can also specify custom AutoArchive settings for a folder. Open the Properties dialog box for the folder, click the AutoArchive tab, and then select the Archive This Folder Using These Settings option. Then specify settings on the AutoArchive tab as desired for the folder. See the section "Configuring Automatic Archiving," on page 765, for details about each of the available settings.

From this point on, the folder for which you have enabled automatic archiving will be archived when Outlook 2010 performs its next automatic archive operation. However, you can also initiate an archive operation any time you need. The next section explains how.

Archiving Your Data Manually

You can archive data not only automatically but also manually—for example, before leaving on vacation, when your mailbox reaches its storage limit, or when you need to move your files to a new machine.

To archive data manually, perform these steps:

1. Choose File, Cleanup Tools, and finally Archive.

In the Archive dialog box, shown in Figure 30-2, select one of the following options:

- **Archive All Folders According To Their AutoArchive Settings** Use this option to archive all folders using preset AutoArchive settings. When you select this option, the remaining options in this dialog box become unavailable. Go to step 7.

- **Archive This Folder And All Subfolders** Select this option if you want to archive individual folders and their subfolders. Go to step 3.

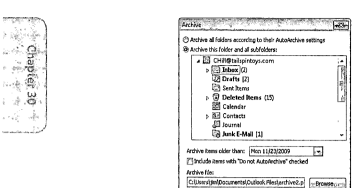

Figure 30-2 Select the way that you want to archive data in all or selected folders.

2. Select the folder you want to archive. If the folder includes subfolders, those folders are archived as well.

3. In the Archive Items Older Than drop-down list, specify the latest date from which Outlook 2010 should start archiving data. For instance, if you want to archive data older than today's date, select that date. Otherwise, all your data in the selected folder will not be archived.

4. If you have specified that a folder should not be archived automatically but you want to archive this folder now, select the Include Items With "Do Not AutoArchive" Checked check box.

5. To change the personal folders file that will store your archive, click Browse, and then specify the file and folder where the archive will be stored. You also can type the path and file name in the Archive File box if you know this information.

6. Click OK.

Outlook 2010 begins archiving your data. If the folder contains a large amount of data, archiving might take several minutes (or longer, depending on the speed of your computer, network connection, and other factors). You can watch the status of the archiving by looking at the Outlook 2010 status bar. When the process has finished, the Archive.pst file (or whichever archive file that you specified in step 6) will contain the data that Outlook 2010 just archived.

Restoring Data After a System Failure or a Reinstallation

Suppose that you've worked on a project for six months and you've been diligent about archiving messages and other items from the project. You come into work one day and find that your system has failed and Outlook 2010 has lost all your data. You need the archived data to get back all your lost information and continue working. How do you get it back?

You can restore data from an archive file in two ways: drag items from a .pst file to a folder, or import a .pst file.

Follow these steps to drag data from a .pst file:

1. After restoring your computer and, if necessary, reinstalling Outlook 2010, choose File, Open, and Open Outlook Data File to open the Open Outlook Data File dialog box, shown in Figure 30-3.

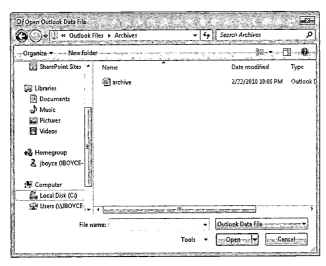

Figure 30-3 Select the .pst file that contains the data you want to restore.

2. Select the file that contains the archived items that you want to restore.

3. Click OK. The archive folder (named Archives by default) now appears in your folder list.

4. Click the plus sign (+) next to Archives (or the name you've given this folder) to expand the folder. Expand subsequent folders if necessary until your data is in the pane on the right.

5. Drag the folder or item to the original folder in which the data was stored.

6. Continue dragging items until all of them are restored. To drag multiple items at one time, hold down the Ctrl key, select the items, and then drag them to the destination.

To restore items by importing a .pst file, follow these steps:

1. Choose File, Open, and Import to open the Import And Export Wizard.

2. Select Import From Another Program Or File, and then click Next.

3. Select Personal Folder File (.pst), and then click Next.

4. On the Import Outlook Data File page, shown in Figure 30-4, type the name of the file that you want to import in the File To Import box, or click Browse to locate the file using the Open Personal Folders dialog box.

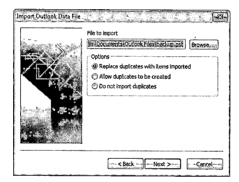

Figure 30-4 On the Import Outlook Data File page, specify the name of the file that you want to import.

5. Select one of the following import options pertaining to duplicate data:

- **Replace Duplicates With Items Imported**   Replaces duplicate items that might be in your folders during import.

- **Allow Duplicates To Be Created**   Lets Outlook 2010 create duplicates in the destination folders.

- **Do Not Import Duplicates**   Outlook 2010 will not create duplicate items.

6. Click Next.

7. Select the folder from which you want to import data.

8. If the archived folder includes subfolders that you want to import as well, select the Include Subfolders option.

9. To filter data, click Filter. You can filter by using search strings, Structured Query Language (SQL), and other advanced querying methods. Click OK after filling in your filter information.

10. Select one of the following destination options:

    - **Import Items Into The Current Folder**   Select this option to import data into the current folder—that is, the folder currently selected.

    - **Import Items Into The Same Folder In**   Choose this option to import data into the destination folder of the same name as the source folder (such as from the Inbox to the Inbox). Then, in the drop-down list under this last option, select the destination personal folders or mailbox.

11. Click Finish.

Outlook 2010 displays a window showing you the progress of the import process. The archive folder appears in the folder list (if the folder list is open), but it is removed when the operation is completed.

Configuring Automatic Archiving

Outlook 2010 provides several ways to configure and manage your data-archiving settings. For example, suppose that you want Outlook 2010 to run AutoArchive every day, but you want to be prompted before it starts. You can configure AutoArchive to do just that. In addition, you might want to delete old items after a specific date (say, after a message sits in the Inbox for six months). This section shows you how to configure AutoArchive to handle many of your archiving needs.

To set AutoArchive options, click File, Options, and Advanced, and then click AutoArchive Settings to open the AutoArchive dialog box. The following sections explain the options that you'll find in the AutoArchive dialog box.

Run AutoArchive Every *n* Days

Outlook 2010 allows you to run AutoArchive on a per-day cycle. For example, if you want to run it each day, set it to run every 1 day. To archive every other day, set AutoArchive to run every 2 days, and so on.

> **Note**
>
> Outlook 2010 has different aging periods for different types of items. Calendar, Notes, Journal, Drafts, and Inbox folders have a default of six months. The default for the Outbox folder is three months, and Sent Items and Deleted Items are two months. Contacts folders do not have an AutoArchive option, so you must archive them manually.

To set the length of time between AutoArchive sessions, set the Run AutoArchive Every *n* Days option to the number of days you want between archiving sessions, as shown in Figure 30-5. The number that you enter must be between 1 and 60.

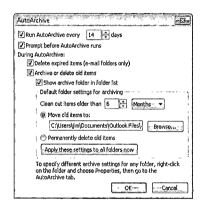

Figure 30-5 Set up Outlook 2010 to run AutoArchive at specified intervals.

Prompt Before AutoArchive Runs

You can have Outlook 2010 display a message before it starts an AutoArchive session. The message includes a Cancel button to let you cancel the AutoArchive session for that day.

To activate this option, select the Prompt Before AutoArchive Runs check box in the AutoArchive dialog box.

Delete Expired Items

In your message folders, AutoArchive can delete messages if they are older than a specified amount of time. To set this option, select the Delete Expired Items check box. Also make sure that the Archive Or Delete Old Items check box is selected.

In the Default Folder Settings For Archiving area, set the amount of time that you want to elapse before AutoArchive automatically deletes email messages. The default is six months, but you can set this to as high as 60 months or as low as one day.

Archive Or Delete Old Items

If you want AutoArchive to archive or delete old Outlook 2010 items, select the Archive Or Delete Old Items check box. Then set the amount of time that should elapse before old items are archived or deleted. Again, the default is six months, but you can set this to as high as 60 months or as low as one day.

> **Tip**
>
> Archiving is based on an item's modified date, not the received date. For example, assume that you have an Outlook add-in that saves your attachments automatically to disk. When the add-in moves the attachment, it causes the Outlook item to be modified. If you run the add-in today on a message that you received a week ago, and then tell Outlook to archive items older than yesterday, that item will not be archived because it was modified today by the add-in.

Show Archive Folder In Folder List

If you want Outlook 2010 to display your archive folder in the Folder List, select the Show Archive Folder In Folder List check box. You might want to select this check box if you think you'd like to be able to see which items have been archived. Also, you might find that some items are removed from your working folders (such as Inbox or Calendar) before you want them removed. By showing the archive folder in the Folder List, you can move items back to a working folder quickly and easily.

Specifying How Archived Items Are Handled

In the Default Folder Settings For Archiving area, you can specify the number of days, weeks, or months that should elapse before email messages or other items are archived or deleted (as described in the preceding two sections).

In addition, this area includes options for the way old items are handled. With the Move Old Items To option, you can specify a .pst file to which Outlook 2010 should move archived items. Click Browse to identify a different location and the .pst file in which you want to store archives.

On the other hand, if you want to delete archived items, select Permanently Delete Old Items, and Outlook 2010 will delete items during the AutoArchive sessions. This option is probably not a good choice if you want to retain information for long periods of time.

Applying Settings to All Folders

If you want these AutoArchive settings to apply to all your folders, click Apply These Settings To All Folders Now. Any settings you establish for individual folders (see the next section) are not overridden by the default settings in the AutoArchive dialog box.

Using AutoArchive Settings for Individual Folders

When you configure AutoArchive settings, you can use the default settings just described, or you can specify options for individual folders.

To take the latter approach, open the Properties dialog box for the folder, click the Auto-Archive tab, and then click Archive This Folder Using These Settings. Then set the following options:

- **Do Not Archive Items In This Folder**   Specify that the current folder should not be archived.

- **Archive This Folder Using These Settings**   Direct Outlook 2010 to archive items in the folder based on the custom settings that you specify.

- **Clean Out Items Older Than** n   This option lets you specify the number of days, weeks, or months that should pass before AutoArchive removes items in the selected folder.

- **Move Old Items To Default Archive Folder**   You can have Outlook 2010 move old items to the folder specified for default AutoArchive settings.

- **Move Old Items To**   This option lets you specify a .pst file in which to archive old items. Click Browse to locate a file.

- **Permanently Delete Old Items**   You can direct Outlook 2010 to delete items in this folder during archiving.

Setting Retention Policy

Your system administrator might enforce company retention policies for your mailbox. If you are running Outlook 2010 with Exchange Server, your administrator can set retention polices that you can't override with AutoArchive settings. For example, your company might require that all email messages be saved and archived to backup tapes or disks and then retained for seven years. As much as you try, you can't change these settings without having the appropriate permissions.

Backing Up and Restoring Data

An important part of working with a computer system is ensuring that you protect any critical data against loss. You protect your data by making a *backup*, a copy of the information that you can store on another disk or on a backup tape. In the event of a critical failure, you can then use this copy to replace or restore any lost information.

Outlook 2010 stores information in two primary ways: in a set of personal folders or in an Exchange Server mailbox. With an Exchange Server mailbox, your message store is located on the server. The network administrator is generally responsible for backing up the server, and with it, the Exchange Server database that contains all the users' information.

If you don't use Exchange Server, Outlook 2010 stores your data in a .pst file, a set of personal folders. In this scenario, each user has his or her own .pst file or even multiple personal folder files. These .pst files can be located either on the local hard disk of your computer or in a home directory on the server. Although server-based .pst files and local .pst files are identical from a functional standpoint, they aren't identical from a backup perspective. Generally, the network administrator regularly backs up server-based user home directories, so if the .pst files are in your home directory, you shouldn't have to do backups on your own (although you can, of course).

With local message stores, however, normal network backup strategies do not apply. Most networks don't back up every hard disk on every machine. It simply isn't efficient. Similarly, if you're a home user, you probably don't have a server to which you can save data or a network administrator to watch over the server. In such cases, you need to take steps on your own to protect your data. Individual backup and restore scenarios apply to these kinds of cases.

Backing Up Your Outlook Data

Three primary options are available for backing up Outlook 2010 data:

- Exporting some or all information to a backup .pst file

- Copying the .pst file to another disk

- Using a backup program to save a copy of the .pst file to tape, another hard disk, or optical media such as CD-R/CD-RW or DVD-R/DVD-RW

Table 30-1 lists the features available in each backup option.

Table 30-1. Backup Options in Outlook 2010

Backup Type	Export	Copy	Backup
Complete backup	Yes	Yes	Yes
Partial backup	Yes	No	No
Automated backup	No	Yes	Yes

The following sections focus on the use of backup programs and .pst copies.

Backing Up Your Personal Folders

If you store your Outlook 2010 data in one or more sets of personal folders, the data resides in a .pst file. This file is usually located on your local hard disk, but it could also be stored on a shared network folder. The first step in backing up your personal folders is to determine where the .pst file is located.

If you are not sure whether you use an Exchange Server account, follow these steps to check your email settings:

1. Click the Mail icon in Control Panel.

2. In the Mail Setup dialog box, click Show Profiles, choose your profile, and then click Properties. Then click E-Mail Accounts to open the E-Mail Accounts dialog box.

If the E-Mail Accounts list includes only Exchange Server, your Outlook 2010 data is stored in your Exchange Server mailbox on the server, and your Exchange Server administrator handles backups. However, you can use the Export method described in the section "Exporting Data," on page 775, to back up your mailbox to a local .pst file. If the E-Mail Accounts list shows an Exchange Server account along with other accounts, look at the mail delivery location specified at the bottom of the dialog box. This area shows where incoming mail is delivered. If it specifies a mailbox, your incoming mail is delivered to your Exchange Server mailbox. If it references a set of personal folders, your incoming mail is stored in a .pst.

If the E-Mail Accounts list shows more than one email account, it's possible that your Outlook 2010 data is stored in more than one set of personal folders. For example, Internet Message Access Protocol (IMAP) and Hotmail accounts store their data in their own .pst files. If you want to back up everything in this situation, you need to back up multiple .pst files.

To determine whether you are using more than one .pst file, click the Data Files tab of the Account Settings dialog box, shown in Figure 30-6. The path name and file name for the .pst are generally long, so it's unlikely that you'll be able to read the full name. Click the vertical bar at the right of the Filename column and drag it to the right until you can view the entire path. Alternatively, simply click Open File Location, which opens the folder where the .pst file is stored and highlights the .pst file in the folder.

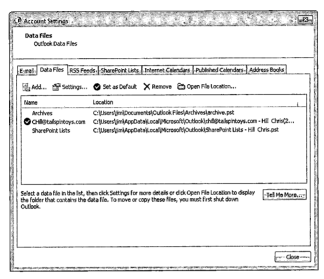

Figure 30-6 The Data Files tab of the Account Settings dialog box lists message stores in use.

After you have verified that the message store is not being backed up elsewhere and is stored in a .pst file, you need to choose which kind of backup to do. Both of the following methods work well, and each has its advantages. Back up each of the .pst files listed in the Data Files tab of the Account Settings dialog box using one of these methods.

Backing Up Using File Copy

Personal folders or archive files can be extremely large—often hundreds of megabytes—so you need to make sure that your backup method can accommodate the size of your .pst file(s). Any of the following options would be acceptable to use with a file backup method:

- Recordable (CD-R) or rewritable (CD-RW) CD drive

- Recordable (DVD-R) or rewritable (DVD-RW) DVD drive

- Flash drive or external universal serial bus (USB) drive

- Network server drive

- A drive on another computer on the network

- A separate hard disk in the machine where the .pst file is stored

INSIDE OUT   Check network backup policies

Be certain to check with your network administrator about the recommended policy for backing up .pst files in your organization. If, for example, .pst files are not allowed on your network because of resource allocation, you'll want to know this and choose another backup method rather than copying your .pst file to the network only to find it deleted the next week. Remember that whatever the merits of a particular backup method, it's critical that your IT staff support it.

If you are saving to a CD or DVD, you can probably use the software that was included with the drive to copy the file. If you're using a flash drive, USB drive, or a network location, simply drag the file to your chosen backup location. Make sure to exit Outlook 2010 before starting the backup copy process.

INSIDE OUT   Don't move the .pst file

When copying, be careful not to *move* the .pst file instead by accident. If you move it, you'll find that you have no message store when you restart Outlook 2010. If you do move your .pst file accidentally, you simply need to copy the file back to the correct location. To avoid this potential problem, automate the copy.

Backing Up Using the Microsoft Backup Utility

Microsoft Windows XP, Windows Vista, and Windows 7 all include a backup application. You can use these applications to identify files for archiving; they offer the following enhancements over a standard file copy:

- Allow simple setup of a backup plan by using wizards

- Have options for verifying the backup

- Have built-in restore and scheduling options

> **Note**
> If you have not used a backup utility in Windows before, take some time to scan through the program's Help content to learn about the program's ins and outs.

Restoring Your Data

Anyone who works with computers long enough will eventually experience a critical error. A drive will become corrupted, a virus will get through your virus software's protection, or you'll accidentally delete something that you need. This is the point when all the time and trouble you've invested in backing up your data will pay dividends.

Depending on how you created your backup file, you will have one of two options: You can simply recopy your backup .pst file from the backup location where you copied it, or you can run the backup utility and use the Restore tab to bring back the missing file or files. From there, you can select the backup file that contains the .pst file and then determine which files to restore and where to put them.

> **Note**
> By default, the backup utility restores a file to its original location. This is generally the best choice because if the .pst file isn't restored to the proper location, Outlook 2010 won't be able to find it.

Whichever method you use, be certain to check the drive carefully for errors and viruses before you restore your data. You don't want to restore the file, only to see it destroyed again a few hours later.

> **INSIDE OUT**   Familiarize yourself with the restore process
>
> It's important to be familiar with the restore process before a disaster recovery process is under way. You should occasionally try restoring your backed-up .pst file to another computer to verify that your backups work. This will help to ensure that the restore process will work and that you know how to perform the necessary tasks.

Using the Offline Folders Option

If you use an Exchange Server account and want to have a backup of your message store available locally, one possible option is to use offline folders. Offline folders allow you to access your message store when your computer is not connected to the server, such as when you're away from the office. To use offline folders, you must create an offline folder (.ost) file, which is stored on the local drive of your computer. If you configure the Exchange Server account to use Cached Exchange Mode, Outlook 2010 creates an .ost file for you automatically and stores your data in that .ost file.

In a sense, .ost files provide backup in reverse: Instead of saving data to a server to back it up, the offline process saves the information from the server to the workstation. Although offline folders don't offer a standard backup, an occasional synchronization to an offline store is an easy way to create a second copy of Outlook 2010 data. (With Cached Exchange Mode, Outlook 2010 always works from the .ost file and synchronizes with the Exchange Server mailbox automatically.) If the Exchange Server mailbox is lost, you need only start Outlook 2010 and choose to work offline to access the lost data. At that point, you can export the data to a .pst file to create a backup.

For more information about setting up and using offline folders, see the section "Working Offline with Outlook and Exchange Server," on page 974.

To be truly useful, your data needs to be portable. You need to be able to move it between applications. For example, maybe you want to copy all your contacts from Microsoft Outlook 2010 to Microsoft Excel 2010 or Microsoft Access 2010. Maybe you need to bring data from Excel 2010 into Outlook 2010. Whatever the case, your Outlook 2010 data is portable, thanks to the import and export features built into the program.

This chapter explains the features in Outlook 2010 that enable you to move data out of Outlook 2010 to other programs and to import data into Outlook 2010 from other programs.

Exporting Data

Sooner or later, you might want to make copies of part of or all the Outlook data store for use in other applications. You can do this by using the export process, in which you save information to a different .pst file or transform data for use in Microsoft Word 2010, Access 2010, or other programs. (The reverse process, importing data, is covered in the next section.)

The export process in Outlook 2010 is straightforward. It allows you to use a wizard to send copies of information from the Outlook 2010 message store. This section looks at three export options in some depth: exporting messages, exporting addresses, and exporting data to a file.

Exporting Outlook Data to a .pst File

You can copy messages and other items into a new or an existing set of personal folders. Unlike backing up, this option lets you choose which items you want to export and which you want to exclude. You can use this method whether your mail is stored in a Microsoft Exchange Server mailbox or in a set of personal folders.

You might already know how to use the AutoArchive feature to move messages out of your message store and into a long-term storage location in another .pst file. You can use the Import And Export Wizard to export messages to a file. Using the Import And Export Wizard to export messages works in a similar way to AutoArchive; the major difference is that when messages in the store are exported, they aren't removed; instead, they are copied, as they are during backup. Another key difference is that archiving is based on modification date of the item, while exporting does not by default consider modification date.

For information about using AutoArchive, see the section "Archiving Your Outlook Data," on page 759.

To export some of or all your Outlook 2010 data, follow these steps:

1. Choose File, Open, and Import to start the Import And Export Wizard, as shown in Figure 31-1.

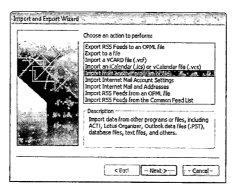

Figure 31-1 Use the Import And Export Wizard to export data to a file.

2. Select Export To A File, and then click Next.

3. The options available on the next wizard page break down into four basic types: text files, databases, spreadsheets, and a personal folders file. Figure 31-2 shows the formats available for exporting. Although you can export your messages in any of these formats, you'll probably find .pst files the most useful. For this example, select Outlook Data File (.pst), and then click Next.

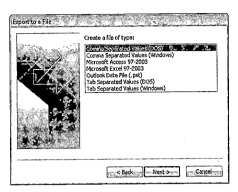

Figure 31-2 You can choose one of these file types for exporting.

4. On the Export Outlook Data File page, select the folder that you want to export. To include subfolders of the selected folder, select the Include Subfolders option. To export all your Outlook 2010 data, select the Mailbox or Personal Folders branch, and then select the Include Subfolders option.

> **Note**
>
> It isn't easy to export just a selection of folders. If you want to export only the Inbox and the Sent Items folders, for example, you must run the export twice: once for the Inbox and then again for Sent Items, specifying the same.pst location each time.

5. If you want to specify a filter, click Filter, and the Filter dialog box appears (see Figure 31-3). By using a filter, you can specify that only certain items be exported. This option could be useful, for example, if you need to send all correspondence with representatives of Wingtip Toys to a new sales representative who will be dealing with that firm. You could export the relevant messages to a .pst file that you could send to the new rep, who could then import them. After you've specified any needed filters, click OK to close the Filter dialog box and return to the wizard page, and then click Next.

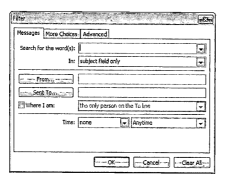

Figure 31-3 Use the Filter dialog box to export only those messages that fit certain criteria.

6. On the final wizard page, specify the location where you want to save exported information, and then specify how duplicate items should be handled. If no export file exists, specify the path and name of the file to be created. If an export file does exist, browse to the file you want to use. When you click Finish, the wizard creates the personal folders file (if it is new), runs the export, and then closes the file.

Exporting Addresses

You can also export address lists out of Outlook 2010 for use elsewhere. Exporting addresses is similar to exporting messages: you use the same Import And Export Wizard. The difference is that addresses are sometimes exported to a database or a spreadsheet to allow easier access to phone numbers, addresses, and other information.

To export the address list to Microsoft Access, for example, first start the Import And Export Wizard. As you work through the wizard, select Export To A File, and then select Microsoft Access. Select the Contacts folder, and then provide a name for the Access database that will be created for the exported addresses.

The primary difference between exporting to a personal folders file and exporting to a database lies in mapping out the fields for the database itself. From the wizard, you can click Map Custom Fields to open the Map Custom Fields dialog box, shown in Figure 31-4. Here, you can specify which fields in Outlook get mapped to fields in the database.

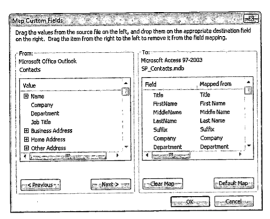

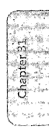

Figure 31-4 Use the Map Custom Fields dialog box to map fields for export into an Access database.

After you've finished the field mapping, click OK, and then click Finish to create the new database file and export the contact information into it.

> **Note**
>
> When you're exporting to a database, you don't have a filter option. Therefore, if you're exporting only certain records, you should create a subfolder to contain the contacts that you want to export. Copy the contacts to this new subfolder, export the subfolder, and then delete the duplicate contacts and the folder containing them.

Exporting Data to a File

Occasionally, data in .pst format simply isn't usable for a particular task. Outlook 2010 gives you a number of options for other export formats, such as Excel, Access, or various text file formats. For example, if you need to export information from Outlook 2010 into a third-party software package, or if you want to use the information in any capacity for which a direct export path is not available, your best option might be to export the needed information to a basic text file, either tab-delimited or comma-delimited. Figure 31-5 shows a text file that was exported from Outlook 2010.

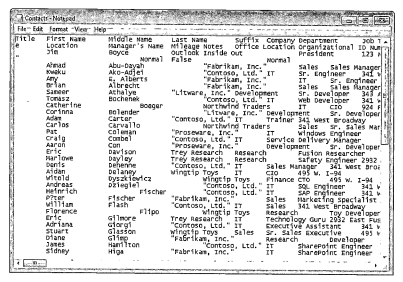

Figure 31-5 This contact information has been exported into a basic text file.

Exporting data to a text file is an easy process, as follows:

1. Choose File, Open, and Import.

2. Choose Export To A File, and then click Next.

3. To export to a comma-delimited file, select Comma Separated Values (Windows). To export to a tab-delimited file, select Tab Separated Values (Windows). Then click Next.

4. Specify a file name for the export file, and then click Next.

5. If you want to change the way fields are mapped, click Map Custom Fields (shown in Figure 31-4). When you have finished mapping fields, click OK, and then click Finish.

Importing Data

Data transfer is a two-way street, of course, and any discussion of how to take information out of Outlook 2010 would be incomplete without a discussion of how to bring information back in as well. Far more options are available for bringing information in than for sending information out.

Importing Data into Outlook

The process of importing data into your Outlook 2010 message store is the same regardless of whether you're importing information into a personal folder or an Exchange Server mailbox. You begin the process by identifying exactly what type of information that you want to import and whether Outlook 2010 can access and import the data properly.

The next sections examine some examples of importing information into Outlook 2010. To begin the import process for any of the examples discussed in these sections, use the Import And Export Wizard.

Importing Internet Mail Account Settings

When upgrading an email system to Outlook 2010, you can often save time and avoid configuration problems by importing the Internet mail settings from the previous system. This process does not bring over any messages or addresses; it simply transfers any existing Internet email account information to the current Outlook 2010 profile. This option works only if the computer on which Outlook 2010 is installed had been using previously a different email client, such as Outlook Express or Eudora.

To start the wizard to import your settings, choose File, Open, and Import. Select Import Internet Mail Account Settings, and then click Next. The wizard is very straightforward, taking you through all the steps of verifying and reestablishing the account (although you'll need to reenter the password). Fields are filled with information taken from the detected settings; you can modify them as needed during the import process. After you have imported the information, the new service will often require you to exit, log off, and restart Outlook 2010 before it will be active. At that point, you should be able to receive and send Internet email through Outlook 2010.

Importing Internet Mail and Addresses

In addition to importing Internet email configuration settings, as just discussed, the other step involved in migrating email data to Outlook 2010 is to bring in any address lists or saved messages that were stored in the previous system. To import an existing message store, follow these steps:

1. Choose File, Open, and Import. When the wizard starts, select Import Internet Mail And Addresses, and then click Next.

2. On the Outlook Import Tool page of the wizard, specify the program from which you are migrating the data. After you select the application, you must specify what to import: messages (Import Mail), addresses (Import Address Book), or both. Then click Next.

3. On the Import Addresses page, specify how Outlook 2010 should handle duplicates. The default entry, Allow Duplicates To Be Created, can create a bit of cleanup work (deleting the duplicate entries that might be created for certain contacts), but it guards against accidental information loss from overwriting the wrong contact entry. Replace Duplicates With Items Imported causes Outlook 2010 to overwrite any existing contacts in Outlook 2010 with matching items from your other mail program. Select Do Not Import Duplicate Items if you want Outlook 2010 to skip any duplicate addresses.

4. Click Finish. The wizard runs the import and then displays the Import Summary dialog box. If the import has gone well, you'll see an indication that all the messages have been imported. If you see that only a portion of the total messages have been imported, you'll know that a problem occurred and not all the information was transferred.

5. In the Import Summary dialog box, click Save In Inbox if you want to save the summary message to your Outlook Inbox folder. Click OK if you just want to close the dialog box.

Importing a vCard File

One of the handiest ways to share contact information is by using vCards, which are a form of electronic business card. When you receive a vCard from someone, you can import the card into your Contacts folder for later use. Start the Import And Export Wizard, select Import A vCard File (.vcf), and then click Next. Browse to the directory where you saved the .vcf file, select the file, and then click Open. The file will be imported as a new contact entry in your Contacts folder.

For details about using vCards to share contact information, see the section "Sharing Contacts," on page 464.

> **Note**
> If you receive the .vcf file as an email attachment, you can double-click the .vcf file icon to import the card into your Contacts folder.

Importing an iCalendar or a vCalendar File

Numerous options, including iCalendar and vCalendar files, are available to users who want to share calendar information. Although they're used for much the same purpose, iCalendar and vCalendar work in different ways.

> **Note**
> iCalendar is a newer standard that is gradually replacing vCalendar. Both are still commonly used, however.

You use iCalendar to send calendar information out across the web to anyone using an iCalendar-compatible system. Users who receive an iCalendar meeting invitation simply accept or decline the meeting, and the information is entered automatically into their calendars. An import process is generally not necessary.

In contrast, you use vCalendar files much as you use vCards: They allow you to create a meeting and send it out as an attachment to other attendees. Attendees can then double-click the attachment or use the import process to bring this meeting into their schedules. If necessary, users can also import iCalendar meetings the same way.

Importing iCalendar and vCalendar files is easy. Choose File, Open, and Import to start the Import And Export Wizard. Select Import An iCalendar (.ics) Or vCalendar File (.vcs), and then click Next. Select the file, and then click OK to complete the import.

> **Note**
> The file name extension used for vCalendar files is .vcs; iCalendar files use an .ics file name extension.

Importing from Another Program File

You've now seen most of the common import options. However, you'll also occasionally encounter situations in which you might need to import other types of information, such as third-party data, text files, and so on. Perhaps the most important of these other possibilities is importing information from another .pst file. This could involve bringing back information from an archive, restoring lost messages from a backup, or even completing the process in the example discussed earlier, in which you need to give a new sales rep copies of all messages sent to or received from Wingtip Toys. If three or four other employees had all exported messages to .pst files, the easiest option for the new rep would be to import the messages back into his or her own message store for easy access.

The following steps describe the process of importing from an existing .pst file. Keep in mind that other file import options are similar, although the particular data and formatting of each file will dictate certain changes in the import process.

To import from an existing .pst file, perform the following steps:

1. Start the Import And Export Wizard. Select Import From Another Program Or File, and then click Next.

2. In the list of file types, select Outlook Data File (.pst).

3. Browse to the .pst file that you want to import. (If you want to import multiple .pst files, you must import each one separately.) Specify how to handle duplicates on the same page, and then click Next.

> **Note**
>
> As mentioned earlier, allowing Outlook 2010 to create duplicates minimizes the risk of overwriting data, but it does increase the size of the store. If you're importing a number of .pst files that might have overlapping data (if many recipients were copied on the same messages, for example), it's often better to avoid importing duplicates.

4. On the page of the wizard shown in Figure 31-6, select the folders to import—either the entire store or only a particular folder or set of folders.

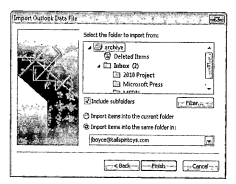

Figure 31-6 Select the folder on the Import Outlook Data File page.

5. The wizard allows you to filter the data that you're importing the same way you filter exported data. Click Filter to open the Filter dialog box, and then add any filters you need.

6. Specify the folder into which the data should be imported.

7. Click Finish to begin the import.

Note

Our fictional sales rep could create a subfolder named Wingtip under the Inbox and then select that folder before starting the Import And Export Wizard. Note that by choosing to import only from the .pst file's Inbox and selecting Import Items Into The Current Folder, the sales rep could bring all the messages from the .pst file into his or her message store without flooding the Inbox with old Wingtip information. Creating subfolders for importing and exporting can be a good way to keep track of where information is coming from and what you are sending out.

Chapter 31

ALTHOUGH some people use Microsoft Outlook 2010 only for email, the majority of people use all the personal information manager (PIM) features the program has to offer. Because a PIM is only as good as its ability to help you search for and organize data, Outlook 2010 offers a solid selection of features to help you do just that.

This chapter shows you how to perform simple and advanced searches to locate data. You'll learn how to search using Instant Search as well as the Find A Contact feature and Advanced Find. This chapter also explores various ways you can organize your Outlook 2010 data—for example, by creating additional folders for storing specific types of messages.

Using Instant Search

The Instant Search feature of the Microsoft Office system provides a simple, unified search interface that is the same across all the Outlook 2010 folders. Instant Search relies on the search subsystem built into Windows, which indexes Outlook 2010 mail folders to deliver search results faster.

Searching in Outlook 2010 is as simple as typing your search terms in the Instant Search box at the top of the Inbox. Outlook 2010 displays results as you type, automatically filtering out older results when there are a large number of items. To focus searches, Outlook 2010 searches only the folder that you have open, although you can easily choose to search all your folders instead.

When you start a search, you first determine the scope of your search. Outlook 2010 sets the search scope as the folder that is selected in the Navigation pane. To change the search scope, you click a different folder in the Navigation pane.

As you type text in the Instant Search box, the search results are displayed in the pane below the Instant Search box. To refine your search and get fewer results, type more text. To widen your search, delete some text. You can also build custom queries based on a wide range of criteria.

Note

If you prefer to use the tools provided in earlier versions of Outlook, you still can. Advanced Find and the Find A Contact feature remain available as options for those who prefer a familiar interface.

Note

Instant Search requires Windows Search, which is part of Microsoft Windows Vista and Windows 7, and is available as a download for Windows XP. For more information about Windows Search, you can visit the Windows Search site at *www.microsoft.com/ windows/products/winfamily/desktopsearch/*.

Using Instant Search with Windows XP

Because Desktop Search is not included with Windows XP, you install Instant Search just a bit differently on a computer that is running Windows XP. You must download and install the Windows Desktop Search software so that you can install it either when you first start Outlook 2010 or later. Once you restart Outlook 2010, Instant Search is enabled. Other than that, Instant Search operates the same way on a computer running Windows XP as on one running Windows Vista or Windows 7.

Configuring Instant Search

While the default configuration of Instant Search should work in most circumstances, you might need to fine-tune things just a bit to optimize Instant Search for how you use Outlook 2010. Using Instant Search might require configuring a few different options, most of which are found in Outlook 2010, although a few options are set with Indexing Options in the Control Panel.

Turning Instant Search On and Off

You turn Instant Search on and off differently depending on whether you are using Windows 7, Windows Vista, or Windows XP.

- **Enabling Instant Search on a Computer Running Windows Vista or Windows 7**   Instant Search is enabled by default on computers running Windows Vista and Windows 7. If you have turned Instant Search off for Outlook, you can enable it again. Open the Indexing Options item from the Control Panel or by clicking in the Instant Search box, and then, on the Search tab, clicking Search Tools, Search Options, and Indexing Options. In the Indexing Options dialog box, click Modify, and then select the content that you want Instant Search to index and search, one of which is Microsoft Outlook. You must exit and restart Outlook 2010 for this change to take effect.

- **Enabling Instant Search on a Computer Running Windows XP**   On computers running Windows XP, you are prompted to download the Windows Desktop Search software the first time that you start Outlook 2010. Once the software is downloaded and installed, you must restart Outlook 2010 to complete the installation process and use Instant Search.

  If you have chosen not to install Windows Search and enable Instant Search, you can always change your mind. To turn on Instant Search, click the Click Here To Enable Instant Search option under the Instant Search box.

> **Note**
> Microsoft must validate your copy of Windows XP before you are allowed to download Windows Desktop Search. If you have not yet installed the validation ActiveX control, you will be prompted to install it. Right-click the information bar, and then choose Install. A security warning dialog box will appear; click Install again. Once the ActiveX control is installed, you will be returned to the download screen.

> **Note**
> If your computer is running Windows XP and you have not downloaded the Windows Desktop Search software, you are prompted repeatedly to install it. If you don't want to see these prompts, you can disable them. To do so, on the Tools menu, choose Options. Choose Other, and then click Advanced Options. In the Advanced Options dialog box, clear the Show Prompts To Download Windows Desktop Search check box, and then click OK.

- **Disabling Instant Search**   Open the Indexing Options dialog box as described previously in this section. Click Modify, and then clear the Microsoft Outlook option. You must exit and restart Outlook 2010 for this change to take effect.

Choosing Search Options

You can determine the initial scope of searches, as well as how Outlook 2010 handles results, in the Search Options dialog box.

To configure Instant Search, click File, Options, and then click Search in the left pane to display the Search page of the Outlook Options dialog box, show in Figure 32-1. The following list explains the options available:

- To have Outlook 2010 show you search results as you type, select When Possible, Display Results As The Query Is Typed. If this option is cleared, Outlook 2010 does not start searching until you click Search or press Enter.

- When your search has a large number of results, Outlook 2010 by default limits the number of items it displays by filtering for the most recent. To view all results of your searches, no matter the number, clear the Improve Search Speed By Limiting The Number Of Results Shown check box.

- To have Outlook 2010 highlight your search terms where they appear in the results, select Highlight Search Terms In The Results. You can also set the highlight color.

- If you want Outlook 2010 to search mail items that have been moved to the Deleted Items folder but not yet actually deleted, select Include Messages From The Deleted Items Folder In Each Data File When Searching In All Items.

- To set the default scope of Instant Search, under Include Results Only From, choose either Current Folder or All Folders.

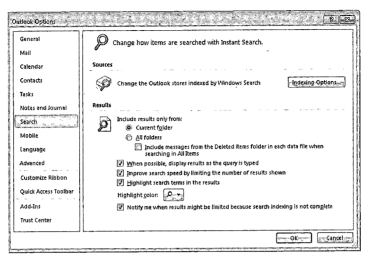

Figure 32-1 You can configure Instant Search using the Search page of the Outlook Options dialog box.

You can also specify which of your Outlook data files (if you have more than one) are indexed by Windows Search, as explained in the next section.

Controlling Which Data Files Are Searched

If you have multiple Outlook 2010 data files, you can tell Outlook 2010 to include only specific data files in an Instant Search without removing them from the list of files that are indexed. This allows you to stop a file from being searched without having to re-create the index for the file when you want it included again—a much faster option. You might use this technique to segregate project or client files, or perhaps to exclude a large archive file from searches most of the time, yet be able to easily include the file when you need to.

To change which data files Outlook 2010 searches, follow these steps:

1. Click in the Instant Search box to open the Search tab, as shown in Figure 32-2.

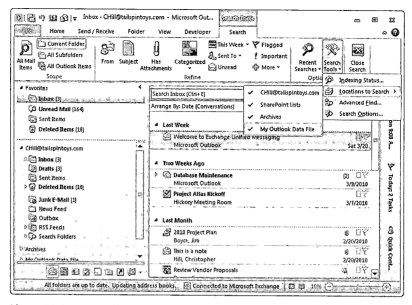

Figure 32-2 You can choose which files are included in Instant Search.

2. Click Search Tools on the Search tab and choose Locations to Search.

3. Select the Outlook 2010 data files that you want included in searches by default. At least one data file must be selected, but you can choose additional files to search as well.

You can also specify whether your Outlook 2010 files are indexed in the Indexing Options item in the Control Panel. For information about using Indexing Options, see the section "Configuring Indexing Options," on page 796.

Performing a Search

Instant Search looks at most fields of Outlook 2010 items when performing searches, making it easy for you to find what you are looking for. This means that you can type almost anything that you think might be in the item you're looking for, even if the item is in an attachment. To search for a message or other Outlook 2010 item, follow these steps:

1. Click in the Instant Search box (or press Ctrl+E), and then type your search text.

2. Outlook 2010 will display the search results as you type, with the search terms highlighted. To narrow the search results, type more text. To widen the results, delete some text.

- If you do not see the items you want, you can broaden your search scope by clicking the link Try Searching Again In All Mail Items (this link changes to reflect the current folder type) in the results pane.

- If your search returns a large number of results, Outlook 2010 might display only the most recent results. If you see a message in the InfoBar similar to the one shown in Figure 32-3, click it to show all results, including the older items.

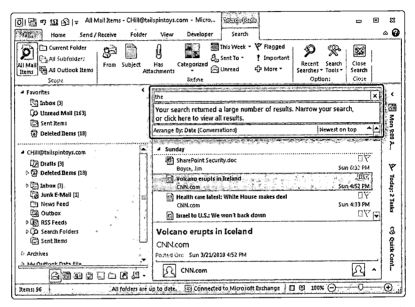

Figure 32-3 Click the message in the InfoBar to display the complete set of search results.

To clear the search and start over, click the X to the right of the Instant Search box.

To repeat a search that you have performed recently, click in the Instant Search box to display the Search tab, and then choose Recent Searches. Select the search that you want to repeat from the list.

> **Note**
> You might find that the results of some of your searches include an item that really doesn't seem to belong there, and in which you can't find the words you searched for. This might be because the item has an attachment that contains the search term.

TROUBLESHOOTING

You don't get any search results

If you repeatedly get fewer results than you expect, or you get no results at all, you should try disabling Instant Search and repeating the search. If you do get results with Instant Search disabled, you might be having problems with Windows Desktop Search indexing.

Check your indexing status by clicking Search Tools on the Search tab and selecting Indexing Status. If a message appears stating that Outlook 2010 is currently indexing your files, note the number of items remaining to be indexed. Check back in a while to see whether the numbers are different. If the numbers are unchanged, you should rebuild the index. For information about rebuilding the index, see the section "Configuring Indexing Options," on page 796.

Refining Your Search

The Refine group on the Search tab shows you a number of extra fields that you can search within to refine your search results. Each type of folder (Mail, Contacts, and so on) displays the most commonly used fields for that type of folder, so each one shows a different list of fields by default. You can also add fields, even those in custom forms, to support searches for exactly the data you want.

> **Tip**
> The Refine group on the Search tab of the ribbon replaces the Query Builder in Outlook 2007.

1. To display the Search tab, click the Instant Search box.

2. Click an item in the Refine group, as shown in Figure 32-4, to add that field to the Instant Search box. Then type the criteria required by the added field, such as a name, word, etc.

3. To add other fields, click More to display the list shown in Figure 32-4.

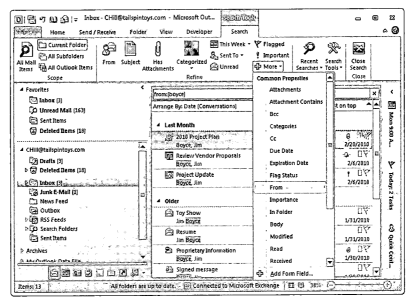

Figure 32-4 Each folder shows a different list of fields in the Refine group.

Tip

Adding fields from the Refine group is a good way to learn about the search syntax that Windows Search uses. After you're familiar with the syntax, you can just type the search keywords yourself, rather than pick them from the list. What's more, you can use the keywords outside Outlook to search for Outlook items. Just click Start and start typing your search criteria. Windows Search will return results in the Start menu based on those criteria.

Making Fields from Custom Forms Available

To add a custom form to the Query Builder list, follow these steps:

1. Click in the Instant Search box.

2. Click More in the Refine group on the Search tab and choose Add Form Field.

3. In the Select Enterprise Forms For This Folder dialog box, choose the type of forms you want to select from.

4. In the list in the left pane, select the form you want to add, and then click Add. Repeat this for each form you want to add. (To display form groups by category, select Show Categories.)

5. Click Close.

> **Note**
>
> If Windows Search is still building the search index, your search results will be incomplete. To check the status of indexing, click the Instant Search field to open the Search tab, and then click Search Tools and choose Indexing Status.

Configuring Indexing Options

While indexing is generally self-maintaining, you can control some settings using the Indexing Options item in the Control Panel. You can also display Indexing Options from Outlook. Click File, Options, and Search, and then click Indexing Options.

To verify that your Outlook 2010 files are being indexed, follow these steps:

1. Click File, Options, and Search.

2. Click Indexing Options. In the Indexing Options dialog box, shown in Figure 32-5, verify that your Outlook 2010 files are listed in the Included Locations list.

3. If your Outlook 2010 files are not listed, click Modify to display the Indexed Locations dialog box. Under Change Selected Locations, select the Microsoft Outlook check box to include the files in the locations that should be indexed. (Outlook 2010 files belonging to other users are also shown, but Outlook will return to you only results from your own data files.) Click OK.

> **Note**
>
> Be patient when you click Modify. It can take quite a while for Windows to display the Indexed Locations dialog box.

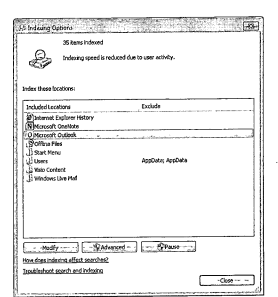

Figure 32-5 You can see the status of indexing across the entire system in the Indexing Options dialog box.

TROUBLESHOOTING

Troubleshooting indexing problems

You might need to rebuild the index due to problems such as empty search results when you know that there are items that match your search. Rebuilding an index takes a while, perhaps even several hours, and is significantly slower if you are also using the computer at the same time. Because of this, you will want to rebuild the index only when you are experiencing ongoing problems with Instant Search, and preferably when you will be away from the computer for a while.

You can rebuild the search index by opening the Indexing Options item in Control Panel and then clicking Advanced. Under Troubleshooting, click Rebuild. Once the index is rebuilt, restart Outlook 2010 to have it use the new index.

Searching for Contacts

If you're like most Outlook 2010 users, your Contacts folder will grow to contain a lot of contact entries—typically, too many to allow you to browse through the folder when you need to find a particular contact quickly. You're also likely to encounter situations in which, for example, you need to locate contact information but can't remember the person's last name. Fortunately, Outlook 2010 makes it easy to locate contact data, providing two convenient ways to search contacts: Instant Search and the Find a Contact box in the Find group on the Home tab on the ribbon.

Instant Search works the same way across all the Outlook 2010 folders, so to locate a contact, begin typing the contact's name in the Search Contacts box. You can use the buttons in the Refine group on the Search tab to add search criteria. If you want to add more fields, you can click More and then select the fields in the list.

You can also use the Find A Contact box on the Home tab on the ribbon, shown in Figure 32-6, to search for contacts. Type the search criterion (such as a first name, last name, or company), and then press Enter.

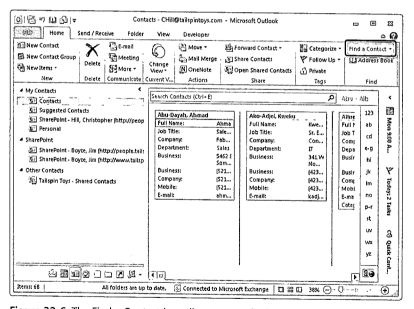

Figure 32-6 The Find a Contact box allows you to find a contact entry quickly.

If Outlook 2010 finds only one contact that matches the search criteria, it opens the contact entry for that person. Otherwise, Outlook 2010 displays the Choose Contact dialog box, shown in Figure 32-7, in which you can select the contact entry to open.

Figure 32-7 Select a contact when Outlook 2010 finds more than one that fits your search criteria.

> **Note**
> The Find A Contact box can be useful when you need to perform a quick search for a contact based on a limited amount of data. To locate contacts and other Outlook 2010 items based on multiple search conditions, use Instant Search or Advanced Find, as discussed in the next section.

Using Advanced Find

In addition to Instant Search, Outlook 2010 still provides the Advanced Find feature for performing advanced searches that require specifying multiple search conditions.

The Advanced Find Dialog Box

To open the Advanced Find dialog box, shown in Figure 32-8, click in the Instant Search box, and then click Search Tools, Advanced Find or simply press Ctrl+Shift+F. You can use this dialog box to search for any type of Outlook 2010 item using multiple search conditions.

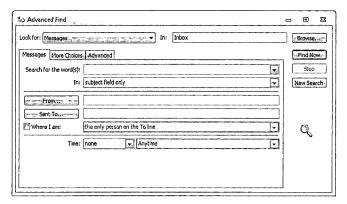

Figure 32-8 Use the Advanced Find dialog box when you need to search using multiple conditions.

The options provided in the Advanced Find dialog box change depending on the type of item that you select in the Look For drop-down list. If you select Contacts, for example, the options change to provide specialized search criteria for contacts, such as restricting the search to a name, a company, or an address. Selecting Messages in the drop-down list changes the options so that you can search the subject field of messages, search the subject and message body, or specify other search criteria specific to messages.

> **Note**
> When you select a different item type in the Look For drop-down list, Outlook 2010 clears the current search and starts a new one. Outlook 2010 does, however, prompt you to confirm that you want to clear the current search.

On the first tab in the Advanced Find dialog box (the title of which changes based on the type of items being searched, for example, Messages in Figure 32-8), you specify the primary search criteria. The following list summarizes all the available options (although not all options appear at all times):

- **Search For The Word(s)**   Specify the word, words, or phrase for which you want to search. You can type words individually, or include quotation marks around a phrase to search for the entire phrase. You also can select from a previous set of search words using the drop-down list.

- **In**   Specify the location in the Outlook 2010 item where you want to search, such as only the subject of a message. The options available in this list vary according to the type of item that you select in the Look For drop-down list.

- **From**   Specify the name of the person who sent you the message. Type the name, or click From to browse the address book for the name.

- **Sent To**   For messages, specify the recipients to whom the message was sent.

- **Attendees**   Specify the people scheduled to attend a meeting.

- **Organized By**   Specify the person who generated the meeting request.

- **E-Mail**   Browse the address book to search for contacts by their email addresses.

- **Named**   Specify the file name of the item for which you're searching. You can specify a single file name or use wildcard characters to match multiple items. The Named box appears if you select Files or Files (Outlook/Exchange) in the Look For drop-down list.

- **Of Type**   Choose the type of file for which to search when using the Files or Files (Outlook/Exchange) options.

- **Journal Entry Types**   Specify the journal entry type when searching the journal for items.

- **Contact**   Browse for a contact associated with an item for which you're searching.

- **Where I Am**   When searching for messages, specify that you are the only person on the To line, on the To line with others, or on the Cc line with others.

- **Status**   Search for tasks based on their status. You can select Doesn't Matter, Not Started, In Progress, or Completed.

- **Time**   Specify the creation or modification time, the start or end time, or other time properties specific to the type of item for which you are searching.

Specifying Advanced Search Criteria

You use the More Choices tab in the Advanced Find dialog box, shown in Figure 32-9, to specify additional search conditions to refine the search.

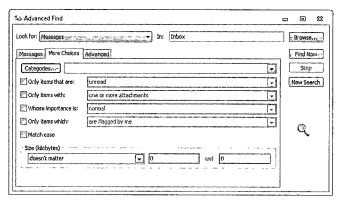

Figure 32-9 Use the More Choices tab to refine the search.

The following options are available on the More Choices tab:

- **Categories**   Specify the category or categories associated with the items for which you are searching. You can type the categories separated by commas, or you can click Categories to open the Categories dialog box and then select categories.

- **Only Items That Are**   Search for items by their read status (read or unread).

- **Only Items With**   Search for items by their attachment status (one or more attachments, or no attachments).

- **Whose Importance Is**   Specify the importance (High, Normal, or Low) of the items for which you are searching.

- **Only Items Which**   Specify the flag status of the items for which you are searching.

- **Match Case**   Direct Outlook 2010 to match the case of the text you entered as the search criterion. Clear this check box to make the search case-insensitive.

- **Size**   Specify the size criterion for the items in your search. You can select one of several options to define the size range in which the item must fall to match the search.

The More Choices tab is the same for all Outlook 2010 items except the Files search item. With Files selected in the Look For drop-down list, the Only Items With option is not available.

You can use the Advanced tab in the Advanced Find dialog box, shown in Figure 32-10, to create more complex searches. On this tab, select the fields to include in the search, as well as the search conditions for each field. You can build a list of multiple fields.

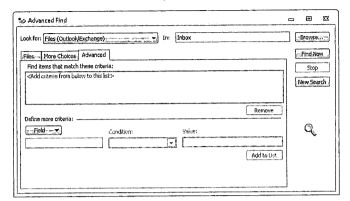

Figure 32-10 On the Advanced tab, select the fields to search and their search criteria.

Organizing Data

Searching for data and organizing data usually go hand in hand. One of the main motivations for organizing your data is that you want to be able to find it easily. Even with perfect organization, however, you'll still need to perform searches now and then because of the sheer amount of data that might be involved. Outlook 2010 provides several ways to organize your data. Whereas other chapters in this book focus on specific ways to organize your Outlook 2010 items, this section provides an overview of ways that you can organize certain types of items and points you to the appropriate chapters for additional information.

Organizing Your Email

Email messages probably make up the bulk of your Outlook 2010 data. For that reason, organizing your messages can be a challenge. Outlook 2010 offers several features that will help you organize your messages so that you can find and work with them effectively and efficiently.

Search Folders

Search folders are the best means in Outlook 2010 to organize messages quickly without moving them around to different folders. A search folder looks and acts like a folder, but it's really a special type of view that displays in a virtual folder view all messages that fit the search condition for the search folder. Search folders offer two main benefits: They can search multiple folders, and they organize messages without requiring that the messages be moved from their current folder.

See the section "Finding and Organizing Messages with Search Folders," on page 288, to learn more about search folders.

Using Folders

Another great way to organize your email messages is to separate them in different folders. For example, if you deal with several projects, consider willcreating a folder for each project and moving each message to its respective folder. You can create the folders as subfolders of your Inbox or place them elsewhere, depending on your preferences. You might even create a folder outside the Inbox named Projects and then create subfolders for each project under that folder.

For more information about creating and managing folders, see Chapter 29, "Managing Outlook Folders and Data."

Using Rules

Rules are one of the best tools you have in Outlook 2010 for organizing messages. You can apply rules to process messages selectively—moving, deleting, copying, and performing other actions on the messages based on the sender, the recipient, the account, and a host of other message properties. You can use rules in combination with folders to organize your email messages. For example, you might use rules to move messages for specific projects to their respective folders automatically. You can apply rules to messages when they arrive in the Inbox or any time you need to rearrange or organize.

For a detailed discussion of rules, see Chapter 11, "Processing Messages Automatically."

Using Color Categories

Outlook 2010 uses color categories to help organize your email messages. If you create rules to apply certain color categories to specified email messages, the color can provide a visual indicator of the sender, the subject, the priority, or other properties of the message. In this way, you can see at a glance whether a particular message meets certain criteria. You can also use automatic formatting in a view to apply color categories.

For more information about color categories, see Chapter 5, "Creating and Using Categories."

Using Views

Views give you another important way to organize your Outlook 2010 data. The default views organize specific folders using the most common criteria. You can customize Outlook Today view using Hypertext Markup Language (HTML) to provide different or additional levels of organization. You can also create custom views of any Outlook 2010 folder to organize your data to suit your preferences.

For more information about customizing views, see the sections "Customizing the Outlook Today View," on page 648, and "Creating and Using Custom Views," on page 653.

Organizing Your Calendar, Contacts, Tasks, and Notes

As with mail folders, you can use categories to organize items in your other folders. For example, you might use categories to identify meetings for specific projects quickly. You can also use conditional formatting to display items in a certain color when those items match your conditional formatting condition. For contacts, you can use multiple folders to separate contacts, such as separating your business contacts from personal contacts.

Organizing Your Outlook Items Effectively

It's far too easy to get swamped in email, but you can make it less of a problem if you learn to use the options that Outlook 2010 offers to help you stay organized. Here are a few tips to get you started:

- **Clean out your Inbox every day**   There is a very real psychological boost when you can leave your office at the end of the day with your Inbox empty—and it's a pretty nice way to start your morning, too. A habitually empty Inbox also means that any mail that is in the Inbox is still unread, so it's easy to tell what you still need to read.

- **Handle each email message only once**   Many time management systems share a similar mantra: Open a message, read it, decide what you have to do about it, and then do it. *Right now.* For most people, a lot of their mail requires no action beyond reading it. If that's the case, delete (or file) mail items immediately. Move any items that require action to a folder other than the Inbox, assigning a color category to make it easier to locate, or set a follow-up flag to remind you of a deadline if needed.

- **Turn off the Reading pane if you have a hard time emptying your Inbox**   While the Reading pane makes it easy to read a piece of mail quickly, the Reading pane also makes it easy to read mail without dealing with it.

- **Use rules to sort mail that you don't need to read immediately into folders as it arrives**   You can also assign categories using rules as messages arrive, providing additional information that you can use to locate those messages later.

- **Use a combination of folders and categories to manage your mail**   Create folders to contain large groups of mail, and then categorize the messages to display a manageable subset of messages.

- **Use search folders to create customized views of your Outlook 2010 items**   Search folders automatically filter the contents of a list of folders that you specify based on the set of criteria found in the Advanced Find dialog box. This lets you see specific sets of messages by simply selecting a folder.

- **Create custom views of messages**   Custom views that filter Outlook 2010 items are another powerful tool, letting you quickly switch between various subsets of messages. Because views can be used in multiple folders, you can create a view once and reuse it in many places.

- **If you have lots of email, consider using multiple .pst files to separate disparate information into discrete data stores**   In addition to segregating data storage, this makes it easy to select specific data sets for Instant Search.

Security and Virus Protection

I F you use Microsoft Outlook 2010 on a daily basis to manage email, appointments, and contacts, losing the information that you've stored in Outlook 2010 could cause significant problems. Outlook 2010 data can be lost in a number of ways, from accidental deletion to file corruption to hard disk failure. In addition, a user who purchases a new computer might leave behind information when transferring data to the new machine.

This chapter examines virus protection for both the server and workstation to help you understand how to protect yourself and your network from email-borne viruses. Outlook 2010 provides features to protect against viruses in attachments, and there are several steps you can and should take to add other forms of virus protection.

Providing Virus Protection

Hardware and software failures are by no means the only source of anguish for the average user or administrator. Viruses and worms have become major problems for system administrators and users alike. When a major virus or worm outbreak hits, companies grind to a halt, systems shut down, system administrators turn off mail servers, and general chaos ensues.

The effects of a particularly virulent virus or worm can be devastating for a company. A virus or worm can bring your mail servers to a quick halt because of the load that it imposes on them with the sheer amount of traffic it generates. Bandwidth, both local and across wide area network (WAN) links, is affected as multiple copies of infected messages flood the network. Files can become infected, rendering them unusable and subjecting users to reinfection. This means that you must recover the files from backups, making an adequate backup strategy even more important than usual.

One often-overlooked effect that viruses have on a company is the public relations night-mare that they can create. How would your customers react if they received a flood of infected messages from your company that brought their mail servers to a screeching halt and damaged their production files? Forget for a moment the ire of your custom-ers' system administrators. Could your company survive the ill will generated by such a catastrophe?

At the least, your company would probably suffer serious consequences. Therefore, devel-oping and implementing an effective virus protection strategy is as important as develop-ing a backup strategy—perhaps even more so. When you examine your antivirus needs, approach the problem from two angles: protecting against outside infection and prevent-ing an outgoing flood of infected messages. You can approach the former through either client-side or server-side solutions, but the latter typically requires a server-side solution.

Implementing Server-Side Solutions

Your first line of defense against viruses and worms should lie between your local area network (LAN) and the Internet. Many antivirus solution vendors offer perimeter security products that monitor traffic coming from the Internet and detect and block viruses in real time. With perimeter protection in place, threats may never reach your network or servers at all.

Stopping viruses before they get into your LAN is a great goal, but even the best products sometimes miss. If your organization uses Microsoft Exchange Server, you should also consider installing an Exchange Server–based antivirus solution. All the major antivirus vendors offer Exchange Server solutions, as does Microsoft, with its Microsoft Forefront suite of protection products.

In addition to detecting and removing viruses from network and Exchange Server traffic, you should implement a solution that provides real-time virus detection for your net-work's file servers. These solutions scan the server for infected files as files are added or modified. For example, a remote user might upload a file containing a virus to your File Transfer Protocol (FTP) server. If local users open the file, their systems become infected and the virus begins to spread across your LAN. Catching and removing the virus as soon as the file is uploaded to the FTP server is the ideal solution. Microsoft SharePoint is another application that should be protected at the application layer. Because documents are stored in Microsoft SQL Server rather than in a file system, the operating system–level antivirus products cannot detect or protect against threats in documents uploaded by users. So you should add a SharePoint antivirus solution in addition to your operating sys-tem protection on the servers themselves.

Consider all these points as you evaluate server-side antivirus products. Some might be more important to you than others, so prioritize them and then choose an antivirus suite that best suits your needs and priorities.

Implementing Client-Side Solutions

In addition to blocking viruses and worms at the server, you should provide antivirus protection at each workstation, particularly if your server-side virus detection is limited. Even if you do provide a full suite of detection services at the server, client-side protection is a vital piece of any antivirus strategy. For example, suppose that your server provides virus filtering, scanning all email traffic coming from the Internet. Even so, the server might miss a new virus in a message with an attached file, perhaps because the virus definition file has not yet been updated. A user opens the infected file and infects his or her system, and the worm begins replicating across the LAN. If the user has a client-side antivirus solution in place, the worm is blocked before it can do any damage.

Use the following criteria to evaluate client-side antivirus solutions:

- **Are frequent updates available?**   On any given day, several new viruses appear. Your antivirus solution is only as good as your virus definition files are current. Choose a solution that offers daily or (at least) weekly virus definition updates.

- **Can updates be scheduled for automatic execution?**   The average user doesn't back up documents on a regular basis, much less worry about whether antivirus definition files are up to date. For that reason, it's important that the client-side antivirus solution you choose provide automatic, scheduled updates.

- **Does the product scan a variety of file types?**   Make sure that the product you choose can scan not only executables and other application files, but also Microsoft Office system documents for macro viruses.

You'll find several client-side antivirus products on the market. Microsoft has two offerings that might be of interest: Microsoft Security Essentials includes antivirus protection in its suite of services for home and small business computer users, and Microsoft Forefront Client Security offers similar protection for computers in an enterprise environment, although it *does not* scan email. Other popular products include Symantec Norton AntiVirus (*www.symantec.com*), McAfee VirusScan (*www.mcafee.com*), and Panda Antivirus for Servers and Desktops (*www.pandasecurity.com*). Many other products are available that offer comparable features.

Virus Protection in Outlook

Virus protection is an important feature in Outlook 2010. You can configure Outlook 2010 to block specific types of attachments automatically, thus helping prevent virus infections. Outlook 2010 provides two levels of attachment protection, one for individual users and one for system administrators.

Outlook 2010 provides features to help protect your system against viruses and other malicious system attacks. For example, Outlook 2010 supports attachment virus protection, which helps protect against viruses you might receive through infected email attachments. Outlook 2010 offers protection against Office system macro viruses, letting you choose when macros run. Control over programmatic access is also configurable, allowing management of how applications interact with the security features in Outlook 2010 as well as their ability to send email.

For information about protecting against malicious HTML-based messages, see the section "Configuring HTML Message Handling," on page 356.

Protecting Against Viruses in Attachments

In the old days, infected boot floppy disks were the most common way computer viruses were spread. Today, email is by far the most common infection mechanism. Viruses range from mostly harmless (but irritating) to severe, sometimes causing irreparable damage to your system. Worms are a more recent variation, spreading across the Internet primarily through email and by exploited operating system flaws. Worms can bog down a system by consuming the majority of the system's resources, and they can cause the same types of damage as viruses.

Outlook 2010 provides protection against viruses and worms by letting you block certain types of attachments that are susceptible to infection. This prevents users from opening attached files that could infect their systems and execute malicious code to damage or steal data. Executable programs (.exe, .com, and .bat files) are also good examples of attachments that are primary delivery mechanisms for viruses. Many other document types are equally susceptible—Hypertext Markup Language (HTML) documents and scripts, for instance, have rapidly become favorite delivery tools for virus creators. Outlook 2010 provides two levels of protection for attachments: Level 1 and Level 2. The following sections explain these two levels, the file types assigned to each, and how to work with attachments.

Protected View

A new feature in Outlook 2010, discussed briefly in Chapter 8, "Sending and Receiving Messages," is designed to limit exposure to threats from Office documents that you receive via email or download from an external location such as a SharePoint site or Internet site. When you open an Office document that is attached to an email, the document's native application (such as Word) opens in a rights-limited sandbox instance. A banner just under the application's ribbon displays a message indicating that the file originated as an email attachment and might be unsafe. The banner also reminds you that the application is running in Protected View.

Limiting the rights that the sandbox application has limits the potential for a virus in the document to be able to "get outside" of the application and do any damage. If you feel comfortable that the document is safe, you can click Enable Editing to open the document in a normal instance and begin making changes, save it, and so on.

Level 1 Attachments

Level 1 attachments are for those that are common vectors for infection, such as executable (.exe) files. When you receive a message containing an attachment in the Level 1 group, Outlook 2010 displays the paper clip icon next to the message header, indicating that the message has an attachment, just as it does for other messages with attachments. When you click the message header, Outlook 2010 displays a message indicating that it has blocked the attachment.

You cannot open Level 1 attachments that are blocked by Outlook 2010. You can open and view the messages, but Outlook 2010 disables the interface elements that otherwise would allow you to open or save the attachments. Outlook 2010 displays a message in the InfoBar informing you that the attachment has been blocked and cannot be opened, as shown in Figure 33-1. If you forward a message with a blocked attachment, Outlook 2010 strips the attachment from the forwarded message.

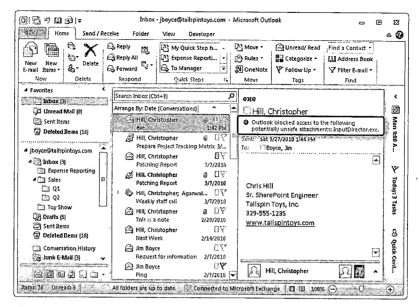

Figure 33-1 Outlook 2010 displays a message informing you that it has blocked an attachment.

For details on how to open attachments that have been blocked by Outlook 2010, see the section "Opening Blocked Attachments," on page 826.

Table 33-1 lists the file name extensions for Level 1 attachments. (Note that this list will change over time.)

Table 33-1 Level 1 Attachments

File Name Extension	Description
.ade	Microsoft Access project extension
.adp	Access project
.app	Executable application
.asp	Active Server Page
.bas	BASIC source code
.bat	Batch processing
.cer	Internet security certificate file
.chm	Compiled HTML help
.cmd	DOS CP/M command file; command file for Windows NT
.cnt	Windows Help file

File Name Extension	Description
.com	Command
.cpl	Control Panel extension
.crt	Certificate file
.csh	csh script
.der	DER-encoded X509 certificate file
.exe	Executable file
.fxp	FoxPro compiled source
.gadget	Windows gadget file
.hlp	Windows Help file
.hpj	Windows Help project file
.hta	Hypertext application
.inf	Information or setup file
.ins	Microsoft Internet Information Services (IIS) Internet communications settings
.isp	IIS Internet service provider (ISP) settings
.its	Internet document set; Internet translation
.js	JavaScript source code
.jse	JScript encoded script file
.ksh	UNIX shell script
.lnk	Windows shortcut file
.mad	Access module shortcut
.maf	Access file
.mag	Access diagram shortcut
.mam	Access macro shortcut
.maq	Access query shortcut
.mar	Access report shortcut
.mas	Access stored procedures
.mat	Access table shortcut
.mau	Media attachment unit
.mav	Access view shortcut
.maw	Access data access page
.mda	Access add-in; Microsoft MDA Access 2 workgroup
.mdb	Access application; Microsoft MDB Access database

File Name Extension	Description
.mde	Access MDE database file
.mdt	Access add-in data
.mdw	Access workgroup information
.mdz	Access wizard template
.msc	Microsoft Management Console (MMC) snap-in control file
.msh	Microsoft shell
.msh1	Microsoft shell
.msh2	Microsoft shell
.mshxml	Microsoft shell
.msh1xml	Microsoft shell
.msh2xml	Microsoft shell
.msi	Microsoft Windows Installer file
.msp	Microsoft Windows Installer update
.mst	Windows SDK setup transform script
.ops	Office system profile settings file
.osd	Open Software Description file
.pcd	Microsoft Visual Test
.pif	Windows program information file
.plg	Microsoft Developer Studio build log
.prf	Windows system file
.prg	Program file
.pst	Exchange Server address book file; Outlook personal folder file
.reg	Registration information/key for Windows 95 and Windows 98; registry data file
.scf	Windows Explorer command
.scr	Windows screen saver
.sct	Windows script component; FoxPro screen
.shb	Windows shortcut into a document
.shs	Shell scrap object file
.ps1	PowerShell
.ps1xml	PowerShell
.ps2	PowerShell
.ps2xml	PowerShell

File Name Extension	Description
.psc1	PowerShell
.psc2	PowerShell
.tmp	Temporary file/folder
.url	Internet location
.vb	Microsoft Visual Basic Scripting Edition (VBScript) file; any Visual Basic source
.vbe	VBScript encoded script file
.vbs	VBScript script file; Visual Basic for Applications (VBA) script
.vsmacros	Microsoft Visual Studio .NET binary-based macro project
.vsw	Microsoft Visio workspace file
.ws	Windows script file
.wsc	Windows script component
.wsf	Windows script file
.wsh	Windows script host settings file
.xnk	Exchange Server public folder shortcut

Level 2 Attachments

Outlook 2010 also supports a second level of attachment blocking. Level 2 attachments are defined by the administrator at the server level and therefore apply to Exchange Server accounts, not to Post Office Protocol 3 (POP3), Internet Message Access Protocol (IMAP), or Hypertext Transfer Protocol (HTTP)–based accounts. Because the Level 2 list is empty by default, no attachments are blocked as Level 2 attachments unless the Exchange Server administrator has modified the Level 2 list.

You can't open Level 2 attachments directly in Outlook 2010, but Outlook 2010 does allow you to save them to disk, and you can open them from there.

Configuring Blocked Attachments

Attachment blocking is an important feature in Outlook 2010 to help prevent viruses from infecting systems. Although you can rely on the default Outlook 2010 attachment security, you can also choose a centrally managed method of customizing attachment handling for Outlook 2010. You can configure attachment blocking in three ways:

- **Using Group Policy**   With Outlook 2010, you can use Group Policy to control how Outlook 2010 handles security, including attachments and virus prevention features. The use of Group Policy also allows the application of these customized security settings in environments without public folders, such as a computer running Exchange Server without public folder deployed, or with clients running Outlook 2010 that are not using Exchange Server. Using Group Policy does, however, require that you be using the Active Directory Domain Services (AD DS) to manage your network.

- **Using the Exchange Security Form**   Earlier versions of Outlook used the Exchange Security Form, which provides essentially the same options as the Group Policy settings now do. The Exchange Security Form relies on Exchange Server shared folders, however, which limits the use of these configuration options to organizations using Exchange Server. You can still use the Exchange Security Form with Exchange Server 2010, for example, to support older Outlook clients.

- **At the user's workstation**   If neither of the preceding options is available to you, a limited amount of customization can be done on an individual workstation. For example, you can modify the client's registry to change the Level 1 list (as explained in the section "Configuring Attachment Blocking Directly in Outlook," on page 825). These modifications also affect non–Exchange Server accounts.

Configuring attachment blocking centrally, either via Group Policy or on a computer running Exchange Server, is the most effective and efficient method; it gives you, as an administrator, control over attachment security. It also allows you to tailor security by groups within your Windows domains.

> **Note**
>
> Because this book focuses on Outlook 2010 used with Exchange Server 2010, the use of the Exchange Security Form is not covered. For detailed information about using the Exchange Security Form, see the Microsoft Office 2003 Resource Kit, available at *office. microsoft.com/en-us/ork2003/*.

In addition to specifying when Outlook 2010 blocks attachments, you can configure other aspects of Outlook 2010 security via Group Policy (or using the Exchange Security Form), letting you limit the behavior of custom forms and control programmatic access to Outlook 2010.

INSIDE OUT   Keep systems safe

Apparently, Microsoft's theory for Level 2 attachments is that the user has a client-side antivirus solution in place that will scan the file automatically as soon as the user saves the file to disk. Alternatively, perhaps the theory is that you can rely on the user to perform a virus check on the file manually. Neither of these scenarios is a sure bet by any means. Even if the user has antivirus software installed, it might be disabled or have an outdated virus definition file. That's why it's important to provide virus protection at the network and server levels to prevent viruses from reaching the user at all.

It's also important to educate users about the potential damage that can be caused by viruses and worms. Too often, these infect systems through user ignorance—users receive an attachment from a known recipient, assume that it's safe (if they even consider that the file could be infected), and open the file. The result is an infected system and potentially an infected network.

Configuring Attachments in Exchange Server

Attachment blocking in Exchange Server can be configured in two ways:

- Group Policy is used by Exchange Server 2010, enabling the configuration of these settings without reliance on public folders, which are optional in Exchange Server 2010, or registry entries on each of the clients.

- The Exchange Security Form, which is configured via an administrative template stored in a public folder, is used in earlier versions of Exchange Server. While the Exchange Security Form can be used only in environments that have public folders, such as Exchange Server 2003, it is still available for configurations, such as using down-level clients, where it is required.

The settings that are configurable in Group Policy and those set via the Exchange Security Form are largely the same, as described in the following section. Whether you choose to use one or the other, or both, depends on the versions of Exchange Server and Outlook that you need to support. Table 33-2 shows which methods can be used by various email servers.

Table 33-2 Security Methods and Types of Email Servers

	Security Method	
EMAIL SERVER	GROUP POLICY	EXCHANGE SECURITY FORM
Exchange Server 2010 (no public folders)	Yes	No
Exchange Server 2010 (with public folders)	Yes	Yes
Exchange Server 2003	Yes	Yes
Non–Exchange Server	Yes	No

Clients running Outlook 2010 can use any of these methods, depending on the Outlook Security Mode set in Group Policy. When you use only Group Policy settings, clients running Outlook 2003 or earlier use the default security settings. If an Exchange Security Form is also available, clients running Outlook 2003, Outlook 2002, and Outlook 2000 (with the security update) will use it. Table 33-3 describes the specific behavior of each client with each security method.

Table 33-3 Security Methods and Versions of Microsoft Outlook

	Security Method		
OUTLOOK VERSION	GROUP POLICY	EXCHANGE SECURITY FORM	BOTH
Outlook 2007 and Outlook 2010	Uses Group Policy settings (by default)	Uses ESF if set in Group Policy (Outlook Security Settings)	Depends on configuration (Group Policy can override ESF, and vice versa)
Outlook 2003, Outlook 2002, and Outlook 2000 with security update	Uses default settings	Uses Exchange Security Form settings	Uses Exchange Security Form settings
Outlook 2000 without the security update and earlier	Uses default settings	Uses default settings	Uses default settings

Outlook Security Mode is set in Group Policy to specify how clients running Outlook 2010 apply security settings. Outlook 2010 can use Group Policy settings, use the Exchange Security Form stored in one of two public folders (Outlook Security Settings or Outlook 10 Security Settings), or use the Outlook 2010 default security settings.

> **Note**
> Using both Group Policy settings and the Exchange Security Form supports the widest range of clients and is particularly useful during upgrades from Outlook 2003 to Outlook 2010 or Exchange Server 2003 to Exchange Server 2010. Clients running Outlook 2010 can retrieve their security information from the appropriate location transparently.

Using Outlook Security Settings

There are three categories of settings you can configure using Group Policy, controlling attachments, forms, and programmatic access to Outlook 2010. These settings are described in the following sections.

> **Note**
> This section covers the settings as described in Group Policy; settings in the Exchange Security Form are similar, even if worded slightly differently.

> **Tip**
> In order to access these security settings, you must add the Office 2010 administrative templates for group policy, which you will find at *http://technet.microsoft.com/en-us/library/cc178992.aspx*.

Attachment Security Settings

Several options are available for customization of attachment handling, including making changes to the blocked attachment lists, specifying when prompts appear, and controlling users' ability to configure their own attachment management.

- **Display Level 1 Attachments**   This option allows users of Outlook 2010 to see and open Level 1 attachments.

- **Allow Users To Demote Attachments To Level 2**   Enabling this option allows users of Outlook 2010 to demote Level 1 attachments to Level 2, which lets a user save the attachments to disk and then open them.

- **Do Not Prompt About Level 1 Attachments When Sending An Item** This setting disables the warning that normally appears when a user tries to send a Level 1 attachment. The warning explains that the attachment could cause a virus infection and that the recipient might not receive the attachment (because of attachment blocking on the recipient's server).

- **Do Not Prompt About Level 1 Attachments When Closing An Item** You can disable the warning that normally appears when the user closes a message, an appointment, or another item that contains a Level 1 attachment.

> **Note**
>
> Disabling warning prompts for Level 1 attachments does not change how Outlook 2010 deals with them. Even without a warning, users are not able to view or open Level 1 attachments in Outlook 2010 items when a setting that disables warning prompts is enabled.

- **Allow In-Place Activation Of Embedded OLE Objects** This option allows users of Outlook 2010 to open embedded Object Linking and Embedding (OLE) objects (such as Microsoft Excel 2010 spreadsheets, Access 2010 databases, and other documents) by double-clicking the object's icon.

- **Display OLE Package Objects** Enable this option to show embedded OLE objects in email messages. Hiding the objects prevents the user from opening them.

- **Add File Extensions To Block As Level 1** Use this setting to modify the Level 1 attachment list. You can enter a list of file name extensions to add to the list.

- **Remove File Extensions Blocked As Level 1** You can specify a list of file name extensions to remove from the Level 1 attachment list.

- **Add File Extensions To Block As Level 2** Use this setting to modify the Level 2 attachment list. You can enter a list of file name extensions to add to the list.

- **Remove File Extensions Blocked As Level 2** You can specify a list of file name extensions to remove from the Level 2 attachment list.

- **Prevent Users From Customizing Attachment Security Settings** This Group Policy setting is used in earlier versions of Outlook to specify whether users can add files to (or remove files from) the Level 1 and Level 2 attachment lists that you have configured. This option overrides other settings; if it is enabled, users cannot configure the lists even if other settings would normally allow them to.

- **Allow Access To E-Mail Attachments**   This setting also is for earlier versions of Outlook. You can create a list of file types that are to be removed from the default Level 1 attachment list. This is functionally equivalent to the Remove File Extensions Blocked As Level 1 setting, just for clients running previous versions of Outlook.

Custom Form Security Settings

There are several options that control the actions that can be taken by scripts and controls in custom forms:

- **Allow Scripts In One-Off Outlook Forms**   Enabling this option allows scripts to be executed if the script and the form layout are contained in the message.

- **Set Outlook Object Model Custom Actions**   This setting determines the action Outlook 2010 takes if a program attempts to execute a task using the Outlook 2010 object model. For example, a virus could incorporate a script that uses the Outlook 2010 object model to reply to a message and attach itself to that message, bypassing the Outlook 2010 security safeguards. The policy setting Prompt User, which you can select from the Options drop-down list when configuring the policy, causes Outlook 2010 to prompt the user to allow or deny the action. Automatically Approve allows the program to execute the task without prompting the user. Automatically Deny prevents the program from executing the task without prompting the user. Prompt User Based On Computer Security uses the Outlook 2010 security settings.

- **Set Control ItemProperty Prompt**   This setting determines the action that Outlook 2010 takes if a user adds a control to a custom Outlook 2010 form and binds that control to any address information fields (To or From, for example). You can select Prompt User to have Outlook 2010 ask the user to allow or deny access to the address fields when the message is received, Automatically Approve to allow access without prompting the user, Automatically Deny to deny access without prompting the user, or Prompt User Based On Computer Security to use the Outlook 2010 security settings.

> **Note**
> You can control which applications can access Outlook 2010 programmatically, to send email or retrieve Outlook 2010 information, using Group Policy. For detailed information about how to do this, see the section "Enabling Applications to Send Email with Outlook," on page 828.

Configuring Security Using Group Policy

There are two steps involved in configuring Outlook 2010 attachment security using Group Policy. First, you configure the security settings for attachments and custom forms. Once you are satisfied with the configuration, you configure Group Policy as the method that Outlook 2010 uses to obtain security information.

> **Note**
>
> Security settings applied via Group Policy do not take effect immediately. Changes will be made after the computer receives a Group Policy update (usually at the next logon) and consequently starts Outlook 2010. Even when a computer receives refreshed Group Policy automatically, settings will not apply to Outlook 2010 until the next time it is started.

You manage Outlook 2010 attachment security using the Outlook 2010 administrative template (Outlk14.adm) and the Group Policy Editor.

For detailed information about using Group Policy templates, go to *support.microsoft.com/ kb/924617*.

To install the administrative template, first download the templates from *www.microsoft. com* and save them to a folder on the local computer or to a file share where you can access them. Then, to add the administrative template to Group Policy, follow these steps:

1. On a server with the Windows Server administrator tools installed, click Start, Run, type **gpedit.msc** in the Open box, and then press Enter.

2. In the Group Policy editor, browse to User Configuration/Administrative Templates.

3. Right-click Administrative Templates, and then select Add/Remove Template.

4. In the Add/Remove Templates dialog box, click Add.

5. Browse to the directory where you downloaded the administrative templates. Select outlk14.adm, and then click Open.

6. In the Add/Remove Templates dialog box, click Close.

To configure the Outlook 2010 attachment security settings, follow these steps:

1. On a server with the Windows Server administrator tools installed, run Group Policy by clicking Start, Run, typing **gpedit.msc**, and then pressing Enter.

2. Browse to User Configuration\Administrative Templates\Classic Administrative Templates (ADM)\Microsoft Outlook 2010\Security\Security Form Settings\ Attachment Security.

3. Configure the settings, using the following list as a guide. The default setting is Not Configured for all items in this policy:

- Enable Display Level 1 Attachments if you want to allow Outlook 2010 users to see and open Level 1 attachments, effectively setting the attachments to Level 2.

- To allow Outlook 2010 users to change Level 1 attachments to Level 2, enable Allow Users To Demote Attachments To Level 2.

- If you want to suppress the warning that usually appears when a Level 1 attachment is sent, enable Do Not Prompt About Level 1 Attachments When Sending An Item.

- To disable the warning that normally appears when the user closes an item that contains a Level 1 attachment, enable Do Not Prompt About Level 1 Attachments When Closing An Item.

- If you want to let Outlook 2010 users open embedded OLE objects (such as Microsoft Word 2010 documents, Excel 2010 spreadsheets, and other documents), enable Allow In-Place Activation Of Embedded OLE Objects.

- Enable Display OLE Package Objects to show embedded OLE objects in email messages and allow users to open them.

- You can block additional file types by enabling Add File Extensions To Block As Level 1. Specify a list of file name extensions, without periods and separated by semicolons (;), in the Additional Extensions field.

- You can specify a list of file name extensions to remove from the Level 1 attachment list by enabling Remove File Extensions Blocked As Level 1 and entering the list in the Additional Extensions field.

- To add file types to the Level 2 list, enable Add File Extensions To Block As Level 2, and then enter a list of extensions.

- Enable Remove File Extensions Blocked As Level 2, and then specify a list of file name extensions to remove from the Level 2 attachment list.

To configure the Custom Form Security settings, follow these steps:

1. In Group Policy, go to User Configuration\Administrative Templates\Classic Administrative Templates (ADM)\Microsoft Outlook 2010\Security\Security Form Settings\Custom Form Security.

2. Select Allow Scripts In One-Off Outlook Forms if you want scripts to be executed when the script and the form layout are contained in the message.

3. Set the Outlook object model Custom Actions execution prompt to specify the action that Outlook 2010 takes if a program attempts to execute a task using the Outlook 2010 object model. Select Prompt User to have Outlook 2010 prompt the user to allow or deny the action. Select Automatically Approve to allow the program to execute the task without prompting the user. Select Automatically Deny to prevent the program from executing the task without prompting the user. Select Prompt User Based On Computer Security to use the Outlook 2010 security settings.

4. You can select Set Control ItemProperty Prompt and then configure the action that Outlook 2010 takes if a user adds a control to a custom Outlook 2010 form and binds that control to an address information field (such as To or From). Select Prompt User to have Outlook 2010 ask the user to allow or deny access to the address fields when the message is received. Select Automatically Approve to allow access without prompting the user. Select Automatically Deny to deny access without prompting the user. Select Prompt User Based On Computer Security to use the Outlook 2010 security settings.

To configure older Outlook settings, follow these steps:

1. In Group Policy, go to User Configuration\Administrative Templates\Classic Administrative Templates (ADM)\Microsoft Outlook 2010\Security.

2. To force Outlook to use Protected View when opening attachments that were received from internal servers (for example, a message from another user of Exchange Server in the same Exchange Server environment), set the Use Protected View For Attachments Received From Internal Senders policy to Enabled.

3. If you do not want users to modify the Level 1 and Level 2 attachment lists, select Prevent Users From Customizing Attachment Security Settings.

Setting the Outlook Security Mode

After you have configured the Outlook 2010 security settings, you have to enable the use of those settings by enabling Exchange Server security and selecting the Outlook Security

Mode. You do this using the same administrative template that you used to configure the security settings. To select the security mode for Outlook 2010, follow these steps:

1. Run Group Policy, and then open Outlk14.adm. Go to User Configuration\ Administrative Templates\Classic Administrative Templates (ADM)\Microsoft Outlook 2010\Security\Security Form Settings.

2. Double-click Outlook Security Mode, and then select Enabled. Select Use Outlook Security Group Policy from the drop-down list, and then click OK.

Configuring Attachment Blocking Directly in Outlook

The preceding sections explained how to configure attachment blocking for Exchange Server users. Non–Exchange Server users can also control attachment blocking, although the method for modifying the attachment list is different. So if you use Outlook 2010 in a workgroup or on a stand-alone computer without Exchange Server, you can still control which attachments Outlook 2010 prevents you from opening. You simply have fewer options for controlling and applying security settings.

> **Note**
> If you modify the registry settings that affect the Level 1 list, you must restart Outlook 2010 for the changes to take effect.

Removing Blocked File Types from the Level 1 List

To change the Level 1 attachment list, you must modify a registry setting on your local computer. You can remove file types from the list as well as add them. To apply the changes across multiple computers, distribute a registry script file. You can distribute this file through a logon script, place it on a network share for users to access, or send users a message containing a shortcut to the file. (For information about how to deploy registry files using a logon script, see the Windows Server help file.)

Follow these steps to create the necessary registry settings and optionally export them as a .reg file for other users:

1. On a system with Outlook 2010 installed, choose Start, Run, and then type **regedit** in the Run dialog box.

2. In the Registry Editor, open the key HKEY_CURRENT_USER\Software\Microsoft\ Office\14.0\Outlook\Security.

3. In that key, type a string value named **Level1Remove**.

4. Set the value of Level1Remove to include the file name extensions of those files that you want removed from the Level 1 attachment list, without leading periods and separated by semicolons. The following example removes Microsoft Installer (.msi) files and Help (.hlp) files from the list:

   msi;hlp

5. If you want to share the customized registry with other users, choose File, Export Registry File. Select a location for the .reg file, and then click Save. You can then distribute the .reg file to the other users, as noted earlier.

Adding Blocked File Types to the Level 1 List

Outlook 2010 is aggressive about which attachments it blocks, but you might want to add other attachment types to the Level 1 list so that Outlook 2010 will block them. Using the same method as in the preceding procedure, add the registry value HKEY_CURRENT_USER\ Software\Microsoft\Office\14.0\Outlook\Security\Level1Add. Set the value of Level1Add to include the file name extensions that you want added to the Level 1 list. You can add multiple file types separated by semicolons. See the preceding section for options for propagating the change to other users.

Opening Blocked Attachments

Although it's useful to block attachments in general, there will undoubtedly still be the occasional legitimate attachment that ends up getting blocked by Outlook 2010. Fortunately, even though attachments are blocked, you can still access them using a few other approaches. The attachment file type (Level 1 or Level 2) and the other email programs available to you determine the best method for opening the file.

Allowing Level 1 Attachments

You can configure Outlook 2010 to allow certain Level 1 attachments (essentially removing them from the Level 1 list) by modifying the registry. (See the section "Configuring Attachment Blocking Directly in Outlook," on page 825, for instructions.) You might want to do this if you find yourself repeatedly having to deal with the same type of blocked Level 1 attachment. If you are using Exchange Server, your ability to do this may be controlled by the administrator as described in the section "Configuring Blocked Attachments," on page 815.

Allowing Level 2 Attachments

Outlook 2010 also uses a list of Level 2 attachments, which are defined by the administrator at the server level (and therefore apply to Exchange Server accounts). You can't open Level 2 attachments in Outlook 2010, but you can save them to disk and open them from there. To open a Level 2 attachment this way, follow these steps:

1. Right-click the attachment, either in the Reading pane or in the message form, and choose Save As.

2. In the Save Attachment dialog box, specify the folder in which you want to save the file, and then click Save.

3. Outside Outlook 2010, browse to the folder where you saved the attachment, and then open the file.

Because the Level 2 list is empty by default, no attachments are blocked as Level 2 attachments unless the Exchange Server administrator has modified the Level 2 list.

For detailed information about configuring attachment blocking under Exchange Server, see the section "Configuring Blocked Attachments," on page 815.

Protecting Against Office Macro Viruses

Like other Office system applications, Outlook 2010 allows you to use macros to automate common tasks. Macros have become an increasingly popular infection mechanism for viruses because most inexperienced users don't expect to have their systems infected by the sort of Office documents they regularly work with. However, Office macros can contain viruses that cause just as much damage as any other virus. Protecting yourself against macro viruses is an important step in safeguarding your system overall.

You can guard against macro viruses by implementing a virus scanner on your computer that checks your documents for macro viruses, by installing an antivirus solution on your email servers or SharePoint farm, or by using both methods. Another line of protection is to control how and when macros are allowed to run. Outlook 2010 provides four security levels for macros that determine which macros can run on the system. To set the level, in Outlook 2010, click File, Options, Trust Center, Trust Center Settings, and finally Macro Settings, and then select one of these levels:

- **Disable All Macros Without Notification**   Macros are totally disabled, and Outlook 2010 does not display any warning that a macro is attempting to run.

- **Notifications For Digitally Signed Macros, All Other Macros Disabled** Your system can run only macros that are digitally signed. This means that some macros— even benign and potentially useful ones—are not available.

- **Notifications For All Macros** You will be prompted as to whether you want to run any macros.

- **Enable All Macros (Not Recommended; Potentially Dangerous Code Can Run)** Macros run automatically, regardless of their signature. This is the most dangerous setting.

For additional information about configuring macro security and specifying trusted sources, see the section "Setting Macro Security," on page 725. To learn how to add a digital signature to your macros so that they don't generate a security warning, see the section "Signing Your Macros to Avoid Security Warnings," on page 727.

Enabling Applications to Send Email with Outlook

Some applications interact with Outlook 2010, most typically using the address book to address and send a message. In most cases, these applications will generate a security warning dialog box. The warning is built into Outlook 2010 to help you identify when unauthorized applications are attempting to access your Outlook 2010 data. For example, a worm that propagates itself by email would likely generate the warning.

The section "Configuring Attachments in Exchange Server," on page 817, explained how Exchange Server administrators can use Group Policy to configure security settings for Outlook 2010 users. That section covered how to configure attachment blocking. You can also use Group Policy to configure the behavior of specific types of applications in relation to the security features in Outlook 2010, as well as specify dynamic-link libraries (DLLs) that should be explicitly trusted and allowed to run without generating a security warning.

If you have not already configured Group Policy to manage security settings, see the section "Configuring Attachments in Exchange Server," on page 817.

Configuring Programmatic Access

Just as with the other security settings that can be configured in Exchange Server, you can control programmatic access to Outlook 2010 via either Group Policy or the Exchange Security Form.

Configuring Programmatic Access Using Group Policy

To configure the settings that determine how Outlook 2010 security features handle various types of applications, follow these steps:

1. Run Group Policy, and then go to User Configuration\Administrative Templates\ Classic Administrative Templates (ADM)\Microsoft Outlook 2010\Security\Security Form Settings\Programmatic Security.

2. Configure the Outlook 2010 object model–related settings as desired. Each of these policy items has the same Guard behavior options. Select Prompt User to have Outlook 2010 prompt the user to allow or deny the action. Select Automatically Approve to allow the program to execute the task without prompting the user. Select Automatically Deny to prevent the program from executing the task without prompting the user. Select Prompt User Based On Computer Security to use the following Outlook 2010 security settings:

   - **Configure Outlook Object Model Prompt When Sending Mail**   Specifies the action that Outlook 2010 takes when an application tries to send mail programmatically with the Outlook 2010 object model.

   - **Configure Outlook Object Model Prompt When Accessing An Address Book**   Specifies the action that Outlook 2010 takes when an application tries to access an address book with the Outlook 2010 object model.

   - **Configure Outlook Object Model Prompt When Reading Address Information**   Specifies the action that Outlook 2010 takes when an application tries to access a recipient field, such as To or Cc, with the Outlook 2010 object model.

   - **Configure Outlook Object Model Prompt When Responding To Meeting And Task Requests**   Specifies the action that Outlook 2010 takes when an application tries to send mail programmatically by using the Respond method on task and meeting requests.

   - **Configure Outlook Object Model Prompt When Executing Save As**   Specifies the action that Outlook 2010 takes when an application tries to use the Save As command programmatically to save an item.

   - **Configure Outlook Object Model Prompt When Accessing The Formula Property Of A UserProperty Object**   Specifies the action that Outlook 2010 takes if a user has added a Combination or Formula custom field to a custom form and bound it to an Address Information field. Blocking access can prevent an application from indirectly retrieving the value of the Address Information field through its Value property.

3. When you have finished configuring programmatic settings, close Group Policy.

Part of the battle of getting an application past the Outlook 2010 security prompts is in understanding what method it is using to access your Outlook 2010 data. If you're not sure, you can simply change one setting, test, and if the change doesn't enable the application to bypass the security prompts, change a different setting. This trial-and-error method isn't the most direct, but it won't take much time to test each of the possibilities. Remember that you must refresh Group Policy and then start Outlook 2010 for these changes to be applied.

Trusting Applications

In addition to (or as an alternative to) configuring security settings to allow various types of applications to bypass the Outlook 2010 security prompts, you can identify specific applications that can bypass the Outlook 2010 security prompts. These applications must be written specifically to use the Outlook 2010 security trust model.

Using Group Policy to Trust Applications

Before an unsigned application (for example, a noncommercial application) can be added to the in, you must generate a hash key value to use when setting Group Policy. The Outlook 2010 Security Hash Generator Tool is available from Microsoft by going to *office.microsoft.com/downloads/* and searching for "Outlook 2010 Security Hash Generator Tool." Once you have downloaded the hash generator, you have to install and register it before using it to create hash keys.

To install the hash generator, follow these steps:

1. Run the Hash Generator Tool Setup program to start installation. Specify a folder for the extracted files, and then click OK.

2. Open a command prompt window, and then go to the folder with the extracted files.

3. Type **CreateHash.bat /register**, and then press Enter.

To register an add-in, follow these steps:

1. Open a command prompt window, and then go to the folder with the extracted files.

2. Type **CreateHash.bat** <filename>**.dll** (where *<filename>* is the name of your file).

3. When the hash value is displayed, copy and paste it into the value field in Group Policy (or save it in a text file).

To add a trusted application, follow these steps:

1. Copy, to a location accessible to the computer where you will be modifying the Outlook 2010 security settings, the DLL or other executable file that loads the application to be trusted.

2. Generate a hash key and note its value for use during installation.

3. Run Group Policy, and then go to User Configuration\Administrative Templates\ Classic Administrative Templates (ADM)\Microsoft Outlook 2010\Security\Security Form\Programmatic Security\Trusted Add-ins.

4. Double-click Configured Trusted Add-ins.

5. Select Enabled, and then click Show.

6. In the Show Contents dialog box, add the DLL name or hash, and then click OK.

7. Repeat the process for any other applications that you want to add to the trusted list, and then close Group Policy.

Tips for Securing Your System

As you have seen, Outlook 2010 has several ways to help keep your system more secure, but there are additional steps that you can take to further ensure that you don't fall victim to viruses or other malicious software.

- **Make sure that your antivirus protection is kept up to date**   The threat from viruses changes on a daily basis, and virus definitions need updating just about as quickly. Set your antivirus software to check for updates automatically, and check it occasionally to make sure that it's doing so.

- **Create exceptions to the standard rules with discretion**   Although there are several ways around the virus protection measures provided in Outlook 2010, you should be careful deciding when you use them. Just because you can demote all Level 1 attachments to Level 2 to get past the Outlook 2010 built-in filtering doesn't mean you should.

- **Get in the habit of storing the file in an archive, such as a compressed (zipped) folder, created using Windows Explorer (or a program such as WinZip) before sending**   Since files with a .zip extension are not blocked by Outlook 2010, you can be sure that your attachment will arrive (unless the recipient server blocks it), allowing the recipient to save it and extract the contents.

> **Note**
>
> To create a zipped folder, in a Windows Explorer window, select the file(s) you want to zip, and then right-click and choose Send To, Compressed (Zipped) Folder. A compressed file will be created in the current folder.

If you have access to a location where you can upload files, such as a file server or a Share-Point site, upload your files there and send email with a link to the site rather than sending the file as an attachment. This method has advantages beyond avoiding unwanted attachment blocking: Mail files are smaller without large attachments, for example, and multiple people can download a file from a single location. Plus, you don't duplicate the file for multiple recipients, which adds to your storage requirements.

When it comes to computer security, a little common sense goes a long way. Pay attention to what you do in email. Don't open unexpected attachments or those from unknown sources.

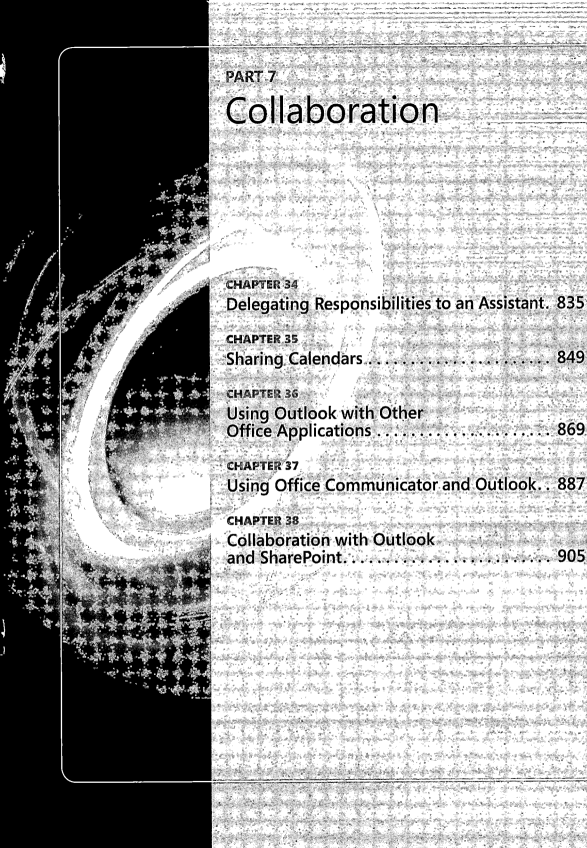

PART 7

Collaboration

Delegating Responsibilities to an Assistant

ICROSOFT Outlook 2010, when used with Microsoft Exchange Server, provides features that allow you to delegate certain responsibilities to an assistant. For example, you might want your assistant to manage your schedule, setting up appointments, meetings, and other events for you; or perhaps you want your assistant to send email messages on your behalf.

This chapter explains how to delegate access to your schedule, email messages, and other Outlook 2010 data, granting an assistant the ability to perform tasks in Outlook 2010 on your behalf. This chapter also explains how to access folders for which you've been granted delegate access.

Delegation Overview

Why delegate? You could simply give assistants your logon credentials and allow them to access your Exchange Server mailbox through a separate profile on their systems. The disadvantage to that approach, though, is that your assistants then have access to all your Outlook 2010 data. Plus, it surely violates at least one security policy at your company and gives your assistants access to everything else secured by your account, such as Microsoft SharePoint sites, line-of-business applications, and much more . . . clearly a horrible idea. By using the Outlook 2010 delegation features, however, you can restrict an assistant's access to your data selectively.

You have two ways of delegating access in Outlook 2010. First, you can specify individuals as delegates for your account, which gives them send-on-behalf-of privileges. This means that the delegated individuals can perform such tasks as sending email messages and meeting requests for you. When an assistant sends a meeting request on your behalf, the request appears to the recipients to have come from you. You can also specify that delegates should receive copies of meeting-related messages that are sent to you, such as meeting invitations. This is required if you want an assistant to be able to handle your calendar.

The second way that you can delegate access is to configure permissions for individual folders, granting various levels of access within the folders as needed. This does not give other users send-on-behalf-of privileges but does give them access to the folders and their contents. The tasks that they can perform in the folders are subject to the permission levels that you grant them.

> **Note**
>
> When a message is sent on your behalf, the recipient sees these words in the From box: <delegate> *on behalf of* <owner>, where *<delegate>* and *<owner>* are replaced by the appropriate names. This designation appears in the header of the message form when the recipient opens the message but doesn't appear in the header in the Inbox. The Inbox shows the message as coming from the owner, not the delegate.

Assigning Delegates and Working as an Assistant

You can assign multiple delegates, so that more than one individual can access your data with send-on-behalf-of privileges. You might have an assistant who manages your schedule and therefore has delegate access to your calendar and another delegate—your supervisor—who manages other aspects of your workday and therefore has access to your Tasks folder. In most cases, however, you'll probably want to assign only one delegate.

Adding and Removing Delegates

You can add, remove, and configure delegates for all your Outlook 2010 folders through the same interface.

Follow these steps to delegate access to one or more of your Outlook 2010 folders:

1. Click File, Account Settings.

2. Choose Delegate Access to open the Delegates dialog box, as shown in Figure 34-1.

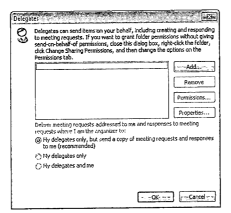

Figure 34-1 The Delegates dialog box shows the current delegates, if any, and lets you add, remove, and configure delegates.

3. Click Add to open the Add Users dialog box.

4. Select one or more users, and then click Add.

5. Click OK. Outlook 2010 displays the Delegate Permissions dialog box, shown in Figure 34-2.

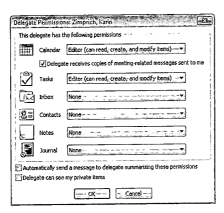

Figure 34-2 Configure delegate permissions in the Delegate Permissions dialog box.

6. For each folder, select the level of access that you want to give the delegate based on the following list:

- **None** The delegate has no access to the selected folder.

- **Reviewer** The delegate can read existing items in the folder but can't add, delete, or modify items. Essentially, this level gives the delegate read-only permission for the folder.

- **Author** The delegate can read existing items and create new ones but can't modify or delete existing items.

- **Editor** The delegate can read existing items, create new ones, and modify existing ones, including deleting them.

7. Set the other options in the dialog box using the following list as a guide:

- **Automatically Send A Message To Delegate Summarizing These Permissions** Sends an email message to the delegate informing him or her of the access permissions that you've assigned in your Outlook 2010 folders, as shown in Figure 34-3.

- **Delegate Can See My Private Items** Allows the delegate to view items that you've marked as private. Clear this option to hide your private items.

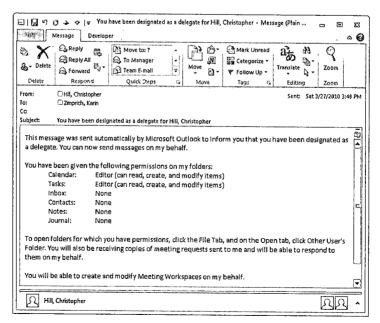

Figure 34-3 Outlook 2010 sends a message to delegates regarding their access privileges.

8. Click OK to close the Delegate Permissions dialog box.

9. Add and configure other delegates as you want, and then click OK.

If you need to modify the permissions for a delegate, open the Delegates dialog box, select the delegate in the list, and then click Permissions to open the Delegate Permissions dialog box. Change the settings as needed, just as you do when you add a delegate. If you need to remove a delegate, select the delegate on the Delegates tab, and then click Remove.

TROUBLESHOOTING

If the Permissions button appears dimmed or you are unable to assign delegate permissions for some other reason, the problem could be that you have designated a local .pst file as the default delivery location for your profile. Make sure that you configure your profile to deliver mail to your Exchange Server mailbox instead. See the section "Configuring Online and Offline Data Storage," on page 57, for details.

Taking Yourself Out of the Meeting Request Loop

If your assistant has full responsibility for managing your calendar, you might want all meeting request messages to go to the assistant rather than to you. That way, meeting request messages won't clog your Inbox.

Taking yourself out of the request loop is easy. Here's how:

1. Click File, Account Settings, and then Delegate Access.

2. Select the My Delegates Only option, and click OK.

Note
The My Delegates Only option appears dimmed if you haven't assigned a delegate.

Opening Folders Delegated to You

If you are acting as a delegate for another person, you can open the folders to which you've been given delegate access and use them as if they were your own folders, subject to the permissions applied by the owner. For example, suppose that you've been given delegate access to your manager's schedule. You can open his or her Calendar folder and create appointments, generate meeting requests, and perform the same tasks that you can perform in your own Calendar folder. However, you might find a few restrictions. For example, you won't be able to view the contents of personal items unless your manager has configured permissions to give you that ability.

Follow these steps to open another person's folder:

1. Start Outlook 2010 with your own profile.

2. Choose File, Open, and Other User's Folder to display the Open Other User's Folder dialog box, as shown in Figure 34-4.

Figure 34-4 Use the Open Other User's Folder dialog box to open another person's Outlook 2010 folder.

3. Type the person's name in the dialog box, or click Name to browse the address list, and then select a name.

4. In the Folder Type drop-down list, select the folder that you want to open, and then click OK. Outlook 2010 generates an error message if you don't have the necessary permissions for the folder; otherwise, the folder opens in a new window.

Depending on the permissions set for the other person's folder, you might be able to open the folder but not see anything in it. If someone grants you Folder Visible permission, you can open the folder but not necessarily view its contents. For example, if you are granted Folder Visible permission for a Calendar folder, you can view the other person's calendar. If you are granted Folder Visible permission for the Inbox folder, you can open the folder, but you can't see any headers. Obviously, this latter scenario isn't useful, so you might need to fine-tune the permissions to get the effect you need.

When you've finished working with another person's folder, close it as you would any other window.

Scheduling on Behalf of Another Person

If you've been given delegate privileges for another person's calendar, you can schedule meetings and other appointments on behalf of that person.

To do so, follow these steps:

1. Start Outlook 2010 with your own profile.

2. Click File, Open, and then select Other User's Folder. Type the user name into the text box, or click Name and select the user name from the Global Address List (GAL). From the Folder Type drop-down list, select Calendar, and then click OK.

3. In the other person's Calendar folder, create the meeting request, appointment, or other item as you normally would for your own calendar.

As mentioned earlier, a meeting request recipient sees the request as coming from the calendar's owner, not the delegate. When the recipient opens the message, however, the header indicates that the message was sent by the delegate on behalf of the owner. Responses to the meeting request come back to the delegate and a copy goes to the owner unless the owner has removed himself or herself from the meeting request loop.

For details about how to have meeting request messages go to the delegate rather than to the owner, see the section "Taking Yourself out of the Meeting Request Loop," on page 839.

Sending Email on Behalf of Another Person

If you've been given Author or Editor permission for another person's Inbox, you can send messages on behalf of that person. For example, as someone's assistant, you might need to send notices, requests for comments, report reminders, or similar messages.

To send a message on behalf of another person, follow these steps:

1. Start Outlook 2010 with your own profile.

2. Start a new message.

3. Click From and choose Other Email Address to open the Send From Other Email Address dialog box.

4. In the From field, type the name of the person on whose behalf you're sending the message, or click From to select an address from the GAL. Then click OK.

5. Complete the message as you would any other, and then send it.

Granting Access to Folders

You can configure your folders to provide varying levels of access to other users according to the types of tasks that those users need to perform within the folders. For example, you might grant access to your Contacts folder to allow others to see and use your contacts list.

Granting permissions for folders is different from granting delegate access. Users with delegate access to your folders can send messages on your behalf, as explained in earlier sections of this chapter. Users with access permissions for your folders do not have that ability. Use access permissions for your folders when you want to grant others certain levels of access to your folders but not the ability to send messages on your behalf.

Configuring Access Permissions

Several levels of permissions control what a user can and cannot do in your folders. These permissions include the following:

- **Create Items**   Users can post items to the folder.

- **Create Subfolders**   Users can create additional folders inside the folder.

- **Edit Own**   Users can edit those items that they have created and own.

- **Edit All**   Users can edit all items, including those that they do not own.

- **Folder Owner**   The owner has all permissions for the folder.

- **Folder Contact**   The folder contact receives automated messages from the folder such as replication conflict messages, requests from users for additional permissions, and other changes to the folder status.

- **Folder Visible**   Users can see the folder and its items.

- **Delete Items**   Depending on the setting that you choose, users can delete all items, only those items they own, or no items.

- **Free/Busy Time**   In the calendar, users can see your free/busy time.

- **Free/Busy Time, Subject, Location**   In the calendar, users can see your free/busy time, as well as the subject and location of calendar items.

- **Full Details**   In the calendar, users can see all details of items.

Outlook 2010 groups these permissions into several predefined levels, as follows:

- **Owner**   The owner has all permissions and can edit and delete all items, including those that he or she doesn't own.

- **Publishing Editor**   The publishing editor has all permissions and can edit and delete all items but does not own the folder.

- **Editor**   Users are granted all permissions except the ability to create subfolders or act as the folder's owner. Editors can edit and delete all items.

- **Publishing Author**   Users are granted all permissions except the ability to edit or delete items belonging to others and the ability to act as the folder's owner.

- **Author**   This level is the same as the Publishing Author level, except that authors can't create subfolders.

- **Nonediting Author**   Users can create and read items and delete items they own, but they can't delete others' items or create subfolders.

- **Reviewer**   Users can view items but can't modify or delete items or create subfolders.

- **Contributor**   Users can create items but can't view or modify existing items.

- **Free/Busy Time**   Users can see your free/busy time.

- **Free/Busy Time, Subject, Location**   Users can see your free/busy time, as well as the subject and location for items on your calendar.

- **None**   The folder is visible, but users can't read, create, or modify any items in the folder.

Follow these steps to grant permissions for a specific folder:

1. Start Outlook 2010, open the Folder List, right-click the folder, and then choose Share, Folder Permissions to display the Permissions tab of the folder, shown in Figure 34-5.

2. Select Default, and then set the permissions that you want users to have if they are not explicitly assigned permissions (that is, if their names don't appear in the Name list).

3. Click Add to add a user with explicit permissions. Select the name in the Add Users list, click Add, and then click OK.

4. From the Name list, select the user that you just added, and then set specific permissions for the user.

5. Click OK to close the folder's Contacts Properties dialog box.

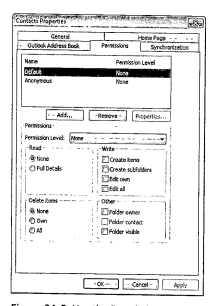

Figure 34-5 Use the Permissions tab to configure access permissions for the folder.

As you can see in Figure 34-5, you can remove the explicit permissions you have given a user by simply removing the user. Just select the user, and then click Remove.

To view (but not modify) a user's address book properties, as shown in Figure 34-6, select the user, and then click Properties.

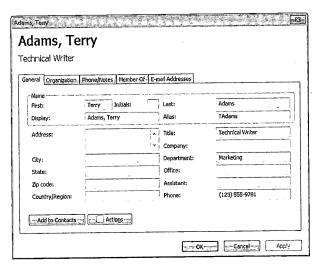

Figure 34-6 You can view a user's address book properties.

Accessing Other Users' Folders

After you've been granted the necessary permissions for another user's folder, you can open the folder and perform actions according to your permissions. For example, if you have only read permission, you can read items but not add new ones. If you've been granted create permission, you can create items.

To open another user's folder, choose File, Open, and Other User's Folder. Type the user's name into the text box, or click Name, select the user in the GAL, and then click OK. Select the folder that you want to open in the Folder Type drop-down list, and then click OK.

For more information about opening and using another person's folder, see the section "Opening Folders Delegated to You," on page 839.

Sharing Folders with Invitations

In addition to the method described in the previous section, you can use email invitations to suggest or request folder sharing. However, this option applies only to non-mail folders, including the Calendar, Tasks, Notes, Contacts, and Journal folders. You cannot share email folders using this method.

To share these types of folders using an email invitation, or to request access to someone else's folder, follow these steps:

1. Click the Folder List icon in the Navigation pane.

2. Right-click the folder that you want to share or request access to in the other person's mailbox, and choose Share, *<folder>*, where *<folder>* is the name of the folder. For example, choose Share, Calendar to share the Calendar folder.

3. Outlook opens a request form, as shown in Figure 34-7.

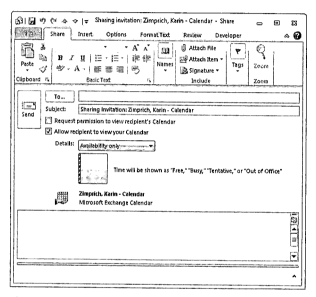

Figure 34-7 Outlook displays a form that you can use to share a folder or request access to one.

4. Enter an email address or click To and select one. This is the email address of the person with whom you are sharing your folder, or for whose folder you want to request access.

5. Choose options based on the following list:

   • **Request Permission To View Recipient's Calendar**   Choose this item if you are requesting access to the other person's folder.

   • **Allow Recipient To View Your Calendar**   Choose this option if you want to share your own calendar.

- **Details** This option applies only to Calendar folders. From the Details drop-down list, choose the level of access you want to grant to the other person to your Calendar folder. You can allow them to see only your free/busy (availability) information, availability and item subjects, or all details.

6. Click Send to send the request.

When you click Send, if you have specified that you are sharing your own folder, Outlook asks you to verify that you want to share it and then sends the message to the specified recipient. When the request arrives, the person receiving the request can click either Allow or Deny in the Respond group on the ribbon (or in the message header if the Reading pane is open) to allow or deny the request. Figure 34-8 shows an example.

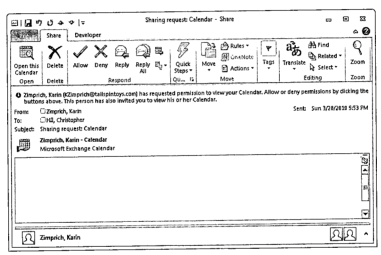

Figure 34-8 Outlook displays a form that you can use to share a folder or request access to one.

M ICROSOFT Outlook 2010 provides a number of ways for you to share your calendar information with others. In addition to using Microsoft Exchange Server to share your calendar with other Exchange Server users, you can publish your calendar to the Internet and invite others to share access to it. You can publish your calendar to Microsoft Office Online or to any Web Distributed Authoring and Versioning (WebDAV) server. You can also send your calendar to someone else via email, save the calendar as a web page and then send it, or post the calendar to a web server.

Sharing Your Calendar

If you use Exchange Server, you can allow other users to access your entire calendar or selected calendar items. To share your calendar and its items, you must set permission levels for various users. In most cases, permissions are set by using built-in roles, as described in Table 35-1, but you can also set custom permissions for the rare cases when the built-in role does not fit the situation. Some permissions allow users only to view your calendar; others allow users to add, or even edit items.

Table 35-1 Folder Permissions

Permission	Description
Owner	The Owner role gives full control of the calendar. An Owner can create, modify, delete, and read folder items; create subfolders; and change permissions on the folder.
Publishing Editor	The Publishing Editor role has all rights granted to an Owner except the right to change permissions. A Publishing Editor can create, modify, delete, and read folder items and create subfolders.
Editor	The Editor role has all rights granted to a Publishing Editor except the right to create subfolders. An Editor can create, modify, delete, and read folder items.

Permission	Description
Publishing Author	A Publishing Author can create and read folder items and create subfolders but can modify and delete only folder items that he or she creates, not items created by other users.
Author	An Author has all rights granted to a Publishing Author but cannot create subfolders. An Author can create and read folder items and modify and delete items that he or she creates.
Nonediting Author	A Nonediting Author can create and read folder items but cannot modify or delete any items, including those that he or she creates.
Reviewer	A Reviewer can read folder items but nothing else.
Contributor	A Contributor can create folder items but cannot delete items.
Free/Busy Time, Subject, Location	A user with these access rights can view the free/busy information, as well as the subject and location.
Free/Busy Time	A user with these access rights can view only the free/busy information.
None	The None role has no rights to access to the folder.

The first step in sharing a calendar is to right-click it in the Navigation pane and then choose Share, Calendar Permissions. Figure 35-1 shows the Permissions tab with the Calendar folder's default permissions.

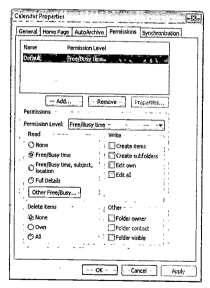

Figure 35-1 The default permissions for a calendar are set to Free/Busy Time.

To allow all users to view details of the calendar, you need to assign Reviewer permission to the default user. A *default user* is any user who is logged in. Select Default in the Name column, and then change the permission level by selecting Reviewer in the Permission Level drop-down list.

INSIDE OUT   Share your calendar for review quickly

You can also right-click the calendar and then choose Share, Share Calendar. An email is generated that grants permission, and you can add people with whom you want to share the calendar to the To line. Reviewer (read-only) status is granted using this method. This approach not only shares the calendar but also automatically generates an email message to inform the recipients that you have made the calendar available to them.

You might assign a permission of Publishing Author to users if they are colleagues who need to be able to schedule items for you as well as view your calendar.

To give users Publishing Author access to the calendar, follow these steps:

1. On the Permissions tab in the Calendar Properties dialog box, click Add to open the Add Users dialog box, shown in Figure 35-2. Alternatively, you can right-click the calendar in the Navigation pane and then choose Share, Calendar Permissions.

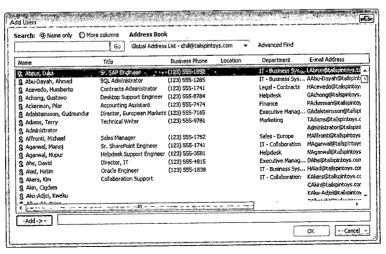

Figure 35-2 Add users to the Permissions tab so that you can specify their permissions for folder sharing.

2. Select a user or distribution list in the Add Users dialog box (hold down Shift and click to select a range of users, or hold down Ctrl and click to select multiple users), and then click Add. After you have selected all the users that you want to add, click OK.

3. By default, Outlook 2010 adds users to the Permissions tab with Free/Busy Time permission. To change the permission of a newly added user to Publishing Author, select the user's name, and then select the permission in the Permission Level drop-down list. Figure 35-3 shows the Permissions tab after these changes have been made.

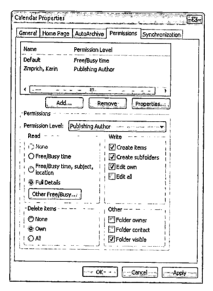

Figure 35-3 A user has been added and the permission level has been changed to Publishing Author.

As you can see in Figure 35-3, the permissions granted to a user can be configured manually using the check boxes in the bottom half of the Permissions tab. However, this is usually unnecessary because you can set most combinations of settings using the Permission Level drop-down list.

You can configure your Free/Busy settings by clicking Other Free/Busy. The Free/Busy Options dialog box is displayed, as shown in Figure 35-4, allowing you to set the amount of free/busy information that you publish on the computer running Exchange Server and specify the frequency of updates. You can also configure your Internet free/busy publishing and search locations to set custom Internet addresses for your free/busy publishing and search locations.

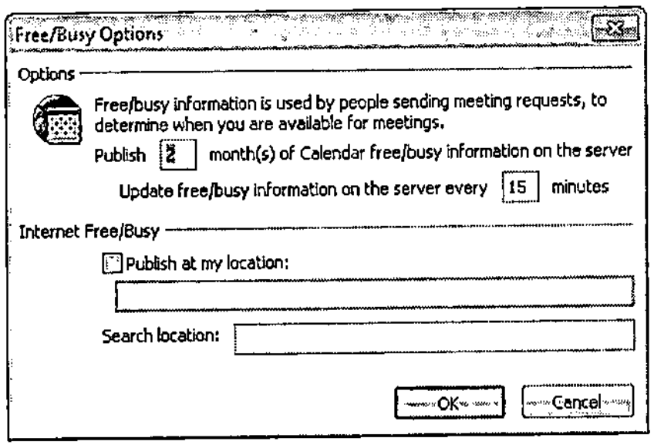

Figure 35-4 Configure your free/busy options for Exchange Server and Internet calendar publishing.

INSIDE OUT   Permissions and delegation are different

Giving someone permission to view or modify your Calendar folder is not the same as assigning them to be a delegate. Delegate permission gives the person the ability to send and receive meeting notices on your behalf. See Chapter 34, "Delegating Responsibilities to an Assistant," for details on assigning delegate permissions.

Managing Your Shared Calendar Information

By default, if you're using Exchange Server, your free/busy information is shared automatically with all other users on that server. If you want users who are not on your server to be able to view that information, or if you do not use Exchange Server at all, you can still share your free/busy information. You can also post your calendar information to Microsoft Office Online or to a web server using WebDAV (including Microsoft SharePoint sites that are configured for anonymous access). For example, your company might set up its own server to enable users to share their calendar information with others, whether within the company (for example, if you don't use Exchange Server) or outside the company.

Note
This section focuses on how to publish your calendar information and configure Outlook 2010 to search for calendar information. See the section "Using Calendar Groups and Schedule View," on page 864, to learn how to view others' calendar information.

TROUBLESHOOTING

Other users don't see your schedule changes

When you make changes to your schedule, those changes might not be visible right away to other users who need to see your free/busy times. By default, Outlook 2010 updates your free/busy information every 15 minutes. To change the frequency of these updates, click File, Options, and then click Calendar. Click Free/Busy Options, and then click Other Free/Busy to access the Update Free/Busy Information On The Server Every n Minutes option (shown in Figure 35-4), which you can use to set the frequency of updates.

Publishing your calendar information makes it possible for others to see your free/busy times in Outlook 2010 when they need to schedule meetings with you or view or manage your calendar. Likewise, the free/busy times of people who publish their calendar information, and who give you access to that information, are visible to you in Outlook 2010. The ability to publish free/busy information to web servers, therefore, brings group scheduling capabilities to users of Outlook 2010 who do not have access to Exchange Server.

Understanding What Status Is Available

Exchange Server provides four free/busy states for a given time period: Free, Tentative, Busy, and Out Of Office. When you publish your calendar to Microsoft Office Online or a WebDAV server, you can specify which level of calendar detail is available to the viewing user. When you publish your free/busy information to a web server or file server via File Transfer Protocol (FTP), Hypertext Transfer Protocol (HTTP), or a file, however, only Free/ Busy or No Information status is available. Consequently, if you view someone's free/busy information that is published to an FTP site, an HTTP site, or a file server, all time that the user has marked as Tentative or Out Of Office appears as Busy when you view his or her schedule in Outlook 2010. The only way to view Tentative and Out Of Office status is to pull that information directly from Exchange Server, from Microsoft Office Online, or from a WebDAV server (if the posting user has chosen to include detail in the calendar).

INSIDE OUT   Prevent free/busy publishing

You can avoid publishing your free/busy information to any servers if you prefer. Choose Tools, Options, click Calendar Options, Free/Busy Options, and then click Other Free/Busy. You can set the Publish n Months Of Calendar Free/Busy Information On The Server option to specify how much of your free/busy information is published. By setting this value to 0, no free/busy information is published, and your free/busy information will appear blank to other users.

Publishing Your Schedule

Microsoft Office Online is a central place on the Internet where you can publish your schedule. Publishing your schedule allows anyone (or only those you specify) to access your calendar information from anywhere on the Internet. This free Microsoft service is useful if you don't use Exchange Server but still want to share your calendar information with others, whether inside or outside your company. You can also use this Microsoft service in conjunction with Exchange Server, publishing your calendar information to the service to allow users outside your Exchange Server organization to view schedule status.

The following sections explain how to publish to the different types of calendar servers. Later in this chapter, you'll also learn how to set up your own free/busy server.

Publishing Your Calendar to Microsoft Office Online

To publish your Calendar folder to Office.com, open the Calendar folder and click Publish Online in the Share group on the Home tab on the ribbon. Then, choose Publish To Office.com or Publish To WebDAV Server, as shown in Figure 35-5.

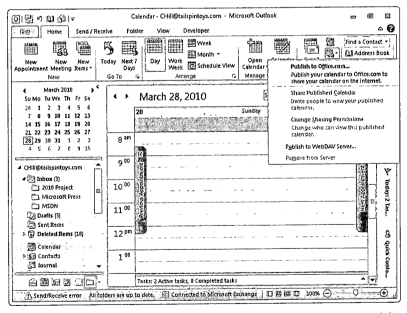

Figure 35-5 To publish your calendar to the Internet, click Publish Online, and then choose Publish To Office.com.

If you choose to publish your calendar to Microsoft Office Online, the Publish Calendar To Office.com dialog box is displayed, as shown in Figure 35-6.

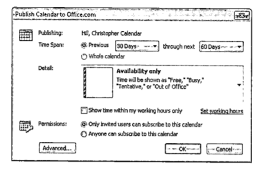

Figure 35-6 You can configure date range, details, access, and updates when publishing your calendar to Microsoft Office Online.

The Publish Calendar To Office.com dialog box contains the following options:

- **Time Span**   In this area, you can specify the range of calendar information by set-ting the Previous and Through Next options.

- **Detail**   In this area, you can select the level of information detail that will be dis-played to users viewing your calendar:

  - **Availability Only**   Only the availability status of the time will be displayed, as Free, Busy, Tentative, or Out Of Office.

  - **Limited Details**   Displays the availability status as well as the Subject line of calendar items.

  - **Full Details**   Includes availability status and all information associated with the calendar items.

  - **Show Time Within My Working Hours Only**   You can limit the display of calendar information to only your working hours by selecting the Show Time Within My Working Hours Only check box. You can configure your working hours by clicking the Set Working Hours link.

- **Permissions**   In this area, you can control the access to your published calendar:

  - **Only Invited Users Can Subscribe To This Calendar**   Limits access to your published calendar to people that you invite (via email).

- **Anyone Can Subscribe To This Calendar**   Allows anyone to view your published calendar.

- **Advanced**   By clicking the Show button in the Advanced area, you can elect to have private items also displayed and to have updates occur with the server's recommended frequency.

- **Upload Method**   In this area, you can control the uploading of your calendar with the following options:

    - **Automatic Uploads**   Enables the automatic updating of your published calendar.

    - **Single Upload**   Enables the one-time publishing of your calendar with no further updates.

    - **Update Frequency**   Choose this option to update the calendar based on the server settings regardless of your configured send/receive settings.

A Few Differences When Publishing to a WebDAV Server

If you are publishing to a WebDAV server instead of to Microsoft Office Online, the dialog box you'll see is slightly different from Figure 35-6, as follows:

- The dialog box title bar reads Publish Calendar To Custom Server.

- The dialog box contains a Location field in which you type the Uniform Resource Locator (URL) location of the WebDAV server and the website or virtual directory where the calendar files (*.ics) are stored—for example, http://server.domain.com/calendars.

- There is no Permissions area.

After you publish your calendar to a WebDAV server, you will be prompted to send email invitations to others with whom you want to share your calendar information.

If this is your first connection to Microsoft Office Online, you will have to register for a Microsoft Windows Live ID (if you don't have one) and go through online registration for the Windows Live service before your calendar is published. You will be prompted to sign in to your Microsoft Office Online account.

After your calendar has been published, you will be asked whether you want to send email notifications to people whom you want to access your calendar.

> **Note**
>
> When sending email invitations to others to access your calendar, Outlook 2010 will include this notice: "This calendar is shared with restricted permissions. To subscribe to this calendar, you need to enroll the email address to which this email message was sent with a Windows Live ID account."

Your calendar information is now shared using Microsoft Office Online, and other users who have received your email invitations can view that information.

Publishing to FTP, HTTP, and File Servers

You can also publish your free/busy schedule to another server using FTP, HTTP, or a share on a file server. For example, if you don't use Exchange Server in your company, you might set up a web server on your network to enable users to publish and share their free/busy information. Using your own server eliminates the need to use the Microsoft Office Online service and the need for users to have a Microsoft Windows Live ID account (which is required to use the Microsoft Office Online service).

You can publish to local or remote FTP or HTTP servers, making it easy to publish free/busy information to servers outside your organization. For example, you might work at a division that doesn't have its own web server, but the corporate office does have a server that you can use to publish your free/busy information. Publishing to a file requires a share on your computer or on a local file server. However, that doesn't mean that users who need to access that free/busy information must be located on the local network. You might publish your free/busy information to a share on your local web server, for example, but remote users can then access that free/busy information through the web server's HTTP-based URL.

You must know the correct URL for the server to configure the free/busy URL in Outlook 2010. Here are three examples:

- *http://www.tailspintoys.com/schedules/chill.vfb*

- *ftp://ftp.tailspintoys.com/schedules/chill.vfb*

- *f:\Schedules\Chill.vfb*

Note that schedule files use a .vfb file name extension. Also, the first two examples assume a virtual or physical folder named Schedules under the root of the specified server URL.

INSIDE OUT   You can specify the URL with replaceable parameters

In addition to specifying the URL string explicitly, you can use two replaceable parameters in the URL string:

- **%server%**   This parameter represents the server portion of the email address. For example, with the address chill@tailspintoys.com, %server% would resolve to tailspintoys.com. If you specified the URL http://%server%/schedules/chill.vfb, Outlook 2010 would resolve the server domain, and the resulting URL would be http://tailspintoys.com/schedules/chill.vfb.

- **%name%**   This parameter represents the account portion of the email address. Using the chill@tailspintoys.com example, %name% would resolve to chill. If you specified the URL http://%server%/schedules/%name%.vfb, for example, Outlook 2010 would resolve the URL to http://tailspintoys.com/schedules/chill.vfb.

If you need to include *www* in the URL, add it like this: http://www.%server%/schedules/%name%.vfb.

If your profile includes an Exchange Server account, specifying *%name%* in the URL string will result in Outlook 2010 trying to use the X.400 address from your Exchange Server account, causing the publishing of the free/busy information to fail. Instead of using the variable, specify an explicit name.

Why provide replaceable parameters if you can just type in the correct URL? You can use Group Policy to control the Outlook 2010 configuration, and one of the policies controls the free/busy publish and search URLs. You can define the publishing URL using replaceable parameters in the policy, and those parameters are then replaced when users log on, resulting in the correct URL for users based on their email address.

Configuring Outlook 2010 to publish to an FTP, an HTTP, or a file URL is easy. Follow these steps to configure Outlook 2010 to publish your free/busy information:

1. Click File, Options.

2. Click Calendar, Free/Busy Options.

3. Click Other Free/Busy.

4. In the Free/Busy Options dialog box, select Publish At My Location.

5. In the Publish At My Location text box, type the fully qualified path to the server on which your free/busy information is to be published.

6. In the Search location box, specify the server to search. This server will be used to view other users' free/busy information. (See the following section for additional details on configuring search locations.)

7. Click OK to close the Free/Busy Options dialog box.

Setting the Search Location for Free/Busy Information

The Free/Busy Options dialog box includes a Search Location box that specifies where Outlook 2010 will search for free/busy information when you create group schedules or meeting requests. Specify the URL or file share where the group's calendars are published, and Outlook 2010 will search the specified URL for free/busy information.

These global settings can work in conjunction with Exchange Server, providing a search location for calendars not stored in Exchange Server. In addition to these global settings, you can specify a search URL for individual contacts. You would specify the search URL in the contact if the contact's free/busy information is not stored on the Microsoft Office Online service or another server specified in the Search Location box.

Follow these steps to set the free/busy search URL for a contact:

1. Open the contact. In the Show group on the Contact tab, click Details.

2. Click in the Address field in the Internet Free-Busy area, and then type the URL as an HTTP, an FTP, or a file share. An FTP URL would look like this:

   ftp://ftp.domain.com/freebusy/JimBoyce.vfb

3. Click Save & Close.

Configuring FTP Authentication in Microsoft Windows XP for Free/Busy Searches

If you publish to an HTTP or a file URL that requires authentication, your web browser or Windows itself will prompt you for a user name and password when Outlook 2010 attempts to connect. If you are publishing to an FTP site, however, you need to use a different method to specify the user name and password for the free/busy server. You cannot simply embed the user name and password in the publish/search string as you would when connecting to an FTP site from Windows Internet Explorer. If you are using Windows XP, you can use the following steps to configure authentication information for connecting to FTP servers. Windows Vista and Windows 7 do not support this operation. However, Windows 7 does allow you to enter the user name and password in the FTP URL using the format *ftp://user:password@ftp.domain.com*.

Perform these steps to add authentication information for an FTP site in Outlook 2010:

1. Choose File, Open, and then Open Outlook Data File.

2. In the Open Outlook Data File dialog box, click the Look In drop-down list, and then select Add/Modify FTP Locations. Outlook 2010 displays the Add/Modify FTP Locations dialog box.

3. Type the FTP server name or Internet Protocol (IP) address in the Name Of FTP Site box.

4. Select the User option, type a user name in the User box, and then type a password in the Password box.

5. Click Add, and then click OK. Click OK to close the Open Outlook Data File dialog box.

Chapter 35

Refreshing Your Schedule

Free/busy information is refreshed automatically at the intervals set in the Free/Busy Options dialog box. (Click File, Options, Calendar, and then Free/Busy Options to configure these settings.)

You can refresh free/busy information manually as well. The command to do so does not by default appear in the ribbon, but you can add it. Right-click the ribbon and choose Customize The Ribbon. From the Choose Commands From drop-down list, choose Commands Not In The Ribbon. Locate the Publish Internet Free/Busy command, add it to the ribbon, and then click OK. When you need to update your free/busy data, click Publish Internet Free/Busy on the ribbon.

Sharing Your Calendar via Email

Outlook 2010 enables you to send your calendar to other people via email, either by clicking the E-Mail Calendar button on the ribbon or by right-clicking the calendar and then choosing Share, E-Mail Calendar. A new mail message form will be opened, and the Send A Calendar Via E-Mail dialog box will be displayed, as shown in Figure 35-7. In this dialog box, you can select the calendar to send and configure the date range and amount of detail that the calendar contains. When you click Show in the Advanced area, you can enable the display of information marked as private, include attachments in the calendar, and specify the layout of the calendar as either Daily Schedule or List Of Events. When you click OK, the calendar is written into the email message as text and as an attachment.

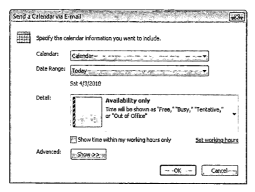

Figure 35-7 You can select a calendar and configure date range, details, and layout when emailing your calendar.

Sending a Link to Your Internet Free/Busy Information Through Email

If you are using an Internet free/busy server to publish your availability, you can use email to send a vCard containing your free/busy URL to others who might need to see your availability. To email your free/busy information to others, you must first link that information to a vCard, as follows:

1. Open a contact item containing your own contact information.

2. In the Show group of the Contact tab, click Details. The Details page appears, as shown in Figure 35-8.

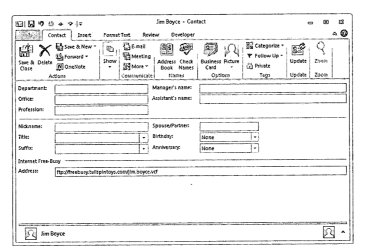

Figure 35-8 On the Details page of a contact form, you can specify the Internet free/busy server.

3. In the Address box in the Internet Free-Busy area, type the address of the server containing your free/busy information.

4. Click Save on the Quick Access Toolbar to save any changes, click File, Save As, and then select vCard Files from the Save As Type dialog box.

5. In the Save As dialog box, type the name of the file, and then select the location where you want to save the file.

6. Click Save to create the vCard.

You can now send the vCard to other users, and they can reference your free/busy information. For more details about using vCards, see the section "Sharing Contacts with vCards," on page 466.

Changing the Free/Busy Status of an Item

You can change the free/busy status of an item easily. One method is to right-click the item, choose Show As, and then select Free, Busy, Tentative, or Out Of Office. The second method is to open the item (by double-clicking it, or right-clicking it and then choosing Open), and then select Free, Busy, Tentative, or Out Of Office from the Show As drop-down list in the Options group on the ribbon.

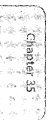

Using Calendar Groups and Schedule View

Outlook 2007 included a feature called Group Schedules that you could use to view the calendars of multiple people at one time, which was handy for seeing availability for a group of people at a glance. This feature has been replaced in Outlook 2010 by calendar groups. Calendar groups offer the same capabilities as Group Schedules, but with the added benefit that some of your calendar groups get created automatically. These include the Team calendar group, which shows the schedules of everyone who reports to you, and the My Peers calendar group, which shows the schedules of everyone who reports to your manager.

Using the Built-In Calendar Groups

To view the default calendar groups, first open the Calendar folder. In the Navigation pane, you should see two groups: Team and My Peers. Place a check beside a group to view the calendars of the group members, as shown in Figure 35-9.

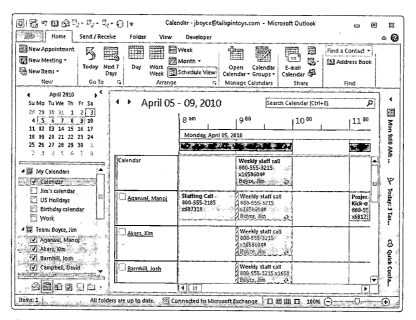

Figure 35-9 Outlook 2010 creates some calendar groups automatically.

As Figure 35-9 shows, the default view for a calendar group is Schedule View, which shows the individuals on the left and their schedules on the right. You can control whose

calendars are shown by selecting or clearing the check boxes beside the names in the Navigation pane. To close the calendar group, clear the check box beside the group name.

In addition to giving you a quick, overall view of the group's availability, you can use calendar groups to schedule calendar items. For example, if you want to schedule a meeting with
someone in a group, just double-click a time slot in someone's schedule. Outlook opens a
new meeting request for the individual using the specified time slot. You can also right-click
in a time slot and choose different types of calendar items from the menu, such as recurring
events and appointments.

You can also view the calendar group using the other standard calendar views, such as day
or week. However, only the Day view is really very useful (and then only if you have suf-
ficient desktop space for Outlook) unless you overlay the calendars. To choose a different
view for the calendar group, simply click a view on the Home tab.

Creating a Calendar Group

The default calendar groups can be very useful, but you might want to create your own
calendar groups. For example, maybe you have people working for you who don't report
directly to you, and therefore their Active Directory Domain Services (AD DS) accounts
don't reflect you as their manager. These people will not show up in your Team calendar.
Alternatively, perhaps you are working on a major project and would like to see the calendars of the other people who are working on the project with you. Whatever the case, you
can create your own calendar groups easily, as follows:

1. Open the Calendar folder, and then, on the Home tab on the ribbon, click Calendar
    Groups and choose Create New Calendar Group.

2. Outlook opens a dialog box to prompt for the name of the group (see Figure 35-10).
    Enter a name of your choice and click OK.

Figure 35-10 Enter a name for the calendar group.

3. In the Select Name dialog box, select the people whose calendars you want to view
    and then click Group Members.

4. Click OK.

The new calendar group appears in the Navigation pane, as shown in Figure 35-11. The calendar group is displayed along with any other individual calendars or groups that you have selected. Use the check boxes beside the groups and individual calendars to control which ones are displayed.

> **Tip**
>
> You can change the order of calendar groups in the Navigation pane. To move a group up or down, right-click the group in the Navigation pane and choose Move Up or Move Down.

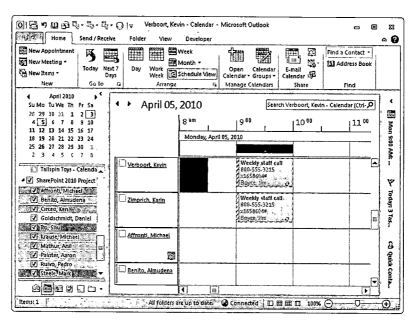

Figure 35-11 The new calendar group appears in the Navigation pane.

Creating a Group from Existing Calendars

If you already have several calendars displayed in Outlook, but they are not part of a group, you can create a group containing those calendars easily. Place a check beside each of the calendars that you want in the group, then click Calendar Groups on the ribbon and choose Save As New Calendar Group. Outlook moves the calendars to the group in the Navigation pane. If you later decide that you want to move some of or all the calendars to different groups, you can. The next section explains how.

Moving/Removing Calendars and Groups

If you want to move a calendar from one group to another, just drag it to the desired group. Note that if you hold down the Ctrl key while dragging the calendar, Outlook displays a plus sign (+) beside the calendar, the standard sign that a program will copy the calendar rather than move it. This is a false indication, however, as the calendar is still moved and not copied. But this could be fixed in a subsequent hotfix or update.

It's easy to remove a calendar group. Just right-click the calendar group in the Navigation pane and choose Delete Group. Outlook displays a dialog box for confirmation. Click Yes to delete the group.

> **Note**
> Deleting a calendar group deletes the group only from Outlook. It does not delete the users' calendars or affect their accounts in any way.

Creating Your Own Free/Busy Server

If you don't have Exchange Server in your organization, you can still publish your free/busy information so that others, whether inside or outside your organization, can view that information for scheduling purposes. As explained earlier in this chapter, Outlook 2010 can publish to FTP, HTTP, or file URLs. Which type you choose depends on the availability of such servers in your network, whether outside users need access to the free/busy information, and firewall and security issues for incoming access to the servers. For example, if your network does not allow FTP traffic through its firewalls but does allow HTTP, HTTP would be the choice for your free/busy server. However, keep in mind that publishing and searching are two different tasks that can use two different methods. You might have users internal to the network publish to a shared network folder, but outside users would access the information by HTTP. Naturally, this means that the target folder for publishing the free/busy information must also be a physical or virtual directory of the URL that outsiders use to view free/busy information. If your free/busy server must be located on the other side of a firewall from your users, FTP or HTTP would be a logical choice for publishing.

After you decide which access methods you need to provide for publishing and viewing free/busy information, it's a simple matter to set up the appropriate type of server. There are no requirements specific to free/busy data for the server, so any FTP, HTTP, or file server will do the trick.

> **Note**
> You can use Microsoft Internet Information Services (IIS) running on Microsoft Windows 2000 Server or later to host free/busy FTP or HTTP virtual servers. If you need no more than a maximum of 10 concurrent connections, you can use Windows XP Professional or Windows Vista to host the site. Windows 7 allows up to 20 concurrent connections. Note that this is a licensing restriction, not a technical restriction.

The following list includes points to keep in mind as you begin planning and deploying your free/busy server:

- **FTP**   Set up the virtual server to allow both read and write permissions for the physical or virtual folder that will contain the free/busy data.

> **Note**
> For the best security, configure the server to require authentication and disallow anonymous access. Passing FTP authentication for free/busy information via Outlook 2010 isn't supported in Windows Vista, but you can do this in Windows XP and Windows 7 (by different methods). Keep in mind that you then need to provide authentication information to everyone who needs to access the server for free/busy information. Remember to configure NTFS file system permissions as needed to control access if the directory resides on an NTFS file system partition.

- **HTTP**   The physical or virtual directory containing the free/busy data must be configured for both read and write permissions. If the directory resides on an NTFS file system partition, configure NTFS file system permissions as necessary to allow access to the directory as needed. You can disallow anonymous access, if desired, for greater security. Users who attempt to access the free/busy data are then required to provide a user name and password when publishing or searching.

- **File**   Configure folder and file permissions as needed to allow users to access the shared directory. For better security, place the folder on an NTFS file system partition and use NTFS file system permissions to restrict access to the folder and its contents as needed.

Integrating Outlook with Other Office Applications

MICROSOFT Outlook 2010 works well as a stand-alone application, but its real strength is realized when you integrate it with other Microsoft Office 2010 system applications. Most of us spend our days working in one or two main programs, such as Microsoft Word or Microsoft Excel, so most of our information is saved in files designed for those programs. For instance, you probably save letters and other correspondence in Word 2010 files; save contact information in Outlook 2010; and save financial or other data in Excel 2010. With the Office system, you can integrate it all, which enables you to choose the best tool for creating your information and the best tool for sharing or producing your data.

Some of the ways to integrate Outlook 2010 with other Office system applications include the following:

- Using Outlook 2010 contacts for a Word 2010 mail merge

- Exporting Outlook 2010 contacts to Word 2010, Excel 2010, or Microsoft Access 2010

- Importing contacts from Word 2010, Excel 2010, or Access 2010 into Outlook 2010

- Using Outlook 2010 notes in other Office system applications

In this chapter, you'll learn about using Outlook 2010 and other Office system applications to share information between applications. Instead of employing standard copy-and-paste or cut-and-paste techniques, you'll find out about ways to reuse your information in Outlook 2010 or another file format without retyping or re-creating the data.

Using Contacts for a Mail Merge in Word

The Outlook 2010 Contacts folder enables you to create contact entries to store information about a person, a group, or an organization. You can then use that contact data to create email messages, set up meetings or appointments, or complete other tasks associated with a contact. Your contacts list can also be used as the data source to provide names, addresses, phone numbers, and other pertinent data to your mail merge documents.

You perform a *mail merge* in Word 2010 when you want to create multiple documents that are all based on the same letter or document but have different names, addresses, or other specific information (referred to as *merge data*). For instance, you might perform a mail merge operation when you want to do a mass mailing to your customers about a new product launch.

You begin by creating and saving a standard letter. Next, you place field codes where you want the recipient's address, the salutation, and other merge data to appear. *Field codes* are placeholders in documents where data will change. For instance, the name of the recipient should be a field code because it will change for each letter you send out.

You then create or assign a database to populate the field codes (that is, to insert the merge data). Word 2010 uses the database and contact information to create separate letters. You can then save these files or print each letter for your mass mailing.

> **Tip**
> Before starting to set up a mail merge using your Outlook 2010 contact data, review your contact entries to make sure that the data is complete and current and that you don't have duplicate entries.

To perform a mail merge using Word 2010, follow these steps:

1. Start Word 2010.

2. Click the Mailings tab on the ribbon.

3. Click Start Mail Merge.

4. Click Step By Step Mail Merge Wizard (see Figure 36-1).

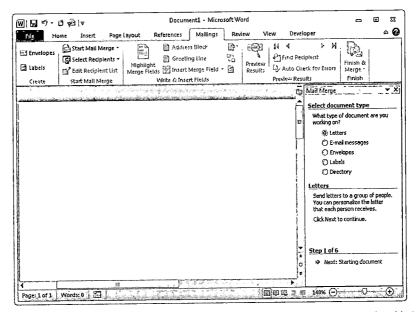

Figure 36-1 Start a mail merge by opening the Step By Step Mail Merge Wizard in Word 2010, which appears in the task pane on the right.

5. In the task pane, select the type of document to create, such as Letters, and then click Next: Starting Document at the bottom of the pane.

6. Select the document to use—for example, the current document. Click Next: Select Recipients.

7. Click Select From Outlook Contacts.

8. Select the Choose Contacts Folder option to open the Select Contacts dialog box (see Figure 36-2). (If you have configured Outlook 2010 to always prompt you for a profile and Outlook 2010 is not open, you are asked to select a profile.)

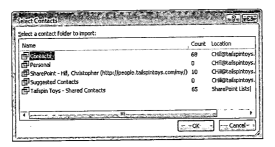

Figure 36-2 Select your Contacts folder here.

9. Select the folder that contains the contacts list that you want to use, and then click OK to open the Mail Merge Recipients dialog box (see Figure 36-3).

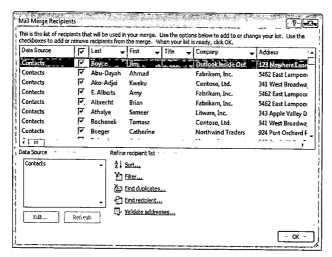

Figure 36-3 Select contacts to include in the mail merge from the Mail Merge Recipients dialog box.

10. Select the contacts that you want to use to populate the mail merge document. All the contacts are selected by default. You can use the following methods to modify the selected list of contacts:

- Select the check box beside the Data Source column to choose all the contacts in the list (the default), or clear the check box to clear all the contacts and then select individual contacts.

- Click Sort to sort the contact list.

- Click Filter to filter the list according to user-specified criteria.

- Click Find Duplicates to locate duplicate names to clear them from the mail merge list.

- Click Find Recipient to locate a specific name in your contact list.

- Click Validate Addresses to use an add-in tool to verify that the addresses are valid.

- Clear the check boxes next to the names of those whom you do not want to include in the mail merge.

> **Note**
> If you want to create a mailing list that is a subset of your Contacts folder, you
> can filter the contacts list with a custom view and then use the custom view to
> perform a mail merge from Outlook 2010.

See the section "Performing a Mail Merge from Outlook," on page 876.

1. Click OK.

2. Click Next: Write Your Letter.

3. Click Address Block to open the Insert Address Block dialog box (see Figure 36-4).

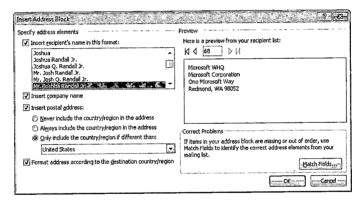

Figure 36-4 Set the address block fields in this dialog box.

4. Using the options in this dialog box, specify the address fields and format that you
   want to include in your letter. Click OK.

5. Press Enter and then click Greeting Line to insert and format a greeting line from
   your Contact information.

6. Click More Items to insert specific fields from your Contact information.

7. Write the body of your letter. When you finish, click Next: Preview Your Letters to
   see how the Outlook 2010 contact data looks in your letter. Figure 36-5 shows an
   example.

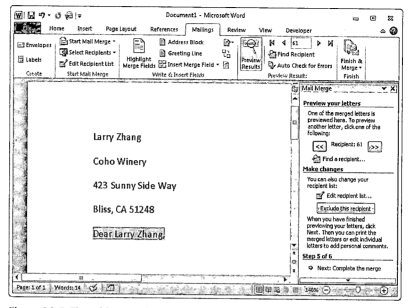

Figure 36-5 The address and salutation data in this letter came from an Outlook 2010 Contacts folder.

> **Note**
>
> As Figure 36-5 indicates, you will probably need to do some formatting of the mail merge fields, such as setting line spacing and spacing before or after paragraphs.

8. In the task pane, click Next: Complete The Merge to finish.

9. Finish editing your letter (or print it, if you want).

For detailed information about performing mail merges in Word 2010 and using other Word 2010 features, see *Microsoft Word 2010 Inside Out,* by Katherine Murray (Microsoft Press, 2010).

Filtering Contacts in or out of the Merge

When you perform a mail merge from Word 2010, you can use selection criteria to deter-mine which of the contacts are included in the mail merge set. For example, assume that you want to send a letter to all your contacts who have addresses in California and whose last names begin with the letter *R*.

In the Mail Merge Recipients dialog box (see Figure 36-3), each data column includes a drop-down button next to the column heading. To specify selection criteria based on a par-ticular column, click the drop-down button and choose one of the following commands:

- **All**   Do not filter based on the selected column.

- **Blanks**   Include only those contacts for which the selected field is blank. For exam-ple, choose this option under the E-Mail Address column to include all contacts who do not have an email address in their contact record.

- **Nonblanks**   Include only those contacts for which the selected field is not blank. For example, select this option under the Last field to include only those contacts whose Last Name field is not blank.

- **Advanced**   Click this button to open the Filter And Sort dialog box, explained next.

If you click Advanced to open the Filter And Sort dialog box, shown in Figure 36-6, you can specify more-complex selection criteria. The following example includes those contacts whose last names start with *R* and whose State value equals *CA:*

1. In the Mail Merge Recipients dialog box, click the drop-down button beside the Last field. Click Advanced.

2. From the first Field drop-down list, choose Last, choose Greater Than from the Comparison drop-down list, and then enter **Q** in the Compare To field.

3. From the second Field drop-down list, choose Last, choose Less Than from the Comparison drop-down list, and then enter **S** in the Compare To field.

4. Select State from the third Field drop-down list, choose Equal To from the Comparison drop-down list, and enter **CA** in the Compare To field. The dialog box should look similar to the one shown in Figure 36-6.

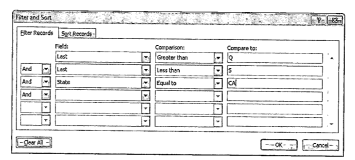

Figure 36-6 These settings select all contacts whose names start with R and whose addresses are in California.

5. Click OK to close the Filter And Sort dialog box. After a few moments, the Mail Merge Recipients list shows only those contacts whose last name begins with *R* and whose State value is listed as *CA*.

As you might have guessed from Figure 36-6, you can select *OR* instead of *AND* in the dialog box for a particular criterion. For example, you would use *OR* for the third criterion (step 4) to cause Outlook 2010 to include contacts in the mail merge if their names started with *R* or if they lived in California. A contact would also be included if both criteria were met.

Performing a Mail Merge from Outlook

As the previous sections illustrated, it's easy to perform a mail merge from Word 2010 and pull contact information from Outlook 2010. You can also filter the contacts to include only those that suit your needs.

You can also perform a mail merge from Outlook 2010. Starting from Outlook 2010 gives you a few advantages:

- **More control over contacts to be included**   You can merge all the contacts in the current view of the Contacts folder or merge only those contacts you have selected in the folder.

- **Control over which fields to include**   You can include all contact fields or only those fields that are visible in the current folder view.

- **Capability to save the contacts for later use**   Outlook 2010 gives you the option of saving the contacts to a Word 2010 document to use for future reference or for future mail merges from Word 2010.

To begin a mail merge from Outlook 2010, select Contacts in the Navigation pane, and then click Mail Merge in the Actions group on the Home tab on the ribbon to open the Mail Merge Contacts dialog box. As Figure 36-7 illustrates, Outlook 2010 offers two options to control which contacts are included in the merge:

- **All Contacts In Current View**   Use this option to include all the contacts in the view, understanding that *all the contacts in the view* is not necessarily the same as *all contacts*. If you create a filtered view of the folder that excludes some of the contacts, those contacts will be excluded from the merge as well.

- **Only Selected Contacts**   Choose this option to include only those contacts that you selected in the Contacts folder prior to clicking Mail Merge. To include contacts selectively, in the Contacts folder, hold down the Ctrl key while clicking to select individual contacts, or press Shift+Click to select a range of contacts.

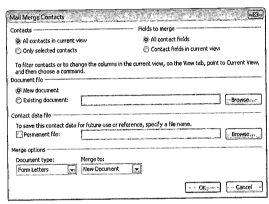

Figure 36-7 Use the Mail Merge Contacts dialog box to choose which contacts and fields to include in the merge.

In addition to specifying which contacts are included, you can control which fields are included, excluding those you don't need. The following two options determine which fields are included:

- **All Contact Fields**   Choose this option to include all the contact fields.

- **Contact Fields In Current View**   Choose this option to include only the fields displayed in the current view. You can customize the view prior to choosing Tools, Mail Merge to include only specific fields.

Creating custom views to filter items in a folder is covered in detail in the section "Creating and Using Custom Views," on page 653.

You can merge the contacts to a new document if you want, or you can choose Existing Document to use a Word 2010 document that you have already created.

The merged contact information can be saved for later or repeated by checking Permanent File under Contact Data File and specifying a file name.

You can choose from a variety of document types for your merged information: form letters, mailing labels, envelopes, and catalogs. The output of the mail merge can be saved as a Word 2010 document, sent directly to a printer, or sent as email to the contacts whom you have selected for the merge.

After you select your options in the Mail Merge Contacts dialog box and click OK, Outlook 2010 opens Word 2010, prepopulating the mail merge contact list and starting the document type that you have specified. The rest of the process depends on the type of document you have selected, as follows:

- **Form letters or catalogs**   To complete the mail merge for a form letter or catalog, click the Mailings tab, click Start Mail Merge, and select the Step By Step Mail Merge Wizard. The wizard opens at step 3, in which you choose the contacts to include in the letter. Because you have already generated a contact list, the Use An Existing List option is selected for you. You can then click Edit Recipient List to verify or fine-tune the list, or you can click Next: Write Your Letter to move to the next step.

- **Mailing labels or envelopes**   Select options in the Mail Merge Helper dialog box to complete the mail merge and create mailing labels or envelopes. You can change the type of document you are creating or click Setup to choose a specific type of mailing label or envelope size. The data source is already selected, but you can change or edit the data source.

See the section "Using Contacts for a Mail Merge in Word," on page 870, for detailed instructions on using the Mail Merge Wizard in Word 2010.

Exporting Contacts to Access

Another way to use Outlook 2010 contact information is to export the data to Access 2010, which is handy if you want to use contact data in database tables or reports. You could spend your time opening individual contact entries in Outlook 2010, copying information from the contact form, and then pasting the information into Access 2010 where you want it. However, Outlook 2010 makes the process much simpler. All you have to do is use the Import And Export Wizard and select Microsoft Access 2010 as the file to export to.

Here's how to export contact information from Outlook 2010 to Access 2010 (the exported file format is for Access 97-2003, which Access 2010 can also read):

1. Click File, Open, and then Import to open the Import And Export Wizard.

2. Select Export To A File and then click Next.

3. On the wizard page shown in Figure 36-8, select Microsoft Access 97-2003 and then click Next.

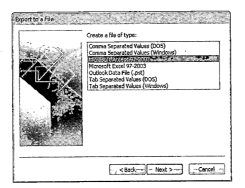

Figure 36-8 The Import And Export Wizard enables you to export to an Access 2010 file.

4. Select the folder from which to export data. In this case, select the Contacts folder (see Figure 36-9) or another folder that includes Outlook 2010 contact information. Click Next.

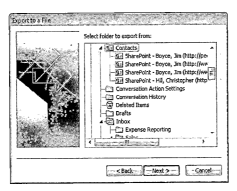

Figure 36-9 Select the folder from which you want to export.

5. Specify the folder and type a name for the export file. You can click Browse to browse to a folder and then click OK to select that folder. When you do this, the file is given an .mdb extension to denote an Access database file. Click Next.

6. In the Export To A File dialog box, click Map Custom Fields. In this dialog box, you can verify that the Contacts fields are mapped properly to the Access database fields, add or remove field items, or modify the way the Outlook 2010 contacts list is saved in the new exported file (see Figure 36-10). When you finish working with field mapping, click OK.

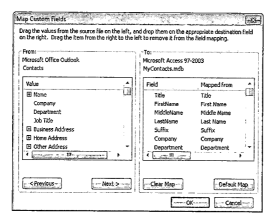

Figure 36-10 Modify field mappings in this dialog box.

7. Click Finish. Outlook 2010 exports the data from the Contacts folder and saves it in the specified file. You can now switch to Access 2010 and open the exported data as a table in that application.

For detailed information on working with Access 2010, see *Microsoft Access 2010 Inside Out,* **by John L. Viescas and Jeff Conrad (Microsoft Press, 2010).**

Importing Contacts from Access

Suppose that you've collected and stored contacts in an Access 2010 database, but now you want to use them in Outlook 2010. You can simply import the data to Outlook 2010 by using the Import And Export Wizard. During the import process, Outlook 2010 can see whether duplicate entries are being added to your contacts list and can then create, ignore, or replace them.

TROUBLESHOOTING

After replacing a duplicate entry in Outlook 2010, you see that you've lost data

Before you choose to allow Outlook 2010 to replace duplicate entries when importing a file, you should make sure that the items really are duplicates. Entries might erroneously appear to be duplicates, for example, if you have two contacts whose names are the same. For that reason, you might want to allow Outlook 2010 to create duplicate entries and then, after the import process is finished, go into the Outlook 2010 Contacts folder and manually remove any true duplicates.

Before you begin, make sure that the database that you want to import is closed in Access 2010. If it isn't closed, you'll receive an error message when Outlook 2010 tries to find the data source.

Then follow these steps to import the data:

1. Switch to Outlook 2010 and choose File, Open, and then Import to open the Import And Export Wizard.

2. Select Import From Another Program Or File, and then click Next.

3. Select Microsoft Access 97-2003 and click Next.

4. In the File To Import text box (see Figure 36-11), specify the Access file (MDB) that you want to import.

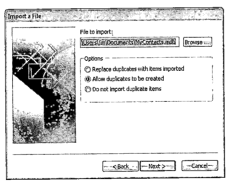

Figure 36-11 Specify the Access file to import and how Outlook 2010 should handle duplicates during the import process.

5. Specify how you want Outlook 2010 to handle duplicates, and then click Next.

6. Select the destination folder in which you want the imported data to be placed, such as the Contacts folder, and then click Next.

7. In the Import A File dialog box, click Map Custom Fields. In this dialog box, you can add or remove field items, modifying the way the Outlook 2010 contacts list is saved in the new imported file. When you finish reviewing or modifying the field mapping, click OK.

8. Click Finish to start the import process.

Exporting Contacts to Excel

You might also find it useful to export Outlook 2010 contact information to Excel 2010 worksheets. In Excel 2010, you can include the data in a spreadsheet of names and addresses for a contact management sheet, sort contact data in various ways, or perform other spreadsheet tasks with the data. Again, you simply use the Import And Export Wizard to create this Excel 2010 file.

Here's how to export contact information from Outlook 2010 to Excel 2010:

1. Choose File, Open, and then Import to open the Import And Export Wizard.

2. Select Export To A File, and then click Next.

3. Select Microsoft Excel 97-2003, and then click Next.

4. Select the folder from which to export data. In this case, select the Contacts folder or another folder that includes Outlook 2010 contact information. Click Next.

5. Specify the folder and type a name for the export file. You can click Browse to browse to a folder, and then click OK to select that folder. When you do this, the file is given an .xls file extension to denote an Excel worksheet file. Click Next.

6. In the Export To A File dialog box, click Map Custom Fields. In this dialog box, you can add or remove field items, modifying the way that the Outlook 2010 contacts list is saved in the new exported file. Click OK when you finish.

7. Click Finish. Outlook 2010 exports the data from the Contacts folder and saves it in the specified file.

> **Note**
> Another reason to export contact information is that you might need to share this data
> with others who do not use Outlook 2010 but do use Excel. Simply export the data to
> an Excel worksheet, open the worksheet, and modify or edit any column information.
> Then save the file and send it to the other users.

For detailed information on working with Excel 2010, see *Microsoft Excel 2010 Inside Out,* by
Mark Dodge and Craig Stinson Douglas (Microsoft Press, 2010).

Importing Contacts from Excel

You import contact information from an Excel 2010 worksheet the same way that you do
from an Access 2010 database. Suppose that your coworker wants to send you contact
information but is not running Outlook 2010. Ask the coworker to save the data in an Excel
2010 worksheet and send that file to you. You can then use the Import And Export Wizard
to import the new contact information into Outlook 2010.

Before you begin the process, make sure that the worksheet that you want to import is
closed in Excel 2010. If it isn't closed, you'll receive an error message when Outlook 2010
tries to find the data source.

Then follow these steps to import the data:

1. Switch to Outlook 2010. Click File, Open, and then Import to open the Import And
   Export Wizard.

2. Select Import From Another Program Or File, and then click Next.

3. Select Microsoft Excel 97-2003, and then click Next.

4. In the File To Import text box, type the name of the file or browse to the Excel 2010
   file (XLS) that you want to import.

5. Specify how you want Outlook 2010 to handle duplicates, and then click Next.

6. Select the destination folder in which you want the imported data to be placed, such
   as the Contacts folder, and then click Next.

7. In the Import A File dialog box, click Map Custom Fields. In this dialog box, you can
   add or remove field items, modifying the way in which the imported items are saved
   in your Contacts list. When you finish verifying or modifying your field mappings,
   click OK.

8. Click Finish to start the import process. You might want to review your contacts to ensure that the data was imported the way you need it. If it wasn't, modify it as necessary in Outlook 2010.

Exporting Tasks to Office Applications

You can use the Import And Export Wizard to export other Outlook 2010 items. For example, you might want to export tasks to a Word 2010 or Excel 2010 file to view past or future assignments in a table format that can be edited easily. You can then use this data in business correspondence, historical documents (such as a travel itinerary), event planning, work assignments, or presentations.

Follow these steps to export tasks from Outlook 2010 to an Excel 2010 file:

1. Choose Click File, Open, Import to open the Import And Export Wizard.

2. Select Export To A File, and then click Next.

3. Select Microsoft Excel 97-2003, and then click Next.

4. Select the folder from which to export data. In this case, choose the Tasks folder or another folder that includes Outlook 2010 tasks. Click Next.

5. Specify the folder and type a name for the export file. You can click Browse to browse to a folder, and then click OK to select that folder. When you do this, the file is given an .xls file extension to denote an Excel 2010 worksheet file. Click Next.

6. In the Export To A File dialog box, click Map Custom Fields. In this dialog box, you can add or remove field items, modifying the way that Outlook 2010 task items are saved in the new imported file. Click OK when you finish.

7. Click Finish to start the export process and open the Set Date Range dialog box (see Figure 36-12).

Figure 36-12 You might need to change the date range to include all the tasks that you want to export.

8. Specify the date range for exported tasks. Some types of tasks are not exported or included directly, such as recurring tasks with recurrences that fall outside the date range you set. Modify the date range as necessary to include the tasks that you want exported.

9. Click OK to start the export process. When it finishes, you can open the worksheet to review your tasks in Excel 2010.

Using Notes in Other Applications

Outlook 2010 notes are great when you need to create electronic "sticky" notes as a reminder of things to do in a document or project or of messages to send out. However, you are limited in how you can store information in notes and how you can use that information in other documents.

One way to reuse the information that you placed in notes is to export the Notes folder and use the note files in another application. Suppose that you have several notes that you want to archive and then remove from the Notes folder. Simply export the Notes folder to a tab-separated file and open the file in Word 2010, creating a document that contains the information.

Here's how to export the file:

1. Click File, Open, and then Import And Export to open the Import And Export Wizard.

2. Select Export To A File, and then click Next.

3. Select Tab-Separated Values (Windows), and then click Next.

4. Select the folder from which to export data. In this case, select the Notes folder or another folder that includes Outlook 2010 notes. Click Next.

5. Specify the folder and type a name for the export file. You can click Browse to browse to a folder and then click OK to select that folder. When you do this, the file is given a .txt extension to denote a text file (which you can open in Word 2010). Click Next.

6. In the Export To A File dialog box, click Map Custom Fields. In this dialog box, you can add or remove field items, modifying the way that Outlook 2010 note items are saved in the new imported file. For example, you might want to remove the Note Color field (just drag it out of the To: list of fields) because this field exports as a numeric value. When you finish verifying or modifying the field mappings, click OK.

7. Click Finish to begin the export process.

NSTANT messaging (IM) and desktop conferencing programs have been around for a long time. Microsoft's first foray into desktop conferencing came with Microsoft NetMeeting, and has changed and grown since then. Other companies have developed competing products, such as AOL Instant Messenger (AIM), Yahoo Messenger, Google Chat, Skype, and others. These applications offer a range of features from simple text-based IM (chat) to full-blow desktop conferencing complete with multi-party video conferencing, Voice-over-IP (VoIP) calling, desktop sharing, and more.

Today, Microsoft's flagship desktop conferencing solution is Office Communications Server, or OCS (formerly Live Communications Server). In much the same way that Outlook serves as a client for Microsoft Exchange Server, Office Communicator serves as the client for OCS. This chapter explores OCS and its integration with Outlook.

Overview of OCS and Office Communicator

OCS, the server-side component of Microsoft's communications environment, provides a wide range of communications features for text, voice, and video conferencing, along with media streaming and desktop application sharing. These features include:

- **Voice**   OCS provides the infrastructure needed to support software-based VoIP calling. Through the client-side application, Office Communicator, users can initiate network-based voice calls through their computers, using either the microphone and speakers built into the computer or a VoIP phone connected to the computer. OCS can integrate with the company's Private Branch Exchange (PBX) system to provide integrated calling, voicemail, and other features.

- **Audio/Video Conferencing**   If you are familiar with desktop conferencing solutions from WebEx, Verizon, and others, then you are already familiar with what OCS provides for audio/video conferencing. Users can participate in online voice conferences, video conferences, and share desktop applications.

- **Group IM**   With Office Communicator on the client side and OCS you are you are youon the server side, you can initiate an IM session with multiple parties. Each participant can participate in the online conversation, sending and receiving messages that all of the participants can see.

- **IM**   In addition to multi-party IM, you can use OCS and Office Communicator for user-to-user instant messaging.

- **Presence**   OCS and Office Communicator work together to provide online status information for people in your organization, and you can view that status within Outlook, Office Communicator, and Microsoft SharePoint.

Just as Outlook serves as the client-side application for Exchange Server, Office Communicator serves as the client-side application for OCS. You can use Office Communicator by itself to start IM sessions, voice calls, and video conferences, and communicate in other ways. The following section explores Office Communicator. Subsequent sections explore the OCS/Office Communicator integration with Outlook.

Configuring Office Communicator

Your computer might already have Office Communicator installed, but if not, it's a simple matter to install it. Therefore, this chapter doesn't cover installation. Instead, let's focus on making the most out of the program. This section covers the basic configuration steps that you will need to accomplish to get Communicator connected to your OCS servers.

> **Note**
> As of this writing, Office Communicator 2007 R2 is the latest available release, although the 2010 version should be out not too long after the release of Office 2010. This chapter is written on the assumption that you are using 2007 R2.

Setting Up the Server Connection

Office Communicator can be configured for either automatic or manual configuration. When set to automatic, Communicator uses your Uniform Resource Indicator (URI); your

Session Initiation Protocol (SIP) address, such as *jboyce@tailspintoys.com*; and Domain Name System (DNS) records to attempt to discover automatically which server it should use. It then goes through a process to attempt to connect to the server based on what it has discovered. If all goes well, Communicator signs you in to OCS.

> **Note**
> The term *automatic* is a little misleading, because there is a lot of configuration that happens on the server side and in DNS to make automatic configuration work. In this context, *automatic* refers to the client configuration, not all the work that is done on the back end to make the automatic client configuration possible.

You can also configure Office Communicator manually, specifying the OCS front-end server to use and other settings. Whether you need to use automatic or manual configuration depends on how the OCS administrators have set up the environment. Your first step, then, is to determine from the OCS team what your settings should be. Then, to configure Communicator, click the Show Menu button near the control menu at the upper-left corner of the window and choose Connect, Change Sign-In Address to open the Office Communicator Options dialog box, shown in Figure 37-1. (You can also click Status and choose Options to open this dialog box.)

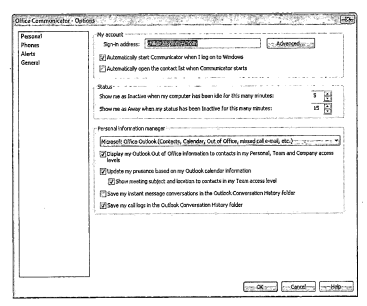

Figure 37-1 Use the Office Communicator Options dialog box to manually configure the Office Communicator.

In the Sign-In Address text box, enter the SIP address assigned to you by your OCS team. Then, click Advanced to open the Advanced Connection Settings dialog box, shown in Figure 37-2. If your OCS environment is set up for automatic configuration, choose the Automatic Configuration option and click OK. If not, click Manual Configuration, and then enter values based on these settings:

- **Internal Server Name Or IP Address** Enter the host name or Internet Protocol (IP) address of the OCS front-end server that Communicator should connect to when you are on the internal network (such as connected to the network at your office).

- **External Server Name Or IP Address** Enter the fully qualified host name or the public IP address of the OCS front-end server that Communicator should connect to when you are outside your office network (such as when you are connecting from the Internet).

- **Connect Using** Choose the connection protocol required by your OCS environment.

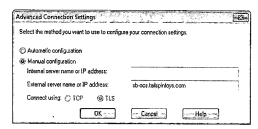

Figure 37-2 Use the Advanced Connection Settings dialog box to configure the connection to OCS.

Configuring Online Presence and Status Behavior

There are some other options you should consider setting on the Personal page of the Options dialog box. In the Status group, for example, you can configure how Communicator adjusts your online status after the computer has been idle for a certain period of time. By default, Communicator sets your status to Inactive when the computer has been idle for 5 minutes. It sets your status to Away when the computer has been idle for 15 minutes. If you frequently don't touch your computer for longer periods of time but are still at your desk (such as when you are on the phone), consider setting these values accordingly.

The Personal Information Manager group contains additional options that control how Communicator handles your online status. These options are:

- **Display My Outlook Out Of Office Information To Contacts In My Personal, Team, And Company Access Levels**   Choose this option to have your Out Of Office message displayed in the Personal Note box in Office Communicator. To set your Out Of Office setting, click File, Automatic Replies.

- **Update My Presence Based On My Outlook Calendar Information**   Choose this option to have Communicator automatically change your status based on your Outlook calendar. For example, when you are online during a scheduled meeting, Communicator changes your status to In A Meeting to reflect that.

- **Show Meeting Subject And Location To Contacts In My Team Access Level**   Choose this option to have your meeting subject and location visible to people for whom you have given Team access level.

Setting Access Levels

Communicator supports five access levels that determine the information that others can see in Communicator. For example, the Team access level enables people to see your published work and mobile numbers, see your schedule and availability, and interrupt you when your status is set to Do Not Disturb. By contrast, people assigned Public access see only limited availability information and some other basic contact information.

To assign an access level to a contact, first right-click the contact and choose Change Level of Access. Then, from the resulting menu, choose the level that you want to assign to that person.

> **Tip**
> If someone has added you as a contact but you don't want them to be able to contact you, right-click the person, choose Change Level Of Access, and then choose Blocked. They will see your contact information, but you will always appear as Offline to them and they won't be able to contact you through Communicator.

Turning on Conversation History

One more configuration step to consider before we look further into using Communicator is to configure conversation history. By default, Communicator does not keep your conversation history. You can turn this feature on, which enables you to see and search through previous conversations. This can be very useful when someone has sent you a piece of information in an IM session and you need to refer to it.

To turn on the conversation history, click Status and choose Options. On the Personal page of the Options dialog box, place a check beside Save My Instant Message Conversations In The Outlook Conversation History Folder. To view the conversation history, in Communicator, click Show Menu and choose Tools, View Conversation History.

Organizing Your Contacts

One additional topic that we'll cover before going into the Outlook/Communicator integration features is your contact list. After all, with no one to talk to, what use would Communicator be?

By default, Communicator creates two groups, Recent Contacts and All Contacts. You can modify the Recent Contacts group's contents, as Communicator uses it to track your recent Communicator sessions. However, you also can create your own groups and use them to organize your contacts. For example, you might create a Team group to contain all the people on your team; or maybe you would like to use a group for a project you are working on, or to group together people who work for various departments.

Creating a group is easy: Click Show Menu and choose Tools, Create New Group. Communicator creates a new group named New Group (see Figure 37-3). Type the name that you want to assign to the group and press Enter.

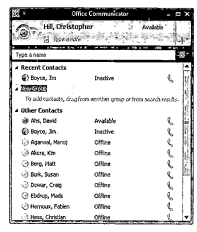

Figure 37-3 Type a name for the new group.

> **Tip**
> When you add a new group, the All Contacts group is renamed to Other Contacts.

After you have created the group, you can simply drag contacts from the Other Contacts group to your new group. You can also add new contacts. To do so, click Show Menu, and choose Tools, Add a Contact to open the Add A Contact wizard. After the wizard adds the contact, it prompts you to choose the group in which the contact should appear (see Figure 37-4). Choose the group from the drop-down list and then click Finish.

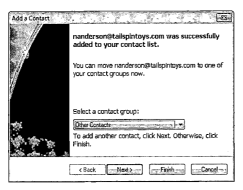

Figure 37-4 The Add A Contact wizard prompts you to select a group for the new contact.

Using OCS and Office Communicator Features in Outlook

Communicator and Outlook work together to provide some great integration features. Not only can you view others' availability, but you can also initiate communication with them in various ways, respond to email with an IM, initiate an online call or desktop conference, and more. This section of the chapter explores these features in Outlook.

Viewing Availability

Outlook and Communicator work together to provide online availability information within Outlook. This online status appears in a various places in Outlook. For example, in the Inbox, you can see online status in the message header, both in the Reading pane and in the message form itself, as shown in Figures 37-5 and 37-6. You can't see all the colors in the screenshots, but you'll see a green square if the person is online and Available, yellow for Away, orange for Busy, and red with a slash through it for Do Not Disturb.

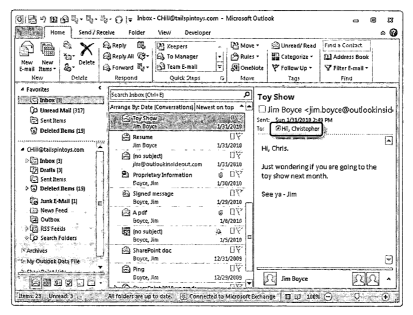

Figure 37-5 You can see online status in the Reading pane.

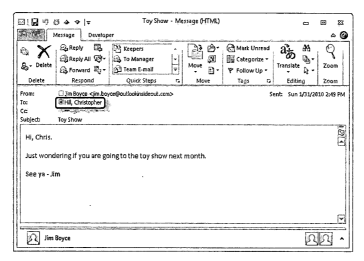

Figure 37-6 You can also see online status in the message form.

You'll also see online status in other places in Outlook. For example, when you are addressing an email message, the recipients' status will appear next to their names in the To, Cc, or Bcc field. This can actually cut down on the amount of email you send because you might decide to open an IM session with someone who is online and available, rather than send an email.

Availability also shows up in meeting request forms. You'll see status not only in the address field, but also in the Scheduling Assistant, as shown in Figure 37-7.

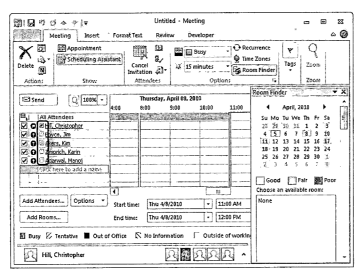

Figure 37-7 You can view online status in a meeting invitation.

Seeing someone's online status is one thing; actually using that status is another. The following sections explain ways in which you can use presence information in Outlook to communicate with others in a handful of ways.

Sending Email

When you pause the mouse over a person's name in the Reading pane or in a message window, Outlook displays a pop-up contact card similar to the one shown in Figure 37-8. The contact card shows the person's online status, as well as the person's department. Clicking Pin Contact Card causes the card to remain open when you move the mouse away from it. Clicking Expand Contact Card expands the card to show phone numbers and other information, as shown in Figure 37-9.

Online status   Pin Open

Expand

Figure 37-8 View online status and basic information in the contact card.

Figure 37-9 Expand the contact card to view more information.

The contact card pulls the person's information from his or her contact information stored in the Global Address List (GAL) or in your Contacts folder. For people in the GAL, the contact card provides two additional tabs, Organization (shown in Figure 37-10) and Member Of. The Organization tab shows organization structure, including the person's manager and direct reports (people who report to him or her). The Member Of tab shows memberships such as distribution lists and SharePoint sites.

Figure 37-10 The Organization tab shows organizational hierarchy for the contact.

You might have realized by now that the contact card lets you do more than just view information about the contact. The buttons on the card let you send an email, start an IM session, place a call, schedule a meeting, view the person's SharePoint MySite, and add him or her to your Outlook Contacts folder. The following two sections explain how to start IMs and voice calls with Communicator from email within Outlook.

Replying with an IM

Although you will often want to reply to an email with another email, there are times when an IM might suffice as well or even better than the email. Outlook 2010 makes it easy to open an IM session with the sender of a message or with the entire group of people who are listed as recipients of the message.

In Outlook, select the message to which you want to reply with an IM. Then, in the Respond group of the Home tab, click IM and choose Reply With IM or Reply All With IM (see Figure 37-11). Use the former to open an IM session to only the sender. Choose the latter to open a group IM to the sender and all recipients.

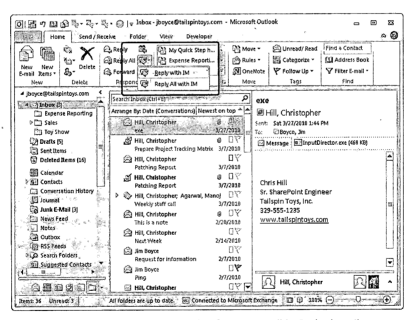

Figure 37-11 You can open an IM session from an email in Outlook easily.

When you choose one of these options, Communicator opens and initiates an IM session with the specified user(s). If you choose Reply With IM, Communicator opens an IM session with the sender. If you choose Reply All With IM, Communicator opens a group IM session, as shown in Figure 37-12. (Note that Communicator includes the users even if their status is set to Offline.)

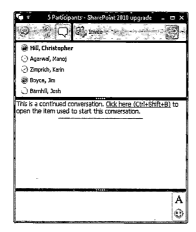

Figure 37-12 You can open a group IM session with everyone in the email conversation.

> **Note**
> If one or more of the people in the group are not available, the IM session will fail.

Making a Call

In addition to starting IM sessions from Outlook, you can initiate voice calls with other Communicator users. As with IM, you can start a call to just the sender of the message or open a call for everyone in the message.

To open a call, select the message whose sender you want to call. Then, in the Respond group of the Home tab, click More and choose Call. From the cascading menu, choose the sender's name to start a call to just that person, or choose Call All to open a call to everyone. Communicator opens and starts a voice conference session. After the other participants have answered, conduct the call as you would if you had initiated it from Communicator. Click End Call when you are finished.

> **Note**
> The call will fail if any of the participants is unavailable.

Using Outlook Features from Office Communicator

Just as there is Communicator integration in Outlook, you'll find Outlook integration in Communicator. For example, if you already have Communicator open, you can send an email to one of your contacts easily. This saves you the time and trouble of opening Outlook to find the contact. The Communicator contact might not even be in your Outlook contacts, so this bit of integration saves you the trouble of adding that person.

> **Tip**
> You can access these integration features from the main Communicator window or from a conversation window.

Sending Email from Communicator

You can send an email from Communicator to one or more Communicator contacts. To send an email to a single contact, right-click that contact and choose Send An E-mail Message. To send an email to multiple contacts, first select those contacts by holding down the Ctrl key and clicking each one in turn, and then right-click and choose Send An E-mail Message. Outlook opens a new message window with the specified recipients already entered into the To field. Compose the message as you would for any other, and then click Send.

If you want to send an email from a conversation window, click Show Menu and choose Actions, Send An E-mail Message. Alternatively, you can right-click a contact and choose Send An E-mail Message. Use this latter option if you are in a multiparty conversation and want to send the email only to one individual. If you want to send an email to a selection of contacts in the current multiparty conversation, hold down the Ctrl key, select the desired contacts, and then right-click and choose Send An E-mail Message.

Scheduling a Meeting from Communicator

It's also handy to be able to schedule meetings from Communicator, particularly if you spend a lot of time with Communicator open. Scheduling a meeting is very similar to sending an email message, and the process is the same whether you are working from the Communicator window or a conversation. Outlook opens a standard meeting request form with the selected contacts added to the form. Complete the meeting request as you normally would, and then click Send.

Adding a Communicator Contact to Outlook

Communicator uses its own contact store to keep track of your Communicator contacts; it doesn't use Outlook contacts. This is because your Communicator and Outlook contacts will not necessarily be the same, among other reasons. You are very likely to have Communicator contacts that are not in Outlook, and vice versa. However, you can add your Communicator contacts to Outlook easily.

To do so, right-click the contact in Communicator and choose Add To Outlook. An Outlook contact form opens with some of the contact information already filled in, as shown in Figure 37-13. Fill in the rest of the information as needed and click Save & Close.

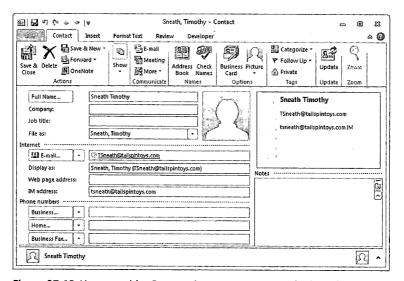

Figure 37-13 You can add a Communicator contact to Outlook easily.

Using Conversation History

Communicator can track your conversation history in Outlook, enabling you to search for, locate, and review previous conversations and calls quickly. Naturally, Outlook won't record voice calls, but you can see when calls were made or received. For IMs, you can view the contents of the conversation. For example, if someone sent you a password for an account by IM and you need to retrieve it, just open the conversation history to find the conversation and the information that you need from it.

Configuring History Behavior in Communicator

To configure Communicator to maintain your conversation history in Outlook, open Communicator, click Status and choose Options to open the Office Communicator Options dialog box previously shown in Figure 37-1. On the Personal page, use the following options to control history behavior:

- **Save My Instant Message Conversations In The Outlook Conversation History Folder**   Choose this option to have your IM sessions copied to the Conversation History folder in Outlook. The information recorded includes the start time and full chat history from the conversation.

- **Save My Call Logs In The Outlook Conversation History Folder**   Choose this option to have your voice calls logged to the Conversation History folder. The information recorded includes the start time, participants, and duration.

Working with the Conversation History Folder

When you install Communicator, it creates a Conversation History folder in Outlook and uses that folder to store your conversation history. After you have configured Communicator to store your conversation history in that folder (as discussed in the previous section), you then can work with your conversation history much like any other Outlook folder, complete with full search capabilities, custom views, and so on.

> ### Tip
> If Outlook doesn't include a Conversation History folder, the problem could be that you did not have a default profile specified in Outlook when you installed Communicator. If that's the case, uninstall Communicator and then configure Outlook to always use the profile that corresponds to your OCS account. Then run Setup again to install Communicator. (To set your default Outlook profile, open the Mail item in the Control Panel, choose Show Profiles, choose the profile that you need to set as the default, choose Always Use This Profile, select the appropriate profile, and click OK.)

Figure 37-14 shows the Conversation History folder. You should see the folder listed in the Navigation pane when you click either the Mail icon or the Folder List icon. The Conversation History folder looks and functions just like your other email folders, and by default, it shows conversations organized by date.

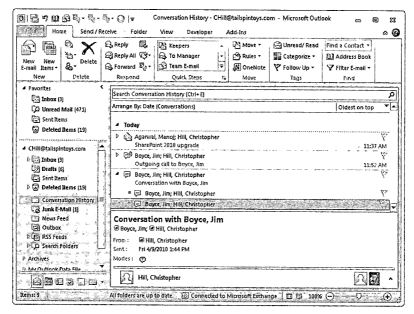

Figure 37-14 Use the Conversation History folder in Outlook to track conversations.

Because the Conversation History folder looks and acts like your other email folders, all the common things that you do to organize, search for, and manage messages also apply. For example, to organize conversations by date, click the Received column header; or if using the compact view, click Newest On Top or Oldest On Top to change the sort order.

If you are just looking for when a particular conversation happened, you can just view the message header in the folder. If you need to see the contents, double-click the message to open it. Figure 37-15 shows an IM history message, and Figure 37-16 shows a call history message. As Figure 37-15 shows, an IM message contains the full content of the IM session.

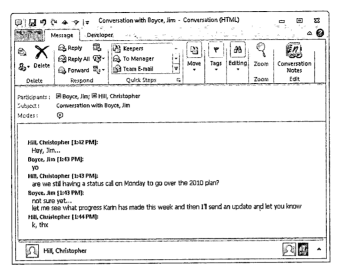

Figure 37-15 Here is an IM history message in the Conversation History folder.

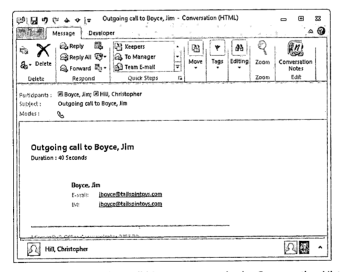

Figure 37-16 Here is a call history message in the Conversation History folder.

Because the Communicator History messages are part of your Outlook data store, they are indexed by default, making them fully searchable. Therefore, if you are looking for a particular message in the history and know a key word or phrase that is likely to be in the message, just click in the Search box and type that word or phrase. Just as Outlook does for your email and other folders, Instant Search will kick in and display results from the Conversation History folder. You can also search on those words or phrases from other folders. For example, if you start a search from the Inbox, you can click Try Searching Again In All Mail Items, and Outlook will include results from your Conversation History folder.

Collaboration with Outlook and SharePoint

ICROSOFT SharePoint is a set of technologies that form a rich collaboration framework for sharing documents, calendars, and other data. SharePoint is much more than just a tool for sharing documents or data, however. Its portal features enable organizations to create a rich portal experience for users, complete with audience targeting and personalization features. The Business Data Catalog (BDC) and Business Connectivity Services (BCS) features, in SharePoint 2007 and SharePoint 2010 respectively, provide the tools needed to integrate SharePoint with back-end line-of-business solutions like SAP, Oracle, Structured Query Language (SQL), Business Objects, and many others. The Web 2.0 features of SharePoint, such as wikis and blogs, enable people to connect and share information in a wide variety of ways. These features are just some of the ones offered by SharePoint. This chapter provides an overview of these features and explains how to use the collaboration features in SharePoint from Microsoft Outlook, how to use Outlook as a tool for creating and consuming SharePoint data, and how to publish Outlook data to SharePoint.

Overview of SharePoint

The SharePoint name actually encompasses multiple services and components. The 3.0/2007 version of SharePoint includes Windows SharePoint Services 3.0 and Microsoft Office SharePoint Server (MOSS) 2007. The latter builds on Windows SharePoint Services 3.0 as a foundational set of services. Windows SharePoint Services provides the framework for document sharing, portals, collaboration features, workflows, and several other core features. MOSS 2007 extends these core services with additional features and functionality. Windows SharePoint Services can stand on its own as a collaboration tool, although it doesn't offer the same breadth of features that MOSS does. Windows SharePoint Services is an included feature of Windows Server 2003 and a separate download for Windows

Server 2008. Windows SharePoint Services is licensed as part of the operating system and requires a Windows Server Client Access License (CAL) to access. MOSS 2007 is licensed separately, requiring a server license and at a minimum a SharePoint Standard CAL. If you will be leveraging the Enterprise features in MOSS, each user also needs an Enterprise CAL in addition to the Standard CAL.

> **Note**
>
> Whether or not you have Windows SharePoint Services or SharePoint Foundation 2010 installed on a server, you will still need a Windows Server CAL for each user who accesses the server for file or print sharing, or for any other service hosted on that server.

As with MOSS 2007, SharePoint Server 2010 builds on a set of core SharePoint services, which in 2010 are named SharePoint Foundation 2010. Also like its predecessor, SharePoint Foundation 2010 is licensed as part of the Windows Server operating system, so each user who accesses SharePoint must have a Windows Server CAL.

INSIDE OUT   2007 versus 2010

If you haven't worked with SharePoint Server 2010 yet, you are probably wondering what the fuss is about. In my "day job," I manage a collaboration practice that, among other things, designs, deploys, and manages SharePoint implementations for a variety of companies and organizations. SharePoint 2010 is not just a new face on SharePoint 2007. Instead, SharePoint 2010 has been redesigned from the ground up to provide better performance and availability, new features, easier customization, and a new user interface that provides much of the same look and feel as the Outlook ribbon.

Because of the new range of solid features that SharePoint Server 2010 provides, my experience has been that many companies are planning rollouts of the initial release of SharePoint Server 2010, rather than waiting for Service Pack 2 (or even Service Pack 1) to come out. The features in SharePoint 2010 are so compelling, and the stability of the product so solid, that many companies are forgoing the "wait and see" period so they can begin using the new features right away.

SharePoint Server 2010 builds on the features and functions in SharePoint Foundation 2010 to offer a much broader breadth of services and features than the basic SharePoint Foundation features. Also like 2007, SharePoint Server 2010 requires a Standard CAL for

all users and the addition of an Enterprise CAL in environments where Enterprise features are enabled.

The Foundations of SharePoint

As mentioned earlier, SharePoint relies on Windows SharePoint Services 3.0 (for the 2007 version) or SharePoint Foundation 2010 to provide its core, foundational features. These features encompass portals for delivering web content, document sharing, sharing of calendars and contacts, workflows for automating processes such as document approvals, and others. The following list describes the key feature areas that underlie SharePoint:

- **Portals**   SharePoint enables you to create portals (web pages) for sharing information, whether as a typical intranet portal that serves relatively static pages, for content that changes dynamically, or for collaboration features like document sharing. SharePoint provides several templates that make it a matter of a few clicks and a few seconds to create various types of websites, such as sites focused on team collaboration, document sharing, and other uses.

- **Document sharing**   Document sharing allows you to store documents on the SharePoint site, which can then be accessed by other team members. This is useful for sharing project-related documents, for example, or any other document that other team members might need access to. In addition to simple document storage, document sharing provides version control tools such as document check-in and checkout so that a document is not accidentally modified by more than one user at a time. Support for metatags enables you to categorize documents for sorting and searching.

- **Picture libraries**   Picture libraries are similar to document libraries in that they store pictures that can be shared among team members. This is basically a web-based photo album.

- **Lists**   Lists are formatted collections of information. The list format can vary based on the type of information being stored. Several lists are predefined, such as Announcements, which are displayed on the main page of a team site by default; Calendar, which can contain events relating to your team or project; Links, which stores web links to pages that your team will find useful or interesting; and Tasks, which helps your team members keep track of work. You can also create your own lists and add new columns to existing lists.

- **Discussion boards**   Discussion boards allow team members to have threaded discussions on specific subjects. Discussion boards are useful to replace email exchanges when more than two people are involved, as those involved can place comments and replies directly in the appropriate thread rather than exchanging a large number of email messages.

- **Surveys**   Surveys are simply a method of polling other team members for information.

- **Workflows**   SharePoint provides basic workflow capability to help you automate processes such as document approvals, moving items between lists, and otherwise automating business processes.

- **Search**   Locate documents, list items, and other information stored in your Share-Point environment quickly and easily.

Extending SharePoint with MOSS or SharePoint Server 2010

Collaboration environments built on Windows SharePoint Services or SharePoint Foundation can be very useful for sharing documents, calendars, and other information, and are often used by large and small companies alike to enable collaboration among groups of people. These foundational features do have some limitations, however, and that's where MOSS and SharePoint Server 2010 come into play.

These products extend SharePoint functionality in several ways:

- **Collaboration and social computing**   Features such as wikis and blogs enable people to share ideas and information in a variety of ways. My Sites adds the capability for each user to have a personal site to share information with others as well as work with his own files, Microsoft Exchange Server mailbox, and other information within a SharePoint web interface. Support for Really Simple Syndication (RSS) feeds enables users to consume RSS content within SharePoint and subscribe to SharePoint content through RSS.

- **Portals**   Additional web parts and support for audience targeting and personalization enable you to tailor and deliver a broader range of information to your users, but in a more targeted fashion.

- **Enterprise content management**   ECM encompasses a range of features, including additional capabilities for document management and sharing and a publishing infrastructure to provide controlled deployment of content with various approval mechanisms.

- **Records Management**   You can use SharePoint to store and manage records, such as email, in addition to documents. Versioning, expiration, and other features help you effectively manage the data.

- **Business processes and forms**   Enhanced workflow capabilities make it easier to use out-of-the-box SharePoint features for multi-party document approval and other business process automation.

- **Enterprise search**   Extend a search across your enterprise to include file servers, websites, line-of-business systems, and other data, making that data searchable and discoverable within SharePoint.

- **Business intelligence**   Use the BDC or BCS to connect to back-end line-of-business systems to expose that data in SharePoint and provide a common interface for users to both consume and modify data stored in those back-end systems. Also use features such as Excel Services to create key progress indicator (KPI) reports, dashboards, and other portal elements that bubble up and organize data from a variety of sources.

As stated earlier, one of the key features of SharePoint is the ability to integrate with Microsoft Office applications. These features include document sharing, which can be done from almost any Office application; lists, which can be synchronized with Microsoft Excel or Microsoft Access files; and Calendar lists, contacts, and alerts, which can be linked to Outlook. In addition, Microsoft SharePoint Designer can be used to edit and customize SharePoint pages. This chapter focuses mainly on the integration of SharePoint and Outlook 2010 to help you consume SharePoint information in Outlook, as well as publish your Outlook data to SharePoint. Before diving into SharePoint and Outlook integration, this chapter explores and explains some common SharePoint tasks and how to accomplish them, starting with setting up alerts.

Setting Up Alerts

Alerts are used when you want to be notified when content on a SharePoint site changes, such as when a document is modified or a new item added to or modified in a list. Alerts are sent through email. For example, if a document changes for which you have configured an alert, you receive an email when someone else has modified the document.

Alerts in WSS 3.0/MOSS

To set up an alert in a WSS 3.0 or MOSS site, follow these steps:

1. Locate the content for which you want to configure the alert. This can be virtually anything on the SharePoint site.

2. Click an item in a library. A menu appears, as shown in Figure 38-1. Select Alert Me to be alerted when that item is changed.

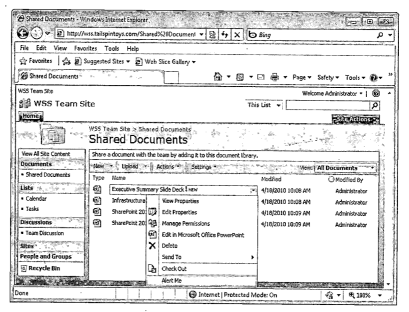

Figure 38-1 Select Alert Me to get an email alert when a specific item has been changed.

3. The New Alert page, shown in Figure 38-2, displays the email address to which alerts will be sent. On this page, select the types of changes you want to be alerted about. Some of the options shown in the figure are not available if you are configuring an alert for a specific item. You can be alerted about all changes; item additions, changes, or deletions; or updates to discussions involving the selected item or library.

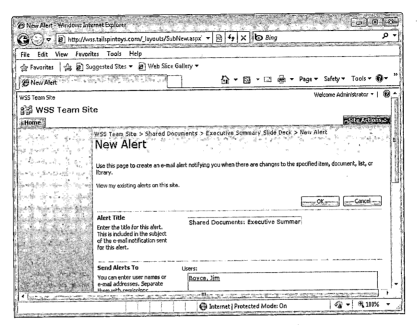

Figure 38-2 The New Alert page is used to configure the alert.

4. Select the frequency for alerts from this item or library. The default setting sends an alert message every time the alert is triggered. You can also elect to receive only a daily or weekly summary of alerts. These options are useful if the item or library for which you are configuring the alert changes often.

5. Click OK, and the alert will be configured.

After you have created an alert, you will be notified each time the alert criteria set on the New Alert page are met. You can view a list of all the alerts you have configured on the site by clicking View My Existing Alerts On This Site on the New Alert page. The My Alerts On This Site page, shown in Figure 38-3, shows all the alerts you have configured on the site. You can delete alerts by selecting the check boxes next to the alerts that you want to delete and then clicking Delete Selected Alerts. It is also possible to add an alert for a list or document library (although not individual items) on the My Alerts On This Site page. To do this, click Add Alert, select the library or list for the alert, and then click Next. Set the options on the New Alert page as described earlier in this section.

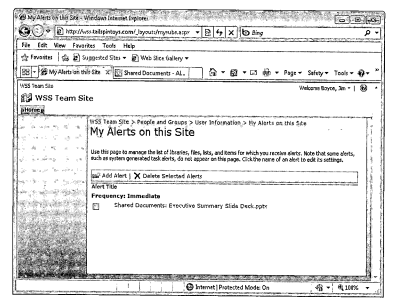

Figure 38-3 You can see all the alerts that you have configured on the site on the My Alerts On This Site page, which is accessible from the New Alert page.

Alerts in SharePoint Foundation/SharePoint Server 2010

You use a somewhat different approach to adding alerts in SharePoint Foundation 2010 and SharePoint Server 2010 sites. This method also is available in WSS 3.0 and MOSS sites for adding alerts to entire lists or libraries, although the interface is somewhat different.

Add an Alert for an Entire List or Library

Follow these steps in SharePoint Foundation 2010 and SharePoint Server 2010 sites to add alerts for an entire list or library:

1. Navigate to the site containing the item for which you want to configure an alert.

2. Click your name (by default in the upper-right corner of the page) and choose My Settings.

3. Click the My Alerts link to show the My Alerts On This Site page.

4. Click Add Alert.

5. On the New Alert page (see Figure 38-4), if you want to receive alerts for an entire list or library, select the item by clicking the radio button beside it.

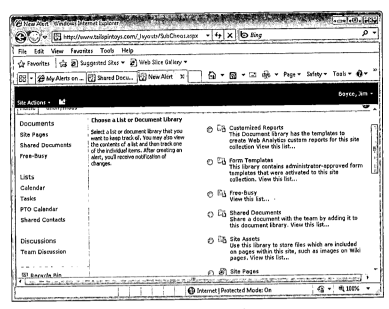

Figure 38-4 Use the New Alert page to set up alerts.

6. Click Next. The resulting page will vary according to the type of list chosen. Figure 38-5 shows the page for a Tasks list.

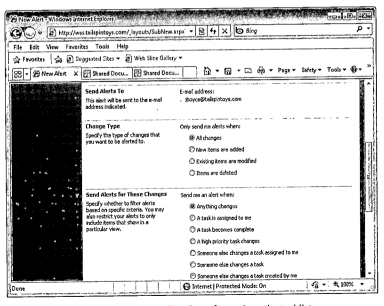

Figure 38-5 Choose the settings for alerts from the selected list.

7. Choose the settings to apply to the alert, including the alert title, change type, and frequency, and then click OK.

Adding an Alert for a Single Item

You use a different process to add an alert for a single item in a SharePoint Foundation 2010 or SharePoint Server 2010 site:

1. Navigate to the list or document library that contains the item for which you want to receive an alert.

2. Pause the mouse over the item and click the drop-down button to open the context menu for the item.

3. Click View Properties.

> **Tip**
>
> You can place a check beside an item and then click View Properties on the ribbon to open the properties for the item. For a SharePoint Server 2010 site, you can choose Alert Me from the item's context menu.

4. In the resulting dialog box (see Figure 38-6), click Alert Me.

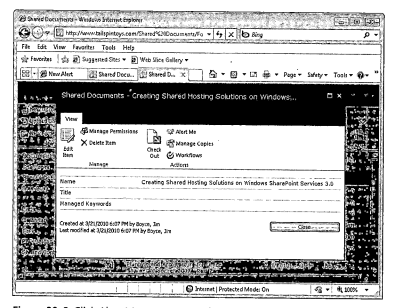

Figure 38-6 Click Alert Me to set up an alert for a single item.

5. In the resulting form (see Figure 38-7), choose the settings for the alert and click OK.

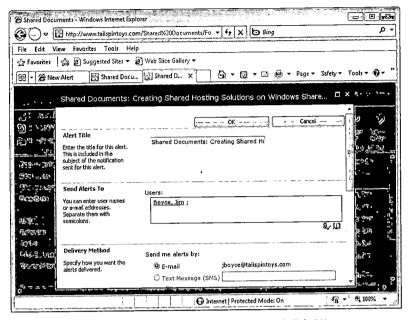

Figure 38-7 Configure the alert settings for the item and click OK.

> **Tip**
> To view all your alerts, click your name and choose My Settings, and then click My Alerts. On the resulting page, you can view, modify, add, and remove alerts.

Working with Shared Documents

Document sharing is simple with SharePoint, and it can be done in one of two ways. If you have an existing Office system document, it is an easy process to add the document to a SharePoint document library. If you don't already have a document created, you can create the document directly on the SharePoint site. When you create a document in a SharePoint site, the appropriate application opens automatically and the template associated with the document type in SharePoint is used. You can then save the document to your local computer or to the SharePoint site.

In addition to creating and adding documents to the SharePoint site, you can do a number of things with existing documents in SharePoint: You can edit or remove existing documents, and you can use features such as document version history, checkout, and check-in to control versions.

Uploading a Document—WSS 3.0/MOSS

To upload a document to a document library, follow these steps:

1. Locate and open the document library.

2. In the document library, click the down arrow next to the Upload button. Click Upload Document to upload a single file, or click Upload Multiple Documents to upload several files at once.

3. On the Upload Document page, shown in Figure 38-8, click Browse, locate the file to upload, and then click Open. You can also click Upload Multiple Files to open a Windows interface–style browser from which you can select multiple files to upload.

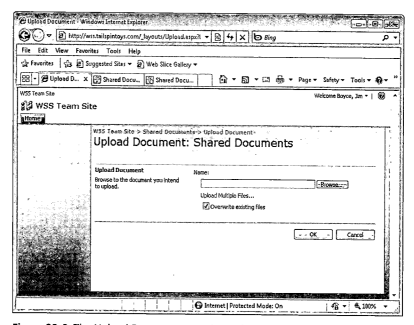

Figure 38-8 The Upload Document page is used to upload files to the document library.

4. Existing files with the same name as the file or files being uploaded are not overwritten by default. If you want to overwrite any existing files, click the Overwrite Existing Files check box (but make sure you really want to overwrite the existing files before doing so).

5. After you have specified or selected the files to upload, click OK. The documents are uploaded, and the Documents page appears.

You will now see the uploaded file listed in the document library.

Uploading a Document—SharePoint 2010

Uploading a document to a SharePoint 2010 site is a little different because of the interface changes. To do this, follow these steps:

1. Open the document library where you want to upload the document.

2. Click Add Document.

3. In the Upload Document form (see Figure 38-9), specify the document and then click OK.

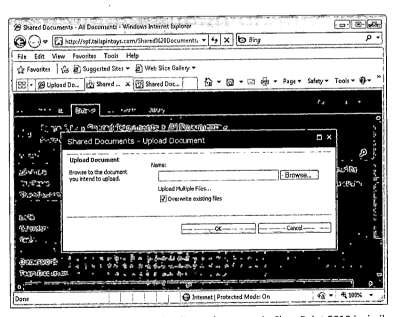

Figure 38-9 The process for uploading a document in SharePoint 2010 is similar to WSS 3.0/MOSS.

Creating a Document from the Site

In addition to uploading an existing document to a document library, you can create a new document directly from the document library. The new document is created using the document template associated with the document library. By default, the Microsoft Word document template is associated with document libraries. The Document Template setting is configured when a new document library is created, and you can set it for an existing document through the settings for the document library (on the Advanced Settings page).

To create a new document, first open the document library in which you want to create the new document. For WSS 3.0 and MOSS, click the down arrow beside New and choose New Document. For a SharePoint 2010 site, click Documents on the Library Tools tab on the ribbon (see Figure 38-10), and then click New Document on the ribbon.

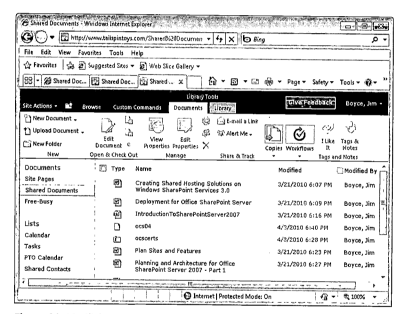

Figure 38-10 Click New Document on the ribbon to create a new document from the SharePoint site.

The Office system application associated with the document template specified for the selected document library is downloaded and opened in its native application, such as Word. Create and then save the new document to the document library (or to your local computer, and then upload it to SharePoint).

Your newly created document will now be shown in the document library.

Working with Existing Documents and Version Control

Document options for each item in a document library are found in the item's drop-down menu. Position the mouse pointer over a document name and a drop-down arrow appears. When you click the arrow, the Item drop-down menu (shown earlier in Figure 38-1) appears. From this menu, you can edit the document (clicking the document name also has this effect); view or edit the document properties, which include the name and a descriptive title for the document; delete the document from the library; manage permissions; start workflows; and check in or check out the document.

The key features in a shared document library are the version control features. In Share-Point, these features include the ability to check a document in and out as well as view its version history. When you check out a document, other users can no longer edit the document until you return it to the document library by checking it in.

To check out a document, simply choose Check Out from the Item drop-down menu, as shown in Figure 38-11. Click OK when warned that you are about to check out the document. The icon in the Type column changes to display a green arrow to indicate that the document is checked out. After you specify that you want to check out the document, click the Item drop-down arrow again and click Edit In Microsoft Word (or whichever application name appears). The document is downloaded to your computer and displayed in the application for editing.

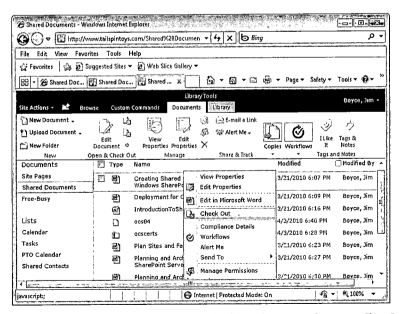

Figure 38-11 Use this drop-down list to check out documents from your SharePoint site.

When you have finished editing, you can save the document with or without checking it in. To save without checking it in, click File, Save. If you then close the document without checking it in, whichever Office application you are using prompts to ask if you want to check in the document. You can click Yes to check it in, or you can choose No and then return to the SharePoint site and check in the document.

Checking a document back into the document library from SharePoint is handled from the same drop-down menu as checking out. Click the Item drop-down arrow, and then click Check In. The Check In page shown in Figure 38-12 is displayed. Enter any comments for the version history, and then click OK. A message box appears, asking whether you want to continue. Click Yes. The document is then checked in.

INSIDE OUT   Force the check-in of a document

A site administrator can force the checking in of a document even if another user has it checked out. This can be useful, for example, if a user checks out a document and forgets to check it back in and then leaves for the day, and other users want to work with it. Changes made while the document was checked out (by the user who forgot to check it back in) might be lost in this case.

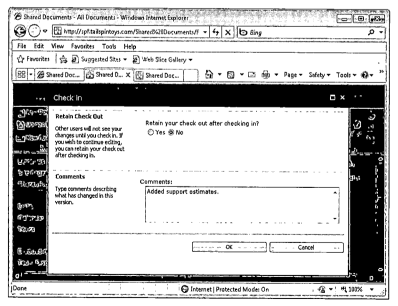

Figure 38-12 The Check In page is used to check in a document.

In the document library, choose Version History from the Item drop-down menu for a document. If version history is enabled for the document library, every time a document is checked in, it will appear in the version history, as shown in Figure 38-13. You can view each version of the document by pausing the mouse pointer over the date and time for a version and then clicking View. You also can restore a document by clicking the Restore option on this drop-down menu. You can delete old versions by clicking Delete Minor Versions, or click the Delete All Versions link to delete all document versions.

INSIDE OUT   Enable version history

Before you can use version history in a SharePoint document library, versioning must be turned on. To do this in WSS 3.0/MOSS, click Settings in the document library and choose Document Library Settings. Click Versioning Settings and choose the desired version settings. To do this in SharePoint 2010, open the library, click the Library tab in the Library Tools group on the ribbon, and click Settings, Library Settings. Click Versioning Settings and set the desired options.

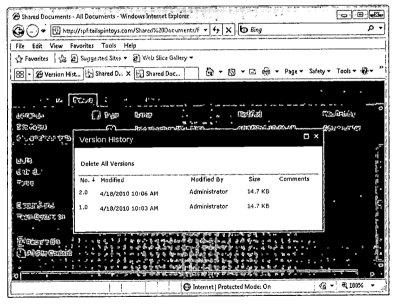

Figure 38-13 The Versions History page shows the document's version history and can be used to manage old versions of the document.

Working with Shared Contacts in Outlook

SharePoint provides lists that can be used to store, manage, and share a variety of information. One of the defined list types is contacts, which is used to store contact information in a way similar to the Contacts folder in Outlook. You can view these shared contacts within SharePoint or connect them to Outlook. This section explains how to use these shared contacts in Outlook.

Start by navigating in SharePoint to the contacts list you want to use in Outlook. Click the List tab in the List Tools group on the ribbon, then click Connect & Export and choose Connect To Outlook (see Figure 38-14). If you are working with a WSS 3.0 or MOSS site, click Actions, Connect To Outlook. (You don't need to click Connect & Export if your screen size is large enough that the Connect To Outlook item appears in the Connect & Export group.)

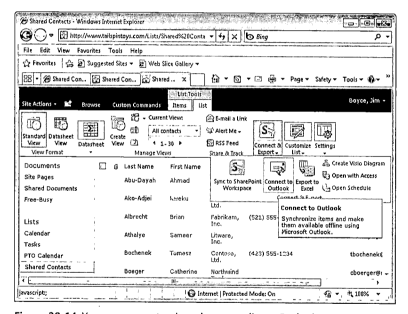

Figure 38-14 You can connect a shared contacts list to Outlook.

A dialog box opens, similar to the one shown in Figure 38-15, prompting you to allow the connection. The dialog box indicates the Uniform Resource Locator (URL) of the site and other information. Click Allow. Outlook then displays a dialog box that prompts you to confirm that you want to add the list to SharePoint. You can simply click Yes to add the list to Outlook without configuring any other settings. Alternatively, click Advanced to display the SharePoint List Options dialog box shown in Figure 38-16.

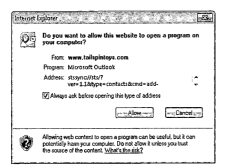

Figure 38-15 You are prompted whether to allow the connection to the SharePoint site.

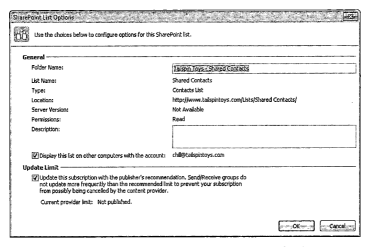

Figure 38-16 Alternatively, configure advanced settings for the connection to the list.

In the SharePoint List Options dialog box, use these two options to control the connection:

- **Display This List On Other Computers With The Account** Choose this option to include the SharePoint list on other computers from which you use Outlook.

- **Update This Subscription With The Publisher's Recommendation** If the Share-Point list is published through RSS, this setting determines how frequently the content is synchronized to Outlook based on the content's Time To Live (TTL) value. If no value is specified, the update defaults to 60 minutes. If you want to synchronize the content more frequently, clear this check box and create a custom send/receive group to update your SharePoint list(s).

When you are satisfied with the settings, click OK, and then click Yes. The SharePoint list appears in the Navigation pane when your Contacts folder is open, and the contents of the SharePoint list appear in Outlook, as shown in Figure 38-17.

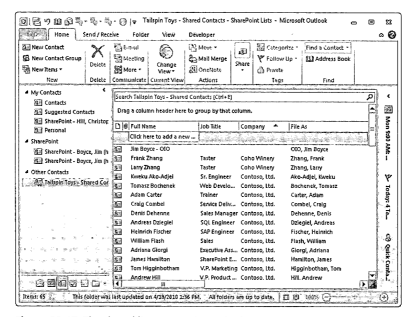

Figure 38-17 The shared list appears in Outlook.

With the list now connected to SharePoint, you can work with it just as you would a local Contacts folder. You can view individual items and even update items, subject to your permissions in SharePoint. Changes that you make in Outlook to the list are synchronized back to the SharePoint list the next time a send/receive action occurs for the list.

Integrating Outlook and SharePoint Calendars

You can connect a SharePoint Calendar list to Outlook 2010, just as you can a Contacts list. SharePoint calendars are typically used to share schedules such as project timelines, vacation schedules, and so on. When you create a team site in SharePoint, the site includes a Calendar by default. When you connect the SharePoint calendar to Outlook, the calendar looks and functions just like the calendars in your local Outlook data store(s). Subject to your permissions in the SharePoint calendar, you can modify the SharePoint calendar in Outlook and the changes are synchronized to SharePoint the next time a send/receive action takes place for the list.

To link a Calendar list to Outlook 2010, follow these steps:

1. Open the SharePoint site and navigate to the calendar you want to connect to Outlook.

2. For WSS 3.0 or MOSS, click Actions, and then click Connect To Outlook. For SharePoint 2010, click the Calendar tab in the Calendar Tools group on the ribbon, and then click Connect To Outlook in the Connect & Export group on the ribbon.

3. If you receive a prompt from Internet Explorer, click Allow. Then click Yes to add the SharePoint calendar to Outlook.

When the calendar is linked to Outlook 2010, it is displayed as shown in Figure 38-18. You can see the new calendar listed in the Navigation pane on the left.

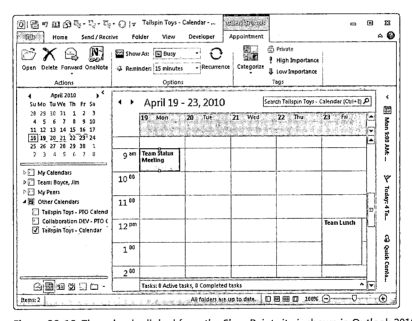

Figure 38-18 The calendar linked from the SharePoint site is shown in Outlook 2010.

If you have Contribute permissions in the SharePoint calendar, you can modify the Share-Point calendar from within Outlook. Just click in or select a time slot and add appointments as you would for a local calendar. The next time a send/receive action occurs for the list, those changes are synchronized to the SharePoint list, where they will be visible by other SharePoint users.

Because SharePoint calendars that are linked to Outlook function like Outlook calendars, you can use the same features for both. For example, you can overlay a SharePoint calendar on one or more of your local calendars for a combined view. Just select the calendars in the Navigation pane to display them, and click the View In Overlay Mode button at the top of the calendar to overlay it with the others.

Managing SharePoint List Connections in Outlook

To manage settings for SharePoint lists in Outlook, click File, Account Settings, and finally Account Settings. In the Account Settings dialog box, click the SharePoint Lists tab, as shown in Figure 38-19.

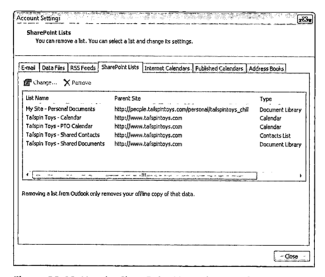

Figure 38-19 Use the SharePoint Lists tab to configure settings for SharePoint lists.

To change the settings for a SharePoint list's connection to Outlook, click the list and then click Change. The SharePoint List Options dialog box, similar to the one shown earlier in Figure 38-16, is shown. You can use this dialog box to change update limits and specify whether the list appears on all computers where you run Outlook. To remove a connected SharePoint list from Outlook, click the list on the SharePoint Lists tab and then click Remove. Removing a list from SharePoint only breaks the connection to SharePoint; it does not delete the SharePoint list itself from SharePoint.

Configuring Alerts from Outlook

We looked at alerts in the section "Setting Up Alerts," on page 909. If you received alerts from multiple sources, you might prefer to manage those alerts from Outlook. Although Outlook doesn't technically provide the features or capabilities to manage your alerts from the Outlook interface, it does enable you to navigate to your alerts from the various sources currently sending you alerts.

To manage SharePoint alerts from Outlook 2010, follow these steps:

1. Configure an alert for a resource on the SharePoint site. The alert notification will be sent to you through email and will appear in your Inbox.

2. Ensure that a mail folder is open.

3. On the Home tab on the ribbon, click Rules, Manage Rules And Alerts. The Rules And Alerts dialog box appears.

4. Click the Manage Alerts tab, shown in Figure 38-20. Wait for Outlook 2010 to retrieve alert information from the SharePoint site(s).

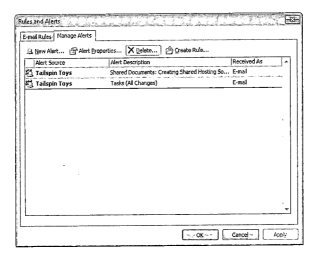

Figure 38-20 The Manage Alerts tab in the Rules And Alerts dialog box is used to manage SharePoint alerts directly from within Outlook 2010.

> **Note**
> You must configure the first alert manually from the SharePoint site because when an alert is processed by Outlook 2010, the site is *trusted*, and you can then manage alerts from the Rules And Alerts dialog box. It is possible to manage alerts without first configuring an alert through the SharePoint site if an administrator adds the site as a trusted domain for alerts.

Adding Alerts from Outlook

You can now work with alerts directly within the client computer running Outlook 2010. To add a new alert, follow these steps:

1. Click New Alert on the Manage Alerts tab in the Rules And Alerts dialog box.

2. Expand Sources Currently Sending Me Alerts in the New Alert dialog box.

3. Select the SharePoint site in the list, as shown in Figure 38-21, and then click Open. You can also type the URL for the SharePoint site in the Web Site Address box and then click Open.

Figure 38-21 Select the SharePoint site in which to create the new alert in the list in the New Alert dialog box.

4. The New Alert page on the SharePoint site opens automatically in a web browser, as shown in Figure 38-22. Select the list or document library for which to set the alert, and then click Next.

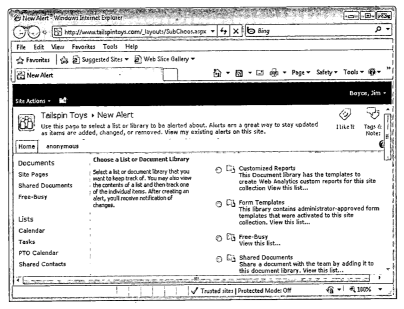

Figure 38-22 The New Alert page on the SharePoint site opens when you select the site from the list in the New Alert dialog box and click Open.

5. Set the alert type and frequency as described in the section "Setting Up Alerts," on page **909**.

6. Click OK to set the alert. You are then taken to the My Alerts On This Site page on the SharePoint site to review your alerts.

7. Switch to Outlook 2010.

8. Click OK to close the Rules And Alerts dialog box.

9. Reopen the Rules And Alerts dialog box.

10. Click the Manage Alerts tab in the Rules And Alerts dialog box. The new alert is shown on the Manage Alerts tab in the Rules And Alerts dialog box.

Editing and Deleting Alerts from Outlook

In addition to adding alerts directly from within Outlook 2010, you can edit existing alerts by following these steps:

1. Select the alert that you want to edit on the Manage Alerts tab in the Rules And Alerts dialog box, and then click Alert Properties.

2. The Alert Properties dialog box opens, as shown in Figure 38-23. This dialog box shows the alert source as a clickable link to the home page of the SharePoint site and includes a link to the main alerts management page in SharePoint. Click Modify Alert to edit the alert.

Figure 38-23 The Alert Properties dialog box is used to edit existing alerts from Outlook 2010.

3. The Edit Alert page on the SharePoint site opens in the web browser. Make any changes you need on the Edit Alert page, and then click OK. You can also click Delete to remove the alert.

You can also remove alerts on the Manage Alerts tab by selecting the alert and then clicking Delete. You are prompted to verify the deletion, and the alert is removed when you click Yes.

Rules Based on Alerts

If you have a lot of alerts configured in a SharePoint site (or multiple sites), they can fill your mailbox quickly and distract from other messages. Outlook 2010 provides a simple way to create rules based on alerts. As you learned in Chapter 11, "Processing Messages Automatically," rules are used to process messages when they arrive in your mailbox. To configure a rule based on an alert, follow these steps:

1. Select the alert for which to configure a rule on the Manage Alerts tab in the Rules And Alerts dialog box.

2. Click Create Rule.

3. The Create Rule dialog box opens, as shown in Figure 38-24. Specify what Outlook 2010 should do when it receives the selected alert. You can have Outlook 2010 display the alert in the New Item Alert window, play a sound, and move the message to a new folder.

4. You can click Advanced Options to open the Rules Wizard and go into more detailed configuration for the rule. Use of the Rules Wizard is explained in Chapter 11. In most cases, this is not necessary for a basic alert.

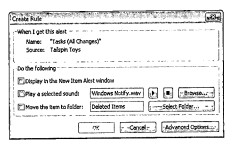

Figure 38-24 The Create Rule dialog box is used to create a rule based on an alert.

5. Click OK to create the rule.

When the rule is created, Outlook displays the Success dialog box, shown in Figure 38-25. You are notified that the rule is a client-side rule and given the option to run the rule against your mailbox immediately to find any messages that fit the rule criteria.

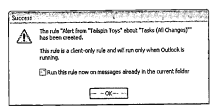

Figure 38-25 When the rule based on an alert is created, the Success dialog box is shown.

After you click OK in the Success dialog box, you can see the newly created rule by clicking the E-Mail Rules tab in the Rules And Alerts dialog box, which is already open.

Using Outlook to Work with SharePoint Libraries and Files

As already explained in previous sections of this chapter, you can connect SharePoint lists and document libraries to Outlook 2010. This makes the library and its items available within Outlook 2010 so that you don't have to use a web browser to view and work with them—you can use Outlook 2010 instead. For example, you might want to have a list of current project documents that have been uploaded to your team's SharePoint site as you create email messages to update your team members, support staff, and management.

By having the list of documents appear in Outlook, you can view the document name, its status, and other information quickly without leaving Outlook. Also, if you open a Share-Point document from within Outlook, that file is stored locally on your hard drive while you view it. This makes the document open faster and reduces network traffic. If you make any edits to the document, you then check in the file to the SharePoint site. Files are stored on your hard drive in your personal folders (.pst) file.

CAUTION

Before you connect a document library to Outlook, make sure you understand the consequences in terms of disk space. If the SharePoint document library contains 2GB of documents, the synchronized copy on your computer will take the same amount of space on your local computer.

Connecting a SharePoint Library to Outlook

To use Outlook 2010 to view and work with your SharePoint documents, first connect the SharePoint library to Outlook 2010. This enables SharePoint and Outlook 2010 to synchronize your files so that you can have them available for offline use in Outlook.

To connect a library to Outlook 2010, follow these steps:

1. Navigate to the document library that you want to connect to Outlook. Click the Library tab in the Library Tools group on the ribbon, click Connect & Export, and then choose Connect To Outlook (see Figure 38-26). For a WSS 3.0 or MOSS site, click Actions, Connect To Outlook.

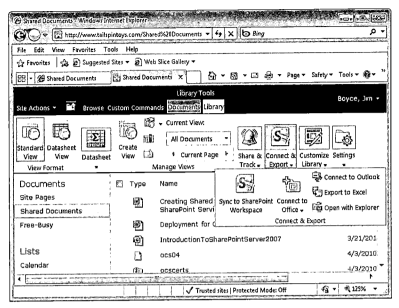

Figure 38-26 You can connect a SharePoint library to Outlook 2010.

2. A warning message might appear, telling you that you should connect lists only from sources you trust. Click Allow if you trust the source. Otherwise, click Cancel.

3. Click Yes. Outlook starts a send/receive action to synchronize the documents. When finished, Outlook 2010 displays the library as a SharePoint list, as shown in Figure 38-27.

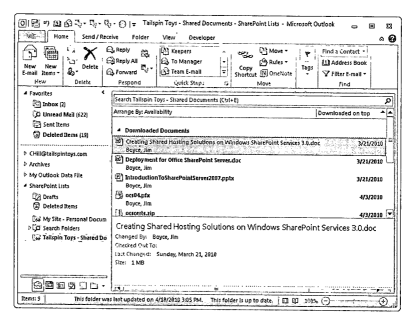

Figure 38-27 Outlook 2010 displays the connected library as a SharePoint Lists item.

The libraries that you connect to Outlook 2010 are in the SharePoint Lists branch in the Navigation pane.

Downloading Individual Files from a SharePoint Library to Outlook

Sometimes when you connect a SharePoint library to Outlook 2010, the library is too large to download to your local hard drive. Instead, Outlook 2010 displays a group named Available For Download in the message list area. You can use this group to select individual files that you want to download to Outlook 2010. You can use the Ctrl key to select multiple files to download. Some files might include a button in the preview window labeled Download This Document. Click that button to download the file.

Opening Files from a SharePoint Site in Outlook

Once you have a SharePoint library connected to Outlook 2010, you can open files stored in that library from within Outlook. Outlook enables you to view a number of different file formats, including the following:

- Word documents

- Excel worksheets

- Microsoft PowerPoint presentations

- Adobe Portable Document Format (PDF) files

- Pictures

To open a SharePoint library file in Outlook 2010, browse to a folder in the SharePoint Lists folder in the Outlook 2010 Navigation pane. Click a folder to display that folder's list of files in the messages list. Files are displayed here just like email messages. Each file, however, includes information about that file, such as name, file format, last user to edit the file, checkout information, modification date and time, and size. Figure 38-28 shows the messages list pane resized to display all the file details for files in a SharePoint document library.

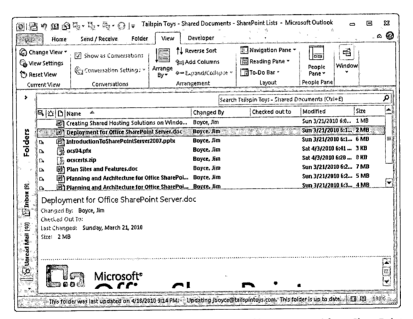

Figure 38-28 Outlook 2007 shows file details for files connected from SharePoint.

To view a file, you can click it to display the file in the Outlook 2010 Reading pane. For example, Figure 38-29 shows a Word file displayed in the Reading pane.

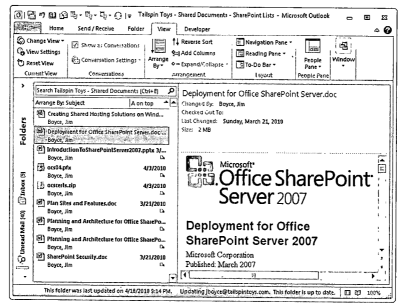

Figure 38-29 Use the Reading pane to preview documents.

Editing Files from a SharePoint Site in Outlook

Not only can you open and view SharePoint files in Outlook 2010, you also can edit them. Before doing so, however, you should return to the SharePoint site and check out the document so that no one else can work on the document while you are working on it. (Outlook 2010 does not provide a way to check out the document locally.)

To edit the file, double-click it. The file opens in the default application for that file format (for example, an .xlsx file opens in Excel 2010, .pptx in PowerPoint 2010, and so on). For applications compatible with SharePoint, a banner appears across the top of the document telling you that the document is an offline server document and that you should save the file to the server later, as shown in Figure 38-30.

Figure 38-30 The Offline Server Document banner reminds you that the file that you are editing needs to be updated to the server later.

Click Edit Offline. A message box appears, telling you that the document will be stored on your computer in the SharePoint Drafts folder. Click OK, and then edit the file. After you complete your edits, click File, Save to save the file, and then close the application. If you are connected to your SharePoint site at this time, the Edit Offline dialog box appears. You can click Update to update the SharePoint site with your edited file. (You also can click Do Not Update Server to update the server later.)

When you click Update, the application (such as Word 2010) saves the changes to the SharePoint site.

If you chose not to update the files using the Update button, return to Outlook 2010 and then click Send/Receive when you are ready to update your files. Outlook 2010 synchronizes with the SharePoint Site to save your changes in the online library.

Removing SharePoint Files in Outlook

You can remove one or more files from a SharePoint library list in Outlook 2010 without actually removing the documents from the SharePoint library. The document remains on the server, but it is removed from your cached list in Outlook. This feature simplifies browsing libraries that contain a large number of items.

To remove files from a SharePoint library that have been connected to Outlook, follow these steps:

1. In the Outlook 2010 Navigation pane, select the library that contains the files you want to remove.

2. Click the file that you want to remove. To remove multiple files, press Ctrl as you click the files.

3. Right-click the file, and then choose Remove Offline Copy, as shown in Figure 38-31.

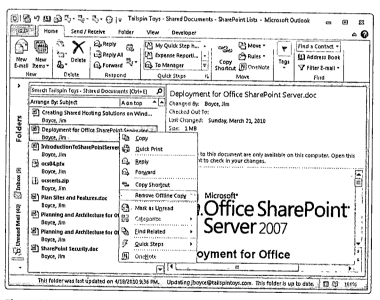

Figure 38-31 You can remove an offline file from Outlook 2010 but keep it on your Share-Point site.

When you remove a file from Outlook 2010, the Reading pane no longer displays the preview of the file, and the file shows as available for download. Outlook 2010 moves the file to the Available For Download group and adds a Download This Document button to the file.

Removing SharePoint Folders in Outlook

If you don't need a particular library anymore, you can remove it from Outlook 2010 easily. Removing the library does not affect it on the SharePoint site; it only removes it from the Navigation pane in Outlook. One thing to keep in mind, however, is that if you have not sent updates to the SharePoint site before you delete the folder, you will lose any edits that you made to the offline files.

To remove a SharePoint folder, right-click it in the Navigation pane. On the shortcut menu that appears, click Delete Folder and then click Yes.

Using Email to Add a File to a SharePoint Library

If the SharePoint document library is configured to accept documents by email, you can add a document to a library simply by sending an email message, with the document attached, to the library. This is handy if you do not want to go through the process of opening your web browser, connecting to your SharePoint site, locating a library, and uploading the file to it.

To use this feature, you need to know the email address for the library to which you plan to send the file. Some organizations include the email address for libraries in their address book. If you have access to the list's settings, look in the List Information area for an E-Mail Address item. If your library is configured to receive files via email, the address will appear here.

Others might include the email address as part of the library's description—for example, placing the address beneath the title of the library so that users can see it while viewing the library in a web browser. After you get the address, if your company does not already include the address in your Contacts folder or in the Outlook Address Book, add it to your Contacts folder.

After you get the email address, return to Outlook 2010 and then create your message. Attach the file that you want to send to the SharePoint site. Add the address of the library in the To box, and then click Send.

> **Note**
> Some organizations use SharePoint groups so that users can send an email message and attachment to other members in a group. When you do this, the attached file is added to the SharePoint site automatically. If this is the case, type the address of the SharePoint group in the To box instead of the library address. The SharePoint group will already have the library address configured.

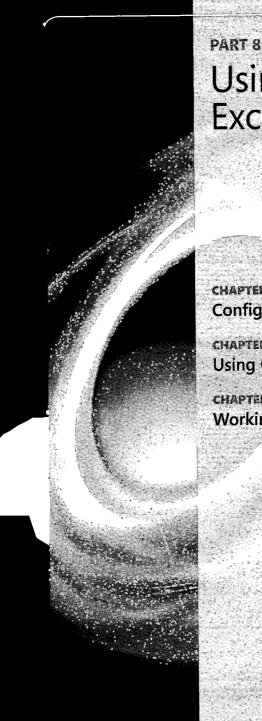

PART 8

Using Outlook with Exchange Server

LTHOUGH you can use Microsoft Outlook 2010 with other types of mail servers, you derive the greatest benefit when you use Outlook 2010 with Microsoft Exchange Server. Added benefits include the Out Of Office Assistant, the ability to recall messages, the ability to delegate functions to an assistant, the use of server-side message rules, and many other collaboration features.

You can connect to Exchange Server using any of several protocols, including Post Office Protocol 3 (POP3), Internet Message Access Protocol (IMAP), and even Hypertext Transfer Protocol (HTTP). This means two things: You can connect to a computer running Exchange Server using email clients other than Outlook 2010 (Microsoft Outlook Express or Windows Mail, for example), and you can use a service provider other than the Exchange Server client within Outlook 2010 (such as POP3) to connect to the server, assuming that the server is configured appropriately. To get all the benefits afforded by the combination of Outlook 2010 and Exchange Server, however, you must use the Exchange Server service provided with Outlook 2010.

This chapter explains how to add the Exchange Server client to an Outlook 2010 profile and configure its settings.

For detailed information about adding other service providers to an Outlook 2010 profile, see Chapter 3, "Configuring Outlook Profiles and Accounts." You'll find additional information about setting up Internet email accounts in Chapter 7, "Using Internet Mail Accounts."

Outlook as an Exchange Server Client

The Microsoft Exchange Server service in Outlook 2010 allows you to use Outlook 2010 as a client for Exchange Server. Of all the services supported by Outlook 2010, Exchange Server offers the broadest range of functionality, providing excellent support for collaboration, information sharing, group scheduling, and more.

The remaining chapters in this part of the book cover a broad range of topics to help you use Outlook 2010 effectively as an Exchange Server client.

Setting up an Exchange Server account in Outlook 2010 isn't difficult, but it does require several steps, as follows:

1. If you are running Outlook 2010 for the first time, in the Outlook 2010 Startup Wizard, go to the Choose E-Mail Service page. To reach this page if you have run Outlook 2010 previously and your profile already includes a mail account, open the Mail item from the Control Panel, select the profile, and then choose Properties. Click E-Mail Accounts, and then click New on the E-Mail tab in the Account Settings dialog box. If Outlook 2010 is already open, click File, Add Account.

2. The Auto Account Setup page, shown in Figure 39-1, gives you a place to specify your name, email address, and password. If AutoDiscover is configured properly for your Exchange Server environment, you can enter your name, email address, and password as it is set on the server, click Next, and have Outlook 2010 determine the necessary settings to connect to your server. However, the following steps assume that you are not able to use AutoDiscover and must configure the account manually.

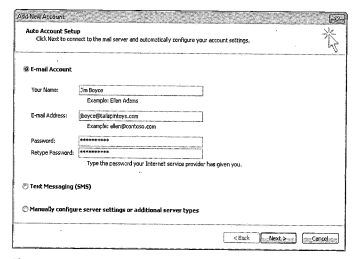

Figure 39-1 Use this page to enter details for your email account.

> **Note**
> AutoDiscover requires that your computer be able to resolve the autodiscover host in your domain. For example, if your computer resides in the tailspintoys. com domain, your computer must be able to resolve autodiscover.tailspintoys. com to the servers on the tailspintoys.com network that are providing AutoDiscover services. For more details on AutoDiscover, see the Exchange Server 2010 documentation.

3. If you don't want to use AutoDiscover, choose Manually Configure Server Settings Or Additional Server Types, and then click Next.

4. Choose Microsoft Exchange Or Compatible Service, and then click Next.

5. On the Server Settings page, shown in Figure 39-2, specify the following information:

- **Server**   Specify the NetBIOS or Domain Name System (DNS) name of the computer running Exchange Server, or its Internet Protocol (IP) address. You don't have to include a double backslash (\\) before the server name.

- **Use Cached Exchange Mode**   Select this check box to have Outlook 2010 create a locally cached copy of your entire Exchange Server mailbox on your local computer. Outlook 2010 creates an offline folder store (.ost) file in which to store the mailbox and works from that cached copy, handling synchronization issues automatically.

- **User Name**   Specify the name of your mailbox on the server. You can specify your logon account name or mailbox name. For example, you might use **chill** or **Chris Hill**.

- **Check Name**   After you enter your logon or mailbox name, click Check Name to check the specified account information against the information on the server. If you specify your logon name, clicking Check Name automatically changes the user name to your mailbox name. Outlook 2010 indicates a successful check by underlining the user name. If you are connecting to the server using Outlook Anywhere (RPC over HTTP), do not click Check Name—you must configure the connection first because Outlook 2010 must be able to communicate with the server to check your name.

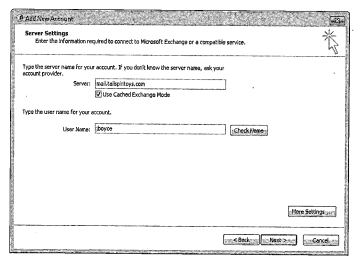

Figure 39-2 Configure basic Exchange Server settings on the Server Settings page.

6. Click More Settings to open the Microsoft Exchange dialog box, shown in Figure 39-3.

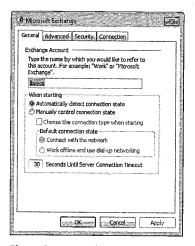

Figure 39-3 Use the Microsoft Exchange dialog box to configure additional options.

7. Use the information in the following sections to configure additional settings if needed, and then click OK to close the Microsoft Exchange dialog box. Click Next, and then click Finish.

Configuring General Properties

You use the General tab in the Microsoft Exchange dialog box (shown in Figure 39-3) to configure the account name, the connection state, and other general settings, as follows:

- **Exchange Account**   This option specifies the name under which the account appears in your Outlook 2010 configuration. This name has no bearing on the Exchange Server name or your account name. For example, you might name the account Office Email, Work Account, or Microsoft Exchange Server.

- **Automatically Detect Connection State**   This option directs Outlook 2010 to detect the connection state (offline or online) at startup and choose the appropriate state. Use this option if your computer is connected to the network all the time. Also use this option if you're setting up an Exchange Server account on a notebook computer under a profile that you use when the notebook is connected to the network.

- **Manually Control Connection State**   This option controls the connection state at startup. Choose this option if you're setting up an Exchange Server account on a computer that is sometimes disconnected from the network (a notebook computer, for example) or that always accesses the computer running Exchange Server remotely. Choose one of the following suboptions, depending on how you want Outlook 2010 to connect to the server:

  - **Choose The Connection Type When Starting**   Specifies which method Outlook 2010 uses to connect to the computer running Exchange Server at startup. If this check box is selected, Outlook 2010 prompts you each time it starts, asking whether you want to connect to the network or work offline. Clear this check box if you want Outlook 2010 to make that determination.

  - **Connect With The Network**   Connects to the computer running Exchange Server through the network rather than initiating a dial-up connection. Use this option if your computer is hard-wired to the network or always online, such as with a Digital Subscriber Line (DSL), cable modem, or other persistent remote connection.

  - **Work Offline And Use Dial-Up Networking**   Use dial-up networking to connect to the computer running Exchange Server. Specify the connection options on the Connection tab.

.**Seconds Until Server Connection Timeout**   This option specifies the time-out for connection attempts to the computer running Exchange Server. If you are working remotely over a slow connection, increase this value to give Outlook 2010 more time to establish the connection to the server.

INSIDE OUT   Increase TCP Time-Out for On-Demand Connections

If you use Internet Connection Sharing (ICS) or demand-dial router connections, you've no doubt had your client computer time out while waiting for the ICS or demand-dial router to establish a connection. This can cause a remote connection to the computer running Exchange Server to fail.

Transmission Control Protocol (TCP) sets a retransmission timer when it attempts the first data transmission for a connection, with an initial retransmission time-out value of 3 seconds. TCP doubles the retransmission time-out value for each subsequent connection attempt, and by default, it attempts retransmission two times. The first attempt is made at 3 seconds, the second at 3 + 6 seconds, and the third at 3 + 6 + 12 seconds, for a maximum time-out of 21 seconds. Increasing the initial retransmission timer to 5 seconds results in a total maximum time-out of 5 + 10 + 20, or 35 seconds.

The initial TCP retransmission time-out is defined by the registry value HKEY_LOCAL_MACHINE\System\CurrentControlSet\Services\Tcpip\Parameters\InitialRtt. The InitialRtt value is a REG_DWORD with a valid range from 0 to 65,535 and specifies the time-out in milliseconds.

The number of connection attempts is defined by the registry setting HKEY_LOCAL_MACHINE\System\CurrentControlSet\Services\Tcpip\Parameters\TcpMaxDataRetransmissions. The TcpMaxDataRetransmissions value is also a REG_DWORD with a valid range of 0 to 65,535.

Configuring Advanced Properties

You use the Advanced tab in the Microsoft Exchange dialog box, shown in Figure 39-4, to configure additional mailboxes to open, as well as security and offline processing settings. Why use additional mailboxes? You might own two mailboxes on the server and need access to both of them. For example, if you are the system administrator, you probably need to manage your own account as well as the Administrator account; or perhaps you've been delegated as an assistant for a set of mailboxes and need to access them to manage someone's schedule (discussed in Chapter 34). The Advanced tab is where you add mailboxes that you own or for which you've been granted delegate access.

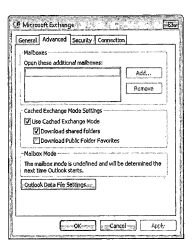

Figure 39-4 Use the Advanced tab to configure additional mailboxes, Cached Exchange Mode, and offline file settings.

The options on the Advanced tab are:

- **Open These Additional Mailboxes** This option defines the set of mailboxes you want Outlook 2010 to open. These can be mailboxes that you own or for which you've been granted delegate access.

- **Use Cached Exchange Mode** This option has Outlook 2010 create and work from a locally cached copy of your mailbox. This setting corresponds to the Use Cached Exchange Mode setting on the Exchange Server Settings page of the E-Mail Accounts Wizard.

- **Download Shared Folders** Select this option if you want Outlook 2010 to download the contents of shared folders, such as other users' Inbox or Calendar folders made available to you through delegate permissions or Microsoft SharePoint folders.

- **Download Public Folder Favorites** Select this check box if you want Outlook 2010 to cache the public folders that you have added to the Favorites folder in the Public Folders branch. Before selecting this check box, consider how much replication traffic you will experience if the folders in your Favorites folder contain a large number of posts and are very active.

- **Outlook Data File Settings** You can use this option to set up an .ost file to use as your data cache while working offline. You need to use an .ost file only if the account is configured to store your data in your Exchange Server mailbox. If your primary data file is a personal folders (.pst) file, or if you don't work offline, you don't need an .ost file.

Configuring Security Properties

The following settings on the Security tab of the Microsoft Exchange dialog box, shown in Figure 39-5, control whether Outlook 2010 encrypts data between the client and the server and how authentication is handled:

- **Encrypt Data Between Microsoft Outlook And Microsoft Exchange**   This setting determines whether Outlook 2010 uses encryption to secure transmission between your system and the server. Select this check box to enable encryption for greater security.

- **Always Prompt For Logon Credentials**   Select this check box if you want Outlook 2010 to prompt you for your logon credentials each time it needs to connect to the server. This is useful if you are concerned that others who have access to your computer might be accessing your mailbox.

- **Logon Network Security**   This setting specifies the type of authentication to use when connecting to Exchange Server. The Password Authentication option causes Exchange Server to use Microsoft Windows NT LAN Manager (NTLM) challenge/ response to authenticate on the server using your current logon account credentials. This is the standard authentication mechanism in Windows NT domains. Kerberos Password Authentication is the default authentication mechanism for Microsoft Windows 2000 Server and later domains. You can choose either of these or choose the Negotiate Authentication option to have Outlook 2010 attempt both.

- **Insert Smart Card**   Use a smart card to authenticate to Exchange Server.

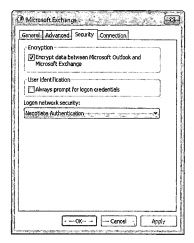

Figure 39-5 Use the Security tab to configure security settings.

Chapter 39

Configuring Connection Properties

The Connection tab in the Microsoft Exchange dialog box, shown in Figure 39-6, allows you to specify how your computer connects to Exchange Server. You can connect through the local area network (LAN), through dial-up networking, or through a third-party dialer, such as the one included with Internet Explorer. The LAN connection option applies if you're connecting over a hard-wired connection—for example, when your computer is connected to the same network as the server. You should also use the LAN option if you connect to the server over a shared dial-up connection hosted by another computer.

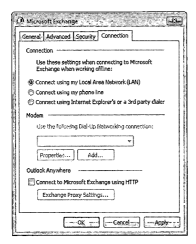

Figure 39-6 Use the Connection tab to specify how Outlook 2010 connects to Exchange Server.

Click Connect Using My Phone Line to use an existing dial-up networking connection or to create a new dial-up connection. Select the desired connection in the drop-down list, and then click Properties if you need to modify the dial-up connection. Click Add if you need to add a dial-up connection.

If you want to connect to the Internet or your remote network using the dialer included in Internet Explorer or a dialer included in a third-party dial-up client, click Connect Using Internet Explorer's Or A 3rd Party Dialer.

The Outlook Anywhere group of controls lets you configure Outlook 2010 to connect to Exchange Server using HTTP. The capability to use HTTP to connect to a remote computer running Exchange Server provides an additional connection option for users of Outlook 2010 and can drastically reduce administrative overhead. Administrators do not need to provide virtual private network (VPN) access to the network or configure VPN client software for users to access the computer running Exchange Server from remote locations.

HTTP access also provides native access to the computer running Exchange Server as an alternative to Outlook Web Access (OWA) for users.

The Connect To Microsoft Exchange Using HTTP check box, if selected, causes Outlook 2010 to connect to the computer running Exchange Server using the HTTP protocol. To configure additional settings, click Exchange Proxy Settings to open the Microsoft Exchange Proxy Settings dialog box, shown in Figure 39-7.

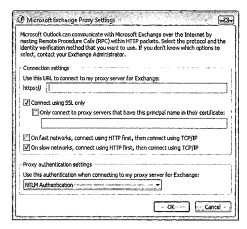

Figure 39-7 Specify settings for the HTTP connection in the Microsoft Exchange Proxy Settings dialog box.

Configure settings in this dialog box using the following list as a guide:

- **Use This URL To Connect To My Proxy Server For Exchange**   This option specifies the Uniform Resource Locator (URL) that serves as the access point for the server. The default is <*server*>/RPC, where <*server*> is the web address of the front-end server running Exchange Server. An example is *httpmail.boyce.us/rpc*. Omit the *https://* prefix.

- **Connect Using SSL Only**   Select this check box to connect to the server using Secure Sockets Layer (SSL). Note that Outlook 2010 changes the URL prefix to *https://* for the URL. (See the preceding option.)

- **Only Connect To Proxy Servers That Have This Principal Name In Their Certificate**   This option specifies the principal name for the remote proxy server for SSL authentication.

- **On Fast Networks, Connect Using HTTP First, Then Connect Using TCP/IP** With this setting, when Outlook 2010 senses a fast connection to the server, it attempts HTTP first and then resorts to TCP/IP if HTTP fails.

- **On Slow Networks, Connect Using HTTP First, Then Connect Using TCP/IP** With this setting, when Outlook 2010 senses a slow connection to the server, it attempts HTTP first and then resorts to TCP/IP if HTTP fails.

- **Use This Authentication When Connecting To My Proxy Server For Exchange** Select the authentication method to use to authenticate on the remote computer running Exchange Server. Choose the type of authentication required by the front-end server.

Verifying Connection Status

After you have finished configuring Outlook 2010 to use RPC over HTTP to connect to your computer running Exchange Server, you can verify the type of connection that it is using. To do this, hold down the Ctrl key, right-click the Outlook 2010 icon in the system tray, and then choose Connection Status to open the Microsoft Exchange Connection Status dialog box, shown in Figure 39-8.

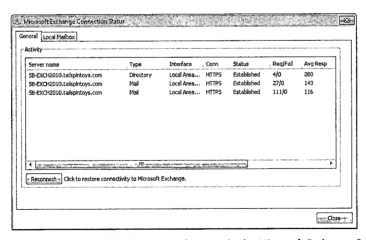

Figure 39-8 Determine the connection type in the Microsoft Exchange Connection Status dialog box.

Testing AutoConfiguration

Outlook 2010 supports automatic account configuration, which means that Outlook 2010 can attempt to determine your account settings automatically. With Exchange Server 2010, Outlook 2010 relies on being able to identify and communicate with the autodiscover host for your domain, such as *autodiscover.tailspintoys.com.* This host corresponds to a virtual server hosted on the computer running Exchange Server. With versions of Exchange Server prior to 2007, you must specify your name, email address, and account password, and then Outlook 2010 attempts to identify the appropriate server based on that information.

To be able to resolve the fully qualified autodiscover host name, your client must be pointed to a DNS server that hosts the records for the autodiscover host or that can forward a query to the appropriate DNS server(s).

After your client is configured appropriately to resolve the autodiscover host, you can use a feature in Outlook 2010 to test the capability to discover account information. If you are having difficulties viewing free/busy information or using the Out Of Office Assistant, the inability of the client to contact the autodiscover host could be the problem.

To test the connection, create an Outlook 2010 profile, with or without a valid email account. To do this, start Outlook 2010, hold down the Ctrl key, and right-click the Outlook 2010 icon in the system tray. Choose Test E-Mail AutoConfiguration to open the Test E-Mail AutoConfiguration dialog box, shown in Figure 39-9.

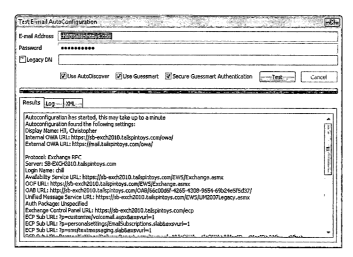

Figure 39-9 Use the Test E-Mail AutoConfiguration dialog box to test AutoDiscover functionality.

Type the email address for your Exchange Server account in the E-Mail Address field, type your email account password in the Password field, and then click Test. If AutoConfigure succeeds, the dialog box will display information similar to that shown in Figure 39-9. If AutoConfigure fails, the dialog box will display an error message indicating that it was unable to determine the correct settings. If you receive the error, verify that the client is configured for the appropriate DNS server(s) and retest.

THIS chapter focuses on some common messaging topics related specifically to Microsoft Exchange Server, such as recalling sent messages, setting messages to expire, and working with the Global Address List (GAL). This chapter also covers voting, which you can use with non–Exchange Server accounts as well as Exchange Server accounts, but which is more likely to be used in a larger organization with Exchange Server in place. Other chapters in this book cover many topics that are more specifically applicable to the Microsoft Outlook 2010 messaging capabilities. For example, see Chapter 8, "Sending and Receiving Messages," to learn about message composition, replies, and using send/receive groups to synchronize your Exchange Server mailbox. Other chapters cover specific features of Exchange Server accounts as well, such as using the Out Of Office Assistant. So, this chapter isn't an all-inclusive look at Exchange Server–specific features, but rather covers useful features that have not already been covered elsewhere.

Sending Messages

When you send messages in Outlook 2010 while connected to Exchange Server, you have more options than you do when you use a regular Internet mail account—for example, you have the ability to recall messages, and you have access to a Global Address List (GAL).

To send a new message, you have a couple of choices:

- In the Inbox or another message folder, click the New button on the ribbon.

- In any folder, click New Items on the ribbon and choose E-Mail Message.

Whichever method that you use, a new message form opens, as shown in Figure 40-1.

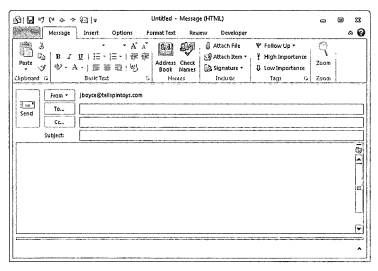

Figure 40-1 Write a message and choose the options for this message using the standard message form.

Addressing Messages

You can designate the recipients of your message in two ways. The first method is to click To or Cc (or Bcc) to open the Select Names dialog adding recipients tobox, shown in Figure 40-2. By default, the GAL is displayed.

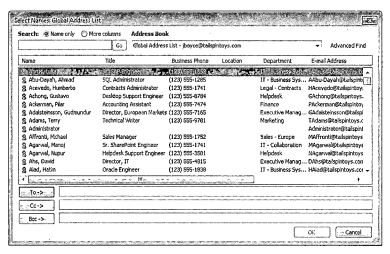

Figure 40-2 The Select Names dialog box displays addresses from the available address books.

The GAL contains all users in the entire organization, except those who are explicitly hidden. An Exchange Server administrator can define other address lists on the computer running Exchange Server to filter addresses by any criteria, such as location, name, or department.

To add a message recipient, select the recipient in the list, and then click To, Cc, or Bcc. Double-click a recipient in the To, Cc, or Bcc field to view the recipient's properties so that you can verify his or her contact information.

One of the most useful features of the Select Names dialog box is the Find feature. Click Advanced Find to open the Find dialog box, shown in Figure 40-3. You can search the address book by any of the criteria shown, such as Title, Company, or Department. The ability to search the address book is most useful when you have a large organization and no additional address lists are defined.

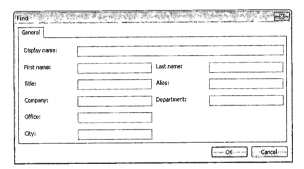

Figure 40-3 You can search the address list for recipients matching specific criteria.

The second way to add recipients to a message is the simplest: Type the recipient's name or alias in the To, Cc, or Bcc field on the message form. An Exchange Server *alias* is another way of referring to an account. The alias might be the user's Active Directory Domain Services (AD DS) account, or it could be the first part of the email address (which could also be the same as the AD DS account).

INSIDE OUT   Cut your typing time

You don't have to type the complete name or alias in an address field, so long as the part of the name that you type is unique. For example, if only one name in the address book matches *Bob*, you can type Bob as the recipient, even if the recipient's name is Bob Smith and the alias is *bob.smith*. If the recipient's name is Robert Smith and the alias is *bob.smith*, you can type either Rob or bob—both will resolve to Robert Smith.

Checking Names

As soon as you finish typing a recipient's name and move the insertion point out of the text box, Outlook 2010 checks the name. If the name is not unique or can't be found, it is underlined in red. When this occurs, you'll need to check the name manually.

You can also check a recipient's name by clicking Check Names in the Names group on the Message tab on the ribbon or by pressing Ctrl+K. When a problem arises, the Check Names dialog box appears, indicating whether the name is not unique or not found. When the name is not unique, all matches are displayed so that you can make a selection.

> **Note**
> If the name you typed is causing a problem, check the spelling of the name. This sounds simple enough, but a small mistake can prevent the name from being resolved. You might need to use the GAL or another address list to find the correct name.

Controlling When Messages Are Delivered

When a message is sent, it is delivered immediately by default. You can, however, delay message delivery until a specified time for an individual message. Delayed delivery is not specific to Exchange Server accounts, but the feature goes hand-in-hand with message expiration (covered next), so it bears discussing here.

To place a message in the Outbox but have it delivered after a certain point, click the More Options button in the More Options group on the Options tab to open the Properties dialog box. Select the Do Not Deliver Before check box, and then set the date and time using the drop-down lists. Click Close, then complete the message and click Send. It will not be sent until after the specified time.

> **Tip**
> If there is enough room on the ribbon, Outlook displays a Delay Delivery button that, when clicked, opens the Properties dialog box, where you can enter the delivery date and time.

Setting Messages to Expire

Just as you can delay the delivery of a message, you can also set a message to expire. The message expires and is removed from the recipient's mailbox after a specified period of time whether or not it has been read. You might want to have a message expire if its contents become outdated after a certain amount of time, or if you want to ensure that the message is deleted. To set this option, open the Properties dialog box by clicking Message Options on the Options tab, select the Expires After check box, and then set a date and time. The message will no longer be available to the recipient after that time.

> **Note**
> The capability to set a message to expire is not a security feature; it simply causes the message to be deleted after the specified period. Use Information Rights Management (IRM), covered in Chapter 14, "Securing Your System, Messages, and Identity," to prevent messages from being forwarded, copied, or printed.

Recalling a Sent Message Before It Is Read

There are many reasons why you might want to recall a message. For example, perhaps the message contains a mistake or is now obsolete. You can recall a message that you have sent so long as the recipient has not read it and the message is still stored on a computer running Exchange Server. Messages sent to recipients using other mail servers cannot be recalled.

To recall a sent message, double-click the message in the Sent Items folder to open it. Click Actions in the Move group on the ribbon, and then click Recall This Message to open the dialog box shown in Figure 40-4. Select whether you want to simply delete all unread copies of the message or delete them and replace them with another message. You can also receive a response reporting the success or failure of each recall attempt.

> **CAUTION**
> For a number of reasons, unread messages often cannot be recalled. You should always take the time to verify the content of a message before sending it.

Figure 40-4 This dialog box is displayed when you attempt to recall a message.

Copying Global Addresses to Your Contacts Folder

On occasion, you might want to copy addresses from the GAL to your personal Contacts folder. For example, maybe you use a Personal Digital Assistant (PDA) or smartphone that synchronizes your Contacts folder to your mobile device, and that device does not support Exchange Server directly. The device would not synchronize the GAL, but you might want a few entries available on your mobile device. You can copy those items to the Contacts folder, and from there, they can be synchronized to your mobile device.

You can copy addresses from the GAL to your Contacts folder easily by following these steps:

1. Click Address Book on the Home tab on the ribbon.

2. Click the address that you want to add to your Contacts folder. You can also select multiple addresses using the Shift and Ctrl keys.

3. Choose File, Add To Contacts. The entry from the GAL opens in a contact form.

4. Make any necessary changes.

5. Click Save & Close. The contact information is now stored in your Contacts folder.

Voting in Outlook

The Outlook 2010 voting feature is useful when you want to solicit input from a group of message recipients. Perhaps you are looking for approval on a proposal, you are holding an informal election in your organization, or you just want to get the group's input on an issue.

You can use Outlook's voting feature with non–Exchange Server accounts as well as with Exchange Server accounts. This feature is typically more useful in a larger organization where Exchange Server is likely to be installed, and that's why the topic is covered in this chapter. However, the functionality is the same.

> **Tip**
>
> The Voting feature supported by Outlook is certainly useful, but it isn't a substitute for a formal approval process. If you have Microsoft SharePoint deployed in your organization, consider using workflows in SharePoint to automate approval processes for documents and other items.

With the voting feature, you solicit and tally votes from the group. Outlook 2010 provides predefined voting responses, but you can also create your own. In this section, you'll learn how to include voting buttons in messages, tally returned votes, and configure voting options.

Here's how voting works in general: You create a message containing the question or document on which the group will be voting. Next, you add voting buttons to the message. Next, you send the message. Recipients cast their vote by clicking the appropriate button. Outlook 2010 prompts them to confirm the vote and then sends the reply back to you.

Sending a Message for a Vote

Sending a message for a vote is simple. In fact, so long as you want to use one of the Outlook 2010 default sets of voting options, the process takes only a few clicks.

Using the Default Voting Responses

Use the following steps to create a message and add voting buttons to it:

1. Start Outlook 2010, and then open a new message or open an existing message from your Drafts folder.

2. On the Options tab, in the More Options group, click Message Options to open the Properties dialog box.

3. In the Voting And Tracking Options area, select the Use Voting Buttons check box. In the drop-down list, select the group of voting buttons that you want to include, as shown in Figure 40-5.

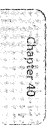

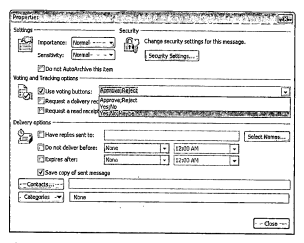

Figure 40-5 Select the voting buttons that you want to include using the Properties dialog box.

4. Click Close.

5. Edit your message. Include any message attachments and configure message options, such as importance level, if needed.

6. Click Send to send the message.

Using Custom Responses

Outlook 2010 doesn't limit you to the default sets of voting options (such as Accept/Reject). You can create your own set that includes the responses that you need for any situation. For example, suppose that you're planning a company appreciation banquet and need to finalize the menu. You want to give everyone a choice of entree and collect those responses for the caterer. What better way to do that than electronically, through Outlook 2010?

Here's how:

1. Compose your message.

2. On the Options tab, in the More Options group, click Message Options to open the Properties dialog box.

3. Select the Use Voting Buttons check box.

4. Click the text field in the Use Voting Buttons drop-down list. Delete the existing text. Type your custom vote options separated by semicolons, as shown in Figure 40-6.

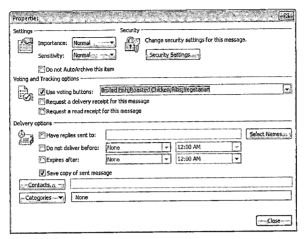

Figure 40-6 You can create custom vote responses in the Use Voting Buttons text field.

5. Click Close.

6. Make any final adjustments to the message as needed.

7. Click Send.

Casting Your Vote

When you receive a message that includes voting buttons, Outlook 2010 displays a message in the InfoBar to indicate that you can vote. Click the InfoBar and then choose an item, as shown in Figure 40-7.

Voting is easy: Just select an option to cast your vote. Outlook 2010 displays a simple dialog box asking whether you want to send the vote now or edit your response. To send the message without modification, select Send The Response Now. To cast your vote and open the message as a reply so that you can include text in your response, select Edit The Response Before Sending.

> **Note**
> Outlook 2010 changes the prompt in the InfoBar to indicate that you responded to the voting request, removing your ability to click the InfoBar link and vote again.

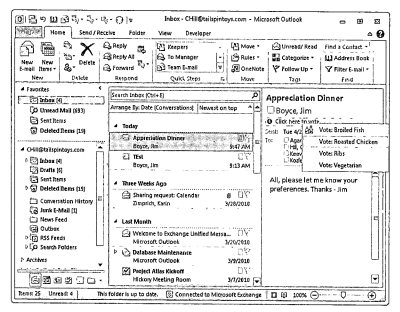

Figure 40-7 The Reading pane shows a message prompting you to vote.

When you cast a vote, Outlook 2010 changes the subject of the message to include your vote. For example, if the original subject is Choose An Entree and you click the Broiled Chicken option, the subject of the reply returned to the sender is Broiled Chicken: Choose An Entree.

Viewing and Sorting Votes

Votes come back to you in the form of messages. You can view the vote summary in a few ways. If the Reading pane is displayed, you can click the message header, click the summary message in the InfoBar, and then choose View Voting Responses, as shown in Figure 40-8. Alternatively, you can open the Sent Items folder, open the original message, and then click the Tracking button in the Show group on the ribbon. Either method displays the Tracking results, as shown in Figure 40-9.

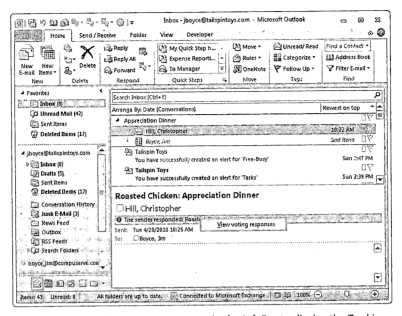

Figure 40-8 Click the summary message in the InfoBar to display the Tracking page.

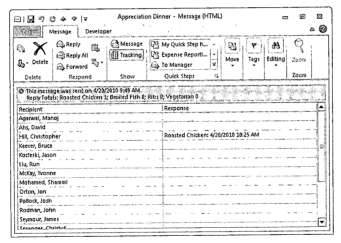

Figure 40-9 Open the message from the Sent Items folder as an alternative way to access the Tracking page.

The Tracking page summarizes the votes, with individual responses displayed one per line. The responses are also totaled in the InfoBar. If you want a printout of the vote responses, print the messages with the Tracking page visible.

Unfortunately, Outlook 2010 doesn't give you a way to sort the vote tally. You can, however, copy the data to Microsoft Excel 2010 to sort it.

To copy voting data to Excel 2010, follow these steps:

1. Select the rows that you want to copy. (Select a row, and then hold down the Shift key to select contiguous responses or hold down the Ctrl key to select noncontiguous ones.)

2. Press Ctrl+C to copy the data to the Clipboard.

3. Start Excel.

4. Select a cell in the worksheet and then press Ctrl+V to paste the data.

5. Choose Data, Sort to open the Sort dialog box, and then click OK to accept the default settings and sort the spreadsheet.

Setting Options for Voting

You can set options in Outlook 2010 to configure how it handles voting. To configure these settings, follow these steps:

1. Start Outlook 2010 (if necessary), and then click File, Options.

2. Click Mail in the left pane.

3. Scroll down to the Tracking group, shown in Figure 40-10.

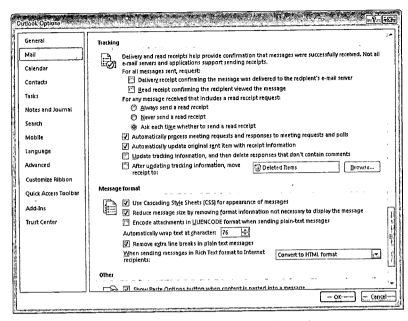

Figure 40-10 Use the Tracking group to configure voting options.

The Tracking group includes the following options that relate to voting:

- **Automatically Process Meeting Requests And Responses To Meeting Requests And Polls** Outlook 2010 processes and tallies responses when they arrive. If you clear this check box, you must open each response to have Outlook 2010 tally it.

- **Update Tracking Information, And Then Delete Responses That Don't Contain Comments** Outlook 2010 deletes voting responses that have no additional comments added to them.

4. Select the options that you want to use, and then click OK to close the Outlook Options dialog box.

TROUBLESHOOTING

Votes aren't being tallied automatically

The Outlook 2010 capability to tally votes automatically, without the user having to open each message, might not be apparent at first. Even on a completely idle system, Outlook 2010 can take several minutes to process the messages. If you need to process the responses more quickly, select all the responses, right-click the selection, and then choose Open Selected Items to open them all at once. Keep in mind, however, that you'll end up with an open message form for each response, which you'll then have to close.

CHAPTER 41

Working Offline and Remotely

Mıcrosoft Outlook 2010 provides several features that enable you to work offline (while you are not connected to your mail server) as well as from a remote location. Using the offline feature and the offline storage of Outlook 2010, which contains copies of all the folders and items in your Microsoft Exchange Server mailbox, you can work with contacts, messages, and other items stored in your mailbox without being connected to the server (except to perform periodic synchronizations). You can create and delete items, add folders, and make other changes while offline; Outlook 2010 synchronizes those changes the next time you connect to the server and perform a send/receive operation.

> **Note**
> This chapter focuses on the offline and remote features in Outlook 2010 used in conjunction with Exchange Server.

If you are looking for ways to work offline and remotely using other types of email servers and accounts, see Chapter 15, "Receiving Messages Selectively."

Offline vs. Remote

Offline use and remote use are two separate aspects of using Outlook 2010, although they typically go hand in hand. When you work offline, your computer is not connected to the server(s) running Exchange Server. This usually means that you're working on a computer that uses a dial-up connection to the server or on a portable computer that you connect to the server through a docking station or a wireless access point on the local area network (LAN). You can be working offline even while your computer is connected to the LAN when the Exchange Server is down for maintenance, or you can set Outlook 2010 offline deliberately.

You can perform most of the same operations offline that you perform when you're connected to the server. You can create messages, contacts, and other Outlook 2010 items; schedule meetings; and carry out other common Outlook 2010 tasks. The items that you create and the changes that you make to your folders and their contents, however, are made to the offline store instead of to your Exchange Server mailbox store. When you reconnect to the server, Outlook 2010 synchronizes the offline store with the mailbox store. Any items that arrived in the mailbox while you were working offline are added to your offline store when Outlook 2010 performs the synchronization. This behavior is the same whether you use Cached Exchange Mode and work from a locally cached copy of your mailbox or simply add an offline store (.ost) file to your profile—the main difference is in how Outlook 2010 synchronizes the online and offline mailboxes.

In contrast, working remotely generally means working with Outlook 2010 from a location other than the LAN on which the server running Exchange Server is located. For example, you might dial in to your LAN with a modem, connect to it through the Internet, or even connect through a demand-dial connection between two offices. Whatever your location, you can be working either offline or online when you work remotely. The only consideration is whether you are connected to the server. If you are not connected to the server, you are working offline. If you are connected to the server, you are simply working remotely.

Establishing a Remote LAN Connection

To work remotely, you need to establish a remote connection to the server. How you accomplish this depends on the connection options available on your LAN and how the network administrator configured the LAN. The following are the most common methods for establishing a remote LAN connection:

- **Dial up access directly to the LAN**   In this scenario, the LAN includes a Remote Access Services (RAS) server that enables clients to dial up directly to the network using a modem or other device, such as an Integrated Services Digital Network (ISDN) connection. The RAS server can be the computer running Exchange Server or another server on the network, depending on the size of the organization and the load on the computer running Exchange Server. Depending on the configuration of the RAS server, dial-up clients might have access to the network or only to the computer running Exchange Server.

- **Connect through a virtual private network connection over the Internet**   If your LAN is connected to the Internet and includes a virtual private network (VPN) server, one of the options for retrieving email messages is to create a VPN connection to the LAN and then connect to the computer running Exchange Server. A

VPN server enables clients to establish secure connections to the network through a public network such as the Internet.

- **Use a demand-dial connection between two networks**   If you have two or more offices, those offices might connect using a demand-dial connection. The connection might take place over a standard dial-up line, or you can use ISDN or another communication method. The demand-dial interface enables the two routers that connect the offices to establish the connection when a client requests it, such as when you connect to synchronize your Outlook 2010 data.

- **Use HTTP to connect to the server**   Outlook 2010 includes support for Hypertext Transfer Protocol (HTTP) as a communications protocol when used with Exchange Server 2003 or later, enabling you to connect to your computer running Exchange Server remotely (such as from the Internet) without using a VPN connection.

CAUTION

You can connect to a computer running Exchange Server through the Internet without configuring Outlook 2010 to use remote procedure call (RPC) over HTTP. However, doing so requires that you open several ports on the firewall that, for security reasons, really should not be opened. For that reason, this method is neither recommended nor explained in this chapter.

Because this book focuses specifically on Outlook 2010 and its integration with Exchange Server, the details of how to set up a RAS or VPN server aren't covered.

Using HTTP to Connect (Outlook Anywhere)

Using HTTP as the communications protocol for your computer running Exchange Server is a useful remote access method that eliminates the need for you to run VPN software on your client. It also eliminates the need for the network administrator to support those VPN connections. Most networks already have port 80 open for HTTP and port 443 open for Hypertext Transfer Protocol Secure HTTP (Hypertext Transfer Protocol)(HTTPS) through Secure Sockets Layer (SSL), so providing HTTP-based access to Exchange Server requires only some setup on the computer running Exchange Server and configuring Outlook to use HTTP.

Note
HTTP-based access to Exchange Server requires Exchange Server 2003 or later and Outlook 2003 or later.

Chapter 39, "Configuring the Exchange Server Client," explains how to configure the Exchange Server client for Outlook 2010, including setting up the account to use HTTP and configuring the server, so that information isn't repeated here. Beyond those steps, there is really nothing else to do to start using HTTP to access your mailbox. However, here is some advice:

- **Use Cached Exchange Mode and synchronize from the LAN at least once**   To reduce the load on the server and the amount of bandwidth that you will use connecting to the server, consider using Cached Exchange Mode, which creates a locally cached copy of your mailbox on your computer. Before connecting remotely, connect to the server on your LAN (if possible) and allow Outlook 2010 to synchronize the cache with your mailbox. By synchronizing from the LAN rather than a remote connection, you will likely decrease the amount of time required to complete the synchronization, particularly if your mailbox contains a large amount of data.

- **Use RPC and TCP/IP when connected locally to the network**   The default settings for using HTTP in Outlook 2010 to connect to your computer running Exchange Server cause Outlook 2010 to attempt a connection with remote procedure call (RPC) rather than Transmission Control Protocol/Internet Protocol (TCP/IP) for a fast connection before it attempts to use HTTP. Leave this setting at its default to provide better performance when you connect to the server from your LAN. Change this setting only if your Exchange Server requires an HTTP connection to the server.

Working Offline with Outlook 2010 and Exchange Server

There are a few specific issues and settings that you need to consider when working with Outlook 2010 offline. This section explains how to configure the Outlook 2010 startup mode and offline folders and how to use an offline address book.

Configuring Startup Options

When you start Outlook 2010, it attempts by default to determine the online or offline status of the server. If the server is unavailable and Outlook 2010 is configured with an .ost file, Outlook 2010 starts in offline mode and uses the offline folder specified in your profile for displaying existing items and storing new items (such as email messages) before synchronizing with Exchange Server. With Cached Exchange Mode enabled, Outlook 2010 automatically uses the local cache (stored in an .ost file) and attempts to synchronize the cached copy with your Exchange Server mailbox if a server connection is available. If you configured autodial in your operating system, Outlook 2010 dials the connection to the Internet service provider (ISP) or RAS server. However, you might want to exercise more control over the Outlook 2010 startup mode and when it connects. For example, you might prefer to have Outlook 2010 start in offline mode so that you can compose messages or perform other tasks before you connect and synchronize with the server.

You configure startup options by setting the properties for the Exchange Server account in your profile, as outlined in the following steps:

1. Open the Mail item in the Control Panel.

2. If you don't use multiple profiles, skip to step 3. If you use multiple profiles, click Show Profiles. Select the profile that you want to change and then click Properties.

3. Click E-Mail Accounts.

4. Select the Exchange Server account and then click Change.

5. If you decide to use Cached Exchange Mode, you can click the Use Cached Exchange Mode option; otherwise, click More Settings and then click the General tab (see Figure 41-1).

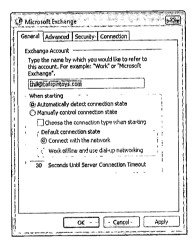

Figure 41-1 Use the General tab to configure startup options for Outlook 2010.

6. Configure the following settings:

   - **Automatically Detect Connection State**   With this setting, Outlook 2010 detects the connection state at startup and enters online or offline mode accordingly (selected by default).

- **Manually Control Connection State**   With this setting, you control the connection state when Outlook 2010 starts. The next three options work in combination with this option.

- **Choose The Connection Type When Starting**   With this setting, Outlook 2010 prompts you to select the connection state when it starts. This enables you to select between online and offline states.

- **Connect With The Network**   With this setting, connect through your local LAN to Exchange Server. You can use this option if you connect to the Internet through a dedicated connection such as a cable modem or a Digital Subscriber Line (DSL) connection (selected by default).

- **Work Offline And Use Dial-Up Networking**   With this setting, you can start in an offline state and use Dial-Up Networking to connect to Exchange Server. On the Connection tab, specify the dial-up connection that you want to use.

- **Seconds Until Server Connection Timeout**   With this setting, specify the timeout, in seconds, for the server (30 seconds by default). Outlook 2010 attempts a connection for the specified amount of time; if Outlook 2010 is unable to establish a connection in the specified period, it times out. You might want to increase the time-out period if you connect to the Internet through a shared dial-up connection hosted by another computer on your LAN.

Increase TCP/IP timeout

You might want to change your TCP/IP timeout values if you change the Seconds Until Server Connection Timeout option in Outlook 2010. Increasing the TCP/IP timeout increases the length of time that your computer waits for TCP/IP connections to succeed before timing out, a feature that is particularly useful with dial-up or unreliable connections.

See the sidebar "Increase TCP Time-Out for On-Demand Connections," on page 948, for details on configuring the TCP/IP timeout.

Using Offline Folders

Although you don't have to use offline folders when you work with Exchange Server over a remote connection, you do need a set of offline folders to work offline. If you haven't set up offline folders and can't connect to the remote server, Outlook 2010 won't start. One of your first tasks after you create your dial-up connection and configure your Exchange Server account should be to configure a set of offline folders. Note, however, that you don't have to perform this step if you configure Outlook 2010 to use Cached Exchange Mode for your Exchange Server account. When you enable Cached Exchange Mode, Outlook 2010 automatically creates an offline store for you.

See Chapter 39 for more information on enabling Cached Exchange Mode.

You can associate one set of offline folders with the Exchange Server account in your profile. The offline file has an .ost file extension and stores a copy of all the folders and items in your Exchange Server mailbox. Outlook 2010 synchronizes the data between the two. For example, suppose that you create an email message and a new contact item while working offline. The message goes in the Outbox folder of the offline store, and the new contact item goes in the Contacts folder of the offline store. When you next connect to the server and perform synchronization, Outlook 2010 moves the message in the local Outbox to the Outbox folder on your computer running Exchange Server, and the message then gets delivered. Outlook 2010 also copies the new contact item in your local Contacts folder to the Contacts folder stored on the computer running Exchange Server. Any additional changes, including those at the server (such as new email messages waiting to be delivered), are copied to your local offline folders.

> **Note**
> The .ost file does not appear as a separate set of folders in Outlook 2010. In effect, Outlook 2010 uses it transparently when your computer is offline.

An .ost file, like a personal folders (.pst) file, contains Outlook 2010 folders and items. One difference, however, is that you can have only one .ost file, but you can have multiple .pst files. Also, Outlook 2010 synchronizes the offline store with your computer running Exchange Server automatically but does not provide automatic synchronization for .pst files.

For more information on adding .pst files to a profile, see the section "Adding Other Data Stores," on page 59.

Follow these steps to configure offline storage with an .ost file:

1. If Outlook 2010 is running, click File, Account Settings, and finally Account Settings. Otherwise, open the Mail item in the Control Panel and click Properties.

2. Select the Exchange Server account and click Change.

3. To use offline folders without Cached Exchange Mode, clear the Use Cached Exchange Mode check box in the Change E-Mail Account dialog box.

4. Click More Settings and then click the Advanced tab.

5. Click Outlook Data File Settings to open the dialog box shown in Figure 41-2.

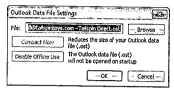

Figure 41-2 Specify the file name and other settings for the .ost file.

6. In the File box, specify a path and name for the .ost file and click OK.

7. On the Advanced tab, click OK.

8. Click Next and then click Finish.

> **Note**
>
> This option to configure the offline folder store might be dimmed (disabled) if you have only an Exchange Server email account configured, yet it can be enabled if you have multiple types of email accounts. If you have a POP3 account configured, for example, and you add an Exchange Server account, the capability to configure the offline storage location is enabled.

Synchronizing with the Exchange Server Mailbox

After you add an .ost file to your profile, you need to synchronize the file with your Exchange Server mailbox at least once before you can work offline.

Follow these steps to synchronize your offline folders:

1. Connect to the remote network where the computer running Exchange Server is located using the Internet, a dial-up connection to a remote access server on the remote LAN, or other means (such as ISDN, cable modem, or DSL). A LAN connection will give you the best performance for the initial synchronization.

2. Open Outlook 2010.

3. Click the Send/Receive tab on the ribbon and click Send/Receive All Folders. Outlook 2010 then synchronizes with the computer running Exchange Server.

Synchronizing with Send/Receive Groups

The preceding section explained how to synchronize your offline folders and your Exchange Server mailbox. Sometimes, though, you might not want to synchronize all folders each time you perform a send/receive operation. You can use send/receive groups to define the actions that Outlook 2010 takes when sending and receiving. For example, you might want to create a send/receive group that sends only mail waiting in your local Outbox and doesn't retrieve waiting messages from the server.

For a detailed discussion of send/receive groups, see the section "Controlling Synchronization and Send/Receive Times," on page 199.

Using an Offline Address Book

Whether you're composing messages offline, scheduling meetings, or creating tasks to assign to others, chances are good that you want access to your Exchange Server address book so that you can address messages to other users in your organization. If the Global Address List (GAL) doesn't change very often on the server (if, for example, employee turnover at your company is low), you can get by with downloading the offline address book infrequently. Otherwise, you'll need to update the offline address book more often.

> **Note**
> You can download additional address lists from the server if the Exchange Server administrator has created additional address books and given you the necessary permissions to access them. Additional address books give you quick access to addresses that are sorted using different criteria than the GAL uses or access to other addresses not shown in the GAL (such as external contacts).

To download the address book manually whenever you want an update, follow these steps:

1. Click the Send/Receive tab, click Send/Receive Groups, and choose Download Address Book to open the Offline Address Book dialog box (see Figure 41-3).

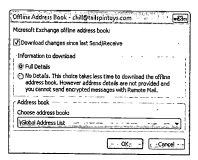

Figure 41-3 Use the Offline Address Book dialog box to specify options for downloading the offline address book.

2. Select options as needed from the following:

- **Download Changes Since Last Send/Receive**   Download only changes made since the last time you performed a send/receive operation. Clear this check box to download the entire address list.

- **Full Details**   Download all address information, including phone, fax, and office location. (You must select this option if you want to send encrypted messages because you need the users' digital signatures.)

- **No Details**   Download only email addresses and no additional address book details.

3. Click OK to download the address book.

In addition to performing manual offline address book updates, you also can configure a send/receive group to download the address book.

Follow these steps to do so:

1. Click the Send/Receive tab, click Send/Receive Groups, and choose Define Send/ Receive Groups.

2. Select the send/receive group in which you want to configure the address book download, and then click Edit.

3. On the Accounts bar of the Send/Receive Settings dialog box, select your Exchange Server account (see Figure 41-4).

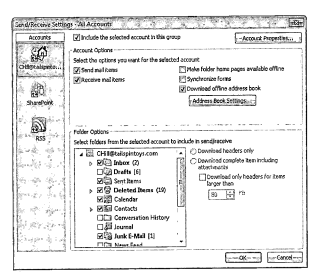

Figure 41-4 You can configure automatic offline address book synchronization.

4. Select the Download Offline Address Book check box and then click Address Book Settings to open the Offline Address Book dialog box.

5. Configure settings as necessary in the Offline Address Book dialog box (discussed in the preceding set of steps) and then click OK.

6. Click OK to close the Send/Receive Settings dialog box.

Each time you synchronize folders using the send/receive group, Outlook 2010 downloads the offline address book according to the settings that you specified. You probably don't want to configure this option for the default All Accounts send/receive group unless you have a fast connection to the server and your offline address book changes frequently. One option is to create a send/receive group that downloads only the offline address book and does not process any other folders. However, this is essentially the same as clicking Send/Receive, Send/Receive Groups, and Download Address Book. Consider how often you need to download the address book and work that task into your send/receive groups as you see fit.

PART 9

Mobility

Accessing Your Outlook Items Through a Web Browser

ICROSOFT first introduced Microsoft Outlook Web Access in Microsoft Exchange Server 5.0 so that clients could access their Exchange Server mailboxes through a web browser. Microsoft has made significant improvements in Outlook Web Access in each new version of Exchange Server to provide support for a larger number of users, better performance, and improved functionality for clients. The latest version of this feature in Exchange Server 2010, now called Outlook Web App, provides most of the functionality of the Microsoft Outlook 2010 client.

This chapter explores Outlook Web App to help you learn why it can be an important feature to implement and how best to put it to work for you, and also to help you put it to work as an alternative or complement to Outlook 2010.

Overview of Outlook Web App

With Outlook Web App and a web browser, users can send and receive messages, view and modify their calendars, and perform most of the other tasks available through Outlook 2010. The features and appearance of Outlook Web App (or Outlook Web Access) depend on the version of Exchange Server that is hosting it. Each successive version of Exchange Server adds a new look and new capabilities.

Outlook 2010 provides full access to an Exchange Server mailbox. Although Outlook Web App isn't intended as a complete replacement for Outlook 2010, it is useful for roaming users who want to access the most common mailbox features when they don't have access to their personal Outlook 2010 installation. Linux, UNIX, and Macintosh users can also benefit from Outlook Web App by being able to access Exchange Server mailboxes and participate in workgroup messaging and scheduling. In addition, Outlook Web App can save the administrative overhead and support associated with deploying Outlook 2010 to users who don't need everything that Outlook 2010 has to offer. These users can use a free web browser to access many functions provided by Exchange Server. However, you must still purchase a Client Access License (CAL) for each user or device that accesses the server running Exchange Server, even if the users do not use Outlook to connect to the server.

Outlook Web App Features

Because email is the primary function of Exchange Server and Outlook 2010, Outlook Web App supports email access. Users can view message headers and read messages (see Figure 42-1) as well as send, reply to, forward, and delete messages. This last capability—deleting messages—might seem commonplace, but it is a useful feature. If your mailbox contains a very large attachment or a corrupted message that is preventing you from viewing your messages in Outlook 2010, you can use Outlook Web App to delete the message without downloading or reading it. Just open your mailbox in your web browser, select the message header, and delete the message.

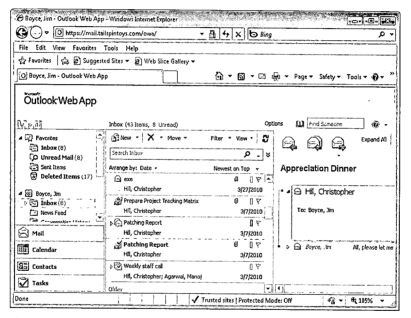

Figure 42-1 Using Outlook Web App, you can access your Inbox through a web browser.

As mentioned earlier, you're not limited to just messaging—you can also access your Calendar folder through Outlook Web App. You can view and modify existing items and create appointments (see Figure 42-2). You can't perform all the same scheduling tasks through Outlook Web App that you can with Outlook 2010, but the ability to view your schedule and add appointments is useful, particularly when you're working from a remote location or on a system without Outlook 2010 installed.

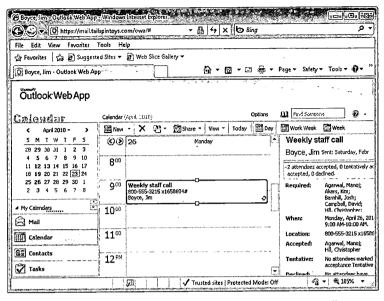

Figure 42-2 Use Outlook Web App to manage your schedule as well as your email messages.

Contacts are another type of item that you can manage through Outlook Web App. You can view and modify existing contact items and add new ones (see Figure 42-3).

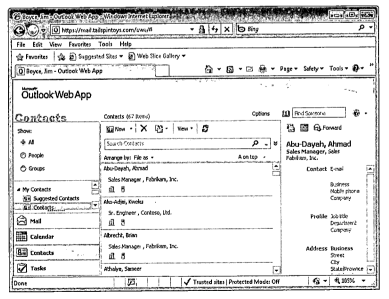

Figure 42-3 You can also work with your Contacts folder through Outlook Web App.

Each successive release of Exchange Server has incorporated changes to Outlook Web Access. These changes have included an interface to match the Outlook interface more closely, addition of spell checking, access to task lists, Secure/Multipurpose Internet Mail Extensions (S/MIME) support, Hypertext Markup Language (HTML) content blocking, scheduling and control of Out Of Office messages, the Scheduling Assistant, access to Microsoft SharePoint documents, Really Simple Syndication (RSS) subscriptions, support for rights management, and many other features. The end result is that Outlook Web App in Exchange Server 2010 provides most of the features offered by the native Outlook client.

Web Browser Options

To access your mailbox through Outlook Web App, you can use any web browser that supports JavaScript and HTML version 3.2 or later, including Microsoft Internet Explorer 4.0 or later and Netscape 4.0 or later. Some features, however, rely on Internet Explorer 5 or later, including drag-and-drop editing, shortcut menus, and native Kerberos authentication. In addition, browsers that support Dynamic HTML (DHTML) and Extensible Markup Language (XML) offer a richer set of features than those that do not. For example, Internet Explorer 5.x and later offer an interface for Outlook Web App that is much closer to the native Outlook 2010 client, including a folder tree for navigating and managing folders, as well as a Reading pane.

> **Note**
>
> Kerberos authentication enables users to access multiple resources across the enterprise with a single set of user credentials, and provides for single sign on (SSO) capability.

Authentication Options

Outlook Web App offers several options for authentication:

- **Basic** Use clear text and simple challenge/response to authenticate access. This option offers the broadest client support, but it also offers the least security because passwords are transmitted as clear text.

- **Integrated Windows** Use the native Windows authentication method for the client's operating system. Integrated Windows authentication provides better security than basic authentication because passwords are encrypted. The client doesn't need to enter authentication credentials because the browser uses the client's Windows logon credentials to authenticate on the Outlook Web App server.

- **Anonymous**   Use anonymous access for public folders in the Exchange Server store. This option can simplify administration.

Exchange Server 2003 and later support some additional options because of additions to Microsoft Internet Information Services (IIS) 6.0:

- **Digest authentication**   This authentication method works only with Active Directory Domain Services (AD DS) accounts. It offers the benefit of sending passwords as a hash rather than in plain text. However, to use digest authentication, you must configure AD DS to allow reversible encryption, which reduces security.

- **Microsoft Passport authentication**   This method enables users to authenticate with their Microsoft Passports.

In addition to these authentication methods, Outlook Web App supports the use of Secure Sockets Layer (SSL) to provide additional security for remote connections.

Using Outlook Web App

After your Exchange Server administrators install and configure Outlook Web App on the server(s), users can begin accessing their mailboxes through their web browsers rather than (or in conjunction with) Outlook 2010. This section explains how to connect to the computer running Exchange Server and use Outlook Web App to access your mailbox.

> **Note**
> This section assumes that you are connecting to Exchange Server 2010 with Outlook Web App. If you have an earlier version of Exchange Server, the features available to you are slightly different, and the look and feel are also different.

Connecting to the Server

Typically, you connect to the computer running Exchange Server through the Uniform Resource Locator (URL) *http://<server>/exchange*, where *<server>* is the Domain Name System (DNS) name, Internet Protocol (IP) address, or NetBIOS name of the server. An example is *https://owa.tailspintoys.com/exchange*. This URL isn't set in stone. The system administrator might have changed the virtual directory name for security purposes. Check with the system administrator if you're not sure what URL to use to connect to the computer running Exchange Server.

> ## Note
>
> Windows Internet Naming Service (WINS) maps NetBIOS names (computer names) to IP addresses, performing a service similar to that provided by DNS (although DNS maps host names, not NetBIOS names). You can use an Lmhosts file to perform NetBIOS name-to-address mapping without a WINS server, just as you can use a Hosts file to perform host name-to-address mapping without a DNS server.

Depending on the server's authentication settings, you might be prompted to log on. Enter your user name and password for the Exchange Server account. If the account resides in a different domain from the one in which the server resides, enter the account name in the form *<domain>\<account>*, where *<domain>* is the logon domain and *<account>* is the user account.

When you connect to your mailbox, you should see a page similar to the one shown in Figure 42-4 for Exchange Server 2010. Earlier versions of Exchange Server show a somewhat different interface (Outlook Web Access 5.5, not shown, is considerably different). Outlook Web App opens your Inbox by default, but you can switch to other folders as needed.

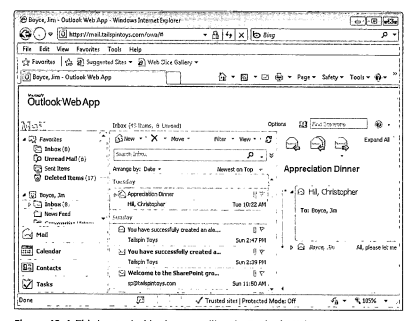

Figure 42-4 This is a typical look at a mailbox in Outlook Web App.

The left pane functions much as the Navigation pane does in Outlook 2010 (or, in the case of Exchange 2000 Server or Exchange Server 5.5, as the Outlook Bar in Outlook 2002 or earlier), and you can select folders from it. (Throughout this chapter, I'll refer to the left pane as the Navigation pane for simplicity.) The right pane changes to show the folder's contents.

> ## Note
>
> The interface for Outlook Web App changed slightly between Exchange Server 5.5 and Exchange 2000 Server, and even more so from Exchange 2000 Server to Exchange Server 2003. The following sections assume that you're using Outlook Web App to access Exchange Server 2010, but the procedures are similar for Outlook Web Access with earlier versions of Exchange Server. Also note that some features are not available with Outlook Web Access and Exchange Server 5.5 or with versions of Internet Explorer earlier than 5.0. Certain other features, such as rules, are only available with Exchange Server 2003 or later.

Sending and Receiving Messages

Outlook Web App automatically shows your current messages when you connect. To read a message, double-click its header to display a window similar to the one shown in Figure 42-5.

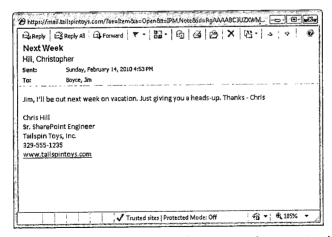

Figure 42-5 Outlook Web App displays messages in a separate window.

As in Outlook 2010, you can reply to or forward email messages. Simply click Reply or Reply To All to reply to a message or click Forward to forward a message. Outlook Web App opens a form similar to the one shown in Figure 42-6. Add addresses as needed and type your text. If you want to add an attachment, click the Attach File button on the toolbar at the top of the form. Outlook Web App opens the window shown in Figure 42-7 so that you can add one or more attachments to the message.

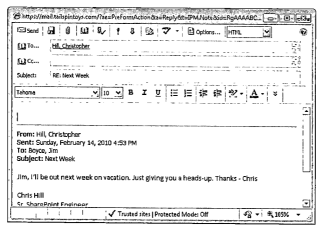

Figure 42-6 This is the Outlook Web App form generated for a reply.

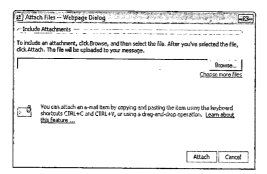

Figure 42-7 Outlook Web App enables you to add attachments to email messages.

When you want to create a message, click the New button on the toolbar (refer to Figure 42-4). Outlook Web App opens a form similar to the one shown previously in Figure 42-6. You can specify addresses, attachments, body text, and other message properties.

Chapter 42

You can set a handful of options for a new message by clicking Options with the new message form open. These options correspond to some of the options available in Outlook 2010 (see Figure 42-8).

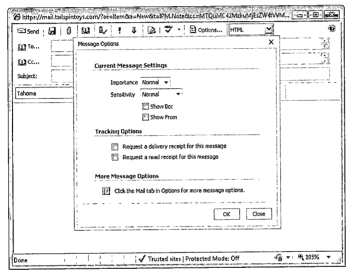

Figure 42-8 Configure message options such as Importance.

Sorting Messages

By default, Outlook Web App displays messages sorted by date and time received in multi-line view. You can sort the messages by other properties as well. To do so, select the drop-down menu beside Arrange By and choose the field by which you want to sort messages (see Figure 42-9).

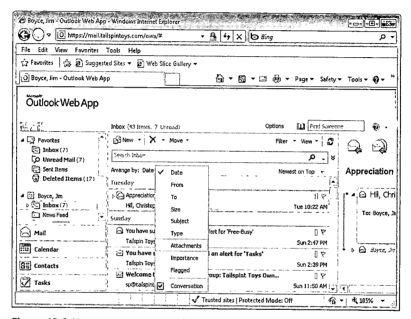

Figure 42-9 You can sort messages by one of several fields.

Copying and Moving Messages

You can copy and move messages by dragging in Outlook Web App. Open the folder containing the messages that you want to copy or move. If the target folder is hidden, scroll and expand folders as needed in the Navigation pane to display the folder in the folder list. To move messages, drag them from the right pane to the destination folder in the folder list. If you want to copy the messages instead of moving them, hold down the Ctrl key while dragging.

Deleting Messages

Deleting messages in Outlook Web App is a good way to clean out your mailbox when you don't have Outlook 2010 handy. It's also particularly useful for deleting large or corrupted messages that would otherwise prevent Outlook 2010 from downloading your messages normally.

To delete messages in Outlook Web App, just select the messages and click the Delete button on the toolbar. Outlook Web App moves the messages to the Deleted Items folder.

Working with Other Folders

Outlook Web App does not limit you to working only with your Inbox. You can work with your Mail, Calendar, Contacts, and Tasks folders. With Outlook Web Access 2007 and Outlook Web App, you can also work with SharePoint libraries and file servers configured on the computer running Exchange Server by the Exchange Server administrator(s). When you select a different folder in the Navigation pane, Outlook Web App 2010 displays the contents of the selected folder in the right pane.

Renaming and Deleting Folders

While in Outlook Web App 2010, you can rename and delete folders in the Exchange Server mailbox that you have created—but note that you cannot rename or delete the default Outlook 2010 folders. To perform either of the first two actions, display the folder in the Navigation pane, right-click that folder, and then choose either Rename or Delete.

Working with Calendar, Contacts, and Other Items

In addition to working with the Inbox or other message folders, you can manage your schedule, tasks, and contacts list on Exchange Server through Outlook Web App.

Calendar Folder

To manage your schedule, click the Calendar icon in the Navigation pane. Outlook Web App updates the right pane to display your Calendar folder. Click the toolbar buttons to choose between Today, Day, Work Week, Week, and Month views. The page also includes a Date Navigator similar to the one in Outlook 2010, which you can use to select dates (see Figure 42-10).

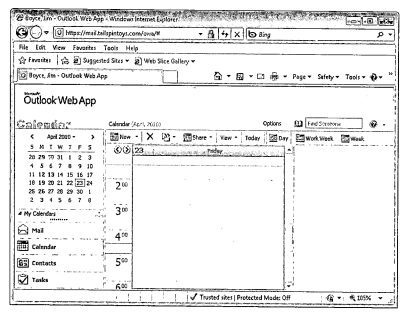

Figure 42-10 You can view and modify your schedule in Outlook Web App.

Click the New button on the toolbar or click the arrow beside the New button and choose Appointment to display an appointment form similar to the one in Outlook 2010. Use the appointment form to specify the title, the time, and other properties for an appointment, just as you would in Outlook 2010.

Contacts Folder

You can also view and manage contacts in Outlook Web App. Click the Contacts icon in the Navigation pane to display the Contacts folder (see Figure 42-11).

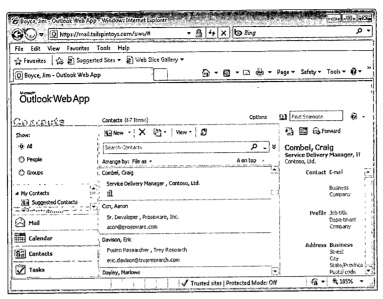

Figure 42-11 You can view and manage the Contacts folder in Outlook Web App.

Simply double-click a contact entry in the list to open a form that contains detailed information for that contact. Click the New button on the toolbar to open the form shown in Figure 42-12, which you can use to create new contact entries. Click Save & Close to save a new contact entry or to save changes to an existing contact entry.

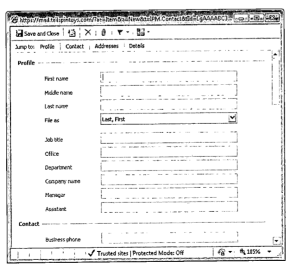

Figure 42-12 The form for creating contact entries in Outlook Web App is similar to the contact form in Outlook 2010.

As when you are working with your mail folders, you can click the drop-down button beside Arrange By to choose a different field for sorting contacts. To locate a contact, click in the Search Contacts text field and click the magnifying glass icon (which turns to a red X icon during the search). Click the red X to clear the search results.

Other Folders

In Outlook Web Access 2007 and Outlook Web App 2010, you can also work with the Tasks folder. With Outlook Web Access 2003, you can also work with the Journal and Notes folders. Outlook Web Access 2003 enables you to create messages, contact items, distribution lists, appointments, tasks, and folders. You can view but not create items in the Journal folder. Earlier versions of Outlook Web Access restrict you to creating messages, contact items, and appointments.

Configuring the Out Of Office Assistant in Outlook Web App

The Out Of Office Assistant automatically responds to messages when you are out of the office. The Out Of Office Assistant functions essentially as a server-side rule, replying to messages as they arrive in your Inbox. Although you usually configure the Out Of Office Assistant in Outlook 2010, you can also configure it in Outlook Web App.

For details on using the Out Of Office Assistant, see the section "Creating Automatic Responses with the Out Of Office Assistant," on page 345.

To configure the Out Of Office Assistant in Outlook Web App, connect to the server using your web browser and click Options to view the Options page. Then click Organize E-Mail, Automatic Replies to view the Out Of Office Assistant (Automatic Replies) properties. To turn on the Out Of Office Assistant, select Send Automatic Replies. Outlook Web App 2010 enables you to specify two different replies: one for people inside your organization and one for people outside the organization. When you are satisfied with the autoreply text, click Save to save the changes. When you want to turn off the Out Of Office Assistant, open the Options page again and select Don't Send Automatic Replies.

> **Note**
> In Outlook Web Access 2000, click the Shortcuts group on the Outlook Bar and then click Options to open the Options page.

Configuring Other Options for Outlook Web App

You can use the Outlook Web App Options page (see Figure 42-13) to set general options for your account. Click Settings to configure many other options for Outlook Web App (see Figure 42-14). You can configure date and time options, calendar options, and contact options; and you can also change your password. You can configure reminders, set up a signature for outgoing messages, set spelling options, and configure many additional options, all of which are essentially the same as those available in Outlook 2010 and covered elsewhere in this book.

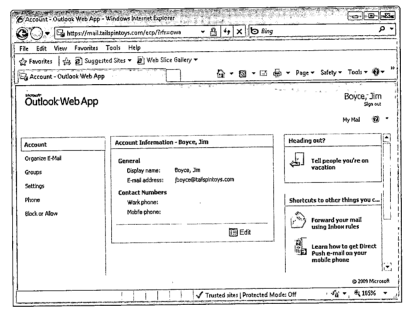

Figure 42-13 Configure the Out Of Office Assistant in Outlook Web App.

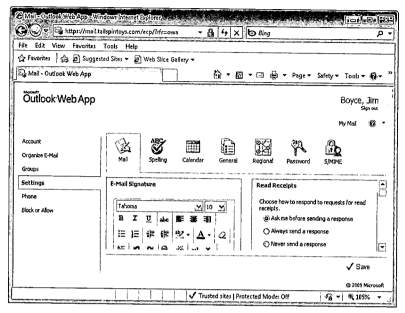

Figure 42-14 Use additional Options pages to configure more Outlook Web App options.

N the past, mobile users were much the exception rather than the rule. Today, users often work from home, from the road, and from remote offices. Personal Digital Assistants (PDAs) and smartphones are more and more common. All these things make the mobility features built into Microsoft Exchange Server and Microsoft Outlook 2010 extremely important.

This chapter covers Outlook 2010 mobility features. For example, the Mobile Service Account provider integrates Outlook 2010 with your mobile phone service. You'll learn in this chapter to configure the Mobile Service Account, send text messages, and use other mobile service features.

This chapter also explores Outlook Anywhere, also known as RPC over HTTP, to enable users to connect to Exchange Server across the Internet. Outlook Anywhere enables administrators to provide remote access to Exchange Server without resorting to virtual private network (VPN) connections or exposing their networks to attack by opening the otherwise-required ports in the firewall.

Before we look at the mobility features offered by Exchange Server and Outlook 2010, let's take a look at mobility in general.

Why Mobility Is Important

In modern offices, the requirement for mobility has increased dramatically with the introduction of technologies such as high-speed broadband Internet connections to the home, the proliferation of wireless Internet connections, and sending data over cellular connections. Employee expectations have changed with these technologies, especially among those workers who are frequently out of the office on business, such as sales teams and executives. These users expect that they will be able to access their email and other collaboration information whether they are in a hotel, at the airport, at a customer site, or at a remote office.

Along with the expectation that they can access their mail, mobile users are looking for more functionality while on the road than simple mail access. With Outlook 2010 and Exchange Server 2010 providing full collaboration functionality as outlined elsewhere in this book, simple web mail is not enough to satisfy these users' requirements. Most mobile users now want full access to all these features from outside the office too.

Mobility features are important for a number of reasons. However, the driving force behind the implementation of all mobility features and products is that they increase the speed of doing business and improve productivity. Mobility solutions, especially those integrated with collaboration products such as Outlook 2010 and Exchange Server, provide this speed and allow employees to conduct business from disparate locations. In a nutshell, email has become the primary mechanism for conducting business in many companies. Anytime/anywhere access to that email, as well as chat and other collaboration capabilities, is crucial.

Overview of Mobility Features in Exchange Server

Microsoft made many changes to Exchange Server to vastly improve mobility features over earlier versions of Microsoft Exchange. Features that were included in a separate product, Mobile Information Server, in Exchange 2000 Server were included in Exchange Server 2003. A number of new features have been added to subsequent Exchange Server versions, and features existing in earlier versions have been improved.

The following list describes many of the mobility features built into Exchange Server:

- **Cached Exchange Mode**   Enables users to cache their mailboxes to their local computers, making it possible to work offline. Changes are synchronized with the computer running Exchange Server the next time Outlook 2010 connects to the server.

- **RPC over HTTP**   A method of providing access to a computer running Exchange Server to remote clients without requiring any kind of VPN connection, RPC over HTTP allows clients to connect using Outlook 2010 directly over the Internet using a publicly accessible port.

- **Outlook Web App**   Microsoft has provided Outlook Web App (and its previous incarnation, Outlook Web Access) with several versions of Exchange and Exchange Server. The latest versions support most of the same functionality as the native Outlook client.

- **Mobile device support**   Mobile devices such as PDAs with wireless network access and mobile phones with PDA-type interfaces have become ubiquitous in many organizations, especially among mobile staff. These devices provide portability because they are much smaller than laptop computers, and they provide much of the functionality of larger systems. Exchange Server 2003 provides a number of tools to integrate with Pocket PC and smartphone devices. Traditionally, handheld devices have had the capacity to synchronize only with an existing application, such as synchronizing mail from Outlook on a laptop or desktop with a PDA. Exchange Server has the capability to work with handheld devices in real time rather than relying on synchronization, using these features:

    - **Exchange ActiveSync**   Enabled by default, Exchange ActiveSync is used to synchronize data from an Exchange Server mailbox to a handheld Pocket PC or smartphone device running Microsoft Pocket Outlook.

    - **Outlook Mobile Access**   Outlook Mobile Access, not enabled by default, is used to provide Exchange Server mailbox access to devices that are Internet-capable but are not Pocket PC or smartphone devices with Pocket Outlook. Although a separate product from Outlook Web App, Outlook Mobile Access is similar to Outlook Web App in that it provides browser-based access to an Exchange Server mailbox. Whereas Outlook Web App runs on web browsers on full-size computers, Outlook Mobile Access runs on Wireless Application Protocol (WAP) browsers on mobile devices.

- **Search improvements**   ActiveSync enables users to query both the local device store and the entire Exchange Server mailbox when searching from a mobile device in an over-the-air search. This capability enables users to retrieve data from the server quickly and efficiently when needed.

- **Direct push**   Mobile devices that support ActiveSync receive updates from the server as soon as the items (such as new email messages) arrive at the server. This capability keeps users' mobile data up to date in an efficient way.

- **Consistent user experience for a variety of devices**   The ActiveSync protocol in Exchange Server 2010 is licensed for use by a variety of mobile providers, ensuring a broad range of mobile device options for organizations.

- **Mobile device security and management**   Administrators can enforce mobile device policies, such as strong personal identification numbers (PINs), and can force a data and application wipe of the mobile device over the air (remotely) if the device is lost or stolen. Exchange Server 2010 supports per-user policies for these operations.

- **Remote access to data hosted by Microsoft SharePoint Services sites and file server resources through LinkAccess** LinkAccess enables administrators to make SharePoint content and documents from file servers available to mobile device users without requiring a VPN connection to these resources.

- **Calendar and Out Of Office improvements** You can access the calendar from a mobile device, manage meeting requests, and send Out Of Office replies from the device.

- **Outlook Web App improvements** As discussed in Chapter 42, "Accessing Your Outlook Items Through a Web Browser," Outlook Web App (formerly Outlook Web Access) gives you access to Out Of Office features, self-service features, and more.

- **Unified messaging** Exchange Server 2010 implements several voicemail capabilities, enabling users to retrieve voice messages and faxes through Outlook 2010, Outlook Web App, and their mobile devices. Users can request a reset of their voicemail PINs and set other voicemail options from Outlook Web App, access their mailboxes by phone, and redirect voice messages to a cell phone or desk phone.

Using Outlook Anywhere for Remote Access to Exchange Server

Outlook Anywhere, called RPC over HTTP in Exchange Server 2003 and Outlook 2003, enables administrators to make Exchange Server connections available to remote users without requiring a VPN connection to the server's network. Outlook Anywhere uses Hypertext Transfer Protocol (HTTP) or Hypertext Transfer Protocol Secure (HTTPS) over ports 80 and 443 to enable Outlook 2010 to communicate with Exchange Server.

Outlook Anywhere offers the following benefits:

- **Simplified remote access** Users do not need to establish a VPN connection to the server's network to connect to Exchange Server. This simplifies the user experience and drastically reduces administrative overhead that would otherwise be required to support those VPN connections.

- **Better security** Without Outlook Anywhere, an Exchange Server administrator would have to open several ports in the organization's firewalls to enable the Outlook 2010 traffic to pass in and out, presenting a large security risk. Because Outlook Anywhere works through ports 80 and 443, which are very likely already enabled for web browsing, the administrator need not open any additional ports.

Outlook 2003 and later support Outlook Anywhere/RPC over HTTP. Chapter 39, "Configuring the Exchange Server Client," explains how to configure an Exchange Server account in Outlook 2010 to use Outlook Anywhere to connect to the server. The combination of Outlook Anywhere and Cached Exchange Mode, also discussed in Chapter 39, gives Outlook 2010 users the combined benefits of easy remote access across the Internet and the capability to work offline.

Using Outlook Mobile Service Accounts

Outlook Mobile Service lets you integrate Outlook 2010 with mobile phones. With Outlook Mobile Service, you can:

- **Send text and multimedia messages from Outlook 2010 to mobile phones.**   Outgoing messages are placed in your Sent Items folder, just as for email messages.

- **Have email messages, reminders, and calendar summaries forwarded to your mobile phone.**   This feature is a great productivity tool for people who are on the move often and need continual access to their Outlook 2010 items.

- **Send messages to email and mobile phone recipients at the same time.**   You do not need to send messages separately to email and phone recipients. Instead, you can choose a selection of recipient addresses, and Outlook 2010 sends the message as needed based on the selected address types.

- **Retrieve cell phone numbers of your existing contacts easily.**   Use the Mobile Address Book to locate the cell phone numbers of your contacts quickly. You don't need to store this information separately. Instead, the Mobile Address Book ties into your existing Contacts folder.

Adding an Outlook Mobile Service Account

Before you can take advantage of Outlook Mobile Service in Outlook 2010, you need to add the service to your profile. Follow these steps to do so:

1. Click File, Add Account.

2. Choose Text Messaging (SMS) as shown in Figure 43-1, and click Next.

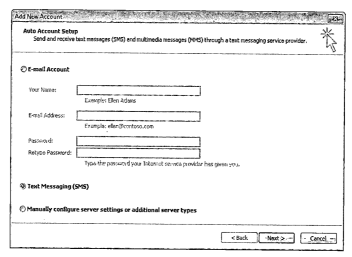

Figure 43-1 Use the Auto Account Setup page to add the Outlook Mobile Service account.

3. On the Account Settings page of the Outlook Mobile Service Account dialog box, shown in Figure 43-2, enter your service provider information. If you don't have a provider set up yet or don't know the appropriate settings, click the link to Microsoft Office Online to browse to a web page where you can select and configure a provider. The resulting web pages will guide you through the setup process.

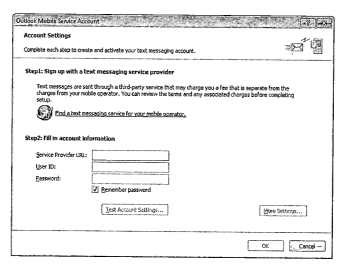

Figure 43-2 Use the Account Settings page to configure your Outlook Mobile Service account.

4. If you want to test the service, click Test Account Settings. Outlook 2010 tests the settings and gives you the option of sending a test message to your mobile phone.

5. Click More Settings to open the Outlook Mobile Service Information and Settings dialog box, shown in Figure 43-3. Here you can change the account name to something other than your mobile device number (such as My Mobile Account) and also change your phone number. Click OK when you've finished.

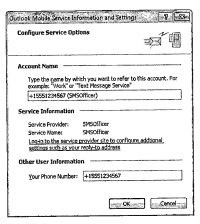

Figure 43-3 Use the Configure Service Options page to configure additional options for your Outlook Mobile Service account.

6. Click OK and close the remaining dialog boxes. Restart Outlook 2010 to access the new mobile features.

Using the Mobile Address Book

Outlook 2010 automatically adds the Mobile Address Book to your profile when you add Outlook Mobile Service to the profile. The Mobile Address Book is not a separate physical address book where contacts are stored. Instead, the Mobile Address Book accesses your existing Contacts folder to retrieve contacts that have mobile device numbers.

To use the Mobile Address Book, click the Address Book icon on the Outlook 2010 ribbon, or click To, Cc, or Bcc in a message form. Either action displays the Address Book dialog box. From the Address Book drop-down list, select Contacts (Mobile). Outlook 2010 then displays all contacts from your Contacts folder that have a mobile number assigned, as shown in Figure 43-4.

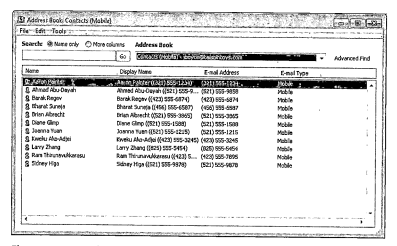

Figure 43-4 Use the Mobile Address Book to access contacts' mobile device numbers quickly.

Because the Mobile Address Book looks up contacts in your Contacts folder, it isn't necessary to add contacts specifically to the Mobile Address Book. Instead, simply make sure that
you specify a device number in the Mobile field of each contact as needed when you create
the contacts.

Sending Text Messages to Mobile Users

Sending a message to a mobile device is essentially the same as sending a message to an
email address. The main difference is that you select the contact in the Mobile Address
Book rather than the Contacts folder, Global Address List (GAL), or other address book.
Outlook actually offers two ways to send a text message. The first uses the Text Message
form, as follows:

1. Click New Items on the Home tab on the ribbon and click Text Message (SMS).

2. In the Text Message form (see Figure 43-5), click To and choose the recipient.
   (Outlook automatically displays your mobile contacts.)

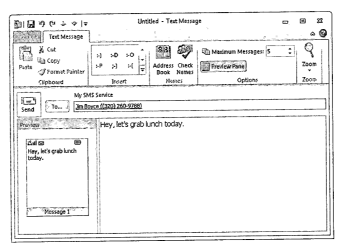

Figure 43-5 Use the Text Message form to send an SMS message.

3. Type the message and click Send.

You can also send a text message from a regular email form. To do so, follow these steps:

1. Start a new email message.

2. Click To, Cc, or Bcc to open the Address Book.

3. Select Contacts (Mobile) in the Address Book drop-down list.

4. Select one or more mobile recipients, and then click To, Cc, or Bcc as needed to add the addresses to the appropriate field.

5. If you need to send the message to email recipients as well, select the appropriate address book in the Address Book drop-down list, and then add addresses to the To, Cc, and Bcc fields as needed.

6. Click OK to close the Address Book.

7. Add subject, message body, and other information as needed, and then click Send.

Note

If you add a mobile recipient to an email, Outlook removes all formatting and nontext content from the message. This means that email and mobile recipients will receive the same text-only message content.

Forwarding Messages to Mobile Devices

You can forward messages as text messages. To forward a message as a text message to a mobile recipient, select the message in Outlook 2010, and then, on the Home tab on the ribbon, click More Respond Actions, Forward As Text Message. Outlook 2010 opens a text message form with the contents of the message in the body of the form. Click To, open the Mobile Address Book, select recipients, and then send the message.

Forwarding Alerts and Messages to Your Mobile Devices

You can configure Outlook 2010 to send alerts to your mobile device. For example, per-haps you want reminders and a calendar summary sent to your mobile device; or maybe you'll be out of the office for several hours and want your new messages redirected to your mobile device. You can accomplish both of these tasks with the Outlook Mobile Service account.

You have two options for sending alerts and forwarding messages to a mobile device. You can have Exchange Server 2010 send the alerts with server-side rules, or you can have Out-look handle the alerts and forwarding using client-side rules. The former lets you receive alerts from your computer running Exchange Server even when Outlook isn't running. The latter lets you use alerts and forwarding if you don't have an Exchange Server account.

Setting Up Alerts for Exchange Server Accounts

You configure server-side alerts and forwarding through Outlook Web App. The following sections explain how to configure server-side alerts.

> **Tip**
> You can navigate directly to Outlook Web App to configure mobile notification settings rather than reach the settings through Outlook. After you log into Outlook Web App, click Options, Phone, and then Text Messaging.

Forward Calendar Alerts and Summaries from Exchange Server

Outlook Mobile Service can forward reminders to your mobile device, as well as a summary of your next day's calendar items. Follow these steps to configure forwarding of these items:

1. Click File, Account Settings, and Manage Mobile Notifications to open a web browser for Outlook Web App.

2. Log in, and then click Phone in the left pane.

3. Click Text Messaging to show the Text Messaging options shown in Figure 43-6.

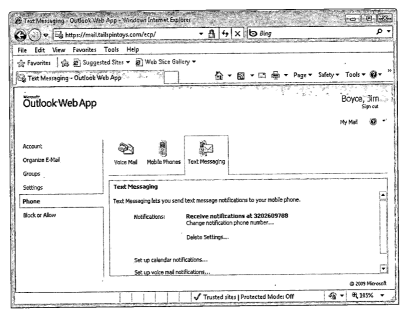

Figure 43-6 Use the Text Messaging page to configure the forwarding of reminders and calendar summaries.

Tip

If you haven't set up your notification phone number yet, click the Change Notification Phone Number link shown in Figure 43-6 and configure your mobile number.

4. Click Set Up Calendar Notifications to access the options shown in Figure 43-7. You can configure options to receive alerts when your calendar is updated, receive meeting reminders, and receive a daily calendar agenda.

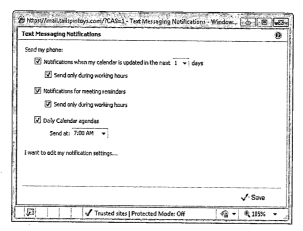

Figure 43-7 Use the Text Messaging Notifications window to configure options for receiving alerts.

5. Click Save.

> **Tip**
>
> To change your mobile number or other mobile settings, click the I Want To Edit My Notification Settings link on the Text Messaging Notifications page.

Forward Email Messages

You can configure Outlook Mobile Service to forward messages to your mobile phone based on conditions that you specify, including how your name appears in the message, the sender, words in the subject, and message importance. For example, you might configure it to forward messages you receive from your manager to your mobile device. Follow these steps to configure message forwarding to your mobile device:

1. Click File, Account Settings, and Manage Mobile Notifications, and log in when prompted.

2. Click Phone in the left pane.

3. Click Text Messaging, and then click Set Up E-mail Notifications to display the options shown in Figure 43-8.

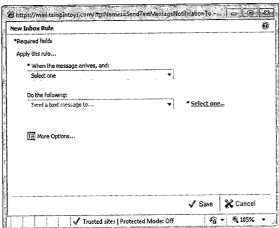

Figure 43-8 Use the New Inbox Rule page to configure message forwarding.

4. Select a condition for the rule from the When The Message Arrives, And drop-down list. For example, choose It Was Received From to have the message forwarded if it is from a specific sender. Another page will open, prompting you to provide more information. For instance, using the example described above, you are prompted to choose a sender from the address book.

5. From the Do The Following drop-down list, choose Send A Text Message To.

6. Click Select One to choose the mobile device to which you want to send the alerts. If you have only one device configured, it is chosen by default.

7. If desired, click More Options to expand the page and add exceptions to the rule.

8. Click Save.

Setting Up Client-Side Alerts and Forwarding

As mentioned previously, you don't need an Exchange Server account to forward messages to your mobile device. You can create client-side rules that use the Outlook Mobile Service to forward alerts and messages. However, Outlook must be running and have an Internet connection available for these features to work.

Forwarding Calendar Alerts and Summaries from Outlook

Follow these steps to configure calendar alerts and summaries from Outlook:

1. Click File, Options to open the Outlook Options dialog box.

2. Click Mobile in the left pane to display the mobile options shown in Figure 43-9.

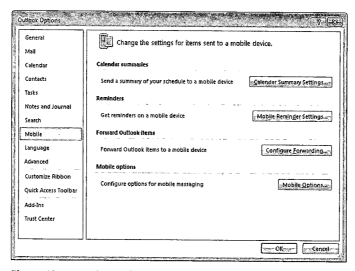

Figure 43-9 Use the Outlook Options dialog box to configure mobile alerts.

3. Click Calendar Summary Settings to open the Calendar Summary dialog box shown in Figure 43-10.

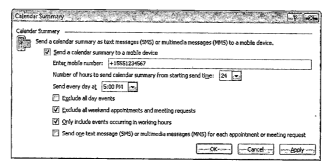

Figure 43-10 Configure calendar alerts in the Calendar Summary dialog box.

4. Configure options as needed and click OK.

5. Click OK to close the Outlook Options dialog box.

Setting Up Mobile Reminders from Outlook

You can configure Outlook to send reminders to your mobile device. Here's how:

1. Click File, Options.

2. Click Mobile in the left pane and then click Mobile Reminder Settings to display the reminder options shown in Figure 43-11.

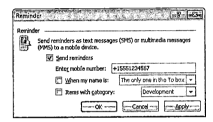

Figure 43-11 Use the Reminder dialog box to configure mobile reminders.

3. Configure options as desired and click OK.

4. Click OK to close the Outlook Options dialog box.

Setting Up Email Forwarding to Mobile Devices from Outlook

Here's how to configure Outlook to forward messages to your mobile device:

1. Click File, Options.

2. Click Mobile in the left pane and then click Configure Forwarding to display the Mobile Notification dialog box shown in Figure 43-12.

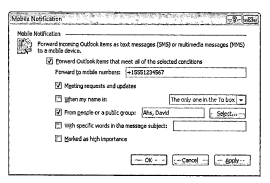

Figure 43-12 Use the Mobile Notification dialog box to configure message forwarding rules.

3. Place a check in the Forward Outlook Items That Meet All Of The Selected Conditions option.

4. Choose the conditions to describe the types of items that you want forwarded to your mobile device.

5. Click OK.

6. Close the Outlook Options dialog box.

Now that you've set up a forwarding rule, you might be wondering how to set up more than one. You can't do it using the process described above, but you can copy the rule created by these steps to use as the basis for another forwarding rule. For example, you might create the first rule to forward messages that you receive from your manager. Then, copy the rule and modify the copy to forward messages that you receive that have high importance. Here's how to copy the rule:

1. Click Rules on the Home tab on the ribbon and choose Manage Rules And Alerts.

2. Click the Forward As Mobile Message (Auto Generated) (Client-Only) rule and then click Copy.

3. Choose the same Inbox as the first rule and click OK.

4. Scroll down to locate the copied rule, click it, and then click Change Rule, Edit Rule Settings. (Alternatively, you can simply click in the Rule Description area of the Rules And Alerts dialog box and modify the rule there.)

5. Make changes to the rule as necessary and click Finish.

6. Place a check beside the rule to enable it, and then click OK to close the Rules And Alerts dialog box.

Creating Rules to Forward Messages to Mobile Devices

In addition to using the methods described above for creating rules to forward messages to your mobile device, you can simply create the rules yourself, just as you create any other rule. To do so, follow these steps:

1. Open the Rules And Alerts dialog box and start a new, blank rule using the Apply Rule On Messages I Receive option.

2. In the Rules Wizard, specify the conditions for the rule, such as received from a particular person, marked as high importance, with specific words in the subject, and so on.

3. Click Next, and in the second page of the wizard shown in Figure 43-13, choose the Forward It To People Or Public Group As An Attachment action.

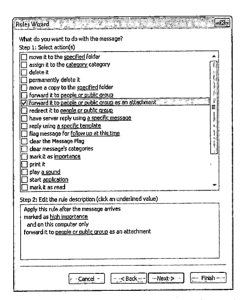

Figure 43-13 You can create a rule to forward messages to a mobile device.

4. In the Edit The Rule Description area, click the People Or Public Group link.

5. When the Rule Address dialog box opens, choose Contacts (Mobile) from the Address Book drop-down list.

6. Choose the mobile device to which you want to send the message and then click OK.

7. Specify other settings for the rule as desired and then click Finish.

Setting Outlook Mobile Service Options

Outlook Mobile Service offers a selection of options that you can use to control how text and multimedia messages are sent. To set these options, click File, Options, Mobile, and finally Mobile Options to open the Mobile Options dialog box shown in Figure 43-14. Set options as desired, click OK, and then click OK again to close the Options dialog box.

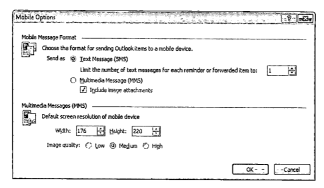

Figure 43-14 Use the Mobile Options dialog box to configure additional mobile messaging options.

Using a Mobile Signature

The section "Using Signatures," on page 273, explains how to add a signature for each email account. For example, perhaps you use one signature for a business account and a different signature for a personal account. Outlook 2010 treats Outlook Mobile Service like any other email account, which means that you can add a signature specifically for your mobile messages. To specify the signature, click File, Options, and then click Mail in the left pane. Click Signatures, and if the signature you want to use for mobile messages doesn't exist yet, click New to create the signature, type a name for the signature, and then click OK. On the E-Mail Signature tab, select Outlook Mobile Service in the E-Mail Account drop-down list, and then select the signature that you want to use for the account. Create or edit the signature, and then click OK twice to return to Outlook 2010.

See the section "Using Signatures," on 273 to learn more about creating and using signatures.

Index to Troubleshooting Topics

Index

Symbols

% Complete (Percentage Complete), setting, 542

... (ellipsis button), in Picture property, 708

! (exclamation point) icon, 187

.ics (iCalendar files), importing, 782–783

.ost files

configuring offline storage using, 62

storing data in, 774

transparency of, 62

using in working offline, 31

working offline, 977–978

.pst files (personal folders)

about, 58–59

archiving items to, 760

backing up, 770–771

eliminating, 12

exporting data to, 775–778

importing from, 783–785

in Exchange Server, 731

limiting access to, 756

moving, 64–65, 772

restoring items using, 764–765

security for, 61

setting up, 30

storing data in, 769

storing rules in, 318–319

using multiple, 754–756

.vcf files (vCard files)

importing, 782

importing from email attachment, 782

.vcs (vCalendar files), importing, 782–783

A

Accept buttons

meeting requests, 105

task assignment, 550–551

Access 2010

exporting contacts to, 878–880

exporting files to, 597

exporting journal items to, 599–600

importing contacts from, 880–882

accounts

configuring advanced settings, 167–168

multiple, 53, 160, 174–177

personal, 57, 198

accounts bar, 200, 202, 980–981

actions group, 325, 493, 877

Active Directory Domain Services (AD DP), 381

Active Directory Domain Services (AD DS). *See* AD DS (Active Directory Domain Services)

ActiveSync protocol, 1003

Active tasks view, 556

Activities button, 441

Activities page, contacts and, 438, 441–442, 443, 586, 597

actual vs. total work, specifying values for, 542, 543–544

Add A Contact Wizard, 893

adding

addresses automatically

to address book, 156

to Contacts Folder, 598

administrative templates to Office, 819

applications to trusted add-in lists, 830–831

blocked file types to level 1 list, 826

columns in message pane, 79

contact groups to Cc field, 153

About the Author

Jim Boyce has authored or coauthored more than 45 books about computer hardware and software, including *Microsoft Office Outlook 2007 Plain & Simple* and *Microsoft Outlook Version 2002 Inside Out*. He is a former contributing editor and monthly columnist for *WINDOWS* Magazine. He has worked with computers as a programmer and systems manager in a variety of capacities since the 1970s, and has a wide range of experience in the MS-DOS, Microsoft Windows, Microsoft Windows NT, and UNIX environments.

What do you think of this book?

We want to hear from you!

To participate in a brief online survey, please visit:

microsoft.com/learning/booksurvey

Tell us how well this book meets your needs—what works effectively, and what we can do better. Your feedback will help us continually improve our books and learning resources for you.

Thank you in advance for your input!

This book belongs to:

For Bridie, Helen and Vincent
- J.L.

Ancient Warriors is © Flying Eye Books 2018.

This is a first edition published in 2018 by Flying Eye Books,
an imprint of Nobrow Ltd. 27 Westgate Street, London E8 3RL.

Illustrations © Joe Lillington 2018.
Joe Lillington has asserted his right under the Copyright, Designs
and Patents Act, 1988, to be identified as the Illustrator of this Work.

Iris Volant is the pen name of the Flying Eye Books in-house writers.
Text written by Hanna Milner.

Published in the US by Nobrow (US) Inc.
Printed in Poland on FSC® certified paper.

MIX
Paper from
responsible sources
FSC® C002795

ISBN: 978-1-911171-93-5
Order from www.flyingeyebooks.com

Iris Volant & Joe Lillington

ANCIENT WARRIORS

FLYING EYE BOOKS
London | New York

CONTENTS

INTRODUCTION

In the beginning, we were all warriors. Our earliest ancestors had to battle for food and survival against the fastest, strongest beasts of the Stone Age. Their first tools were used for hunting, but were soon turned against other humans as they began to fight for territory.

Ancient battles have shaped our world over thousands of years of warfare, and countless lives have been lost to history. It was only through great strategic planning, incredible strength and bravery that ancient warriors were able to survive. In this book, you'll journey from the age of bronze until moments before gunpowder and firearms changed the world, and along the way, you'll meet some of the world's greatest military minds and discover the legendary battles of ancient times.

THE FIRST WARRIORS

Mesopotamian Bronze Age: 3300–1200 BC

Thousands of years ago, a beautiful land in the eastern Mediterranean was home to the world's first cities. Mesopotamia, as the region was known, was home to people from many different cultures. Peace was not easy and the people of these cities were constantly fighting over control of their fertile land. Higher and higher walls were built to protect against attack. Locked in a struggle to develop bigger and better weapons, the race to master the battlefield was on!

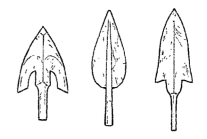

Bronze arrowheads

Bronze spearhead

Bronze sword

THE WORLD'S FIRST SUPER WEAPON

Bronze was harder, stronger and sharper than the flint that had been used before. It could be easily molded into different shapes and was used to do many different jobs. Bronze arrows could punch through animal skin armor and shields, and bronze swords could slice up just about anything.

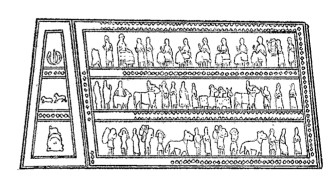

STANDARD OF UR

An ancient Mesopotamian box decorated with mosaic war scenes, known as the Standard of Ur, shows that the most common weapons were spears and bows, probably because they used less metal and were cheaper to make than swords and axes.

MAYA WARFARE

Preclassic to Classic Period c. 2600 BC–900 AD

Ruling over the wide plains and dense forests of Mesoamerica for thousands of years, the Maya people were one of the greatest ancient civilizations on Earth. After winning their battles, the Maya captured high-ranking enemies to sacrifice to their gods, believing that this would lead to more fortune in war.

The spear-throwing technique of a Maya warrior.

THE SPEAR-THROWER

Spears and darts were the favored weapons of a Maya warrior. Skilled fighters used an ingenious tool called the atlatl, or spear-thrower. The atlatl was a long stick with a notch at one end for the spear. With this tool, warriors could throw spears much further and more accurately than ever before.

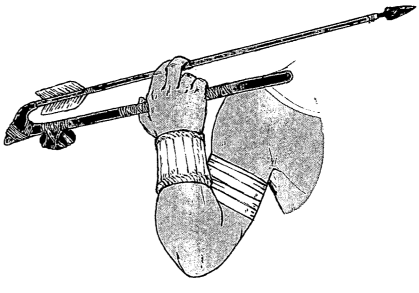

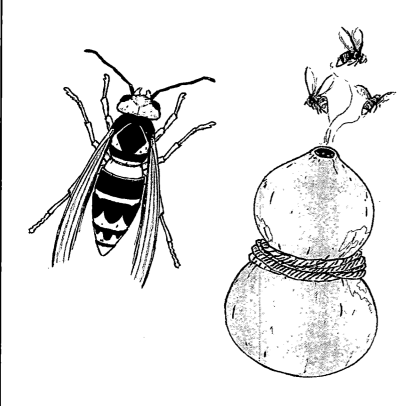

The hornets inside these 'bombs' were aggravated and ready to attack.

DEADLY STING

When defending a valuable settlement, the K'iche Maya people devised a clever 'natural bomb'. Filling gourd fruits with live hornets, they flung them over the fortress walls at the unsuspecting enemy attackers. The invaders had no choice but to flee the poisonous onslaught, and the settlement was protected.

ARMIES OF THE PHARAOH

1674–1069 BC

The pharaohs of ancient Egypt were fabulously wealthy. Their beautiful cities and marvelous temples made them tempting targets for rival kingdoms.

The Egyptians had no choice but to learn from their enemies. It didn't take them long to start borrowing techniques from the people they met. For instance, Egyptian warriors first saw the chariot being used by the invading Hyksos people and soon started using it themselves.

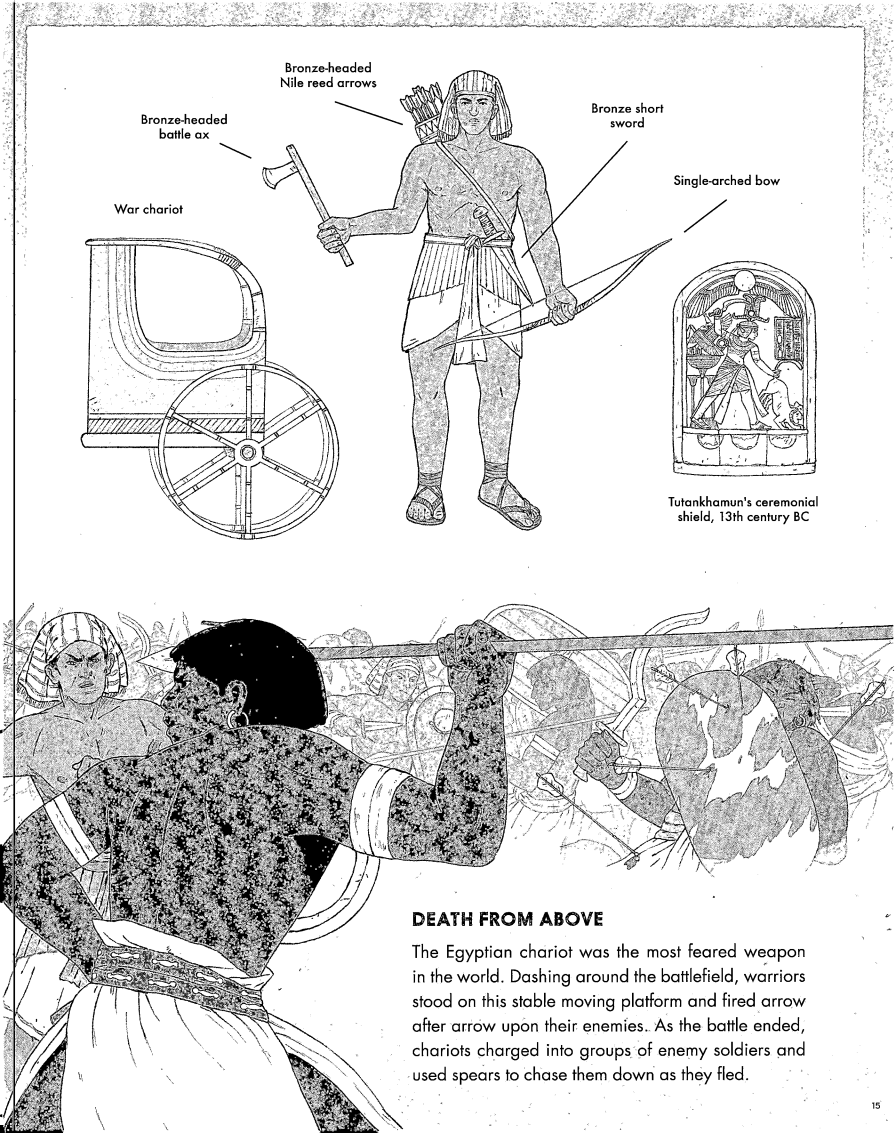

Bronze-headed
Nile reed arrows

Bronze-headed
battle ax

Bronze short
sword

Single-arched bow

War chariot

Tutankhamun's ceremonial
shield, 13th century BC

DEATH FROM ABOVE

The Egyptian chariot was the most feared weapon
in the world. Dashing around the battlefield, warriors
stood on this stable moving platform and fired arrow
after arrow upon their enemies. As the battle ended,
chariots charged into groups of enemy soldiers and
used spears to chase them down as they fled.

· GREAT LEADERS ·

RAMESSES II

Ruled 1279–1213 BC

Known to Egyptians as the 'Great Ancestor', Ramesses II was the most powerful pharaoh in history. Leading countless battles, defeating sea pirates and building new cities, Ramesses II ruled until his death at the grand age of 90 years old and made Egypt incredibly rich.

BATTLE OF KADESH

One of the most famous battles to take place during Ramesses II's reign was the Battle of Kadesh, fought against ancient Egypt's long-standing enemy, the Hittites. With around 6,000 chariots on the battlefield, it was the largest chariot battle the ancient world had ever seen.

At a crucial moment in the battle, Ramesses II was led into a trap that separated him from his troops, leaving him surrounded by enemy soldiers. But the great pharaoh was more skilled than his enemies. He single-handedly drove back the Hittites until the rest of his army returned to deliver the final blows. The Hittites were forced to flee into the river and Ramesses II was heralded for his bravery.

THE GREAT WALL

Construction started c. 771 BC

The largest armies of the ancient world were Chinese. Hundreds of thousands of warriors were led by generals who were appointed not for their wealth but for their skill.

Chinese soldiers were masterful engineers. They built the Great Wall across China's northern borders: a huge 13,170-mile-long barrier to keep out invaders. It was so large that 10,000 men with rapid-fire repeating crossbows could stand guard on its towers.

SUN TZU 544–496 BC

Sun Tzu was a wise Chinese general whose teachings on warfare are collected in a book called *The Art of War*. His theories on strategy and tactics have been read around the world. Sun Tzu always advised that countries should avoid going to war whenever possible.

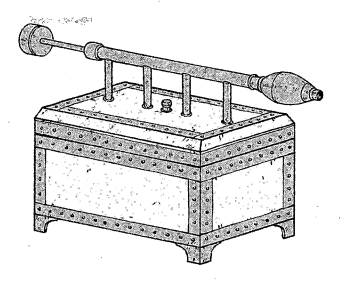

FLAMES OF FURY

The most deadly weapon in the Chinese arsenal was the flamethrower. Warriors pumped a terrible burning oil onto their enemies. They had to make sure that the wind was blowing the right way, or they could end up burning themselves!

499–449 BC

The Persian emperor Xerxes had always desired the Greek cities across the sea. Now that he finally had an army big enough to seize them, nothing could stand in his way... apart from 7,000 brave Greek hoplites from Sparta, Thebes and other allied cities.

BATTLE OF THERMOPYLAE

For three days, 7,000 Greeks held off roughly 150,000 Persians in a narrow mountain pass. The hoplites were armed with long spears and the secret to their strength was the phalanx formation. As the Persians approached, the Greeks arranged their shields and spears into a terrifying wall of spikes. They could have won if it hadn't been for a traitor who told the Persian army of a secret path.

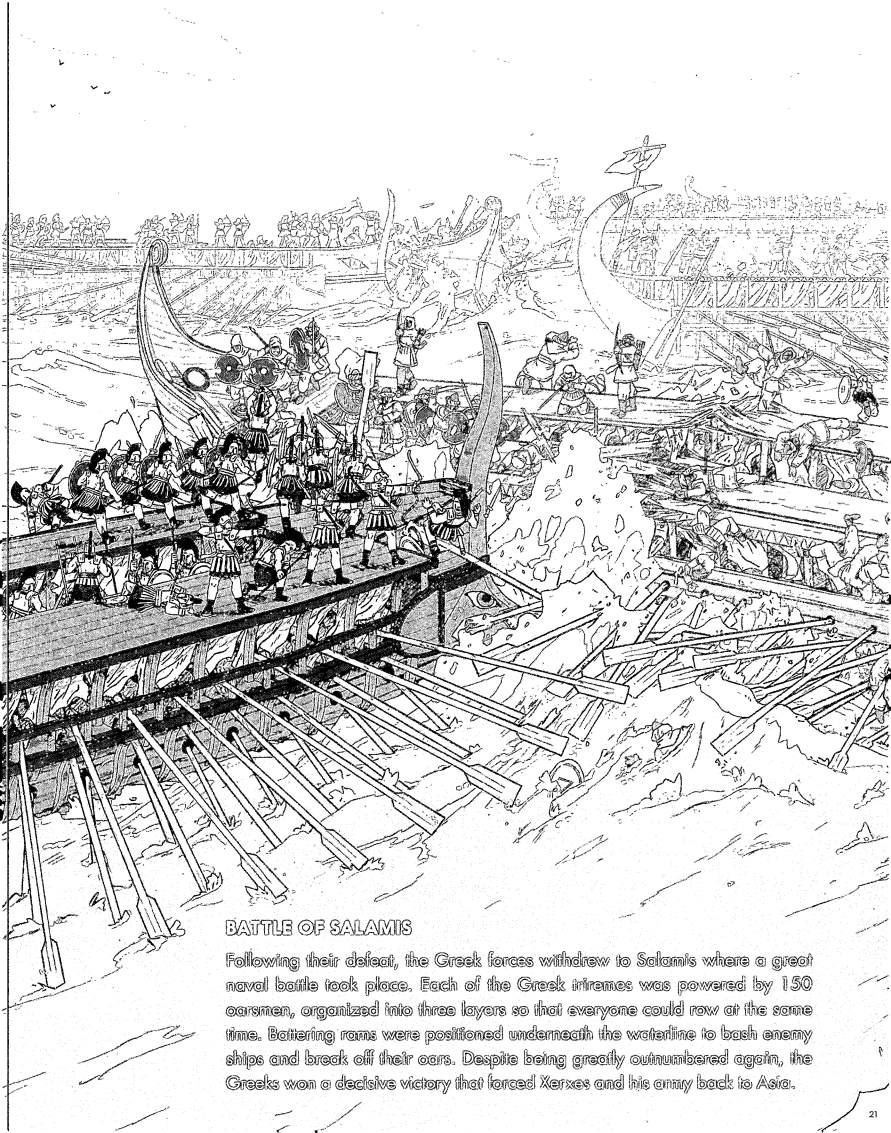

BATTLE OF SALAMIS

Following their defeat, the Greek forces withdrew to Salamis where a great naval battle took place. Each of the Greek triremes was powered by 150 oarsmen, organized into three layers so that everyone could row at the same time. Battering rams were positioned underneath the waterline to bash enemy ships and break off their oars. Despite being greatly outnumbered again, the Greeks won a decisive victory that forced Xerxes and his army back to Asia.

ALEXANDER THE GREAT

356–323 BC

From the mountains of Greece to the river Ganges in India, none could stand in his way. In his ten years of fighting he never lost a single battle. His name was Alexander and he was probably the greatest general who ever lived.

MIXED UNITS

Alexander's willingness to take risks and try new tactics was the secret to his success. He was one of the first generals to fight with mixed-unit tactics, which meant using different types of warriors to outsmart the enemy. As the battle began, archers harassed the enemy with volley after volley of arrows. Then the indestructible phalanx locked their opponents in battle, pinning them in place while the Companion cavalry maneuvered around to deliver the final deadly charge.

THE COMPANIONS

Alexander's Companions were the first shock troops in history. They rode the best horses and carried the best equipment. Using a wedge formation, they charged into their enemies' flanks, shattering formations and spreading terror.

THE RISE OF ROME

Founded 753 BC, peaked 117 AD

Against a horde of enemies, one man on his own can do little, even if he is strong, brave and skilled. But one thousand men, trained to know exactly when to march, when to fire and when to charge, were enough to set any barbarian trembling. That was the strength of the Roman legions.

A legionary's discipline made him the toughest fighting man in the world. All legionaries used the same weapons and armor, which meant they could perfectly coordinate their tactics.

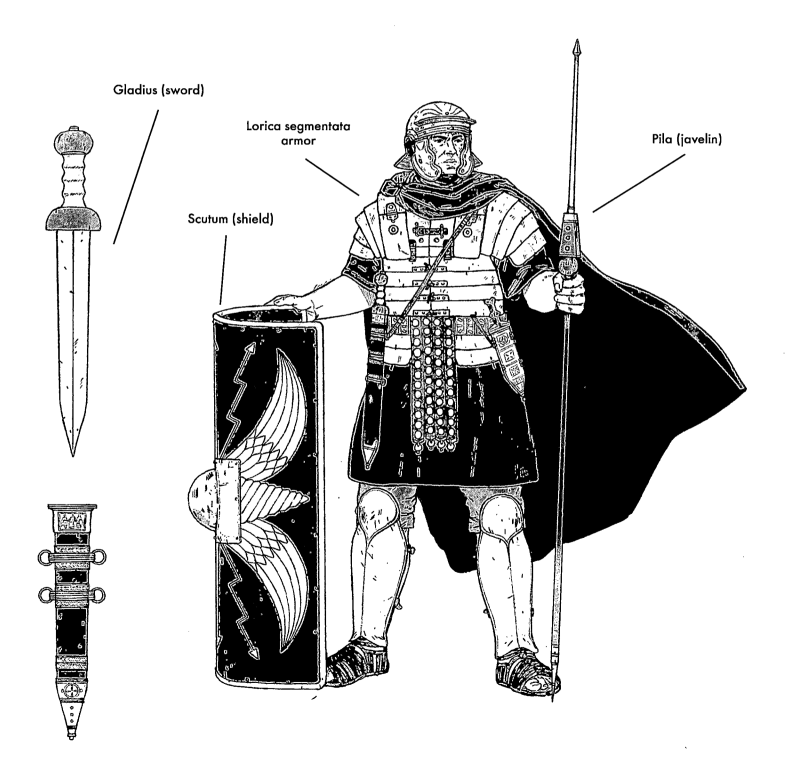

Gladius (sword)

Lorica segmentata armor

Pila (javelin)

Scutum (shield)

LEGIONARY TACTICS

While other soldiers rushed straight into the fight, Roman legionaries lined up
and waited until the enemy was almost upon them. Then at the last minute,
they hurled their spears and charged into battle. When Roman soldiers were
being attacked by archers, they formed a 'tortoise' by joining together and
lifting their shields above their heads. This kept them safe from enemy arrows.

Tortoise formation

Cannae formation

Wedge formation

264–241 BC

As the Roman Empire grew, so did conflicts over territory with Carthage in North Africa. A great Empire in its own right, Carthage dominated the Mediterranean Sea with its unbeatable navy. It was only a matter of time before a great battle between these two superpowers erupted around Sicily, a strategically important island off the coast of modern Italy.

CORVUS

The Romans were not used to sea battles, so they devised a way to fight the Carthaginians on their own terms. The Roman ships got as close as they could to the enemy vessels and then lowered a special bridge called a corvus onto them. Storming on board over the bridge, the Romans now had the advantage and fought face-to-face on the ship's deck. The Roman army emerged victorious and now held the strongest navy in the Mediterranean.

HANNIBAL BARCA

247–183 BC

Those who stood up to Rome needed a fresh strategy if they wanted to survive. No one's plan was grander than that of Hannibal Barca, a general from Carthage.

Hannibal had a secret weapon: elephants. He hoped that these huge African beasts would smash through the Roman legions. Hannibal planned to drag his elephants around the Spanish coast and over the Alps to surprise the Romans in northern Italy.

FALL FROM GLORY

Hannibal's plan paid off... at first. In a series of battles, he beat the Romans on their own ground. At Cannae in southern Italy he won one of the bloodiest battles ever, trapping and killing more than 50,000 Roman soldiers. But before long, Hannibal began to run out of supplies. The Romans retreated to the hills, refusing Hannibal the chance to defeat them in battle. Eventually, with his army exhausted and starving, Hannibal had to leave Italy and admit defeat.

CELTIC WARRIORS

Celtic uprising 60 AD

Celtic warriors and their weapons were both beautiful and terrible. Great artistry went into blades, armor and even humans, who were painted in blue war paint.

Charging into war on foot, Celtic warriors played a loud instrument called a carnyx to announce their arrival on the battlefield. The terrible wailing sound it made struck fear into their opponents' hearts. Most Celts fought with little more than a helmet, a shield and a lot of bravery for protection. Some nobles used chariots as a stable platform to throw javelins from.

BOUDICCA

Boudicca was the Queen of the Celtic Iceni tribe of East Anglia at the time of Roman conquest of Britain. She led an uprising against Roman rule. Her soldiers stormed the ancient towns of Londinium and Verulamium, killing thousands, including an entire Roman legion. They were only defeated when a large, organized Roman force drove them back.

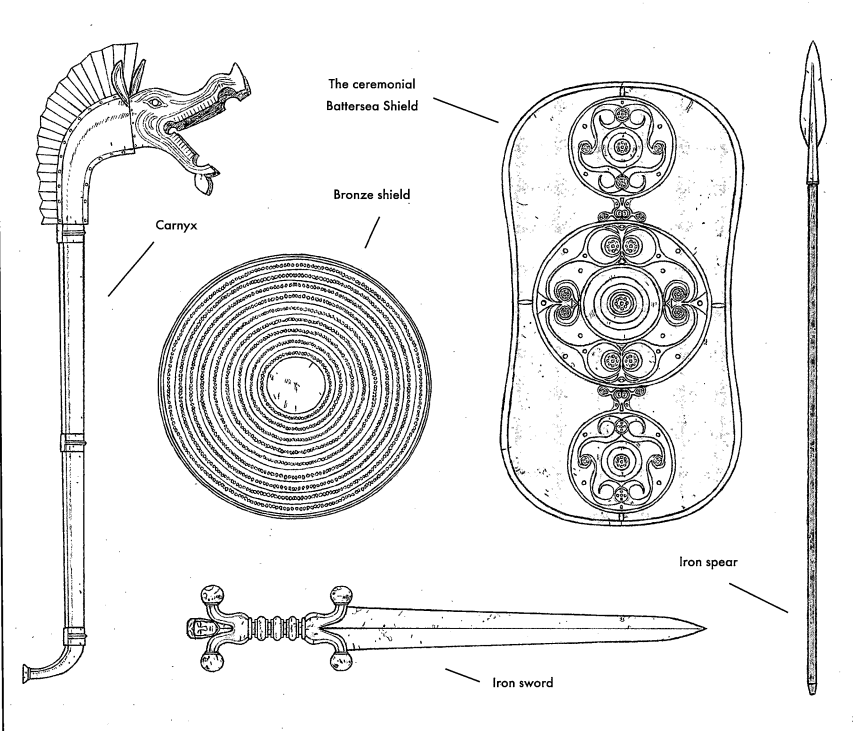

The ceremonial Battersea Shield

Bronze shield

Carnyx

Iron spear

Iron sword

THE TRUNG SISTERS

c. 12–43 AD

For hundreds of years, the Chinese occupied their neighboring country of Vietnam. But they never could have suspected that two brave women would lead the first resistance.

THE PEOPLE'S RESISTANCE

Trung Trac and Trung Nhi were daughters of a military family. They were trained in martial arts and understood tactical warfare from a young age. After her husband's murder, Trac raised a great army of around 80,000 people. The generals and leaders were almost all women, including the Trung sisters' own mother. The sisters rode out on great elephants to face the Chinese, and within a few months they drove the occupying forces from their land. Trac was crowned queen and Nhi became her chief advisor.

Although the Trungs' reign lasted only three years, their legacy is remembered to this day. There are ceremonies and temples across Vietnam that honor the sisters as symbols of the country's independence.

HUNS

Attila the Hun c. 406–453 AD

Savage, brutal, beastly. This was how the Huns were described by their enemies. Their ferocious army was both renowned and feared across the ancient world.

Led by their ruthless ruler Attila, the nomadic Huns dominated Europe and Asia in the 5th century. They were excellent at military strategy and staging surprise attacks. Aside from their weapons, the Huns' most important companions in battle were their horses. Huns were so attached to their horses that Westerners compared them to mythical centaurs.

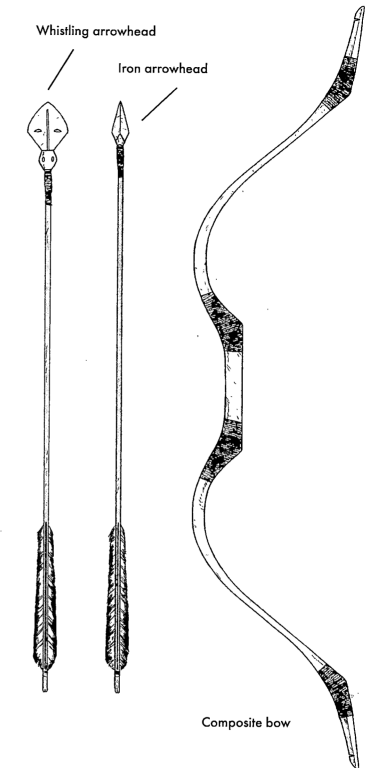

Whistling arrowhead

Iron arrowhead

Composite bow

THE HUNNIC BOW

Firing arrows relentlessly from horseback, an army of Huns were formidable opponents on the battlefield. Their skill as archers was unmatched at the time. They used distinctive curved bows made from horn and wood, and a well-crafted bow was passed down from generation to generation.

SHAOLIN MONKS

Shaolin monastery first established 477 AD

Many warriors were brave and strong, but few treated fighting as an art. The monks of the Shaolin monastery were the most skilled warriors in all of China. It was said that seeing them fight was like watching a beautiful dance.

Shaolin monks learned martial arts as a form of defense against bandits who roamed the lands around the monastery. Not only were the monks trained in unarmed combat, but they could also fight with the 18 fabled weapons of their order. These were deadly versions of the farm tools the monks had used for centuries.

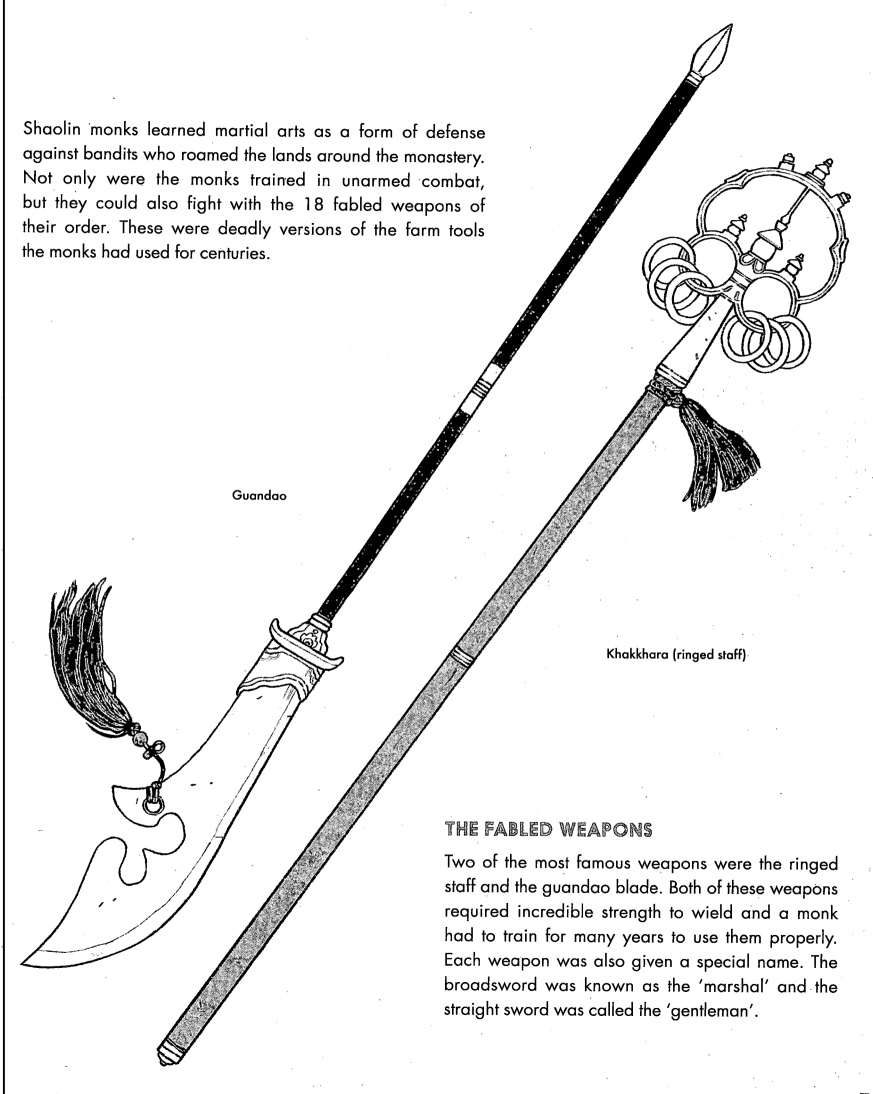

Guandao

Khakkhara (ringed staff)

THE FABLED WEAPONS

Two of the most famous weapons were the ringed staff and the guandao blade. Both of these weapons required incredible strength to wield and a monk had to train for many years to use them properly. Each weapon was also given a special name. The broadsword was known as the 'marshal' and the straight sword was called the 'gentleman'.

FLAVIUS BELISARIUS

500–565 AD

The Roman Empire was in danger. On all sides its enemies were closing in. Even the city of Rome had been lost. But the Romans weren't giving up without a fight. General Belisarius, once a bodyguard to the Emperor himself, set out to reconquer Italy. But hundreds of years had passed since Rome's power was at its height, and now the legions looked very different.

DROMON

The Roman navy had come a long way since the days of the trireme. The most dangerous ship on the high seas was now the dromon. The dromon's deadliest weapon was called Greek fire, a mysterious mixture whose composition is still not known and which was legendary at the time. Its flames were even said to set the sea alight.

ELITE UNIT: CATAPHRACT

Belisarius' success was mostly due to his heavily armored cataphract cavalry. Like Alexander's Companions, this well-organized group of heavy shock troops terrified their opponents. Heavily armored and wielding lances along with long, double-edged swords, this unit was the most powerful force on the battlefield.

LEGENDARY BATTLES: YARMOUK

636 AD

Belisarius may have triumphed, but he only bought Rome a few more years. A new force was rising in the Arabian deserts. Appearing out of nowhere, striking with lightning speed and vanishing beyond the sands, the great Arabian armies defeated all who challenged them.

Desperate to slow the Arab advance, the Roman emperor sent his soldiers south to force a pitched battle. On a flat plain high above the desert, at a place called Yarmouk, the two armies met. It was a battle that would decide the fate of the Middle East.

IT'S A TRAP!

The battle raged for six days before the Arabs eventually claimed victory. The Arab general Khalid ibn al-Walid maneuvered his powerful cavalry unit around the Roman army, sealing the trap. At the same time, his camel warriors scared the Roman horses into bolting and running away. They had never seen such strange animals before!

VIKINGS

793–1066 AD

In the Dark Ages, few sights were more feared than a troop of Vikings arriving at your door. Vikings sailed in their longships from their home in Scandinavia, stealing the riches of towns and monasteries for themselves.

They were masters of the raid, racing ashore to take whatever they wanted and sailing away before an army could respond. Vikings fought with many different types of iron axes, including the two-handed Dane ax. Their swing was so powerful that they could even chop through armor and bone.

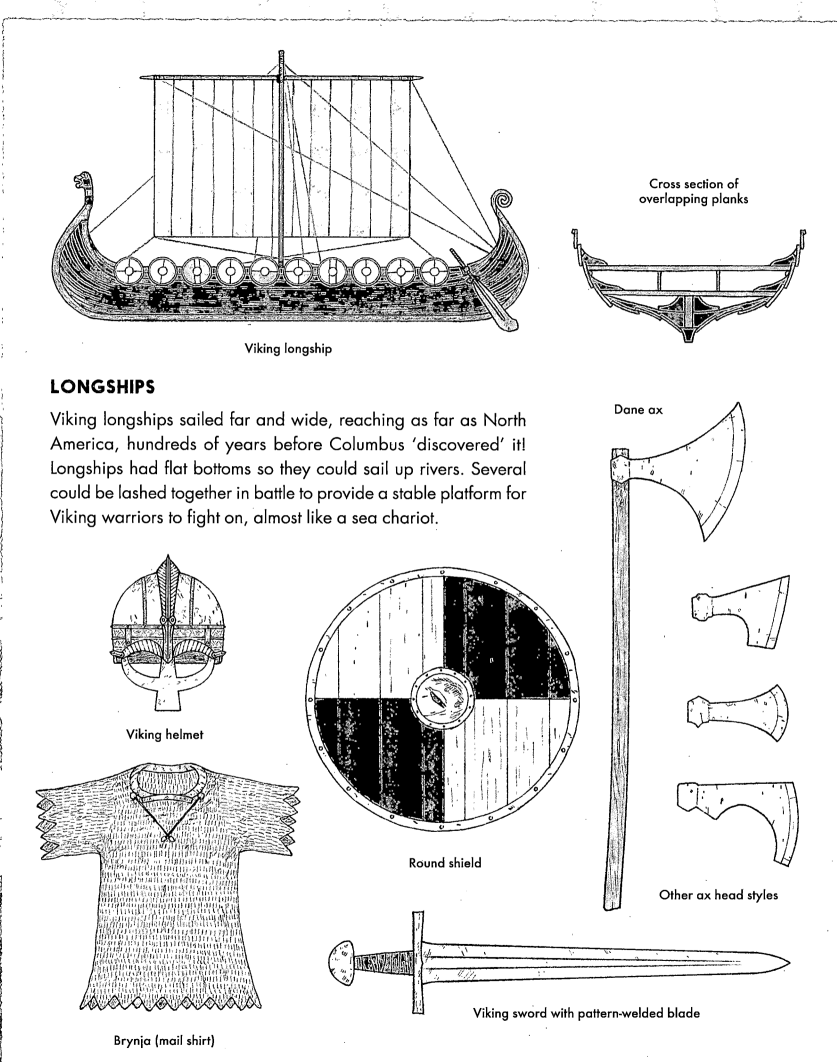

Cross section of
overlapping planks

Viking longship

LONGSHIPS

Viking longships sailed far and wide, reaching as far as North America, hundreds of years before Columbus 'discovered' it! Longships had flat bottoms so they could sail up rivers. Several could be lashed together in battle to provide a stable platform for Viking warriors to fight on, almost like a sea chariot.

Dane ax

Viking helmet

Round shield

Other ax head styles

Brynja (mail shirt)

Viking sword with pattern-welded blade

GENGHIS KHAN

1162–1227 AD

The Vikings may have been fierce, the Romans disciplined and the Shaolin monks beautiful, but no warriors were as deadly as the Mongol horsemen of Genghis Khan.

Genghis Khan united the warring tribes of Mongolia into the most powerful fighting force the world had ever seen. He and his warriors swarmed over the Great Wall and conquered the empire of China.

TACTICS

Most of Genghis Khan's men were horse archers. They used hit-and-run tactics, riding up close to their enemies before firing their arrows, then fleeing away to a safe distance. Once the archers had softened them up, the toughest horsemen closed in. Using lances, maces and scimitars, these warriors smashed into the enemy ranks before they had a chance to recover.

KNIGHTS

Order first founded 1099 AD

The rumble of hooves, the clash of steel on steel. That could only be the sound of the medieval knight.

Knights wore full suits of armor that protected them from all but the strongest of blows. At first this was a mail shirt, made up of many small, connected rings, sometimes as many as 30,000 separate links. Over time, this developed into a full outfit of heavy metal plates that were much stronger, but much heavier than chainmail.

KNIGHTLY TACTICS

The main tactic used by knights was the charge. Standing in their stirrups and leaning forward, knights spurred their horses into a gallop and drove their lances into the heart of enemy formations. Lances usually shattered on impact, so once they got into close combat, knights hacked and chopped with weapons like the poleax or the longsword. Knights wore a variety of different styles of helmet as well, each with a different approach to the same problem: protecting their head while still allowing them to see and breathe with ease.

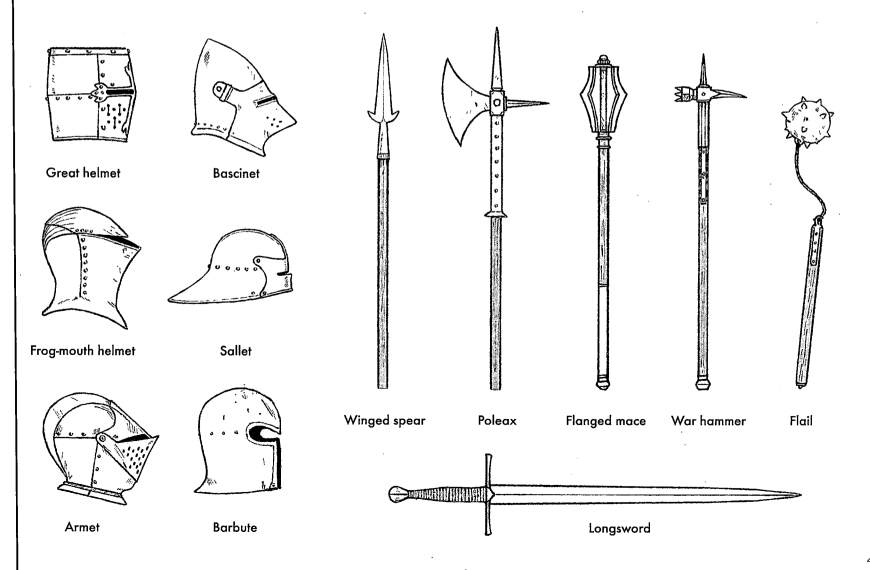

Great helmet

Bascinet

Frog-mouth helmet

Sallet

Armet

Barbute

Winged spear

Poleax

Flanged mace

War hammer

Flail

Longsword

· GREAT LEADERS ·

SALADIN

1138–1193 AD

Saladin was a famous Arab general who fought during the religious wars called the Crusades. He was respected by both Christians and Muslims for his military skill, his wisdom and his willingness to show mercy.

Saladin led his armies into many battles against the crusaders, who were led by the English King Richard the Lionheart. By using lightly armored and fast-moving troops like horse archers and camel warriors, Saladin outmaneuvered the heavy, overheated crusader forces.

THE BATTLE OF HATTIN

Crusader horses were terrified of Saladin's camels and sometimes fled the battlefield instead of fighting. His warriors harassed crusader battle lines, exhausting them before launching the final strike that destroyed the crusader army.

The crusaders had spent the night without water and were being driven mad by the heat. They could barely find the strength to fight back as Saladin's armies pushed them back against two steep hills called the Horns of Hattin. With the defeat of the Christian army at Hattin, the Muslims were able to re-conquer Jerusalem.

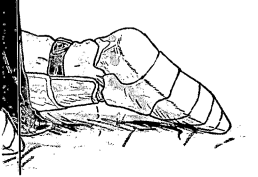

THE AGE OF THE SAMURAI

1185-1868 AD

The earliest samurai were horseback archers, just like the Mongols across the sea. When they fought, samurai would announce their rank and achievements as a challenge to their enemies before charging at each other, shooting arrows as they raced into battle.

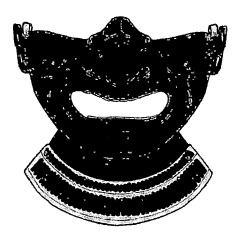

Menpō (facial armor)

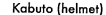
Kabuto (helmet)

Ō-yoroi (full armor)

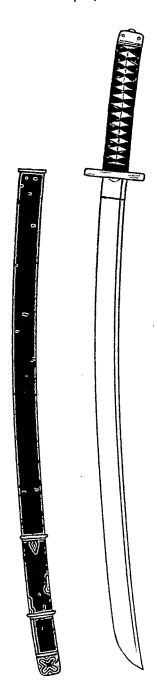

Saya (scabbard)
Katana (curved sword)

Hidden behind a terrifying death mask and protected by armor covered in images of dragons and lions, the samurai prepared for war. Carrying huge bows and wielding the finest swords in the world, samurai dominated the battlefields of their homeland Japan.

ULTIMATE SWORDSMITHS

Over time, the sword replaced the bow as the main weapon of the samurai. Samurai swords were the finest blades ever made. The hard cutting edge was sharp enough to cut at the lightest touch, while the inner core was soft and flexible to keep the sword from breaking.

· GREAT LEADERS ·

TOMOE GOZEN

c. 1157–1247 AD

Almost a thousand years ago, the greatest war between two samurai families was raging in Japan. Female samurai were common, and one of the most famous was a woman named Tomoe Gozen. She was an incredibly skilled swordswoman and rider, renowned throughout the country for her bravery and intelligence in battle.

THE GENPEI WAR

Tomoe was one of the finest warriors in general Yoshinaka's army and was highly trained in martial arts and archery. When it came to war, she was chosen to ride out as his first captain. During the battle, Tomoe defended a bridge single-handed against dozens of warriors and courageously led a few hundred samurai against a hoard of 2,000 attackers.

Tomoe fought with a naginata, which was a female samurai's favored weapon. Made of a long wooden shaft with a curved blade at the end, Tomoe would have swung this light and elegant staff at her enemies with deadly force.

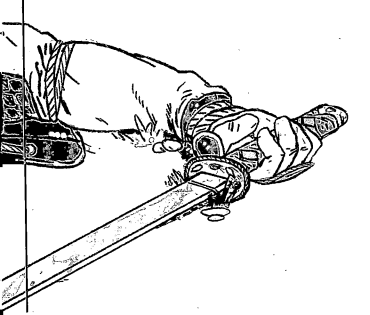

LEGENDARY BATTLES: CRÉCY

1346 AD

The greatest knights in the world were French. But they certainly weren't invincible. Sometimes a skilled army, using the simplest of weapons, could cut down a much better armed and armored group of men. This is exactly what happened at the battle of Crécy.

RAIN OF ARROWS

In the middle of a French forest, a small army of around 10,000 Englishmen defeated at least 20,000 French warriors.

The French knights, tired from the day's march and forced into a muddy field between two forests, let out their battle cry and launched an all-out charge at the English position. But the English longbowmen, trained to fire one arrow every five seconds, aimed a great cloud of arrows at the lightly armored French horses. As their mounts collapsed, the French knights started to panic and flee the battlefield, trampling their own men as they scrambled to escape.

JOAN OF ARC

1412–1431

The bloody Hundred Years' War between the English and the French had been raging for 92 long years, when a young woman named Joan declared that she would lead the French to victory.

HOLY MISSION

Joan had no doubt in her mind about her mission. After all, she believed the saints had spoken to her directly. Her bravery soon impressed military leaders, so they sent her to Orléans as a challenge. If she could win back the besieged city, she would prove her divine visions.

THE SIEGE OF ORLÉANS

Joan arrived at Orléans to crowds of cheering supporters. After several days of battle, a French commander advised the tired troops to leave the final assault until the following morning. But Joan rallied the French soldiers to attack immediately. Inspired by her courage, the men followed her lead. Clambering up ladders, they plunged straight into the English fortress and demolished the English forces with an onslaught of swords and arrows. Young Joan had commanded the greatest French victory in thirteen years.

THE EVOLUTION OF WEAPONS

Hard rock, like flint or obsidian, was used for thousands of years to make simple handheld blades and daggers. The eventual discovery of metals like iron, bronze (a mixture of copper and tin) and steel (a mixture of iron and carbon), meant that weapon technology would quickly begin to change. With each improvement in material and craftsmanship, blades could be made sharper, lighter, and more durable than earlier weapons, which meant a great advantage on the field of battle.

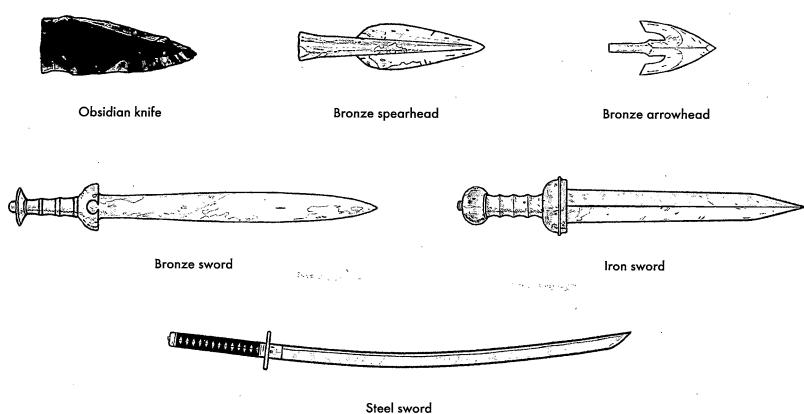

Obsidian knife

Bronze spearhead

Bronze arrowhead

Bronze sword

Iron sword

Steel sword

FOCUS ON: OBSIDIAN

One of the first stones used to make weapons was a type of dark volcanic glass called obsidian. When fractured, its edges are sharper than even the best metal knife today. The Maya people used obsidian for spearheads and swords, like the deadly macuahuitl: a wooden club surrounded by razor-sharp blades of obsidian.

THE EVOLUTION OF ARMOR

Early forms of armor were made from tanned animal skins or cloth, which offered minimal protection against sharp blades. Bronze and iron were used in different ways to create tougher armor: as small plates laced together in rows, or as overlapping scales. The full-body steel plates of the medieval knight offered maximum protection, and their clever design did not restrict movement.

Tanned skins

Lamellar armor

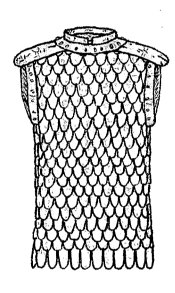
Scale armor

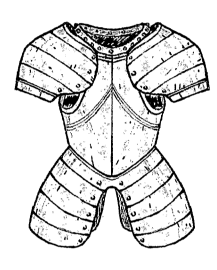
Plate armor

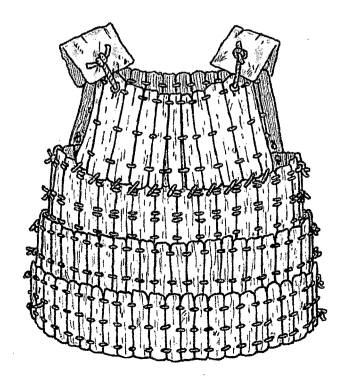

FOCUS ON: BONE ARMOR

An unusual suit of armor made entirely of bones was recently discovered by archaeologists in Siberia. Small pieces of animal bone were sewn together with strips of leather, and would have provided excellent protection against the stone and bronze weapons used at the time.

 # INDEX